Developing Leaders

Research and Applications in Psychological Type and Leadership Development

Integrating Reality and Vision, Mind and Heart

Catherine Fitzgerald and Linda K. Kirby
Editors

DAVIES-BLACK PUBLISHING
Palo Alto, California

Published by Davies-Black Publishing, an imprint of Consulting Psychologists Press, Inc., 3803 East Bayshore Road, Palo Alto, California 94303; 1-800-624-1765.

Special discounts on bulk quantities of Davies-Black Publishing books are available to corporations, professional associations, and other organizations. For details, contact the Director of Book Sales at Davies-Black Publishing, 3803 East Bayshore Road, Palo Alto, California 94303; 650-691-9123; Fax 650-988-0673.

Myers-Briggs Type Indicator, MBTI, and *Introduction to Type* are registered trademarks of Consulting Psychologists Press, Inc.

California Psychological Inventory, CPI, *Fundamental Interpersonal Relations Orientation–Behavior,* and FIRO-B are trademarks of Consulting Psychologists Press, Inc.

02 01 00 99 98   6 5 4 3 2

Library of Congress Cataloging-in-Publication Data
Developing leaders : research and applications in psychological type and leadership
        development : integrating reality and vision, mind and heart / Catherine
        Fitzgerald and Linda K. Kirby, editors.
        p.   cm.
        Includes bibliographical references and index.
        ISBN 0-89106-082-0
        1. Leadership—Psychological aspects.   2. Myers-Briggs Type Indicator.   I.
        Fitzgerald, Catherine.   II. Kirby, Linda K.
        HD57.7.D497   1997
        658.4′07124—dc20   95–44376
                                                                                                      CIP

FIRST EDITION
First printing 1997

Contents

Preface

BACKGROUND

Since the publication of the *Myers-Briggs Type Indicator®* (MBTI®) by Consulting Psychologists Press in 1975[1], practitioners and researchers interested in the MBTI have had access to an increasing number of valuable resources. Published resources include:

- the MBTI *Manual* (Myers & McCaulley, 1985)
- the booklet *Introduction to Type* (Myers, 1993) and more specialized booklets (e.g., *Introduction to Type in Organizations*, Hirsh & Kummerow, 1990)
- books describing psychological type and its applications (e.g., *LIFETypes*, Hirsh & Kummerow, 1989; *Type Talk*, Kroeger & Thuesen, 1988)
- *The Atlas of Type Tables* (Macdaid, McCaulley, & Kainz, 1987), which provides extensive type distribution data
- books on special topics regarding psychological type, such as type and learning (Lawrence, 1993), the inferior function (Quenk, 1993), and type and organizational change (Barger & Kirby, 1995)
- training guides, with reproducible material for use in workshops (e.g., *Using the MBTI in Organizations*, Hirsh, 1991)

In addition, the international Association for Psychological Type (APT) has sponsored biennial international conferences, regional organizations, and local chapters that have increased the level of interest, knowledge, and expertise about psychological type and its various

---

[1]Educational Testing Service (ETS) was actually the first publisher of the MBTI and the first edition of the MBTI *Manual* (1962). However, until 1975, the use of the MBTI was restricted to research.

applications. Specialized, intensive training programs, known as "qualifying programs," have been developed by APT and other organizations[2] to train practitioners in the sound and ethical use of the MBTI. APT's publications, the *Journal of Psychological Type* and the *Bulletin of Psychological Type,* have published articles on various aspects of psychological type research and practice. The Center for Psychological Type (CAPT), founded in 1975 by Isabel Myers and Mary McCaulley and now headed by Mary McCaulley, has contributed enormously to knowledge and expertise in the MBTI through its research, publications, training programs, conferences, and technical assistance to researchers.

Since 1975, the MBTI has been increasingly used in management and leadership development. Researchers and practitioners have developed hypotheses and explored questions about type differences in the style and impact of leaders. To allow a dialogue about emerging research approaches and findings, in 1994, the National Leadership Institute of the University of Maryland University College sponsored an International Research Conference on the MBTI and Leadership, with cosponsorship from APT and CAPT (see Fitzgerald, 1994). At the conference, researchers from around the world presented and discussed a rich variety of research findings—and the implications of those findings for practice.

PURPOSE AND OVERVIEW
OF THE BOOK

The purpose of this book is to build on past research and writing by assembling the work of authors from a variety of settings and roles who have done thoughtful, in-depth work on one or more aspects of psychological type and leadership. This book has three parts: overview, research, and application. Each of these parts is described briefly below.

Part I, the overview section, consists of two chapters: the first an overview/introduction of psychological type and the MBTI; the second an overview of the history, background, and rationale for the use of the MBTI in leadership development. Chapter 1, by Linda Kirby, is intended to be particularly useful to readers who are not familiar with the MBTI and to provide a review for readers who are more knowledgeable

---

[2]Contact the publisher of the MBTI, Consulting Psychologists Press, Inc. (Palo Alto, California) for additional information about approved qualifying programs.

about the MBTI. In addition to an overview of the MBTI, the chapter
summarizes current data on type distribution in leaders—a topic that is
likely to be of interest to both new and experienced users. Chapter 2,
by Catherine Fitzgerald, explores the question, "Why use the MBTI in
leadership development?" from a number of perspectives, and discusses the MBTI in relation to recent research in personality. It also examines the unique characteristics of the MBTI relative to current perspectives on leadership and leadership development.

Part II focuses on research and attempts to build on the work of the
1994 International Research Conference. A variety of presenters at the
conference were asked to elaborate on and extend some of the research
presented there. Part II begins with an extensive review of the literature
by Christa Walck (Chapter 3). Walck concludes her review with some
provocative suggestions for rethinking our approach to conducting
research on the MBTI and leadership. In Chapter 4, drawing on extensive data from the Center for Creative Leadership (Greensboro, North
Carolina) as well as other sources, John Fleenor summarizes research
relating the MBTI to other psychological instruments used in leadership
development. In Chapter 5, Ellen Van Velsor and John Fleenor compare
research on the MBTI and four 360-degree feedback instruments. They
discuss the implications of the findings for the development of leaders
and for the selection of the instruments used to provide feedback to
leaders. Paul Roush, in Chapter 6, reports data from ongoing research
on type and military leadership and addresses the issue of the differential impact on different types of feedback from subordinates. In Chapter
7, Usha Haley explores the relationship between the MBTI "function
pairs" (i.e., ST, SF, NF, NT) and strategic decision-making styles in managers, and suggests approaches to increasing the effectiveness of decisions for managers of all types. Eric Sundstrom and Paul Busby, in
Chapter 8, present type-specific profiles of feedback from co-workers
on SYMLOG®, a 360-degree feedback instrument, and examine gaps
between each of these profiles and the research-based profile of the
most effective leader.

For Part III, the application section, senior practitioners experienced
in areas related to leadership development and type were invited to provide in-depth guidance for practitioners on one or more aspects of the
application of psychological type to leadership development. The first
two chapters in this part focus on two in-depth levels of interpreting
and using the MBTI in leadership development. Chapter 9, by
Catherine Fitzgerald and Linda Kirby, focuses on how to use type

dynamics, particularly in work with individual leaders. Chapter 10, by Catherine Fitzgerald, explores the topic of type development in leaders and particularly focuses on the midlife process (i.e., late thirties and beyond) and its implications for leadership development. In Chapter 11, Nancy Barger and Linda Kirby address the needs of different types during organizational change and offer guidance to leaders about how knowledge and use of psychological type can facilitate change. Betsy Kendall and Sally Carr, in Chapter 12, describe a variety of ways that psychological type can be used with management simulations to help both participants and staff explore links between behavior and type. In Chapter 13, through an overview of the instrument and with a variety of case examples, Jean Kummerow and Dick Olson demonstrate how the MBTI Step II can be used to enhance a leader's understanding of his or her leadership style. In Chapter 14, Sue Clancy provides guidance in understanding and responding to the reactions and needs of managers and staff with Sensing, Thinking, and Judging (STJ) preferences as they participate in organizational change. Through a variety of case examples, in Chapter 15, Geno Schnell and Allen Hammer explore the joint use of the MBTI with the FIRO-B™, a psychological instrument that is widely used in leadership development. In Chapter 16, Susan Brock provides strategies to help leaders be more effective in their communication by understanding and responding to the differential needs of different types. Finally, in Chapter 17, Reg Lang describes ways in which knowledge of psychological type can contribute to the effectiveness of strategic planning and change.

AUDIENCE

This book was designed to be of value to a variety of audiences, such as:

- practitioners who currently use the MBTI in leadership development or related application areas, or those interested in exploring the potential use of the MBTI
- researchers interested in the MBTI generally or in MBTI and leadership particularly, as well as researchers exploring various aspects of leadership and personality
- managers and leaders familiar with psychological type who have a special interest in deepening their knowledge of type and leadership

Although we believe that much of the book will be useful to beginning or prospective users of the MBTI, a primary goal was to be of value to advanced practitioners. Our hope is that even the most advanced users of the MBTI in leadership development will find new and useful information and insight. For some chapters, specialized knowledge of the MBTI and/or other leadership tools and techniques is helpful or required; examples include chapters on the MBTI Step II (Chapter 13), and on the joint use of the MBTI and FIRO-B (Chapter 15). An advanced application topic, the use of type dynamics in leadership development (Chapter 9), is particularly aimed at experienced users of the MBTI; beginning MBTI users are encouraged to review other sources (e.g., Myers & McCaulley, 1985; Myers & Kirby, 1994) before tackling Chapter 9.

Readers who have *not* been through MBTI qualifying programs or equivalent training are encouraged to read Chapter 1 of this book and to review the MBTI *Manual* (Myers & McCaulley, 1985) to understand the unique characteristics of the MBTI as a type-based (vs. trait-based) instrument and to understand the theory underlying the MBTI.

ACKNOWLEDGMENTS

We are grateful to a large number of people without whom this book could not have been produced. We would especially like to thank Jennifer Berger for her invaluable suggestions, feedback, and assistance in editing the book, Michael Berger for his essential calm and persistent help with producing the book, and Laura Benedict for all her help and support. We are very grateful to the following colleagues and friends who have contributed their ideas, feedback, and support: Nancy Barger, Liz Berney, Sally Carr, David Coleman, Allen Hammer, Dee Hahn-Rollins, Jean Kummerow, Joe Mancini, Mary Parish, Jody Olsen, Naomi Quenk, Geno Schnell, Charlie Seashore, and Pat Stocker. We are also very grateful to the contributors to this book for the quality of their work, their thoughtfulness in expanding upon and communicating their work, and their flexibility and patience in dealing with our crowded schedules and emergent deadlines. The influence of Lee Langhammer Law, head of Davies-Black Publishing, is noteworthy. This book could not have been produced without Lee's early encouragement; later patience; and overall intelligence, judgment, and support. Her colleagues at Davies-Black Publishing, particularly Melinda Merino and John Walker, were also very helpful and supportive.

We would like to thank our current and past clients—those leaders and staff within the organizations in which we have been privileged to work who have shared their stories and insights. We would also like to thank members of the faculty of the Association for Psychological Type

MBTI qualifying training program—whose commitment, experience, and professionalism as cotrainers have substantially expanded our understanding and use of psychological type.

Catherine Fitzgerald would like to thank teachers who have been particularly influential in her intellectual and professional development: Sister Cecilia Madeleine, Patricia Plante, Edward Katkin, and Murray Levine. Catherine would also like to express her deepest appreciation and gratitude to her husband, Derek Updegraff, Sr., for his unfailing help and support; and her son, Derek Updegraff, Jr., for his patience and ability to provide comic relief during the process.

Linda Kirby would like to thank those who introduced her to psychological type many years ago and mentored her through the long process of developing understanding and expertise: Nancy Barger and Naomi Quenk. Finally, Linda deeply appreciates the unfailing support—both practical and emotional—that she receives from her parents and children: Barrett Kirby, Jeanne Kirby, Ruth Johnson, Pamela Kirby, and Zachary Kirby.

Catherine Fitzgerald and Linda Kirby

REFERENCES

Barger, N. J., & Kirby, L. K. (1995). *The challenge of change in organizations: Helping employees thrive in the new frontier.* Palo Alto, CA: Davies-Black.

Fitzgerald, C. (Ed.). (1994). *Proceedings of the Myers-Briggs Type Indicator and Leadership: An International Research Conference.* College Park, MD: University of Maryland University College National Leadership Institute.

Hirsh, S. K. (1991). *Using the Myers-Briggs Type Indicator in organizations: A resource book* (2d ed.). Palo Alto, CA: Consulting Psychologists Press.

Hirsh, S. K., & Kummerow, J. M. (1989). *LIFETypes.* New York: Warner Books.

Hirsh, S. K., & Kummerow, J. M. (1990). *Introduction to type in organizations* (2d ed.). Palo Alto, CA: Consulting Psychologists Press.

Kroeger, O., & Thuesen, J. M. (1988). *Type talk.* New York: Delacorte Press.

Lawrence, G. (1993). *People types and tiger stripes* (3d ed). Gainesville, FL: Center for Applications of Psychological Type.

Macdaid, G. P., McCaulley, M. H., & Kainz, R. I. (1987). *Myers-Briggs Type Indicator atlas of type tables.* Gainesville, FL: Center for Applications of Psychological Type.

Myers, I. B. (1993). *Introduction to type* (5th ed.). Edited by K. D. Myers and L. K. Kirby. Palo Alto, CA: Consulting Psychologists Press.

Myers, I. B., & McCaulley, M. H. (1985). *Manual: A guide to the development and use of the Myers-Briggs Type Indicator.* Palo Alto, CA: Consulting Psychologists Press.

Myers, K. D., & Kirby, L. K. (1994). *Introduction to type dynamics and development.* Palo Alto, CA: Consulting Psychologists Press.

Quenk, N. (1993). *Beside ourselves: Our hidden personality in everyday life.* Palo Alto, CA: Davies-Black.

PART ONE

Overview

1 | Introduction

Psychological Type and the Myers-Briggs Type Indicator

Linda K. Kirby

The *Myers-Briggs Type Indicator*® personality inventory is one of the most popular self-report instruments in leadership and management development programs; in team-building, communications training, and career enhancement programs; and in other organizational development training in the United States and around the world. It is designed to provide information about respondents' Jungian psychological type preferences.

Swiss psychiatrist Carl Jung developed his theory of psychological type from his work with individual clients and his study of both primitive and developed societies. His theory, he believed, described the structure of human consciousness. Human beings, as a species, are born with certain mental and emotional possibilities, Jung believed, and he identified the two primary ones this way:

- The ability to gather, store, and retrieve information by observing the world around them as well as their own memories and inner states
- The ability to reflect upon that information and organize it coherently to understand and make decisions

These are the mental tools humans need to pursue what Jung saw as their natural impulses to relate meaningfully to the world and people through productive work and significant relationships and to develop personally toward integration.

3

Jung believed that although all humans have these capacities to observe and to organize, there are natural, inborn differences in the ways people prefer to use these capacities. These natural differences developed as the human brain evolved through increasing specialization, and they lead to very different structures of consciousness in normal human beings.

Isabel B. Myers and Katharine Briggs studied and applied Jung's theories to their understanding of individuals for 18 years, from the publication of Jung's *Psychological Types* in English in 1923 to the early 1940s. In 1941, they began developing and testing questions that they hoped would assist people in identifying their own Jungian type preferences. Their goal was construction of an instrument that would assist people in developing self-understanding and increasing their understanding and appreciation of others. The eventual result was the *Myers-Briggs Type Indicator* (MBTI®) personality inventory. The MBTI instrument operationalizes Jung's theories and makes it possible to develop practical applications. Using the instrument and the theory provides a structured, systematic way of recognizing individual differences—one's own and those of other people.

NORMAL DIFFERENCES AMONG PEOPLE

Jung's picture of human functioning portrayed people as having access to all of the mental tools he identified and using each of them to some extent to function effectively (more about this in Chapter 9). Nevertheless, an individual's natural preferences for certain ways of approaching these tools, he believed, shape the ways in which they will develop and be used, thus creating different normal patterns of development and of operating in the world.

The Importance of Opposites

It is important to understand Jung's idea of preferences and opposites. Preferences are best defined as inborn, natural ways of using a particular mental tool that shape a person's perspective and development, much as a preference for right- or left-handedness shapes the ways in which people learn to perform physical tasks. For each of the mental tools, Jung identified two opposite preferences:

- Perception (gathering information) may be exercised through *Sensing* or *Intuition;*

• Judgment (structuring and prioritizing) may be exercised through *Thinking* or *Feeling*.

Because the two kinds of perception (Sensing or Intuition) and the two ways of judgment (Thinking or Feeling) are opposite and one of each is preferred from early in life, Jung believed that people do not typically use both with equal ease or facility. Instead, one of the opposites will be used more often, developed more completely, and will remain more comfortable for an individual. Correspondingly, the nonpreferred mental tool will be less developed, less comfortable, often ignored, and take more energy to use.

Both kinds of perception and judgment have value and are needed for the most effective leadership, but, according to theory and to research, it is virtually impossible for one person to have developed both of the opposites equally well. As Jung put it, human beings can strive for "completion," but only God is perfect! One of the hopes of Myers and Briggs as they developed the MBTI instrument was that knowledge of one's own natural and developed way of gathering information and of making decisions would include recognition of their opposites—what is potentially being overlooked—and therefore encourage exploration of ways to balance oneself.

Perception (Sensing or Intuition): Two Ways of Gathering Information

Jung identified two ways of gathering information, modes that he named *Sensing* and *Intuition*. Each individual will have a natural preference and developed facility in one of these opposites.

Those who prefer to gather information through Sensing focus on what is actual in the present, on data available to the senses. As leaders, they tend to be realistic and pragmatic, have a good grasp of what is actually happening in their organization, and like to use factual data in forecasting the future and making decisions.

Those who prefer to gather information through Intuition focus on the connections between sensing data. They are drawn to the overall patterns and meanings or theoretical explanations that will put specific data into context. As leaders, they tend to be visionary and imaginative, have an accurate "feel" for what is going on, and like to make decisions based on a theoretical projection of future possibilities that they "see."

Each preferred way of gathering information has its own strengths, as the above descriptions indicated, but each also has characteristic blind spots and weaknesses. Leaders with a Sensing preference may be so focused on present reality and their own experience that they have difficulty dealing with quickly changing environments that require radical rethinking of present procedures. They typically want to collect a lot of data before accepting that a pattern or meaning is real and should be acted upon. They can miss important, more global connections in their focus on their more immediate environment.

Leaders with an Intuitive preference may be so persuaded of their perceptions of underlying patterns and future possibilities that they fail to give proper weight to current realities. They can "go with their hunches" without giving enough consideration to the resources that will be required, the impact this will have on day-to-day work, or modifications of their vision that could make it more achievable.

Judgment (Thinking or Feeling): Two Ways of Making Decisions

Jung identified two different ways in which people organize and structure information and make decisions. He named these different modes *Thinking* and *Feeling*. Each individual will prefer one of these opposites to the other.

Those who prefer Thinking like to apply logical principles to make objective decisions. As leaders, they tend to take a detached, analytical approach to problem solving; to value clarity and accuracy; and to ask tough questions. They typically believe that problems have correct solutions that can be found through analysis, and that these logical, reasonable analyses are the best bases for decisions.

Those who prefer Feeling like to make decisions by a process of valuing. They filter situations through their own values, the values of other people important to them, and the values of the organizations to which they are committed. As leaders, they tend to encourage participation and consensus in decision making; to value the contributions of others; and to compassionately put themselves in the other person's shoes during the process.

Both Thinking and Feeling are rational processes for deciding what information to use in decision making and how much weight to give to different kinds of information. Those preferring Thinking want to include information that is directly relevant and objective by their standards. Those preferring Feeling want to include everything that is important to the people involved in the situation, without requiring that it be logical; they are much less inclined to apply the same objective standard, even to similar situations, because for them, each situation is different due to the specific values and people involved.

As with the differences in perception, each of these bases for decision making has value, and each has some blind spots and potential weaknesses for leaders. Leaders preferring Thinking may focus so much energy on logical analysis and tasks that they do not give enough weight to the impacts of their decisions on people. They can be overly competitive, seeing it as most important to determine who or what is "right," and less important to find common ground. Those preferring Feeling can focus so much energy on including others and empathizing with their positions that they lose track of some of the tough decisions they may need to make. They can also, at times, overidentify with people who are important to them, allowing their decisions to seem to be biased or personal.

Differences in Orientation
(Extraversion or Introversion)

In addition to the basic mental tools Jung identified, he also described differences in orientation and direction of energy. People may direct their energy and attention primarily to the external world, which Jung called *Extraversion;* or primarily to their inner world of ideas, values, and experience, which Jung called *Introversion.*

Those preferring Extraversion are drawn toward people and things outside themselves. They tend to actively pursue external interaction, drawing mental and emotional energy from these exchanges. As leaders, those preferring Extraversion tend to initiate contact and seek out others, to be action oriented, and to like processing their thoughts out loud. They are often gregarious, enthusiastic, and expressive leaders.

Those preferring Introversion tend to direct their energy and attention toward reflection and to draw energy from quiet, introspective time. As leaders, those preferring Introversion tend to like receiving information in written form and then to have time to process it internally before arriving at decisions. They typically prefer one-on-one interactions and may be contained and reserved—hard to "read."

Each of these orientations makes contributions to leadership and each has some potential weaknesses for leaders. Leaders preferring Extraversion may take quick action before giving enough reflection time. Their external processing of ideas can be confusing to colleagues and followers who may not recognize that these are ideas in process and are not final decisions. Others may feel that the Extraverted leader is inconsistent or doesn't know his or her own mind because they do not understand the thinking-out-loud process. Extraverted leaders may also "crowd" their Introverted colleagues or followers, failing to give them sufficient time for internal processing or space for their contributions.

Leaders preferring Introversion, on the other hand, may continue to reflect when it is time for action. Their internal processing and decision making may exclude others who feel they have a right to participate in the process. The Introvert's eventual announcement of a decision may seem to come from out of the blue because he or she has not explained the process or shared the information on which the decision is based. The Introverted leader's reserve and containment may seem to others to be aloofness or even snobbishness and may cause others to feel not only excluded, but also judged by the leader.

Different Approaches to Structure
(Judgment or Perception)

A final set of opposites indicated by the MBTI personality inventory refers to how people like to organize their external environment. The MBTI reports this dimension as a preference for Judging or Perceiving.

Some people direct the mental tool they use in making decisions (whether Thinking or Feeling) toward the external world (whether they prefer Extraversion or Introversion). Myers and Briggs termed these people Judging. These people use their Judging to organize and structure the world around them, preferring that their environment be orderly, clear, planned, and scheduled. As leaders, those who prefer Judging tend to be uncomfortable with ambiguity and impatient with process. They focus on achieving the desired results as quickly as possible and then moving on. They like to plan both long-range and short-term and to stick to plans and schedules. They trust their ability to get things done.

Others direct the mental tool they use in information gathering (whether Sensing or Intuition) toward the external world (whether they prefer Extraversion or Introversion). Myers and Briggs termed these people Perceiving. Because they direct this Perceiving process externally, they prefer to keep their environment as open and unstructured as possible. As leaders, those who prefer Perceiving typically want a great deal of information before making decisions and want their decisions to emerge from the information-gathering process. To them, goals are moving targets, temporary and changeable as new information arises. They enjoy flexibility and spontaneity in their environment, and they trust their ability to respond quickly to changing circumstances.

Both ways of organizing the external world have value, and both have potential problem areas for leaders. Judging leaders can push for closure and decisions before enough information has been gathered, stick with plans when they need to be reevaluated and changed, and oversimplify complex situations for the sake of clarity. Their drive for structure and schedules can straitjacket Perceiving followers, and their emphasis on following plans and time frames can feel controlling to others. Perceiving leaders can continue to gather information when decisions need to be made, waiting too long for the decision to emerge. They can so trust their ability to respond quickly to crises that they actually encourage crises, and their spontaneity and flexibility can place undue stress on others, especially their Judging followers. For both, there is a tendency to deprecate and be critical of the process of their opposites.

USING COMBINATIONS OF PREFERENCES

The four sets of opposites identified by the MBTI personality inventory result in 16 possible combinations, which the MBTI identifies by letters: E (Extraversion) or I (Introversion); S (Sensing) or N (Intuition); T (Thinking) or F (Feeling); J (Judging) or P (Perceiving). The number that accompanies the letter result is an indication of how clearly this preference was reported. (A later section of this chapter will give more information on interpreting MBTI results.)

A leader may determine that his or her preferences are, for example, for ISTJ. ISTJ leaders would typically show the following characteristics:

- A calm, reserved, and contained manner, with a desire for quiet processing time (I)
- Emphasis on hard, realistic data, on experience, on what is practical and doable (S)
- Use of logical analysis and rational criteria for decisions, a "toughness" in choices (T)
- Desire for an orderly, structured environment (J)

Together, these preferences lead to leaders who emphasize the bottom line, take a realistic and organized approach to their work and require that of others, and insist on a no-nonsense attitude. They approach new ideas with tough questions, tend to be skeptical of suggested changes that are not firmly grounded, and require thorough exploration of initiatives before accepting them.

The Type Table Format

MBTI group data is normally displayed on a type table consisting of 16 squares, each representing one of the 16 MBTI types. Table 1 is such a display. The type table is arranged so that types with similar preferences are next to each other. This allows one to look at sections of the type table and recognize patterns within a group.

Combinations of Sensing, Intuition, Thinking, and Feeling

Each column of a type table such as Table 1 is made up of four types that have the same two middle letters. The four types, then, share a preference for kinds of information (S or N) and ways of making decisions (T or F). The far left column in the type table consists of the four ST types; the next column is the four SF types; the third is the four NF types; and the far right column is the four NT types. Though the four types in each column differ on their E–I and J–P preferences, the fact that they share preferences for a particular way of gathering information and one way of making decisions means that there typically will be important similarities. For example,

- STs (ISTJ, ISTP, ESTP, and ESTJ) tend to share a focus on the bottom-line realities. They are practical, logical, and tend to be drawn to technical concerns.
- SFs (ISFJ, ISFP, ESFP, and ESFJ) tend to share a focus on practical service to people. They are sympathetic, friendly, and warm, and tend to be drawn to areas where they can support others on a day-to-day basis.
- NFs (INFJ, INFP, ENFP, and ENFJ) usually focus on people more globally, wanting to find ways to improve the long-range well-being of all. They tend to be insightful and enthusiastic, and they value effective communication.

TABLE 1 MBTI Type Table

	S	S	N	N	
I	ISTJ	ISFJ	INFJ	INTJ	J
I	ISTP	ISFP	INFP	INTP	P
E	ESTP	ESFP	ENFP	ENTP	P
E	ESTJ	ESFJ	ENFJ	ENTJ	J
	T	F	F	T	

- NTs (INTJ, INTP, ENTP, and ENTJ) tend to focus more on developing and using conceptual frameworks. Their strength is analyzing systems and seeing ways to improve them.

Combinations of Extraversion–Introversion and Judging–Perceiving

Each row of the type table consists of four types that share the same preferences on the E–I and J–P dimensions. Thus, the four types in a particular row have similar orientations to the world and similar preferences for organizing their external environment. For example,

- IJs (ISTJ, ISFJ, INFJ, and INTJ), who make up the top row in Table 1, are the decisive Introverts. When new information or ideas are presented to them, they take time to process the information in their inner world—to check whether it fits with their internal picture and understanding. If it does, they will move ahead in an organized fashion to try to implement their perception. If the ideas don't fit their internal data or picture, however, they can be immovable.
- IPs (ISTP, ISFP, INFP, and INTP) make up the second row of Table 1. These types appear flexible and tolerant externally, preferring to keep things open on the outside. When new information or ideas are presented to them, however, they take them inside to evaluate them with their preferred judging function, either Thinking or Feeling. For

Thinking types, new ideas must pass their logical analysis. For Feeling types, new ideas must meet their values standards.

- EPs (ESTP, ESFP, ENFP, and ENTP) make up the third row in Table 1. These types are typically resourceful and energetic. They usually are excellent networkers and gatherers of information, and their enthusiasm carries others along with them. They typically greet new information or ideas by "trying them out," plunging into action to see how they work.
- EJs (ESTJ, ESFJ, ENFJ, and ENTJ) make up the bottom row in Table 1. EJs love to take action to organize and structure the environment. They typically are decisive and energetic in making things happen. They respond to new information or ideas by focusing on the goals, making plans, and implementing them.

Other Combinations

The four quadrants of the type table are used by many researchers and other type experts to look at issues of organizational change (Hirsh, 1992).

- In the top left-hand quadrant of a type table are four types that share preferences for Introversion and Sensing. The quick phrase used to describe the IS reaction to proposals for change is, "Let's keep what we have."
- The types in the top right-hand quadrant of the type table share preferences for Introversion and Intuition. The quick phrase used to describe the IN reaction to proposals for change is, "Let me go away and think about it—I'll get back to you."
- In the bottom left-hand quadrant of the type table are types that share preferences for Extraversion and Sensing; these types respond to change proposals by saying, "Let's just do it."
- The types in the bottom right-hand quadrant of the type table share preferences for EN and typically respond to change by saying, "Whatever there is, let's change it."

The four types in the corner squares of the type table share a preference for Thinking and Judging, types that Isabel Briggs Myers referred to as "tough-minded executives." The combination of Thinking and Judging means that these types Extravert their Thinking, using it to plan, structure, and systematize their external environment. They rationally analyze likely consequences of various alternatives and make quick decisions based on logic.

Using Type Combinations
to Understand Leaders

As this discussion of preference combinations has illustrated, the four-letter type is more than a simple addition of the four preferences: Each of a person's preferences influences how all the others will be used.

Chapter 9 provides additional information about preference interactions. We also recommend *Introduction to Type®* (Myers, 1993), which gives complete descriptions of each of the 16 types. *Introduction to Type in Organizations* (Hirsh & Kummerow, 1990) also includes excellent information on work style for the 16 types.

All 16 types are found in leadership positions. As we have indicated, each preference and each combination of preferences will typically bring special strengths as well as potential blind spots to leadership. Research about leaders indicates that although all types are represented, they are not represented equally. The tendency in organizations of all kinds is for leaders to be predominantly Thinking and Judging—people who use their logical decision making to organize their external environment.

THE MBTI INSTRUMENT

Comparison with Other Instruments

The MBTI assessment tool is different from most of the others that are used today, including those with which it is compared in the research chapters of this book, for three reasons:

First, it is one of the oldest assessment tools, with development beginning in 1941, extensive testing and revision undertaken throughout the 1940s and 1950s, a research edition (Form F) published in 1962, and availability for more general use beginning in 1975.

Second, it is a theory-based instrument, designed to give information about a psychological construct—type preferences. Though descriptions, behaviors, attitudes, and activities associated with MBTI type are based on empirical research, the instrument itself is designed to operationalize a theory.

Most of the other instruments normally used in leadership and management development are based on empirical evidence gathered about specific values and behaviors that this evidence indicates are connected to positive or negative leadership behaviors. The theory behind the MBTI instrument sees specific values and behaviors as habits that tend to develop as people exercise their underlying type preferences. Though the MBTI uses common behaviors in its questions to indicate type, it does not claim, nor should it be used, to measure specific behaviors, values, attitudes, or skills.

Third, the MBTI instrument is designed to sort people into presumed preexisting categories (that is, the 16 types), rather than to measure how much or how little of a particular human characteristic a respondent possesses or uses. Most other instruments used in leadership development are *trait* measures in which it is assumed that everyone possesses a particular trait or traits, and the instrument reveals how much. Trait measures generally are reported using a normal curve, which reveals the average amount of the trait possessed by people. This kind of approach includes an evaluative aspect.

For example, an instrument assessing the trait of dominance will show a *normal* range; a *high* range, which may indicate domineering or even abusive behaviors; and a *low* range, which may indicate lack of self-confidence and assertiveness. These results tend to be used to help leaders identify and develop new attitudes and behaviors that will move them into the normal range of behavior. Subsequent ratings on the same instrument might be used to evaluate how successfully the leader has changed on his or her dominance trait.

In contrast, the MBTI is intended to indicate a category—a natural preference for one or the other of two opposite modes. Leaders will normally have developed skills and behaviors related to both of the opposites, but the intention is to clarify respondents' "home base." The MBTI, then, does not directly measure behavior nor give information about how much Extraversion, for example, a particular individual has.

Reliability and Validity

The MBTI *Manual* (Myers & McCaulley, 1985) includes extensive information on split-half and test-retest reliabilities. For educated U.S. adults (such as most of those in leadership positions), the reliability coefficients are consistently +.80, indicating excellent reliability.

The *Manual* also includes the following kinds of validity evidence:

- Correlations of MBTI preferences with other reliable instruments are in the direction that would be predicted by psychological type theory.
- Observer reports of behavior by type are consistent with the underlying theory.

- Studies of type distributions in occupations, in major fields of study, and in specializations within occupations are consistent with what psychological type theory would predict. (These studies use self-selection ratio [chi-square] to reveal significant differences from a comparative population.)
- Studies indicate that respondents choose their own type description rather than other alternative type descriptions at a statistically highly significant rate.

The research and applications chapters in this book provide additional validity evidence for the MBTI.

Interpretation and Ethical Use

The MBTI requires extensive introduction and interpretation by a trained professional: It is an *indicator*, and determining a respondent's "true type" is a process that involves MBTI results, the professional's interpretation, and the respondent's self-knowledge and judgment. In practice, respondents agree with their MBTI results about 75% of the time. When they disagree, it is most often on a dimension where their numerical score (indicating degree of confidence that the respondent identified his or her true preference) was low.

The MBTI personality inventory indicates psychological type preference and does *not* give information about how well developed a particular preference is, how skillfully it is used, nor specific aptitudes. Because of this, it is impractical and unwise, as well as unethical, to use numerical scores or MBTI results for selection to a particular job, assignment of tasks, inclusion on a team, hiring, firing, or promotions.

Instead, MBTI type is appropriately used to assist individuals in developing their self-understanding and their understanding and appreciation of differences. The remainder of this book, especially Part III, includes a great deal of information about appropriate applications of psychological type and the MBTI. We also include here a list of basic references dealing with type and the MBTI.

TYPE DISTRIBUTION OF LEADERS

One of the first questions leaders ask when they are introduced to psychological type is, "So am I the right type?" It's an understandable response, but not the right question to ask. Thousands of reports on the MBTI types of leaders and managers illustrate that all types occupy leadership positions.

Experience using the MBTI with leaders suggests that all types can be effective leaders, illustrating one of the basic principles of psychological type: that all types are valuable and have important contributions to make.

On an individual level, leaders' type preferences are useful for understanding likely strengths and potential weaknesses; for developing a personal understanding of their own functioning and their impact on others; and for identifying potential areas for development. Every type of leader can use psychological type for these purposes.

Nevertheless, the question of leader and manager types *as a group* is an important one to consider for several reasons:

- Type distributions of leaders and managers provide evidence for the validity of the MBTI.
- A type distribution of leaders that is different from the type distribution of the general population or from that of the employees in an organization provides information about leadership characteristics valued in that organization.
- Recognition of the frequency (or infrequency) of a particular type among leaders can validate the experience of individuals.
- Information about the common types of leaders provides a perspective for understanding current definitions of leadership.

This chapter provides information about the MBTI types of leaders and managers in the United States and internationally, primarily in the form of type tables. In the discussion and conclusions, I address some of the issues mentioned above. Although researchers and writers often make a theoretical distinction between leaders and managers, type distribution data does not generally distinguish between them. In this chapter, "leaders" and "managers" are used interchangeably.

TYPE TABLES OF LEADERS

The following type tables come from a variety of studies using the MBTI in organizational settings. Those using such tables need to be aware of some additional interpretation points.

Reported Type Versus "True" Type

The tables reproduced in this chapter consist of reported type; that is, they are based on leaders' and managers' results on the MBTI. In practice, after the process of interpretation and verification of type, about 75% of respondents agree that their MBTI results accurately describe them, while 25% disagree with the results. When respondents disagree with the results, it is most often on one preference, and usually one on which they received a low numerical score (Myers and McCaulley, 1985).

There are some indications that respondents may be influenced by the demands of their environment when the MBTI is administered in a work setting (Kummerow, 1988; Hammer, & Yeakley, 1987). This raises issues for practitioners using the MBTI in organizational settings and suggests that caution should be exercised in interpreting type tables of reported type. Some respondents may be unintentionally responding to MBTI questions with the values of their organization in mind, skewing their results somewhat toward behaviors that meet the organization's expectations. This factor needs to be taken into account when interpreting type table data.

Comparing Distributions

Another important consideration in interpreting type distributions of leaders and managers is that their reported type needs to be compared to type distributions in a wider population in order to determine whether they are similar in distributions or whether some types or preferences are over- or underrepresented. If a group of leaders reports 25% ISTJ, it needs to be determined what the percentage of ISTJs is in that culture or in that organization in order to know how to interpret these data. For example, if a culture as a whole has 50% of its people reporting ISTJ, we would interpret the leader percentage of 25% as indicating that ISTJs were less likely to be in leadership positions than one would expect, based on their presence in the overall population. If, on the other hand, the culture as a whole seems to have about 10% of its population reporting ISTJ, then we would interpret the leaders' types as indicating that ISTJ tends to be preferred in leadership positions over other types.

Some researchers report such comparisons with a number referred to as the *self-selection ratio*, which is a comparison of the percentage of a particular type in a sample group to the percentage of the same type in a base group. Such a numerical comparison allows the researcher to indicate the statistical significance of any difference found between the percentage of a particular type in leadership and the percentage of that same type in some population group used for comparison.

In the absence of such information from the person reporting the type distribution, those interpreting type tables need to remember to assess the data with such comparisons in mind. Because of this, the type tables in this chapter will begin with attempts by researchers to estimate type distributions in general populations. These data can be used to assess whether a particular distribution of leaders and managers seems to be indicating a pattern of selection of certain preferences or combinations of preferences into these roles. Tables 2 through 8 display type percentages for groups ranging from college students to business managers and school administrators.

DISCUSSION

The tables in this chapter reveal patterns in the majority types of managers and leaders. One pattern, in particular, is consistently reported in Tables 2 through 8 and in other research:

- Thinking and Judging types (ISTJ, INTJ, ESTJ, and ENTJ) are in the majority in management across a variety of cultures and types of organizations.

This overrepresentation of the Thinking and Judging combination remains consistent, even in professions or organizations that are oriented toward service to people such as schools and various social service agencies.

The Prevalence of Thinking and Judging

The clear majorities and overrepresentation of Thinking and Judging leaders and managers in most samples seem to indicate that the structure and values of organizations favor the logical and decisive behaviors most comfortable to those preferring Thinking and Judging, but are less natural or comfortable to the three other comparable combinations of preferences—Feeling and Judging, Feeling and Perceiving, and Thinking and Perceiving. Because the Thinking and Judging types are so prevalent in organizational leadership, it may be that Thinking and Judging behaviors have become the accepted definition of what it means to lead, and, therefore, people displaying these behaviors are seen as "leadership material." Other styles of leading may then not be seen as "leadership" because they do not fit the standard definition. Some experts have suggested that changing requirements and expectations of leaders in the present—such as describing the leader

TABLE 2 Males: College Graduates (*N* = 6814)

Sensing		Intuition				N	%
Thinking	Feeling	Feeling	Thinking				

ISTJ	ISFJ	INFJ	INTJ
n = 1210	n = 293	n = 238	n = 671
% = 17.76	% = 4.30	% = 3.49	% = 9.85
■■■■■	■■■■	■■■	■■■■■
■■■■■			■■■■■
■■■■■			
■■■			

ISTP	ISFP	INFP	INTP
n = 217	n = 115	n = 337	n = 418
% = 3.18	% = 1.69	% = 4.95	% = 6.18
■■■	■■	■■■■■	■■■■■
		■	■

ESTP	ESFP	ENFP	ENTP
n = 183	n = 99	n = 391	n = 357
% = 2.69	% = 1.45	% = 5.74	% = 5.24
■■■	■	■■■■■	■■■■■
		■	

ESTJ	ESFJ	ENFJ	ENTJ
n = 1025	n = 239	n = 272	n = 749
% = 15.04	% = 3.51	% = 3.99	% = 10.99
■■■■■	■■■■	■■■■	■■■■■
■■■■■			■■■■■
■■■■■			■

Judgment — Introversion — Perception — Perception — Extraversion — Judgment

Note. ■ = 1% of sample   8631509

	N	%
E	3315	48.65
I	3499	51.35
S	3381	49.62
N	3433	50.38
T	4830	70.88
F	1984	29.12
J	4697	68.93
P	2117	31.07
IJ	2412	35.40
IP	1087	15.95
EP	1030	15.12
EJ	2285	33.53
ST	2635	38.67
SF	746	10.95
NF	1238	18.17
NT	2195	32.21
SJ	2767	40.61
SP	614	9.01
NP	1503	22.06
NJ	1930	28.32
TJ	3655	53.64
TP	1175	17.24
FP	942	13.82
FJ	1042	15.29
IN	1664	24.42
EN	1769	25.96
IS	1835	26.93
ES	1546	22.69
ET	2314	33.96
EF	1001	14.69
IF	983	14.43
IT	2516	36.92
S dom	1785	26.20
N dom	1657	24.32
T dom	2409	35.35
F dom	1963	14.13

This table is one of a series of tables from the CAPT-MBTI Data Bank of MBTI records submitted to CAPT for computer scoring between 1971 and December 1982. The subjects were males who, at the time of testing, were 25 years of age and older, not enrolled in school and had completed four years of college. This sample was drawn from 55,971 Form F records and 32,671 Form G records. These two data banks were comprised of 56% females and 44% males; education level completed: 6% some grade school, 30% high school diploma, 25% some college, 18% bachelor degrees, 11% masters degrees, 3% doctoral or postdoctoral work, and 6% unknown. Age group percentages were: 11% under 18, 29% 18 to 20, 12% 21 to 24, 10% 25 to 29, 16% 30 to 39, 10% 40 to 49, 5% 50 to 59, 2% 60 plus, and 5% unknown.

From *Atlas of Type Tables,* by G. P. Macdaid, M. H. McCaulley, and R. I. Kainz, 1986, Gainesville, Florida: Center for Applications of Psychological Type. Copyright 1986 by Center for Applications of Psychological Type. Reprinted with permission.

TABLE 3 Females: College Graduates (N = 7952)

	Sensing		Intuition			N	%
Thinking	Feeling	Feeling	Thinking				

ISTJ	ISFJ	INFJ	INTJ		E	3935	49.48
n = 855	n = 869	n = 562	n = 486		I	4017	50.52
% = 10.75	% = 10.93	% = 7.07	% = 6.11		S	3721	46.79
■■■■■	■■■■■	■■■■■	■■■■■		N	4231	53.21
■■■■■	■■■■■	■■	■		T	3416	42.96
■	■				F	4536	57.04
					J	5371	67.54
					P	2581	32.46
ISTP	ISFP	INFP	INTP				
n = 128	n = 214	n = 608	n = 295		IJ	2772	34.86
% = 1.61	% = 2.69	% = 7.65	% = 3.71		IP	1245	15.66
■■	■■■	■■■■■	■■■■		EP	1336	16.80
		■■■			EJ	2599	32.68
					ST	1748	21.98
					SF	1973	24.81
ESTP	ESFP	ENFP	ENTP		NF	2563	32.23
n = 84	n = 208	n = 729	n = 315		NT	1668	20.98
% = 1.06	% = 2.62	% = 9.17	% = 3.96				
■	■■■	■■■■■	■■■■		SJ	3087	38.82
		■■■■			SP	634	7.97
					NP	1947	24.48
					NJ	2284	28.72
					TJ	2594	32.62
ESTJ	ESFJ	ENFJ	ENTJ		TP	822	10.34
n = 681	n = 682	n = 664	n = 572		FP	1759	22.12
% = 8.56	% = 8.58	% = 8.35	% = 7.19		FJ	2777	34.92
■■■■■	■■■■■	■■■■■	■■■■■				
■■■■	■■■■	■■■	■■		IN	1951	24.53
					EN	2280	28.67
					IS	2066	25.98
					ES	1655	20.81

Note. ■ = 1% of sample   8631516

ET	1652	20.77	
EF	2283	28.71	
IF	2253	28.33	
IT	1764	22.18	

This table is one of a series of tables from the CAPT-MBTI Data Bank of MBTI records submitted to CAPT for computer scoring between 1971 and December 1982. The subjects were females who, at the time of testing, were 25 years of age and older, not enrolled in school and had completed four years of college. This sample was drawn from 55,971 Form F records and 32,671 Form G records. These two data banks were comprised of 56% females and 44% males; education level completed: 6% some grade school, 30% high school diploma, 25% some college, 18% bachelor degrees, 11% masters degrees, 3% doctoral or postdoctoral work, and 6% unknown. Age group percentages were: 11% under 18, 29% 18 to 20, 12% 21 to 24, 10% 25 to 29, 16% 30 to 39, 10% 40 to 49, 5% 50 to 59, 2% 60 plus, and 5% unknown.

S dom	2016	25.35
N dom	2092	26.31
T dom	1676	21.08
F dom	2168	27.26

From *Atlas of Type Tables,* by G. P. Macdaid, M. H. McCaulley, and R. I. Kainz, 1986, Gainesville, Florida: Center for Applications of Psychological Type. Copyright 1986 by Center for Applications of Psychological Type. Reprinted with permission.

TABLE 4 Managerial Type Table Compared to Male High School Students' Type Table With Selection Ratio Index (*I*)

The Sixteen Complete Types

ISTJ	ISFJ	INFJ	INTJ
n = 1115 % = 14.9 I = 1.71*** ■ ■ ■ ■ ■ ■ ■ ■ ■ ■ ■ ■ ■ ■ ■	n = 469 % = 6.3 I = 1.40*** ■ ■ ■ ■ ■ ■	n = 232 % = 3.1 I = 1.94*** ■ ■ ■	n = 421 % = 5.6 I = 1.53*** ■ ■ ■ ■ ■ ■
ISTP	ISFP	INFP	INTP
n = 201 % = 2.7 I = 0.44*** ■ ■ ■	n = 189 % = 2.5 I = 0.49*** ■ ■ ■	n = 340 % = 4.6 I = 1.31** ■ ■ ■ ■ ■	n = 267 % = 3.6 I = 0.75*** ■ ■ ■ ■
ESTP	ESFP	ENFP	ENTP
n = 202 % = 2.7 I = 0.30*** ■ ■ ■	n = 209 % = 2.8 I = 0.39*** ■ ■ ■	n = 517 % = 6.9 I = 1.16* ■ ■ ■ ■ ■ ■ ■	n = 365 % = 4.9 I = 0.76*** ■ ■ ■ ■ ■
ESTJ	ESFJ	ENFJ	ENTJ
n = 1272 % = 17.0 I = 1.00 ■ ■ ■ ■ ■ ■ ■ ■ ■ ■ ■ ■ ■ ■ ■ ■ ■	n = 546 % = 7.3 I = 0.89 ■ ■ ■ ■ ■ ■ ■	n = 367 % = 4.9 I = 1.73*** ■ ■ ■ ■ ■	n = 751 % = 10.1 I = 1.89*** ■ ■ ■ ■ ■ ■ ■ ■ ■ ■

Note. N = 7463 ■ = 1% of N I = Selection Ratio Index
*p<.05 **p<.01 ***p<.001

Dichotomous Preferences

E	4229	56.7	***I=0.92
I	3234	43.3	***I=1.14
S	4203	56.3	***I=0.85
N	3260	43.7	***I=1.28
T	4594	61.6	I=1.01
F	2869	38.4	I=0.99
J	5173	69.3	***I=1.33
P	2290	30.7	***I=0.64

Pairs and Temperaments

IJ	2237	30.0	***I=1.62
IP	997	13.4	***I=0.68
EP	1293	17.3	***I=0.61
EJ	2936	39.3	***I=1.18
ST	2790	37.4	***I=0.92
SF	1413	18.9	***I=0.76
NF	1456	19.5	***I=1.40
NT	1804	24.2	***I=1.20
SJ	3402	45.6	***I=1.18
SP	801	10.7	***I=0.39
NP	1489	20.0	I=0.97
NJ	1771	23.7	***I=1.76
TJ	3559	47.7	***I=1.37
TP	1035	13.9	***I=0.53
FP	1255	16.8	***I=0.77
FJ	1614	21.6	***I=1.26
IN	1260	16.9	***I=1.24
EN	2000	26.8	***I=1.30
IS	1974	26.5	*I=1.08
ES	2229	29.9	***I=0.72
ET	2590	34.7	I=n.a.
EF	1639	22.0	I=n.a.
IF	1230	16.5	I=n.a.
IT	2004	26.9	I=n.a.

Jungian Types (E)			Jungian Types (I)			Dominant Types		
	N	% Index		N	% Index		N	% Index
E-TJ	2034	27.1 n.a.	I-TP	468	6.2 n.a.	Dt.T	2491	33.4 n.a.
E-FJ	913	12.2 n.a.	I-FP	529	7.1 n.a.	Dt.F	1442	19.3 n.a.
ES-P	411	5.5 n.a.	IS-J	1584	21.2 n.a.	Dt.S	1995	26.7 n.a.
EN-P	882	11.8 n.a.	IS-J	653	8.7 n.a.	Dt.N	1535	20.6 n.a.

From "Psychological Type and Management Research: A Review," by Christa Walck, 1992, *Journal of Psychological Type, 24*, p. 18. Copyright 1992 by *Journal of Psychological Type.* Reprinted with permission.

TABLE 5 *Myers-Briggs Type Indicator* Percentages for Managers in Business and Industry in the United States

	ISTJ	ISFJ	INFJ	INTJ
A Managers	14.9	6.3	3.1	5.6
B Retail	26.3 +	2.2	0.3	3.2
C Banking	16.9	3.8	1.1	4.9
D Executives	10.4	0.0	1.5	10.4

	ISTP	ISFP	INFP	INTP
A Managers	2.7	2.5	4.6	3.6
B Retail	1.3	0.3	0.0	1.6
C Banking	3.8	2.1	2.8	3.3
D Executives	0.0	0.0	1.5	10.4

	ESTP	ESFP	ENFP	ENTP
A Managers	2.7	2.8	6.9	4.9
B Retail	2.5	1.0	0.3	1.6
C Banking	4.2	2.0	3.7	6.6
D Executives	3.0	1.5	7.5	10.4

	ESTJ	ESFJ	ENFJ	ENTJ
A Managers	17.0	7.3	4.9	10.1
B Retail	46.5 +	2.5	0.3	10.1
C Banking	25.5 +	6.6	2.9	9.7
D Executives	16.4	1.5	4.5	20.9 +

Note. Numbers preceding bar graphs represent the percent of the sample falling in that type. In bar graphs, one inch represents 20% of sample. If percentage exceeds 20%, a + follows the bar.

Note.
A. A composite group of managers and administrators (*N* = 7,463)
B. Managers in a national chain of retail stores (*N* = 316)
C. A composite group of financial managers and bank officers (*N* = 756)
D. Executives (*N* = 67)

From *Atlas of Type Tables,* by G. P. Macdaid, M. H. McCaulley, and R. I. Kainz, 1986, Gainesville, Florida: Center for Applications of Psychological Type. Copyright 1986 by Center for Applications of Psychological Type. Reprinted with permission.

TABLE 6 *Myers-Briggs Type Indicator* Percentages for Managers in Business and Industry in Japan, England, and Latin America

	ISTJ	ISFJ	INFJ	INTJ
A Japan	7.1	7.1	1.8	12.5
B Japan	5.9	4.2	1.7	16.1
C England	23.8 +	6.5	2.4	6.5
D Latin Am.	28.6 +	1.5	0.0	7.3

	ISTP	ISFP	INFP	INTP
A Japan	0.0	3.6	0.0	3.6
B Japan	0.8	1.7	0.0	2.5
C England	4.4	1.2	3.1	2.9
D Latin Am.	2.8	0.0	1.0	1.0

	ESTP	ESFP	ENFP	ENTP
A Japan	10.7	5.4	7.1	3.6
B Japan	8.5	5.9	4.2	2.5
C England	3.9	1.2	2.9	4.2
D Latin Am.	4.4	0.5	1.5	1.9

	ESTJ	ESFJ	ENFJ	ENTJ
A Japan	19.6	3.6	3.6	10.7
B Japan	21.2 +	5.1	3.4	16.1
C England	20.7 +	5.9	1.6	8.8
D Latin Am.	39.3 +	1.0	2.9	6.3

Note. Numbers preceding bar graphs represent the percent of the sample falling in that type. In bar graphs one inch represents 20% of sample. If percentage exceeds 20%, a + follows the bar. Data summarized from published and unpublished sources described in the text.

Note.
A. "Top managers" in large Japanese companies (N = 56)
B. Chief executives of "Japan's leading companies" (N = 118)
C. Managers in England (N = 849)
D. Latin American managers in Center for Creative Leadership programs (N = 206)

From *Atlas of Type Tables,* by G. P. Macdaid, M. H. McCaulley, and R. I. Kainz, 1986, Gainesville, Florida: Center for Applications of Psychological Type. Copyright 1986 by Center for Applications of Psychological Type. Reprinted with permission.

TABLE 7 *Myers-Briggs Type Indicator* Percentages for Consultants to Organizations (*N* = 192)

Sensing		Intuition			N	%
Thinking	Feeling	Feeling	Thinking			

ISTJ	ISFJ	INFJ	INTJ
n = 18	n = 8	n = 10	n = 12
% = 9.38	% = 4.17	% = 5.21	% = 6.25
■■■■■ ■■■■	■■■■	■■■■■	■■■■■ ■

ISTP	ISFP	INFP	INTP
n = 3	n = 3	n = 12	n = 7
% = 1.56	% = 1.56	% = 6.25	% = 3.65
■■	■■	■■■■■ ■	■■■■

ESTP	ESFP	ENFP	ENTP
n = 7	n = 3	n = 22	n = 16
% = 3.65	% = 1.56	% = 11.46	% = 8.33
■■■■	■■	■■■■■ ■■■■■ ■	■■■■■ ■■■

ESTJ	ESFJ	ENFJ	ENTJ
n = 16	n = 9	n = 22	n = 24
% = 8.33	% = 4.69	% = 11.46	% = 12.50
■■■■■ ■■■	■■■■■	■■■■■ ■■■■■ ■	■■■■■ ■■■■■ ■■■

Side labels: Judgment / Perception (Introversion); Perception / Judgment (Extraversion)

	N	%
E	119	61.98
I	73	38.02
S	67	34.90
N	125	65.10
T	103	53.65
F	89	46.35
J	119	61.98
P	73	38.02
IJ	48	25.00
IP	25	13.02
EP	48	25.00
EJ	71	36.98
ST	44	22.92
SF	23	11.98
NF	66	34.38
NT	59	30.73
SJ	51	26.56
SP	16	8.33
NP	57	29.69
NJ	68	35.42
TJ	70	36.46
TP	33	17.19
FP	40	20.83
FJ	49	25.52
IN	41	21.35
EN	84	43.75
IS	32	16.67
ES	35	18.23
ET	63	32.81
EF	56	29.17
IF	33	17.19
IT	40	20.83
S dom	36	18.75
N dom	60	31.25
T dom	50	26.04
F dom	46	23.96

Note. ■ = 1% of sample   8629302

This table is one of a series of tables from the CAPT-MBTI Data Bank of MBTI records submitted to CAPT for computer scoring between 1971 and June 1984. This sample was drawn from 59,784 records with useable occupational codes from the total data bank of 232,557. This data bank has 51% Form F cases from 1971 to March 1978, 35% Form F cases from 1978 to June, 1984 and 14% Form G cases from 1978 to December, 1982. An analysis of Form F and G data banks were comprised of 56% females and 44% males; education level completed: 6% some grade school, 30% high school diploma, 25% some college, 18% bachelor degrees, 11% masters degrees, 3% doctoral or postdoctoral work, and 6% unknown. Age group percentages were: 11% under 18, 29% 18 to 20, 12% 21 to 24, 10% 25 to 29, 16% 30 to 39, 10% 40 to 49, 5% 50 to 59, 2% 60 plus, and 5% unknown.

From *Atlas of Type Tables,* by G. P. Macdaid, M. H. McCaulley, and R. I. Kainz, 1986, Gainesville, Florida: Center for Applications of Psychological Type. Copyright 1986 by Center for Applications of Psychological Type. Reprinted with permission.

TABLE 8 MBTI Types for Participants in the CCI's Leadership Development Program in Percentages (N = 26,477)

ISTJ	ISFJ	INFJ	INTJ
18.2	3.1	1.7	10.5
ISTP	ISFP	INFP	INTP
3.5	1.1	2.5	6.9
ESTP	ESFP	ENFP	ENTP
3.4	1.2	4.5	8.0
ESTJ	ESFJ	ENFJ	ENTJ
16.0	3.2	3.0	13.1
E: 52.5	S: 49.6	T: 79.6	J: 68.9
I: 47.5	N: 50.3	F: 20.4	P: 31.1

From "The Relationship Between the MBTI and Measures of Personality and Performance in Management Groups," by John W. Fleenor, Chapter 4 in this volume. Reprinted with permission.

as "coach" or as "meaning maker," or choosing a team member as a leader—may lead to increasing numbers of other type combinations in leadership.

Types of Women in Management and Leadership

The major difference in type distributions of men and women in the general population is on the Thinking–Feeling dimension. In the United States, about 65% of males typically report a preference for Thinking on this dimension, while only about 35% of females report a preference for Thinking. Though the percentages differ in other cultures, the pattern of males reporting a preference for Thinking that is 20%+ higher than that of females remains consistent (Kirby & Barger, 1996).

Reports on the types of women in management sometimes show a greater percentage of Feeling types than in male management groups, but typically Thinking is preferred by a majority of women (McCaulley, 1992).

Types in Studies of Managers Outside the United States

Studies of MBTI types of leaders and managers in countries and cultures outside the United States show trends similiar to those seen in samples of U.S. managers (see Table 6). Thinking–Judging appears to be the most common type preference combination in large samples of managers from a wide variety of cultures (for further information on MBTI studies of managers and organizations outside the U.S., see Kirby & Barger, "Multiculturalism" in Hammer, 1996).

Management Trends in Sensing and Intuition

Some studies report a statistically significant increase in preferences for Intuition at higher management levels in organizations. This trend, while statistically significant, is slight, and type tables of chief executives still typically show at least a slight majority of Sensing types.

It may be that behaviors and skills natural to Intuition—such as future vision and long-range planning—are seen by organizations as particularly valuable at higher levels in organizations. Intuitive types more naturally deal with broader issues, which can also be seen by organizations as "leader" behavior. Correspondingly, the practical, present-oriented focus of Sensing types may be seen as more relevant to the tasks of managers responsible for the day-to-day tasks of the organization.

Impacts of Type Distributions of Leaders and Managers

The consistency of the patterns described above—across cultures and different kinds of organizations—tends to support the validity of the MBTI and the significance of psychological type as an explanatory pattern for human behavior. These patterns also raise some issues for organizations, leaders, and consultants who work with them.

Group Imbalance

Psychological type asserts that every type is valuable and has essential contributions to make. From a type perspective, then, groups such as leaders and managers would ideally consist of a variety of types, all valued for their particular kinds of contributions to the organization.

When groups show a significant imbalance in their type preferences, as do the samples of managers and leaders shown in the tables here, there is a tendency for some of the following effects to occur as a result of the group imbalance:

- The dominant types have a great deal of influence on how "reality" is defined.
- Dominant type individuals tend not to see a need to modify their expressions of their type preferences, and may, in fact, exaggerate them.
- The group may verbalize and demonstrate a definite bias for the imbalance and see no need for the other preferences.
- People of minority types—even those who have learned to deal successfully with differences in one-on-one collegial relationships—may be annoyed and angry at dominant type characteristics, and may resent not being able to be themselves.
- Those who do not share the dominant type may mask their true preferences and unconsciously adapt their style to match the style of the majority; then the individual(s) and the group run the risk of losing the real strength of those preferences.

These effects of group type imbalance are similar to the effects of other types of group imbalance, such as that which occurs as a result of gender and ethnicity. What is missing in all these cases is the diversity of perspective that can help organizational leaders gather more diverse information and make more balanced decisions.

The Overrepresentation of TJ Managers and Leaders

Based on quantitative and qualitative research, those with a preference for Thinking and Judging typically display some of the following strengths related to the tasks of managing and leading:

- Focusing on creating order and structure in the organization and its processes
- Using logic to quickly analyze problems and arrive at decisions
- Moving to implement decisions quickly
- Focusing on tasks
- Emphasizing efficiency and completion

Thinking Judging types may pay less attention to—and be less skilled at—some other valuable behaviors related to managing and leading. For example, they may demonstrate the following weaknesses in relating to colleagues or to those they supervise:

- Not soliciting information and perspectives from others who are affected by the problem
- Not including others in the process of structuring and organizing

They may also compromise their effectiveness by the following tendencies:

- Sometimes making decisions before they have gathered enough information from enough sources
- Moving to action so quickly that others feel they are being steamrollered

The Underrepresentation of the Feeling Preference in Leadership and Management

People with a preference for Feeling are in a minority in management and leadership. The strengths of leaders and managers that we would expect to see in those with a preference for Feeling are the following:

- Focussing on meeting and supporting the needs of people, both employees and customers
- Including others in the processes of information gathering and decision making
- Evaluating alternatives by the values of an organization, a culture, and the people in it
- Evaluating alternatives by the impacts they will have on those involved
- Working for consensus and win–win decisions
- Feeling comfortable in the role of "coach" and persuader rather than "boss"

Because of the small percentage of leaders and managers with a Feeling preference in most groups and the effects brought about by this imbalance, these natural strengths and perspectives of Feeling types may be missing or, when they exist, may be ignored.

As would be expected, leaders who prefer Feeling also have potential blind spots, including:

- Avoiding conflict
- Needing consensus before making decisions—even when that is not possible

- Feeling overwhelmed by the emotions of people impacted by decisions or external events
- Overpersonalizing decisions
- Focusing on the needs of people to the detriment of long-range, strategic plans and decisions

Most organizations have so few leaders with a preference for Feeling that what is obvious at the present time is the absence of the positive potential of the Feeling perspective. This issue and possible solutions to the dilemmas it creates have been discussed by many leadership development practitioners (see Chapter 2 in this book).

Cautions in Applying Group Data to Individuals

In interpreting all of these discussion comments and the tables in this chapter, it is important to remember the perspective introduced at the beginning of this chapter. *First,* common characteristics of types and type combinations are derived from groups. Individuals within these groups will most often display some of the characteristics of the particular type preferences, but there are many factors outside psychological type preference that influence an individual's style of leadership or management. Individuals within a particular type normally demonstrate a wide variety of behaviors and skills. Type analysis, while insightful, identifies only group patterns.

Second, psychological type preferences do not directly indicate skills and abilities. For example, some Intuitive types do not use their Intuition well, while some Sensing types may have developed their skills in areas normally associated with Intuition. The MBTI was not designed to assess the level of skill with which an individual uses a preference, and MBTI results will not be a reliable indicator of skills and abilities.

Third, the type development process also influences how any individual will experience and express type preferences. People at different stages of life and of psychological growth may demonstrate quite different use of the same preferences.

Because of these factors, it is unwise, as well as unethical, to use MBTI results or even an individual's verification of type preferences to select people for particular positions. Group type data provide interesting information about group patterns, but they should not be applied directly to any individual.

A Psychological Type Perspective
on One-Sided Groups

Isabel Briggs Myers summarized the goal of psychological type knowledge as constructively using the normal differences in people defined by psychological type and indicated by the MBTI. Her belief was that this approach to differences was ethically and morally right and would lead to more effective functioning for individuals and organizations. Type distributions of managers and leaders indicate some of the challenges organizations face in using differences to create stronger and more effective workforces and leadership.

A FINAL NOTE

Our most fundamental reason for undertaking this book is our own experience of using the MBTI in decades of work with groups and individuals. We have found the perspective, knowledge, and values of the MBTI remarkably useful to us and our clients. These understandings have enhanced our work and personal lives, and we are convinced that they have the potential to make a real difference to leaders, managers, and employees in many types of organizations. We hope that the information in this book will make your work and personal development more productive and enjoyable.

REFERENCES

Hammer, A. L. (Ed). (1996). *Research supplement to the MBTI manual*. Palo Alto, CA: Consulting Psychologists Press.

Hammer, A. L., & Yeakley, F. R., Jr. (1987). The relationship between "true type" and reported type. *Journal of Psychological Type, 13*, 52–55.

Hirsh, S. K. (1992). *MBTI team building program*. Palo Alto, CA: Consulting Psychologists Press.

Hirsh, S. K., & Kummerow, J. M. (1989). *LIFETypes*. New York: Warner Books.

Hirsh, S. K., & Kummerow, J. M. (1990). *Introduction to type in organizations*. Palo Alto, CA: Consulting Psychologists Press.

Kirby, L. K., & Barger, N. J. (1996). Multiculturalism. In Hammer, A. L. (Ed.), *Research supplement to the MBTI manual*. Palo Alto, CA: Consulting Psychologists Press.

Kummerow, J. (1988). A methodology for verifying type: Research results. *Journal of Psychological Type, 15*, 20–25.

Macdaid, G. P., McCaulley, M. H., & Kainz, R. I. (1986). *Myers-Briggs Type Indicator atlas of type tables*. Gainesville, FL: Center for Applications of Psychological Type.

McCaulley, M. H. (1990). The Myers-Briggs Type Indicator and leadership. In K. E. Clark and M. B. Clark (Eds.), *Measures of leadership,* pp. 381–418. West Orange, NJ: Leadership Library of America.

McCaulley, M. H. (Spring 1992). Asking the right questions. *Bulletin of Psychological Type, 15:2,* pp.1, 5–6.

Myers, I. B., with Myers, P. B. (1980). *Gifts differing.* Palo Alto, CA: Consulting Psychologists Press.

Myers, I. B. (1993). *Introduction to type* (5th edition). Palo Alto, CA: Consulting Psychologists Press.

Myers, I. B., & McCaulley, M. H. (1985). *Manual: A guide to the development and use of the Myers-Briggs Type Indicator.* Palo Alto, CA: Consulting Psychologists Press.

Walck, C. L. (1992). Psychological type and management research: A review. *Journal of Psychological Type, 24,* 13–23.

FURTHER READING

For additional information about type distributions, the most complete source is the data bank of the Center for Applications of Psychological Type (CAPT) in Gainesville, Florida. Many of these data are collected and reported in the *Atlas of Type Tables.*

The *Journal of Psychological Type,* edited by Tom Carskadon and published at Mississippi State University, includes numerous articles about type distributions in a variety of management groups and cultures.

The most comprehensive discussion of leaders, managers, and type distributions in different cultures is in a paper delivered by Mary McCaulley for the Conference on Psychological Measures and Leadership and printed in *Measures of Leadership.*

2 | The MBTI and Leadership Development

Personality and Leadership Reconsidered in Changing Times

Catherine Fitzgerald

The following are assumptions about the current state of application and research on the *Myers-Briggs Type Indicator* (MBTI) and leadership and leadership development:

- The MBTI is being very widely used in the area of leadership and leadership development in the United States and internationally.
- The five-factor model of personality is beginning to influence leadership research and practice, and most researchers and practitioners, even those familiar with the MBTI, are unaware of the relationship between the MBTI and the Big Five and do not understand the implications behind the differing philosophies that underlie the MBTI versus more traditional five-factor instruments.
- At first glance, the MBTI appears to be a simple instrument, and can indeed be used in fairly basic ways (e.g., giving managers some interesting information about their problem-solving and decision-making styles; providing a context for deriving strategies for more effective interpersonal interactions). However, the theory underlying the MBTI—the theory of psychological type—is one of the most coherent and comprehensive theories of individual difference and individual development and has components that could make an invaluable contribution to leadership development application and

research. These components are largely unknown and unexploited by practitioners and researchers.

The purpose of this chapter is to revisit the issue of leadership and personality and to look at the MBTI and its use in leadership development in the context of currently occurring and widely anticipated changes in organizations, and in the leadership that organizations require. Specifically, this chapter:

* Articulates the potential usefulness of a coherent framework for understanding personality in relationship to leadership and describes progress toward an overriding model of personality
* Describes the relationship between the MBTI and the five-factor model
* Identifies the unique characteristics of the MBTI and the theory of psychological type and describes how these unique characteristics offer promise for enhanced application and for new approaches to research

LEADERSHIP AND PERSONALITY

Reviewers of the extensive literature on leadership and personality (e.g., Bass, 1981; McCall & Lombardo, 1978; Yukl & Van Fleet, 1992) have typically expressed disappointment, or even dismay, about the array of confusing and contradictory results and have detailed once widely pursued but now outmoded approaches (e.g., the pursuit of the characteristics of the "great man"). Research in personality generally has also had a checkered recent history, as the earlier search for robust personality characteristics was deflated in the 1960s by influential research that found substantial impacts of the situation, but not of personality dispositions (Mischel, 1968).

The Emergence of the Five-Factor Model

In the last 10 years or so, however, with the emergence of the Big Five model of personality, there has been a rekindling of interest in and research on personality, with research findings that are beginning to influence thought and practice in many applied fields (e.g., Barrick & Mount, 1991; Hogan, 1994; Miller, 1991), including the field of leadership and leadership development (e.g., Hogan, Curphy, & Hogan,

1994). The development of the five-factor model has resulted in substantial agreement about five key "domains" of normal human difference. In a remarkable history of the emergence and testing of the five-factor model, Goldberg (1993) concluded:

> It might be argued that the hallmark of a compelling structural model is that it is initially disliked, thereby stimulating numerous attempts to replace it with something more attractive—all of which fail. In any case, so it has been with the Big Five model of perceived personality trait descriptors. Most of the present proponents of the model were once its critics, and some of its present critics contributed to its success. (p. 27)

Perhaps the most influential and extensively researched version of the five-factor model is the five NEO-PI factors (Costa & McCrae, 1992), which are presented in Table 1, along with examples of the traits associated with each.

The Development of the MBTI

During the time that personality research was losing and regaining favor, the MBTI was being developed, refined, researched, and, later, applied—in relative isolation from the mainstream of traditional personality research. The relative isolation has been linked to the following factors:

- The MBTI was theory based at a time when an atheoretical, empirical approach to psychological test development was in favor.
- The theory underlying the MBTI was based on the work of Carl Jung, who has been viewed as very far removed from the mainstream of psychological research and theory.
- The MBTI was not developed by psychologists.

Although there has been more than 50 years of research on the MBTI (Myers & McCaulley, 1985) and the MBTI is widely used in a variety of settings (e.g., counseling, leadership development, team development), until very recently it was virtually unknown to most academic researchers. Even academic researchers who are familiar with the MBTI are often unaware of the depth and breadth of the research on the reliability and validity of the instrument. (See Chapter 1 for a definition of the MBTI dimensions; the history of the MBTI and its underlying theory; and reliability, validity, and interpretation information.)

TABLE 1 Examples of Traits From the Five NEO-PI Factors

Neuroticism	Extraversion
Calm — Worrying	Reserved — Affectionate
Even tempered — Temperamental	Loner — Joiner
Self-satisfied — Self-pitying	Quiet — Talkative
Comfortable — Self-conscious	Passive — Active
Unemotional — Emotional	Sober — Fun/Loving
Hardy — Vulnerable	Unfeeling — Passionate
Openness	**Agreeableness**
Down-to-earth — Imaginative	Ruthless — Soft-hearted
Uncreative — Creative	Suspicious — Trusting
Conventional — Original	Stingy — Generous
Prefer routine — Prefer variety	Antagonistic — Acquiescent
Uncurious — Curious	Critical — Lenient
Conservative — Liberal	Irritable — Good-natured
Conscientiousness	
Negligent — Conscientious	
Lazy — Hardworking	
Disorganized — Well-organized	
Late — Punctual	
Aimless — Ambitious	
Quitting — Persevering	

From "Personality Stability and Its Implications for Clinical Psychology" by R. R. McCrae and P. T. Costa, Jr., 1986, *Clinical Psychology Review, 6.* Reprinted with kind permission from Elsevier Science Ltd, The Boulevard, Langford Lane, Kidlington OX5 1GB, U.K.

A Remarkable Convergence

In the late 1980s, as part of an ongoing series of research studies exploring the relationship between the NEO-PI and other psychological instruments, McCrae and Costa (1989) researched the relationship between the NEO-PI and the MBTI. They found strikingly high correlations between the MBTI and four of the five NEO-PI factors, as Table 2 illustrates. The correlations between MBTI Extraversion–Introversion and NEO-PI Extraversion and between MBTI Sensing–Intuition and NEO-PI Openness, in particular, were so high that McCrae and Costa pointed out that "corrected for unreliability, they would approach unity" (p. 30).

That there should be such strong agreement between instruments with such different development histories and philosophies is remarkable and seems to provide additional support that these instruments are capturing basic human differences.[1]

Table 2 Correlations of Self-Reported NEO-PI Factors
With MBTI Continuous Scores in Men and Women

MBTI	NEO-PI Factor				
	N	E	O	A	C
Men					
EI	.16**	−.74***	.03	−.03	.08
SN	−.06	.10	.72***	.04	−.15*
TF	.06	.19**	.02	.44***	−.15*
JP	.11	.15*	.30***	−.06	−.49***
Women					
EI	.17*	−.69***	−.03	−.08	.08
SN	.01	.22**	.69***	.03	−.10
TF	.28***	.10	−.02	.46***	−.22***
JP	.04	.20**	.26***	.05	−.46***

Note. N = 267 for men and 201 for women. NEO-PI N = Neuroticism, E = Extraversion, O = Openness to Experience, A = Agreeableness, and C = Conscientiousness
*p < .05, **p < .01, ***p < .001

From "Reinterpreting the Myers-Briggs Type Indicator From the Perspective of the Five-Factor Model of Personality," by R. R. McCrae and P. T. Costa, Jr., 1989, *Journal of Personality, 57,* p. 30. Copyright 1989 by Duke University Press. Reprinted with permission.

THE MBTI'S CONTRIBUTIONS TO LEADERSHIP AND LEADERSHIP DEVELOPMENT

As was suggested earlier, the convergence of research findings, first across empirically derived instruments and then between a major empirically derived instrument and the theory-based MBTI, provides persuasive evidence regarding the basic domains of human difference. The identification of these basic domains of difference provides an opportunity to bring coherence to the understanding of the relationship between personality and many areas of human functioning. In fact, the extensiveness of the research conducted on the MBTI and on the NEO-PI and other five-factor instruments represents a solid foundation for validation, comparison, and further elaboration. One of the most important similarities between the two bodies of research, for example, is the consistent finding that personality in all five domains is remarkably stable over time (McCrae & Costa, 1990; Myers & McCaulley, 1985), a finding that is very consistent with the theory of psychological type.

In spite of their similarities, however, there are substantial differences in the way that the MBTI and empirically derived instruments like the

NEO-PI describe and assess the domains/dimensions of difference and the theory or lack of theory on which they are based. These differences have profound implications for the effectiveness of the use of these instruments in leadership development application and research. Some of the unique characteristics of the MBTI potentially provide valuable solutions to some current and emerging dilemmas and needs in leadership development and organizational change.

These unique characteristics of the MBTI include:

- The MBTI's description of all eight "preferences" (i.e., the two possible choices for each of its four dimensions) in positive terms and the underlying belief that all eight preferences are "normal" and that each makes an invaluable contribution to any human enterprise
- An approach to the administration of the MBTI that presents individual results as "indicators" of the person's preferences and provides a process for individual consideration and validation—a process that considers the individual to be the final judge of his or her type
- The MBTI's dialectical approach to each dimension, which defines two alternative constructs or "preferences" that are psychologically "opposed" (e.g., Extraversion and Introversion)
- A theory of the predictable interplay or dynamics among the preferences, which results in characterizations of 16 distinct types—characterizations that have differential implications for leadership development
- A theory of development that specifies differences in developmental paths and challenges for each of the 16 types and provides guidance on leadership development strategies for different age groups (e.g., younger managers vs. managers in midlife)

Each of these characteristics and their potential implications for leadership and leadership development are discussed below.

Valuing Differences Versus Evaluating Them

Although the MBTI and the NEO-PI deal with the same domains of human difference, one of the most important distinguishing characteristics of the MBTI in relation to the NEO-PI and other personality instruments is its philosophy regarding the valuing of differences. The overriding impetus to the development of the MBTI was the desire to provide everyday people with information and a way of thinking about differences that encouraged them to honor and work well across these differences. The goal of the MBTI is to provide positive descriptions of each preference and each type and to encourage people to understand

TABLE 3   Characteristics Associated With the Eight MBTI Preferences

Extraversion	Introversion
• Attuned to external environment	• Drawn to their inner worlds
• Prefer to communicate by talking	• Prefer to communicate by writing
• Learn best through doing or discussing	• Learn best by reflection, mental "practice"
• Breadth of interests	• Depth of interest
• Tend to speak first, reflect later	• Tend to reflect before acting or speaking
• Sociable and expressive	• Private and contained
• Take initiative in work and relationships	• Focus readily

Sensing	Intuition
• Focus on what is real and actual	• Focus on "big picture," possibilities
• Value practical applications	• Value imaginative insight
• Factual and concrete, notice details	• Abstract and theoretical
• Observe and remember sequentially	• See patterns and meanings in facts
• Present-oriented	• Future-oriented
• Want information step-by-step	• Jump around, leap in anywhere
• Trust experience	• Trust inspiration

Thinking	Feeling
• Analytical	• Sympathetic
• Logical problem-solvers	• Assess impact on people
• Use cause-and-effect reasoning	• Guided by personal values
• "Tough-minded"	• "Tender-hearted"
• Strive for impersonal, objective truth	• Strive for harmony and individual validation
• Reasonable	• Compassionate
• Fair	• Accepting

Judging	Perceiving
• Scheduled	• Spontaneous
• Organized	• Open-ended
• Systematic	• Casual
• Methodical	• Flexible
• Plan	• Adapt
• Like closure—to have things decided	• Like things loose and open to change
• Avoid last-minute stresses	• Feel energized by last-minute pressures

and see the inherent value in each preference and each type (Myers & Myers, 1980). Table 3 contains descriptions of the contrasting characteristics of each set of the four MBTI dimensions.

This focus on positive description versus evaluation presents a contrast to the traditions of psychological testing. No doubt influenced by its origins in the measurement of intelligence (where more is clearly superior to less) and by a dominant focus on identifying pathology (e.g., the *Minnesota Multiphasic Personality Inventory*), the approach of traditional psychological testing has tended to be evaluative in nature and has typically focused on identifying better versus worse attributes. Notwithstanding their focus on normal human differences, the NEO-PI and other five-factor models are still very much affected by the tradition of better versus worse attributes.

For example, as reported earlier, the MBTI Sensing–Intuition dimension and the NEO-PI Openness dimension are strikingly strongly correlated ($r = .74$ in men and .69 in women). However, the ways in which the two instruments frame and interpret their constructs are remarkably different. Consistent with its focus on defining each dimension by two qualitatively different but equally valuable approaches, the MBTI states that those who prefer Sensing "like to take in information through their eyes, ears, and other senses to find out what is actually happening" (Myers, 1993) and that those who prefer Intuition "like to take in information by seeing the big picture, focusing on the relationship and connections between facts" (Myers, 1993).

In contrast, the NEO-PI identifies its construct as "Openness to Experience," with the equivalent of the MBTI Intuition side clearly superior to the MBTI Sensing side. Those who score on the Intuitive side are characterized as imaginative, creative, original, curious, and preferring variety, while those who score on the Sensing side are seen in a much less positive light as uncreative, conventional, uncurious, down-to-earth, and preferring routine (McCrae & Costa, 1986). A contrast between the ways that the MBTI and the NEO-PI characterize differences on all four of the related dimensions can be seen by comparing the contents of Table 1 and Table 3.

That psychologists would have such a positive view of Intuition is not surprising in light of what MBTI research reveals about those of us who choose to become psychologists. Intuitives are disproportionately attracted to the profession of psychology: In contrast to the general U.S. population, of whom about 30%–35% are Intuitive, psychologists as a group are overwhelmingly Intuitive, with studies revealing an Intuitive–Sensing split, of 85% Intuitive and 15% Sensing (Myers & McCaulley, 1985). Psychologists' focus on the positive qualities of

Intuition while underplaying the positive qualities of Sensing was high-lighted by attendance at a session of the 1992 American Psychological Association convention in which a number of five-factor model proponents discussed the varying definitions of the Openness to Experience dimension. Throughout the lengthy, energetic, and thoughtful discussion there was little indication of a recognition of the positive attributes of Sensing. Given the likely distribution on the Sensing–Intuition dimension of the psychologists involved in the discussion, this unrecognized bias is understandable and offers a good example of how differences can, with the best of intentions, be shaded with subtle and not-so-subtle forms of better versus worse attributes. As 65–70% of the population and a majority of managers at all levels (McCaulley, 1990) are Sensing types, it is not surprising that psychologists are sometimes disappointed by their lack of impact on and respect from organizations (e.g., Hogan, Curphy, & Hogan 1994).

The evaluative focus of the five-factor approach has been reflected in the early attempts to apply the five-factor model to areas of practice. In an article about the application of the model to psychotherapy, Miller (1991) asserted that the five-factor model made it possible for the first time for psychologists to "understand the relationship between personality and complex networks of thinking, behavior and feeling" (p. 416). His summary of the status of understanding human differences—without this new framework—sounds remarkably similar to conclusions about the status of the understanding of leadership and personality: "Psychotherapy is difficult to practice and impossible to master because real-world people are astoundingly diverse. Despite the advances in every branch of social science over the past century, the human landscape remains a wilderness" (p. 416). In discussing the application of the five-factor model to psychotherapy, Miller demonstrated the evaluative slant of the five-factor model, characterizing patients who score low on Conscientiousness (i.e., MBTI Perceiving types) as "impervious to therapeutic attempts" (p. 430) and perhaps "represent[ing] one of the absolute limits to the power of psychotherapy" (p. 430). He described patients who scored low on Openness (i.e., MBTI Sensing types) in this way: "They seem unable to fantasize or symbolize; their speech seems boring, pedantic, and overly conventional; and they do not easily understand or accept elementary psychodynamic interpretations" (p. 425). In a similar vein, not surprisingly, the first attempts to apply the five-factor model to leadership and organizational issues (e.g., Barrick

& Mount, 1991; Hogan, Curphy, & Hogan 1994) have focused primarily on the evaluation-focused issues of personnel selection and leadership selection.

As they continue their research, it is interesting to note that some five-factor researchers are struggling with their evaluative perspective—and discovering some qualitative differences within their dimensions. In discussing the NEO-PI Extraversion dimension, for example, Costa and McCrae (1992) explained:

> While it is easy to convey the characteristics of the extravert, the introvert is less easy to portray. In some respects, introversion should be seen as the absence of extraversion rather than what might be assumed to be its opposite. Thus, introverts are reserved rather than unfriendly, independent rather than followers, even-paced rather than sluggish. Introverts may say they are shy when they mean that they prefer to be alone: they do not necessarily suffer from social anxiety. Finally, although they are not given to the exuberant high spirits of extraverts, introverts are not unhappy or pessimistic. *Curious as some of these distinctions may seem, they are strongly supported by research and form one of the most important conceptual advances of research on a five-factor model* [Emphasis added]. (p. 15)

The Potential Impact of Valuing
Versus Evaluating Differences

A great deal has been written in recent years that describes a major shift in how organizations and their leaders need to function to thrive—and even to survive—in an increasingly fast-paced, technology-driven, globally competitive marketplace (e.g., Drucker, 1993; Handy, 1994; O'Hara-Devereaux & Johansen, 1994; Mitroff & Linstone, 1993). There is widespread agreement that the past organizational focus on high management control, closely held information, narrow roles, decision making concentrated at high levels, and individual achievement is being replaced by a focus on leadership and influence, widely shared information, knowledge and learning as key organizational assets, diversity of people and perspectives, decision making at all levels, and team achievement (Kouzes & Posner, 1993; Lawler, 1992; Pasmore, 1994; Pinchot & Pinchot, 1994; Senge, 1990).

Organizations of the past tended to be slow-moving bureaucratic organizations that operated with a narrow set of organizational "players" (typically white males), with a clear pecking order based primarily on positional power, and with an emphasis on homogeneity and conformity in ways of thinking and behaving. A key element of transforming organizations (and their leaders) involves increasing their capacity to understand, value, and deal well with many dimensions of difference (e.g., gender, race and ethnic origin, age, professional affiliation, organizational function), as well as with the essential human variety represented by the MBTI preferences.

Understanding, valuing, and dealing well with the differences represented by the MBTI as well as other key differences is important because

- The workplace is expected to become increasingly diverse.
- There has been simultaneously enormous expansion in scope (i.e., to global markets) and refinement in focus (i.e., to highly segmented and diverse niche markets) of target markets that need to be understood and served.
- As organizations reduce their staff size and face stiffer competition, there is an increased need for exceptional performance from all staff, and staff whose unique contributions are not recognized and/or who don't feel valued (for whatever reason) are unlikely to perform at their highest level.
- To deal with increasingly complex external environments, organizations have been required to become correspondingly more internally complex, which requires managing well across many dimensions of difference.

The last point regarding the requirement for internal organizational complexity has been increasingly discussed by experts in organizational change and leadership development as external complexity and change have become critical themes in organizational survival. The discussions often reference work done by Ashby (1952) in defining the "law of requisite variety." In a chapter from the book *The Executive Mind,* Fry and Pasmore (1983) addressed the implications that Ashby's law has for executives:

> Ashby's (1952) law of requisite variety states that for a system to survive, it must be capable of adapting to changes in its environment; to do so requires that somewhere within it the system must possess a wide enough variety of behaviors to provide an appropriate response to each significant change. Hence, as the environment of a system becomes more complex, meaning that the environment is changing more rapidly in ways that could threaten the system's survival, the system must also become more complex internally in order to continue to adapt. . . . By virtue of their positions, executives are primarily responsible for ensuring that varieties of internal capabilities are developed in those areas most crucial to the organization's survival. (p. 282)

Although effectively increasing internal organizational complexity involves many components, a perspective on valuing and accommodating differences of many kinds seems essential to obtaining the "requisite" variety.

In the past, organizations have attempted to minimize differences (i.e., by fostering homogeneity of both people and perspectives) or to explicitly or implicitly evaluate them (i.e., by limiting promotion to those with similar characteristics and by establishing clear pecking orders). As organizations attempt to change in the ways that were described earlier, there are a number of key advantages for leaders and organizations of shifting from minimizing or evaluating differences to valuing and making positive use of them.

Use of the MBTI potentially makes a substantial contribution to this shift through, first, its coverage of the basic domains of human difference and, second, its focus on describing and valuing all of the differences that it addresses. Potential advantages of the MBTI to organizations and their leaders include the following:

• By highlighting that we each have a set of personality preferences and that all of the preferences make a critical contribution to organizations, a focus on valuing differences potentially reframes and redirects the frustrating and ill-fated search for the "perfect" leader. In an article on the MBTI and leadership, McCaulley (1992) emphasized this point by asserting that

> we might dream of the perfect leader who will have all the answers, but there are no perfect people and no perfect leaders. There is always room, therefore, for each of us, with our gifts and our imperfections, to make a difference in our changing world. (p. 6)

Abandoning the search for perfection in our leaders might allow us to give up the cycles of hope and disappointment that organizations desperate for leadership are currently experiencing. In addition, a "post-perfection" perspective might allow creative problem solving and experimentation with other approaches, such as the development of complementary top management teams and the crafting of support systems for individual leaders that are tailored to the leader's strengths and limitations.

• An emphasis on valuing differences reinforces the importance of enhanced self-awareness in leaders—awareness that reflects accurate assessments of an individual leader's predispositions, strengths, and blind spots.

- A focus on valuing differences is philosophically and practically consistent with the emphasis on dialogue versus discussion as a critical element of the learning organization (Senge, 1990).
- An emphasis on valuing differences supports the reframing of a manager's role from evaluating staff to developing them—a reframing that is consistent with current thinking about learning organizations, the failure of traditional performance evaluation systems, and the flattening of organizational hierarchies.
- A focus on valuing differences supports the shift from an emphasis on the individual achievement to an emphasis on collaboration and team achievement.

At a more global level, a focus on valuing differences potentially refocuses leadership development to highlight the higher-order skills of managing a complex field of differences. Components of these higher-order skills might include:

- An ongoing search for and articulation of the dimensions of difference that are essential to organizational success (e.g., reality versus vision, control versus flexibility)
- The development of organizational strategies that identify and correct—without overcorrection—imbalances in perspective (e.g., organizations are seeking to become more flexible and "emergent" but must make wise choices about what kinds of planning and control systems to keep, change, or develop to achieve an optimal balance of flexibility and control)
- An understanding of the dynamics of majorities and minorities (e.g., that majorities tend to shape the dominant view of what is acceptable, that minorities may have difficulty having their perspectives heard, that minorities typically have greater insight into the culture of the majority than do more mainstream majority members, that organizational innovation often comes from minority perspectives)

In addition, at a practical level, the focus of the MBTI on valuing and describing differences has led to the compilation and availability of the type distributions of a wide range of occupations and professions (e.g., accountants, lawyers, scientists, secretaries). Organizations and their leaders can use these data as a working "blueprint" of differences and through them can form hypotheses and develop strategies to enhance effective communication and collaboration across internal and external organizational parties.

The MBTI's Focus on Individual
Understanding and Choice

The goal of the MBTI is to make the theory of psychological type "understandable and useful in people's lives" (Myers & McCaulley, 1985). The MBTI was deliberately designed to be accessible to a wide range of people and to focus on the individual. The instrument's somewhat unusual approach to administration and interpretation reflects this focus on the individual. During interpretation of MBTI results, although it is the responsibility of the interpreter of the MBTI to provide information about the instrument and its dimensions, the discussion of MBTI results is always seen as a collaborative exploration between the interpreter and the person who is receiving the results. As the MBTI *Manual* (Myers & McCaulley, 1985) stresses: "The interpreter's role is not to determine the accuracy of the MBTI. The interpreter's task is to provide ways in which respondents can understand their best and most trustworthy way of functioning" (p. 62). The *Manual* also cautions: "As with all psychological instruments, the interpreter should keep in mind that self-report from a limited number of questions, no matter how carefully validated, cannot completely describe any human being" (p. 62). In contrast to the approach used with many other instruments of providing authoritative (or at best, statistically "qualified") results, with the MBTI the individual is considered to be the final judge of his or her results.

The ethics of administering and interpreting the MBTI in organizations, as in other settings, stress the voluntariness and confidentiality of MBTI results and the obligation of the MBTI interpreter to use the MBTI only in situations and settings in which differences can be addressed in a constructive way. It is also the interpreter's obligation to present each preference as equally valuable and to tactfully reframe and counter expressions of bias on the part of managers or staff.

The individual focus and accessibility of the MBTI to people who are not experts in test interpretation was addressed by McCrae and Costa (1989):

> Those who develop and employ personality measures can learn a good deal from the strategies of application that have been used with the MBTI. Decades of experience show that it is possible and sometimes useful to describe personality in lay terms, to teach individuals the nature and value of individual differences, and to increase understanding among people who interact by sharing information on personality and explaining differences in styles. (p. 37)

The Potential Impact of Focusing
on Individual Understanding and Choice

The primary focus on individual understanding and individual control over MBTI results may seem counter to the trend in organizations toward collaboration and teamwork. However, it seems that almost paradoxically, it is this individual focus that has made the MBTI so popular and effective in supporting teamwork. Moreover, the instrument's interpretation focus (i.e., on the individual) and its administration approach (i.e., involving joint interpretation between the interpreter, who brings knowledge of type theory, and the individual, who brings his or her experience and knowledge of self) are consistent with and supportive of important trends within organizations. Among these trends are the following.

First, there is decreasing focus on mere compliance with authority and an increasing value placed on individual initiative and responsibility. The MBTI focus on the individual highlights the ability of individuals to understand themselves, to take responsibility for understanding and dealing with differences, and to learn to interact with others in increasingly skillful ways.

Second, the traditional model of the "expert," who, in communication that is primarily one way, communicates a "diagnosis" and then a solution, is being reframed across many areas of practice, including organization development (e.g., Weisbord, 1991; Bunker & Alban, 1992). The new approach to helping individuals and organizations change focuses on collaboration between practitioners and the individuals and organizations they serve. The collaborative approach to the interpretation of MBTI results is very consistent with this trend.

Third, as teamwork and collaboration become more essential, there is an increasing recognition of the inevitable tension between individual freedom and flexibility and the requirements of coordinated collective action. Experience with effective teamwork suggests that respecting individual contributions and differences is a necessary prelude to collaboration. By giving control of results to individuals, the MBTI supports individual differences, while providing a rich, nonjudgmental platform for communicating about teamwork.

A Theory of Opposites

A key aspect of the theory of psychological type is its focus within each dimension on two different constructs that are in "psychological opposition" to each other. The MBTI *Manual* (Myers & McCaulley, 1985) describes this opposition, in reference to Extraversion and Introversion:

> Jung regarded extraversion and introversion as "mutually complementary" attitudes whose differences "generate the tension that both the individual and society need for the maintenance of life." Extraverts are oriented primarily toward the outer world; thus they tend to focus their perception and judgment on people and objects. Introverts are oriented primarily toward the inner world; thus they tend to focus their perception and judgment upon concepts and ideas. (p. 2)

The concept of the tension of opposites is critical for understanding the MBTI and how it differs from many other psychological instruments, including the five-factor instruments. Using the Sensing–Intuition dimension as an example, type theory asserts that

- Sensing and Intuition are essential aspects of *every* person.
- Sensing and Intuition both involve ways of perceiving the world, but these ways are diametrically opposed, with Sensing focusing on "perceptions observable by way of the senses" and Intuition "focusing on the perceptions of possibilities, meanings, and relationships by way of insight" (Myers & McCaulley, 1985).
- These opposite mental processes *cannot* be used at the same time, although they *can* be used sequentially.
- Individual development involves a natural inclination (called a preference) for either Sensing or Intuition. Unless the environment interferes with the natural inclination, the preferred process will be used more—at the expense of the other—and will over time become more developed, refined, and conscious.

Because of the underlying focus within each MBTI dimension on the tension of opposites, there are subtle but very important differences between the MBTI and the five-factor instruments. Like most other psychological instruments, the NEO-PI, for example, involves "traits that approximate normal, bell-shaped distributions," with individual scores "representing degrees of the personality trait" (Costa & McCrae, 1992, p. 13). The MBTI, in contrast, is designed to sort, or *indicate,* to respondents their likely preference on each dimension. MBTI scores are *not* designed to indicate *how much* of, say, Extraversion, a person has, as such a focus on amount is incompatible both with the underlying view of personality as a process involving the tension of opposites and with the instrument's goal of sorting as opposed to measuring. This apparently subtle difference between the MBTI and other psychological instruments leads to errors in interpretation by practitioners who do not understand the difference between a trait-based instrument and a type-based one.

A critical implication of the type versus trait difference involves the link between a particular construct and a person's behavior. Traits are seen as being linked casually to behaviors, but the link is more complex with type. Psychological type theory assumes that all people use both Sensing and Intuition but that each individual prefers (and therefore is likely to differentially use and develop) one preference at the expense of the other. However, type theory also assumes that Sensing types, for example, can—and do—use and develop their Intuition (and conversely) and that both types have the ability to consciously choose, based on their assessment of the requirements of a situation, to use either Sensing or Intuition, although probably not with equal ease, facility, or enjoyment. It is therefore entirely "natural" for Introverts to be skilled presenters, for Sensing types to be creative, for Feeling types to do logical analysis, for Perceiving types to be organized, and so on, *if and when they choose to devote the time and effort to do so.*

Because of the theory of opposites embedded within it and because of additional complexities involving the dynamic across dimensions and involving development over time (both of which are discussed below), relative to the five-factor model, the theory of psychological type *is* a complex model. However, we know both from the research and from our own experience that human personality *is* complex and that simplicity for its own sake is not necessarily an advantage.

Moreover, the MBTI's focus on the tension of opposites, while atypical in the arena of psychological testing, is based on a dialectical view of human functioning—a view that has a long history in philosophical thought and in psychological theory and research. Within psychology, dialectical approaches have been applied to such arenas as interpersonal communication (Werner & Baxter, 1994), environmental psychology (Altman & Gauvain, 1981), and interpersonal relationships (Altman, Vinsel, & Brown, 1981). In addition, Altman and Gauvain (1981) have argued that dialectical approaches are implicit in other psychological theories (e.g., Freud's constructs of id versus superego, and Piaget's notions of assimilation and accommodation).

In applying dialectical thinking to some current themes in psychology, Altman (1987) argued that some key features of dialectical thinking are that it assumes that phenomena are composed of oppositional features that exist in a dynamic condition of tension [and that these] . . . oppositional process-es form a unity or whole, with each pole of the dialectic lending meaning to the other, and with the whole dependent on the existence of some amount of the opposite. (p. 1058)

Type theory seems very consistent with the features that Altman described.

The Potential Impact of a Theory of Opposites

As organizations and their leaders struggle to deal with escalating amounts of change and complexity, experts in leadership and organiza-tional change are proposing more complex and more comprehensive models of the effective functioning of organizations and their leaders. For example, in *The Age of Paradox,* Handy (1994) asserted that

we used to think that we knew how to run organizations. Now we know better. More than ever they need to be global and local at the same time, to be small in some ways but big in others, to be centralized some of the time and decentralized most of it. They expect their workers to be both more autonomous and more of a team, their managers to be more delegating and more controlling. (p. 35)

Similarly, Aram (1990) addressed the issue of overly simple approaches to complex organizational problems:

Managerial ideas and tools are often ill-suited to address the complex char-acter of large organizations. We have theories and practices of innovation and concepts and policies of control; rarely do we seek conceptually or practically to integrate innovation and control. Many extol the virtues of change. Why isn't comparable emphasis placed on benefits of stability, and why not address ourselves more to the important challenge of balancing sta-bility and development? Some persons seek to make our organizations more efficient. Others want to make them more humane. A "yes/and" perspective is a valid and valuable approach to addressing the theory and practice of management. (p. 186)

Aram further asserted that a critical task for managers is "to capture the benefits of seemingly opposing elements" (p. 185).

With the explicit goal of "challenging managers to think at a higher level of intellectual complexity," Pascale (1990), in *Managing on the Edge,* described the elements of the well-known management consult-ing framework, the *Seven-S Framework,* and identified the underlying polarities—what he called "contending opposites"—within each ele-

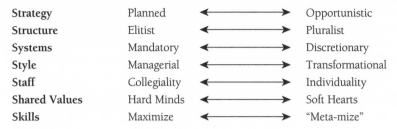

Strategy	Planned ⟵⟶	Opportunistic
Structure	Elitist ⟵⟶	Pluralist
Systems	Mandatory ⟵⟶	Discretionary
Style	Managerial ⟵⟶	Transformational
Staff	Collegiality ⟵⟶	Individuality
Shared Values	Hard Minds ⟵⟶	Soft Hearts
Skills	Maximize ⟵⟶	"Meta-mize"

Figure 1 "Contending Opposites" of the Seven-S Framework

From *Managing on the Edge* (p. 53) by R. Pascale, 1990, New York: Simon & Schuster. Copyright 1990 by Richard Pascale. Reprinted with permission.

ment. Figure 1 illustrates the contending opposites that Pascale identified. Pascale elaborated on the need to integrate within these elements by asserting that

> the forces that we have historically regarded as locked in opposition can be viewed (through a different mindset, or paradigm) as apparent opposites generating inquiry and adaptive responses. This is because each point of view represents a facet of reality, and these realities tend to challenge one another and raise questions. (p. 51)

He proposed that organizations require a "dynamic synthesis—not a compromise or mathematical halfway house of strategic and opportunistic tendencies, but a paradoxical embrace that contains both poles" (p. 53).

The dialectical approach of the MBTI, integrated with some of the dialectical approaches to leadership and organizational functioning, potentially offers us an opportunity for the first time to have complex but coherent models that are illuminating and homologous at a number of different levels of analysis (i.e., intrapersonal, interpersonal, team, organizational). Table 4 contains an illustrative set of questions at different levels of analysis regarding working well with both sides of the Sensing–Intuition dimension.

In contrast to the potential richness of interconnections across levels of analysis and the coherent complexity of the dialectical approach of the MBTI, five-factor models are static, evaluative, and limited. Chapter 10 provides further detail about the link of the MBTI to current models in leadership and organizational change and, in addition, demonstrates how key elements of such models are often closely related to the MBTI dimensions.

TABLE 4   Questions Regarding the Sensing–Intuition Dimension
                    at Different Levels of Analysis

Intrapersonal level
- As a Sensing type, am I making an effort to see possibilities, pay attention to trends, and be creative when it's appropriate?
- As an Intuitive type, am I making an effort to pay attention to the present, focus when appropriate on the facts, and take care of real-world matters?
- Do I really value and appreciate the other preference?

Interpersonal level
- When I am communicating with someone who has a different preference on Sensing–Intuition, can I truly listen to the other person's approach and perspectives?
- Can I communicate regarding *my* preference effectively, without disparaging the other side?
- Do I actively look for things to admire and appreciate in the approach and perspectives of the other side?
- In my language and my actions, do I demonstrate respect to both people with the other preference and their perspectives?

Team level:
- Do we understand and value Sensing enough to notice and support its essential contribution to team effort?
- Do we understand and value Intuition enough to notice and support its essential contribution to team effort?
- Do we use constructive language for describing the characteristics and perspectives of each preference?
- Do we have the awareness and skills to engage in a constructive, ongoing dialogue about both short-term, practical, factual matters (Sensing), and trends, possibilities, theories (Intuition)?
- Does our relative focus on Sensing considerations (i.e., facts, present reality, short-term goals, and experience-based approaches) versus Intuitive considerations (i.e., theories and concepts, future possibilities, long-term goals, and creative approaches) fit our goals, tasks, and environment?
- Have we created an environment in which both Sensing and Intuition perspectives can be freely articulated and respected?
- Do we truly value both Sensing and Intuitive staff members?

TABLE 4   Questions Regarding the Sensing–Intuition Dimension
at Different Levels of Analysis (continued)

Organizational level

- Do we recognize that, in dealing with Sensing and Intuitive business considerations (i.e., short term and long term, reality and vision), we are managing a polarity and not just solving a problem? Do we understand the dynamics of managing a polarity? (See Johnson, 1992; Pascale, 1990.)
- At the organizational level and between and within organizational units, do we have constructive language for characterizing both Sensing and Intuitive considerations and perspectives?
- Do we continually emphasize the essential contributions of both Sensing and Intuitive perspectives to our success as an organization?
- Do our leaders each understand their own preference and their likely blind spots and do they freely solicit and welcome input on the other side?
- Do we provide opportunities for staff to learn about and continually enhance their constructive use of Sensing–Intuition differences?

A Theory of Inner Dynamics

In a recent critique of the five-factor model, Block (1995) asserted that an important limitation of the five-factor model is its focus on unconnected variables discovered "robotically" through factor analysis techniques and its lack of a "coherent *intra-individual* theoretical framework" (p. 210). Block considered the model's inability to represent a "personality structure" a serious flaw:

> It is the personality structure of an individual that, energized by motivations, dynamically organizes perceptions, cognitions, and behaviors so as to achieve certain "system" goals. No functioning psychological "system," with its rules and bounds, is designated or implied by the "Big Five" formulation: it does not offer a sense of what goes on within the structured, motivation-processing, system-maintaining individual. (p. 188)

The MBTI, in contrast, has a complex but coherent underlying theory, the theory of type dynamics, that describes the interplay among the four MBTI dimensions. Type dynamics theory proposes that:

- The second and third dimensions of the MBTI, known as the *functions,* are literally cognitive processes that all people use *some* of the time; that is, everyone takes in sense data about the world (Sensing), sees patterns and possibilities (Intuition), applies logic to decisions (Thinking), and applies personal values to decisions (Feeling).
- For each of the 16 types, there is a particular order and way in which the functions are used.
- Of the two most preferred functions, one will be a perceiving function (either Sensing or Intuition) and one will be a judging function (either Thinking or Feeling); one will be *the* most preferred function (the dominant function) and one will be the second most preferred (the auxiliary function).
- The two less-preferred functions are referred to as tertiary (i.e., the third most preferred) and inferior (i.e., the least preferred). The two functions will generally be less developed, less conscious, more primitive, and harder to use than the dominant and auxiliary functions.
- Of the two most preferred functions, one will be used primarily in the outer world and one will be used primarily in the inner world. Extraverts will use their dominant function primarily in the outer world, while Introverts will use their dominant function primarily in the inner world. For a more complete explanation of type dynamics and its application to leadership development, see Chapter 9.

The Potential Impact of a Theory
of Inner Dynamics

The theory of type dynamics has been successfully used in leadership development settings by advanced practitioners of the MBTI. Unfortunately, however, most practitioners who use the MBTI in leadership development are not knowledgeable about the theory or skilled in its application. Chapter 9 is intended to provide an introduction to the topic as well as information on various aspects of the theory and its general application (see also Myers & Kirby, 1994; Myers & McCaulley, 1985; Myers & Myers, 1980; Quenk, 1993).

The theory of type dynamics can provide a unique and valuable contribution to leadership development by providing leaders, and those who work with them, with a more refined sense of their characteristic ways of collecting information and making judgments. Specific potential advantages of this refined sense include:

- The theory highlights the relationship between a leader's inner and outer worlds and expands our notions of Extraversion and Introversion by noting that both Extraverts and Introverts have characteristic ways of relating to both their inner and outer worlds. The theory can bring understanding to the experiences of individual leaders, and those who work with them, with regard to how different processes occur during interactions with others (e.g., meetings) versus during private time.
- The theory also highlights the critical relationship between perception (i.e., collecting information) and judgment (i.e., making decisions on the basis of that information). The theory can thus provide an elaborated framework for understanding differences in the pace, timing, form, and relative emphasis on data collection versus decision making in leaders of different types.
- Elaborations of the theory (e.g., Quenk, 1993) provide differential descriptions of behaviors likely to be exhibited by different types of leaders under conditions of extreme stress and fatigue.
- The theory leads to specific, targeted recommendations and remedies for leadership development challenges in different types, in different situations. See Chapter 9 for specific examples.
- Explicit use of the theory in helping individual leaders analyze their own type dynamics increases their awareness and appreciation of the complexity and richness of other people. This effect may be particularly valuable to technically oriented leaders, who can be intrigued by the elegance, complexity, and accuracy of their own type dynamics description and can begin to see other people as more interesting, complex, and potentially understandable.

A Theory of Development

As mentioned earlier, proponents of both the MBTI and the NEO-PI consider that the characteristics the instruments measure are stable within individuals over time, and research has supported this stability (McCrae & Costa, 1990; Myers & McCaulley, 1985). A unique characteristic of the MBTI, however, relative to the five-factor instruments, involves the developmental focus of the theory of type development. Elaborating on the theory of type dynamics, which, as noted earlier, describes a predictable dynamic interaction of the four MBTI functions—Sensing, Intuition, Thinking, and Feeling—for each type, the theory of type development addresses the typical timing and pattern of the development of the functions for each type. Chapter 10 explains type development in substantial detail and elaborates on its link to leadership development.

The Potential Impact of a Theory of Development

There are a variety of advantages of the developmental focus of the theory of psychological type. First, as a theory that focuses on both stability (i.e., that type does not change over time) and development (i.e., that development of both the preferred and the less-preferred functions is a lifelong process), the theory of psychological type offers a framework for understanding the seemingly contradictory sense we have that people are surprisingly consistent (in some ways) over time and yet are capable of remarkable development and change. This framework of stability and change is a helpful context for understanding leadership development research and practice in which we encounter otherwise difficult-to-understand patterns of leaders exhibiting both a remarkable consistency over the course of their careers and noteworthy development over time.

Second, the theory sets the stage for a much-needed discussion and refinement of the concept of maturity—a concept about which experienced leadership development practitioners have a great deal of working knowledge. Refinement of our understanding of maturity and its development is very important in understanding and promoting leadership development. The theory of psychological type offers an invaluable framework for understanding maturity both within and across types.

Third, the theory potentially provides guidance to practitioners who are working with managers who are in midlife (late 30s and beyond)—a group that includes a great many middle- and upper-level managers. The theory also enhances and expands our views of the differing developmental tasks of the first and second half of life—differences that have profound implications for leadership and leadership development.

SUMMARY

This chapter has synthesized recent research on the basic factors of normal personality, contrasted approaches to these basic personality factors that are used by the MBTI versus five-factor instruments, and argued that some unique characteristics of the MBTI and the theory of psychochologial type make the MBTI potentially especially valuable for leadership development. The unique characteristics of the MBTI include the focus on valuing differences versus evaluating them, the focus on individual understanding and choice, the underlying theory of opposites, the theory of type dynamics, and the theory of type development. This chapter has argued that these characteristics are consistent with and supportive of shifts in organizations toward increasing workplace diversity, an emphasis on teamwork and participation in decision making, knowledge and learning as key organizational assets, and the need for "requisite" internal variety within organizations to match increasingly complex external environments. Leadership development practitioners who use the MBTI are encouraged to learn more about the advance levels of analysis and use of the MBTI—type dynamics and type development—as applying these levels can make an enhanced contribution to leadership development and constructive organizational change.

NOTES

1. Although the MBTI does not have a dimension equivalent to Neuroticism, Isabel Briggs Myers, the codeveloper of the MBTI, was very aware of the fifth factor but chose for both theoretical reasons, which are elaborated later in this chapter, and practical reasons (i.e., her desire to make the MBTI accessible and widely available) not to include such a component (McCaulley, personal communication, 1989).

REFERENCES

Altman, I. (1987). Centripetal and centrifugal trends in psychology. *American Psychologist, 42,* 1058–1069.

Altman, I., & Gauvain, M. (1981). A cross-cultural and dialectic analysis of homes. In L. Liben, A. Patterson, & N. Newcombe (Eds.), *Spatial representation and behavior across the life span: Theory and application* (pp. 283–320). New York: Academic.

Altman, I., Vinsel, A., & Brown, B. B. (1981). Dialectic conceptions in social psychology: An application to social penetration and privacy regulation. In L. Berkowitz (Ed.), *Advances in experimental social psychology* (Vol. 14, pp. 107–160). New York: Academic Press.

Aram, J. D. (1990). Appreciative interchange: The force that makes cooperation possible. In S. Srivasta, D. L. Cooperrider, & Associates (Eds.), *Appreciative management and leadership* (pp. 175–204). San Francisco: Jossey-Bass.

Ashby, W. (1952). *Design for a brain.* New York: Wiley.

Barrick, M. R., & Mount, M. K. (1991). The Big Five personality dimensions and job performance: A meta-analysis. *Personnel Psychology, 44,* 1–26.

Bass, B. M. (1981). *Stogdill's handbook of leadership: A survey of theory and research.* New York: Free Press.

Block, J. (1995). A contrarian view of the five-factor approach to personality description. *Psychological Bulletin, 117*, 187–215.

Bunker, B. B., & Alban, B. T. (1992). The large group intervention—A new social innovation? *Journal of Applied Behavioral Science, 28*, 473–479.

Costa, P. T., Jr., & McCrae, R. R. (1992). *The revised NEO Personality Inventory and NEO Five Factor Inventory: Professional manual.* Odessa, FL: Psychological Assessment Resources.

Drucker, P. F. (1993). *Post-capitalist society.* New York: Harper Business.

Fry, R. E., & Pasmore, W. A. (1983). Strengthening management education. In S. Srivasta & Associates (Eds.), *The executive mind: New insights on managerial thought and action* (pp. 269–296). San Francisco: Jossey-Bass.

Goldberg, L. R. (1993). The structure of phenotypic personality traits. *American Psychologist, 48*, 26–34.

Handy, C. (1994). *The age of paradox.* Boston: Harvard Business School Press.

Hogan, R., Curphy, G. J., & Hogan, J. (1994). What we know about leadership. *American Psychologist, 49*, 493–504.

Johnson, B. (1992). *Polarity management: Identifying and managing unsolvable problems.* Amherst, MA: HRD Press, Inc.

Kouzes, J. M., & Posner, B. Z. (1993). *Credibility: How leaders gain and lose it, why people demand it.* San Francisco: Jossey-Bass.

Lawler, E. E., III. (1992). *The ultimate advantage: Creating the high-involvement organization.* San Francisco: Jossey-Bass.

McCall, M. W., Jr., & Lombardo, M. M. (1978). *Leadership: Where else can we go?* Durham, NC: Duke University Press.

McCaulley, M. H. (1990). The Myers-Briggs Type Indicator and leadership. In K. E. Clark & M. B. Clark (Eds.), *Measures of leadership* (pp. 381–418). West Orange, NJ: Leadership Library of America.

McCaulley, M. H. (1992). Leadership and psychological type: Asking the right questions. *Bulletin of Psychological Type, 15*(1), 5–6.

McCrae, R. R., & Costa, P. T., Jr. (1986). Personality stability and its implications for clinical psychology. *Clinical Psychology Review, 6*, 407–423.

McCrae, R. R., & Costa, P. T., Jr. (1989). Reinterpreting the Myers-Briggs Type Indicator from the perspective of the five-factor model of personality. *Journal of Personality, 57*, 17–40.

McCrae, R. R., & Costa, P. T., Jr. (1990). *Personality in adulthood.* New York: Guilford Press.

Miller, T. (1991). A psychotherapeutic utility of the five-factor model of personality: A clinician's experience. *Journal of Personality Assessment, 57*, 415–433.

Mischel, W. (1968). *Personality assessment.* New York: Wiley.

Mitroff, I. I., & Linstone, H. A. (1993). *The unbounded mind: Breaking the chains of traditional business thinking.* New York: Oxford University Press.

Myers, I. B., & McCaulley, M. H. (1985). *Manual: A guide to the development and use of the Myers-Briggs Type Indicator.* Palo Alto, CA: Consulting Psychologists Press.

Myers, I. B., with Myers, P. B. (1980). *Gifts differing.* Palo Alto, CA: Consulting Psychologists Press.

Myers, I. B. (1993). *Introduction to type: A guide to understanding your results on the Myers-Briggs Type Indicator.* Palo Alto, CA: Consulting Psychologists Press.

Myers, K. D. & Kirby, L. K. (1994). *Introduction to type dynamics and development: Exploring the next level of type.* Palo Alto, CA: Consulting Psychologists Press.

O'Hara-Devereaux, M., & Johansen, R. (1994). *Globalwork: Bridging distance, culture, and time.* San Francisco: Jossey-Bass.

Pascale, R. T. (1990). *Managing on the edge.* New York: Simon & Schuster.

Pasmore, W. A. (1994). *Creating strategic change: Designing the flexible, high-performing organization.* New York: Wiley.

Pinchot, G., & Pinchot, E. (1994). *The end of bureaucracy and the rise of the intelligent organization.* San Francisco: Berrett-Koehler.

Quenk, N. L. (1993). *Beside ourselves: Our hidden personality in everyday life.* Palo Alto, CA: Davies-Black.

Senge, P. M. (1990). *The fifth discipline: The art and practice of the learning organization.* New York: Doubleday/Currency.

Weisbord, M. R. (1991). *Productive workplaces.* San Francisco: Jossey-Bass.

Werner, C. M., & Baxter, L. A. (1994). Temporal qualities of relationships: Organismic, transactional, and dialectical views. In M. L. Knapp & G. R. Miller (Eds.), *Handbook of interpersonal communication* (pp. 323–379). London: Sage.

Yukl, G., & Van Fleet, D. D. (1992). Theory and research on leadership in organizations. In M. D. Dunnette & M. H. Leaetta (Eds.), *Handbook of industrial and organizational psychology* (2nd ed., pp. 147–197). Palo Alto, CA: Davies-Black.

PART TWO

Research on the MBTI and Leadership Development With Implications for Practice

3 | Using the MBTI in Management and Leadership

A Review of the Literature

Christa L. Walck

When people want to understand organizations, they usually turn to the people at the helm of organizations—managers. Managers get credit (or blame) for organizational outcomes based on their competence at planning, organizing, and controlling the use of organizational resources to meet customer needs. Managers are also judged on their leadership, defined as their ability to interact with others in a way that influences and inspires them to work together to meet organizational goals.

When individual managers are held responsible for organizational outcomes, psychology becomes a tool for understanding managers and the process of management and leadership. Psychologists have long probed the motives, cognitive abilities, skills, attitudes, and behaviors of managers to attempt to link them to organizational success or failure. They have also looked at how managers interact in groups and tried to measure congruence between managers and the organizations they serve.

Jungian psychological type, sometimes referred to as *cognitive style, decision-making style,* or *problem-solving style,* is another psychological construct that can be used to understand managers. The *Myers-Briggs*

Type Indicator (MBTI) has operationalized the Jungian construct of type so that it can be quickly and fairly reliably identified, quantified, and compared to other measures of management, leadership, and organizational effectiveness (see Fleenor, Chapter 4 for a discussion of correlations of MBTI with *California Psychological Inventory*™, FIRO-B™, *Kirton Adaption-Innovation Inventory,* Leadership Style Indicator, and Leaderless Group Discussion in a large sample from the Center for Creative Leadership). The easy availability and use of the MBTI has made it an exceptionally popular instrument for management consulting. It has also been widely used in management research.

There are two streams of research on type and management. The first stream focuses on populations of managers: The researcher finds a sample of managers or leaders, determines their types, and makes inferences from the type distributions about managers as a category, or about the organizations, industries, professions, or countries from which the sample is drawn. Some of this research is qualitative, using interviews and observational studies of managers' behavior. This research is primarily descriptive, and a significant amount is done by researchers with expertise in psychological type. (See Chapter 1 for summary of some of the descriptive data.)

The second stream of research is predictive, rather than descriptive. It identifies skills, capacities, and behaviors associated with management and leadership and tests predictions about how they relate to type. Subjects consist of managers and students. Because MBA students tend to have management experience, for the purposes of this review, studies involving MBA students were included. In addition, studies using undergraduate students were included when the research focused on general cognitive issues that are relevant to management. Some of this research is done by researchers with expertise in management but not in psychological type.

Researchers involved in these two lines of research, descriptive and predictive, occasionally misunderstand one another. Since psychological type indicates preferences, not behaviors, type experts are often uncomfortable with research that tries to predict individual behavior based on type (Walck, 1992), particularly if the results can be used to discriminate against people with certain preferences. Conversely, management specialists are often frustrated by the lack of success in using type to predict behavior. This is partly due to methodological problems: Many studies use simulations rather than real behavior; real behavioral variables are difficult to separate from other variables; and students rather than working adults are often used for research (Furnham & Stringfield, 1992). However, researchers have failed to see alternative ways in which type can be used to enhance management and leadership.

This chapter reviews a wide range of research on using the MBTI in management and leadership, building and expanding on two previous reviews (McCaulley, 1990; Walck, 1992). This review is divided into the following sections:

- Measuring Psychological Type for Management Research
- Building Hypotheses About Type and Management
- Type and the Manager as Decision Maker
- Type and the Manager as Leader
- Type and Organizational Success
- Applying Type to Management

It should be noted that this research is generally limited to studies of U.S. managers, and the results may not transfer across cultures.

MEASURING PSYCHOLOGICAL TYPE FOR MANAGEMENT RESEARCH

Psychological type is complex. Not only do the eight preferences combine to form sixteen types, but the less-preferred preferences, type development, and interaction of preferences all are theorized to have an impact on which preferences get enacted in behavior. Coe (1992), for example, cautions about potential misuse of the MBTI (particularly in regard to the *shadow*, or less-preferred preferences) and offers a useful table of suggestions for using it. Research seeking relationships between type and management, however, often reduces psychological type to function pairs (ST, NT, SF, NF), single preferences, and occasionally temperaments (SJ, NT, SP, NF). There are advantages and disadvantages to using type this way.

The obvious advantage of using the function pairs or temperaments is simplicity: There are fewer variables with which to compare management concepts. Another advantage is that function pairs, defined as preferences for information gathering (S–N) and information evaluating (T–F), can be linked to cognition and strategic decision making rather than "the more global meaning implicit in personality" (Hellriegel & Slocum, 1980, p. 152). Depending on the nature of the problem under inquiry, the function pairs have been variously called *problem-solving styles, decision-making styles, choice styles* (Nutt, 1986a), *leadership styles,* and *cognitive styles.*

A disadvantage of using function pairs is that they eliminate valuable information about attitudes (E–I and J–P) that affect both functions. For example, although ESTPs and ISTJs are both STs (and S dominant), they express and operationalize the Sensing and Thinking functions differently, which draws them disproportionately to different functional units of organizations—ESTPs to sales and ISTJs to accounting (Myers & McCaulley, 1985). Nutt (1986a) noted that limiting research to the function pairs not only excludes half the classification categories that Jung considered important, but also "fails to deal with the sequential nature of choice making, and does not account for implementation preferences implicit in Jungian theory" (p. 342). To rectify this, Nutt developed a classification scheme that involved two sets of pairs, *choice styles* (combinations of S–N and T–F) and *implementation styles* (combinations of E–I and J–P). Wilson and Wilson (1994) also cautioned researchers about using single preferences, showing that pairs such as ES and EN have yielded significant relationships when IS and IN did not.

In this chapter, the term *type* will be used to refer to any aspect of type (single preference, preference pairs, or four-preference types), unless a more specific designation is necessary.

BUILDING HYPOTHESES
ABOUT TYPE AND MANAGEMENT

The dominant model for management research is management science. Management science, like science in general, is concerned with observable outcomes. What is the observable outcome of psychological type? We can observe behavior, but how tightly is type linked to behavior? What is the effect of other mediating variables, both demographic (age, gender, education, culture) and situational, on behavior? The need to distinguish between the effects of multiple variables on behavior has led to a primacy of quantitative analysis that employs sophisticated statistical techniques to discover relationships between variables.

Management science, like science in general, proceeds by establishing hypotheses and then testing them. Management science seeks to predict dependent variable B from the independent variable A. For example, does psychological type (independent variable A) predict how a manager will resolve conflict (dependent variable B)—will ENTJs resolve conflict directly while ISFPs avoid resolving conflict? The early work relating type to management, called *theory building* in a previous literature review (Walck, 1992), could more accurately be called *hypothesis building*. Researchers draw inferences from detailed, normative descriptions of types and preferences and then hypothesize relationships with established concepts in management and leadership.

Research on type and management began in the early 1970s. Much of the early research generated hypotheses about how function pairs were linked to managerial and organizational behaviors such as goal setting, planning, problem solving, and decision making (Hellriegel & Slocum, 1975; Kilmann & Herden, 1976; Kilmann & Mitroff, 1976; Mason & Mitroff, 1973; Mitroff, Barabba, & Kilmann, 1977; Mitroff & Kilmann, 1975a, 1975b; Nutt, 1979; Taggart & Robey, 1981). Since type is a system of dichotomous variables, researchers dualized such concepts as productivity (efficiency vs. effectiveness), planning (operational vs. strategic), time frame (present vs. future), and orientation (internal vs. external, social vs. technical) and matched them against S–N and T–F preferences to generate four-cell matrices. These hypotheses were refined and extended by later research (Haley & Stumpf, 1989; Mullen & Stumpf, 1987; Nutt, 1986a, 1986b). A common product of this type of hypothesis building is a four-cell matrix that relates two aspects of type to two aspects of management. The four cells represent predictions that seek to relate various aspects of type and management. A summary of the hypothesized relationships is presented in Table 1.

Empirical evidence for many of these hypotheses was qualitative. Mitroff and Kilmann (1975a, 1975b) developed a projective technique for revealing managers' preferences through storytelling. Stories written by managers about their ideal organizations were analyzed for content, matched with Jungian preferences, and compared with the MBTI results of the managers who wrote them (Hellreigel & Slocum, 1980; Steckroth, Slocum, & Sims, 1980). Mullen & Stumpf (1987) also coded language used by managers as they interacted in a simulation called Looking Glass.

These early studies concluded that the four function pairs revealed preferences for information (S–N) and action (T–F) that influence how managers would perform in organizations. To perform well, managers were hypothesized to need information and organizations aligned with their own psychological types, as well as awareness of their own and their co-workers' preferences. For example, Mitroff and Kilmann

TABLE 1 Hypothesized Relationships Between Type and Management

Relationship	Type: ST	NT
Ideal Organization (1)	Bureaucratic: Impersonally realistic Detailed and factual Narrowly economic goals	Matrix, R & D: Impersonally conceptual Broad, ill-defined Macro-economic issues
Planning (2)	Operational problem solving	Long-range strategic planning
Problem Solving (3)	Real-time operational-technical problem solvers	Future-time strategic-technical problem generators
Organizational Effectiveness (4)	Internal efficiency: Inventory cost Units produced per hour	External efficiency: Cost of capital New product development
Decision Style (5)	Systematic Information: Quantitative measures Warrant: Statistical significance Decision aids: Cost-benefit analysis	Speculative Information: Future possibilities Warrant: Assumptional flux, stochastic parameters Decision aids: Decision trees with sensitivity analysis
Decision Making: Strategic Issues (6)	Identifier/Analytic	Evolver/Conceptual
Biases (7)	Anchoring, functional fixedness, impute regularity of structure	Perseverance, positivity, representativeness
Action Orientation (5)	Action averse Prefer to deal only with ST	Action oriented Prefer to deal with SF
Ways of Doing Science (8)	Hard Experimentalist	Abstract Theorizer

Relationship	Type: SF	NF
Ideal Organization (1)	Familial: Personally realistic Human qualities of specific people Work roles	Organic Adaptive: Personally idealistic People and human goals Flexible and adaptive
Planning (2)	Day-to-day human relations	Long-range human goals
Problem Solving (3)	Real-time social problem solvers	Future-time strategic-social problem generators
Organizational Effectiveness (4)	Internal effectiveness: Employee turnover Employee commitment	External effectiveness: Consumer satisfaction Social responsibility
Decision Style (5)	Judicial Information: Current situation Warrant: Acceptance by interested parties Decision aids: Decision groups	Heuristic Information: Current possibilities Warrant: Experience and judgment Decision aids: Mutual adjustment
Decision Making: Strategic Issues (6)	Convergent/Direct	Searcher/Behavioral
Biases (7)	Availability, social desirability, fundamental attribution error	Vividness, reasoning by analogy, illusory correlations
Action Orientation (5)	Action oriented Prefer to deal with NT	Action oriented Prefer to deal with ST
Ways of Doing Science (8)	Human Scientist	Intuitive Synthesizer

Note. (1) Mitroff & Kilmann (1987); Mitroff (1983); (2) Mitroff & Kilmann (1975a); (3) Mitroff et al. (1977); (4) Kilmann & Herden (1976); (5) Nutt (1986a); (6) Mullen & Stumpf (1987); (7) Haley & Stumpf (1989); (8) Mitroff & Kilmann (1975b).

(1975a) hypothesized that if asked to identify their "ideal" organization, STs would prefer impersonally (T) realistic (S) organizations, while NFs would prefer personally (F) idealistic (N) organizations. If a manager were asked to plan, NT managers were hypothesized to gravitate toward long-range (N) strategic (T) planning, while SF managers would plan for day-to-day (S) human relations (F). Even the concept of information was considered preference driven: When Sensing types asked for information, it was hypothesized that they wanted raw data, while Intuitive types wanted stories, Thinking types wanted abstract and symbolic information, and Feeling types wanted artistry (Mason & Mitroff, 1973).

Although management researchers claimed to be drawn to Jungian type because of its nonjudgmental nature (Hellreigel & Slocum, 1975; Hellreigel, Slocum, & Woodman, 1989; Mason & Mitroff, 1973), they often generated hypotheses that created dualities and hierarchies of function pairs in which some preferences were more equal than others. Mason and Mitroff (1973), Mitroff and Kilmann (1975a), and Kilmann and Mitroff (1976) concluded that one function pair, ST, was privileged over the others in management, and that NTs played a supporting role. They reasoned that science, and by extension, management based on management science, is an ST activity, and that management information systems provided ST information in ST form. They suggested that STs value quantitative analysis and deny the value of qualitative, humanistic approaches represented by NT, NF, and SF. This was echoed by Hellreigel and Slocum's (1975) assertion that Western industrialized society is characterized by S and T, while N and F are "disregarded, undeveloped, and repressed" (p. 31). The negative impact of this one-sidedness was demonstrated in a case study in which a federal agency charged with long-range planning got stuck in the normative, quantitative ST mode and couldn't value the qualitative input of NFs and NTs (Mitroff et al., 1977).

Ramaprasad and Mitroff (1984) attempted to shift the privileged position to NT, when they claimed NT was superior under conditions valuing strategic problem solving. They likened the Piagetian process of simple abstraction to S–N, and Piagetian reflexive abstraction to T–F. Combining the two produced *logico-mathematical structures*, which they hypothesized moved through logical stages of development from SF to ST, NF, and finally NT. SF thus reflected rudimentary thinking and NT refined thinking. Ramaprasad and Mitroff also attempted to change the way MBTI scores would be used to assess strategic capability. They stated that people should be classified based on their strength of preference, not their dominant or overall preference. This led them to develop a hierarchy in which people with strong preferences in all four functions (Sensing and Intuition and Thinking and Feeling) were considered ideal strategists, or synthesizers, while those with strong preferences for fewer functions were less flexible and limited and could only play support roles such as technicians. It should be noted that these researchers did not present any empirical evidence to support these hypotheses and that their normative approach is antithetical to the approach outlined in the MBTI *Manual.* Hypotheses about strategic decision making will be discussed in the next section.

TYPE AND THE MANAGER AS DECISION MAKER

Traditional management theory divides the work of the organization into making decisions and implementing decisions. Managers make decisions and others implement them. As a result, research on strategic decision making is a staple of management science. Even postmodern management theory, which flattens the organization by pushing planning and decision making down to employees, still reserves strategic decision making for executives.

Early research on type and management conducted in the 1970s was primarily qualitative and hypothesized relationships between type and management concepts such as planning and decision making. The results are summarized in Table 1. Subsequent research tested these hypotheses empirically with a variety of measurement strategies.

Building Hypotheses

Many management researchers, searching for reliable predictors of managerial performance, have hypothesized relationships between psychological type, problem-solving and decision-making behaviors, and decision outcomes. Empirical research linking type to decision making has tended to use function pairs, which combine perception (information gathering) and judging (evaluating): ST, NT, SF, NF.

Numerous hypotheses have been generated (see Table 1). Taggart and Robey (1981) hypothesized a link between cognitive styles and brain hemispheres—ST and NT were linked to the left hemisphere and NF and SF to the right hemisphere. Ramaprasad and Mitroff (1984) privileged NT as the best strategists. Mullen and Stumpf (1987) hypothesized links between type and their empirically identified strategic-issues styles (identifier, evolver, searcher, and convergent) and with Rowe and Boulgarides' (1983) decision styles.

Nutt (1986a, see also 1979; Henderson & Nutt, 1980) developed the most elaborate hypothesis, identifying preferred types of information, justifications for action (warrants), and decision aids for each *choice style* (function pair), which he then linked to *implementation styles* (E–I and J–P combinations) to generate hypothesized *decision styles* for all 16 types (e.g., ESTJ is *Procedural* while INFP is *Committed*). Arguing against Ramaprasad and Mitroff's (1984) ideal strategist who would synthesize various psychological functions as needed to adapt to a given situation, Nutt (1986a) claimed that such a strategist would be "merely confused, switching from one posture to another without any means for synthesis" (p. 361). Instead, he argued that synthesis would be achieved when teams of managers with opposite decision styles engaged in dialogue.

Empirical research has confirmed some hypotheses about strategic decision making, but often the results are mixed. Moreover, synthesizing the results of this research is problematic for several reasons. First, sample sizes are generally small (less than 100) and sometimes consist of students with minimal management experience. Second, a variety of simulations substitute as proxy for decision-making activity; as Patz (1990) notes, closed-system simulations are not like the open-ended "real world" and can be biased toward certain preferences. Third, researchers do not all study the same preference combinations. Fourth, researchers have not always carefully separated the results of preference from other independent variables, primarily situational ones such as task type. Finally, it is not always clear whether we have accurately identified what kind of traits or behavior, broadly speaking, Jungian type is supposed to point to.

For example, Catford (1987) assumed that S and T would point to *rational* behavior and N and F would point to *nonrational* behavior. Yet in an experiment in which business professionals described how they would solve problems using innovation, Catford discovered that MBTI categories of S, N, T, and F do not predict the use of strategies that she had classified as rational or nonrational. Moreover, training (a situational variable) was a better predictor than type: Professionals who had taken creative problem-solving courses tended to use nonrational strategies, while those who took courses with traditional structured approaches used rational strategies.

Decision making is usually conceptualized as a multiple-step process: defining the problem, gathering information, and evaluating information to make a decision. We can divide empirical research on type and decision making into these categories.

Defining the Problem

Before one can solve a problem, one has to recognize that a problem exists. There is some evidence that N and T assist with problem definition. Regardless of organizational size, structure, and managerial style, N managers were significantly more likely than S managers to recognize strategic problems in written case scenarios (Hunt, 1986). When Phillips-Danielson (1985) tried to differentiate problem definers from nondefiners along a series of variables, only 12 of 77 managers sampled in four diverse organizations were problem definers. They were primarily T, and the majority held upper-level management positions or oversaw special projects. However, Malley (1982) found no relationship between type and problem recognition activity.

Gathering Information

Type theory suggests that perception preferences (S–N) influence what one attends to. As a result, management theorists have hypothesized that certain types would attend to certain kinds of information, and that the kinds of information provided by management information systems (MIS), decision aids, and other decision support systems (DSS), including the format in which that information is presented, should be designed specifically to meet the needs of different types (De Waele, 1978) or varied enough to meet the needs of many types (Nutt, 1986b).

There is some support for this hypothesis. NTs sought more quantitative data than NFs when they tried to solve a problem in an unstructured case study (Kerin & Slocum, 1981). Fs preferred and performed better with graphical representation of information, while Ts preferred and performed better with tabular information (Ghani, 1981).

Interviews with 20 nurse executives (10 S, 10 N) revealed that Ss were more likely to use information from others and described themselves more as rapid decision makers, while Ns relied more on observation and used the literature as an information resource for decision making (Kerlin, 1992). This may be related to findings from a simulation exercise with MBA students in which STs looked at the fewest reports and were the most satisfied information users, while Ns looked at the largest number of reports and NFs were the least satisfied users (Garceau, 1986). With respect to report format, these MBA students all preferred tabular reports, but STs had the strongest preference for them and NF the weakest; all subjects preferred aggregated reports, but STs requested them more frequently, and NTs requested disaggregated reports most frequently. Based on his research, Davis (1981) suggested any kind of information could be presented to NTs, but graphical raw data was most appropriate for STs, tabular raw data for SFs, tabular statistical summaries for SFs, and tabular raw data or graphical statistical summaries for NFs. More generally, Crothers (1990) found that ESTJs were the most positive about using statistical methods, while IPs and EPs were the least positive.

From this research, it can be concluded that there is some relationship between type, quantity of information desired, and speed of decision making. Ns appear less satisfied with information that is presented to them and thus cast a wider net for information. This may impede their ability to make decisions as quickly as Ss, who are satisfied with less information and can make a quicker decision with what they have. However, because several studies used function pairs, it is somewhat difficult to separate the effects of S–N from T–F. T–F appears to have some influence on information preferred for strategic decision making, particularly a T preference for quantified, well-structured data.

Preference for information content can also vary with type: In order to diagnose organizations, change agents of all types wanted information about task, organizational structure, and people, but information on organizational structure seemed more important to NTs, and information on people seemed more important to SFs and NFs (Slocum, 1978).

Despite this evidence of relationship between type and information preferences, two other simulations (Macrides, 1981; Nutt, 1986b) as well as a survey conducted in Singapore of higher education managers' satisfaction with office information technology (Tan & Lo, 1991) found no relationship between type and information usage.

Evaluating Information and Making the Decision

Type theory suggests that judging preferences (T–F) influence how one makes decisions. Management research suggests that elements in the decision-making environment such as task type, structure, and risk affect decision process and outcomes. Several management science studies have attempted to find relationships between type, the decision making process, elements in the environment, and decision outcomes.

Several studies revealed no relationship between type and decision making. Interviews with nurse executives revealed that Ss and Ns use the decision-making process in similar ways (Kerlin, 1992). Psychological type had no impact on the cognitive process used to process information in a simulation with 101 undergraduate students, although task type did have a significant impact (Tsai, 1991). Task type also had a significant impact on outcomes, while type did not, in an experiment using the Multiple-Cue Probability Learning Paradigm (MCPLP): 162 students performed better on human resources tasks than financial tasks, but STs did not predict financial performance better than NFs, nor did NFs predict employee performance better than STs (Ruble & Cosier, 1990). A large-scale "total enterprise" simulation (CORPORATION) yielded no correlation between type and performance (Patz, 1990, 1992).

Type did have some impact on decision making when the structure of the decision-making environment was taken into account. When the decision-making environment was complex and open-ended, N and T outperformed S and F. When the decision-making environment was moderately well-structured, S and F outperformed N and T. In one experiment, 80 students with clear S, N, J, and P preferences, grouped by NP, NJ, SP, and SJ and controlled for gender, engaged in two problem-solving activities: Dunker's box problem and Witkins' embedded figures problem (Hunter & Levy, 1982). Ns outperformed Ss: NJs developed significantly more possible solutions to the box problem than SJs; NPs attempted to find the most figures in the Witkins' problem, and SJs the least; NPs also did better at the task. In a second experiment, Patz (1990, 1992) ran "total enterprise" simulations MICROMATIC and Multinational Management Game (MMG) with 332 MBA students. Groups with dominant N and T performed best, and groups with S and F performed worst. Patz explained these results, compared to a lack of results for the simulation CORPORATION, by the fact that in MICRO-MATIC and MMG, the algorithm for success was known, while for CORPORATION the algorithm was unknown. He reasoned that NTs were able to figure out the algorithm and thus knew where to direct their long-range (N), fact-oriented (T) preferences in the former and win. Patz cautioned that this does not necessarily reflect real-world problem solving. Conversely, when 96 graduate students, evenly divided by cognitive style (ST, NT, SF, NF), engaged in a computer simulation (SIMPRO) in which they acted as production managers trying to achieve the lowest cost of production (Davis, Grove, & Knowles, 1990), the rank order of performance was SF, ST, NF, NT; NTs performed significantly worse than SF and ST and substantively but not significantly worse than NF on this task. Davis hypothesized that S outperformed N because of the moderately well-structured decision environment.

Type also had a significant impact on risk tolerance, but results were contradictory. In a study of risky shift in small groups comprised of 101 undergraduate students, only S–N affected risk: Ns made initial and group choices in the direction of greater risk, while Ss made them in the direction of less risk (Rifkind, 1975). Conversely, when middle managers (Henderson & Nutt, 1980) and top executives (Nutt, 1986b) were asked whether they would adopt proposals to make capital expenditures under eight scenarios that varied by level of uncertainty, SFs showed the most risk tolerance, adopting proposals regardless of the uncertainty of the situation, while STs showed the most risk avoidance, unwilling to adopt even under conditions of low uncertainty. NTs and NFs took an intermediate position of nominal risk taking. Among top executives, IJs were also least likely to take risk. The fact that education was also positively correlated with risk taking in Nutt's research may explain the difference in the outcomes between the student and managerial samples.

The impact of type on risk tolerance also appears to be affected by the fit between the decision maker and the decision-making environment. The eight scenarios in the study of top executives (Nutt, 1986b) were also rated for fit with type. Results showed that STs were more inclined to take risk (adopt proposals) when they were in an environment consistent with their type, while NTs, NFs, and SFs were more likely to take risk when operating in environments incompatible with their type. Nutt hypothesized that "compatible environments may create implementation problems for the SF, NT, and NF executives because their arguments may be more transparent to people who understand them," (p. 59) and interpreted STs as "inherently conservative" (p. 60).

Type also appears to be associated with biases that impair evaluation. Haley and Stumpf (1989) hypothesized that type leaves a cognitive "trail" of heuristics (rules of thumb) and biases that impairs the ability of decision makers to reach correct conclusions. To test the hypothesis, they observed 43 bank managers during six-hour runs of the Looking Glass management simulation and coded their behavior by heuristics and biases. STs showed *anchoring* bias and NTs *perseverance* bias more than other types. Given the preponderance of STs and NTs in management, Haley and Stumpf concluded that organizations may succumb to biases for conservatism (anchoring) and perseverance in beliefs against the weight of new evidence. Other relationships between cognitive style and bias were hypothesized (see Table 1) but not substantiated due to the small sample size for SFs and NFs (see Chapter 7 for further information on this research).

In summary, results regarding the impact of type on decision making are not conclusive. While some studies found relationships between type and problem definition, information gathering, and evaluation, other studies found none. Perhaps the most significant conclusion regarding type is that we should not assume that S–N affects information gathering and T–F affects information processing; all four functions may have some impact on all steps in the decision-making process. Moreover, task type seems more important than psychological type in determining the kinds of information people choose and the kinds of information for solving the specific problems that face them.

There was some evidence to suggest that Ns and Ts are better able than Ss and Fs to make decisions in unstructured environments. Ns and Ts may be more likely to recognize problems and patterns, request more information and quantitative information for problem solving, and outperform Ss and Fs in complex, open-ended situations. This may in part be a result of N's association with *integrative complexity* (Tetlock, Peterson & Berry, 1993, discussed below), which is defined as seeking out information about the world and identifying creative and integrative solutions to problems. It may also be related to an ability to take risk and overcome biases that affect judgment. While Ns seem to take the middle road on handling risk and exhibit a perseverance bias, Ts are more conservative than Fs. STs are more risk-averse than NTs, NFs, and SFs, which may be explained by their anchoring bias.

TYPE AND THE MANAGER
AS LEADER

Leadership theory has come full circle, starting with and returning to charismatic theories of leadership, in which leadership is the result of exceptional qualities possessed by the individual rather than the result of authority vested in the individual by tradition or position. Theories of leadership traits and attitudes possessed by the individual leader gave way in the 1970s and 1980s to contingency theories in which situational factors determined what type of leadership to exercise and reciprocal influence theories in which followers attributed leadership to others. Contingency theory has started to wane in the 1990s as leadership theory introduces a new version of the charismatic leader, the *transformational* leader. The transformational leader articulates and focuses attention on a clear vision of the future, derives charisma from interaction with followers while attending to their individual needs, transforms followers to transcend self-interest for the sake of collective purpose, and manages change, complexity, and teams. This transformational leader is usually contrasted with a *transactional* leader, conceptualized as a leader who maintains the status quo by clarifying roles and tasks, satisfies the needs of subordinates in exchange for performance, and works within the existing culture. (See DuBrin, 1995, and Yukl, 1989, for a discussion of the overlap between charismatic and transformational leadership, and theorists such as Bass, 1985, Burns, 1978, Bennis and Nanus, 1985, and Tichy and Devanna, 1986, who have contributed to the theories of charismatic and transformational leadership.)

Research relating type to leadership theory relies primarily on correlating MBTI scores with scores on instruments designed to measure leadership. While most of these instruments ask people to rate themselves, some also ask subordinates, peers, and occasionally superiors for ratings. A few studies use interviews and observational data. These are discussed below. In addition, two activities associated with leadership are also addressed: managing subordinates and managing conflict.

Situational Leadership

The contingency theory of leadership, which has been popularized in Hersey and Blanchard's (1988) situational leadership model, suggests that leadership style should vary with the characteristics of the tasks and subordinates. For example, in a structured situation with low-ability employees, a directive style of leadership may be most appropriate, whereas in a complex situation with high-ability employees, a participative style may be most appropriate. Good leaders will be able to apply the style that is appropriate to the situation. Since research suggests that most managers have a limited repertoire of leadership styles (both dominant and backup), managers need to learn more varied leadership behaviors in order to practice situational leadership.

The questions for type research are whether type predisposes a manager to a certain leadership style and whether type makes it difficult to learn new styles of leadership. Management scientists have designed various questionnaires to measure leadership styles. All attempts to find relationships between psychological type and leadership style, using the *Leadership Effectiveness and Adaptability Description* (LEAD-Self) questionnaire and the *Fiedler Contingency Model Questionnaire* (CMQ), have failed (Berg, 1993; Davis, 1981; Dietl, 1981; Dobbs, 1988; Flores, 1987; Frankowski, 1992; Pierson, 1984; Savelsbergh, 1989; Vail, 1991). Nor has any relationship been found between type and communication style as measured by the Audit of Administrator Communication Instrument in a sample of 117 public school administrators (Bueler, 1984).

However, a study of 159 Finnish managers using Reddin's 3-D model and Hersey and Blanchard's model did find some relationships: Es were more *executive,* Ss more *bureaucratic,* and Fs more *missionary* (Routamaa & Ponto, 1994). Another study by Hammer and Kummerow (1996) compared MBTI continuous scores to the Leadership Style Scale of the 1994 *Strong Interest Inventory.* There was some evidence (correlations between .37 and .42) that E and N were correlated with "leading by delegating" and "taking charge," while I and S were correlated with "leading by example."

Even though there is little evidence that certain types prefer one leadership style over another, research has found that some preferences are associated with certain leader behaviors, including participative decision making, managing subordinates, and managing conflict. These topics are addressed below.

Participative Decision Making

While the research on decision making described earlier attempted to discover how managers themselves behave as they make decisions, another aspect of decision making is whether and how a manager involves others in the decision-making process. Autocratic managers make decisions by themselves, while participative managers involve others in the decision-making process.

There is some evidence that managers with preferences for Sensing and Feeling are more participative than those who prefer Intuition and Thinking. Ss chose more participative methods than Ns, Ns chose more autocratic methods, and the T–F scale was unrelated to participative decision making in a study using Vroom and Yetton's (1973) decision-making exercise (Schweiger & Jago, 1982). However, the researchers concluded that situational factors impacted decision making more than type did. In another study, the S–N preference appeared to influence whether human resource professionals were included in the strategic decision-making process: Questionnaires administered to CEOs and human resource managers revealed that CEOs were more likely to include their HR managers in the strategic decision-making process if both had the same S–N preferences; T–F congruence did not affect inclusion (Nutter, 1991). However, in a case study analysis performed by 168 undergraduate students, Walck (1991) discovered that even though all types learned to use the philosophy of participative management well, Fs used it better than others and different types emphasized different parts of the philosophy. Most interestingly, the effect of T–F preference on performance was mediated by gender: F females performed significantly better than the rest of the sample, and T males performed significantly worse in their use of participative management.

Nonetheless, an attempt to find a relationship between type and participative leadership behaviors as measured by the *Group Environment Scale* failed (Conlen, 1992). Nor was there empirical evidence that type was related to observer ratings of Leaderless Group Discussions (N = 5793 managers), which require frequent interaction with group members and a high level of participative decision making (Grant, 1993, cited in Fleenor, Chapter 4).

Managing Subordinates

Research suggests that E, N, and F are associated with facilitating and interactive leader behaviors, while S, T, and J are associated with administrative skills.

In a structured interview study (Chung, 1986) of corporate planners (primarily ENTs), Ns characterized themselves as facilitators and process managers, while Ss tended to characterize themselves as planners. This self-report dichotomy was confirmed by an exploratory study of two school superintendents with high scores on N and two with high scores on S who were observed on-site over 20 days: N superintendents verbalized their unexplainable feelings a great deal, fostered a climate where Intuitive thinking styles were nurtured, and displayed a more caring attitude toward personnel and a preference for new challenges;

but they had less concern for facilities and finances and were impatient with routine and detail work (Brown, 1990).

Subordinates perceived similar differences. In research conducted on coaching activities of corporate middle managers (Hein, 1989), subordinates considered Es and Ns more effective at coaching; Ns gave more positive feedback, and Ns and Ts attended more to development needs of subordinates, while Js emphasized being on a tight schedule. There was no relationship between type and difficulty with coaching. Managers with E, N, and F preferences also received higher ratings from subordinates on motivation and morale measures in a study of 208 managers from several industries (Johnson & Golden, 1994). In a study of counseling directors using the *Leadership Practices Inventory* (Anderson, 1992), N was significantly related to challenging, E to encouraging, and IJ and TJ to modeling; interview data supported the survey findings. In a study of first-line supervisors at an Alaskan oil company, N and F were significantly positively related to subordinate perception of effective decision making, and F to empathic feedback; however, SJs were rated higher than NTs by subordinates for empathic feedback (Bablonka, 1992). Supervisors as well as subordinates gave N, as well as P, high marks for effective managerial behaviors and job success in a study of 62 engineering managers (Hay, 1966). However, in self-reports of 386 managers on the Management Skills Profile, only E was correlated with human relations and leadership skills and communication skills, and even this finding was not confirmed by subordinate and peer ratings (Fitzgerald, 1994). Other research suggests that Es tend to overrate themselves in comparison to subordinate ratings (Wilson & Wilson, 1994).

Although Fitzgerald's (1994) study showed few relationships between type and leadership, it did reveal that subordinate and peer ratings showed a significant correlation between S, T, and J and administrative skills such as planning, organizing, and time management; cognitive skills such as problem analysis and quantitative skills; delegating and controlling (except for T); and results orientation. Similarly, a study of predominantly STJ park managers found a relationship between SJ and subordinates' perceptions of a high level of initiation of structure and a high level of budgetary participation (Mackie, 1986).

Much of the data about the relationship between type and leaders' ability to manage subordinates comes from subordinate feedback on various instruments (*Management Skills Profile, Survey of Management Practices, Benchmarks®*, and SYMLOG®) which may be measuring different things. Van Velsor and Fleenor (Chapter 5) review in detail five studies of multirater feedback, some of which were briefly summarized above (Fitzgerald, 1994; Sundstrom, Koenigs, & Huet-Cox, 1994; Johnson & Golden, 1994; Van Velsor & Fleenor, 1994). They conclude that the perspective of the rater as a peer, subordinate, or supervisor affects the MBTI dimension to which the rater relates a leadership skill, but that there appears to be more of a relationship between type and subordinate and peer ratings than between type and supervisor ratings. Fs seem to make more of a favorable impression on peers and subordinates than on supervisors, but Ns tend to make a more favorable impression on their supervisors than they do on peers or subordinates. One of the most consistent findings reported by Van Velsor and Fleenor (Chapter 5) was that Es tend to overrate themselves relative to how they are seen by others. The authors suggest that this may reflect the prevalence of Es in the U.S. population and the social desirability of extraverted approaches.

Subordinates tend to rate managers in ways that are consistent with the managers' personalities (Sundstrom & Busby, Chapter 8). In a study by Sundstrom, Koenigs and Huet-Cox (1994), subordinates used SYMLOG to rate 381 managers in a manufacturing firm as dominant or submissive, friendly or unfriendly, and authority-aligned or authority-opposed. Results were consistent with type predictions: Es were associated with dominance (personal power, popularity, assertiveness, individualism, having a good time), Ns were associated with creativity, Fs were associated with friendliness, and Js were somewhat associated with conventional practice and efficiency. In a study by Pearman and Fleenor (cited in Chapter 4), peers and subordinates rated 150 managers for each of the 16 types using the Leadership Style Indicator (adjective list), and chose significantly different adjectives for each type. ISTJs, for example, were guarded and pressuring, while ENFPs were appreciative, easygoing, energetic, resourceful and understanding.

Another factor that influences superior-subordinate relationships is type congruence (the amount of similarity between types). A case study of four women college administrators and their women subordinates revealed that opposites on MBTI tended to have a more positive management relationship than those with similar types (Duley, 1989). This was confirmed in a study of 107 leader-member dyads in the aerospace industry in which perceived leader effectiveness was higher when dyads were dissimilar on the T–F scale. This echoes Nutt's (1986a) contention that *action-oriented types* SF, NT, and NF prefer to deal with their opposites rather than with others of the same style, although *action-averse* STs have difficulty coping with other styles. On the other hand, DiMarco and Tate's (1994) study of superior-subordinate dyads in the United States and Ireland found that the smaller the difference in type, the higher the superior rated the subordinate on the *Minnesota Satisfactoriness Scale*. Roush's (1992) research suggested that the likelihood of higher ratings varies with type; in a study of Naval Academy midshipmen, ESFPs and ENFJs rated like-type superiors high, while TJs rated like-type superiors quite low.

Managing Conflict

Although S–N preferences appear to have a significant impact on management style of interaction with subordinates, they do not appear to impact conflict management style. T–F preferences seem to have some impact, however. On three instruments measuring conflict handling modes, Fs had an increased tendency to use accommodation and cooperation, Es were more integrative and assertive, Js tended to compromise, and Ts were competitive; the S–N scale was unrelated to conflict handling (Kilmann & Thomas, 1975; Mills, Robey, & Smith, 1985). Another sample of managers, evenly distributed by gender, found that personality (E–I, T–F, and J–P) was a better predictor of integrating and compromising strategies than gender, while gender was a better predictor of obliging and dominating strategies; S was positively associated with avoiding conflict (McIntyre, 1991). However, no relationship was found between T–F and the conflict management style reported by 198 college students in an open-ended questionnaire (Nolan, 1985). The only preference that was associated with conflict management in a study of 40 project management students from the People's Republic of China was F, which was correlated with conflict avoidance; cross-cultural differences may account for the differences in results (Smith & Haar, 1990).

Managing Change and the Transformational Leader
Contemporary leadership studies and postmodern management theory seem to privilege one type of leadership: transformational leadership. Broadly conceived, transformational leaders have vision, creativity, flexibility, and the ability to integrate complexity, which enables them to generate substantial organizational commitment from followers in order to transform organizations and thus "manage change."

The demand for transformational leaders can be viewed as a response to a world that is increasingly complex, rapidly changing, and global in scope. In the good old days of stable environments and plenty, organizations were thought to need managers who steadfastly guided the ship (transactional leaders); but in today's rapidly changing and complex environment, organizations are thought to need people who can respond to change by developing new visions and renewing their organizations. This leadership role is usually assigned to top management and increasingly to top teams, whose tasks are to envision creative strategies that integrate complexity and build teams to enact those strategies.

When this shift from "managers" to "leaders" is framed in type terms, it emerges as a call for a shift from the ST and SJ managers who dominate most organizations to NF and NP leaders who can develop a vision of the future and arouse the excitement of organizational members to pursue it. Some research has found Intuition, Perceiving, and possibly Feeling associated with various measures of transformational leadership.

Three studies found a relationship between type and measures of transformational leadership. In a study of 128 senior executives of a major pharmaceutical company, for example, Ns and Ps were more likely than Ss and Js to self-report a disposition for transformational leadership; moreover, the more strongly a leader held a transformational disposition, the more likely subordinates were to rate the leader positively (Van Eron, 1991). The authors concluded that individual differences (type) were associated with leadership disposition (in this case, transformational leadership), and that leadership disposition was significantly associated with leadership practices related to transformational leadership, as measured by subordinates. However, the low correlations of the latter suggested to the researchers that other situational factors also influence leadership practices. In a study of 249 Executive Directors of YMCAs and YWCAs, type rather than situation explained the largest amount of variation in transformational leadership behavior, as measured by the Leadership Behavior Questionnaire (Sanchez, 1988).

Roush and Atwater (1992) found that S and F preferences had a high association with transformational leadership as measured by the Multifactor Officer Questionnaire, in a sample of Naval Academy midshipmen, and Roush (1992) found that Fs were significantly more likely to receive higher scores on transformational leadership as measured by a Leadership Feedback Questionnaire constructed for his study of approximately 2,000 Naval Academy midshipmen. Roush interpreted this as a result of the questionnaire's emphasis on interpersonal interaction between leader and follower. However, the range of variation in scores between types (1.92 to 2.11 on a five-point scale with 1 as the high rating) was so small that it is difficult for this reviewer to draw the conclusion that one type was more *transformational* than another.

Two key aspects of transformational leadership are creativity and ability to manage change. N and P were associated with innovation, the creativity style that searches for wholly new solutions, in four studies (Fleenor, Chapter 4, N = 12,115 managers; Carne & Kirton, 1982; Gryskiewicz & Tullar, 1995, N = 54 middle managers; Van Rooyen, 1994, N = 87 South African female managers) that compared type to the *Kirton Adaption-Innovation Inventory.* The relationship between innovation and E, reported in Carne and Kirton (1982), was not verified by the other studies. Sundstrom, Koenigs, and Huet-Cox (1994) found that subordinates' ratings of creativity in their supervisors (N = 361) were associated with N. Conversely, ESTJ was related to *adaption,* the methodical and incremental approach to change (Van Rooyen, 1994).

Managing change is also associated with N. People who actively create change in organizations were studied in situ in a management education setting (Evered, 1977). They were significantly more likely to be Ns, which was also significantly associated with the world of dreams and fantasies, rather than with the sensate world. A survey of school superintendents revealed that only ENTs implemented a significantly high percentage of changes during their tenure; however, there were only two ENTs in the sample (Crawford, 1991). On the other hand, high school principals and assistant principals who were successful change leaders, according to input gathered from subordinates using the *Change Facilitator Style Questionnaire,* were predominantly either NT or SJ (McGhee, 1992).

Change agents (organizational development, or OD, consultants) have been the subject of several studies involving type. Hamilton (1988) defined effectiveness of OD consultants as openness and responsiveness to others, comfort with ambiguity, and comfort with oneself in relation to others—traits associated with transformational leadership. In her study of U.S. Navy OD consultants, she found N positively related, S negatively related, and T–F unrelated to consultant effectiveness as rated by peers and superiors. Bushe and Gibbs (1990) also found only N predictive of trainer ratings (but not peer ratings) of OD consultant effectiveness. However, they concluded that higher levels of ego development as measured by the Washington University Sentence Completion Test (SCT) Form 11/68 (Loevinger and Wessler, 1970) were a better predictor of effectiveness, and that whatever information the N preference carried was better captured by ego development. Another study did not find Ns better able to tolerate ambiguity, according to the *Rydell-Rosen Ambiguity Tolerance Scale* (Durow, 1987).

A survey of change agents revealed that different types chose different tactics for creating organizational change (Slocum, 1978). Although all types use a similar repertoire of tactics, only NTs tended to use survey feedback and only STs tended to use behavior modification. Group- and people-oriented techniques, including decision centers, T-groups, and confrontation meetings, were used more by NFs, and transactional analysis was used almost exclusively by SFs.

Integrative Complexity

An interesting measure of transformational leadership is *integrative complexity*, defined by Tetlock, Peterson, and Berry (1993) as *evaluative differentiation* (the capacity and willingness to tolerate different points of view) and *conceptual integration* (capacity and willingness to generate linkages between points of view). In a thorough study, they found a high correlation between integrative complexity and N and P preferences. Assessing 131 MBA students with self-report measures (including MBTI), observations by trained experts in personality and management, and semiprojective tests, Tetlock et al. found an impressive consistency of correlations across these various methods. Integratively complex personalities were positively defined as those who are open-minded, open to new experiences, and good listeners, and who seek out information about the world and identify creative integrative solutions to problems. In self-reports, they had creativity, independence, flexibility, and empathy.

But there was a negative side as well: integrative complexity was negatively correlated with conformity, socialization, work motivation, responsibility, and orderliness; projective tests showed a correlation with power (not achievement or affiliation) motivation. While management observers rated their performance during an in-basket exercise as high in initiative and self-objectivity, and Tetlock et al. concluded there was a striking correlation with classic studies of scientific and artistic creativity, personality observers reported the *integratively complex* as unpredictable, hostile, rebellious, distrustful, undependable, and critical. Tetlock et al. interpreted the divergent portrait as the interpersonal price to be paid for self-assertive open-mindedness; these complex individuals are seen as narcissistic, hostile, exploitative of weakness of others, and even power hungry. The negative side of NP echoes Sundstrom and Busby's (Chapter 8) findings from a study using SYMLOG that INTPs were seen by co-workers as undervaluing friendly social relationships and expressing unfriendly values detrimental to teamwork, while overemphasizing self-interest, self-oriented assertiveness, resistance to authority, rejection of popularity, going it alone, and noncooperation with authority.

Tetlock et al. did not discuss in detail the portrait of *integratively simple* thinkers, who deny ambiguity, see things dichotomously, and don't synthesize divergent viewpoints; but they depicted them as practical, decisive, and principled, and as good team players who accept the rules of the collective. Personality observers viewed them as warm, giving, orderly, and socially compliant, but also unimaginative, suggestible, and prone to premature closure. While Tetlock et al. did not report any MBTI correlations, the presumption is that they are not NPs.

In light of the continuing call for visionary leaders with ability to function in ambiguous situations, Tetlock et al.'s (1993) identification of such leaders as integratively complex NPs shows there may be a dark side or downside to the vaunted NP leader. They reported that

> it remains to be seen . . . whether (a) the integratively complex MBAs will prosper as creative executives in corporations that value innovation or fail because they antagonize key persons critical to career success and (b) the integratively simple MBAs will prosper in corporate hierarchies that require conformity or fail because they do not display the capacity for flexible and innovative thinking critical to success in an increasingly global economy. (p. 510)

In summary, there is little evidence that certain types prefer one leadership style over another. There is some evidence that Ss and Fs are more participative decision makers than Ns and Ts. Research also suggests that N, E, and F are associated with facilitating and interactive leader behaviors with subordinates, while S, J, and T are associated with administrative skills. S–N appears to have no impact on conflict management, while Fs appear more likely to avoid, accommodate, or compromise than Ts. N and P appear to be positively associated with creativity, managing change, and transformational leadership.

Since the perspective of the rater as a subordinate, peer, or supervisor and the similarity of type of rater to ratee appear to influence the rater's perception of a manager's leadership ability, results of multirater feedback should be used with some caution.

TYPE AND ORGANIZATIONAL SUCCESS

Leaders and managers are embedded within organizations and workplaces. Individual differences such as type can impact their ability to succeed in these organizations and workplaces in a variety of ways (Furnham, 1993). This section addresses how type affects managers' ability to learn and self-manage, achieve goals and move up the organizational ladder, adapt to changing job requirements, and fit into the organizational culture

Self-Management and Learning

Self-management is often considered the first step toward managing others. A study of 347 students using the *Lifestyle Approaches Inventory* to measure self-management found that only J was significantly correlated with self-management, and specifically with the dimension of organization of physical space; S also appeared to be positively related to self-management (Williams, Verble, Price, & Layne, 1995).

Several researchers have examined the link between type and learning in management settings. Much of the early research was done on learning in laboratory settings, such as T-groups (training groups), where N and F preferences clearly predicted sensitivity to and ability to learn in these settings. Steele (1968) found that Ns learned more and were more effective than Ss in laboratory situations like National Training Labs (NTL) T-groups. Since NTL staff members in Steele's study were exclusively Ns, he concluded that laboratory learning attracted Ns, who probably trained others in a way that reached Ns more than Ss. Kilmann and Taylor (1974) built on Steele's work by hypothesizing that T-group norms were E, N, F, and P—interpersonally engaging (E) rather than intrapersonally engaging (I), associating (N) rather than describing (S), valuing (F) over conceptualizing (T), and processing (P) over seeking closure (J). Their empirical study showed that people with I, S, T, and J preferences tended to reject T-group experiences, and TJs most strongly rejected T-group norms. Haber (1980) discovered that Jungian attitudes (E–I) and dominant functions (S, N,

T, F) were related to evaluations of nonverbal and fantasy experiences, which are often used in laboratory learning. Haber found that Es and Ns evaluated nonverbal and fantasy experiences more positively than Is and Ts, and Fs preferred fantasy to nonverbal, while Ns preferred nonverbal to fantasy.

Conversely, in a production simulation that required learning well-defined, structured procedures, STs and SPs maintained a high interest throughout the simulation, while NTs and NFs lost interest rapidly and "dropped out" (Blaylock, 1983).

Not surprisingly, training and feedback can ameliorate the effects of type through learning. Training in entrepreneurship significantly affected individuals' perceptions of efficacy, ameliorating low confidence initially felt by Is, Fs, and Ps (Porter, Peacock, & Rabinowitz, 1994). However, in a program to improve attitudes toward quality, significant improvement was achieved, but these attitude shifts could not be related to type (Procopio, 1991).

Satisfaction, Self-Esteem, and Stress

There is some evidence that managers who prefer Extraversion are more satisfied with their jobs than are those who prefer Introversion. Extraverted managers reported significantly more job satisfaction than introverted managers on the Managerial Job Satisfaction Questionnaire (Fitzgerald, 1994; $N = 386$), and E and J students were more satisfied than I and P students with their role as student, as reported on the *Brayfield and Rothe Index of Job Satisfaction* (Rahim, 1981). Es also exhibited a more positive sense of well-being in a sample of health care executives (Shewchuk & O'Connor, 1995). This may be related to the fact that Es are better able to manage stress, according to both self-reports of stress (Fitzgerald, 1994) and the *Holistic Stress Test* (Short & Grasha, 1995; $N = 252$ research and development managers). (P was also significantly correlated positively with stress and negatively with self-care, according to Fitzgerald, 1994). On the other hand, in a sample of oil refinery engineering managers (Hay, 1966; $N = 62$), congruence between descriptions of actual and ideal job selves (self-ideal congruence) was significantly related to I; this was interpreted as a measure of job adjustment or self-in-job actualization.

Job satisfaction is often positively influenced by person–job fit and person–organization fit. Measuring job or organization in type terms is problematic. If the "type" of the job or organization is measured by the aggregate percentage of people in the job or organization, then fit seems to point to some measure of well-being, if not satisfaction. Shewchuk and O'Connor (1995) found that ETJs had a more positive sense of well-being than non-TJs in a sample of 522 health care executives, of which 63% were TJs. Another study of health care managers found that managers whose personality preferences were similar to the majority preferences in their organization had higher self-esteem, as measured by the *Inventory of Self-Actualizing Characteristics and Attitudes Checklist,* but they did not express more satisfaction with their jobs than those who were not congruent (Marcic, Aiuppa, & Watson, 1989). The researchers suggested that people with high fit tend to be rewarded by organizations, which increases their self-esteem. However, Rahim (1981) found no confirmation that people whose personality was aligned with their occupation were more satisfied in their jobs.

A study of employee turnover at long-term care facilities ($N = 320$) found no relationship between type and turnover (Bradshaw, 1986); turnover could also be a measure of job satisfaction.

Organizational Level

Studies of managers consistently reveal that, while managers in general exhibit a remarkably constant predominance of S, T, and J at all levels of management and across all kinds of organizations, movement up through managerial ranks reveals some predictable changes in frequency of preferences, most notably an increased frequency of N, which is usually interpreted as a process of selection (Hay, 1964; Johnson, 1992; Nordwick, 1994; Reynierse, 1993, 1995; Roach, 1986). Reynierse (1993) compared independent samples of personnel from three management levels across several industries ($N = 1,952$) and found that selection from pools of typologically diverse college students into lower-level supervisory ranks revealed a selection for I, N, T and J; at the middle-management level, I and N were increasingly selected; and at the executive level E, N, and T were selected.

Searching for predictors of promotion, Johnson (1992) fine-tuned our understanding of the increasing preference for N at the top in a fine-grained MBTI-TDI (Type Differentiation Indicator) analysis of 22 top achievers in the wholesale grocery business. Compared to other managers in the same industry, these achievers were significantly more N on all five subscales: abstract, imaginative, intellectual, theoretical, and original. They also were significantly higher in the T subscale of questioning, the P subscale of spontaneity, and the leader measure.

Regardless of type, some research has suggested that successful managers may be significantly clearer about their preferences (Johnson, 1992; Rytting, Ware, & Prince, 1994a). Knowing yourself well may be the best path to success.

Success Due to Performance

Even though E and N are somewhat overrepresented among executives, there is little evidence that type predicts performance that leads to success. In fact, a field study that compared type to internal performance appraisal ratings found that ISTJ, the modal type in the organization (38%), was negatively correlated with performance; this was true even though T alone was positively correlated with performance (Markham & Murry, 1994). In a study of women administrators in community colleges (predominantly E, N, T, and J), Julian (1992) concluded that situational or organizational factors were more highly related to career achievement than personal characteristics. Other variables interact with type to affect performance. In one interesting example, Es with a low degree of subject knowledge outperformed Es with a high degree of subject knowledge in a week-long simulation with medical students, while Is with a high degree of subject knowledge outperformed Is with a low degree of subject knowledge (Cloutier, 1986).

Ns were higher performers and had been promoted at an earlier age, in a sample of 66 managers with identical job descriptions (Loehr, 1983), yet N school superintendents were not more likely to be exemplary (Durow, 1987); and in a regional study of business founders, NTJs were both the most successful and most unsuccessful at running high-tech firms (Blumenthal, 1994). A study of high-school principals found STJs more likely to be high performers (Gardner & Martinko, 1990).

Es earned significantly more income than Is, and Ts more than Fs, in a sample of 102 white male small-business owner/managers in Mississippi (Rice & Lindecamp, (1989), but they did not make significantly more than could be expected, and the sample was too small to draw clear conclusions. Cultural factors may influence which preferences lead to performance: In a study of European and Chinese managers who were rated by their supervisors, Furnham and Stringfield (1992) found that E tended to be correlated with high job performance ratings for Europeans, and I associated with job success for Chinese managers, but these correlations were not statistically significant.

At the bottom of the ladder, screening and training did not help to select for success by type. An attempt to relate type to administrative abilities using a simulated assessment center procedure failed (Smith, 1991). Training did not benefit one type more than another in a study of 57 management trainees of a major retail firm; after 14 weeks of training and 3 months on the job, no type was more successful than another and there was also no significant relationship between successful types and perceptions of success (Burlew, 1987). At the top of the ladder, no one type outshone the others: No particular type preference characterized the CEOs of 348 successful companies (Rytting et al., 1994a).

However, training in type followed by feedback from lower-ranked students at the U.S. Naval Academy resulted in significant positive behavioral change among upperclassmen, as reflected in improved ratings by subordinates on seven items eight weeks later (see Chapter 6; Roush, 1992; Roush & Barry, 1994). The greatest change occurred among Fs, then Ps; specifically, ENFPs, ESFPs, ESTJs, ISFJs, INFPs, and ESTPs showed significant change on at least four of the seven items. ISTJs, however, were rated more negatively after feedback on all seven items, even though they had initially been rated more positively than most other types. Roush interpreted the results by suggesting that the required behavioral changes were more comfortable for ENFPs than for ISTJs; another interpretation may be that the minority population of Fs and Ps were more motivated to respond to feedback than the majority STJs (Roush & Barry, 1994; also see Roush, Chapter 6 in this book).

Although type is not a global predictor of performance in organizations, it may predict success at specific things. Although Js did not outperform Ps on goal attainment using planning methods (Fitzgerald, 1987), successful implementers of management by objectives (MBO) were more likely to be S, T, and J, while unsuccessful implementers were more likely to be N, F, and P (Jaffe, 1980). Nonetheless, Hoy and Hellreigel (1982) used goal setting as a measure of effectiveness in a survey of 150 small-business CEOs, but concluded that since all types chose the same ST goal of *internal efficiency*, there was no relationship between type and goal setting.

Type may be a more reliable guide to how managers spend their time. When Gardner and Martinko (1990) observed principals on site and coded their behavior using Luthans and Lockwood's (1984) Leader Observation System, they discovered that Is devoted more time to paperwork, problem solving, and interacting with outsiders; Es spent more time socializing and politicking; Ts engaged in more staffing activities; and Js spent more time on paperwork, exchanging routine information, and interacting with outsiders. Whether these activities lead to success depends on the demands of the specific organization.

Success Due to Changing Job Requirements

Movement up the management ladder can be seen as a process of selection for jobs with new and different requirements, rather than a result of successful performance. Church and Alie (1986) tested the relationship between type, position in the organization, and job content, using the *Functional Job Analysis Self-Report*. Surveying 110 managers at two manufacturing plants, which they characterized as traditional mechanistic environments, they found a larger proportion of NTs at the upper levels where jobs were more people focused; at middle-management levels, jobs that were data focused had significantly more Ss, while jobs that were people focused were equally S and N.

Reynierse (1993, 1995; Reynierse & Harker, 1995) drew on Jaques' (1976) theory of bureaucracy to interpret type changes as a process of managerial flow through hierarchical bureaucratic organizations. Lower-level managerial functions—characterized by operational responsibilities, short time horizons, and expected outputs expressed in specific terms—were hypothesized to require S; whereas middle manager and executive functions—characterized by strategic and institutional responsibilities, longer time horizons, and abstraction—were hypothesized to require more N. This selection process operated virtually identically in Japan, except at the entry level, where Japanese entry-level managers were more type diverse (Reynierse, 1995). Reynierse interpreted this as the result of differential hiring practices: While U.S. companies make a critical selection at initial hiring, Japanese companies hire a diverse pool and slowly evaluate and socialize their managers over time. Reynierse and Harker's (1995) findings that line managers tended to be J while staff managers tended to be more N and P led them to hypothesize that J represents a tendency toward bureaucracy and P a tendency toward entrepreneurism and change.

A continuing selection process may have been responsible for the outplacement of senior executives with significantly more I, S, and J than those who remained employed (Reynierse, 1991). Reynierse hypothesized that this *deselection* could have been a function of behaviors (Is were out touch with the organization's political reality, Ss were preoccupied with immediate activities, and Js were inflexible) or strategy (strategic shifts in a business may have left "cash cow" ISJ managers without a business unit to manage, which could be related to type).

Organizational Culture and Climate

Organizational culture theory suggests that cultures are reflections of founder's or leader's preferences. Studies that use type to measure leader preference and a variety of measures including Likert's Profile of Organizational Characteristics for organizational culture find no support for this hypothesis (Hagerman, 1991; Matteson, 1987; Klusendorf, 1985). High school principals with NF preferences were not perceived to have higher "morale" at their organizations and SJ managers did not have higher "goal focus" at their organizations than did principals or managers with other types (Hagerman, 1991).

There is some evidence that organizational culture encourages managers of all types to accept certain core values regardless of type, and that those values reflect the majority preferences in the organization. A study of managers' stories of ideal organizations revealed that managers of all types learned to value the organizational culture of the majority managerial type, ST—and that STs valued it the most (Walck, 1992; Hellreigel & Slocum, 1980). In a manufacturing organization, 361 managers, regardless of individual MBTI preferences, appeared to express core organizational values of individual prominence, active reinforcement of authority, tough-mindedness, obedience, dedication, and quiet contentment, as measured by subordinates using SYMLOG (Sundstrom and Busby, Chapter 8). These managers were predominantly I, S, T, and J, preferences that appear to this author to be aligned with the organization's core values. When Sundstrom and Busby (Chapter 8) compared these organizational values with an ideal culture (the "most effective profile" for teamwork as measured by SYMLOG), they found that, while the organization's leaders' profiles were roughly parallel with the ideal, there were statistically significant departures on the majority of items: Teamwork and cooperation was less valued, while authority, convention, and self-interest were more valued. The MBTI type that deviated furthest from teamwork was INTP. Sundstrom and Busby suggested that the TJ majority overestimated the differences between themselves and the NPs, leading to polarization of values and scapegoating.

Bridges (1992) has developed an Organizational Culture Index (OCI), which claims to measure culture in type terms. Rytting, Ware, and Prince (1994b) found no psychometric support for the OCI. They did find that family firms are more likely to have CEOs with I and IF preferences than nonfamily firms, which have more E and S. They hypothesized that family firms were more likely to give IFs a chance than non-family firms.

A study of type and organizational climate (Collins, 1965) found that Ns favored open climates and had low satisfaction with closed climates, while Ss had high satisfaction with both and were more adjustable. Adding T sharpened the level of acceptance: NTs most strongly favored open climates and rejected closed climates, while STs were more accepting of closed climates.

In summary, although S, T, and J are the dominant preferences in upper management (reflecting the dominant preferences in the male population in the U.S.), there is an increasing selection for N as one moves up through the ranks. While there is some evidence that Ns are high achievers and get promoted earlier, type does not appear to predict success in organizations. No one type stands out at the top. While training may be a better indicator of success than type, training does not seem to differentially impact people with different types.

The findings that Ns seem more comfortable learning in less-structured situations and favor open environments may contribute to their selection, or self-selection, for executive jobs, which are fairly unstructured. There is also evidence of selection for E in the executive ranks; Es have a more positive sense of well-being that may help them manage the stress of executive positions better than Is.

While type may not predict success, it may predict what people tend to spend their time on, such as Is spending more time on paperwork and Es more on politicking. These activities may lead to more or less success, depending on the specific organizational requirements or culture. There is some evidence that managers of all types learn to value "managerial culture," which can be characterized in type terms as STJ, practical and results oriented.

APPLYING TYPE TO MANAGEMENT

There is a large and growing industry of consultants who use type to help managers identify their strengths and weaknesses as managers and leaders in order to improve their managerial and leadership skills. Experts in type have published many guides to help consultants and managers apply type (e.g., Barr & Barr, 1989; Hirsh, 1991; Hirsh & Kummerow, 1990; Roach, 1989). Leadership programs, such as those offered by the Center for Creative Leadership, regularly include the

MBTI as one of a battery of instruments used to help managers examine their leadership style. Consultants also target team building as a useful application of type (Hirsh, 1992). Self-help books have even reached out to managers to help them apply type in the workplace (e.g., Kroeger with Thuesen, 1992; Kummerow, Barger, & Kirby, 1997).

This widespread knowledge and use of type has spawned many articles on how to apply type to specific work settings or improve leadership in organizations. Most of these articles do not go beyond hypotheses already developed about type and do not approach application from the perspective of research.

Two studies that do approach application from a research perspective are Campbell (1988) and Hoyer and Huszczo (1994). Campbell (1988) studied a search conference on participative community planning in Montana in which there was an extreme preponderance of NTJs. Since NTJs tend to inhibit cooperation, she used this knowledge to enhance the effectiveness of the conference, and concluded that understanding the interplay of types among individuals can help to understand and design search conferences and thus facilitate social change. Hoyer and Huszczo (1994) looked at two groups that are traditionally in conflict: union and management. They designed an instrument to measure the quality of union and management relations and found that there was no relationship between subjects' reports of relationship quality and subjects' type. Both union and management subjects in their workshops were primarily E, S, T, and J. Using this knowledge, they worked with unions and management in an OD effort to improve their ability to work together.

Type may also help people attend to the results of feedback from other sources. A trainer reported (in Wilson, Wilson, Booth, & Shipper, 1992) that when the MBTI was used after participants had received results from the Survey of Management Practices, the participants got much more out of MBTI feedback than any other time he had used it. The trainer reasoned that having learned their impact on co-workers from the first instrument, the participants became more motivated to study the MBTI results to understand the reasons for this impact. I also found the same effect with undergraduate students in a leadership course; when they received their MBTI results in the middle of the course rather than at the beginning, they had a much more positive response to the MBTI and could compare it to other knowledge gained in the course as well as feedback from fellow students.

More research on application and intervention using type theory in management settings is needed.

CONCLUSION

Despite considerable research conducted on type and management over the past 30 years, results, as Furnham and Stringfield (1992) have noted, remain limited and equivocal. Although research on type distributions in organizations has produced robust results (see Chapter 1), research that attempts to predict behavior from type, and therefore adopts the hypothesis-building and hypothesis-testing model of management science, has produced mixed results. Research testing hypothesized relationships between type and information processing, decision making, conflict management, and leadership have produced results that sometimes confirm and sometimes conflict with prior research. This makes it difficult to predict with confidence the impact of type on managerial and leadership behaviors. Reasons why this stream of research is problematic are discussed in the next section, along with implications for future research.

After 30 years of research on type and management, we can draw the following conclusions. When it comes to decision making, all four functions (S, N, T, and F) may have some impact on all steps in the decision-making process; we should not assume that only S–N affects information gathering and only T–F affects information processing, as has been hypothesized. Nonetheless, psychological type seems less important than task type in determining the kinds of information people choose and the kind of process they use to evaluate it, and situational factors appear more important than type in decision making. People of all types seemed to want similar kinds of information for solving the specific problems that faced them.

With respect to leadership, there is little evidence that certain types prefer one leadership style over another. There is some evidence that Ss and Fs are more participative decision makers than Ns and Ts. However, research also suggests that N, as well as E and F, are associated with facilitating and interactive leader behaviors with subordinates, while S, J, and T are associated with administrative skills. N and P appear to be positively associated with creativity, managing change, and transformational leadership. When facing conflict, Fs appear more likely to avoid, accommodate, or compromise than Ts.

Type does not appear to predict success in organizations. No one type stands out at the top. Training appears to affect success, and some types seem more disposed to certain kinds of training than others (Ns to laboratory training). Training that raised confidence levels and provided feedback on leadership behavior differentially impacted people with different types.

Although S, T, and J are the majority preferences in upper management, there is an increasing selection for N as one moves up through the ranks and for E and T at the executive level. While this movement up the ranks may in part be due to superior performance (there is some evidence that Ns are high achievers and get promoted earlier), it can also be interpreted as a selection process for jobs with new and different requirements, such as a higher tolerance for or adaptability to the open-ended, higher-risk environment of upper management.

NTs appear less risk-averse than STs, and there is some evidence that Ns and Ts are better able than Ss and Fs to make decisions in unstructured environments. Ns seem more comfortable learning in less-structured situations and favor open environments. In complex, open-ended situations, Ns and Ts have been more likely to recognize problems and patterns, request more and quantitative information for problem solving, and outperform Ss and Fs. Ns and Ps are more likely to seek out information about the world and identify creative and integrative solutions to problems. Finally, Es have a more positive sense of well-being that may help them manage the stress of executive positions better than Is.

While type may not predict success, it may predict what people tend to spend their time on, such as Is spending more time on paperwork and Es more time on politicking. These activities may lead to more or less success, depending on the specific organizational requirements or culture.

There is some evidence that managers of all types learn to value "managerial culture," which can be characterized in type terms as STJ, practical and oriented to goal-setting and results.

The Future for Research in the Management Science Paradigm

The difficulty of predicting behavior from type with confidence has led some management scientists to dismiss psychological type as a meaningful concept for addressing issues of managerial behavior. However, prediction is a problem for research in the social sciences in general and for the study of organizational behavior in particular. As Mohr (1982) noted, there is "a lack of reasonable and warranted *stability* in results [in social science research]. . . . We keep getting different answers to similar questions" (p. 8).

Mohr suggested several sources of instability. First, we use radically different methods or devices for measuring something. The foregoing review demonstrated the bewildering variety of instruments that have been used to measure leadership and other management behaviors in relationship to type. A second source of instability is the confusion between process theory and variance theory: "An explanation of the process of acquiring power within an organization—how this process works—is not the same as the explanation for the distribution of power—why one person or unit has more than another" (Mohr, 1982, p. 13). We could say the same of type: An explanation of the process for utilizing intuition in management and leadership—how intuition works—is not the same as explaining the distribution of Ns in executive ranks—why there are more Ns among executives than middle managers and supervisors. A third source of instability is interaction, which Mohr defines as the dependence of the impact of one phenomenon on the presence or level of another. Inadequate research designs for separating situational and demographic variables that interact with type may be partly to blame for inconclusive research results.

Even if we resolved some of these sources of instability raised by Mohr, we would still need to question the premise: Does type predict behavior? Type theory states that type involves preference, not ability and skill. Preference may lead to certain observable behaviors, but ability, skill, education, and situational variables such as opportunity also impact behavior. Behavior is thus a complex outcome of multiple variables. Whereas the lack of skill will not only influence but even preclude certain behaviors (for example, if I have not learned to speak French fluently, it is unlikely that I can successfully conduct a business negotiation with native French speakers who do not speak English), the lack of a preference does not preclude behaviors associated with that preference. For example, a preference for Extraversion does not preclude the practice of behaviors associated with Introversion; an Extravert can close her office door and "manage by concentrated desk time," a behavior associated with Introversion. The Extravert may close his door less often, however, which suggests that we should be investigating the degree to which a preference impacts a desired behavior and under what conditions, rather than whether the preference impacts it or not in an absolute sense.

If type cannot predict behavior in a simple, direct way, this is not necessarily a bad thing. Management science has the explicit goal of rationalizing organizations—making them more efficient and effective. Research on type and management that follows the paradigm of management science would have an implicit goal of using the predictive power of type to make organizations function more efficiently and effectively. While this may seem like a reasonable organizational goal, consider the implications for individuals if type were employed in this overly simplified and prescriptive way.

If we "know," for example, that ESTJs resist change, then the efficient thing to do may be to remove ESTJs from positions that require adaptation and flexibility. If we "know," for example, that type-heterogeneous groups solve open-ended problems more effectively than type-homogeneous groups, then the effective thing to do may be to create type-heterogeneous groups when we have an open-ended problem to solve. Both scenarios imply maintaining a record of employees' types for organizational purposes and using psychological type as a tool for selection, assignment, and even appraisal of managers and employees. This approach to using type in management generates ethical problems. It fails to consider how people develop and use type along with other knowledge and skills acquired during their lifetimes to improve their practice of management. A better approach is the one suggested by McCaulley (1990): Instead of asking which type is the best leader, one should ask how each type shows leadership and what strategies can be used to enhance leadership in each type.

Another problem with following in the footsteps of traditional management science is that management science, like the concept of management itself, is bound up with our notion of the modern. Yet we live in a world that is increasingly postmodern, in which the modern concepts of stable principles of management and unitary personality functioning in a fixed universe are giving way to the concepts of flexible leadership and multiple selves adapting to a universe in flux (Wheatley, 1992). When type is viewed as a stable personality construct, it may keep us locked into a modern and therefore static view of management and leadership. A better understanding of and emphasis on type dynamics, type development, and the interactive effects of type and management could lead us to a postmodern perspective on type and leadership that would help us to unlock other paradigms for research.

Alternate Paradigms for Research

Although management science is the dominant paradigm, or conceptual framework, in management research today, it is not the only paradigm. Put another way, management science is not the only reliable way of knowing about the relationships between type, management, and leadership. Management science is embedded in the *functionalist* paradigm, which tries to reduce one variable to being a function of another—that is, autocratic leadership is a function of TJ preferences. There are other paradigms for researchers to explore in order to understand the relationship between type and management. In some ways, type practitioners and management consultants are already implicitly using these other ways of knowing.

One paradigm, or way of knowing, that is starting to challenge management science successfully is called *naturalistic inquiry* (Lincoln, 1985) or the *interpretive paradigm* (Burrell & Morgan, 1979), and is what anthropologists call *ethnographic research*. Naturalistic inquiry asks the researcher to explore human behavior in natural settings, such as the workplace, and describe that behavior as accurately as possible. Instead of using questionnaires that attempt to capture behavior with the researcher's predetermined categories for behavior, the researcher observes behavior as it emerges in the workplace and uses methods like in-depth interviews to get open-ended responses and the subject's point of view on what is happening. This kind of inquiry can explore process, and it produces a way of knowing about behavior that anthropologists have traditionally considered reliable.

A few researchers have begun to use this paradigm to explore the relationships between management and type (Brown, 1990; Kerlin, 1992). They start by identifying managers and employees with clear preferences, and then observe them in the workplace and interview them. Questions that a researcher might try to answer through interviews and observation might include:

- What do Sensing, Intuitive, Thinking, and Feeling managers do to motivate their subordinates?
- How do they describe their methods for motivating employees, and what do they think is successful?
- How do Sensing, Intuitive, Thinking, and Feeling managers differentially construct their roles as managers and leaders?
- Do managers at different levels describe leadership the same way, and does type help to explain this?

- How do subordinates perceive and respond to their leaders, and does the interaction of subordinate and leader types affect this perception?
- When does similarity in type bind managers and employees together, and when does it render them apart?

The interpretive paradigm described above, like the previously described functionalist paradigm in which management science is embedded, tries to understand the world as it is. It seeks to understand the status quo and to promote order and improve cohesion. However, two other paradigms, which Burrell and Morgan (1979) call the *radical humanist* and *radical structuralist* paradigms, seek to understand how the world can be changed (hence the label *radical*) rather than how it can be maintained. Radical humanism tries to understand how individual humans can create change by altering their own consciousness. If people can change their understanding of their situation, can alter how they perceive reality, then they may be able to transcend social and organizational constraints and realize their full human potential.

Researchers using this paradigm might ask the following questions:

- How can type knowledge enable people to see their organizations, their managers and subordinates, and themselves in new ways—how can it change their consciousness of who they are and allow them to transcend the limits placed on them by their organizations?
- How can type knowledge help leaders change organizations so that all employees will be able to achieve their potential?
- Do some types find it easier to alter their perceptions than others, and are they more likely to be certain kinds of leaders?
- What kinds of interventions do different types of leaders introduce and why?

Research on organization-employee fit and OD interventions would benefit from this new way of knowing, as would career counseling applications of type, particularly if the researcher focused primarily on the perspective and needs of the employee rather than the needs of the organization. Action research that intervenes in an organization and studies the consequences of that intervention would also be a way of using the radical humanist way of knowing.

The paradigm of *radical structuralism* seeks change through altering organizational and social structures, rather than altering individual consciousness. This way of knowing steps back from the individual manager or leader and looks squarely at the organization or society in which the manager is embedded. Questions that a researcher in this paradigm might ask include:

• What are the structures of power in organizations? Does type play a role in creating these power structures?
• How does one group dominate another? Does one type dominate another in organizational settings, and how does it maintain that dominance?
• Does conflict create change? Does type explain some of the conflicts in organizations?
• What kinds of networks distribute power and information? Does type play a role in how those networks are constructed, and how they are maintained?

Research on type distributions may be a first step in answering these questions. Research suggests that there are structural impediments to change in organizations: Does the preponderance of TJs in management across diverse organizations help to maintain stable organizational structures, even when change is required? How do TJ managers maintain stable structures, and what do NPs do to change structures?

In conclusion, in light of our limited success linking type to management and leadership behaviors, we should be cautious about how we apply type concepts to management practice. Despite limited research results, hypotheses about type and management generated by normative type theory are often presented as unvarying truths. Modern management's tendency to look for tools to rationalize practice makes unethical practices such as stereotyping and "type casting" all too easy. If we look to rectify some of the sources of instability in the management science paradigm while branching out into new paradigms for research, we can take type into the postmodern era and have a significant impact on management and leadership practice.

REFERENCES

Allen, N. H. (1986). *In search of a mix for excellence: An exploratory study of the possible relationship between organizational performance and the psychological type of key group members.* Unpublished doctoral dissertation, George Washington University, Washington, DC.

Anderson, S. J. (1992). *Psychological type and leadership (Counselling directors).* Unpublished doctoral dissertation, University of Calgary, Calgary, Alberta, Canada.

Bablonka, J. P. (1992). *The relationship between interpersonal effectiveness and psychological type of first-line supervisors*. Unpublished doctoral dissertation, The Fielding Institute, Santa Barbara, CA.

Barr, L., & Barr, N. (1989). *Leadership Equation*. Austin, TX: Sunbelt Media.

Bass, B. M. (1985). *Leadership and performance beyond expectations*. New York: Free Press.

Bennis, W., & Nanus, B. (1985). *Leaders: The strategies for taking charge*. New York: Harper & Row.

Berg, K. H. (1993). *Leadership styles and personality types of Minnesota school superintendents*. Unpublished doctoral dissertation, University of Minnesota, Minneapolis.

Blaylock, B. K. (1983). Teamwork in a simulated production environment. *Research in Psychological Type, 6,* 58–67.

Blumenthal, R. A. (1994). Winners and losers: Types that found businesses and that succeed or fail in their businesses. In C. Fitzgerald (Ed.), *Proceedings from the Myers-Briggs Type Indicator and Leadership: An International Research Conference* (pp. 209–217). College Park, MD: University of Maryland University College National Leadership Institute.

Boreham, N. C. (1987). Causal attribution by sensing and intuitive types during diagnostic problem solving. *Instructional Science, 16,* 123–126.

Bradshaw, S. L. (1986). *Myers-Briggs personality types of administrative managers in long-term care facilities and their relationship to employee turnover rates and resident occupancy rates*. Unpublished doctoral dissertation, The University of Texas at Austin.

Breeding, B. E. (1988). *Positive synergy in the design, development and implementation of successful management information system: Individual differences revisited*. Unpublished doctoral dissertation, University of Houston, Houston, TX.

Bridges, W. (1992). *The character of organizations: Using Jungian type in organizational development*. Palo Alto, CA: Davies-Black.

Brittain, K. H. (1981). *Analysis and comparison of communication styles of executive styles of executive women and women in traditional roles*. Unpublished doctoral Dissertation, Memphis State University, Memphis, TN.

Brocato, T. C. (1985). *Psychological type and task accomplishment in the public school management team*. Unpublished doctoral dissertation, University of Oklahoma, Norman.

Brown, A. R. (1990). *The use of intuition in the decision-making processes of public school superintendents*. Unpublished doctoral dissertation, Texas A&M, College Station.

Bueler, C. M. (1984). *A study of relationships among personality traits and communication styles of secondary and elementary school principals*. Unpublished doctoral dissertation, University of Missouri, Columbia.

Burlew, L. D. (1987). *The relationship between MBTI types and the actual and perceived success of entry-level retail managers*. Unpublished doctoral dissertation, George Washington University, Washington, DC.

Burns, J. M. (1978). *Leadership*. New York: Harper & Row.

Burrell, G., & Morgan, G. (1979). *Sociological paradigms and organizational analysis*. Portsmouth, NH: Heinemann.

Bushe, G. R., & Gibbs, B. W. (1990). Predicting organization development consulting competence from the *Myers-Briggs Type Indicator* and stage of ego development. *Journal of Applied Behavioral Science, 26 (3),* 337–357.

Cabral, G., & Joyce, M. H. (1991). Managers and psychological type in an industrial setting: Sex differences and similarities, managerial level, and age. *Journal of Psychological Type, 21,* 40–53.

Campbell, D. P., & Van Velsor, E. (1985). *The use of personality measures in the leadership development program.* Greensboro, NC: Center for Creative Leadership.

Campbell, K. Q. (1988). *A Jungian view of the search conferences process.* Unpublished doctoral dissertation, The Fielding Institute, Santa Barbara, CA.

Carne, G. C., & Kirton, M. J. (1982). Styles of creativity: Test-score correlations between *Kirton Adaption-Innovation Inventory* and *Myers-Briggs Type Indicator. Psychological Reports, 50,* 31–36.

Catford, L. R. (1987). *Creative problem solving in business: Synergy of thinking, intuiting, sensing and feeling strategies.* Unpublished doctoral dissertation, Stanford University, Stanford, CA.

Chung, I. K. (1986). *An investigation of the relationship between the corporate planner's personal characteristics and the successful functioning of the corporate planning process.* Unpublished doctoral dissertation, University of Minnesota, Minneapolis.

Church, L. M., & Alie, R. E. (1986). Relationships between managers' personality characteristics and their management levels and job foci. *Akron Business and Economic Review, 17 (4),* 29–45.

Cloutier, M. G. (1986). *The relationship of medical knowledge and psychological type to aggressive leadership performance of senior medical students in a stressful environment.* Unpublished doctoral dissertation, The University of Texas at Austin.

Coe, C. K. (1992). The MBTI: Potential uses and misuses in personnel administration. *Public Personnel Management, 12(4),* 511–522.

Collins, J. A. (1965). *Individual personality and organizational climate.* Unpublished doctoral dissertation, Claremont Graduate School and University Center, Claremont, CA.

Conlen, J. J. (1992). *The psychological typologies and leadership behaviors of first-line supervisors in a large automotive company.* Unpublished doctoral dissertation, Western Michigan University, Kalamazoo.

Craig, D. L., Craig, C. H., & Sleight, C. (1988). Type preferences of decision makers: Corporate and clinical. *Journal of Psychological Type, 16,* 33–37.

Crawford, S. G. (1991). *Leadership types and second-order change (superintendents).* Unpublished doctoral dissertation, University of North Carolina at Greensboro.

Crothers, H. L. (1990). *The relationship of Myers-Briggs types to the perceived usefulness of statistical methodology by managers.* Unpublished doctoral dissertation, The Union Institute, Cincinnati, OH.

Davey, J. A., Schell, B. H., & Morrison, K. (1993). The Myers-Briggs personality indicator and its usefulness for problem solving by mining industry personnel. *Group and Organization Management, 18(1),* 50–65.

Davis, D. L., Grove, S. J., & Knowles, P. A. (1990). An experimental application of personality type as an analogue for decision-making style. *Psychological Reports, 66,* 167–175.

Davis, D. L. (1981). *An experimental investigation of the form of information presentation, psychological type of the user, and performance within the context of a management information system.* Unpublished doctoral dissertation, University of Florida, Gainesville.

Davis, T. L. (1981). *Personality type, leadership style and leadership training: A study of secondary school principals.* Unpublished doctoral dissertation, Auburn University, Auburn, AL.

De Waele, M. (1978). Managerial style and the design of decision aids. *Omega, the International Journal of Management Science, 6(1),* 5–13.

Dietl, J. A. (1981). *Study reflecting the dominant personality style most successful in exemplifying effective situational leadership within a corporate organization.* Unpublished doctoral dissertation, United States International University, San Diego, CA.

DiMarco, N., & Tate, R. M. (1994). A cross-cultural comparison of superior-subordinate MBTI preferences and their relationship with performance ratings. In C. Fitzgerald (Ed.), *Proceedings from the Myers-Briggs Type Indicator and Leadership: An International Research Conference* (pp. 61–71). College Park, MD: University of Maryland University College National Leadership Institute.

Dobbs, R. L. (1988). *The relationship between leadership effectiveness and personality type for a group of urban elementary school principals.* Unpublished doctoral dissertation, Memphis State University, Memphis, TN.

Doering, R. D. (1972, March–April). Enlarging scientific task team creativity. *Personnel, 43*–52.

DuBrin, A. J. (1995). *Leadership: Research findings, practice, and skills.* Boston: Houghton Mifflin.

Duley, S. I. (1989). *Characteristics and human skills of women who manage women: A community college case study.* Unpublished doctoral dissertation, Western Michigan University, Kalamazoo.

Durow, W. P. (1987). *Ambiguity tolerance and intuition in the management styles of selected Iowa school administrators.* Unpublished doctoral dissertation, Iowa State University, Ames.

Evered, R. D. (1977). Organizational activism and its relation to "reality" and mental imagery. *Human Relations, 30(4),* 311–334.

Flores, M. (1987). *Relationship between personality types and effective leadership styles.* Unpublished doctoral dissertation, University of Nevada, Las Vegas.

Fitzgerald, C. (1994). The relationship between the MBTI and ratings of management skills, occupational stress, and managerial job satisfaction. In C. Fitzgerald (Ed.), *Proceedings from the Myers-Briggs Type Indicator and Leadership: An International Research Conference* (pp. 163–176). College Park, MD: University of Maryland University College National Leadership Institute.

Fitzgerald, C. (1987). *Daily versus monthly planning: The effect on adult goal pursuit and attainment.* Unpublished doctoral dissertation, State University of New York at Buffalo.

Frankowski, R. J. (1992). *Relationships of selection method, leadership style, and personality type among chairpersons in engineering departments (Department chairperson selection).* Unpublished doctoral dissertation, Marquette University, Milwaukee, WI.

Furnham, A. (1993). *Personality at work: The role of individual differences in the workplace.* New York: Routledge.

Furnham, A., & Stringfield, P. (1993). Personality and occupational behavior: *Myers-Briggs Type Indicator* correlates of managerial practices in two cultures. *Human Relations, 46 (7),* 827–848.

Furnham, A., & Stringfield, P. (1992). Personality and work performance: *Myers-Briggs Type Indicator* correlates of managerial performance in two cultures. *Personality and Individual Differences, 14(1),* 145–153.

Futrell, D. A. (1992). *Cognitive ability and Myers-Briggs Type Indicator preferences as predictors of group performance: An empirical study (work teams).* Unpublished doctoral dissertation (1992), University of Tennessee, Knoxville.

Garceau, L. R. (1986). *The relationship of cognitive style and usage environment to decision-making performance, user satisfaction and information preferences: A contingency model.* Unpublished doctoral dissertation, Boston University, Boston, MA.

Garden, A. M. (1989). Organizational size as a variable in type analysis and employee turnover. *Journal of Psychological Type, 17,* 3–13.

Gardner, W. L., & Martinko, M. (1990). The relationship between psychological type, managerial behavior, and managerial effectiveness: An empirical investigation. *Journal of Psychological Type, 19,* 35–43.

Gauld, V., & Sink, D. (1985). The MBTI as a diagnostic tool in organization development interventions. *Journal of Psychological Type, 9,* 24–29.

Ghani, J. A. (1981). *The effects of information representation and modification on decision performance.* Unpublished doctoral dissertation, University of Pennsylvania, Philadelphia.

Ginn, C. W., & Sexton, D. L. (1988). Psychological types of *Inc.* 500 founders and their spouses. *Journal of Psychological Type, 16,* 3–12.

Grant, L. D. (1993). The *Myers-Briggs Type Indicator* and ratings of leadership behavior. Unpublished master's thesis, North Carolina State University, Raleigh, NC.

Gryskiewicz, N. D., & Tullar, W. T. (1995). The relationship between personality type and creativity style among managers. *Journal of Psychological Type, 32,* 30–35.

Haber, R. A. (1980). Different strokes for different folks: Jung's typology and structured experience. *Group and Organization Studies, 5(1),* 113–121.

Hagerman, S. F. (1991). *A comparative analysis of leader personality type and work environment.* Unpublished doctoral dissertation, University of Arkansas, Fayetteville.

Hai, D. M. (1983). Comparisons of personality dimensions in managers: Is there a management aptitude? *Akron Business & Economic Review, 14(1),* 31–36.

Haley, U. C. V., & Pini, R. (1994). Blazing international trails in strategic decision-making research. In C. Fitzgerald (Ed.), *Proceedings from the Myers-Briggs Type Indicator and Leadership: An International Research Conference* (pp. 19–30). College Park, MD: University of Maryland University College National Leadership Institute.

Haley, U. C. V., & Stumpf, S. A. (1989). Cognitive trails in strategic decision making: Linking theories of personalities and cognitions. *Journal of Management Studies, 26(5),* 477–497.

Hammer, A. L., & Kummerow, J. M. (1996). *Strong and MBTI Career Development Guide.* Palo Alto, CA: Consulting Psychologists Press.

Hamilton, E. (1988). The facilitation of organizational change: An empirical study of factors predicting change agents' effectiveness. *The Journal of Applied Behavioral Science, 24(1),* 37–59.

Hay, J. E. (1964). *The relationship of certain personality variables to managerial level and job performance among engineering managers.* Unpublished doctoral dissertation, Temple University, Philadelphia.

Hay, J. E. (1966, June). Self-ideal congruence among engineering managers. *Personnel and Guidance Journal,* 1085–1088.

Hein, H. R. (1989). *Psychological type, coaching activities, and coaching effectiveness in corporate middle managers.* Unpublished doctoral dissertation, University of Bridgeport, Bridgeport, CT.

Hellriegel, D., & Slocum, J. W., Jr. (1975). Managerial problem-solving styles. *Business Horizons, 18(6),* 29–37.

Hellriegel, D., & Slocum, J. W., Jr. (1980). Preferred organizational designs and problem-solving styles: Interesting companions. *Human Systems Management, 1,* 151–158.

Hellriegel, D., Slocum, J. W., Jr., & Woodman, R. (1989). *Organizational behavior* (5th ed.). St. Paul, MN: West.

Helms, M. M. (1987). *Strategy and the impact of environmental pressures: An analysis of the expedited small package industry.* Unpublished doctoral dissertation, Memphis State University, Memphis, TN.

Henderson, J. C., & Nutt, P. C. (1980). The influence of decision style on decision-making behavior. *Management Science, 26(4),* 371–386.

Hersey, P., & Blanchard, K. H. (1988). *Management of organizational behavior: Utilizing human resources.* (5th ed.). Englewood Cliffs, NJ: Prentice Hall.

Hirsh, S. K. (1992). *MBTI team building program.* Palo Alto, CA: Consulting Psychologists Press.

Hirsh, S. K. (1991). *Using the Myers-Briggs Type Indicator in organizations: A resource book* (2d ed.). Palo Alto, CA: Consulting Psychologists Press.

Hirsh, S. K., & Kummerow, J. M. (1990). *Introduction to type in organizations* (2d ed.). Palo Alto, CA: Consulting Psychologists Press.

Hoy, F., & Hellreigel, D. (1982). The Kilmann and Herden model of organizational effectiveness criteria for small business managers. *Academy of Management Journal, 25(2),* 308–322.

Hoyer, D. T., & Huszczo, G. E. (1994). Union leaders and joint union-management organizational development efforts: An MBTI perspective. *Journal of Psychological Type, 31,* 3–9.

Huitt, W. G. (1992). Problem solving and decision making: Consideration of individual differences using the *Myers-Briggs Type Indicator. Journal of Psychological Type, 24,* 33–44.

Hunt, T. G. (1986). *An investigation of problem recognition: Developing a measure of problem recognition ability and assessing its usefulness to strategic managers.* Unpublished doctoral dissertation, The Florida State University, Tallahassee.

Hunter, F., & Levy, N. (1982). Relationship of problem-solving behaviors and Jungian personality types. *Psychological Reports, 51,* 379–384.

Hurst, D. K., Rush, J. C., & White, R. E. (1989). Top management teams and organizational renewal. *Strategic Management Journal, 10,* 87–105.

Jaffe, J. M. (1980). *The relationship of Jungian psychological predispositions to the implementation of management by objectives: A sociotechnical perspective.* Unpublished doctoral dissertation, University of Southern California, Los Angeles.

Jannes, J. D. (1984). *The effect of choice preferences and psychological type differences on group problem solving effectiveness.* Unpublished doctoral dissertation, University of Pittsburgh, Pittsburgh, PA.

Jaques, E. (1976). *A general theory of bureaucracy.* London: Heinemann.

Johnson, D. A. (1992). Predicting promotion to management in the wholesale grocery industry using the type differentiation indicator. *Journal of Psychological Type, 23,* 51–59.

Johnson, D. A., & Golden, J. P. (1994). How psychological type influences effective leadership: The Survey of Management Practices and the Type Differentiation Indicator (TDI). In C. Fitzgerald (Ed.), *Proceedings from the Myers-Briggs Type Indicator and Leadership: An International Research Conference* (pp. 89–97). College Park, MD: University of Maryland University College National Leadership Institute.

Julian, A. A. (1992). *Selected factors related to career achievement of women administrators in community colleges.* Unpublished doctoral dissertation, North Carolina State University, Raleigh.

Kandell, J. J. (1991). *The effects of group homogeneity-heterogeneity based on cognitive style on the quality of group decision-making.* Unpublished doctoral dissertation, University of Maryland, College Park.

Kerin, R. A., & Slocum, J. W., Jr. (1981). Decision-making style and acquisition of information: Further exploration of the *Myers-Briggs Type Indicator. Psychological Reports, 49,* 132–134.

Kerlin, M. P. (1992). *Decision-making practices of sensing and intuitive nurse executives.* Unpublished doctoral dissertation, University of Pittsburgh, PA.

Kilmann, R. H., & Herden, R. P. (1976). Toward a systematic methodology for evaluating the impact of interventions on organizational effectiveness. *Academy of Management Review, 1 (3),* 87–98.

Kilmann, R. H., & Mitroff, I. I. (1976). Qualitative versus quantitative analysis for management science: Different forms for different psychological types. *Interfaces, 6 (2),* 17–27.

Kilmann, R. H., & Taylor, V. (1974). A contingency approach to laboratory learning: Psychological types versus experiential norms. *Human Relations, 27 (9),* 891–909.

Kilmann, R. H., & Thomas, K. W. (1975). Interpersonal conflict-handling behavior as reflections of Jungian personality dimensions. *Psychological Reports, 37,* 971–980.

Klusendorf, D. J. (1985). *A study of the relationship between central administrative teams' psychological type variables and their perception of the management system.* Unpublished doctoral dissertation, Vanderbilt University, Nashville, TN.

Kroeger, O., with Thuesen, J. M. (1992). *Type talk at work.* NY: Delacorte Press.

Kummerow, J. M., & McAllister, L. W. (1988). Team-building with the *Myers-Briggs Type Indicator:* Case studies. *Journal of Psychological Type, 15,* 26–32.

Kummerow, J. M., Barger, N. J., & Kirby, L. K. (1997). WORKtypes. NY: Warner Books.

Leuder, D. C. (1986a). Psychological types and leadership styles of the 100 top executive educators in North America. *Journal of Psychological Type, 12,* 8–12.

Leuder, D. C. (1986b). The "rising stars" in educational administration: A corollary to psychological types and leadership styles. *Journal of Psychological Type, 12,* 13–15.

Lincoln, Y. S., Ed. (1985). *Organizational theory and inquiry: The paradigm revolution.* Beverly Hills: Sage.

Lindsley, D. H., & Day, D. V. (1994). Effects of team leader-member MBTI type similarity on perceived leader effectiveness. In C. Fitzgerald (Ed.), *Proceedings from the Myers-Briggs Type Indicator and Leadership: An International Research Conference* (pp. 73–79). College Park, MD: University of Maryland University College National Leadership Institute.

Loehr, H. T. (1983). *Individual differences in managers' perceptions of their work.* Unpublished doctoral dissertation, University of Massachusetts,

Loevinger, J., & Wessler, R. (1970). *Measuring ego development: Vol. 1. Construction and use of a sentence completion test.* San Francisco: Jossey-Bass.

Luthans, F., & Lockwood, D. L. (1984). Toward an observational system for measuring leader behavior in natural settings. In J. G. Hunt, D. Kosking, C. A. Schreisheim, & R. Seward (Eds.), *Leaders and managers: International perspectives on managerial behavior and leadership* (pp. 117–141). New York: Pergamon Press.

Macdaid, G. P., McCaulley, M. H., & Kainz, R. I. (1987). *Myers-Briggs Type Indicator atlas of type tables.* Gainesville, FL: Center for Application of Psychological Type.

Mackie, J. J. (1986). *An empirical investigation of the impact of personality type on supervisor-subordinate relationships in a budgetary setting.* Unpublished doctoral dissertation, Texas A&M University, College Station.

Macrides, G. A. (1981). *The relationship of psychological type and other personal variables to the decision-making behavior of administrators.* Unpublished doctoral dissertation, University of Wisconsin-Madison.

Malley, J. C. (1982). *An exploratory investigation into managerial, organizational and strategic planning correlates of problem recognition.* Unpublished doctoral dissertation, The Florida State University, Tallahassee.

Marcic, D., Aiuppa, T. A., & Watson, J. G. (1989). Personality type, organizational norms and self-esteem. *Psychological Reports, 65,* 915–919.

Markham, S. E., & Murry, W. D. (1994). Predicting leadership outcomes through the MBTI: A field study. In C. Fitzgerald (Ed.), *Proceedings from the Myers-Briggs Type Indicator and Leadership: An International Research Conference* (pp. 142–150). College Park, MD: University of Maryland University College National Leadership Institute.

Mason, R. O., & Mitroff, I. I. (1973). A program for research on management information systems. *Management Science, 19 (5),* 475–487.

Matteson, C. J. (1987). The relationships among environmental uncertainty, cognitive style, organicity and organizational culture in small growing public companies. Unpublished doctoral dissertation, University of Pittsburgh, Pittsburgh, PA.

McCaulley, M. H. (1990). The *Myers-Briggs Type Indicator* and leadership. In K. E. Clark & M. B. Clark (Eds.), *Measures of leadership* (pp. 381–418). West Orange, NJ: Leadership Library of America, Inc.

McCaulley, M. H. (1987). The *Myers-Briggs Type Indicator:* A Jungian model for problem-solving. In J. Stice (Ed.), *Developing critical thinking and problem-solving abilities* (pp. 37–54). San Francisco: Jossey-Bass.

McClure, L. (1985). *Leaders' responses as functions of reciprocal determinism: A comparison between female and male leaders.* Unpublished doctoral dissertation, Arizona State University, Tempe.

McGhee, M. J. (1992). *Relation of leadership temperament to change facilitator effectiveness.* Unpublished doctoral dissertation, University of Texas at Austin.

McIntyre, S. E. (1991). *Conflict management by male and female managers as reported by self and by male and female subordinates.* Unpublished doctoral dissertation, Georgia State University, Atlanta.

Mills, J., Robey, D., & Smith, L. (1985). Conflict handling and personality dimensions of project management personnel. *Psychological Reports, 57,* 1135–1143.

Mitroff, I. I. (1983). *Stakeholders of the organizational mind.* San Francisco: Jossey-Bass.

Mitroff, I. I., Barabba, V. P., & Kilmann, R. H. (1977). The application of behavioral and philosophical technologies to strategic planning: A case study of a large federal agency. *Management Science, 24 (1),* 44–58.

Mitroff, I. I., & Kilmann, R. H. (1975a, July). Stories managers tell: A new tool for organizational problem solving. *Management Review, 19–28.*

Mitroff, I. I., & Kilmann, R. H. (1975b). On evaluating scientific research: The contribution of the psychology of science. *Journal of Technological Forecasting and Social Change, 8,* 163–174.

Mitroff, I. I., & Kilmann, R. H. (1976). Qualitative versus quantitative analysis for management science: Different forms for different psychological types. *Interfaces, 2 (6),* 17–27.

Mohr, L. B. (1982). *Explaining organizational behavior: The limits and possibilities of theory and research.* San Francisco: Jossey-Bass.

Mullen, T. P., & Stumpf, S. A. (1987). The effect of management styles on strategic planning. *Journal of Business Strategy, 7,* 60–75.

Myers, I. B., & McCaulley, M. H. (1985). *Manual: A guide to the development and use of the Myers-Briggs Type Indicator.* Palo Alto, CA: Consulting Psychologists Press.

Nolan, L. L. (1985). *Conflict management: Effects of perception and personality on strategies for handling conflict.* Unpublished doctoral dissertation, Ohio State University, Columbus.

Nordwick, H. (1994). Type, vocation, and self-report personality variables: A validity study of a Norwegian translation of the MBTI, Form G. *Journal of Psychological Type, 29,* 32–36.

Nutt, P. C. (1986a). Decision style and its impact on managers and management. *Journal of Technological Forecasting and Social Change, 29,* 341–366.

Nutt, P. C. (1986b). Decision style and strategic decisions of top executives. *Journal of Technological Forecasting and Social Change, 30,* 39–62.

Nutt, P. C. (1979). Influence of decision styles on use of decision models. *Journal of Technological Forecasting and Social Change, 14,* 77–93.

Nutter, J. R. (1991). *The effect of cognitive behavioral style congruence on the chief executive officer's inclusion of the chief human resource management officer in the strategic planning process.* Unpublished doctoral dissertation, Nova University, Fort Lauderdale, FL.

Ohsawa, T. (1993). *Introduction to characteristics of Japanese management style: For better understanding of cultural differences in comparing MBTI data of Japan with other countries.* Paper presented at meeting of Psychological Type and Culture—East and West, Honolulu, HI.

Oswick, C., & Mahoney, J. P. (1993). Psychological types of first-line supervisors in the United Kingdom: A comparison to U.S. and U.K. managers. *Journal of Psychological Type, 25,* 31–38.

Patz, A. L. (1990). Group personality composition and total enterprise simulation performance. *Developments in business simulation and experiential exercises, 17,* 132–137.

Patz, A. L. (1992). Personality bias in total enterprise simulations. *Simulation & Gaming, 23 (1),* 45–76.

Phillips-Danielson, W. H. (1985). *Managerial problem definition: A descriptive study of problem definers.* Unpublished doctoral dissertation, University of North Texas, Denton, TX.

Pierson, J. F. (1984). *Leadership styles of university and college counseling center directors: Perspectives from the field.* Unpublished doctoral dissertation, University of Georgia, Athens, GA.

Porter, G., Peacock, P., & Rabinowitz, S. (1994). The MBTI and entrepreneurial confidence: Initial comparisons and changes after training in small business management. In C. Fitzgerald (Ed.), *Proceedings from the Myers-Briggs Type Indicator and Leadership: An International Research Conference* (pp. 123–130). College Park, MD: University of Maryland University College National Leadership Institute.

Procopio, A. J. (1991). *Relationships of cognitive styles and training program structure to changing attitudes toward quality improvement.* Unpublished doctoral dissertation, University of Bridgeport, Bridgeport, CT.

Rahim, A. (1981). Job satisfaction as a function of personality-job congruence: A study with Jungian psychological types. *Psychological Reports, 49,* 496–498.

Ramaprasad, A., & Mitroff, I. I. (1984). On formulating strategic problems. *Academy of Management Review, 9 (4),* 597–605.

Reynierse, J. H. (1991). The psychological types of outplaced executives. *Journal of Psychological Type, 22,* 27–32.

Reynierse, J. H. (1993). The distribution and flow of managerial types through organizational levels in business and industry. *Journal of Psychological Type, 25,* 11–23.

Reynierse, J. H. (1995). A comparative analysis of Japanese and American managerial types through organizational levels in business and industry. *Journal of Psychological Type, 33,* 19–32.

Reynierse, J. H., & Harker, J. B. (1995). The psychological types of line and staff management: Implications for the J–P preference. *Journal of Psychological Type, 34,* 8–16.

Rice, G. H., & Lindecamp, D. P. (1989). Personality types and business success of small retailers. *Journal of Occupational Psychology, 62,* 177–182.

Rideout, C. A., & Richardson, S. A. (1989). A teambuilding model: Appreciating differences using the *Myers-Briggs Type Indicator* with developmental theory. *Journal of Counseling and Development, 67,* 529–533.

Rifkind, L. J. (1975). *An analysis of the effects of personality type upon the risky shift in small group discussions.* Unpublished doctoral dissertation, The Florida State University, Tallahassee.

Roach, B. (1986). Organizational decision makers: Different types for different levels. *Journal of Psychological Type, 12,* 16–24.

Roach, B. (1989). *Strategy styles and management types: A resource book for organizational and management consultants.* Stanford, CA: Balestrand Press.

Robertson, P. E. (1990). *An investigation of personality characteristics and demographic profiles of women and men in management positions.* Unpublished doctoral dissertation, The University of North Carolina at Greensboro.

Roush, P. E (1992). The *Myers-Briggs Type Indicator,* subordinate feedback, and perceptions of leadership effectiveness. In K. E. Clark, M. B. Clark, & D. P. Campbell (Eds.), *Impact of leadership* (pp. 529–544). Greensboro, NC: Center for Creative Leadership.

Roush, P. E., & Atwater, L. (1992). Using the MBTI to understand transformational leadership and self-perception accuracy. *Military Psychology, 4 (1),* 17-33.

Roush, P. E., & Barry, J. (1994). Type, leadership feedback and willingness to change. In C. Fitzgerald (Ed.), *Proceedings from the Myers-Briggs Type Indicator and Leadership: An International Research Conference* (pp. 199–203). College Park, MD: University of Maryland University College National Leadership Institute.

Routamaa, V., & Ponto, V. (1994). Situational leadership and the MBTI types of certain Finnish managers. In C. Fitzgerald (Ed.), *Proceedings from the Myers-Briggs Type Indicator and Leadership: An International Research Conference* (pp. 189–198). College Park, MD: University of Maryland University College National Leadership Institute.

Rowe, A. J., & Boulgarides, J. D. (1983). Decision styles—A perspective. *London Organizational Development Journal,* 3–9.

Ruble, T. L., & Cosier, R. A. (1990). Effects of cognitive styles and decision setting on performance. *Organizational Behavior and Human Decision Processes, 46,* 283–295.

Rytting, M., Ware, R., & Prince, R. A. (1994a). Bimodal distributions in a sample of CEOs: Validating evidence for the MBTI. *Journal of Psychological Type, 31,* 16–23.

Rytting, M., Ware, R., & Prince, R. A. (1994b). The impact of family ownership and CEO type on the character of companies. *Journal of Psychological Type, 31,* 32–40.

Sample, J. A., & Hoffman, J. L. (1986). The MBTI as a management and organizational development tool. *Journal of Psychological Type, 11,* 47–50.

Sanchez, A. L (1988). The contribution of personality type (preference) and selected situational factors to visionary leadership behavior. Unpublished Doctoral dissertation, University of Colorado at Denver.

Savelsbergh, M. C. (1989). *A study of effective consultant teachers' leadership styles and personality preferences.* Unpublished doctoral dissertation, Oregon State University, Corvallis.

Scarbrough, D. P. (1993). Psychological types and job satisfaction of accountants. *Journal of Psychological Type, 25,* 3–10.

Schweiger, D. M. (1985). Measuring managerial cognitive styles: On the logical validity of the *Myers-Briggs Type Indicator. Journal of Business Research, 13,* 315–328.

Schweiger, D. M., & Jago, A. D. (1982). Problem-solving styles and participative decision making. *Psychological Reports, 50,* 1311–1316.

Shewchuk, R. M., & O'Connor, S. J. (1995). Health care executives: Subjective well-being as a function of psychological type. *Journal of Psychological Type, 32,* 23–29.

Short, G. J., & Grasha, A. F. (1995). The relationship of MBTI dimensions to perceptions of stress and coping strategies in managers. *Journal of Psychological Type, 32,* 3–10.

Slocum, J. W., Jr. (1978). Does cognitive style affect diagnosis and intervention strategies of change agents? *Group and Organization Studies, 3 (2),* 199–210.

Smith, F. H. (1991). *Personality types and administrative potential.* Unpublished doctoral dissertation, University of Houston, Houston, TX.

Smith, L., & Haar, J. (1990). An assessment of conflict-handling and personality characteristics of project management personnel in the People's Republic of China. *Journal of Social Behavior and Personality, 5 (3),* 61–76.

Steckroth, R. L., Slocum, J. W., & Sims, H. P. (1980). Organizational roles, cognitive roles, and problem-solving styles. *Journal of Experiential Learning and Simulation, 2,* 77–87.

Steele, F. I. (1968). Personality and the "laboratory style." *Journal of Applied Behavioral Science, 4 (1),* 25–45.

Sundstrom, E., Koenigs, R. J., & Huet-Cox, D. (1994). Personality and expressed values in management teams: MBTI and co-worker ratings on SYMLOG values. In C. Fitzgerald (Ed.), *Proceedings from the Myers-Briggs Type Indicator and Leadership: An International Research Conference* (pp. 131–141). College Park, MD: University of Maryland University College National Leadership Institute.

Taggart, W., & Robey, D. (1981). Minds and managers: On the dual nature of human information processing and management. *Academy of Management Review, 6 (2),* 187–195.

Tan, B. W., & Lo, T. W. (1991). The impact of interface customization on the effect of cognitive style on information system success. *Behavior & Information Technology, 10 (4),* 297–310.

Tetlock, P. E., Peterson, R. S., & Berry, J. M. (1993). Flattering and unflattering personality portraits of integratively simple and complex managers. *Journal of Personality and Social Psychology, 64 (3),* 500–511.

Tichy, N. M., & Devanna, M. A. (1986). *The transformational leader.* New York: Wiley.

Tsai, R. J. (1991). *An investigation on the impact of task characteristics and cognitive style on cognitive process in a decision-making environment (information systems).* Unpublished doctoral dissertation, University of North Texas, Denton, TX.

Vail, J. F. (1991). *Leadership styles and personality types of superintendents in South Carolina.* Unpublished doctoral dissertation, University of South Carolina, Columbia, SC.

Van Eron, A. M. (1991). *Key components of the transformational/transactional leadership model: The relationship between individual differences, leadership disposition, behavior and climate.* Unpublished doctoral dissertation, Columbia University, New York.

Van Eron, A. M., & Burke, W. W. (1992). The transformational/transactional leadership model: A study of critical components. In K. E. Clark, M. B. Clark, & D. P. Campbell (Eds.), *Impact of leadership* (pp. 149–167). Greensboro, NC: Center for Creative Leadership.

Van Rooyen, J. (1994). Creativity: An important managerial requirement. A South African perspective. In C. Fitzgerald (Ed.), *Proceedings from the Myers-Briggs Type Indicator and Leadership: An International Research Conference* (pp. 49–59). College Park, MD: University of Maryland University College National Leadership Institute.

Van Velsor, E., & Fleenor, J. W. (1994). Leadership skills and perspectives, gender and the MBTI. In C. Fitzgerald (Ed.), *Proceedings from the Myers-Briggs Type Indicator and Leadership: An International Research Conference* (pp. 109–122). College Park, MD: University of Maryland University College National Leadership Institute.

Vroom, V. H., & Yetton, P. W. (1973). *Leadership and decision making.* Pittsburgh: University of Pittsburgh Press.

Walck, C. L. (1992). Psychological type and management research: A review. *Journal of Psychological Type, 24,* 13–23.

Walck, C. L. (1991). Training for participative management: Implications for psychological type. *Journal of Psychological Type, 21,* 3–12.

Williams, R. L., Verble, J. S., Price, D. E., & Layne, B. E. (1995). Relationship of self-management to personality types and indices. *Journal of Personality Assessment, 64 (3),* 494–506.

Wilson, C. L., Wilson, J., Booth, D., & Shipper, F. (1992). The impact of personality, gender, and international location on multilevel management ratings. In K. E. Clark, M. B. Clark, & D. P. Campbell (Eds.), *Impact of leadership* (pp. 345–358). Greensboro, NC: Center for Creative Leadership.

Wilson, J. L., & Wilson, C. L. (1994). Exploring MBTI type relationships to management skills. In C. Fitzgerald (Ed.), *Proceedings from the Myers-Briggs Type Indicator and Leadership: An International Research Conference* (pp. 81–88). College Park, MD: University of Maryland University College National Leadership Institute.

Wheatley, M. J. (1992). *Leadership and the new science.* San Francisco: Berrett-Koehler.

Yukl, G. A. (1989). *Leadership in organizations.* (2d ed.). Englewood Cliffs, NJ: Prentice Hall.

4 | The Relationship Between the MBTI and Measures of Personality and Performance in Management Groups

John W. Fleenor

The *Myers-Briggs Type Indicator* (MBTI) has become increasingly popular as a measure of personality in leadership development programs, team-building efforts, organizational change work, and one-on-one coaching sessions (e.g., Hirsh & Kummerow, 1990). In these efforts, the MBTI instrument often is used in conjunction with other personality measures, 360-degree rating instruments (Van Velsor & Leslie, 1991), behavioral assessment exercises, and other measures to provide feedback to managers about various aspects of their management style and skills.

According to Myers and McCaulley (1985), we can increase our understanding of the dimensions of the MBTI by studying relationships between it and other psychological measures. With this in mind, Myers and McCaulley presented correlations between the MBTI and various personality and interest inventories in the MBTI *Manual*. Similarly, Thorne and Gough (1991) suggested that the MBTI can be better understood by examining relationships between its scales and other measures with meanings that are known. They reported correlations between MBTI scores and several other instruments, including the

Adjective Check List, the *California Psychological Inventory,* and the *Minnesota Multiphasic Personality Inventory.*

The purpose of this chapter is to describe relationships between the MBTI and several measures of personality and performance used with management groups. An understanding of these relationships is valuable information for people who work with the MBTI in various leadership settings and are interested in understanding individual differences as they relate to leadership.

USE OF THE MBTI IN LEADERSHIP DEVELOPMENT PROGRAMS

The MBTI is frequently used as a means of increasing the self-insight of participants in leadership development programs. Two previous studies investigated relationships between the MBTI and instruments used in leadership development programs. In the first study, Campbell and Van Velsor (1985) examined relationships between the MBTI and other measures using a sample of 1,002 participants who attended Center for Creative Leadership (CCL) programs between 1979 and 1982. In the second study, Fitzgerald (1991) investigated correlations between the MBTI and several other instruments using 386 participants from a leadership development program at the University of Maryland. Some of the results from the Fitzgerald study will be presented later in this chapter.

CCL's Leadership Development Program

The Leadership Development Program (LDP) at the Center for Creative Leadership is a six-day training program in which participants receive feedback on a number of personality and performance measures, including the MBTI. (For a historical overview of the LDP, see Campbell, 1992.) Since 1985, scores from the instruments used in these programs have been stored in a computer database. Using this database, it was possible to investigate relationships between the MBTI and other instruments with a large sample of practicing managers. When possible, the results of the present study are compared to the two earlier studies that used samples from leadership development programs (Campbell & Van Velsor, 1985; Fitzgerald, 1991). By comparing these studies, the generalizability of the results across different managerial samples can be investigated.

Study Participants

MBTI scores were available for 26,477 participants who attended CCL programs from 1985 to 1993. These participants generally were middle- and upper-level managers. Demographic data, available for 95% of this sample, are presented in Table 1. The average age of the participants was 41, and the average level of education was 16.8 years. The sample demographics in the present study are similar to those reported in the two earlier studies discussed previously (Campbell & Van Velsor, 1985; Fitzgerald, 1991). The primary difference is in the percentage of women in the samples. The two previous studies contained about 10% fewer women (in relation to men) than the current sample.

Scores on every instrument were not available for all participants in this sample. Because they vary from instrument to instrument, sample sizes will be reported separately for each analysis discussed in this chapter.

Participants' MBTI Types

The distribution of the 16 MBTI types for the total sample of 26,477 participants is presented in Table 2. As can be seen in the table, the percentages were highest for ISTJs (18%), ESTJs (16%), and ENTJs (13%). Percentages were very low for ISFPs (1%), ESFPs (1%), and INFJs (2%). This managerial sample showed strong preferences for Thinking over Feeling and for Judging over Perceiving. However, for this group, preferences for Extraversion and Introversion and for Sensing and Intuition were about the same (see Chapter 1 for information about type distributions in management samples more generally).

THE INSTRUMENTS

Several instruments were administered to the participants as part of the CCL Leadership Development Program, as described below. The participants completed paper-and-pencil versions of the instruments several weeks before attending the program and mailed them to CCL for scoring.

Myers-Briggs Type Indicator (MBTI)

MBTI continuous scale scores were used in all of the analyses reported in this chapter. Intercorrelations among the MBTI continuous scores are

TABLE 1 Sample Demographics for CCI's Leadership Development Program
in Percentages (N = 26,477)

Gender		Educational Degree	
Male	72.4	High school	12.8
Female	27.6	Associate degree	4.7
		Bachelor's degree	39.0
Ethnicity		Master's degree	31.1
Native American	0.4	Doctorate/Professional	12.3
Asian	2.4		
African American	4.4	Job Function	
Hispanic	2.6	Accounting	4.2
White	89.0	Administration	22.8
Other	1.2	Advertising/Public relations	1.6
		Education	2.8
Organization Type		Engineering	4.9
Business/Industry	59.1	Human resources	7.8
Business/Service	15.5	Information services	4.6
Educational	7.5	Law	1.4
Military	0.9	Manufacturing	5.2
Government	7.3	Marketing	7.6
Other nonprofit	3.8	Purchasing	1.9
Other	5.9	Medicine	0.8
		Operations	6.3
Organizational Level		Product development	2.1
Not relevant	3.6	Quality control	1.5
Hourly worker	3.0	Research	1.5
First-level manager	3.3	R & D	4.4
Middle manager	30.0	Sales	5.8
Upper-middle manager	8.7	Secretarial/Support	2.6
Executive	17.6	Security	0.5
Top	3.8	Social service	0.3
		Systems analysis	0.7
		Other	6.4

shown in Table 3. As can be seen in the table, the correlation between
the S–N and J–P scales was .41, indicating that Intuition was fairly highly correlated with Perceiving. This finding has been reported in other
studies. When interpreting MBTI scores, therefore, users should be
aware that the S–N and J–P scales are not entirely independent dimensions.

TABLE 2   MBTI Types for Participants in CCL's Leadership Development Program in Percentages (N = 26,477)

ISTJ	ISFJ	INFJ	INTJ
18.2	3.1	1.7	10.5
ISTP	ISFP	INFP	INTP
3.5	1.1	2.5	6.9
ESTP	ESFP	ENFP	ENTP
3.4	1.2	4.5	8.0
ESTJ	ESFJ	ENFJ	ENTJ
16.0	3.2	3.0	13.1

E: 52.5	S: 49.6	T: 79.6	J: 68.9
I: 47.5	N: 50.3	F: 20.4	P: 31.1

California Psychological Inventory (CPI)

The *California Psychological Inventory*™ (CPI; Gough, 1987) is a 468-item self-report personality inventory that measures behavioral tendencies on 20 scales that are important for normal functioning in adults. It is designed to measure *folk concepts*, that is, aspects of interpersonal relationships and behavior that are described in familiar, commonsense terms.

The CPI also provides scores on three factors called structural scales or vectors (*v*; Gough, 1987, p. 16). The three structural scales are Internality (*v.*1), Norm-Favoring (*v.*2), and Self-Realization (*v.*3).

Fundamental Interpersonal Relations Orientation–Behavior (FIRO-B)

The FIRO-B™ (Schutz, 1967) is a 54-item instrument that measures six dimensions of an individual's behavior toward others: Expressed Inclusion, Expressed Control, Expressed Affection, Wanted Inclusion, Wanted Control, and Wanted Affection. (For more information on the FIRO-B and the MBTI, see Schnell, Hammer, Fitzgerald, Fleenor, & Van Velsor, 1994, and Chapter 15 in this book.)

TABLE 3 Intercorrelations Among MBTI Continuous Scores (*N* = 26,477)

	EI	SN	TF	JP
EI	–			
SN	–.15	–		
TF	–.13	.14	–	
JP	–.08	.41	.25	–

Kirton Adaption-Innovation Inventory (KAI)

The *Kirton Adaption-Innovation Inventory* (KAI; Kirton, 1987) is a 33-item self-report inventory designed to measure cognitive style in creativity, problem solving, and decision making. The KAI locates the respondent on a continuum ranging between high adaption and high innovation, corresponding with low to high scores. Adaptors tend to use available procedures and approaches to problems, while innovators try to restructure problems and use less conventional approaches. The KAI also yields scores on three subscales: Rule/Group Conformity (R), Sufficiency of Originality (O), and Efficiency (E). KAI scores have been found to demonstrate acceptable levels of reliability (DeMauro, 1992, p. 443).

Leadership Style Indicator (LSI)

The *Leadership Style Indicator* (LSI) is a multirater instrument developed by Bailey (1991) to help managers understand how they relate to others when taking on a leadership role. On the LSI, co-workers rate the target manager on 48 adjectives using a three-point scale ranging from "does not describe this person" to "strongly describes this person." The LSI contains adjectives relevant to a leadership role, such as appreciative, critical, delegating, demanding, and understanding.

Leaderless Group Discussion (LGD)

On the first day of the Leadership Development Program, the participants take part in two behavioral assessment exercises. These assessments are typical of the Leaderless Group Discussion (LGD) exercises used in assessment centers (Bray, Campbell, & Grant, 1974). The development of the exercises was based on research by MacKinnon (1975) and is described by Campbell (1992). The first LGD is a competitive exercise in which each of six participants is assigned a different candidate to support for a leadership position. The group members compete to gain the group's endorsement for their candidate. The second LGD is a cooperative exercise in which each group member is given a different piece of information essential to solving a problem, and the participants must work together to arrive at the best solution. Eight dimensions are rated in each exercise: Activity Level, Led Discussion, Influenced Others, Problem Analysis, Task Orientation, Motivated Others, Verbal Effectiveness, and Interpersonal Skills.

Using behaviorally anchored rating scales, two trained observers rated each participant's performance on the eight dimensions in each exercise with a 50-point scale (10 = low performance; 50 = high performance). The assessors were not aware of the participants' scores on the MBTI before rating their behavior in the LGD. After making their individual ratings, the observers met to reach a consensus rating for each dimension. An overall rating was calculated by taking the mean of the dimension ratings for each participant.

Using ratings for a sample of 2,285 LDP participants, interrater reliabilities for the individual dimension ratings were calculated for the two exercises. For the competitive exercise, interrater reliabilities ranged from .68 to .79; for the cooperative exercise, the reliabilities ranged from .57 to .77.

RESULTS FROM THE CCL LEADERSHIP DEVELOPMENT PROGRAM

Factor Analysis of MBTI, CPI, and FIRO-B Scores

Scores from the MBTI, CPI, and FIRO-B were factor analyzed using a sample of 12,074 CCL participants. The results of this analysis indicated that all of the variance in these test scores could be accounted for by six factors. The scales that loaded on each of the factors and the amount of variance accounted for by each factor are presented in Table 4. Factor 1 was defined by MBTI Extraversion, CPI Dominance, FIRO-B Expressed Control, CPI negative Femininity/Masculinity, and CPI negative Internality (v.1). Factor 2 was defined by MBTI Intuition and CPI Achievement via Independence. Factor 3 was defined by MBTI Judging and CPI Norm-Favoring (v.2). Factor 6 was defined by MBTI Feeling. All of the FIRO-B scales except for Expressed Control loaded on Factor 4, indicating that the FIRO-B does not share a large amount of variance with MBTI and CPI scores. Factor 5, defined by CPI Good Impression and Self-Control, could be interpreted as a social desirability factor.

Table 4 Factor Analysis of MBTI, CPI, and FIRO-B Scores (N = 12,074)

	Factor 1	Factor 2	Factor 3	Factor 4	Factor 5	Factor 6
MBTI	Extraversion	Intuition	Judging			Feeling
CPI	Dominance	Ach. via Independence	Norm-Favoring (v.2)		Good Impression	
	Sociability	Self-Realization (v.3)	Socialization		Self-Control	
	Self-Acceptance	Intellectual Efficiency	Achievement via Conformance			
	Social Presence	Tolerance	Responsibility			
	Independence	Psychological-Mindedness	Communality			
	Capacity for Status	Flexibility				
	– Feminine/Masculine	Well-Being				
	– Internality (v.1)	Empathy				
FIRO-B	Expressed Control			Wanted Affection		
				Wanted Inclusion		
				Expressed Affection		
				Expressed Inclusion		
				Wanted Control		
Variance accounted for	29%	27%	16%	12%	10%	6%

Similar to other analyses (e.g., Johnson & Saunders, 1990), the factor analysis confirms the factor structure underlying the MBTI. As noted elsewhere in this volume (Chapter 2), the MBTI dimensions are closely related to four of the Big Five factors of personality (McCrae & Costa, 1989), which researchers believe represents an extremely robust taxonomy of personality (Goldberg, 1993). Neuroticism, the one factor of the Big Five not present in the MBTI, was not found in our factor analysis.

Users of the MBTI, CPI, and FIRO-B, such as those giving feedback in leadership development programs, may find the results of the factor analysis in Table 4 useful. When presenting scores from personality measures to participants, practitioners can use this structure to integrate and organize the data.

The MBTI and the CPI

Correlations were calculated for a sample of 12,971 participants in CCL programs for whom both MBTI and CPI data were available. These correlations are presented in Table 5. Because of the large sample size, many very small correlations (e.g., $r < .03$) were statistically significant. Because such correlations are not likely to be meaningful in practice, the results discussed in this chapter will focus on correlations greater than or equal to .20 (a similar level of significance was used by Myers & McCaulley, 1985, in the MBTI *Manual* to highlight meaningful results).

Correlations between MBTI and CPI scores are presented in Table 5. Extraversion was related to CPI scores on Dominance (.44), Capacity for Status (.41), Sociability (.66), Social Presence (.52), Self-Acceptance (.46), Independence (.32), Empathy (.52), and Self-Realization (v.3; .23). Introversion was correlated with Internality (v.1; .56).

Sensing was related to Internality (v.1; .30) and Norm-Favoring (v.2; .26). Intuition was correlated with Capacity for Status (.38), Sociability (.24), Social Presence (.33), Self-Acceptance (.25), Achievement via Independence (.32), Intellectual Efficiency (.28), Psychological-Mindedness (.28), Flexibility (.42), Independence (.33), Empathy (.42), and Self-Realization (v.3; .28). The Thinking–Feeling dimension of the MBTI appeared to be unrelated to CPI scores.

Judging was related to Socialization (.22), Self-Control (.26), Achievement via Conformity (.29), and Norm-Favoring (v.2; .38). Perceiving was correlated with Social Presence (.23), Flexibility (.43), and Empathy (.23).

TABLE 5 Correlations Between MBTI Scores and CPI Scales ($N = 12,971$)

CPI Scales	MBTI Scores			
	EI	SN	TF	JP
Dominance (Do)	−.44	.18	−.07	−.02
Capacity for Status (Cs)	−.41	.38	.05	.13
Sociability (Sy)	−.66	.24	.06	.06
Social Presence (Sp)	−.52	.33	.03	.23
Self-Acceptance (Sa)	−.46	.25	.00	.11
Well-Being (Wb)	−.15	.01	−.08	−.07
Responsibility (Re)	−.05	.04	.01	−.14
Socialization (So)	−.02	−.18	−.06	−.22
Self-Control (Sc)	.14	−.17	−.08	−.26
Tolerance (To)	−.14	.19	.05	.02
Good Impression (Gi)	−.17	−.03	−.06	−.18
Communality (Cm)	.02	−.17	−.02	−.16
Achievement via Conformity (Ac)	−.13	−.03	−.06	−.29
Achievement via Independence (Ai)	.00	.32	.08	.11
Intellectual Efficiency (Ie)	−.16	.28	−.01	.07
Psychological-Mindedness (Py)	−.06	.28	−.08	.05
Flexibility (Fx)	−.13	.42	.18	.43
Independence (In)	−.32	.33	−.12	.16
Empathy (Em)	−.52	.42	.16	.23
Femininity/Masculinity (Fm)	.13	−.03	.13	−.09
Internality (v.1)	.56	−.30	.00	−.15
Norm-Favoring (v.2)	−.08	−.26	−.13	−.38
Self-Realization (v.3)	−.23	.28	.05	.05

Note. Positive correlations with MBTI scales are associated with I, N, F, and P. Negative correlations with MBTI scales are associated with E, S, T, and J.

Because of the very large sample size in this table, small correlations are statistically significant but are not likely to be meaningful in practice. In interpreting results, an arbitrary cutoff of .20 or higher is used for interpreting meaningful results.

The following CPI scales did not appear to be related to any of the MBTI dimensions: Well-Being, Responsibility, Tolerance, Good Impression, Communality, and Femininity/Masculinity. When presenting CPI and MBTI results, it is recommended that those giving feedback emphasize the scores on these CPI scales because they appear to be furnishing information not provided by the MBTI.

The correlational results are similar to those reported by Fitzgerald (1991) and Thorne and Gough (1991). This provides some evidence that the relationships between the MBTI and the CPI are consistent across different samples.

To help practitioners understand and apply these results, the data in Table 6 are presented. This table, modeled after McCaulley (1990, p. 406), shows which MBTI types scored significantly higher or lower on the CPI scales in relation to the sample mean. As indicated by McCaulley, this table allows the reader to evaluate clusters of CPI characteristics for each MBTI type. For example, Extraverts tended to score higher on Dominance, Capacity for Status, Sociability, Social Presence, and Self-Acceptance. Intuitive types tended to score higher on Achievement via Independence, Flexibility, Intellectual Efficiency, Independence, and Empathy. Feeling types tended to score higher on Femininity/Masculinity, and Judging types tended to score higher on Socialization, Self-Control, and Achievement via Conformity.

In general, the results presented in Table 6 are in agreement with McCaulley (1990). There are, however, some differences. McCaulley reported that ESFJs scored lower on Capacity for Status, Sociability, and Social Presence. In the present study, ESFJs scored higher on Sociability, and there were no differences on Capacity for Status and Social Presence. Because of the larger sample size, some of the differences in CPI scores in the present study were statistically significant, whereas similar differences were not significant in McCaulley's results.

The MBTI and the FIRO-B

Correlations were calculated for a sample of 26,430 participants in CCL programs for whom FIRO-B and MBTI data were available. The results of this analysis are presented in Table 7. Correlations that met the .20 criterion discussed previously are described below.

Extraversion was related to Expressed Inclusion (.49), Wanted Inclusion (.29), Expressed Affection (.42), and Wanted Affection (.27). Thinking was related to Expressed Control (.21). Feeling was correlated with Expressed Affection (.25) and Wanted Affection (.23). Both the Sensing–Intuition and the Judging–Perceiving dimensions of the MBTI appear to be unrelated to FIRO-B scores.

As can be seen from the results of the factor analysis shown in Table 4, several FIRO-B scales that are correlated with MBTI scores did not load on the factors corresponding to those scales. For example, although Expressed Inclusion is correlated with MBTI Extraversion, it

TABLE 6　MBTI Types Scoring Significantly Higher or Lower on the CPI (N = 15,102)

ISTJ			ISFJ			INFJ			INTJ		
n = 2,680　17.7%			n = 397　2.6%			n = 281　1.9%			n = 1,702　11.3%		
H	L		H	L		H	L		H	L	
So	Do	Ai	Sc	Do	Ai	Ai	Do		Re	Do	
Sc	Cs	Ie	Fm	Cs	Ie	Fm	Sy		Sc	Sy	
Cm	Sy	Py		Sy	Py		Sp		Ac	Sp	
Fm	Sp	Fx		Sp	Fx		Sa		Ai	Sa	
	Wb	In		Sa	In		Wb		Ie	Gi	
	To	Em		Wb	Em		Gi		Py	Em	
				To			In		Fm		

ISTP			ISFP			INFP			INTP		
n = 514　3.4%			n = 153　1.0%			n = 398　2.6%			n = 1,129　7.5%		
H	L		H	L		H	L		H	L	
	Do	Gi	Fm	Do	Gi	Ai	Do	So	Ai	Do	So
	Cs	Ac		Cs	Ac	Fx	Sy	Sc	Ie	Sy	Sc
	Sy	Ai		Sy	Ai	Fm	Sp	Gi	Py	Sa	Gi
	Sp	Ie		Sp	Ie		Sa	Cm	Fx	Wb	Cm
	Sa	Py		Sa	Py		Wb	Ac	In	Re	Ac
	Wb	In		Wb	In						
	Re	Em		Re	Em						
	To			To							

ESTP			ESFP			ENFP			ENTP		
n = 530　3.5%			n = 156　1.0%			n = 779　5.2%			n = 1,344　8.9%		
H	L		H	L		H		L	H		L
Do	Re	Ai	Sy	Sc		Do	Ai	So	Do	Ai	Re
Sy	Sc	Ie		Ac		Cs	Ie	Sc	Cs	Ie	So
Sp	To	Py		Py		Sy	Fx	Gi	Sy	Py	Sc
Sa	Ac	Fm				Sp	In	Cm	Sp	Fx	Cm
Fx						Sa	Em	Ac	Sa	In	Ac
						To			To	Em	Fm

ESTJ			ESFJ			ENFJ			ENTJ		
n = 2,223　14.7%			n = 401　2.7%			n = 474　3.1%			n = 1,944　12.9%		
H		L	H	L		H		L	H		L
Do	Sc	Ai	Sy	Ai		Do	Gi		Do	To	Fm
Sy	To	Ie	So	Ie		Cs	Ac		Cs	Gi	
Sp	Gi	Py	Cm	Py		Sy	Ai		Sy	Ac	
Sa	Cm	Fx	Ac	Fx		Sp	Ie		Sp	Ai	
Wb	Ac	Fm	Fm	In		Sa	Py		Sa	Ie	
So						Re	Fx		Wb	Py	
						To	Em		Re	Fx	
									So	In	
									Em		

Note. H indicates CPI scale means significantly higher (*p* < .001) than sample mean; L indicates scale means significantly lower (*p* < .001) than sample mean.

TABLE 7 Correlations Between MBTI Scores and FIRO-B Scales (N = 26,430)

FIRO-B Scales	MBTI Scores			
	EI	SN	TF	JP
Expressed Inclusion	−.49	.04	.14	−.01
Wanted Inclusion	−.29	.07	.12	.04
Expressed Control	−.16	.08	−.21	−.01
Wanted Control	.02	−.03	.16	.00
Expressed Affection	−.42	.07	.25	.03
Wanted Affection	−.27	.02	.23	.02

Note. Because of the very large sample size in this table, small correlations are statistically significant but are not likely to be meaningful in practice. An arbitrary cutoff of .20 or higher is used for interpreting meaningful results.

did not load on the Extraversion factor. This is an indication that the FIRO-B scales have more in common, that is, they share more variance, with each other than they do with MBTI or CPI scores. In interpreting joint results of the MBTI and the FIRO-B, it may be helpful for interpreters to remember both the extent of correlation of the FIRO-B scores with the MBTI and the factor analysis results that suggest that the FIRO-B, as a separate factor, may contribute additional information.

Again, the correlational results are very similar to those reported by Fitzgerald (1991), indicating that these findings are supported by a separate study and a different sample of practicing managers. For an in-depth discussion of the joint use of the MBTI and the FIRO-B, see Schnell, Hammer, Fitzgerald, Fleenor, and Van Velsor (1994) and Chapter 15 of this volume.

The MBTI and Creativity—the KAI

Correlations between MBTI scores and KAI scores were calculated on a sample of 12,115 CCL participants for whom scores from both instruments were available. These correlations are presented in Table 8. Once again, only scores of .20 and above will be discussed here.

Extraversion was correlated with the total score (.23) and with Sufficiency of Originality (.30). The Thinking–Feeling dimension of the MBTI did not appear to be related to the KAI scores.

Intuition was correlated with the total score (.54), Rule/Group Conformity (.45), Sufficiency of Originality (.47), and Efficiency (.34). Perceiving was related to the total score (.49), Rule/Group Conformity (.40), Sufficiency of Originality (.32), and Efficiency (.48).

TABLE 8 Correlations Between MBTI Scores and KAI Scores (*N* = 12,115)

KAI Scores	MBTI Scores			
	EI	SN	TF	JP
Rule/Group Conformity	−.11	.45	−.01	.40
Sufficiency of Originality	−.30	.47	−.05	.32
Efficiency	−.11	.34	.13	.48
Total Score	−.23	.54	.01	.49

Note. Because of the very large sample size in this table, small correlations are statistically significant but are not likely to be meaningful in practice. An arbitrary cutoff of .20 or higher is used for interpreting meaningful results.

When presenting results from the MBTI and the KAI, users should be aware of the high correlation between Intuition and Perceiving and KAI scores. Managers with high preference scores on these MBTI dimensions have a strong tendency to score toward the Innovative end of the KAI continuum.

The MBTI and the LSI

Using the CCL database, Pearman and Fleenor (1995) selected a random sample of 150 managers for each of the 16 MBTI types. (For two of the types, INFP and ENTP, only 149 managers were available for inclusion in the study). MBTI type and ratings from subordinates and peers on the LSI adjectives were analyzed using analysis of variance. This analysis indicated that there were significant differences among the MBTI types on the LSI adjectival ratings.

Table 9 shows, for each MBTI type, which LSI adjectives were rated significantly higher relative to the other types. For example, ISFJs were seen by their subordinates and peers as being more conservative, conventional, guarded, and reserved than the other types. The results of this study provide some evidence that observers in the workplace view each of the MBTI types differently. These findings also provide additional information about each of the MBTI types for those providing feedback to managers.

MBTI and LGD Ratings

In collaboration with CCL researchers, Grant (1993) investigated the relationship between MBTI scores and LGD ratings using data from a sample of 5,793 LDP participants. The correlations between MBTI scores and Competitive LGD ratings are presented in Table 10, and the correlations between MBTI scores and Cooperative LGD ratings are

TABLE 9 MBTI Types Rated Significantly Higher on LSI Adjectives by Peers and Subordinates (N = 2,398)

ISTJ n = 150	ISFJ n = 150	INFJ n = 150	INTJ n = 150
Guarded Pressuring	Conservative Conventional Guarded Reserved	Delegating Dependable Easygoing Fair Guarded Initiating Patient Permissive Reflective Reserved Supportive	Adaptable Analytical Appreciative Deliberate Determined Fair Independent Initiating Methodical Organized Resourceful Self-Confident Supportive Understanding

ISTP n = 150	ISFP n = 150	INFP n = 149	INTP n = 150
Critical Detached Guarded Independent Resourceful	Easygoing	Appreciative Easygoing	Dogmatic Easygoing Energetic Fair Independent Initiating Resourceful Understanding

ESTP n = 150	ESFP n = 150	ENFP n = 150	ENTP n = 149
Demanding	Changeable Energetic Forceful Initiating Resourceful	Appreciative Easygoing Energetic Resourceful Understanding	Independent Initiating

ESTJ n = 150	ESFJ n = 150	ENFJ n = 150	ENTJ n = 150
Dogmatic Impatient Impulsive Initiating Manipulating Pressuring	Changeable Energetic Forceful Initiating Resourceful	Appreciative Compromising Delegating Energetic Fair Resourceful Supportive	Adaptable Energetic Fair Impersonal Independent Initiating Opinionated Resourceful

Note. Adjectives listed for each type were rated significantly higher (*p* < .05) relative to the other types.

Adapted from "Differences in Perceived and Self-Reported Qualities of Psychological Type," by R. R. Pearman and J. W. Fleenor. Copyright 1995 by R. R. Pearman and J. W. Fleenor, Center for Creative Leadership, Greensboro, NC. Reprinted with permission.

presented in Table 11. As can be seen from these tables, none of the correlations met the .20 criterion discussed above.

Because effective performance in the LGD requires frequent interaction with group members and a high level of participation and little time to reflect prior to the group activity, a strong relationship between Extraversion and LGD ratings was anticipated. An Extravert's focus of energy toward people and events was expected to be reflected in their LGD ratings. The correlations between Extraversion scores and LGD ratings, however, were only in the .05 to .15 range. These correlations were similar for both the competitive and the cooperative exercises.

Intuition scores showed the strongest relationships to the LGD ratings. These correlations were in the .10 to .17 range and were similar for both exercises. It was expected that the novel nature of the LGD tasks and the fact that participants are not provided with substantial factual preparation for those tasks might hinder the performance of participants who preferred Sensing.

Effective performance in the LGD required that the participants guide the group toward a decision. It was expected, therefore, that a Judging type's preference for making decisions and reaching closure might be related to high LGD ratings. However, the correlations between Judging scores and LGD ratings were very low.

Overall, correlations between the MBTI scores and the LGD ratings were lower than anticipated. Because the ratings were made by expert observers using a well-known assessment method, it was expected that correlations with Extraversion, Intuition, and Judging would exceed the .20 criterion.

One possible explanation for these results is that participants were able to manage their behavior within the context of the LGD. A participant, therefore, may have appeared more Extraverted in the exercises than suggested by his or her MBTI scores. In other words, savvy participants may have recognized that the observers would rate Extraverted behavior more positively and acted accordingly.

In previous studies, Campbell and Van Velsor (1985) found that managers who performed well in LGD tended to be more Extraverted and Intuitive; however, they did not indicate if these differences were significant. Thorne and Gough (1991) reported correlations between MBTI scores and observer ratings of 411 individuals who were assessed at the Institute for Personality Assessment and Research (IPAR). The observers rated these assessees after a 90-minute interview using the

TABLE 10 Correlations Between MBTI Scores and Leaderless Group Discussion Ratings, Competitive Exercise (N = 5,793)

LGD Ratings	MBTI Scores			
	EI	SN	TF	JP
Activity Level	−.15	.16	.00	.04
Led Discussion	−.15	.17	.00	.03
Influenced Others	−.12	.16	.00	.03
Problem Analysis	−.11	.16	.00	.03
Task Orientation	−.13	.16	.00	.02
Motivated Others	−.12	.15	.02	.03
Interpersonal Skills	−.06	.10	.04	.01
Verbal Effectiveness	−.09	.16	.01	.06
Overall Rating	−.13	.17	.01	.03

Note. Because of the very large sample size in this table, small correlations are statistically significant but are not likely to be meaningful in practice. An arbitrary cutoff of .20 or higher is used for interpreting meaningful results.

Adapted from *The Myers-Briggs Type Indicator and Ratings of Leadership Behavior,* by L. D. Grant, 1993, unpublished master's thesis, North Carolina State University, Raleigh. Copyright 1993 by L. D. Grant. Reprinted with permission.

TABLE 11 Correlations Between MBTI Scores and Leaderless Group Discussion Ratings, Cooperative Exercise (N = 5,793)

LGD Ratings	MBTI Scores			
	EI	SN	TF	JP
Activity Level	−.12	.16	.01	.06
Led Discussion	−.12	.17	.00	.07
Influenced Others	−.10	.16	.00	.06
Problem Analysis	−.07	.15	.01	.05
Task Orientation	−.10	.15	.01	.06
Motivated Others	−.11	.16	.04	.07
Interpersonal Skills	−.05	.11	.05	.04
Verbal Effectiveness	−.07	.17	.03	.06
Overall Rating	−.10	.17	.02	.07

Note. Because of the very large sample size in this table, small correlations are statistically significant but are not likely to be meaningful in practice. An arbitrary cutoff of .20 or higher is used for interpreting meaningful results.

Adapted from *The Myers-Briggs Type Indicator and Ratings of Leadership Behavior,* by L. D. Grant, 1993, unpublished master's thesis, North Carolina State University, Raleigh. Copyright 1993 by L. D. Grant. Reprinted with permission.

Interviewer's Check List (ICL). The ICL captures ratings on nine dimensions, including Activity, Movement, Speech, and Reaction to the Interview. Overall, the correlations between the ICL ratings and the MBTI scores were low. The highest correlation for each MBTI scale was .19 for EI, .20 for SN, .22 for TF, and .27 for JP. Although slightly higher, these correlations are comparable to the relationships found between MBTI scores and LGD ratings in the CCL's LDPs.

These findings do not provide much guidance for presenting the results of MBTI and LGD scores for feedback purposes. Although one would intuitively expect these measures to be related, the empirical evidence does not support this hypothesis. Some light may be shed on these findings by recent research on the discrepancy between self-ratings and the ratings of others. According to Van Velsor, Taylor, and Leslie (1993), managers' self-ratings are often very different from the ratings provided by their co-workers on 360-degree feedback instruments. A similar phenomenon may be occurring with the MBTI and the LGD ratings. A participant's self-perception of his or her preference for Extraversion, for example, may differ from the perception of an observer who is rating that person's behavior. In light of the different methods of gathering the data (paper-and-pencil responses versus observational ratings) and the different perspectives of the respondents (self versus other), these findings do not seem to be exceptional.

RESULTS FROM THE UNIVERSITY OF MARYLAND LEADERSHIP DEVELOPMENT PROGRAM

Fitzgerald (1991) investigated the relationships between the MBTI and several other measures using 386 participants from the Leadership Development Program (LDP) at the University of Maryland University College. This sample was mostly male (83%) upper-middle-level managers (51%), with an average age of 41. Seventy-three percent were from business organizations, and the majority (85%) had at least a bachelor's degree.

Fitzgerald (1991) reported findings of the relationships between the MBTI and two instruments used in the University of Maryland University College LDP: the *Occupational Stress Inventory* (OSI) and the *Managerial Job Satisfaction Questionnaire* (MJSQ). The OSI (Osipow & Spokane, 1987) contains 14 scales that measure three dimensions of occupational adjustment: occupational stress, psychological strain, and coping resources. The reliability (alpha coefficients) of the OSI scales ranges from .71 to .94. The MJSQ (Celucci & DeVries, 1978) is a 20-item questionnaire designed to measure one's satisfaction with five components of a job: the work itself, supervision, co-workers, pay and benefits, and promotion opportunity. The reliability of the MJSQ scales ranges from .61 to .85.

The results of Fitzgerald's (1991) correlational analysis of MBTI continuous scores with OSI scores are presented in Table 12. Using the .20 criterion, three of the Personal Strain scales (Vocational Strain, Psychological Strain, and Interpersonal Strain) were related to Introversion, and one of the Personal Resources scales (Social Support) was related to Extraversion. The Role Insufficiency scale from the Occupational Roles dimension was correlated with Intuition, and Physical Strain from the Personal Strain dimension was related to Perceiving. Overall, these results indicate that Introverts who are managers appear to be more susceptible to occupational stress than Extraverts in the same kinds of positions.

The results of the correlational analysis between the MBTI and the MJSQ (Fitzgerald, 1991) are presented in Table 13. Using the .20 criterion of Myers and McCaulley (1985), several meaningful relationships were found. Extraversion was meaningfully related to two MJSQ scales: The Work Itself and Supervision. Additionally, Extraversion was related to one item on the Co-Worker scale, "I enjoy working with people here." The correlation between Extraversion and the average of all MJSQ items was .24. These results indicate that there is a positive relationship between job satisfaction and Extraversion. In general, Extraverts appear to be more satisfied than Introverts with their jobs and their supervisors.

CONCLUSION

According to Hirsh and Kummerow (1990), the MBTI is a useful tool for helping managers in organizations increase their own self-insight, understand individual differences, improve teamwork, and solve organizational problems. Because the MBTI is descriptive in nature (Hirsh & Kummerow, 1990, p. 3), other measures that are more prescriptive are sometimes used in conjunction with it. Some of the instruments employed for this purpose have been discussed in this chapter.

TABLE 12 Correlations Between MBTI and OSI Scores (*N* = 386)

OSI Scales	MBTI Scores			
	EI	SN	TF	JP
Occupational Roles				
Role Overload	.02	.06	−.03	.03
Role Insufficiency	.11	.22	.06	.15
Role Ambiguity	.15	.13	.02	.14
Role Boundary	.08	.11	.11	.17
Responsibility	.16	−.08	−.06	−.07
Physical Environment	.04	−.05	.00	.03
Personal Strain				
Vocational Strain	.20	.05	.09	.16
Psychological Strain	.21	.00	.09	.08
Interpersonal Strain	.20	.08	.06	.11
Physical Strain	.15	.05	.11	.22
Personal Resources				
Recreation	−.16	.09	.09	.01
Self-Care	−.15	.17	.10	−.15
Social Support	−.20	.06	.06	−.06
Rational/Cognitive Coping	−.07	.09	−.03	−.15

Note. Because of the large sample size in this table, small correlations are statistically significant but are not likely to be meaningful in practice. An arbitrary cutoff of .20 or higher is
used for interpreting meaningful results.

Adapted from *The MBTI and Managers: Research Findings and Implications for Management
Development,* by C. Fitzgerald, 1991, College Park, MD. Copyright 1991 by C. Fitzgerald.
Reprinted with permission.

Knowledge of the relationships between the MBTI and these other
instruments should increase the effectiveness of the user in applying
insights gained through these measures.

The data contained in this chapter may help make useful connections between instruments for practitioners who use the MBTI in conjunction with the other instruments presented here. In addition, it may
prevent practitioners from overstating relationships between the MBTI
and other measures by contributing data to refine and perhaps correct
hypotheses about relationships (e.g., Extraversion and performance
in LGD).

TABLE 13 Correlations Between MBTI Scores and MJSQ Scores (N = 386)

MJSQ Items	MBTI Scores			
	EI	SN	TF	JP
The Work Itself				
1. My job is interesting.	−.22	.01	−.03	−.07
2. I feel good about the amount of responsibility in my job.	−.16	−.15	.00	−.09
3. I would rather be doing another job.[a]	−.19	−.11	−.04	−.05
4. I get little sense of accomplishment from doing my job.[a]	−.16	−.09	−.03	−.09
Average	−.23	−.12	−.03	−.10
Supervision				
5. The managers I work for back me up.	−.15	−.10	.02	−.12
6. The managers I work for are top-notch.	−.17	−.07	−.04	−.07
7. My supervisors don't listen to me.[a]	−.17	−.02	−.05	−.08
8. My management doesn't treat me fairly.[a]	−.19	−.06	−.03	−.03
Average	−.21	−.07	−.02	−.09
Co-Workers				
9. The people I work with do not give me enough support.[a]	−.12	−.06	−.03	−.06
10. When I ask people to do things, the job gets done.	−.07	−.10	−.09	−.11
11. I enjoy working with the people here.	−.22	−.13	.01	−.02
12. I work with responsible people.	−.14	−.07	.01	−.02
Average	−.18	−.08	−.03	−.08
Pay and Benefits				
13. My organization pays better than competitors.	−.10	−.07	−.15	.01
14. I am underpaid for what I do.[a]	−.01	.02	−.01	−.01
15. My pay is adequate, considering the responsibilities I have.	−.03	.00	−.06	.00
16. My fringe benefits are generous.	.03	.04	.14	.05
Average	−.04	.00	−.03	.02

TABLE 13 Correlations Between MBTI Scores and MJSQ Scores (N = 386) (continued)

MJSQ Items	MBTI Scores			
	EI	SN	TF	JP
Promotion				
17. I do not like the basis on which my organization promotes people.[a]	−.08	−.11	−.13	−.04
18. Promotions are infrequent in my organization.[a]	−.10	.05	.03	.04
19. If I do a good job, I'm likely to get promoted.	−.13	.07	.01	.03
20. I am satisfied with my rate of advancement.	−.07	−.16	.04	−.08
Average	−.13	−.10	−.02	−.02
Average across all items	−.24	−.11	−.03	−.08

Note. Because of the large sample size in this table, small correlations are statistically significant but are not likely to be meaningful in practice. An arbitrary cutoff of .20 or higher is used for interpreting meaningful results.

Adapted from *The MBTI and Managers: Research Findings and Implications for Management Development*, by C. Fitzgerald, 1991, College Park, MD. Copyright 1991 by C. Fitzgerald. Reprinted with permission.

[a]Ratings for these items were reverse scored.

The *Managerial Job Satisfaction Questionnaire* is copyrighted by the Center for Creative Leadership, Greensboro, NC. Reprinted with permission.

For practitioners who use the MBTI with managers without other instruments, knowledge of MBTI correlates that were reported in this chapter may help them develop and explore hypotheses with their clients about differences based on type preferences. One example of potentially applicable information is that managers who prefer Extraversion tend to be higher in dominance than Introverted managers. Another might be that Introverted managers tend to report more stress and less job satisfaction than Extraverted managers. It should be remembered, however, that the results presented in this chapter are based on managerial samples and may not be applicable to other groups.

In this chapter, relationships between the MBTI and several measures of personality and performance were discussed. Meaningful relationships between the MBTI and two well-known personality measures, the CPI and the FIRO-B, were reported. The MBTI also was found to be correlated with the KAI, a measure of creativity in problem solving. Ratings from co-workers on the descriptors from the LSI were found to differentiate among the MBTI types. On the other hand, the MBTI did not appear to be strongly related to ratings from two LGD exercises. Using measures of occupational stress (the OSI) and job satisfaction (the MJSQ), it was reported that Introverts seem to be more susceptible to occupational stress and experience less job satisfaction than Extraverts.

REFERENCES

Bailey, R. S. (1991). *The Leadership Style Indicator.* Greensboro, NC: Center for Creative Leadership.

Bray, D., Campbell, R., & Grant, D. (1974). *Formative years in business: A long-term AT&T study of managerial lives.* New York: Wiley.

Campbell, D. (1992, August). *The Center for Creative Leadership's Leadership Development Program (LDP): An historical overview.* Paper presented at the meeting of the Academy of Management, Las Vegas.

Campbell, D., & Van Velsor, E. (1985). *The use of personality measures in the Leadership Development Program.* Greensboro, NC: Center for Creative Leadership.

Celucci, A., & DeVries, D. L. (1978). *Measuring managerial satisfaction: A manual for the MJSQ* (Tech. Rep. No. 11). Greensboro, NC: Center for Creative Leadership.

DeMauro, G. (1992). Review of the Kirton Adaption-Innovation Inventory. In J. Kramer & J. Conoley (Eds.), *The eleventh mental measures yearbook.* Lincoln: University of Nebraska Press.

Fitzgerald, C. (1991). *The MBTI and managers: Research findings and implications for management development.* Unpublished manuscript.

Goldberg, L. (1993). The structure of phenotypic personality traits. *American Psychologist, 48,* 26–34.

Gough, H. (1987). *California Psychological Inventory administrator's guide.* Palo Alto, CA: Consulting Psychologists Press.

Grant, Lisa D. (1993). *The Myers-Briggs Type Indicator and ratings of leadership behavior.* Unpublished master's thesis, North Carolina State University, Raleigh, NC.

Hirsh, S. K., & Kummerow, J. M. (1990). *Introduction to type in organizations* (2d ed.). Palo Alto, CA: Consulting Psychologists Press.

Johnson, D. A., & Saunders, D. R. (1990). Confirmatory factor analysis of the Myers-Briggs Type Indicator—Expanded Analysis Report. *Educational and Psychological Measurement, 50,* 562–571.

Kirton, M. J. (1987). *Kirton Adaption and Innovation Inventory (KAI) manual* (2d ed.). Hatfield, UK: Occupational Research Centre.

MacKinnon, D. (1975). *An overview of assessment centers* (Tech. Rep. No. 1). Greensboro, NC: Center for Creative Leadership.

McCaulley, M. (1990). The *Myers-Briggs Type Indicator* and leadership. In K. Clark & M. Clark (Eds.), *Measures of leadership.* West Orange, NJ: Leadership Library of America.

McCrae, R., & Costa, P. T. (1989). Reinterpreting the *Myers-Briggs Type Indicator* from the perspective of the five-factor model of personality. *Journal of Personality, 57,* 16–39.

Myers, I. B., & McCaulley, M. H. (1985). *Manual: A guide to the development and use of the Myers-Briggs Type Indicator.* Palo Alto, CA: Consulting Psychologists Press.

Osipow, S. & Spokane, A. (1987). *Occupational Stress Inventory.* Odessa, FL: Psychological Assessment Resources.

Pearman, R. R., & Fleenor, J. W. (1995). Differences in perceived and self-reported qualities of psychological type. Greensboro, NC: Center for Creative Leadership.

Schutz, W. C. (1967). *The FIRO scales manual.* Palo Alto, CA: Consulting Psychologists Press.

Schnell, E. R., Hammer, A. L., Fitzgerald, C., Fleenor, J. W., & Van Velsor, E. (1994). Relationships between the MBTI and the FIRO-B: Implications for their joint use in leadership development. In C. Fitzgerald (Ed.), *Proceedings of the Myers-Briggs Type Indicator and Leadership: An International Research Conference* (pp.177–188). College Park, MD: University of Maryland University College National Leadership Institute.

Thorne, A., & Gough, H. (1991). *Portraits of type: An MBTI research compendium.* Palo Alto, CA: Davies-Black.

Van Velsor, E., & Leslie, J. (1991). *Feedback to managers: Vol. 2, A review and comparison of sixteen multi-rater feedback instruments.* Greensboro, NC: Center for Creative Leadership.

Van Velsor, E., Taylor, S., & Leslie, J. (1993). An examination of the relationships among self-perception accuracy, self-awareness, gender, and leader effectiveness. *Human Resource Management, 32,* 249–264.

5 | The MBTI and Leadership Skills

Relationships Between the MBTI and Four 360-Degree Management Feedback Instruments

Ellen Van Velsor

John W. Fleenor

The *Myers-Briggs Type Indicator* (MBTI) is one of the most widely used instruments in human resource development efforts of many kinds and is frequently used in leadership development programs for managers from supervisory to senior levels. Its popularity is rooted in its accessible presentation of personality-related preferences and the ease with which it can be related, in training and development settings, to work preferences and leadership style.

The use of 360-degree, or multirater, feedback instruments in leadership development programs also has grown over the years and has proven to be a valuable method of assessment-for-development. This kind of instrument allows managers to rate themselves and to be rated by their supervisors, direct reports, and peers on multiple domains of managerial work or leadership effectiveness (Tornow, 1993; Van Velsor & Leslie, 1992).

The MBTI is often used in conjunction with a 360-degree instrument, in a group setting or in individual development counseling.

Feedback consultants or training staff have frequent opportunities to provide background information and to field questions about the empirical
relationship between MBTI preferences and leadership capacities or
development needs. Yet these professionals have had little research-based
information on which to rely. Although there is a long history of research
on personality and job performance, until recently, little research has been
done on the relationship between frequently used measures such as the
MBTI and instruments that assess leadership capacities from a variety of
perspectives. This kind of research is important to interpreting both the
MBTI and leadership skills instruments with managers.

Fitzgerald (1994a) reported in the proceedings of an international
conference on the MBTI and leadership on several studies that focused
on relationships between MBTI preferences and leadership capacities as
measured by different 360-degree instruments.[1] All of the studies
showed some significant relationships between rated leadership skills
and personality-based preferences, whether measured by the MBTI or
the *Type Differentiation Indicator* (TDI), a method of scoring Form J of
the MBTI to produce subscales.[2] The purpose of this chapter is not to
review these individual studies in depth, but to go beyond them by
comparing and integrating their results and discussing implications for
the use of these instruments in leadership development.

This chapter has five sections. The first describes the methods and
focus of five studies on the MBTI and leadership effectiveness (the five
studies focus on four different leadership instruments). The second section looks at the relationship between MBTI scores and ratings of leadership skills, covering three areas: (a) skills related to Sensing,
Thinking, and Judging versus those related to Intuition, Feeling, and
Perceiving; (b) how managers with different MBTI preferences are seen
by others; and (c) self versus rater differences on leadership and MBTI
preferences. The third section compares the results of studies that relate
the TDI subscales to leadership skills, while the fourth focuses on type
and rated leadership effectiveness. Implications for the use of these
instruments in leadership development are addressed in the last section
of the chapter.

METHODS AND FOCUS OF FIVE STUDIES
ON THE MBTI AND LEADERSHIP EFFECTIVENESS

Table 1 outlines the method and focus of five studies on the MBTI and
leadership effectiveness: Fitzgerald (1994b) on the *Management Skills*

TABLE 1 Methods and Focus of Five Studies on the MBTI and Leadership Effectiveness

	Fitzgerald (1994b)	Sundstrom et al. (1994)	Wilson & Wilson (1994)	Johnson & Golden (1994)	Van Velsor & Fleenor (1994)
Instrument Used	Management Skills Profile[3]	SYMLOG[4]	Survey of Management Practices[5]	Survey of Management Practices[5]	Benchmarks[6]
MBTI Form	Form G	Form G	Form G	Form J	Form F
Sample Size	386 middle/upper-middle managers	380 senior executives	914 managers	208 managers	788 upper-middle or executive-level managers
Sample Source	Leadership Development Program	Division of international manufacturing company		Various industries	Leadership Development Program
Demographics	83% male; college educated; average age 41; average 8 years' management experience	96% male; 86% college educated; median age 48		68% male; Average age 37	73% male; 82% White; college educated; average age 46
MBTI Percentage Distribution	I 54% S 53% T 82% J 69%	I 55% S 60% T 89% J 79%		I 41.3% S 66.7% T 59.5% J 75.8%	I 41.8% S 65.7% T 78.1% J 91.4%

Profile; Sundstrom, Koenigs, and Huet-Cox (1994) on SYMLOG; Wilson and Wilson (1994) and Johnson and Golden (1994) on the *Survey of Management Practices;* and Van Velsor and Fleenor (1994) on *Benchmarks.* A description of each of the instruments appears in Table 2.

Fitzgerald (1994b) related MBTI continuous scores (Form G) to ratings on the *Management Skills Profile* (MSP) using a sample of 386 managers attending a leadership development program in which these instruments were administered. The sample was primarily male, college-educated, upper-middle and middle-level managers, with an average age of 41 and an average of eight years of managerial experience. The preferences of these participants tended toward Introversion (54%), Sensing (53%), Thinking (82%), and Judging (69%). The purpose of Fitzgerald's research was, in part, to explore the relationships between MBTI preferences and leadership skills and to examine the correlation between MBTI preference scores and the discrepancy between self-ratings and others' ratings on the MSP.

Sundstrom, Koenings, and Huet-Cox (1994) related MBTI continuous scores (Form G) to co-worker perceptions of 26 expressed values on SYMLOG using a sample of 380 upper-middle managers and senior executives in one division of an international manufacturing company. The sample was mostly male, with an average age of 48, and primarily college educated. The purpose of their research was to look at the relationship between personality preferences and expressed values related to leadership and teamwork. Self-ratings on SYMLOG were not reported in this research. Instead, results focused on the relationships between the MBTI dimensions and co-worker ratings of expressed values.

Two papers that compared scores on the *Survey of Management Practices* (SMP) to MBTI preference scores were authored by Wilson and Wilson (1994) and Johnson and Golden (1994). Although Wilson and Wilson focused their research on both MBTI (Form G) continuous scores and on categories created using a 10% grouping on either side of the sample median, for the sake of comparability across studies, only results using continuous MBTI scores are reported here. Their sample consisted of 914 managers, and their studies focused on self-ratings, boss ratings, and subordinate ratings on the SMP.

Johnson and Golden used the *Survey of Management Practices* as the measure of leader effectiveness and looked at its relationship to the TDI. Their sample was comprised of 208 managers from a variety of

TABLE 2 Summary of Four Management and Leadership Feedback Instruments

Instrument	Description	Categories/Scales/Dimensions Include	Method of Assessment
Management Skills Profile	122-item questionnaire that provides feedback on 19 categories of management skill	Planning Organizing Personal Organization and Time Management Informing Oral Communications Listening Written Communications Problem Analysis and Decision Making Financial and Quantitative Human Relations Conflict Management Leadership Style and Influence Motivating Others Delegating and Controlling Coaching and Developing Personal Motivation Personal Adaptability Occupational/Technical Knowledge Results Orientation	Managers are assessed on a five-point scale (1 = not at all; 5 = to a very great extent) that focuses on how frequently they use each behavior.

TABLE 2 Summary of Four Management and Leadership Feedback Instruments (continued)

Instrument	Description	Categories/Scales/Dimensions Include	Method of Assessment
System for Multiple Level Observation of Groups (SYMLOG)	26-item questionnaire designed to measure values important for teamwork that tap three bipolar dimensions	Dominance vs. Submissiveness Friendliness vs. Unfriendliness Acceptance vs. Opposition to the Task Orientation of Established Authority	Managers receive feedback based on averaged responses by five co-workers regarding their expression of 26 values using a three-choice format (0 = rare; 1 = sometimes; 2 = often). Managers are compared against the empirically based most effective profile of values for teamwork effectiveness.
Survey of Management Practices	Multirater feedback instrument covering 15 areas of management practice	Clarifying Goals Encouraging Work Participation Orderly Planning Organization Expertise Work Facilitation Giving Feedback Time Emphasis Control of Details Goal Pressure Delegation (Permissiveness) Recognition Approachability Teambuilding Interest in Subordinate Growth Building Trust	Respondents are asked to rate the manager on a scale of 1 to 7. Anchors are provided at the midpoint and the ends of each scale (1 = Extremely small extent, "Never" or "Not at all"; 4 = Average extent, "Normal in degree or frequency"; 7 = Extremely high degree, "Without fail").

Instrument	Description	Categories/Scales/Dimensions Include	Method of Assessment
Benchmarks	Multirater feedback instrument that provides managers feedback from supervisors, peers, and direct reports on 16 leadership skills and perspectives as well as 6 "derailment" factors	*Skills and Perspectives* Resourcefulness Doing Whatever It Takes Being a Quick Study Decisiveness Leading Subordinates Setting a Developmental Climate Confronting Problem Subordinates Work Team Orientation Hiring Talented Staff Building and Mending Relationships Compassion and Sensitivity Straightforwardness and Composure Balance Between Personal Life and Work Self-Awareness Putting People at Ease Acting with Flexibility *"Derailment" Factors* Problems with Interpersonal Relationships Difficulty in Molding a Staff Difficulty Making Strategic Transitions Lack of Follow-Through Overdependence Strategic Differences with Management	Respondents rate the extent to which the manager displays the 16 skills and perspectives (5 = To a very great extent; 4 = To a great extent; 3 = To some extent; 2 = To a little extent; 1 = Not at all). Persons are rated according to the extent to which they display characteristics that can lead to derailment (5 = Strongly agree; 4 = Tend to agree; 3 = Hard to decide; 2 = Tend to disagree; 1 = Strongly disagree).

industries. The purpose of their work was to look at the correlation between MBTI type and the difference between self-ratings and ratings by subordinates.

A series of studies conducted at the Center for Creative Leadership over the past two years (Van Velsor & Fleenor, 1994; Fleenor, 1995; see also Chapter 4 by Fleenor in this volume) focused on the relationship of *Benchmarks* scores to MBTI (Form F) continuous scores and to MBTI type for a sample of 788 managers who attended leadership development programs. These studies also addressed the relationship of TDI subscale scores to leadership skills as measured by *Benchmarks* and assessed the relationships from a variety of rater perspectives. The sample used in this research was 73% male and 82% White. Sixty-two percent were upper-middle or executive-level managers, with a mean age of 46. The educational level of this sample was higher than the overall norm for participants in these programs, with 79% having a graduate degree.

At least one note of caution is in order before comparing the results of studies using different leadership instruments. Most 360-degree leadership instruments represent models that are related to effective leadership. Yet these models can be quite different, depending on how they were derived or the premises on which they are based. A model can represent any of the following:

- Components of managerial work (e.g., what managers need to do)
- Skills and perspectives that effective senior executives report learning from their career experiences (e.g., what they are aware of having developed)
- Skills that differentiate successful from derailed executives (e.g., what do the successful have that the derailed do not)
- Ideal or "personal best" characteristics (e.g., what are the characteristics of the most effective leader I've ever known)
- Values displayed by leaders who are viewed as effective

Although these differences can be subtle, they are important when comparing scores on these instruments to MBTI preferences in that the relationship between MBTI scores and one model of leadership might be very different from the relationship between MBTI scores and another model of leadership skills.

In terms of the instruments compared here, we consider both the *Management Skills Profile* and the *Survey of Management Practices* to be based on models of managerial work (what managers need to do). *Benchmarks* represents skills and perspectives executives report learning from their experience, as well as skills that differentiate successful from derailed executives. SYMLOG assumes that leaders' values are expressed in behaviors and that a leader's effectiveness depends on the expression of values related to teamwork.

RELATIONSHIP BETWEEN MBTI DIMENSIONS AND CO-WORKER RATINGS OF LEADERSHIP SKILLS

In this section, we will report on the findings in the studies: first, in terms of skills related to Sensing, Thinking, and Judging versus those skills related to Intuition, Feeling, and Perceiving; second, in terms of how managers with different MBTI preferences were seen by others; and third, in terms of self and rater differences on leadership and MBTI preferences.

Skills Related to Sensing, Thinking, and Judging Versus Intuition, Feeling, and Perceiving

Table 3 summarizes the leadership scales most strongly related to each of the MBTI preferences for each of the studies. In looking across studies of the MBTI and leadership skills, it is clear that all MBTI preferences relate to skills and perspectives as assessed by at least one leadership instrument.

In comparing the relationship of preference scores on the MBTI to leadership skills as measured by various instruments, it is clear that managers with a preference for Sensing, Thinking, and/or Judging tend to be seen by others as more skilled in typical domains of administrative and/or task management, such as planning and decision making.

In Fitzgerald's (1994b) analysis of the *Management Skills Profile* data, for example, managers with an MBTI preference for Sensing, Thinking, or Judging received higher scores than their opposites on a number of MSP scales, including Planning, Organizing, Problem Analysis and Decision Making, and Results Orientation. (Note: Table 3 contains statistically significant correlations greater than .15. Some of the correlations discussed here are statistically significant, but smaller.) In addition, managers with a preference for Sensing or Judging received higher scores on the Personal Organization and Time Management scale, as well as on the Delegating and Controlling scale. Thinkers received higher ratings from others on Planning and on Financial and Quantitative. Finally, managers with a preference for Judging also received higher ratings on Planning, as well as on Written Communications.

TABLE 3 Leadership Scales (Rating by Others) Most Strongly Related ($r > .15$) to MBTI Preferences

MBTI Preference	Instrument				
	Management Skills Profile	SYMLOG	Survey of Management Practices (Wilson & Wilson)	Survey of Management Practices (Johnson & Golden)	Benchmarks
E		Personal Prominence, Popularity, Relaxing Control, Friendship, Self-Interest	Recognition, Encouraging Participation, Feedback	Clarification of Goals, Upward Communication, Recognizing Good Performance, Teambuilding, Interest in Subordinate Growth	Putting People at Ease
I		Efficiency, Conservative, Passivity			
S		Reinforcement of Authority, Conservative, Loyalty, Obedience, Passivity	Orderly Work Planning		
N		Creativity	Clarification of Goals		
T		Assertiveness, Rejecting Popularity	Goal Pressure	Control of Details Goal Pressure	Problems with Interpersonal Relationships

Instrument

MBTI Preference	Management Skills Profile	SYMLOG	Survey of Management Practices (Wilson & Wilson)	Survey of Management Practices (Johnson & Golden)	Benchmarks
F		Popularity, Trust	Delegation, Recognition	Approachability	Acting with Flexibility, Balance, Hiring Talented Staff, Work Team Orientation, Leading Subordinates, Setting a Developmental Climate, Compassion and Sensitivity, Self-Awareness, Putting People at Ease, Building and Mending Relationships
J	Planning, Organizing, Time Management, Written Communication, Problem Analysis and Decision Making, Results Orientation	Reinforcement of Authority, Conservative, Obedience		Making Control Adjustments Planning	
P		Relaxing Control	Expertise, Feedback		

In the Wilson and Wilson (1994) research using the *Survey of Management Practices,* fewer leadership scales were related to Sensing, Thinking, or Judging. Yet Sensors were rated higher by their direct reports on Orderly Work Planning, and Thinkers were seen as exercising more Goal Pressure. Thinking types received higher ratings on Control of Details and on Goal Pressure in the Johnson and Golden (1994) research as well (also using the SMP). In addition, managers with a preference for Judging were rated more favorably in Johnson and Golden's research on Making Control Adjustments and on Planning.

Finally, using SYMLOG as an assessment of the values expressed by leaders, Sundstrom et al. (1994) reported that managers with a preference for Sensing or Judging were seen by others as expressing authority-aligned values more often (e.g., efficiency, authority, conventional ways of doing things).

In contrast to the other instruments, *Benchmarks* appears not to be measuring most of the skills and perspectives that come naturally to Sensing, Thinking, or Judging managers. Perhaps because of this, Thinking managers were rated significantly lower by others on many *Benchmarks* scales.

Although managers with a preference for Sensing, Thinking, or Judging tend to be strong in the traditional domains of task management and administration, managers with a preference for Intuition, Feeling, and/or Perceiving have other strengths related to people management and team leadership. Although the *Management Skills Profile* may not be measuring skills more typically found in Intuitive, Feeling, or Perceiving managers (Fitzgerald, 1994b), most of the other instruments used in these analyses do show such relationships.

On the SMP, supervisors tended to rate Intuitive managers higher on Clarification of Goals and to give Feeling managers higher scores on Delegation and Recognition skills. Managers with a preference for Perceiving were given higher ratings by direct reports on Expertise and on Feedback (Wilson & Wilson, 1994). In Johnson and Golden's (1994) research, 12 small but significant differences favor Intuition over Sensing on the SMP. Intuitives were rated higher by others on six of the task cycle ratings (Clarification of Goals, Orderly Work Planning, Expertise, Work Facilitation, Feedback, Recognizing Good Performance), as well as on all four of the interpersonal relations scales (Approachability, Teambuilding, Interest in Subordinate Growth, Building Trust). In addition, managers with a preference for Feeling were rated highly by others on people-oriented scales such as Work

Facilitation, Approachability, Teambuilding, and Interest in Subordinate Growth.

With SYMLOG, Sundstrom et al. found that managers with a preference for Intuition were seen by others as expressing values for creativity more often (e.g., creativity, friendship, less obedience). In addition, managers with a preference for Feeling were seen as expressing friendly values more often (e.g., popularity, teamwork, protection).

From the perspective of raters, the most important relationships between MBTI preference scores and the skills measured by *Benchmarks* have to do with the Thinking–Feeling dimension. Managers with a preference for Feeling were rated significantly higher by their peers and direct reports on Leading Subordinates, Setting a Developmental Climate, Compassion and Sensitivity, Self-Awareness, and Putting People at Ease. In addition, they were rated higher by direct reports on Work Team Orientation, Hiring Talented Staff, Balance Between Personal Life and Work, Building and Mending Relationships, and Acting with Flexibility. Managers with a preference for Feeling were seen by both peers and direct reports as significantly less likely to have Problems with Interpersonal Relationships, a "derailment" factor.

Rater Perspective Differences Across Instruments

Whenever studies used more than one rater perspective (e.g., the manager's supervisor, peers, and direct reports), the relationship of rated leadership skills to the manager's personality preferences varied by rater perspective. That is, peer ratings of some leadership skills may be related to one MBTI dimension, while direct report ratings of other leadership skills are correlated with a different dimension of the MBTI. Or supervisor ratings may be uncorrelated with MBTI scores when leadership ratings by direct reports clearly differentiate between managers with different MBTI preferences.

On the SMP, for example, where supervisors tended to rate Intuitive managers more favorably, the correlations of that dimension with peer or direct report ratings were much lower, suggesting that Intuitive types may tend to make a more favorable impression on their supervisors than they do on their peers or direct reports (Wilson & Wilson, 1994). Yet in the research reported using *Benchmarks,* there appeared to be no relationship between supervisor ratings and MBTI preference scores, while peer and subordinate ratings were frequently and significantly related to a preference for Feeling. In other words, Feeling types may make more of an impression on their peers and direct reports than they do on their supervisors. People in a lateral or a reporting relationship to the target manager may see a preference for Feeling as more relevant to the leadership skills measured by *Benchmarks* than do people in a supervisory relationship to the manager. Finally, the relative lack of relationship of MBTI preference to supervisors' ratings may indicate that managers of all types exert extra energy to demonstrate leadership skills and values in the presence of higher-ranking people.

MBTI Dimensions and Self/Rater Difference

Extraversion–Introversion

One of the most consistent findings across the research on leadership skills and the MBTI was that Extraverts rated themselves higher than Introverts rated themselves on a wide variety of leadership skills and behaviors, but they were typically not given significantly higher ratings by others on these same skills and behaviors. Four of the five studies compared here used self-ratings of leadership skill in their analyses, and, of the four, three found that Extraverts tended to overrate themselves relative to how they were seen by others.

For example, managers who report a preference for Extraversion on the MBTI rated themselves higher on the majority of skills and perspectives on *Benchmarks* (Van Velsor & Fleenor, 1994). Extraverts rated themselves higher than Introverts on Resourcefulness, Doing Whatever It Takes, Decisiveness, Leading Subordinates, Setting a Developmental Climate, Building and Mending Relationships, Compassion and Sensitivity, Putting People at Ease, and Acting with Flexibility. Extraverts also rated themselves more favorably (reported less difficulty) on Difficulty in Molding a Staff. Yet raters did not share the perception that Extraverts have many skills that set them apart. Peer ratings for Extraverts were higher on only one scale, Putting People at Ease, while neither direct reports nor superiors rated Extraverts more favorably on any of the 16 skills and perspectives or on any of the "derailment" scales.

Fitzgerald's (1994b) research using the MSP indicated that Extraverts rated themselves higher on 8 of the 19 scales—Informing, Oral Communications, Human Relations, Leadership Style and Influence, Motivating Others, Coaching and Developing, Personal Motivation, and Personal Adaptability—although they were not rated as more effective on any scale by their co-workers. In fact, on the MSP, Extraverts were rated by others as significantly less effective on four scales—Personal Organization and Time Management, Problem Analysis and Decision Making, Financial and Quantitative, and Occupational/Technical Knowledge.

Wilson and Wilson (1994) also found that managers with a preference for Extraversion rated themselves higher than Introverts did on 9 of the 11 SMP scales. Although most of the Extraverts' high self-ratings were not supported by more favorable ratings from their co-workers, Wilson and Wilson did find that Extraverts were more inclined to be seen by their supervisors as giving Recognition for Good Performance and were seen by the people they supervised as better at Encouraging Participation, Feedback, and Recognition for Good Performance.

The one study in which Extraverts did not demonstrate a tendency to overrate their leadership skills was the Johnson and Golden (1994) research, also using the SMP. In their study, Extraverted managers rated themselves higher on nearly all aspects of the SMP and were given more favorable ratings by others on most all of the skills as well. It is unclear at this point whether the divergent results are related to the domains measured by the instrument or to characteristics of their sample.

Although the SYMLOG research did not report self-ratings of values expressed by leaders, Sundstrom et al. (1994) reported that raters saw managers with a preference for Extraversion as expressing dominance values more often (e.g., personal prominence, popularity, tough-minded assertiveness). Values such as these could easily relate to a tendency to overrate one's own skills and abilities.

Sensing–Intuition, Thinking–Feeling, and Judging–Perceiving

Although Extraverts may have the greatest tendency to overrate themselves, other preferences were occasionally related to inflated self-ratings on specific skills. For example, in Wilson and Wilson's (1994) research on the SMP, self-ratings on three scales were related to a preference for Intuition. Although the higher ratings were borne out on one scale by supervisor ratings, Intuitives were not rated more favorably by other rater groups on any scale. Managers with a preference for Thinking or Judging rated themselves higher on Planning and Making Control Adjustments. Again, these groups were not rated higher by others on any scale of the SMP. Instead, Feeling types were more likely to receive favorable supervisor ratings. Yet there appeared to be no relationship between the Thinking–Feeling dimension and subordinate ratings on the SMP. On the Judging–Perceiving dimension, managers with a preference for Judging gave themselves higher ratings on several SMP scales, with supervisor and subordinate ratings on two scales supporting their self-rating.

In the *Benchmarks* analyses, managers who reported a preference for Intuition rated themselves higher on Doing Whatever It Takes, while individuals with a preference for Feeling rated themselves higher on Compassion and Sensitivity and on Putting People at Ease. Managers with a preference for Perceiving rated themselves less favorably on Lack of Follow Through. Although Perceiving managers were significantly more likely to believe they had a problem with Lack of Follow Through, this deficit was not perceived by any of their rater groups. As described earlier, the most important relationships between MBTI preferences and raters' views of managers' skills as measured by *Benchmarks* had to do with the Thinking–Feeling dimension. Although managers with a preference for Feeling did not tend to rate themselves higher on *Benchmarks* scales, they were rated more favorably by others on 10 of the 22 scales.

THE TDI AND LEADERSHIP SKILLS

The results of analyses using MBTI continuous scores have been mixed. While some researchers have found many scales related to rater assessments of leadership skills, others have found few relationships.[7] Two of the studies compared here sought to investigate the added value of using the TDI subscale analyses in studying correlates of leadership effectiveness. Table 4 shows the TDI subscales that related to leadership skills.

In Johnson and Golden's (1994) research using the SMP, six of the twenty-seven TDI subscales related to SMP scores, including three subscales of Extraversion–Introversion. In particular, managers who were rated highest on Upward Communication and Participation tended to have higher subscale scores on the Initiator subscale (E), as well as on Accepting (F), Affective (F), and Optimistic (Comfort). Higher ratings on the SMP Feedback scale were also positively related to the Initiator subscale (E). Delegating was related to higher scores on the Affective subscale (F), while more favorable ratings on Recognizing Good Performance related to higher Initiator (E), Accepting (F), and Optimistic (Comfort) subscale scores. Approachability was positively related to the Feeling subscales Accepting, Tender, and Affective, as well as to the Comfort subscale Optimistic. Managers who scored high on the subscales Initiator (E), Accepting (F), Affective (F), and Optimistic

(Comfort) were likely to be seen as most effective in the area of Teambuilding. Similarly, Interest in Subordinate Growth on the SMP was related to three of the same subscales—Initiator, Accepting, and Optimistic. Lower ratings on Goal Pressure were related to higher scores on the four Feeling subscales—Accepting, Tender, Accommodating, and Affective.

The study of *Benchmarks* data (Fleenor, 1995) used a large sample (*N* = 1134) of managers, as well as a reduced scale scoring system for the TDI subscales, due to the fact that Form F of the MBTI does not contain all the items necessary for complete scoring of all subscales. Overall, 20 items are missing from the complete set comprising all TDI scales. However, the missing items are distributed across scales in such a way that most reduced scales missing items are missing only one (i.e., 18 scales are missing one item each, one scale (Initiator-Receptor) is missing two items, and eight scales are missing no items).

Many significant correlations were found between *Benchmarks* self-ratings and TDI subscales. The Extraversion subscales Initiator and Expressive were related to high self-ratings on the scales Doing Whatever It Takes, Decisiveness, and Putting People at Ease. In addition, Expressive (E) was related to high self-ratings on the Building and Mending Relationships, Compassion and Sensitivity, and Acting with Flexibility. The Intuitive subscale Intellectual was related to high self-ratings on the *Benchmarks* scale Being a Quick Study. The Feeling subscales Accepting, Tender, Affective, and Compassionate were all related to high self-ratings on Compassion and Sensitivity and Putting People at Ease. The Perceiving subscales Polyactive, Open-Ended, and Emergent were related to lower self-evaluations (i.e., more perceived problems) on Lack of Follow Through on *Benchmarks*. In addition, high scores on the Perceiving subscale Casual were related to lower self-ratings on Confronting Problem Subordinates.

Several of the psychological Comfort subscales were also significantly related to high self-ratings on *Benchmarks*, including Intrepid (related to higher Resourcefulness, Doing Whatever It Takes, and Decisiveness, and to less Difficulty Making Strategic Transitions); Decisive (related to higher Doing Whatever It Takes, Decisiveness, Confronting Problem Subordinates, and less Difficulty Making Strategic Transitions); and Leader (related to high self-ratings on the *Benchmarks* scale Decisiveness).

In addition to the *Benchmarks* self-ratings relationships to TDI subscale scores, this research found that subscale scores added value from

TABLE 4 TDI Subscales and Others' Ratings of Leadership Skills ($r > .15$)

SMP	Initiator-Receptor	Expressive-Contained	Gregarious-Intimate	Pragmatic-Intellectual	Critical-Accepting
Upward Communication	−.18				.16
Feedback	−.16				
Goal Pressure					−.17
Delegation					
Recognizing Good Performance	−.21				.15
Approachability					.15
Teambuilding	−.17				.15
Interest in Sub-ordinate Growth	−.20				.17
Benchmarks					
Decisiveness		−.15			
Compassion & Sensitivity					.21
Putting People at Ease		−.22	−.16		.22
Doing Whatever It Takes		−.18			
Being a Quick Study				.19	
Confronting Problem Employees		−.17			
Building & Mending Relationships					.16

the point of view of understanding rater perspectives (See Table 4). Superior ratings on seven *Benchmarks* scales were related to higher TDI subscale scores. For example, Decisive (Comfort) correlated with Decisiveness; Accepting (F), Tender (F), Affective (F), and Compassionate (F) correlated with Compassion and Sensitivity; and Expressive (E), Gregarious (E), Accepting (F), Tender (F), Affective (F), Compassionate (F), and Optimistic (Comfort) correlated with Putting People at Ease. None of the TDI subscales were related to any of the *Benchmarks* ratings from either peers or direct reports.

Although research on the Big Five personality factors indicates that the five broad personality dimensions are more closely related to work and performance than are the more specific scales of other personality

TABLE 4 TDI Subscales and Others' Ratings of Leadership Skills ($r > .15$) (continued)

Tough-Tender	Questioning-Accommodating	Logical-Affective	Reasonable-Compassionate	Guarded-Optimistic	Decisive-Ambivalent
		.16		.22	
-.22	-.19	-.21		-.20	
		.16			
				.16	
.16		.19		.20	
		.16		.18	
				.20	
					-.20
.17		.18	.17		
.16		.20	.18	.17	

measures (Ones, Schmidt, & Viswesvaran, 1994), the studies reviewed here do show evidence of the added value of the TDI subscales in the study of leadership skills.

TYPE AND LEADERSHIP SKILLS

To the extent that MBTI dimensions interact with each other in their relationship to leadership skills, type may have explanatory value beyond the four preference dimensions in the study of leadership. Of the studies compared here, only two looked at the relationship between entire type (all four preferences) and rated leadership skills, and the approach taken in the two studies differed substantially.

Sundstrom et al. (1994) studied the interactions among the MBTI continuous scores to look for evidence that type has added explanatory value. They did, in fact, find many significant interactions in their analysis of MBTI and SYMLOG dimensions. For example, co-workers tended to see INTPs as expressing significantly more unfriendly values (e.g., self-oriented individualism, rejection of conformity, going it alone) than any other Introverted or Thinking type.

Van Velsor and Fleenor (1994) looked at the mean *Benchmarks* scores for each of the 16 skills and found that one type, INFJ, consistently had the highest *Benchmarks* ratings from direct reports. This type was rated more favorably on all but one scale. The second highest *Benchmarks* ratings from direct reports were most often received by ESFJ or ENFJ managers.

Wilson and Wilson (1994) looked at type in a more limited way, focusing only on self-rater discrepancy for two types that were particularly well represented in their sample, ESTJ and ISTJ. However, this comparison was particularly interesting in light of what we've seen in comparing results across all these instruments. That is, while there were few significant differences between the co-worker ratings for these two types (and those that there were favored ISTJs), ESTJs consistently tended to rate themselves more favorably than did ISTJs.

DISCUSSION

Comparing analyses of MBTI and leadership instruments seems to reveal at least three important points:

- Self-ratings and others' ratings of leadership are related to MBTI preferences in different ways.
- MBTI preference may be related to the likelihood of overrating or underrating self on domains of leadership capacity.
- MBTI preferences do not rule out effectiveness as a manager, but the strengths and development needs of managers may differ in ways that relate to preference.

It may seem obvious that the correlations between scores that are all self-ratings (MBTI and the other instrument) will be more numerous and higher than the correlations between one set of self-ratings (MBTI) and one set of ratings by others (the other instrument). After all, it makes sense that the way one sees one's preferences should be related to the way one sees one's skills.

Yet that is not all of what we see when we look across leadership instruments. The MBTI is related to both self-ratings and to ratings by others, but in different ways. People who have a preference for Extraversion on the MBTI (i.e., they like to spend their time and energy in the world of people, things, and activity) also tend to see themselves as skilled in many areas of managerial work and leadership behavior. The preferences that related to favorable leadership skills ratings from others tended to be Sensing, Intuition, Thinking, Feeling, and Judging, depending on the kinds of skills assessed by the instrument. Since managers tend to frequently be ESTJs or ISTJs, one might expect that ESTJs would see themselves more favorably than ISTJs. Co-workers, however, probably see them as equally skilled, especially in administrative or task management. Co-workers also tend to see and appreciate the interpersonal skills of managers with a preference for Feeling, regardless of whether these managers are Introverts or Extraverts.

Although it may seem a paradox that Extraverts, who are likely to be more comfortable and to spend more time interacting with others, seem less likely to see themselves as others see them, there are several possible explanations:

- Extraverts tend to have other personality characteristics that may lead them to see their skills as more well developed than others see them. Extraversion is related to other measures of personality, such as dominance, social presence, capacity for status, and self-acceptance on the *California Psychological Inventory* (see Chapter 4).
- Although Extraverts may enjoy their interactions with others more than Introverts, they tend not to be as comfortable spending long periods of time reflecting on their experiences and may therefore miss opportunities to integrate others' views into their self-assessment.
- Extraverts' higher self-ratings may also reflect the fact that Extraverts are more numerous in the U.S. population and that Extraverted approaches and styles are often considered more desirable (Myers & McCaulley, 1985).

It is clear from this comparison that MBTI preference is related to the kinds of leadership strengths and development needs of managers. Managers with a preference for Sensing, Thinking, and Judging are more likely to get relatively favorable ratings from others on instruments and scales that assess the administrative or task management side of their worlds. These areas tend to represent their strengths, and receiving feedback on this kind of instrument will probably be relatively easy for them. The skills measured by such instruments are skills they tend to believe are important, and the adjustments they will be asked to make may be small. The areas where these managers are likely to need improvement will be interpersonally oriented, especially for managers with a preference for Thinking.

Skills and practices such as recognition of employees' work, putting people at ease, and building relationships are likely to be seen as less important to Thinking managers and to be experienced as more difficult to master. Although Thinking managers predominate in organizations (usually about 80% of any sample), they are not likely to be the managers who deal the best with the people side of management. What's more, their potential to derail will be higher unless attention is focused on the development of heightened interpersonal skills.

Although one might expect that the developmental task of managers with a Feeling preference would tend to focus on the administrative or task management arena, this assumption is not supported by the results of the studies compared here. Feeling managers did show development needed in terms of exerting on subordinates an adequate amount of goal pressure, but no other inadequacies showed up relative to Thinking managers. Given the underrepresentation of Feeling managers in middle and upper levels of management, one might conclude that a group of potentially very effective managers is being seriously underutilized in organizations.

The most difficult and important developmental feedback a manager can receive relates to areas where development is really needed. Because leadership development needs often relate to the most underdeveloped part of one's personality, these areas for development tend to be ones that the manager does not enjoy or may actually devalue, making change particularly difficult. To some extent, then, managers with a preference for Perceiving are apt to gain more good information about areas for improvement from instruments that focus on skills related to Judging. Similarly, Thinking managers are likely to benefit most from feedback on surveys that focus on skills related to a preference for Feeling. Although the experience of receiving this feedback may not be pleasant, and the task of trying to improve will be difficult, the potential benefits of targeted development efforts will most likely be substantial.

NOTES

1. This chapter compares all the studies of leadership skills and the MBTI reported by Fitzgerald (1994a) that were based on sample sizes greater than 100 managers. For a detailed look at the interrelationships between the MBTI and leadership effectiveness as measured by a particular instrument, see Fitzgerald,
1994a.
2. Form J of the MBTI contains a total of 290 questions, which comprise all the
questions Isabel B. Myers tested in constructing the MBTI. Factor analysis of
responses to Form J found four general categories, corresponding to the preferences of the MBTI, with five to seven subcategories associated with each of the
preference dimensions (see Table 4, which lists the TDI subscales). Seven of the
27 TDI subscales refer to dichotomies that Myers and David Saunders, the
developer of the TDI method of scoring, believed were related to psychological
comfort, or how effectively a person was able to use his or her type. The TDI
lists these seven scales under a fifth dimension called Comfort–Discomfort. For
further information about the TDI, see Saunders, 1987.
3. *Management Skills Profile.* Copyright 1982, Personnel Decisions, Inc.
4. SYMLOG. Copyright 1983, R. F. Bales.
5. *Survey of Management Practices.* Copyright 1981, 1995, Clark Wilson Group, Inc.
6. *Benchmarks.* Copyright 1988, Center for Creative Leadership.
7. A third study (Quast & Hansen, 1994), not covered in this chapter because of
the relatively small sample size, also investigated the relationship of MBTI subscales to leadership skills. See Fitzgerald (1994a) for more detail on this
research.

REFERENCES

Bales, R. F. (1988). A new overview of the SYMLOG system: Measuring and chang-
ing behavior in groups. In R. B. Polley, A. P. Hare, & P. J. Stone (Eds.), *The
SYMLOG practitioner* (pp. 319–344). New York: Praeger.
Fleenor, J. W. (1995). *Type Differentiation Indicator and leadership skills as assessed by
Benchmarks.* Unpublished report, Center for Creative Leadership,
Greensboro, NC.
Fitzgerald, C. (Ed.). (1994a). *Proceedings from the Myers-Briggs Type Indicator and
Leadership: An International Research Conference.* College Park, MD: University
of Maryland University College National Leadership Institute.
Fitzgerald, C. (1994b). The relationship between the MBTI and ratings of manage-
ment skills, occupational stress, and managerial job satisfaction. In C.
Fitzgerald (Ed.), *Proceedings from the Myers-Briggs Type Indicator and Leadership:
An International Research Conference* (pp. 163–176). College Park, MD:
University of Maryland University College National Leadership Institute.
Johnson, D. A., & Golden, J. P. (1994). How psychological type influences effective lead-
ership: The Survey of Management Practices and the Type Differentiation
Indicator (TDI). In C. Fitzgerald (Ed.), *Proceedings from the Myers-Briggs Type
Indicator and Leadership: An International Research Conference* (pp. 89–98). College
Park, MD: University of Maryland University College National Leadership
Institute.
Myers, I. B., & McCaulley, M. H. (1985). *Manual: A guide to the development and use of
the Myers-Briggs Type Indicator.* Palo Alto, CA: Consulting Psychologists Press.

Ones, D. S., Schmidt, F. L., & Viswesvaran, C. (1994). *Do broader personality variables predict job performance with higher validity?* Paper presented at the Conference for the Society for Industrial and Organizational Psychology, Nashville.

Quast, L. N., & Hansen, T. L. (1994). The relationship between MBTI Expanded Analysis Report (EAR) scores and leaders' management behaviors. In C. Fitzgerald (Ed.), *Proceedings from the Myers-Briggs Type Indicator and Leadership: An International Research Conference* (pp. 151–162). College Park, MD: University of Maryland University College National Leadership Institute.

Saunders, D. (1987). *TDI manual.* Palo Alto, CA: Consulting Psychologists Press.

Sundstrom, E., Koenigs, R. J., & Huet-Cox, D. (1994). Personality and expressed values in management teams: MBTI and co-worker ratings on SYMLOG values. In C. Fitzgerald (Ed.), *Proceedings from the Myers-Briggs Type Indicator and Leadership: An International Research Conference* (pp. 131–142). College Park, MD: University of Maryland University College National Leadership Institute.

Tornow, W. W. (1993). Perceptions or reality: Is multiperspective measurement a means or an end? *Human Resource Management, 32,* 221–229.

Van Velsor, E., & Fleenor, J. W. (1994). Leadership skills and perspectives, gender and the MBTI. In C. Fitzgerald (Ed.), *Proceedings from the Myers-Briggs Type Indicator and leadership: An International Research Conference* (pp. 109–122). College Park, MD: University of Maryland University College National Leadership Institute.

Van Velsor, E., & Leslie, J. B. (1992). *Feedback to managers: A review and comparison of sixteen multirater feedback instruments.* Greensboro, NC: Center for Creative Leadership.

Wilson, J. L., & Wilson, C. L. (1994). Exploring MBTI type relationship to management skills. In C. Fitzgerald (Ed.), *Proceedings from the Myers-Briggs Type Indicator and Leadership: An International Research Conference* (pp. 81–88). College Park, MD: University of Maryland University College National Leadership Institute.

6 | Type, Leadership Feedback, and Willingness to Change

Paul E. Roush

W e all receive feedback from a wide variety of sources. Often the feedback is given with the intent of bringing about some form of change in our lives—for example, feedback from parents, teachers, or coaches. Similarly, feedback in the workplace, if done appropriately, has enormous potential for enhancing both the quality of work and the quality of life for workers.

There have been a number of attempts to study workplace feedback. Van Velsor, Ruderman, and Phillips (1991) found that when managers received low evaluations from followers, they improved their subsequent performance. Bass and Yammarino (1989) found that Navy enlisted followers gave higher ratings to those officers who were assessed highest by their seniors and who were subsequently more likely to be selected for promotion. There is a burgeoning industry in what has come to be known as 360-degree feedback, in which the raters include subordinates, peers, supervisors, and, sometimes, customers (London & Beatty, 1993; London, Wohlers, & Gallagher, 1990). Unfortunately, there have been relatively few studies of situations that provide systematic feedback and then observe, quantify, and analyze subsequent change.

One such ongoing system of feedback has been in operation at the U.S. Naval Academy for a number of years. In this approach, the student leaders assess their own leadership behaviors and are assessed in terms of those same leadership behaviors by student followers. This process is repeated at intervals, thus providing the leaders the opportunity to modify both their behaviors and their own self-assessments. The approach assesses the way leaders deal with their followers, as the leaders attempt to influence the incoming students in the direction of certain values, skills, knowledge, and abilities associated with competent functioning as officers in the naval service. Our approach has the research advantage of continuity, as we have administered the same feedback instrument for five years. The key to the process, of course, is not the feedback itself, but in the subsequent change that occurs as a result of the feedback.

ASSIMILATION INTO
THE NAVAL ACADEMY

The traditional system for assimilation at the U.S. Naval Academy requires midshipmen[1] to pass through a number of rather demanding gates. On initial entry, at the end of June or the beginning of July each year, the newly arriving midshipmen are designated as plebes, also known as fourth-classmen. They immediately embark on the transition from civilian to military society. This process begins during the summer, culminating in mid-August with the return of the rest of the brigade of midshipmen and the start of the academic year.

During the summer, the plebes are assigned to a military unit called a squad with approximately a dozen other plebes, all under the direct supervision of a squad leader—a carefully selected midshipman who has been at the academy for at least two years. Under the supervision of the squad leader, the plebes learn basic military skills such as marching, proper wearing of uniforms, knowledge of regulations, and receiving and carrying out orders. The total experience constitutes an orientation to the culture of the naval service.

When the academic year begins in late August, the plebes are assigned to one of 36 companies comprising approximately 120 people each. While a commissioned officer heads up each company, the plebes are under the more direct supervision of other midshipmen who themselves had begun the process one, two, or three years earlier. Although the responsibility is shared among all upperclass students (i.e., all nonplebes), it is the midshipmen beginning their third year (juniors in civilian institutions) who are primarily charged with the professional development of the new plebes. It is these midshipmen in their third year (known as second-classmen) who make the most extensive time investment in the further professional development of the plebes. These second-classmen have had the benefit of two years' experience at the Naval Academy and two summer cruises with the fleet, so they bring a fairly extensive background to the process. Since they have undergone the rigors of plebe year, they also have comprehensive knowledge of the various facets of that endeavor.

Positive and Potentially Negative Aspects of the System

There are many positive aspects to such an approach. The plebes have the benefit of the experience of persons who have successfully negotiated the same journey on which they are now embarked. They receive much well-considered advice. They encounter role models—persons who have demonstrated their ability to perform well under difficult circumstances—at every turn.

Unfortunately, the system has the potential for several unintended consequences as well. Upperclass students have enormous power relative to the plebe. In the exercise of that power, they sometimes behave inappropriately. Sometimes they "do unto plebes" what was done to them when they were plebes, even if such acts were inappropriate or impermissible. The situation is somewhat analogous to the abused child syndrome—the abuser is often a person who was abused as a child. Just as there is a natural tendency for inappropriate abusive behavior to be passed down through generations, so is there a danger of inappropriate leadership behavior being passed on to multiple generations of midshipmen in the absence of intervention to break the cycle.

Encouraging Positive Leadership

In an effort to counter the potentially negative elements while retaining the positive aspects of the system, a number of relatively unobtrusive initiatives were undertaken in recent years in the professional development of midshipmen. Among them were these three: (a) expanded use of the *Myers-Briggs Type Indicator* (MBTI) in the leadership curriculum, (b) the Leadership Feedback Program, and (c) an emphasis on a particular approach to counseling.

All midshipmen completed Form G of the MBTI within a week of arrival at the naval academy. During the period covered by this study, the results were interpreted for them early in the first semester of the academic year as a part of their first leadership course. They completed Form J of the MBTI a year later and received the MBTI *Expanded*

Analysis Report as part of their second leadership course. The objectives included understanding and appreciating individual differences, acquiring a modicum of skill at typewatching (Kroeger & Thuesen, 1988), and applying type theory to other activities such as counseling (Provost, 1987), team building, and conflict resolution. They also were given materials intended to help them study more effectively by linking approaches to study with their psychological preferences.[2]

During this process, we placed considerable emphasis on explaining in class the MBTI type of the Naval Academy as an institution.[3] Here the intent was to help midshipmen understand that they were in a system in which people perceived both rewards and levels of stress differentially, partially as a function of their psychological preferences. The objective was to explain why certain activities were viewed positively by some and negatively by others as a consequence of their preferences.

For those whose type matched that of the Academy, the passage was often less unpleasant than for those whose type was in contrast to the institutional preferences.[4] The important point was that differences between the Academy's preferences and an individual's preferences did not signify that anything was wrong with the person. Certainly, it would have been inexcusable for an instructor to infer that certain types were better than others or that a midshipman should attempt to change his or her type-related behaviors. To the contrary, if change is required, it is often the case that institutional change is more necessary than individual accommodation to institutional mores.

THE LEADERSHIP FEEDBACK PROGRAM

The Leadership Feedback Program arose out of the desire to shape behavior of midshipmen toward their subordinates in a more positive direction. Twenty-six statements (listed in Appendix A following this chapter), all reflecting positive leadership behaviors, became the criteria on which the leadership competency of the second-classmen was assessed by the plebes. A number of the statements followed a model developed by Bass (1985), in which the leader articulates a vision of the future, stimulates the follower intellectually, and attends to differences among followers. Bass labeled such behavior *transformational*, as distinguished from *transactional* leadership, the latter being an approach in which the leader provides a reward in exchange for specified follower behavior.

Studying Specific Leadership Behaviors

While all 26 leadership behaviors were important in that they addressed areas in which deficiencies had been noted, factor analysis has shown that several of the leadership behaviors could be subsumed by a more fundamental underlying factor (Atwater, Roush, & Fischthal, 1995). Factor loadings identified seven of the items on the leadership feedback instrument that loaded above .4 on one factor and did not load above .4 on any other factor. These seven items, taken together, were called *positive fleet leadership*. The remaining 19 items addressed specific areas of concern at the academy but did not cluster in the factor analysis to indicate the presence of other fundamental underlying factors. Midshipmen still seek to emulate those other behaviors, but the items describe 19 discrete, independent areas rather than one or more global factors.

Accordingly, the analysis in this study was limited to the seven items that clustered together to constitute positive fleet leadership. Those items are as follows:

- "No matter how upsetting the situation, this second-classman never loses self-control."
- "When I am a second-classman, I would like to lead in the same manner as this leader."
- "Even though the plebe indoctrination program is very demanding, this second-classman treats me with respect."
- "The leadership techniques used by this second-classman would be very appropriate if applied to enlisted sailors in the fleet."
- "Most of the time, this second-classman tries to motivate me by using positive leadership techniques."
- "As a general rule, this second-classman praises in public and reprimands in private."
- "This second-classman treats me in a consistent rather than an erratic manner."

Podsakoff and Organ (1986) point out a shortcoming that occurs in many feedback instruments, namely, asking raters to engage in higher-order cognitive processes such as weighting, inference, prediction, interpretation, and other abstract tasks, rather than reporting specific facts or events. The items in positive fleet leadership are weighted toward reporting of specific behaviors in order to minimize that problem.

The Feedback Process

All midshipmen had computers in their rooms, and all were linked together on the Naval Academy's time-sharing network. The plebes used their personal computers to respond anonymously to the 26 survey items about leadership behaviors of the second-classmen. The second-classmen, after rating themselves on the same 26 behaviors, called up on their computer screens the aggregated averages of the ratings supplied by the plebes in their respective squads. The process was repeated both semesters of the second-class year, thus providing the opportunity to assess behavioral change by the leaders as well as changes in the accuracy of their self-perception following the initial feedback. Mabe and West (1982) point out that self-assessment accuracy can be enhanced by clarity about expected performance, keeping self-assessments confidential, and the absence of personal gain resulting from favorable self-reports. All of the above conditions were met in the current study.

Using a Counseling Approach to Leadership

The genesis for the counseling approach was an earlier study done at the academy (Roush & Atwater, 1992), in which it was determined that the follower perception of leader behavior was enhanced in direct proportion to the extent to which that leadership was hands-on rather than laissez-faire or by exception. In other words, the greater the direct involvement by the leader in the individual life of the follower, the greater the likelihood that the follower saw the leader as effective and as one worthy of additional effort from the follower.

The counseling program, properly monitored, was one in which hands-on leadership was the norm. In the current study, the counseling occurred four times per semester and required fairly intensive involvement between the plebe and the second-classman. The process involved the joint setting of goals, agreement by both parties on indicators of goal accomplishment, and development of a strategy whereby the leader received from the follower or some other source the appropriate feedback. The feedback needed to provide information about progress toward the agreed-upon goals, and it had to be received in sufficient time to determine whether there might be a need to revise the goals, indicators, or feedback methods. The idea was that the follower would perceive that the second-classman who worked with him or her to set goals had a vested interest in the progress achieved, was making a substantial investment in the follower's life, and was, in fact, exercising positive leadership.

It was the confluence of these three factors in 1991—increased use of the MBTI, development of the Leadership Feedback Program, and the counseling requirement—that provided the underpinning for the current investigation into the relationship between feedback, willingness to change, and psychological type. The purpose of the investigation was to determine the extent to which psychological preferences, as indicated by the MBTI, and feedback from subordinates would be factors in the increasing acquisition of positive leadership behaviors.

STUDY OF THE FEEDBACK

The Leadership Feedback Program began in the fall semester of 1990. The plebes rated the second-classmen at the 8-week point of the semester and again at the 16-week point using a leadership feedback survey. Each plebe rated the four second-classmen who were in his or her 13-person squad, the basic organizational unit at the academy. The squad members lived in the same area within the dormitory, ate at the same table for all meals, and were together for formations and other military activities. Accordingly, the raters knew the ratees exceedingly well. Ratings were accomplished by indicating one's measure of agreement with a series of positive statements (e.g., "this second-classman always treats me with respect") that were linked to positive leadership practices. The rater indicated agreement (or lack of the same) by using a scale of 1 through 5, with 1 indicating strongly agree and five indicating strongly disagree. Hence, low scores are more positive.

The second-classmen rated themselves against the same criteria the first week of their second semester (January 1991) in terms of how well they believed they had performed against the criteria during the preceding semester. Following the entry of their self-assessments into the computer, they were able to see how they were rated by their followers. They retrieved on their computers a single number for each of the 26 questions. That number represented eight entries, that is, two entries each by four plebes. Thus, they were able to view their computer screens in the privacy of their own rooms and compare their self-assessments with the assessments their followers had made of them.

The second-classmen knew the process would be repeated later in the semester. In the interim, they could change their leadership behaviors if they were so inclined. Since no one other than the individual second-classman knew his or her aggregated ratings, there was no extrinsic pressure to make any changes. If changes were to occur, they would be intrinsically based changes. In other words, if the second-classmen were to change, it would be solely because they wanted to.

Three months after the initial ratings were made, the plebes assessed the second-classmen again, and the second-classmen then did another self-assessment, after which they were able to see the new aggregated feedback from the plebes. This assessment was identical to the earlier one, except that six additional items were added to the leadership feedback survey for the purpose of assessing specific counseling skills. There were no changes to the seven items that constituted the positive fleet leadership factor.

Study Selection

The brigade of midshipmen comprises six battalions of roughly 700 persons each. The population selected as ratees for the study was a subset of the entire student population. First, it comprised only those students who were second-classmen. Second, only the second-classmen from a single battalion were selected. A total of 163 midshipmen constituted this population. Of these, 15 were women and 24 were minority midshipmen. The study was conducted with the prior approval of the Commandant of Midshipmen for the specific purpose of ascertaining whether the counseling approach would have a discernible effect on the leadership behaviors of the second-classmen as inferred from the results of the Leadership Feedback Program.

Leadership instructors monitored the second-classmen in the study group as they carried out their counseling obligations. Plebes in the battalion were to be given a written agenda for each counseling session 24 hours in advance of its occurrence. They could request additions to the agenda and had time to prepare for a discussion of the items they were provided. Second-classmen in the study population submitted written reports of each of four formal counseling sessions as a major part of a course grade. Those reports included a copy of the counseling agenda, a narrative of the substance of the counseling interaction, strengths and weaknesses they noted in the counselee, goals agreed on by both parties, indicators of goal accomplishment, and methods of acquiring the necessary feedback. The instructors critiqued the goal setting, indicators of goal accomplishment, modification of goals, and all other parts of the counseling process. The result was to virtually assure a particular kind of interaction between second-classman and plebe: fairly intensive and relatively positive. It is reasonable to infer that the interaction represented a significant, responsible investment by the leader in the life of the follower.[5]

Yammarino and Bass (1990) have shown that intensive (hands-on) interaction yields the perception among followers that overall leadership is more effective. Followers indicated a willingness to make greater effort when given such leadership. Roush (1992) had also shown that there were significant differences in leadership ratings following feedback and as a function of the MBTI type of the second-classmen being rated, the MBTI type of the plebe doing the rating, and the interaction between the MBTI types of rater and ratee.

The Question for This Study

Accordingly, the issue in this study was not about differences in the ratings received by the leaders as a function of MBTI type. The question was this: *Do people have a differential propensity to change as a function of their MBTI types?* The focus, then, was on change over time rather than feedback scores received at any given time. The hypothesis for the current study was that there would be significant differences in the willingness of the second-classmen in the study population to change their leadership behavior following feedback as a function of their MBTI type.

Two-factor analysis of variance was calculated for each of the seven items that comprised positive fleet leadership. The MBTI type of the second-classmen was one factor. The other factor was time of assessment of the second-classmen by the plebes. The first time of assessment was at the 8-week point in the first semester; the second was at the 16-week point in the second semester; and the third was during the second semester at the 32-week point of the academic year. Results are shown in Table 1.

Each MBTI type was organized into its own data set and analyzed using analysis of variance. The independent variable was time of assessment and the dependent variable was the item number of the positive fleet leadership factor. In Table 2, the mean score for each item is shown by MBTI type for each of the three times the second-classmen were assessed by the plebes. One to three asterisks are used to indicate if the score attained by the second-classmen after receiving feedback[6] was statistically significant with respect to either of the prefeedback

TABLE 1 *F* Values and *P* Values for Each Factor in the Two-Factor Analysis of Variance by Positive Fleet Leadership Item Number

Survey Item	Factor	F Value	P Value
Item 1	MBTI type	3.658	.0001
Item 1	Time of assessment	7.683	.0005
Item 2	MBTI type	2.207	.0048
Item 2	Time of assessment	4.255	.0143
Item 3	MBTI type	1.586	.0703
Item 3	Time of assessment	7.685	.0005
Item 4	MBTI type	1.352	.1629
Item 4	Time of assessment	8.227	.0003
Item 5	MBTI type	2.066	.0093
Item 5	Time of assessment	6.177	.0021
Item 6	MBTI type	1.714	.0423
Item 6	Time of assessment	25.376	.0001
Item 7	MBTI type	0.881	.5856
Item 7	Time of assessment	2.300	.1005

Note. MBTI type of the second-classmen was significant at $p < .05$ for item 6, at $p < .01$ for items 2 and 5, and at $p < .001$ for item 1. It was not statistically significant for items 3, 4, and 7. Time of assessment was statistically significant for all but item 7. The interaction of MBTI type and time of assessment, while not shown in the table, was statistically significant for items 5 and 7, in each case at $p < .05$.

ratings.[7] In reading the data in the table, keep in mind that low scores are more positive.

When the mean initial ratings of second-classmen received by each of the MBTI types were compared with the mean ratings they received after feedback, the following findings were obtained from the data in Table 2:

- The second-classmen, in the aggregate, were rated higher after receiving feedback than they were prior to receiving feedback. The trend was evident on all seven items selected for the study. They had modified their leadership behavior in the direction called for by the criteria represented by the positive fleet leadership items on the leadership feedback survey.
- One MBTI type, the ISTJs, were rated less positively after feedback than they were before feedback on all seven items of the leadership feedback survey.
- The statistically significant changes on rating scores following feedback are summarized as follows by MBTI type for each item number.

Item 1: "No matter how upsetting the situation, this second-classman never loses self-control." INFPs, ESFPs, ENFPs, and ESTJs were more positive ($p < .05$); ISTJs were less positive ($p < .05$).

Item 2: "When I am a second-classman, I would like to lead in the same manner as this leader." ISFJs were more positive ($p < .05$); ISTJs were less positive ($p < .05$).

Item 3: "Even though the plebe indoctrination program is very demanding, this second-classman treats me with respect." ENFPs were more positive ($p < .01$); ISFJs and ESTJs were more positive ($p < .05$); ISTJs were less positive ($p < .05$).

Item 4: "The leadership techniques used by this second-classman would be very appropriate if applied to enlisted sailors in the fleet." ENFPs were more positive ($p < .001$); ESTJs were more positive ($p < .01$); INFPs and ESFPs were more positive ($p < .05$); ISTJs were less positive ($p < .05$).

Item 5: "Most of the time, this second-classman tries to motivate me by using positive leadership techniques." INFPs, ESTPs, ESFPs, ENFPs, and ESTJs were more positive ($p > .05$); ISTJs were less positive ($p < .01$).

Item 6: "As a general rule, this second-classman praises in public and reprimands in private." ENFPs were more positive ($p < .001$); ISTPs, ENTPs, and ESTJs were more positive ($p < .01$); ISFJs, INFPs, INTPs, ESTPs, and ESFPs were more positive ($p < .05$).

Item 7: "This second-classman treats me in a consistent rather than an erratic manner." ESFPs were more positive ($p < .01$); ISFJs, ISTPs, and ESTPs were more positive ($p < .05$); ISTJs were less positive ($p < .001$).

Categorizing the MBTI types in terms of the number of items from the positive fleet leadership factor for which a given MBTI type achieved positive change at statistically significant levels, the following results were attained:

- ESFPs, ENFPs, and ESTJs (five of seven items)
- ISFJs, INFPs, and ESTPs (four items)
- ISTPs (two items)
- INTPs and ENTPs (one item)

On the negative side, ISTJs represented change that moved away from all seven of the evaluative criteria, and at statistically significant levels on six of the seven.

TABLE 2 Mean Ratings Received by Second-Classmen for Each Item on the Positive Fleet Leadership Factor by MBTI Type and Time of Rating

	ISTJ	ISFJ	INFJ	INTJ	ISTP	ISFP	INFP	INTP
Item 1								
8 weeks	1.698	1.737	2.000	2.062	1.868	2.545	2.692	1.979
16 weeks	1.952	1.684	2.000	2.188	1.961	2.565	2.385	2.234
32 weeks	2.189*	1.294	2.000	2.071	1.653	2.263	1.840*	1.833
Item 2								
8 weeks	2.143	2.421	2.364	2.688	2.434	2.318	2.808	2.447
16 weeks	2.270	2.263	2.600	2.188	2.451	2.043	2.692	2.787
32 weeks	2.623*	1.588*	2.200	2.214	2.408	2.000	2.320	2.429
Item 3								
8 weeks	1.540	1.798	1.545	2.062	1.774	1.545	2.154	1.702
16 weeks	1.714	1.947	1.800	1.750	1.843	1.826	1.923	2.170
32 weeks	1.962*	1.176*	1.600	1.750	1.755	1.526	1.720	1.786
Item 4								
8 weeks	2.032	2.263	2.545	2.531	2.094	2.682	2.808	2.362
16 weeks	2.143	2.158	2.300	2.219	2.314	2.348	2.385	2.723
32 weeks	2.491*	1.588	2.300	2.107	1.918	2.158	2.000*	2.310
Item 5								
8 weeks	1.667	2.158	2.000	2.438	1.887	2.000	2.462	2.191
16 weeks	1.873	1.842	2.300	1.875	2.176	1.783	2.192	2.383
32 weeks	2.321**	1.471	1.800	2.000	1.776	1.579	1.640*	2.000
Item 6								
8 weeks	2.302	2.632	2.636	2.750	2.491	2.864	2.692	2.745
16 weeks	2.206	2.053	2.300	2.344	2.235	2.478	2.615	2.702
32 weeks	2.245	1.412*	1.900	2.429	1.898**	2.368	1.960*	2.190*
Item 7								
8 weeks	1.333	1.895	1.545	2.031	1.830	1.909	2.115	1.723
16 weeks	1.794	1.947	1.900	1.719	1.902	1.913	1.962	2.064
32 weeks	2.038***	1.176*	1.900	1.929	1.429*	2.105	1.600	1.929

	ESTP	ESFP	ENFP	ENTP	ESTJ	ESFJ	ENFJ	ENTJ
Item 1								
8 weeks	1.795	1.938	1.857	2.105	2.379	2.000	2.182	2.089
16 weeks	2.079	1.733	2.000	2.088	2.400	2.056	2.909	2.070
32 weeks	1.744	1.214*	1.596*	1.878	1.982*	1.933	2.214	1.690
Item 2								
8 weeks	2.436	2.250	2.224	1.912	2.500	2.444	2.636	2.333
16 weeks	2.684	2.333	2.188	2.158	2.477	2.833	2.909	2.419
32 weeks	2.256	1.857	1.809	2.224	2.263	2.333	2.500	2.310
Item 3								
8 weeks	1.744	1.500	1.776	1.667	2.136	1.889	1.818	1.822
16 weeks	2.053	1.800	1.771	1.684	2.062	1.944	2.727	1.674
32 weeks	1.590*	1.357	1.277**	1.612	1.667*	1.800	1.714	1.667
Item 4								
8 weeks	2.205	1.750	2.490	2.035	2.455	2.333	2.000	2.178
16 weeks	2.368	2.400	2.438	2.105	2.631	2.389	2.727	2.419
32 weeks	2.128	1.571*	1.638***	2.163	2.000**	1.867	2.286	2.238
Item 5								
8 weeks	2.051	2.000	2.000	1.807	2.379	2.000	1.818	2.089
16 weeks	2.289	1.933	1.875	1.667	2.169	2.222	2.818	2.023
32 weeks	1.667*	1.214*	1.553*	1.776	1.912*	2.200	2.286	2.048
Item 6								
8 weeks	2.538	2.250	3.000	2.649	2.970	2.500	2.727	2.644
16 weeks	2.421	2.467	2.667	2.351	2.708	2.500	2.727	2.256
32 weeks	2.000*	1.714*	1.702***	1.980**	2.140**	2.200	2.143	2.476
Item 7								
8 weeks	1.821	1.938	2.020	1.772	1.803	1.667	1.545	2.067
16 weeks	1.947	1.600	2.083	1.789	1.815	1.778	1.909	1.791
32 weeks	1.436*	1.071**	1.702	1.694	1.860	1.867	1.929	1.690

*indicates significance at the level of $p > .05$, **indicates significance at the level of $p > .01$, ***indicates significance at the level of $p > .001$

TABLE 3 Gain Scores of the Positive Fleet Leadership Factor After Feedback
by MBTI Preference and by Item Number

Preference	Item 1	Item 2	Item 3	Item 4	Item 5	Item 6	Item 7
Extraversion	.36	.18	.29	.32	.24	.57	.18
Introversion	.18	.09	.07	.17	.14	.37	.05
Sensing	.18	.11	.16	.23	.18	.44	.13
Intuition	.32	.16	.20	.26	.20	.51	.14
Thinking	.18	.03	.11	.12	.10	.37	.06
Feeling	.41	.36	.34	.51	.37	.70	.24
Judging	.13	.09	.16	.16	.03	.32	.06
Perceiving	.35	.17	.21	.31	.32	.60	.26

Table 3 shows the average change in mean rating score by MBTI preference and item number on the positive fleet leadership factor. The difference is obtained by comparing the rating score received by the
second-classmen after feedback with the average of the mean scores
they received before feedback, that is, the average of the mean scores
attained on the 8-week and 16-week assessments.

Clearly, when all seven items are taken into account, the greatest
change occurs for those midshipmen with the Feeling preference.
Midshipmen with a Perceiving preference are close behind, and those
with a preference for Extraversion have the third largest magnitude of
change. Only the Sensing–Intuition scale shows approximately equivalent amounts of change for its constituent preferences.

OBSERVATIONS FROM THE STUDY

Feeling and Perceiving, Thinking and Judging

One of the more intriguing facets of the study is the extent to which the
midshipmen with Feeling and Perceiving preferences are given high
leadership ratings by their followers. The Feeling preference appears in
only about 25% of the midshipmen, while the remaining 75% exhibit
the Thinking preference. In fact, the combination of both the Thinking
and Judging preferences occurs in more than half of all academy midshipmen since 1987, the year in which the MBTI was first administered
to entire entering classes. Yet the Thinking preference had the smallest
amount of positive change, and the Judging preference had the second
lowest gain scores in this study.

McCaulley (1990) reported an overrepresentation of Thinking Judging types (TJs) among leaders in a wide range of occupations across geographic and cultural boundaries. Campbell (1987) found that 72% of army brigadier generals who attended the Leadership Development Program offered by the Center for Creative Leadership had both Thinking and Judging preferences.

Since these officers represent the epitome of success in military society, it is interesting to speculate about why the TJ midshipmen were not rated more highly by their followers. The same dilemma arises in terms of a particular TJ type, namely, ISTJs. Campbell found that 28% of the generals in his sample were ISTJs. ESTJs constituted an additional 28% of the sample. No other type exceeded 9%, so evidently ISTJs, as a group, perform superbly as military officers. What, then, explains the phenomenon just discussed regarding the current study? Perhaps the issue can be explained by the nature of (a) the counseling task and (b) the items on the positive fleet leadership factor.

The Counseling Task

In considering this issue, let's look first at the counseling task. Counseling, in the sense it was practiced for this study, is no doubt facilitated by certain skills and hindered by the absence of certain others. Myers and McCaulley (1985) pointed out a number of type differences among providers of psychological services. Intuitive types, for example, are much more facile at identifying inferred meanings than Sensing types. Feeling types are more comfortable than Thinking types in interacting with people. Extraverts are more likely to prefer dealing with issues involving the outer world than are Introverts, who would prefer intrapsychic pursuits. Perceiving types are more likely to want to understand their clients than Judging types, who are more interested in directive and structured approaches.

Myers, Kirby, and Myers (1993) described a number of characteristics of the eight preferences of the MBTI. Those descriptions shed light on the problems faced by TJs in general, and ISTJs in particular, when called upon to do counseling activities. The Thinking preference seeks impersonal, objective truth, takes a tough-minded approach to situations, and relies on logic and cause-and-effect reasoning. The Judging preference wants closure, structure, and systematic and methodical approaches to life. While there is merit to such an approach in some counseling situations, counselees are frequently not searching for an impersonal, objective relationship aimed at early closure.

While it is true that counseling, as it was done in this study, hardly qualifies as provision of psychological services, it is reasonable, nonetheless, to presume that the counseling issues described above are applicable in varying degrees in the midshipmen's counseling interactions. The counseling task is generally more amenable to the Extraverted types, Intuitive, Feeling, and Perceiving in our midst. In the type of counseling done for this study, scores for the Intuitive preference were only mildly higher than those for the Sensing preference, probably due to the counseling tasks assigned the midshipmen; that is, identifying inferred meaning was a relatively minor part of the process.

Nature of Items Rated

With respect to the nature of the items on which the second-classmen were rated, several points should be made. The 26 leadership feedback items from which the positive fleet leadership factor was derived constituted a small subset in a very large spectrum. Those items certainly do not represent the totality of leadership. The items were developed to address a particular problem, namely, shortfalls in the leadership practices of upperclass midshipmen during their interactions with plebes. Congressional legislation in effect prohibits hazing at the naval academy and defines hazing as "any unwarranted assumption of authority by a midshipman whereby another midshipman suffers or is exposed to any cruelty, indignity, humiliation, hardship, or oppression, or the deprivation or abridgment of any right."[8] It is precisely these and similar behaviors that the Leadership Feedback Program was intended to curb. Had the focus been on attention to detail, ability to persevere in the face of obstacles, loyalty to the organization, willingness to keep commitments, fidelity in meeting deadlines, and willingness to be held accountable and to set and abide by standards, ISTJs would no doubt have been rated more positively.

There is considerable merit in Deming's (1991) statement that it is not possible to assess an individual. Every effort to do so necessarily includes within it an assessment of the system within which the individual functions. Generally, within the military system, ISTJs are assessed very favorably. Within a system focusing on a particular set of leadership behaviors that may be related to skill in a particular form of counseling, the assessment may be less positive.

Overall ISTJ Ratings

Finally, it is worth remembering that ISTJs were not given unfavorable ratings by their followers. They were, in fact, rated more positively than most of their peers in the prefeedback ratings, especially at the eight-week point. The problem occurred in the postfeedback ratings, where they were rated less positively than midshipmen with other MBTI types in almost all instances. While feedback seemed to help their peers improve, it was associated with more negative ratings for ISTJs. Instead of progressive improvement, ISTJs experienced a progressive decline in the ratings they received, the reverse trend from what was experienced by all other MBTI types.

Even on the postfeedback ratings, however, ISTJs were not rated negatively in absolute terms. They were simply rated less favorably than they had been previously on the positive fleet leadership items. On the scale of 1 to 5 that was employed on the Leadership Feedback Program, average ratings were better than 3, a neutral appraisal, for all MBTI types. The study, in other words, revealed varying degrees of positive assessment of the second-classmen by the plebes, including every MBTI type.

The Value of Feedback

A second observation pertains to feedback, which appears to be a change enhancer for the great majority of people, even when the new tasks are not necessarily aligned with their psychological preferences. When followers provide feedback to leaders about follower perceptions of leader behavior, leaders tend to change their behavior in the direction of the specified evaluative criteria.

If this apparent trend can be widely replicated, the knowledge is very powerful. Establishing consensus-based criteria could potentially have the power to move people, and eventually institutions, toward the behaviors specified in the criteria. The downside, of course, is that inappropriate criteria could move individuals and institutions in inappropriate directions.

Leaders With a Preference for Feeling

A third observation involves the positive feedback regarding leaders with the Feeling preference. Midshipmen who prefer Feeling over Thinking are in the distinct minority at the Naval Academy. That minority status has often caused those midshipmen to question whether they were suited for a career in the military. The data from the study have been useful in suggesting that there are leadership competencies that are enhanced by the exercise of the Feeling preference. Anecdotal evidence abounds that when midshipmen with a predisposition for the Feeling preference are made aware of the findings of this study, it results in a very dramatic sense of validation for them.

Use of the Ratings

A fourth observation has to do with the ways in which the ratings are used. Midshipmen do not fear the rating process. In fact, they look forward with great anticipation to seeing how their leadership behaviors are perceived by their followers. In my judgment, this state of affairs could not prevail if the chain of command had access to the ratings. If decisions were made about midshipmen on the basis of how their subordinates rated them, the process would be very counterproductive.

Ilgen, Fisher, and Taylor (1979) point out that feedback can create a perception of the feedback provider as exercising control over the feedback recipient. Since only the rated midshipman knows his or her rating scores, no threat is involved in the current study. There is no pressure to inflate ratings or to otherwise refrain from telling the truth, and the choice of whether or not to modify one's behavior based on feedback is a personal one.

Impact on Leadership Development

Finally, the study offers evidence that the system used has the potential for modifying the traditional approach to leadership development. The combination of counseling, feedback from subordinates, and awareness of and appreciation for individual differences has provided objective evidence of an increasingly positive approach to leadership. As a by-product of the process, the midshipmen are acquiring skills with long-term utility in their profession.

CONCLUSIONS

First, a program in which the subordinates assess the leadership skills of those in supervisory capacities seems to have considerable promise of wider application for organizations seeking more predictable behavioral changes among their supervisors. The evidence from this and other cited studies is that leadership behavior will change following feedback. More important, the change is not random but appears to occur in the direction of the criteria for the feedback program.

Second, such a program should be one in which the feedback data are not used against the person being rated. If the ratings were used as part of a promotion system or became part of the rated person's permanent record, the resultant system would have the potential to do great harm. The raters could experience considerable pressure from the ratees to award higher ratings than would be deserved. Entire organizational entities, perhaps competing with each other for aggregated ratings, could push for inflated assessments. The results could potentially destroy the integrity and utility of the system.

Third, a key to managing change may be the realization that change may be necessary for both the individual and the institution. For example, should the inappropriate behaviors that constitute hazing continue to occur, however infrequently, the problem must be attacked on both fronts. The study has described some approaches to modifying the behaviors of individual persons. It is also true, however, that the change process will be more effective and less transient if there are conscious efforts at changing the institution in ways that encourage and reward positive leadership in every aspect of academy life. This study describes an initiative from a single department. Using the approach described in the study can make a difference for particular people during a particular time, but it will not bring about enduring change unless the concepts are institutionalized more broadly.

Fourth, feedback scores varied with regard to differences in MBTI type. The nature of the tasks being assessed may have influenced the amount of change that occurred. The meaning of this phenomenon as it applies to organizations may be that when accomplishing a particular task requires a person to act "out of type," institutional intervention may be appropriate. For example, training programs may be developed that will take the type bias of the task into account and shape the training to accommodate individual differences.

The evidence in this study seems to clearly suggest that MBTI type differences play an important part in willingness to change. It is less certain that the types who changed most in this study would be equally willing to change in other circumstances. For example, analysis of the data shows that ENFPs, the type most opposite to ISTJs, made the greatest amount of positive change. The change at issue in this study required behaviors with which ISTJs are likely to be less comfortable and ENFPs are likely to be very comfortable. It remains an open question as to whether ENFPs would be more willing to exhibit positive change than ISTJs if the behavior at issue had called for working alone in highly concrete tasks requiring impersonal, cost-benefit analysis as the decision-making model in a highly structured arrangement that rewarded early closure.

Nevertheless, it would probably be making an unwarranted assumption to infer that the study simply confirms that people are more likely to change when asked to move in the direction of tasks for which they are already ideally suited by their psychological preferences. Other MBTI types that shared three of the four preferences of ISTJs were not rated less positively with the passage of time and the provision of feedback. In the same way, other types sharing three of the preferences of ENFPs did not experience the same level of movement in a positive direction as did the ENFPs. Evidently, there is a particular combination of responses only activated by the predisposition for all four of the preferences that constitute each of these MBTI types.

Fifth, the power of counseling as a vehicle for creating intensive interaction between leader and follower appears to be confirmed. This is especially likely to be true if the manner of counseling includes joint goal setting, agreement concerning indicators that will be accepted as evidence of movement toward the goals, and overt efforts to arrange for feedback. Under these circumstances, the follower is likely to interpret the process as one in which the leader is making a significant investment in the life of the follower.

FOLLOW-UP: IMPACT ON
ACADEMY LEADERSHIP DEVELOPMENT

The combination of the use of the MBTI in leadership instruction, the Leadership Feedback Program, and monitored counseling was continued annually through the spring semester of 1995. When those data are analyzed, there will be the opportunity to learn the extent to which the results of the current study will be replicated. Because the program was so successful, it has been expanded to include all midshipmen. In other words, the sample size increased sixfold. It should, therefore, be possible to expand future analyses to include such factors as gender and minority status.

It is even possible that the dilemmas such as those posed by the ISTJs and ENFPs will be seen as a matter of differential resistance to systemic change. With the passage of time, the experimental nature of the counseling approach may have come to be viewed as traditional, and ISTJs may be more amenable to changing when the process has been institutionalized. If so, the results of subsequent iterations of the approach described in this study may well yield substantially different results.

NOTES

1. *Midshipmen* is the academy's term for its students. The title is a military rank, not an indicator of gender; hence, it refers equally to men and women. Second-classmen is also a term used in the academy to refer to both men and women in their third year.

2. Lawrence (1982) is an excellent reference for type differences in learning.

3. The academy's "type" is ESTJ.

4. Bridges (1992) has a splendid discussion of organizational "type."

5. Six items that addressed the issue of counseling competencies were added to the Leadership Feedback Program in the spring semester of 1991. Since they were not part of the program at the beginning of the study, the results are not included in this study's analysis. For the reader's information, they are listed in Appendix B following this chapter.

6. That is, the score received in midspring at approximately the 32-week point of the academic year.

7. The prefeedback ratings occur at the 8-week and 16-week points in the fall semester. The initial feedback is seen by the upperclassmen at the start of the spring semester, roughly 22 weeks from the start of the academic year.

8. Title 10 U.S. Code § 6964.

REFERENCES

Atwater, L., Roush, P., & Fischthal, A. (1995). The influence of upward feedback on self- and follower ratings of leadership. *Personnel Psychology, 48,* 35–59.

Bass, B. M. (1985). *Leadership and performance beyond expectations.* New York: Free Press.

Bass, B. M., & Yammarino, F. J. (1989). *Transformational leaders know themselves better* (Tech. Rep. No. ONR-TR-5). Arlington, VA: Office of Naval Research.

Bridges, W. (1992). *The character of organizations: Using Jungian type in organizational development.* Palo Alto, CA: Davies-Black.

Campbell, D. (1987). *The psychological test profiles of brigadier generals: Warmongers or decisive warriors?* Paper presented at the annual meeting of the American Psychological Association, New York.

Deming, Edwards W. (1991, December). *A day with Dr. Deming.* Remarks given to Navy, Marine Corps, and Coast Guard flag officers and senior executive service members, Washington, DC.

Ilgen, D., Fisher, C., & Taylor, M. (1979). Consequences of individual feedback on behavior in organizations. *Journal of Applied Psychology, 64*(4), 349–371.

Kroeger, O., & Thuesen, J. M. (1988). *Type talk.* New York: Delacorte Press.

Lawrence, G. (1982). *People types and tiger stripes: A practical guide to learning styles* (2d ed.). Gainesville, FL: Center for Applications of Psychological Type.

London, M., & Beatty, R. (1993). 360-degree feedback as a competitive advantage. *Human Resource Management, 32,* 353–372.

London, M., Wohlers, A., & Gallagher, P. (1990). A feedback approach to management development. *The Journal of Management Development, 9*(6), 17–31.

Mabe, P., & West, S. (1982). Validity of self-evaluation of ability: A review and meta-analysis, *Journal of Applied Psychology, 67*(3), 280–296.

McCaulley, M. (1990). The *Myers-Briggs Type Indicator* and leadership. In K. Clark & M. Clark (Eds.), *Measures of leadership.* West Orange, NJ: Leadership Library of America.

Myers, I. B., & McCaulley, M. H. (1985). *Manual: A guide to the development and use of the Myers-Briggs Type Indicator.* Palo Alto, CA: Consulting Psychologists Press.

Myers, I. B., with Kirby, L. K., & Myers, K. (Eds.). (1993). *Introduction to type* (5th ed.). Palo Alto, CA: Consulting Psychologists Press.

Podsakoff, P., & Organ, D. (1986). Self-reports in organizational research: Problems and prospects. *Journal of Management, 12*(4), 531–544.

Provost, J. (1987). Psychological counseling. In J. Provost & S. Anchors (Eds.), *Applications of the Myers-Briggs Type Indicator in higher education.* Palo Alto, CA: Davies-Black.

Roush, P. E. (1992). The *Myers-Briggs Type Indicator,* subordinate feedback, and perceptions of leadership effectiveness. In K. Clark, M. Clark, & D. Campbell (Eds.), *Impact of leadership.* Greensboro, NC: Center for Creative Leadership.

Roush, P. E., & Atwater, L. (1992). Using the MBTI to understand transformational leadership and self-perception accuracy. Military Psychology, *4*(1), 17–33.

Van Velsor, E., Ruderman, M., & Phillips, D. (1991). *Enhancing self-objectivity and performance on the job: The developmental impact of feedback.* Unpublished manuscript.

Yammarino, F., & Bass, B. (1990). Long-term forecasting of transformational leadership and its effects among naval officers: Some preliminary findings. In K. Clark & M. Clark (Eds.), *Measures of leadership.* West Orange, NJ: Leadership Library of America.

APPENDIX A

Leadership Feedback Statements

1. This second-classman knows how I am doing academically.
2. This second-classman shows me ways to do better academically.
3. It seems to me that this second-classman is concerned about my personal welfare.
4. No matter how upsetting the situation, this second-classman never loses self-control.
5. This second-classman treats me as an individual rather than a number.
6. This second-classman is willing to listen to me when I am having a problem.
7. This second-classman seems to enjoy the respect and camaraderie of his or her peers and seniors.
8. The uniform appearance of this second-classman is as good as or better than that of the fourth-classman.
9. The room standards of this second-classman are as good as or better than those of the fourth-classman.
10. When I am an upperclassman, I would like to lead in the same manner as this second-classman.

11. The compliance with regulations by this second-classman serves as a good model for me to follow.
12. This second-classman gives me feedback about both the good and bad aspects of my performance.
13. This second-classman advises me on how I can improve my performance in weak areas.
14. This second-classman requires me to back up my opinions with good reasoning.
15. This second-classman helps me by providing new ways of thinking about problems.
16. Even though the plebe indoctrination system is very demanding, this second-classman treats me with respect.
17. The leadership techniques used by this second-classman would be very appropriate if applied to enlisted sailors in the fleet.
18. Most of the time this second-classman tries to motivate me by using positive leadership techniques.
19. As a general rule, this second-classman praises in public and reprimands in private.
20. This second-classman holds me accountable for the highest personal, uniform, and room standards.
21. This second-classman consistently takes advantage of opportunities to acknowledge my successes.
22. The statements of this second-classman about orders issued by higher authority reflect loyalty to that authority.
23. This second-classman treats me in a consistent rather than an erratic manner.
24. This second-classman clearly communicates what is expected of me.
25. This second-classman follows up on assignments he or she has directed me to accomplish.
26. I feel motivated to make an extra effort in the tasks assigned to me by this second-classman.

APPENDIX B

Feedback Items Addressing Counseling Competencies

1. In our counseling sessions, this second-classman and I worked together to develop goals.
2. In our counseling sessions, this second-classman reviewed with me my progress toward goal accomplishment.
3. In our counseling sessions, this second-classman helped me to see ways to accomplish goals.
4. The counseling sessions with this second-classman seemed relaxed and conducive to open discussion.
5. This second-classman made obvious efforts to ensure that I was an active participant in the counseling process.
6. The counseling techniques this second-classman demonstrated are ones I will emulate with my subordinates when I am a second-classman.

7 | The MBTI and Decision-Making Styles

Identifying and Managing Cognitive Trails in Strategic Decision Making

Usha C. V. Haley

Global innovation and change place enormous information-processing demands on managers; opportunities abound for confusion and conflict. Frequently, managers are required to make strategic decisions with less information and time than they had just a few years ago. Research on strategic decision making often provides little guidance to managers on how to improve decisions. Generally, researchers understand well-structured, deliberative, isolated decisions better than loose-structured, opinion-based, interactive ones. Yet, executives' decisions often occur in chaotic environments, seem to rely on confidently held beliefs, and usually require face-to-face interactions (Simon, 1987). Individual managers' decision-making styles can also influence greatly and differentiate strategic decisions (Haley, 1995; Hambrick & Mason, 1984). This chapter shows how managers can use research findings associated with the *Myers-Briggs Type Indicator* (MBTI) to identify systematic cognitive errors and to improve strategic decisions.

Humans are born with well-formed brains whose 100 billion neurons are linked through genetic programming into functional paths. As an infant develops, experiences activate, reinforce, or obliterate specific neural paths. For example, frequently used responses invoke structural alterations in neurons (Restak, 1984). Brains appear as evolving highway systems: Experiences add new roads, broaden popular roads, and abandon less traveled roads. Therefore, variations in experiences, captured by variations in brain structures, may lie beneath many individual differences. Road maps of brains form documented phenomena (Aoki & Siekevitz, 1988). In this chapter, we will deal with an undocumented aspect of these maps—the trails, or cognitions, that people use (Haley & Stumpf, 1989). Different personality types develop different decision-making styles: They display discrete preferences for modes of gathering data, generating alternatives, and evaluating alternatives. Managers' personality types may indicate the cognitive trails that they most frequently traverse. Personality types' cognitive trails may involve *heuristics* that affect strategic decision making. Heuristics constitute rules of thumb, or cognitive tools, to organize information. As the heuristics that managers use seem to vary systematically, cognitive trails provide metaphors to understand why and how managerial decisions vary.

The first section of this chapter discusses current theory and research that relate personality types to decision making. The next two sections review heuristics and cognitive trails that form parts of decision making; they also link personality types with decision heuristics in a strategic-decision-making framework. The ensuing section explores cognitive trails' implications for managerial decision making, corporate strategies, and environmental influences. The final section indicates the cognitive trails that managers may traverse in an international business situation and identifies how managers can improve strategic decisions.

PERSONALITY TYPES' DECISION-MAKING PREFERENCES

Managerial decisions reflect unconscious cognitions. Managerial preferences determine the experiences and information that managers will store and apply to strategic decisions. These managerial preferences reveal themselves in characteristic decision styles: The preferences prompt managers to search selectively for information, emphasizing and recognizing some kinds of information and ignoring others (Weick, 1979). In this fashion, the searches enable managers to identify and to verify important information when making complex strategic decisions; however, the searches also reveal managers' unique preferences and may vary widely across managers. This section explores different managerial preferences for data and for reaching decisions as revealed by the MBTI and research on decision making.

Jungian personality types' preferences provide information on the heuristics that managers most often use; thus, they shed light on links between cognitions and strategic decisions (Haley, 1995; Haley & Stumpf, 1989). Jung (1923) argued that the two ways in which people obtain data (Sensing and Intuition) and the two ways in which they evaluate data (Thinking and Feeling) define personality types. Myers (1980) clarified the influence of combinations of these Jungian mental functions, identifying four: Sensing Thinking (STs), Intuition Thinking (NTs), Sensing Feeling (SFs), and Intuition Feeling (NFs). Jung viewed these personality types as dominant, not absolute, modes of expression. Many people exhibit all types of behaviors in their perceiving and judging activities; but most people have preferred styles—styles that they use more often, particularly in ill-structured situations (Simon, 1987). STs and NFs may anchor the two ends of an information-processing continuum (Taggart & Robey, 1981): STs appear predominantly left-brained, depending on analytical techniques; NFs seem predominantly right-brained, emphasizing intuition and judgment; NTs and SFs may form intermediate types. Researchers' observations about each personality type's decision-making preferences follow.

Sensing Thinking Types (STs)

STs stress systematic decision making with hard data (Nutt, 1986a). They want to establish order, control, and certainty (Mitroff & Mitroff, 1980). They place importance on tasks and structured information. They also take fewer risks than other types do (Behling, Gifford, & Tolliver, 1980). STs appear to focus on immediate problems, to prefer quick returns, and to use standard operating procedures to solve problems (Hellriegel & Slocum, 1975). They delve into details and specifics and use logical, step-by-step processes to reason from causes to effects. Doubts or opposition may not deter STs, who may not reanalyze their positions in such circumstances. They may seem to concentrate on the problems of today, sometimes of yesterday.

Intuitive Thinking Types (NTs)

NTs erect nonlinear problems by studying patterns in data (Nutt, 1986a, 1986b). They prefer general information rather than specific, detailed information. Like STs, NTs stress analysis, but their constructions undertake bolder leaps into the unknown: NTs emphasize longer-range plans and new possibilities. They enjoy tackling complex problems and reducing them to simpler ones. However, they often seem more interested in planning than in implementation. Their styles can be impersonal and idealistic, and they may ignore naysayers. They stress needs for innovation, risk taking, and discovery (Mitroff & Mitroff, 1980).

Sensing Feeling Types (SFs)

SFs stress people's opinions in decision making. They concentrate on affective and evaluative parts of communication: Facts about people interest them more than facts about things (Hellriegel & Slocum, 1975). Like STs, they appear to focus on problems facing them today; but SFs' problems have human implications: SFs deal with how to make people get along in more harmonious manners. They attempt to reconcile individual differences by improving interpersonal communication (Slocum, 1978). For SFs, actions seem to become feasible when people endorse them (Nutt, 1986a).

Intuitive Feeling Types (NFs)

NFs stress their judgment and experience, which may result in their portraying their personal views as facts (Nutt, 1986a, 1986b). They rely on gestalt and intuitive perceptions, and maintain few decision-making rules (Mitroff & Mitroff, 1980). They construct open, nonlinear problems. Their interests in new, institutional forms and fresh, human possibilities structure their problems. They concentrate more on broad themes rather than specifics. Longer-term goals engage their attention. NFs like working on ill-defined problems that require innovative concepts and theories. Sometimes NFs test their hunches; at other times they may just state their preferences (Henderson & Nutt, 1980).

The studies referred to above suggest that Jungian personality types display discrete cognitive and behavioral preferences. The next section explores some heuristics that managers may use when making strategic decisions.

THEORIES OF DECISION HEURISTICS IN STRATEGIC PROCESSES

Since Simon (1947) noted that decision makers rarely use complete information or exhibit total rationality, researchers have recognized that cognitive limitations affect decisions. Managers' perceptions fill information gaps to help them to interpret their environments and to steer their organizations (Starbuck, 1976). Mintzberg's (1978) research indicated that managers' a priori perceptions cause them to favor certain strategies—yet these intended strategies rarely approximate the strategies that their organizations finally pursue. Early laboratory studies identified several decisional *biases,* or systematic errors, that increase the gaps between perceptions and actualities. Recent research suggests that these biases permeate strategic decisions as well (Barnes, 1984; Schwenk, 1984, 1986).

Many important reviews of decision processes already exist (Hogarth, 1980; Hogarth & Makridakis, 1981; Markus & Zajonc, 1985; Slovic, Fischhoff, & Lichtenstein, 1977). These reviews highlight numerous heuristics, or rules of thumb, that individuals use to make decisions. Managers use heuristics constantly in strategic and mundane decisions. Assume a situation where a manager has to decide on a new corporate hire. For example, Dr. Smith has to decide if her company should hire Mr. Romano as a middle-level manager. She has a variety of information on Mr. Romano. His academic credentials look good and he seems to have the relevant work experience. However, she also discovers that his colleagues at his old corporation speak disparagingly of him and do not seem to like him. She places more emphasis on the tangible or hard information and ignores his colleagues' opinions. She decides to hire Mr. Romano on his credentials and work experience. Dr. Smith has used a decision heuristic to select, and to limit, the information on Mr. Romano to which she pays attention.

Heuristics affect the strategic alternatives that managers generate, select, and evaluate. Managers often make strategic decisions in novel, complex, and uncertain situations (Mintzberg, Raisinghani, & Theoret, 1976). Consequently, some researchers have pointed out that heuristics may actually improve decisions (Tversky & Kahneman, 1982): Managers use heuristics to filter and to organize information, thereby clarifying situations and simplifying decisions. But sometimes heuristics may lead to biases or systematic errors.

Researchers often use the terms *bias* and *heuristic* interchangeably; but important differences distinguish these concepts. For managers, biases may occur when their capacities to comprehend completely are affected by cognitive inclinations. Biases generally result in inferior or wrong decisions. Decision heuristics form organizing tools that *may, or may not,* result in inferior or wrong decisions. If inferior or wrong decisions do result, they stem from inaccurate premises about the data, or from the processes by which managers make inferences. In other words, decision heuristics just form tools—but their use may lead to biases that subsequently affect premises and inference processes; consequently, ambiguities distort distinctions between decision heuristics and biases. This chapter categorizes some errors caused by managers' uses of decision heuristics into *three sequential biases* that may occur in strategic decision making (Haley & Stumpf, 1989):

- *Input biases*—or errors that occur when managers collect data
- *Output biases*—or errors that occur when managers generate alternatives
- *Operational biases*—or errors that occur when managers evaluate alternatives

Simon (1987) contended that managers' intuitive (Note: Simon's use of "intuitive" does *not* refer to Jungian Intuition; instead, he means "natural" or "instinctive") responses often indicate recognizable chunks of organized information; as these responses become habitual, they come to represent characteristic decision styles. Similarly, Haley and Stumpf (1989) showed that managers habitually use specific heuristics to guide searches and to make evaluations; eventually these heuristics become associated with managers' preferences. Sequentially connected decision heuristics form cognitive trails that managers frequently travel. Managers' personality types reveal the decision heuristics and biases that they habitually use (Haley & Stumpf, 1989).

The heuristics may display themselves in snap judgments. For example, although idiosyncratic differences prevail, some evidence indicates that managers revert to instinctive behaviors when under stress: Stress decreases control over behavioral responses (Brief, Schuler, & Van Sell, 1981). Many top-level, strategic decisions occur in stressful situations (Kotter, 1982). Therefore, heuristics may explain significant portions of the variations in strategic decisions.

Traces abound of systematic cognitive processes in decision making. Managers perceive data differently: Paine and Anderson (1977) observed that managers see varying amounts of uncertainty in similar environments. Managers' perceptions of problems affect the strategic alternatives that managers and organizations consider. For example, Khandwalla (1976) learned that when managers perceive their corporate environments as complex, managerial strategies become more complex. Managers' strategic actions also limit subsequent strategic choices. For example, Bower (1970) noted that the choices already made by managers significantly influence the choices they will make. Other researchers have noted links between information gathering, alternative

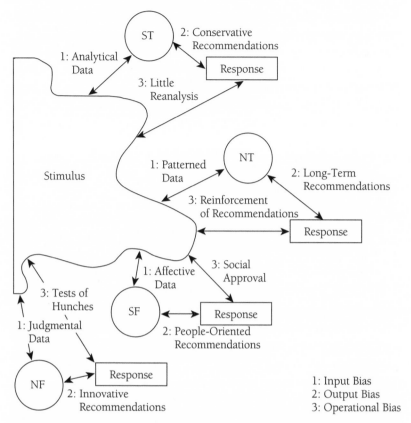

From "Cognitive Trails in Strategic Decison Making" by U. C. V. Haley and S. A. Stumpf, 1989, *Journal of Management Studies, 26,* p. 482. Copyright 1989 by Blackwell Publishers Ltd. Reprinted with permission.

Figure 1 Personality Types' Cognitive Trails

generation, and evaluation (Dutton, Fahey, & Narayanan, 1983; Lyles & Mitroff, 1980; Mintzberg et al., 1976). Consequently, Dutton et al. (1983) suggested that managers' beliefs about causes and effects shape how they identify strategic issues and assign corporate resources.

Drawing on researchers' observations, Haley and Stumpf (1989) argued that the personality types demonstrate distinct preferences for collecting data, generating alternatives, and evaluating alternatives. Therefore, personality types provide opportunities to observe habitual, cognitive trails in decision processes. These cognitive trails result in systematic input, output, and operational biases. Figure 1 outlines the personality types' cognitive trails.

Input biases occur when decision makers rely on data selectively and give some kinds of data more weight than others (Markus & Zajonc, 1985). As data biases that occur because of the availability, accessibility, or saliency of some information, these input biases cause decision makers to use inappropriate methods in dealing with information. Our research (Haley, 1995; Haley & Pini, 1994; Haley & Stumpf, 1989) showed that managers of different personality types demonstrate distinctly different preferences for data. These preferences may result in well-known decision heuristics that result in input biases in managerial decision making. Haley and Stumpf (1989) identified the following *four input biases* in strategic decision making:

- *Anchoring*—or adjusting data around some initial values
- *Perseverance*—or adhering to prior beliefs about data despite disconfirming evidence
- *Availability*—or using data that come easily to mind
- *Vividness*—or using memorable, vivid data

Output biases reflect preferences for certain types of responses; these preferences can affect adversely the quality of the alternatives that managers generate. Decision makers laboring under output biases fail to evaluate data appropriately: They supply guesses in the absence of data, or pad insufficient data. Our research (Haley, 1995; Haley & Pini, 1994; Haley & Stumpf, 1989) showed that managers of different personality types may systematically generate alternatives based on inaccurate evaluations of data. These preferences may result in erroneous responses that constitute output biases in managerial decision making. Haley and Stumpf (1989) identified the following *four output biases* in strategic decision making:

- *Functional fixedness*—or relying excessively on selected methods to generate alternatives
- *Positivity*—or generating unduly positive, confirming alternatives
- *Social desirability*—or generating alternatives that one thinks people want
- *Reasoning by analogy*—or generating relatively simplistic alternatives through analogies and metaphors

Operational biases deal with how managers evaluate the effectiveness of the generated alternatives. Operational biases stem from inferences made by decision makers (Markus & Zajonc, 1985). These erroneous uses of data occur when managers draw conclusions either from inap-

propriate samples or in the absence of data that such conclusions normally require. To gauge operational biases, one measures what decision
makers intend to achieve against what they actually achieve. In corporations, this requires measuring individual managers' goals against corporate goals. Research has offered inconclusive evidence on links
between decision makers' intentions and organizational outcomes: The
repetitive nature of managerial decisions confounds the influence of any
individual on organizational decisions (Blaylock & Rees, 1984).
Generally, researchers attribute only around 10% of the variance to
decision makers' cognitive styles (Huber, 1983). Indeed, circumstances
often explain more variance in outcomes than personalities do (Vroom
& Yetton, 1973; Zmud, 1979). Different decision environments, one-
time experiments, and instruments that measure cognitive or political
ability rather than style (Huber, 1983) may distort the influences of personality on decision making. However, though the effects on organizational decisions may be weak, we have discovered that personality types
may evaluate alternatives in different fashions. These preferences may
result in erroneous inferences that constitute operational biases in managerial decision making. Haley and Stumpf (1989) identified the following *four operational biases* in strategic decision making:

- *Imputation of regularity and structure*—or unduly favoring the status
  quo and quantifiable alternatives
- *Representativeness*—or unduly favoring alternatives that can be categorized easily
- *Fundamental-attribution error*—or unduly favoring alternatives
  regarding persons rather than situations
- *Illusory correlation*—or unduly favoring alternatives based on coincidental associations

Haley and Stumpf (1989) first identified cognitive trails through a
large-scale, behavioral simulation. The simulation revolved around a
hypothetical, large, commercial bank with several hierarchical managerial roles. After selecting managerial roles, participants received information on the financial-service industry, the bank, their roles, and policy issues. Then participants managed the bank as they saw fit. Specific
roles had critical information to diagnose and to resolve different issues.
To yield unobtrusive information on the biases, Haley and Stumpf
(1989) used structured observations in the simulation. With operational measures of the biases, trained observers noted the information-
gathering methods that participants used and tracked participants' dis-

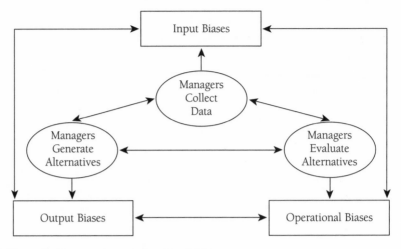

Figure 2 Biases in Strategic Decision Making

cussions of key issues. The observers did not know of participants' MBTI preferences. The simulation provided opportunities for over a hundred recommendations (Haley & Stumpf, 1989) that did not necessarily reveal biases. Recommendations covered aspects of capitalizing on strengths, resolving problems, exploiting opportunities, reducing threats, and simultaneously exploiting opportunities and increasing threats. Yet, through statistical tests, Haley and Stumpf (1989) demonstrated that the different personality types significantly fell prey to a pattern of linked biases or cognitive trails. These findings, and other related research, form the basis for identifying and exploring the implications of personality types' cognitive trails.

Through our research, we concluded (Haley, 1995; Haley & Pini, 1994; Haley & Stumpf, 1989) that heuristics etch cognitive trails through the processes of strategic decision making. When managers use certain heuristics to gather information, they subsequently rely on other heuristics hinged to those to generate and to evaluate alternatives. These cognitive trails may result in systematic biases that increase gaps between where corporations are and where they want to be. Haley and Stumpf (1989) showed that managers' input biases have subsequent output biases, which may lead to operational biases. Figure 2 displays how these biases may seep through strategic decisions.

The next section translates personality types' cognitive trails into sequential heuristics and biases. It deals only briefly with organizational actions, implementation techniques, or effectiveness. Instead, it concentrates on the cognitive processes by which managers may make judgments and thus highlights a portion of the instinctive influences that shape strategic decisions.

DECISIONAL BIASES
IN COGNITIVE TRAILS

Studies on heuristics have delivered many insights into how people make decisions. However, most of these studies have occurred in controlled laboratories, and most have little applicability to the chaotic situations that managers encounter. Studies of personality types fall prey to different problems. Personality types provide excellent thumbnail sketches of actors and situations, but these studies fail to incorporate recent theoretical advances in cognitive research. As such, personality studies have benefited little from research on decision making, and vice versa.

By identifying different personality types' preferences, researchers may track heuristics' effects on managerial performances. As the previous sections outlined, in our research, STs, NTs, SFs, and NFs exhibited distinct information-screening and behavioral preferences. This section links personality types' preferences to cognitive heuristics. Specifically, this section shows how managers use certain heuristics to gather data and to identify problems. These heuristics influence managers' choices of strategic alternatives. Managerial choices, in turn, may affect evaluations of possible effects. In this manner, uses of some heuristics result in subsequent uses of other, connected heuristics and may result in biases.

A Hypothetical Strategic-Decision Situation

Imagine that managers from the four personality types are considering a strategic alliance between their company and another; each personality type would probably emphasize different types of information when gathering data on the other company, generate different strategic alternatives for their company, and evaluate these alternatives differently. We will use a hypothetical strategic-decision situation to illustrate input, output, and operational biases for the four personality types. Our hypothetical case is one in which the top managers at Fiat, the largest Italian automobile manufacturer in the early 1990s, have highlighted Chrysler, one of the top three U.S. automobile manufacturers, as a takeover target, a merger possibility, or a strategic alliance.

International strategic relationships have large potential benefits for automobile manufacturers. Strategic relationships can help to defray the immense price tags, often running into billions of dollars, that manufacturers pay to develop new models. Through strategic relationships, manufacturers can gain valuable access to new markets or to new technologies and manufacturing techniques. The right relationships allow smaller companies to realize big economies of scale when ordering components. Alternatively, international relationships encounter huge costs. Cross-cultural factors like managerial style and workers' expectations can create problems and compound uncertainties and risks. Consequently, most international strategic relationships fail.

In the early 1990s, the time frame for our strategic decision, the U.S. government had rescued Chrysler from bankruptcy and some optimism had surfaced regarding Chrysler's future. Chrysler introduced a range of excellent new models all aimed at higher-end markets. Chrysler also cut costs to become among the most cost-efficient manufacturers in the global automobile industry, especially in new-product development. Despite some problems with quality control, Chrysler had introduced Japanese-style innovations in work methods and management techniques to reduce product-development time and to cut costs. Against Chrysler's efforts lay the backdrop of an increasingly militant labor force in Detroit's automobile industry, and some of the highest real interest rates in history, casting doubts on continuing high auto sales in the U.S.

Historically, both Fiat and Chrysler have failed at international strategic relationships in the automobile industry. Fiat and Chrysler have also failed in each others' home markets of the United States and Europe. How might Fiat's managers from the four personality types make the strategic decision on a relationship with Chrysler? With 20/20 hindsight, we can gauge the potentials and pitfalls of their cognitive trails.

Sensing Thinking Type Managers

Anchoring Input Biases: When Decision Makers
Erroneously Adjust Data Around Some Initial Values

Our research (Haley & Stumpf, 1989) disclosed that ST managers' preferences for data predispose them to *anchoring* biases. Tversky and Kahneman (1982, p. 14) noted that when decision makers use anchoring heuristics, they "make estimates by starting from an initial value that is adjusted to yield the final answer. . . . [Final] estimates . . . are biased towards the initial values." Some indicators suggest that ST managers may bias decisions by failing to alter their judgmental criteria sufficiently in light of new information: Nutt (1979) noticed that STs perform best when they use models to represent decision problems; these models specify the relevant data and provide formats for logical analysis. When decision makers use anchoring heuristics, they prefer more of the same type of data and avoid different types of data that require more interpretation (Wright, 1980). Researchers have recorded STs' preferences for quantitative, aggregate data and distaste for qualitative data (Blaylock & Rees, 1984; Henderson & Nutt, 1980). Nutt (1986a) contended that STs oversimplify and quantify decisions to give order and meaning to data: Qualitative information adds uncertainty; it disrupts the order, structure, and concreteness of the previously preferred situation. Thus, ST managers may stumble on anchoring biases by failing to incorporate new data that do not conform to initial specifications.

In our hypothetical strategic-decision situation, an ST manager at Fiat may analyze Chrysler's financial statements to gather data on Chrysler. The data that the ST manager may consider may include working capital, retained assets, earnings, market value of equity divided by book value of debt, dividend rates paid to shareholders, and sales—all quantitative data. However, financial statements just capture one aspect of Chrysler's strengths and weaknesses. Qualitative data, such as top management's vision, may help to interpret the quantitative data or to put it in perspective. Even when later given relevant, qualitative data, the ST manager at Fiat may concentrate on the financial data as most important for a decision on a strategic relationship. The ST manager may thereby greatly oversimplify the strategic decision: Studies show that top management's vision, or corporate history, can explain whether a company can extricate itself from declining profits or how it can survive a strategic relationship. The ST manager may succumb to an anchoring bias when gathering data.

Functional-Fixedness Output Biases:
When Decision Makers Rely Excessively
on Selected Methods to Generate Alternatives

Our research (Haley & Stumpf, 1989) showed that for STs, anchoring may also lead to *functional-fixedness* output biases (Higgins & Chaires, 1980). Functional-fixedness biases can reflect excessive reliance on certain problem-solving methods. ST managers often use standard operating procedures to solve problems; these procedures provide continuity and structure by helping STs to reject unusual alternatives (Nutt, 1986a). However, standard procedures may sometimes prove inappropriate, and functional-fixedness biases may arise. ST managers may reject novel or innovative solutions when their procedures fail to support them. Schwenk (1984) noticed that decision makers who used anchoring when formulating goals also erroneously inferred that some alternatives were unfeasible. Similarly, Steinbruner (1974) posited that decision makers may deal with alternatives they do not prefer by inferring that they may prove unworkable. Thus, functional-fixedness biases may result in prematurely rejecting more feasible alternatives and choosing less effective ones. Behling, Gifford, and Tolliver (1980), in a study on betting behaviors, found that Sensing types bet much more conservatively than Intuitive types. Simulation studies on capital-expansion projects also demonstrated that STs form the most action-averse and risk-averse personality type, rejecting the most proposals (Henderson & Nutt, 1980; Nutt, 1986b). Nutt (1986b) attributed STs' conservative attitudes to quantitative data that often fail to provide the analytic precision that STs desire. Thus, STs seem trapped by their initial preferences for data (Nutt, 1979).

In our hypothetical strategic-decision situation, the ST manager at Fiat might use a standard operating procedure, such as Altman's formula, to generate strategic alternatives regarding Chrysler. (Edward Altman developed a Z score to measure a corporation's financial health: Z incorporates quantitative data such as working capital/total assets, retained earnings/total assets, earnings before interest and taxes/total assets, market value of equity/ book value of total debt, and sales/total assets.) Using Altman's formula, financially strong corporations have Z scores over 2.99; corporations in serious financial trouble have Z scores below 1.81; corporations between 1.81 and 2.99 form question marks that can go either way. Suppose that in the early 1990s, Chrysler has a Z score of 1.9, indicating that it has uncertain chances of financial success. The ST manager may decide to reject any strategic relationship with Chrysler: Chrysler's Z score shows that it may go bankrupt and increase Fiat's financial burden. A strategic relationship with Chrysler, though financially risky, may constitute the more-acceptable strategic alternative for Fiat—regardless of Chrysler's Z score. A merger could provide Fiat with Chrysler's technologies and markets. However, a strategic relationship with Chrysler incurs the high risks, uncertainties, and mortality that international business affords; it may not generate immediate profits. Consequently, the ST manager would probably reject the alternative. The ST manager could precisely identify cutoff points for strategic alternatives: low Z scores for Chrysler indicated unnecessary financial risks for Fiat. In this fashion, the ST manager may succumb to a functional-fixedness bias when generating alternatives.

Imputation-of-Regularity-and-Structure
Output Biases: When Decision Makers
Unduly Favor the Status Quo and
Quantifiable Alternatives

Our research (Haley and Stumpf, 1989) revealed that as ST managers evaluate alternatives, functional-fixedness biases may also predispose them to impose *erroneous regularity and structure* on random events (Galanter & Smith, 1958). Nutt (1979) noted that STs see decisions as closed, definable systems; they become uncomfortable when alternatives resist quantification or acquire open, incalculable characteristics. This tendency reinforces STs' preferences for established, well-known practices and the status quo. Nutt (1986b) found that ST managers become more decisive in well-defined and regulated environments. To the extent that STs avoid reanalysis, their logic structures do not evolve (Nutt, 1986a). By structuring problems, managers may underassess how ambiguous situations really are: Slocum (1978) found that ST change agents concentrate on tasks; when policies fail, STs recommend using behavior-modification techniques with people rather than changing the characteristics of the tasks.

   In our hypothetical strategic-decision situation, the ST manager at Fiat may prefer the status quo, established practices, and their already proposed strategic alternatives—regardless of new evidence—when evaluating strategic alternatives regarding Chrysler. Brisk sales of its new models have enhanced Chrysler's attractiveness in a strategic relationship. Yet, when evaluating the alternative, the ST manager may reject this new data as an aberration and continue to search for other investment opportunities for Fiat. If Chrysler's Z score increases, the ST manager may even recommend changing the people who gathered the new data on Chrysler, rather than change the decided alternative. In this fashion, the ST manager may impose erroneous regularity and structure when evaluating alternatives.

Intuitive Thinking Type Managers

Perseverance Input Biases: When Decision Makers
Erroneously Adhere to Prior Beliefs About Data
Despite Disconfirming Evidence

Our research (Haley & Stumpf, 1989) disclosed that NT managers' preferences for data predispose them to *perseverance* biases. Researchers suggest that individuals bias cognitions by assuming causal linkages between initial and subsequent information. When the initial information is proven wrong, cognitions about causal links endure and affect individuals' perceptions (Carroll, 1978). Individuals fall prey to perseverance biases in data gathering when they adhere to their prior beliefs and ignore subsequent disconfirming evidence (Ross, Lepper, & Hubbard, 1975). NT managers tend to see patterns in structured data (Nutt, 1986a; Slocum, 1978), ignoring cases that negate their beliefs: They often deny the counsel of people with pertinent facts—especially when these facts contradict NTs' notions (Nutt, 1986a). They may also resort to quick, superficial studies that fail to indicate ideas' limits (Nutt, 1986a). Thus, NT managers may persevere in their beliefs in spite of contradictory evidence.

In our hypothetical strategic-decision situation, an NT manager at Fiat may look for patterns of performance when gathering data on Chrysler. The NT manager may notice that Chrysler has a record of rebounding from crises. Despite contradictory evidence, such as the permanent restructuring of the U.S. economy, the NT manager may view Chrysler's past performance as evidence that Chrysler will survive. In this fashion, the NT manager may succumb to a perseverance bias when gathering data.

Positivity Output Biases: When Decision Makers Generate Unduly Positive, Confirming Alternatives

Our research (Haley & Stumpf, 1989) showed that NT managers' preferences for holistic information, and their nonlinear problem constructions also encourage *positivity* biases. Positivity biases form parts of selective recall; positive, confirming information weighs more heavily than negative, disconfirming information with respect to given alternatives (Matlin & Stang, 1978). Positivity biases generally operate when little specific data exist; when generating alternatives, decision makers affected by positivity biases may assign positive, confirming information more importance. NT managers favor longer-term, open-ended projects; they move from abstract needs and opportunities to specific solutions (Nutt, 1986a). They tend to test their ideas on hypothetical possibilities (Nutt, 1986a, 1986b). In the process, they may deny the importance of gaps between objectives and performances, and cling to their strategies. For example, Nutt (1986a) argued that NTs tend to ignore or to discount arguments based on principles different from their own. They fail to notice policies' weaknesses because they often disregard ideas and data that contradict their policies. Nutt (1986b) also found that NTs selected analytical techniques that seem to account for important contingencies; thus, NT managers try to make their risky actions look defensible and their failures seem superficial. These processes may cause NTs to weigh confirming arguments more heavily than disconfirming ones.

In our hypothetical strategic-decision situation, the NT manager at Fiat may favor a longer-term relationship when generating strategic alternatives regarding Chrysler. The NT manager may see Chrysler's ability to rebound from crises as a great investment opportunity. Unlike the ST, the NT may propose a strategic alliance between Fiat and Chrysler despite the high risks and uncertainty. NTs often display less conservatism than STs, and a strategic alliance with Chrysler has potential; the alliance could open markets for Fiat and could provide Fiat with new technologies. The NT manager may test this strategic alternative on hypothetical possibilities and favorable evidence, such as Chrysler's higher new car sales. The NT manager may recall that Chrysler has a history of cooperating with suppliers; this pattern would make easier a potential strategic alliance with Fiat. Clinging to the strategy of a long-term relationship, the NT manager may unintentionally omit from consideration the gaps between Fiat's cost-cutting objectives and Chrysler's actual cost-cutting relations with suppliers. Additionally, the NT manager may unconsciously disregard discomfiting events, such as rising U.S. interest rates, that could hurt future sales of all Chrysler's expensive new models. The NT manager may also inadvertently ignore operational synergies between Fiat and Chrysler. To generate the strategic alternatives, the NT may select an analytical technique, such as time-series analysis, that incorporates Chrysler's performance swings. Long-term views of performance may also justify the strategic alliance's risks and reduce its failure's importance. In this fashion, the NT manager may succumb to a positivity bias when generating alternatives.

Representativeness Operational Biases:
When Decision Makers Unduly Favor
Alternatives That Can Be Categorized Easily

Our research (Haley & Stumpf, 1989) revealed that as NT managers evaluate alternatives, their previous input and output biases may also lead to *representativeness* biases. Representativeness highlights similarities between specific instances and the categories to which they belong; it involves finding patterns in the structured data that NTs use (Tversky & Kahneman, 1982). As NTs operate with little specific data, they may depend on analytical techniques, like sensitivity analysis, to identify similarities between categories (Nutt, 1986a). However, NTs may limit themselves by thinking of information as belonging to single categories; thus, they may ignore the nuances caused by data belonging to multiple categories, thereby causing biases. For example, Henderson and Nutt (1980) found NTs in firms more likely to adopt feasible capital-expansion projects than NTs in hospitals: Henderson and Nutt (1980) concluded that firms generate more sequential, organized data, and therefore more certainty, enabling NTs to categorize the data and to take action; simultaneous, sometimes chaotic events, as in hospitals, provide uncertainty, hindering NTs from categorizing the data and taking actions.

In our hypothetical strategic-decision situation, the NT manager may look for patterns in structured data when evaluating strategic alternatives regarding Chrysler. The NT manager may see Chrysler's range of new models as evidence of its viability and of its proving a strong strategic ally for Fiat. Generally, viable, growing organizations do innovate and introduce new products. However, manufacturers in the U.S. automobile industry have often violated this conventional wisdom. Many U.S. automobile manufacturers have created some of their best models before collapsing. For example, Willys Jeep, Kaiser Steel, and American Motors (developers of the Jeep); Studebaker (developer of the Avanti); and Nash (developer of the Metropolitan) all withered after developing their highly acclaimed models. However, the NT may limit options by thinking of Chrysler as belonging to one category, that of a potential strategic ally; consequently, the NT may ignore the nuances of Chrysler's belonging to multiple categories, including the U.S. automobile industry, which has a distinct pattern of its own. In this fashion, the NT manager may succumb to a representativeness bias when evaluating alternatives.

Sensing Feeling Type Managers

Availability Input Biases: When Decision Makers
Erroneously Use Data That Come Easily to Mind

Our research (Haley & Stumpf, 1989) disclosed that SF managers' preferences for data predispose them to *availability* biases. Managers use availability heuristics when they estimate how often problems may occur, or how workable solutions may prove, by the ease with which they can bring these problems and solutions to mind (Tversky & Kahneman, 1973). Availability heuristics use some cues and problem-solving routines as substitutes for other characteristics (Tversky & Kahneman, 1973); however, these substitutes may prove inappropriate. Slocum (1978) found that SF change agents place more importance on people-oriented information. Similarly, Nutt (1986a) noticed that SFs often suggest consultative, group-process solutions; he argued that such solutions provide means to process and to reconcile facts that gave rise to feelings. Nutt (1986a) highlighted the inherent weakness of this style: SF managers often seem more interested in promoting discussions about premises than in exploring any of the premises in detail. Thus, SFs may exhibit availability biases by concentrating on people at the expense of ideas.

In our hypothetical strategic-decision situation, an SF manager at Fiat may look for people-oriented information when gathering data on Chrysler. The SF manager may remember that cross-cultural strategic relationships, such as a possible one between Fiat and Chrysler, often fail: Strategic alliances have failed for Chrysler and Maserati as well as for Fiat and Nissan; both these alliances produced as much bitterness as reward. The SF may look for cultural indicators, like the top manager's flexibility, that may affect this strategic relationship's fate. Consequently, the SF manager may ignore financial and operational factors that may have a greater influence on the relationship's survival. In this fashion, the SF manager may succumb to an availability bias when gathering data.

Social-Desirability Output Biases: When Decision Makers
Generate Alternatives That They Think People Want

Our research (Haley & Stumpf, 1989) showed that these traits may also lead SF managers to *social-desirability* biases. As noted above, SF managers place importance on interpersonal relations and social approval. Social-desirability biases have less cognitive and more motivational origins. Managers enact social-desirability biases when they do what they think other people want them to do, rather than what they actually feel (Warner, 1965). Nutt (1986a) proposed that SF managers' acute needs for acceptance by others prompt them to promote others' ideas instead of their own. Decision makers succumb to social-desirability biases when they believe that solutions become more effective as more people support the solutions. In a study of capital-expansion projects,

Henderson and Nutt (1980) found that SF managers are most likely to act when they expect support from their groups. Another study of capacity-expansion projects found that SFs' actions require members' consensus and endorsements: SFs co-opt members to make strategic acts look risk free (Nutt, 1986b). Nutt (1986a) contended that SF managers, in their zeal to achieve consensus and acceptance, often restate viewpoints to shape arguments used by others.

In our hypothetical strategic-decision situation, the SF manager at Fiat may place importance on interpersonal relations and social approval when generating strategic alternatives regarding Chrysler. For example, in a consultative group situation, if the NT manager expresses conviction about a strategic alliance with Chrysler, the SF may concur with the alternative. Privately, the SF manager may reject a strategic alliance with Chrysler based on people-oriented data regarding similar alliances. However, through the group situation, the SF manager may feel that more managers favor a strategic alliance with Chrysler; consequently, this alternative appears as more effective for the SF. In this fashion, the SF manager may succumb to a social-desirability bias when generating alternatives.

Fundamental-Attribution Error Operational Biases:
When Decision Makers Unduly Favor Alternatives
Regarding Persons Rather Than Situations

As SF managers evaluate alternatives, our research (Haley & Stumpf, 1989) disclosed their previous input and output biases may lead to *fundamental-attribution errors*. SF managers collect detailed facts; yet facts about people absorb them more than facts about things. Fundamental-attribution errors arise when decision makers erroneously see persons, rather than situations or circumstances, as more influential in determining outcomes (Nisbett & Ross, 1980). Fundamental-attribution errors stem from availability biases to which SFs may succumb: "[people are seen] as dynamic and interesting, while situations more commonly are static and pallid. . . . The [person] and his action are 'figural' against the 'ground' of the situation" (Nisbett & Ross, 1980, pp. 122–123). Nutt (1986a) suggested that SFs see facts as the tangible views of people; consequently, they may often jump to conclusions on faulty premises.

In our hypothetical strategic-decision situation, the SF manager may assign greater importance to persons than to situations when evaluating strategic alternatives regarding Chrysler. For example, labor unrest in Detroit may intensify after Fiat announces interest in a strategic alliance with Chrysler; the SF manager may conclude that the strategic alternative violates cultural synergies and proves inadequate. However, labor unrest may occur because of the U.S. recession, and ignorance about the two companies' specific plans for maintaining production facilities in the United States. The SF manager may reject a strategic alliance with Chrysler based on faulty inferences about people. In this fashion, the SF manager may succumb to a fundamental-attribution error when evaluating alternatives.

Intuitive Feeling Type Managers

Vividness Input Biases: When Decision Makers Erroneously Use Memorable, Vivid Data

Our research (Haley & Stumpf, 1989) disclosed that NF managers' preferences for data predispose them to *vividness* biases. Vividness forms a type of availability heuristic that causes individuals to favor memorable data over other data. NFs often rely on relevant anecdotes, catchy symbols, and vivid imagery to make points (Mitroff & Kilmann, 1975; Nutt, 1986a). They use their personal evaluations of situations to reduce uncertainty (Nutt, 1986a). Experiments reveal that individuals may ignore statistical evidence in favor of highly vivid instances (Borgida & Nisbett, 1977). Product advertisements rely on vivid memories. As vivid and conspicuous features are easier to recall, individuals may attribute greater causal significance to them than to less flagrant features. Using vivid data, NFs may overestimate their ability to work through plans or to implement them. For example, NF managers would be more likely to remember successful than unsuccessful plans, thus exhibiting vividness biases.

In our hypothetical strategic-decision situation, an NF manager at Fiat may look for successful, memorable instances when gathering data on Chrysler. In 1979, the U.S. government rescued Chrysler from bankruptcy. Chrysler made a tremendous financial recovery with a range of excellent cars. The NF manager at Fiat may recall the government's rescue of Chrysler more than the creditors that refused to support Chrysler. The NF manager may also remember vivid imagery about Chrysler more than operational details. For example, in the early 1990s, the NF manager likely recalls Chrysler's flashy new models more than the reason why Chrysler had to introduce them hurriedly: Through poor management, Chrysler had become entirely dependent on one product, the minivan, which faced fierce competition. In this fashion, the NF manager may succumb to a vividness bias when gathering data.

Reasoning-by-Analogy Output Biases:
When Decision Makers Generate Relatively
Simplistic Alternatives Through Analogies
and Metaphors

Our research (Haley & Stumpf, 1989) showed that vividness heuristics may lead NFs to see *analogies* in dissimilar situations—analogies that they feel they can exploit. NFs enjoy creative problem solving. They reject traditional methods and standard operating procedures in favor of novel, ingenious solutions. Nutt (1979) indicated that NFs often excel at poorly structured decisions: NFs try several dissimilar approaches to problems to see where each approach leads; several false starts, followed by periods of thought and reflection, often lead to insights and novel, effective alternatives (Nutt, 1979). NFs also like reducing complex problems to simpler ones. Steinbruner (1974) identified simplifying processes that help in formulating problems; he called these processes *reasoning by analogies.* When using this heuristic, NF managers apply analogies from simple, vivid situations to more complex ones. Images and metaphors dominate this process. For example, McKenney and Keen (1974) showed how NF operators of paper mills controlled papermaking processes by "tasting the broth." Reasoning by analogies helps reduce environmental uncertainty, and even yields creative solutions to problems (Gordon, 1961; Huff, 1980). However, NF managers may mistakenly think of their problems as more simple, or more familiar, than they really are. Relying on this heuristic, NF managers may instill rigidity into their decision making by using sets of unquestioned assumptions (Mason & Mitroff, 1981). Reasoning by analogies may contribute to managerial mystiques and even help NF managers to stay in power. However, such tactics may provide scant help or continuity to organizations.

In our hypothetical strategic-decision situation, the NF manager at Fiat may place importance on analogies and metaphors when generating inventive strategic alternatives regarding Chrysler. The NF manager may propose an alternative that encourages the U.S. government to support the strategic alliance's push into new markets; or the NF may propose a friendly takeover of Chrysler. In these alternatives, the NF may see Fiat as bearbaiting U.S. governmental assistance or may see Fiat as the white knight saving a damsel in distress. However, the NF's alternatives may rest on faulty assumptions: When national sentiments oppose governmental intervention, as they did in the early 1990s, the U.S. government probably would not help Chrysler—or Chrysler may not wish to be rescued. In this fashion, the NF manager may succumb to a reasoning-by-analogy bias when generating alternatives.

Illusory-Correlation Operational Biases:
When Decision Makers Unduly Favor
Alternatives Based on Coincidental Associations

As NF managers evaluate alternatives, our research (Haley & Stumpf, 1989) revealed that their previous input and output biases can lead to confusion between correlations and causations among variables. This bias, known as *illusory correlation*, causes individuals to form erroneous links around important events (Chapman & Chapman, 1969). NF managers construct fluid problems that deal with new possibilities. Additionally, NFs may not subject their ideas to rigorous testing (Nutt, 1986a, 1986b). Prior expectations of relationships between variables may culminate in illusory correlations between variables. Or, more restrictively, NF decision makers, drawing on vivid data and analogies, may perceive coincidental associations between variables as causal connections (McArthur & Friedman, 1980). Uncertain situations may hinder NFs from forming these causal connections. Thus, although NFs generally appear adventurous and risk-taking (Behling et al., 1980), as projects become more uncertain, NFs appear more action-averse than any other type (Henderson & Nutt, 1980).

In our hypothetical strategic-decision situation, uncertainty surrounding alternatives may greatly affect the NF manager when evaluating strategic alternatives regarding Chrysler. For example, if the recession intensifies and the Government seems unlikely to help Chrysler, the NF manager may abandon the alternative of a strategic alliance with Chrysler. Yet, the NF may display misplaced risk-aversion under uncertainty: In an effort to keep jobs, governmental assistance to Chrysler may intensify as the recession deepens. In this fashion, the NF manager may succumb to an illusory-correlation bias when evaluating alternatives.

TABLE 1 Personality Types' Cognitive Biases

Input Bias	⇔	Output Bias	↔	Operational Bias
STs: Anchoring	⇔	Functional Fixedness	↔	Imputation of Regularity and Structure
NTs: Perseverence	⇔	Positivity	↔	Representativeness
SFs: Availability	⇔	Social Desirability		Fundamental-Attribution Error
NFs: Vividness	⇔	Reasoning by Analogy	↔	Illusory Correlation

From "Cognitive Trails in Strategic Decison Making" by U. C. V. Haley and S. A. Stumpf, 1989, *Journal of Management Studies, 26,* p. 489. Copyright 1989 by Blackwell Publishers Ltd. Reprinted with permission.
⇔ = strong links, ↔ = weak links

Table 1 summarizes these results on decision heuristics and personality types. The next section examines some implications of the cognitive trails that managers use.

IMPLICATIONS OF COGNITIVE TRAILS

This chapter has attempted to show that decision heuristics and their related biases may nest within Jungian personality types; the information on these cognitive trails could help both managers and researchers. Ideally, decision tasks should dictate the decision-making styles managers use. Managers should be able to switch to ST, NT, SF, and NF styles as situations require. Good managers should at least be able to apply and to understand conclusions drawn from different decision models and processes, or to understand when their specific skills should come into play and when they may prove counterproductive. However, these ideal, decision-making approaches may not be possible. Only about 17% of U.S. managers see things in personal and interpersonal dimensions; 83% tend to see things in technical and structural dimensions (Campbell & Van Velsor, 1985). Cognitive trails in strategic decision making have implications for managerial decision making, corporate strategies, and environmental influences.

Managerial Decision Making

Evidence indicates that managers use decision models consistent with their decision styles: Executives of the four personality types make different choices even when given identical information (Nutt, 1979; 1986b). Such demonstrations of personality-type preferences inevitably lead to poor strategic decisions, as each decision model has specific strengths and weaknesses. Thus, STs and SFs may subject open-system tasks to rigorous analyses, even when the analyses cannot capture critical criteria. Similarly, NFs and NTs may tinker with clear-cut tasks instead of subjecting them to straightforward analyses. Mapping the cognitive trails that managers travel may insure against some erroneous decisions that managers may make in strategic situations.

Research on expert problem-solving techniques demonstrates that managers often arrive rapidly at problem diagnoses and solutions in strategic situations without being able to report their procedures (Simon, 1987); studies show that managerial choice sequences may form recognizable patterns stored in long-term memory. If personality types do consistently use certain cognitive trails, some insight into managers' problem-solving techniques may be garnered. For example, personality types' heuristics may help in building strategic expert systems. Slocum (1978) concluded that different personality types' decision styles lead to heterogeneous strategies, with varying degrees of effectiveness. Tools for improving managerial judgment can then specify the knowledge and recognition capabilities that managers in a given domain need to acquire as bases for crafting appropriate strategies. Researchers may also be able to design expert systems capable of automating this expertise, or alternatively, of providing managers with expert consultants. Thus, strategic expert systems could indicate the choices different personality types may ordinarily make, the information that managers may leave out of their calculations, and the environmental conditions under which managers' predominant styles may lead to good strategies. Such information could benefit managers by sensitizing them to sequential biases in decision making and identifying appropriate and erroneous tactics. For example, strategic expert systems can identify when analyses, decision groups, and politics should or should not be applied.

Corporate Strategies

Corporations have interests in closing gaps between intended and realized strategies. By identifying the cognitive trails that managers use, corporations can ascertain what information managers may systematically miss in formulating and implementing strategies.

The different personality types probably accentuate contrasting corporate goals. For example, STs may pursue goals of profitability; NTs may seek advantages over competing organizations; SFs may want to respond to constituencies' wants and needs; and NFs may pursue service to the community. These managerial goals require different resources and support systems. Consequently, corporations may want to identify managers' cognitive trails to control long-term resource allocations in pursuit of goals.

Managers' cognitive trails also indicate how managers may gather data and generate and evaluate strategic alternatives: Consequently, when some personality types dominate corporate boardrooms, the managers' decision-making styles probably mold corporate abilities to scan, understand, and shape environments. Managers with different personality types probably collect different information (Haley, 1995). For example, STs may emphasize financial market information; NTs may link demand projections and economic trends; SFs may see their projects' people-oriented features; and NFs may see prospects to increase corporate influence.

Managers with different personality types probably generate different alternatives (Haley, 1995). For example, STs may generate alternatives from planning models using data; NTs may use various kinds of planning models, pose what-if questions, and generate the most-likely alternatives; SFs may use results from planning models to initiate discussion with trusted colleagues who make estimates; and NFs may use the results from planning models to stimulate discussions among trusted colleagues who state their beliefs. When discussing alternatives, STs may use projections by experts who review the data; NTs may seek opinions from managers with comparable experience; SFs may use predictions from trusted colleagues, familiar with the projects, who can review the estimates; and NFs may also use estimates from trusted colleagues familiar with the projects.

Managers with different personality types probably evaluate differently the strategic alternatives (Haley, 1995). For example, to determine performance, STs may use objective measures of cost centers and check calculations' details; NTs may compare departmental performances against departmental potentials to gauge responses to economic trends and consumer whims; SFs may use subordinates' objective measures and monitor key groups' support; and NFs may compare departmental heads' views against the NF's view of their potentials to gauge opportunities for improving organizational prestige.

TABLE 2 Managers' Risk-Taking Propensities

Managerial	Risk-Taking	Preferred Team Type
ST	Conservative risk-averse	STs
NT	Intermediate risk-taking	STs, NFs, and SFs
NF	Intermediate risk-taking	STs, NTs, and SFs
SF	High risk-taking	STs, NTs, and NFs

The cognitive trails that managers employ may also indicate the levels of risks to which managers may expose the corporations. STs form the most conservative and risk-averse managers, generally rejecting more alternatives than they accept; ST managers also display the greatest risk-taking propensities, and least tension, in teams composed primarily of other STs. SFs form the most risk-taking managers, probably because they acquiesce to other managers' opinions. NT and NF managers have intermediate risk levels. Unlike ST managers, SF, NT, and NF managers often exhibit more adventurousness and creativity in teams of managers with personality types divergent from theirs. As risk generally correlates positively with returns, corporations may work with managers to help them understand their own risk-taking propensities and potentials. Drawing on managers' cognitive trails, Table 2 outlines risk-taking propensities for managers from the four personality types.

Environmental Influences

Environments provide corporations with opportunities and constraints; strategic management involves decisions that align corporations with their environment (Haley, 1991). Different environments may accentuate or obliterate the cognitive trails that managers use, thereby affecting managerial decisions and consequently corporate strategies. Future research could inquire further into environmental characteristics and their effects on cognitive trails. Corporate environments can range from very stable to extremely volatile—depending on the amount and types of changes that their industries experience.

Some environments display technological, economic, social, and political stability: In the United States, the soft-drink industry could provide such a stable environment for managers because it displays minor and largely predictable changes. ST managers may excel in such environments. The environments' order and concreteness minimize the managers' biases and highlight their strengths. ST managers do not have to generate creative solutions in these environments; they can rely on orderly analyses.

Some environments display primarily technological or economic change: In the United States, the insurance industry could provide such an intermediate environment for managers. The insurance industry has gone through economic cycles that refined its operating technologies. However, social circumstances, as captured in labor-management relations and regulation, have remained fairly constant for the industry. NTs may excel as top managers in such environments: They can provide continuity for companies, see patterns in data, take risks, and do not have to calculate for many specific contingencies.

Other environments display primarily social change: In the United States, the food-product industry could provide such an intermediate environment for managers. Social changes have greatly affected tastes; preferences for fish over red meats and emphases on low-fat and healthy foods have influenced the industry. Also, increases in dual-career families have reduced time spent on preparing foods. Few technological, political, or economic changes have hit this industry. SFs may excel as top managers in such environments: Their sensitivities to values and to people might prove very helpful; their desires for social approval may not hinder as much.

Still other external environments display social, economic, political, and technological changes: In the United States, the computer industry could provide such a volatile environment for managers. International strategic alliances, developments in artificial intelligence, widespread usage of personal computers, and political issues surrounding national competence in producing and developing computers have all affected the industry. NFs may excel as top managers in such environments. They provide creative solutions to old problems, see analogies from dissimilar situations, and seize opportunities; their inability to give continuity to organizations does not hinder them as much.

Table 3 summarizes the kinds of environments that may facilitate managerial uses of some cognitive trails. Environments could help some managers' decision-making styles more than others. Future research may elaborate on the links between cognitive trails and environments; however, *this chapter does not advocate one type of manager for any one corporation in any specific environment*. Differing managerial types see

TABLE 3 Possible Environmental Influences

Environment	Environmental Characteristics	Preferred Manager Type
Stable	Minor technological, economic, and political changes	ST
Intermediate	Some technological and economic changes	NT
Intermediate	Some social changes	SF
Volatile	Major technological, economic, and political changes	NF

diverse aspects of complex realities. Corporations fare best when they can capture as much of their reality as possible—when different personality types function as managers regardless of the environments and when these managers work collaboratively together. Even the most stable environments have characteristics that managers cannot perceive. For example, the probably predominantly ST managers in Coca-Cola, part of the stable soft-drink industry, may have drawn on extensive data and research to recommend a "New Coke" formula to replace the old one. The managers ignored the emotional association between the American public and the all-American soft drink. In blind taste tests, four Americans to one preferred the new formula over the old one. However, New Coke proved a disaster. Profits dropped and Coca-Cola had to return to its old formula.

The next section indicates the cognitive trails that managers may journey in an international business situation; it identifies how managers may use knowledge of cognitive trails to make better decisions for corporations.

USING COGNITIVE TRAILS
IN STRATEGIC MANAGEMENT

As industries become increasingly global, cross-national strategic alliances increase. Yet increased risks and returns attend international strategic decisions and strategic platforms composed of different nationals; most cross-national strategic alliances fail (Haley, 1995). This section proposes how understanding the cognitive trails that managers traverse can help to reduce the risk of such failures.

Research and work with managers indicate that identifying personality types through the MBTI, and understanding cognitive trails that the MBTI helps to highlight, may provide an efficient way for managers to recognize their habitual biases (Haley, 1995). However, managers must also pay attention to the informational texture that they favor (statistics, anecdotes, or experiences), whether they focus on the short or long term, and whether they emphasize people or things. Knowledge of these patterns may help managers to guard against possible dangers, build better teams, and thereby make better decisions.

A recent unpublished sample of the MBTI types of 16,398 U.S. managers (from the Center for Creative Leadership) was consistent with Campbell and Van Velsor's (1985) national findings. These two studies suggest that STs comprise about 40% of U.S. managers, and NTs comprise about 37%. The sample of middle and top-level managers, from a representative cross-section of industrial sectors, participated in the Center for Creative Leadership's executive-development programs. The sample suggests that over 70% of U.S. managers may be STs and NTs; the biases in these two personality types' cognitive trails probably infiltrate U.S. strategic processes. U.S. corporations probably adopt conservative recommendations, or recommendations based on patterned data, more than people-oriented recommendations.

One cannot assume that the personality-type distributions for U.S. managers will apply to managers from other countries; indeed, a study conducted in Italy indicated that differences may in fact exist between countries (Haley & Pini, 1994). We (Haley & Pini, 1994) did a pilot study among Italian managers to identify the cognitive trails that the managers use in international strategic decisions; the research, though exploratory, yields some propositions for U.S. and Italian team-building efforts in strategic planning. After conducting validity tests, we translated the MBTI personality inventory into Italian for the first time and administered it to managers. Sixty-six middle and top-level managers, from nine discrete industrial sectors, comprised the preliminary sample of Italian managers; the managers participated in Olivetti's forum for executive training and most of them headed planning divisions and had engineering degrees. Figure 3 provides a distribution of the U.S. and Italian managers by personality types.

The Italian preliminary sample indicates that NTs may comprise about 37% of Italian managers, and NFs may comprise about 24%.

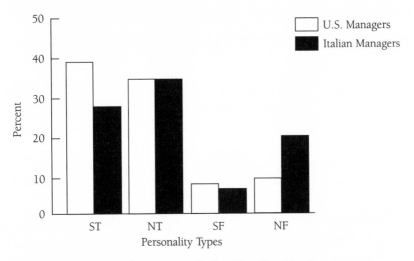

Source: Center for Creative Leadership; Elea, Olivetti S.p.A.

Figure 3   U.S. and Italian Managers' Personality Types

If these percentages hold up among Italian managers as a whole, the biases in these two personality types' cognitive trails may infiltrate Italian strategic processes. Future research could corroborate these distributions that could have profound implications for international business interactions. Italian corporations may adopt recommendations based on patterned data or on vivid recollections more than people-oriented recommendations. Intuitive types appear to dominate: Their biases may partly explain some Italian corporations' innovativeness and apparent riskiness (Haley, 1995).

Let us examine the implications of these findings for international strategic alliances. In a joint U.S.-Italian undertaking, the clearest vision of the future may come from the Intuitive types—the NTs and the NFs that may dominate Italian corporations. The most practical vision may come from the Sensing types—the STs that dominate U.S. corporations, and the SFs. The most incisive vision may come from the Thinking types—the STs and NTs that dominate U.S. corporations, and the NTs that may dominate Italian corporations. And the most skillful handling of people may come from the Feeling types—the SFs and the NFs that may form a significant proportion of Italian corporations. Future research could test these propositions with larger samples from Italy as well as from other countries.

Managing International Cognitive Trails

Our preliminary findings (Haley & Pini, 1994) indicated that top managers from different countries may represent differing personality types—and consequently, may gather different sorts of data, generate different sorts of alternatives, and evaluate these alternatives in diverse fashions. Inadequate understanding and managing of these differences may partially explain why many international strategic alliances fail. As international strategic alliances proliferate, corporations should try to increase the chances that these alliances succeed by managing their cognitive trails. For effective strategic management, despite the increased risks, this chapter has recommended the following:

- Building strategic expert systems to identify and to compensate for potential biases in strategic decision making
- Building heterogeneous teams composed of managers from different personality types and different countries to shape better strategic decisions
- Incorporating managers from different personality types and countries at different stages of alliances to view differing aspects of realities
- Understanding that social, political, and technological environments may influence managers' decision-making styles and effectiveness

Strategy formulation provides a good example to highlight the effective management of cognitive trails in international strategic decisions: Errors or biases in formulating strategic problems can result in solving the wrong problems—with global ramifications. To form complex and evolving pictures of reality, teams should incorporate managers with different skills at different stages of strategy formulation. Strategy formulation can then move from gut feelings about problems and solutions to abstract theorizing. Managers using different cognitive heuristics and biases can help at each stage. For example, one hypothetical corporate scenario, as outlined in Figure 4, shows that over time, strategy formulation may move from SFs, through STs and NFs, and finally culminate with NTs.

Using the managers' diverse strengths at different stages in strategy formulation limits managerial biases: SFs generally avoid long-range plans and are affected by biases that emphasize availability of information, social desirability, and fundamental-attribution error. STs can effectively use the data that are now available and gathered; however,

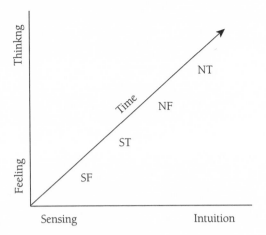

Figure 4   Ideal Strategy Formulation

they may want premature closure as they can be affected by biases emphasizing anchoring, functional fixedness, and imputation of regularity and structure. NFs can break with the STs' logic through intuitive leaps; however, they can endanger the continuity of corporate strategies as they are affected by biases that emphasize vividness, reasoning by analogy, and illusory correlation. Finally, NTs excel at long-range plans, tend not to see the differences in specific situations, and are affected by biases that emphasize perseverance, positivity, and representativeness. Abstract strategies may, however, lose touch with local conditions and local subsidiaries: SFs may be needed again to reformulate the problems and, with their understanding of people, to gain acceptance for the strategic plans through management structures.

Let us examine the implications of Haley's (1995) conclusions for one solution to the hypothetical strategic-decision situation of Fiat and Chrysler. Initially, strategy formulation depends on feedback based on personal experiences and values: Italian and U.S. managers may use heuristics that emphasize these factors; the managers may also have ready repertoires of solutions. As the process develops, U.S. managers may dominate with their tendencies to reason from cause to effect and to build rationales. Further along in the process may come other Italian managers with their ability to break with the rationales, to reason intuitively, and to generalize. Finally, both Italian and U.S. managers may participate with their abilities to generalize and to see long-term patterns.

This section provides one scenario, and some propositions, to chart and to use managers' cognitive trails to improve corporate strategies; others exist. Today, successful managers must learn to cope with international, complex, and evolving business environments; more importantly, they must learn to manage the environments efficiently. This chapter has shown how teams of managers from the four personality types can generate different alternatives for the same, though evolving, problems at different stages of strategy formulation. This approach, acknowledging that managers journey across cognitive trails, can give corporations competitive and creative edges in a world that values time as well as innovativeness. Consequently, one point to start to make better strategic decisions would revolve around understanding managers' cognitive trails.

ACKNOWLEDGMENTS

The author thanks Jennifer Berger, Rod Davies, Catherine Fitzgerald, George Haley, and Linda Kirby for their helpful comments and suggestions, and Comet for being there through the writing.

REFERENCES

Aoki, C., & Siekevitz, P. (1988, December). Plasticity in brain development. *Scientific American*, 56–64.

Barnes, J. H. (1984). Cognitive biases and their impact on strategic planning. *Strategic Management Journal, 5*, 129–137.

Behling, O., Gifford, W. E., & Tolliver, J. M. (1980). Effects of grouping information on decision making under risk. *Decision Sciences, 11*(2), 272–283.

Blaylock, B. K., & Rees, L. P. (1984). Cognitive style and the usefulness of information. *Decision Sciences, 15*, 74–91.

Borgida, E., & Nisbett, R. E. (1977). The differential impact of abstract versus concrete information on decisions. *Journal of Applied Social Psychology, 7*, 258–271.

Bower, L. J. (1970). *Managing the resource allocation process: A study of corporate planning and investment*. Boston: Division of Research, Harvard Business School.

Brief, A. P., Schuler, R. S., & Van Sell, M. (1981). *Managing job stress*. Boston: Little, Brown.

Campbell, D. P., & Van Velsor, E. (1985). *The use of personality measures in the leadership development program*. Greensboro, NC: Center for Creative Leadership.

Carroll, J. S. (1978). The effect of imagining an event on expectations for the event: An interpretation in terms of the availability heuristic. *Journal of Experimental Social Psychology, 14*, 88–96.

Chapman, L. J., & Chapman, J. P. (1969). Illusory correlation as an obstacle to the use of valid psychodiagnostic signs. *Journal of Abnormal Psychology, 74*, 271–280.

Dutton, J. E., Fahey, L., & Narayanan, V. K. (1983). Towards understanding strategic issue diagnosis. *Strategic Management Journal, 4*, 307–324.

Galanter, E. H., & Smith, W. A. (1958). Some experiments on a simple thought-problem. *American Journal of Psychology, 71*, 359–366.

Gordon, W. J. (1961). *Synectics.* New York: Harper & Row.

Haley, U. C. V. (1991). Corporate contributions as managerial masques: Reframing corporate contributions as strategies to influence society. *Journal of Management Studies, 28*(5), 485–509.

Haley, U. C. V. (1995). *Managing cognitive biases in international strategic decisions.* Paper presented at the international conference of the Institute for Operations Research and the Management Sciences (INFORMS), Singapore.

Haley, U. C. V., & Pini, R. (1994). Blazing international trails in strategic decision-making research. In C. Fitzgerald (Ed.), *Proceedings of the Myers-Briggs Type Indicator and Leadership: An International Research Conference* (pp. 19–28). College Park, MD: University of Maryland University College National Leadership Institute.

Haley, U. C. V., & Stumpf, S. A. (1989). Cognitive trails in strategic decision making: Linking theories of personalities and cognitions. *Journal of Management Studies, 26*(5), 477–497.

Hambrick, D. C., & Mason, P. A. (1984). Upper echelons: The organization as a reflection of its top managers. *Academy of Management Review, 9*, 193–206.

Hellriegel, D., & Slocum, J. W. (1975, December). Managerial problem-solving styles. *Business Horizons*, 29–37.

Henderson, J. C., & Nutt, P. C. (1980). The influence of decision style on decision-making behavior. *Management Science, 26*(4), 371–386.

Higgins, E. T., & Chaires, W. M. (1980). Accessibility of interrelational constructs: Implications for stimulus encoding and creativity. *Journal of Experimental Social Psychology, 16*, 348–361.

Hogarth, R. M. (1980). *Beyond static biases: Functional and dysfunctional aspects of judgmental heuristics.* Chicago: Center for Decision Research, University of Chicago, Graduate School of Business.

Hogarth, R. M., & Makridakis, S. M. (1981). Forecasting and planning: An evaluation. *Management Science, 27*, 115–138.

Hoy, F., & Hellriegel, D. (1982). The Kilman and Herden model of organizational effectiveness criteria for small business managers. *Academy of Management Journal, 25*, 308–322.

Huber, G. P. (1983). Cognitive style as a basis for MIS and DSS designs: Much ado about nothing? *Management Science, 29*(5), 567–579.

Huff, A. S. (1980). Evocative metaphors. *Human Systems Management, 1*, 1–10.

Jung, C. (1923). *Psychological types.* London: Rutledge.

Kelley, H. H. (1973). The process of casual attribution. *American Psychologist, 28*, 107–128.

Khandwalla, P. N. (1976). The technoeconomic ecology of corporate strategy. *Journal of Management Studies, 13*, 62–75.

Kotter, J. P. (1982). *The general managers.* New York: Free Press.

Lyles, M. A., & Mitroff, I. I. (1980). Organizational problem formation: An empirical study. *Administrative Science Quarterly, 25*, 102–119.

Markus, H., & Zajonc, R. B. (1985). The cognitive perspective in social psychology. In G. Lindzey & E. Aronson (Eds.), *The handbook of social psychology* (pp. 137–230). New York: Random House.

Mason, R. O., & Mitroff, I. I. (1981). *Challenging strategic planning assumptions.* New York: Wiley.

Matlin, M., & Stang, D. (1978). *The Pollyanna principle.* Cambridge, MA: Schenkman.

McArthur, L. Z, & Friedman, S. (1980). Illusory correlations in impression formation: Variations in the shared distinctiveness effect as a function of the distinctive person's age, race, and sex. *Journal of Personality and Social Psychology, 39,* 615–624.

McKenney, J. L., & Keen, P. (1974). How managers' minds work. *Harvard Business Review, 52*(3), 79–90.

Mintzberg, H. (1978) Patterns in strategy formation. *Management Science, 24,* 934–949.

Mintzberg, H., Raisinghani, D., & Theoret, A. (1976). The structure of "unstructured" decision processes. *Administrative Science Quarterly, 21,* 246–275.

Mitroff, I. I., & Kilmann, R. H. (1975). Stories managers tell: A new tool for organizational problem-solving. *Management Review, 64*(7), 18–28.

Mitroff, I. I., & Mitroff, D. D. (1980). Personality and problem solving: Making the links visible. *Journal of Experiential Learning and Simulation, 2,* 111–119.

Myers, I. B., with Myers, P. B. (1980). *Gifts differing.* Palo Alto, CA: Consulting Psychologists Press.

Nisbett, R. E, & Ross, L. (1980). *Human inferences: Strategies and shortcomings in social judgment.* Englewood Cliffs, NJ: Prentice Hall.

Nutt, P. C. (1979). Influence of decision styles on use of decision models. *Technological Forecasting and Social Change, 14,* 77–93.

Nutt, P. C. (1986a). Decision style and its impact on managers and management. *Technological Forecasting and Social Change, 29,* 341–366.

Nutt, P. C. (1986b). Decision style and strategic decisions of top executives. *Technological Forecasting and Social Change, 30,* 39–62.

Paine, F. T., & Anderson, C. R. (1977, May). Contingencies affecting strategy formulation and effectiveness: An empirical study. *Journal of Management Studies,* 147–158.

Restak, R. (1984). *The brain.* New York: Bantam Books.

Ross, L., Lepper, M. R., & Hubbard, M. (1975) Perseverance in self-perception and social perception: Biased attributional processes in the debriefing paradigm. *Journal of Personality and Social Psychology, 32,* 880–892.

Schwenk, C. R. (1984). Cognitive simplification processes in strategic decision-making. *Strategic Management Journal, 5,* 111–128.

Schwenk, C. R. (1986). Information, cognitive biases, and commitment to a course of action. *Academy of Management Review, 11,* 298–310.

Simon, H. A. (1947). *Administrative behavior.* New York: Macmillan.

Simon, H. A. (1987, February). Making management decisions: The role of intuition and emotion. *Academy of Management Executive,* 57–64.

Slocum, J. W. (1978). Does cognitive style affect diagnosis and interventions strategies of change agents? *Group and Organization Studies, 3*(2), 199–210.

Slovic, P., Fischhoff, B., & Lichtenstein, S. (1977). Behavioral decision theory. *Annual Review of Psychology, 28,* 1–39.

Starbuck, W. H. (1976). Organizations and their environments. In M. D. Dunnette (Ed.), *Handbook of industrial and organizational psychology* (pp. 1069–1123). Chicago: Rand McNally.

Steinbruner, J. D. (1974). *The cybernetic theory of decision.* Princeton: Princeton University Press.

Taggart, W., & Robey, D. (1981). Minds and managers: On the dual nature of human information processing and management. *Academy of Management Review, 6,* 187–195.

Tichy, N. (1974). Agents of planned social change: Congruence of values, cognitions and actions. *Administrative Science Quarterly, 19,* 164–182.

Tichy, N., & Nisberg, J. (1976). Change agent bias: What they view determines
what they do. *Group and Organization Studies, 1*(3), 286–301.

Tversky, A., & Kahneman, D. (1973). Availability: A heuristic for judging frequency and probability. *Cognitive Psychology, 5,* 207–232.

Tversky, A., & Kahneman, D. (1982). Judgment under uncertainty: Heuristics and
biases. In D. Kahneman, P. Slovic, & A. Tversky (Eds.), *Judgment under uncertainty: Heuristics and biases* (pp. 3–20). New York: Cambridge University
Press.

Vroom, V. H., & Yetton, P. W. (1973). *Leadership and decision-making.* Pittsburgh:
University of Pittsburgh Press.

Warner, S. L. (1965). Randomized response: A survey technique for eliminating
evasive answer bias. *Journal of the American Statistical Society, 60,* 63–69.

Weick, K. E. (1979). *The social psychology of organizing.* Menlo Park, CA: Addison-
Wesley.

Wright, W. F. (1980). Cognitive information processing biases: Implications for pro-
ducers and users of financial information. *Decision Sciences, 11,* 284–298.

Zmud, R. W. (1979). Individual differences and MIS success: A review of the empirical literature. *Management Science, 25*(10), 966–979.

8 | Co-Workers' Perceptions of Eight MBTI Leader Types

Comparative Analysis of Managers' SYMLOG Profiles

Eric Sundstrom

Paul L. Busby

This chapter uses an established measurement system for assessing leader effectiveness, called SYMLOG®, to analyze differences in co-workers' perceptions of leaders in eight MBTI classifications. SYMLOG, or *Systematic Multiple-Level Observation of Groups,* grew out of four decades of research by Robert F. Bales (1983). After introducing the system and its application to leadership development, we describe a study of the leaders of a single manufacturing organization, each of whom had co-workers rate the teamwork values he or she demonstrated at work. We compare the resulting SYMLOG profiles of co-workers' perceptions against the empirically derived Most Effective Profile for leadership effectiveness and analyze the differences by MBTI type.

We then analyze eight Thinking types separately. Unfortunately, our leader group did not contain enough of any one Feeling type to analyze them separately, so we combined all of the Feeling managers into one group to contrast them with the eight Thinking types. Our analysis showed that the eight Thinking types differed from Feeling types and from one another on SYMLOG in ways consistent with their preferences.

LEADERSHIP DEVELOPMENT
AND SYMLOG

SYMLOG is both a measurement system for leader effectiveness and an empirically derived field theory of group dynamics based on the behavioral expression of values found important to teamwork. The values measured by SYMLOG emerged from systematic observation of small group interaction by Bales (1950a), directed toward finding the predictors of group effectiveness. Bales (1950b) developed a set of categories for observing and recording behavior in group discussions, which eventually became one of the most widely used tools for studying groups (McGrath, 1984). The categories he developed were then used to identify specific behaviors and values important to teamwork and to develop a system for ratings by team members (Bales, Cohen, & Williamson, 1979).

Bales (1970) proposed an integrative framework based on three basic dimensions of group interaction:

- Dominance
- Friendliness
- Acceptance of the task orientation of established authority

The third dimension combined two other dimensions often seen in research on leadership and group interaction: task orientation and authority acceptance, which Bales found to be correlated.

SYMLOG Dimensions

Bales' descriptive dimensions differed from those of other researchers in that they extended to undesirable as well as desirable extremes. Earlier approaches, such as Blake and Mouton's (1978) grid, included only the desirable ends of the dimensions of task orientation and friendliness. In SYMLOG, the dimension *friendliness* extends to unfriendly and negative; *dominance* extends to submissiveness; and *accepting the task orientation of established authority* includes opposition to authority and/or task.

Together, SYMLOG's three dimensions are intended to deal with the full range of values relevant to teamwork, including desirable values identified in many current models of leadership—dominance, friendliness, and task orientation—as well as the undesirable extremes that usually interfere with teamwork: passivity, unfriendliness, and task and/or authority opposition.

Applying this framework to leadership and teamwork, Bales et al. (1979) developed a measure that assesses the expression of the teamwork values as seen by the individual leader or by other people observing the leader. The measure, which can be applied to groups or cultures as well as individuals, uses 26 carefully worded items. Each item represents a pole or extreme end of one or more bipolar dimensions. The measure, "Individual and Organizational Values for Teamwork," uses an innovative approach: Most items deliberately represent two or even three of the bipolar extremes instead of just one dimension per item. The result is a compact series of 26 items in which the three dimensions are each tapped by 18 items.

Table 1 shows the 26 items and the dimensions they measure. Each item is coded to indicate the dimension and pole with which it is associated, using the following codes:

Dominance dimension

    U indicates upward or dominant

    D indicates downward or submissive

Friendliness dimension

    P indicates positive and friendly

    N indicates negative and unfriendly

Accepting the task orientation of established authority dimension

    F indicates forward or accepting authority

    B indicates backward or rejecting authority

Some items tap all three dimensions by representing three poles. For example, active teamwork toward common goals, organizational unity (item 3) indicates all three poles—dominant, friendly, and authority aligned. This item is labeled *UPF* because higher ratings indicate dominance, friendliness, and acceptance of the task orientation of established authority.

Codes indicate an item's theoretical relationship to the coordinates. For example, the first nine items all measure dominance, indicated by *U*. Item 1 is designed to represent pure dominance and to be neutral on other dimensions, neither friendly nor unfriendly, neither accepting nor rejecting authority, and is therefore coded with a *U*. Item 4 represents a dominant, authority-aligned value, neither friendly nor unfriendly, and is therefore coded *UF*.

The 26 items include all combinations of nonopposing poles, allowing assessment of an individual's expression of values along the full range of the three dimensions of interpersonal interaction seen as critical for leadership and teamwork.

TABLE 1 SYMLOG Dimensions and Values Items Associated With Each

		SYMLOG Dimensions		
SYMLOG Values Items		Dominant/ Submissive	Friendly/ Unfriendly	Accepting/ Opposing Authority
1. U	Individual financial success, personal prominence and power	X		
2. UP	Popularity and social success, being liked and admired	X	X	
3. UPF	Active teamwork toward common goals, organizational unity	X	X	X
4. UF	Efficiency, strong impartial management	X		X
5. UNF	Active reinforcement of authority, rules, and regulations	X	x	X
6. UN	Tough-minded, self-oriented assertiveness	X	x	
7. UNB	Rugged, self-oriented individualism, resistance to authority	X	x	x
8. UB	Having a good time, releasing tension, relaxing control	X		x
9. UPB	Protecting less able members, providing help when needed	X	X	x
10. P	Equality, democratic participation in decision making		X	
11. PF	Responsible idealism, collaborative work		X	X
12. F	Conservative, established, correct ways of doing things			X
13. NF	Restraining individual desires for organizational goals		x	X
14. N	Self-protection, self-interest first, self-sufficiency		x	
15. NB	Rejection of established procedures, rejection of conformity		x	x
16. B	Change to new procedures, different values, creativity			x
17. PB	Friendship, mutual pleasure, recreation		X	x
18. DP	Trust in the goodness of others	x	X	
19. DPF	Dedication, faithfulness, loyalty to the organization	x	X	X

TABLE 1 SYMLOG Dimensions and Values Items Associated With Each (continued)

	SYMLOG Dimensions		
SYMLOG Values Items	Dominant/ Submissive	Friendly/ Unfriendly	Accepting/ Opposing Authority
20. DF Obedience to the chain of command, complying with authority	x		X
21. DNF Self-sacrifice if necessary to reach organizational goals	x	x	X
22. DN Passive rejection of popularity, going it alone	x	x	
23. DNB Admission of failure, withdrawal of effort	x	x	x
24. DB Passive noncooperation with authority	x		x
25. DPB Quiet contentment, taking it easy	x	X	x
26. D Giving up personal needs and desires, passivity	x		

Note. X indicates first pole (e.g., dominant) and x indicates second pole (e.g., submissive). (Adapted from Bales, 1983). SYMLOG items copyright by R. F. Bales, 1983. Reprinted with permission.

Leader Effectiveness, Situational Balance, and the Most Effective Profile

SYMLOG defines leader effectiveness as "the ability to unify a diverse group of people to work effectively as a team toward a common purpose under varied and often difficult conditions" (Bales & Koenigs, 1992). Bales' research found that groups were most effective when they demonstrated a balance of task orientation and socioemotional orientation (Bales, 1958). The premise of SYMLOG is that unification of a group depends on a leader's situationally appropriate balance in expressing values for dominance, friendliness, and authority alignment (Bales, 1988).

In the short term, balance translates as expression of the specific values that the leader's situation requires. Some situations call for friendly advocacy of teamwork and collaboration. A crisis may require tough-minded assertion of authority or relaxation of tension through humor. At times, a leader may have to advocate protection of less able members. Other situations require adherence to established procedures; still others demand creativity.

In the long term, however, situational balance is seen as calling for a demonstration of moderately dominant, moderately positive, and moderately authority-aligned values. Figure 1 shows the Most Effective Profile on the 26 values (indicated by Es) constructed from data reported by Bales (1990) on 567 individual ratings concerning the most effective leader of a task-oriented team each person had known. The profile agreed closely with the optimal profile found in earlier research (Bales et al., 1979) and with 1,666 averaged ratings of values ideal for group effectiveness (Bales, 1990). For comparison, the figure also shows the average response to the question "In general, what kinds of values are currently shown in the culture of your organization?" from a random sample drawn from a cross-section of U.S. manufacturing, service, military, and religious organizations (Koenigs, 1990). The cross-sectional sample departs substantially from the Most Effective Profile for teamwork.

A related study examined six U.S. Navy commanders who were judged "superior" on readiness and performance by a panel of experts (Bachman, 1988). Compared with six "average" commanders, subordinate ratings of the "superior" commanders on the 26 SYMLOG items came significantly closer to the moderately dominant, friendly, authority-aligned values represented by the Most Effective Profile in Figure 1.

Leadership Development

The SYMLOG system promotes leadership development by providing a vehicle for feedback from co-workers, who provide ratings of how often the leader demonstrates each of the 26 values. Feedback takes the form of summarized ratings by multiple co-workers, including subordinates, peers, and/or superiors. As in most current leader-feedback systems, SYMLOG provides leaders with a profile describing how they are perceived, with specific areas for development. Feedback includes a bar graph of averaged ratings by co-workers on the 26 values, along with a detailed Bales Report, comparing each with the Most Effective Profile.

RESEARCH DESIGN AND METHOD

The present study addressed two research questions:

- How do co-workers' perceptions of leaders' expressed values, as measured by SYMLOG, vary with leaders' MBTI types?
- How does each MBTI type's SYMLOG profile differ from the empirically derived Most Effective Profile for leader effectiveness?

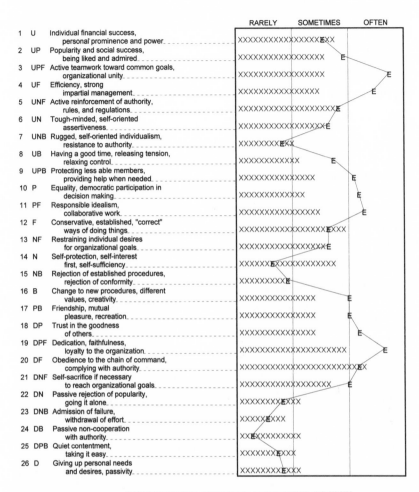

			RARELY	SOMETIMES	OFTEN
1	U	Individual financial success, personal prominence and power.			
2	UP	Popularity and social success, being liked and admired.			
3	UPF	Active teamwork toward common goals, organizational unity.			
4	UF	Efficiency, strong impartial management.			
5	UNF	Active reinforcement of authority, rules, and regulations.			
6	UN	Tough-minded, self-oriented assertiveness.			
7	UNB	Rugged, self-oriented individualism, resistance to authority.			
8	UB	Having a good time, releasing tension, relaxing control.			
9	UPB	Protecting less able members, providing help when needed.			
10	P	Equality, democratic participation in decision making.			
11	PF	Responsible idealism, collaborative work.			
12	F	Conservative, established, "correct" ways of doing things.			
13	NF	Restraining individual desires for organizational goals.			
14	N	Self-protection, self-interest first, self-sufficiency.			
15	NB	Rejection of established procedures, rejection of conformity.			
16	B	Change to new procedures, different values, creativity.			
17	PB	Friendship, mutual pleasure, recreation.			
18	DP	Trust in the goodness of others.			
19	DPF	Dedication, faithfulness, loyalty to the organization.			
20	DF	Obedience to the chain of command, complying with authority.			
21	DNF	Self-sacrifice if necessary to reach organizational goals.			
22	DN	Passive rejection of popularity, going it alone.			
23	DNB	Admission of failure, withdrawal of effort.			
24	DB	Passive non-cooperation with authority.			
25	DPB	Quiet contentment, taking it easy.			
26	D	Giving up personal needs and desires, passivity.			

Figure 1 The Most Effective Profile on 26 SYMLOG Values

Note. E = the "optimum" location for most effective teamwork; Bar of Xs = the average rating on each item. Bar graph ratings made in response to "In general, what kinds of values are currently shown in the culture of your organization?"

From *A SYMLOG Profile of American Business: Leaders, Teams and Organizations*, by R. J. Koenigs, 1990. Reprinted with permission.

We expected differences in perceptions of various MBTI types to reflect issues related to preference and type development. For the leaders with Thinking preferences, for example, we expected relatively infrequent expression of friendly values such as item 17, friendship, in comparison to the Most Effective Profile, particularly for Introverts with dominant Thinking (ISTPs and INTPs). We expected SYMLOG profiles to reflect these and to reveal more subtle issues related to type development.

Research Setting and Participants

This study involved a division of an international manufacturing organization with more than 12,000 employees at multiple U.S. sites. Participants in the study, comprising 529 people, came from the top three tiers of management:

- Vice presidents who reported to the president
- Directors who reported to vice presidents
- Managers who reported to directors

Their 85 overlapping management groups each consisted of a manager and the people who reported directly to that manager. Each group leader belonged—as a member—to the next higher-ranking group. Group size ranged from three to eighteen, with an average of seven, counting the leader. While most groups had worked together for years, about 10% had been formed or reorganized within the previous six months.

All top managers were invited to one of a series of off-site training sessions conducted during a six-month period. Of those invited, 487 attended (92%) and, as part of the process, rated the expressed values of other group members. Of those, 401 completed the MBTI and arranged for ratings on their own expressed values by members of their groups (84% of attendees). Of those, 361 had complete ratings returned by three or more co-workers, which comprised the population for the present study. Participants represented five small departments (fewer than 20 people each) and 76 management groups.

The 361 mostly male (96%) managers ranged in age from 25 to 64 years, with a median age of 48. Most had college degrees (86%), and almost half (46%) reported having some postgraduate education.

Procedures

Managers scheduled for training received an MBTI test booklet, answer sheet, and instructions via company mail. An accompanying letter explained that a personal profile would be provided during training. The envelope held SYMLOG rating forms for all members of the management group and instructions to solicit ratings from other group members with whom they had worked at least six months. Each invitee designated a person to receive completed ratings in sealed envelopes and put them in the mail.

Training sessions occurred four to six weeks after materials were mailed. At the sessions, participants received MBTI profiles and copies of *Introduction to Type* (Myers, 1987). Each also received a SYMLOG bar graph summary of co-workers' ratings and a narrative Bales Report comparing individual summary ratings against the Most Effective Profile.

Measures

SYMLOG Ratings

Participants were rated by co-workers on the 26-item SYMLOG Values form (see Table 1). They were asked to consider their work-related experience with this person and to answer the following question on actual behavior in the workplace: "In general, what kinds of values does this person actually show in his or her behavior?" For each item, the rater could mark "rarely," "sometimes," or "often." Instructions stated that if not all of an item seemed to apply, respondents were to answer for the part that did.

Myers-Briggs Type Indicator

Participants completed either the 126-item Form G or the 94-item Form G Self-Scorable version (*n* = 54) of the MBTI.

Variables

Expressed Values: 26 SYMLOG Items

Co-workers' ratings of expressed values were scored on the following scale: "rarely" = 0, "sometimes" = 1, or "often" = 2. Ratings were averaged across all raters; averages ranged from 0 (all raters said the person

	←——— Sensing ———→		←——— Intuitive ———→	
Judging	ISTJ n = 107 30%	ISFJ n = 5 1%	INFJ n = 7 2%	INTJ n = 51 14%	**Introvert**
Perceiving	ISTP n = 12 3%	ISFP n = 5 1%	INFP n = 5 1%	INTP n = 10 3%	
Perceiving	ESTP n = 10 3%	ESFP n = 3 1%	ENFP n = 4 1%	ENTP n = 26 7%	**Extravert**
Judging	ESTJ n = 65 18%	ESFJ n = 6 2%	ENFJ n = 8 2%	ENTJ n = 37 10%	
	Thinking	←——— Feeling ———→		Thinking	

Figure 2 Distribution of MBTI Types (N = 361)

expressed the value "rarely") to 2.0 (all said "often") for 26 SYMLOG values.

MBTI Classifications

Individuals received dichotomous classifications on the four MBTI preference pairs using standard scoring techniques for Form G or the Form G Self-Scorable form.

RESULTS AND DISCUSSION

The data allowed us to assess differences among MBTI types on SYMLOG values as perceived by co-workers.

Leaders' MBTI Types

Figure 2 shows the MBTI types for the 361 managers of the organization who returned completed MBTI inventories and participated in the SYMLOG ratings. As in other populations of executives and top managers (Kroeger with Thuesen, 1992), they were predominantly Thinking Judging types (72%), the most common type being ISTJ. Introverts (53%) were more prevalent than they are in the U.S. population. Thinking (89%) was far more common than among U.S. males (about 60%); Judging (79%) was similarly overrepresented.

In this aerospace manufacturing firm, with its emphasis on engineering and technology, the predominance of TJ types among leaders is not surprising. It probably reflects career choices based on individual preferences and organizational selection based on cultural compatibility. If the leadership culture of the organization reflected the preferences of top managers, it might be characterized as an ISTJ culture in MBTI terms.

Cultural Context

The cultural context can also be assessed by combining the ratings of all leaders participating in the study. The combined ratings of all leaders by their co-workers on the 26 SYMLOG items appear in Table 2. The average SYMLOG ratings can be seen as employees' collective perception of the values expressed by their leaders, or perhaps as a summary of the leadership culture of the organization.

The cultural profile (average ratings for all leaders) roughly paralleled the SYMLOG Most Effective Profile, but showed statistically significant departures on a majority of the items. For the population of 361, item standard errors of the mean ranged from .012 to .023. These averages differed from the Most Effective Profile by three or more standard errors on 20 items. Many of these departures from the Most Effective Profile are similiar to those shown in ratings of a cross-section of U. S. organizations, as illustrated in Figure 1.

As a group, these managers showed the following departures from the Most Effective Profile at a level of three or more standard errors. The managers underemphasized the following values:

- Active teamwork toward common goals (3)
- Efficiency, strong impartial management (4)
- Releasing tension (8)
- Equality, democratic participation in decision making (10)
- Collaboration (11)
- Creativity (16)

TABLE 2 Average Ratings on 26 SYMLOG Values and Results of Univariate Tests of Differences Among MBTI Types

SYMLOG Values Items	Population Statistics		Univariate F for Differences Across MBTI Types	Significant Differences Among MBTI Types Shown by Student–Newman Keuls Tests
	Mean	SD		
1. U Individual financial success, personal prominence and power	0.91	0.45	1.93	ESTJ > INTJ
2. UP Popularity and social success, being liked and admired	1.08	0.38	4.71***	ISTJ, INTJ < ESTJ, ENTP, ••F•
3. UPF Active teamwork toward common goals, organizational unity	1.41	0.37	1.30	
4. UF Efficiency, strong impartial management	1.19	0.35	1.66	
5. UNF Active reinforcement of authority, rules, and regulations	1.34	0.34	3.23**	ENTP < ESTJ, ISTJ
6. UN Tough-minded, self-oriented assertiveness	1.15	0.46	4.63**	INTP > all; ENTJ > ••F•; INTJ < ESTJ, ENTJ, ISTJ; INTP > all; ENTJ > INTJ
7. UNB Rugged, self-oriented individualism, resistance to authority	0.63	0.38	4.11**	
8. UB Having a good time, releasing tension, relaxing control	0.87	0.41	4.38***	••F• > ENTJ, INTJ, ISTJ; ENTP > ENTJ, ISTJ
9. UPB Protecting less able members, providing help when needed	1.16	0.36	2.25*	••F• > ENTJ
10. P Equality, democratic participation in decision making	1.19	0.36	1.86	
11. PF Responsible idealism, collaborative work	1.23	0.32	1.70	
12. F Conservative, established, correct ways of doing things	1.35	0.34	3.05**	ISTJ > ENTP
13. NF Restraining individual desires for organizational goals	1.11	0.31	0.72	

SYMLOG Values Items	Population Statistics		Univariate F for Differences Across MBTI Types	Significant Differences Among MBTI Types Shown by Student–Newman Keuls Tests
	Mean	SD		
14. N Self-protection, self-interest first, self-sufficiency	0.87	0.41	2.77**	INTP, ENTJ > INTJ; INTJ > ISTJ
15. NB Rejection of established procedures, rejection of conformity	0.55	0.34	2.05*	INTP > ISTJ
16. B Change to new procedures, different values, creativity	1.10	0.33	1.13	
17. PB Friendship, mutual pleasure, recreation	1.09	0.37	3.84*	••F• > ENTJ, INTJ, ISTJ
18. DP Trust in the goodness of others	1.12	0.37	2.29*	••F• > ENTJ, ISTJ
19. DPF Dedication, faithfulness, loyalty to the organization	1.63	0.31	0.78	
20. DF Obedience to the chain of command, complying with authority	1.64	0.28	3.70***	INTP < all but ESTP, ENTP ISTJ, INTJ > ENTP
21. DNF Self-sacrifice if necessary to reach organizational goals	1.24	0.34	0.71	
22. DN Passive rejection of popularity, going it alone	0.76	0.35	5.44***	INTP > all; ••F• < ISTJ< ENTJ, INTP
23. DNB Admission of failure, withdrawal of effort	0.41	0.24	1.04	
24. DB Passive noncooperation with authority	0.40	0.29	2.04*	INTP > ISTJ, INTJ
25. DPB Quiet contentment, taking it easy	0.59	0.35	1.46	
26. D Giving up personal needs and desires, passivity	0.74	0.27	1.56	

Note. U = dominant, D = submissive, P = friendly, N = unfriendly, F = authority aligned, and B = authority opposed. $N = 361$. For univariate Fs for differences across MBTI types, $df = 8$ and 352. "•• F•" represents all MBTI Feeling types combined.

$*p < .05$, $**p < .01$, $***p < .001$

The managers overemphasized the following values:

- Reinforcement of authority (5)
- Established ways of doing things (12)
- Self-interest and self-protection (14)
- Obedience (20)
- Going it alone (22)
- Passivity (26)

In brief, the culture, as seen in the combined SYMLOG ratings, emphasized teamwork and cooperation less and authority, convention, and self-interest more than the SYMLOG optimum profile of values for teamwork.

MBTI TYPES AND CO-WORKER PERCEPTION OF VALUES FOR TEAMWORK

In this chapter we have focused on leader MBTI types common enough in the organization to provide subgroups of sufficient size for reliable SYMLOG profiles. The four TJ categories were well represented with sample sizes of at least 30. Of the TP categories, only ENTP had a sizable subgroup ($n = 26$); others ranged from 8 to 12, just sufficient to test for differences from other profiles. For contrast, we also examined all leaders with Feeling preferences in a combined group ($n = 43$). This led to a total of nine type groups for analysis: ISTJ, INTJ, ISTP, INTP, ESTP, ENTP, ESTJ, ENTJ, and Feeling types combined.

Differences Among MBTI Types in Co-Workers' Perceptions

To address the question of whether the eight common MBTI leader types differed from one another in terms of co-workers' perceptions of their expressed values, we conducted an initial multivariate test. A one-factor multivariate analysis of variance (MANOVA) was conducted with MBTI type as the factor (nine categories, including one category for all Feeling types combined) and averaged co-worker ratings on the 26 SYMLOG values as the measured variables. MANOVA revealed significant multivariate differences among the MBTI types ($N = 361$; $F = 1.32$; $df = 208$ and 2,602; $p < .01$). This test answered the first research question: Co-workers definitely saw leaders of differing MBTI types expressing different profiles of values.

For more specific answers, we conducted follow-up univariate tests of significance, which are summarized in Table 2. They revealed significant differences on 14 of the 26 values. The table shows the results for items with significant differences, with indications of specific differences between the MBTI types. We will discuss the significant differences separately for each leader MBTI type later in the chapter.

Leaders' MBTI Types and
SYMLOG Most Effective Profile

We also addressed the question of how perceptions of each MBTI type compared to the SYMLOG Most Effective Profile of values. To do this, we averaged co-workers' ratings for the separate MBTI types and created bar graphs that appear in the subsections for each leaders' type. The bar graphs show ratings from 62 to 781 raters, many of whom gave data for more than one leader.

We used two tests to detect differences between each MBTI type's profile of means on the 26 values and the SYMLOG Most Effective Profile. First, we calculated standard errors of the mean for each item for each MBTI type (based on the standard deviation of ratees' scores averaged across raters) and identified items for which the co-workers' average differed by at least three standard errors from the Most Effective Profile (*univariate p* < .002). Second, we applied a more conservative test of differences—the SYMLOG Consulting Group's test—based on absolute differences on the response scale of approximately one-third of the range. This corresponds with plus or minus 5 Xs on the bar graphs.

Table 3 displays the number of standard errors on each of the 26 values by which each MBTI type differed from the SYMLOG Most Effective Profile when they differed by three or more standard errors. Differences that exceeded the more conservative SYMLOG Consulting Group's absolute margin are indicated on the table by an asterisk. In most cases, the second test was considerably more conservative because relatively large Ns used to calculate the standard errors made that test highly sensitive to small differences. For interpretation, we relied more on patterns of differences than on specific items and preferred to interpret those that showed significant differences by both tests.

Table 3 shows two patterns worth describing as context for analysis of the separate profiles. The first, which we call *cultural constants*, refers to values that all leaders were seen expressing with about the same frequency, regardless of individual preferences as indicated by the MBTI.

TABLE 3 Leader MBTI Types and Departure of Co-Worker Average Rating from SYMLOG Most Effective Profile

		Leader's MBTI Type and Differences from M.E.P. in Standard Errors								
		ESTJ	ESTP	ENTJ	ENTP	ISTJ	ISTP	INTJ	INTP	••F•
	Ratees	n = 65	n = 10	n = 37	n = 26	n = 107	n = 12	n = 51	n = 10	n = 43
SYMLOG Value Items	Raters	n = 512	n = 62	n = 249	n = 203	n = 781	n = 101	n = 379	n = 62	n = 326
1. U Individual financial success, personal prominence and power		–	–	–	–	–5	–	–5	–	–
2. UP Popularity and social success, being liked and admired		–3	–	–	–	–9*	–	–8*	–3*	–
3. UPF Active teamwork toward common goals, organizational unity		–9*	–3*	–8*	–6*	–11*	–7*	–6*	–5*	–7*
4. UF Efficiency, strong impartial management		–12*	–5*	–9*	–7*	–11*	–4*	–9*	–5*	–9*
5. UNF Active reinforcement of authority, rules, and regulations		+3	–	–	–	+7	–	–	–	–
6. UN Tough-minded, self-oriented assertiveness		–	–	–	–	–	–	–	+5*	–
7. UNB Rugged, self-oriented individualism, resistance to authority		–	–	–	–	–	–	–	+3*	–
8. UB Having a good time, releasing tension, relaxing control		–5	–	–6*	–	–11*	–4*	–5*	–3*	–
9. UPB Protecting less able members, providing help when needed		–6	–	–5*	–	–8	–	–4*	–3*	–
10. P Equality, democratic participation in decision making		–7*	–4*	–6*	–3	–8	–5*	–3	–3	–
11. PF Responsible idealism, collaborative work		–8*	–3*	–8*	–5*	–10	–4	–4	–4*	–4*
12. F Conservative, established, correct ways of doing things		+6	–	+3	–	+11*	+4	+11*	–	+4

Leader's MBTI Type and Differences from M.E.P. in Standard Errors

SYMLOG Value Items	ESTJ $n=65$ $n=512$	ESTP $n=10$ $n=62$	ENTJ $n=37$ $n=249$	ENTP $n=26$ $n=203$	ISTJ $n=107$ $n=781$	ISTP $n=12$ $n=101$	INTJ $n=51$ $n=379$	INTP $n=10$ $n=62$	••F• $n=43$ $n=326$
13. NF Restraining individual desires for organizational goals	—	—	—	—	—	—	—	—	—
14. N Self-protection, self-interest first, self-sufficiency	+9*	+4*	+9*	+7*	+11*	+3*	+5*	+6*	+6*
15. NB Rejection of established procedures, rejection of conformity	—	—	—	—	—	—	—	—	—
16. B Change to new procedures, different values, creativity	−7	−4	−3	−3	−9	−3	−5	—	−4
17. PB Friendship, mutual pleasure, recreation	−4	—	−5*	—	−8*	−4*	−7*	−3*	—
18. DP Trust in the goodness of others	−8*	—	−6*	−4*	−11*	−5*	−6*	−5*	−3
19. DPF Dedication, faithfulness, loyalty to the organization	—	—	−5	−3	−3	—	−3	—	—
20. DF Obedience to the chain of command, complying with authority	+6	—	—	—	+9	+5	+8	—	+4
21. DNF Self-sacrifice if necessary to reach organizational goals	—	—	−3	—	—	—	—	—	—
22. DN Passive rejection of popularity, going it alone	+5	—	+5	—	+7	+3	+4	+10*	—
23. DNB Admission of failure, withdrawal of effort	—	—	—	—	—	—	—	—	—
24. DB Passive noncooperation with authority	+6	—	+6	+5	+7	—	+5	+3*	+3
25. DPB Quiet contentment, taking it easy	—	—	—	—	—	—	+4	—	+5
26. D Giving up personal needs and desires, passivity	+5	+3	+4	—	+9	+4	+8	—	+5
Total Number of Departures*	6	5	9	5	8	6	9	13	4

Note. "••F•" represents all MBTI Feeling types combined. *Average rating differed from the Most Effective Profile by ±0.3030, the conservative margin used by SYMLOG Consulting Group.

A second pattern reflects differences among leaders of various MBTI types who departed from the cultural constants to either match or deviate from the Most Effective Profile.

Cultural Constants

Table 3 shows that although perceptions of leaders' values varied significantly by MBTI type, type was not a factor for some values. On these values, leaders of all MBTI types were seen as matching the Most Effective Profile or as uniformly departing from it. We interpreted these results as indicating the organization's core values, which all leaders were strongly (perhaps only implicitly) encouraged to express: the *cultural constants.*

Values on which the culture approximately matched the optimum profile across all or most MBTI types included:

- Individual prominence (1)
- Active reinforcement of authority (5)
- Tough-minded, self-oriented assertiveness (6)
- Resistance to authority (7)
- Restraining individual desires for organizational goals (13)
- Rejection of established procedures (15)
- Obedience (20)
- Dedication, faithfulness, loyalty to the organization (21)
- Quiet contentment (25)

These values are indicated in Table 3 by rows in which all or most types show no significant difference from the optimum (noted by a dash).

The culture *consistently* deviated from the optimum profile on a few other values, indicated by rows in which all MBTI types differed in approximately the same way from the optimum. These cultural constants included overemphasis of:

- Self-interest (14)

The cultural constants included underemphasis of:

- Teamwork (3)
- Efficiency and strong, impartial management (4)

When using the most conservative test, the three values described above were unanimously shared by all types. As Table 3 shows, a number of other departures from the Most Effective Profile were shared by a majority of types, but not by all types in our study.

We thought the uniform overemphasis of self-interest (14) probably reflected a lack of impartiality more than a lack of efficiency, because several employees privately complained about the prevalence of favoritism and political favor-trading in the selection of people for promotions and desirable work assignments. This is consistent with the pervasive overemphasis on self-interest, a value that Bales (1988) identifies as one that almost always interferes with teamwork.

These cultural constants, determined by analyzing each type's fit or lack of fit with the Most Effective Profile, are in keeping with the cultural context described earlier. Together, they describe the values of the culture of this organization.

Leadership Style Differences by Type

A second pattern in Table 3 involves departures from the cultural constants, apparent in the columns. Against the backdrop of the culture, the leaders of various MBTI types differentiated themselves on the number of values in which they matched and differed from the Most Effective Profile. Counting the departures from the optimal profile detected by both tests, the leader MBTI category seen as closest to optimal was the group that combined all Feeling types. As shown at the bottom of the table, Feeling types deviated from optimal on just four values:

- Active teamwork toward common goals (3)
- Efficiency, strong impartial management (4)
- Responsible idealism, collaborative work (11)
- Self-protection, self-interest first (14)

It is important to note that three of these four are cultural constants, and all eight Thinking types also deviated substantially from optimal on these. Among the Thinking types, those seen as closest to expressing the optimal profile of values were ESTPs and ENTPs, who were seen as departing from optimal on just five values. In contrast, INTPs were seen as deviating from optimal on 13 values.

Figure 3 shows the SYMLOG bar graph for all the Feeling leaders combined. This profile came closer to matching the Most Effective Profile than any of the others. Because it combines the profiles of eight Feeling types, however, it does not suggest that individuals in any one of the type categories necessarily matched the Most Effective Profile more closely than any one of the Thinking types.

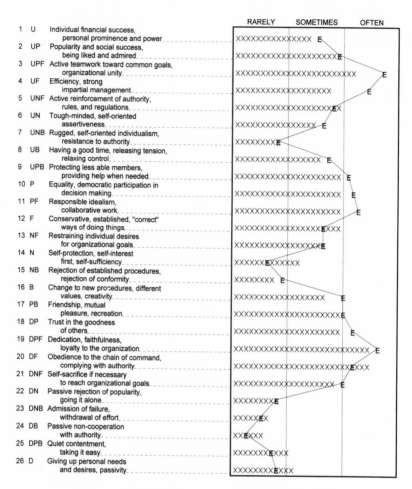

Figure 3 Ratings for All Feeling Types on 26 SYMLOG Values

Note. Bar of Xs = the average rating on each item; E = the "optimum" location for most effective teamwork.

The differences among the MBTI types in their fit with the optimum profile of values for teamwork are directly related to the research questions and are consistent with the results of the multivariate test of differences among MBTI types: Co-workers clearly saw differences among leaders with varying MBTI types in expression of some values.

For example, the four Thinking Judging types were consistently seen as underemphasizing trust in the goodness of others (18), while all but one other type were seen as close to optimal on this value. Similarly, three of four Introverted types, but none of the Extraverted types, were seen underemphasizing popularity (2).

LEADERS' PERCEIVED VALUES BY TYPE

To get a more complete picture of leaders' values as perceived by their co-workers, we separated the leaders into their MBTI type categories and constructed a SYMLOG bar graph of the average rating for all leaders of a particular type. The following analyses are based on Table 3 and the bar graph for each type.

ESTJ Leaders

The SYMLOG bar graph for one of the most common MBTI types among the leaders of this organization, ESTJ, appears in Figure 4. Labeled by Kroeger and Thuesen (1992) as "natural administrators," these 65 leaders matched the Most Effective Profile exactly on nine values (despite the sensitivity of the standard error tests with such a large N) and approximately matched on all but six of them. So, the ESTJs were probably seen as highly effective leaders in this culture.

These leaders departed from the SYMLOG Most Effective Profile on six values. As a group, ESTJ leaders were seen as underemphasizing the following:

- Active teamwork toward common goals (3)
- Efficiency, strong impartial management (4)
- Equality (10)
- Responsible idealism, collaborative work (11)
- Trust in the goodness of others (18)

ESTJ leaders were seen as overemphasizing:

- Self-protection, self-interest first (14)

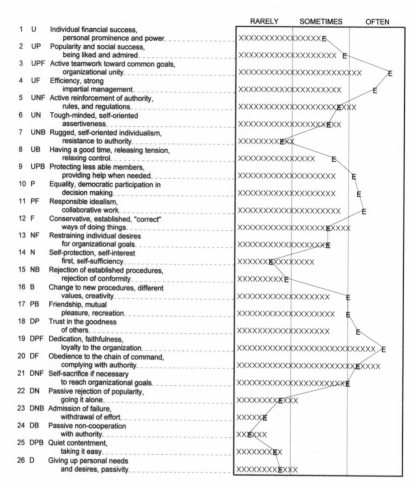

Figure 4 Ratings for ESTJs on 26 SYMLOG Values

Note. Bar of Xs = the average rating on each item; E = the "optimum" location for most effective teamwork.

Their pattern of underemphasizing values 3 and 4 and of overemphasizing value 14 followed the culture. The other three departures for ESTJs are all underemphasizing of friendly values and are consistent with a decisive, action-oriented approach that may fail to fully consider the views of others before taking action. This decisive, action-oriented approach has been attributed to ESTJs' Extraverted Thinking (Hirsh & Kummerow, 1989). Except for these departures, the bar graph closely paralleled the Most Effective Profile.

In comparison with leaders with Feeling preferences, ESTJs were seen as similar in frequency of expression of friendly values—only a small, insignificant difference favored the Feeling types on item 17, friendliness, for example. While the ESTJs apparently occupied an environment that reinforced their dominant Thinking judgment, they seem to have developed some of the skills needed to establish friendly relationships. It is possible that their co-workers saw their authority-aligned, detailed initiatives as both friendly and focused. This is consistent with the perceptions of ESTJs, in Thorne and Gough's (1991) study, reported as being aware of the correct thing to do, oriented to power in self and others, and gregarious.

ESTP Leaders

The SYMLOG bar graph for ratings of 10 ESTP leaders appears in Figure 5. Counting items that departed from the Most Effective Profile on both tests, the bar graph shows significantly different values on only five items, including the three departures on cultural constants that all leader MBTI types shared in common.

ESTP leaders were seen as underemphasizing the following:

- Active teamwork toward a common goal (3)
- Efficiency, strong impartial management (4)
- Equality (10)
- Responsible idealism and collaborative work (11)

ESTP leaders were seen as overemphasizing:

- Self-protection, self-interest first (14)

The two departures from optimum that were not cultural constants were shared by most of the Extraverted and Thinking types (the only exception is ENTPs on item 10), suggesting that co-workers may have noticed a tendency more toward individual decisiveness than cooperativeness among these Extraverted and Thinking leaders.

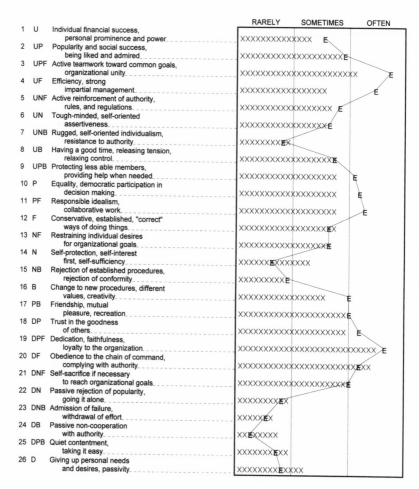

Figure 5 Ratings for ESTPs on 26 SYMLOG Values

Note. Bar of Xs = the average rating on each item; E = the "optimum" location for most effective teamwork.

ESTPs were among the leaders seen as closest to expressing the optimum values for teamwork in a culture where leaders with Judging preferences predominated. ESTPs also tended to be seen in the middle of the range on most SYMLOG values and were seen as significantly different from other types on few items. (They only differed from INTPs where INTPs were outliers.) Perhaps ESTPs' dominant Sensing function and its practical, grounded approach helped them stay focused on the organization's tasks and avoid what for them may have been a temptation to offer alternatives to authoritative directives. Another explanation for ESTPs' effectiveness is that they may have reached leadership positions only after mastering the Judging skills needed to succeed in a structured, deadline-conscious organization.

ENTJ Leaders

The SYMLOG bar graph for 37 ENTJ leaders appears in Figure 6. Co-workers' ratings on their expressed values departed from the Most Effective Profile on both tests on nine items, including six departures that differentiated them from some of the other MBTI types. Overall, their SYMLOG profile suggests that they were seen as effective leaders, but not as effective as most other Thinking types. While perhaps able to realize their label as "life's natural leaders" in some settings (Kroeger with Thuesen, 1992), ENTJs were perhaps seen here as they were in Thorne and Gough's (1991) study—as ambitious and power oriented.

Compared with the SYMLOG Most Effective Profile, ENTJ leaders were seen as underemphasizing the following:

- Active teamwork toward a common goal (3)
- Efficiency, strong impartial management (4)
- Having a good time (8)
- Protecting less able members (9)
- Equality (10)
- Collaborative work (11)
- Friendship (17)
- Trust in the goodness of others (18)

ENTJ leaders were seen as overemphasizing:

- Self-protection, self-interest first (14)

Underemphasizing having a good time (8) is consistent with the serious approach expected of dominant Extraverted Thinking. The ENTJs

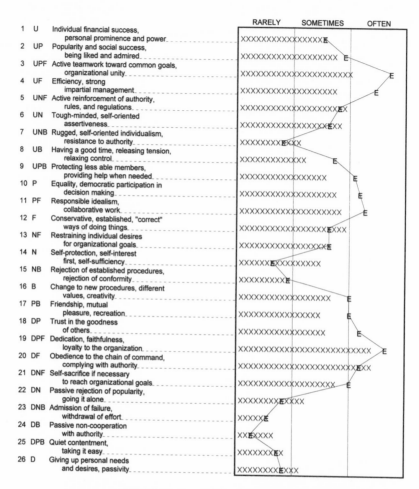

			RARELY	SOMETIMES	OFTEN
1	U	Individual financial success, personal prominence and power			
2	UP	Popularity and social success, being liked and admired			
3	UPF	Active teamwork toward common goals, organizational unity			
4	UF	Efficiency, strong impartial management			
5	UNF	Active reinforcement of authority, rules, and regulations			
6	UN	Tough-minded, self-oriented assertiveness			
7	UNB	Rugged, self-oriented individualism, resistance to authority			
8	UB	Having a good time, releasing tension, relaxing control			
9	UPB	Protecting less able members, providing help when needed			
10	P	Equality, democratic participation in decision making			
11	PF	Responsible idealism, collaborative work			
12	F	Conservative, established, "correct" ways of doing things			
13	NF	Restraining individual desires for organizational goals			
14	N	Self-protection, self-interest first, self-sufficiency			
15	NB	Rejection of established procedures, rejection of conformity			
16	B	Change to new procedures, different values, creativity			
17	PB	Friendship, mutual pleasure, recreation			
18	DP	Trust in the goodness of others			
19	DPF	Dedication, faithfulness, loyalty to the organization			
20	DF	Obedience to the chain of command, complying with authority			
21	DNF	Self-sacrifice if necessary to reach organizational goals			
22	DN	Passive rejection of popularity, going it alone			
23	DNB	Admission of failure, withdrawal of effort			
24	DB	Passive non-cooperation with authority			
25	DPB	Quiet contentment, taking it easy			
26	D	Giving up personal needs and desires, passivity			

Figure 6 Ratings for ENTJs on 26 SYMLOG Values

Note. Bar of Xs = the average rating on each item; E = the "optimum" location for most effective teamwork.

were also seen as underemphasizing protecting less able members (9), perhaps reflecting impatience growing out of the Judging preference. Other TJ types also tended to underemphasize items 8 and 9, and all were lower on these values than Feeling types and the TP leaders in the study. ENTJs were also seen expressing self-interest significantly more often than INTJs, consistent with perceptions of ENTJs as ambitious for themselves. Some ENTJ individuals in the group privately described clear and specific political aspirations for advancement in the organization.

These perceptions suggest that ENTJs may have found themselves in a culture that reinforced their dominant Thinking more than it fostered type development. These ENTJs apparently faced a continuing challenge to incorporate what Hirsh and Kummerow (1989) have called the "human element" into their leadership styles.

ENTP Leaders

The bar graph for 26 leaders whose MBTI type is ENTP appears in Figure 7. It reveals that ENTP leaders were seen by co-workers as matching the Most Effective Profile more closely than any other Thinking type besides ESTP. The ENTP leaders approximately matched the optimal profile on all but five values, three of which were cultural constants. Like the ESTPs, ENTPs apparently were seen as highly effective leaders in this Judging culture. EPs are typically described as enjoying and being stimulated by interaction with others, which may contribute to their being seen as effective leaders of teams.

ENTP leaders were seen as underemphasizing:

- Active teamwork toward a common goal (3)
- Efficiency, strong impartial management (4)
- Collaborative work (11)
- Trust in the goodness of others (18)

In underemphasizing items 3 and 4, ENTPs were following the cultural constants in the organization. In underemphasizing items 11 and 18, ENTPs are like other Extraverted and Thinking types.

Co-workers saw ENTPs expressing some values more or less than other MBTI types. ENTPs were seen as overemphasizing the following:

- Self-protection, self-interest first (14)
- Popularity and social success (2) more than ISTJs and INTJs, who were low on this value

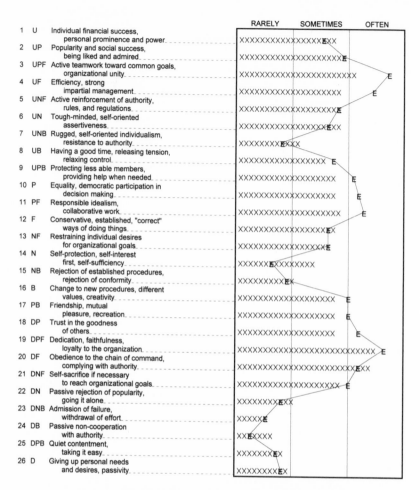

			RARELY	SOMETIMES	OFTEN
1	U	Individual financial success, personal prominence and power	XXXXXXXXXXXXXXXXXXEXX		
2	UP	Popularity and social success, being liked and admired	XXXXXXXXXXXXXXXXXXXXXE		
3	UPF	Active teamwork toward common goals, organizational unity	XXXXXXXXXXXXXXXXXXXXXXXX		E
4	UF	Efficiency, strong impartial management	XXXXXXXXXXXXXXXXXXXXX		E
5	UNF	Active reinforcement of authority, rules, and regulations	XXXXXXXXXXXXXXXXXXXXE		
6	UN	Tough-minded, self-oriented assertiveness	XXXXXXXXXXXXXXXXXEXX		
7	UNB	Rugged, self-oriented individualism, resistance to authority	XXXXXXXXEXXX		
8	UB	Having a good time, releasing tension, relaxing control	XXXXXXXXXXXXXXXXX E		
9	UPB	Protecting less able members, providing help when needed	XXXXXXXXXXXXXXXXXX	E	
10	P	Equality, democratic participation in decision making	XXXXXXXXXXXXXXXXXX	E	
11	PF	Responsible idealism, collaborative work	XXXXXXXXXXXXXXXXXX		E
12	F	Conservative, established, "correct" ways of doing things	XXXXXXXXXXXXXXXXXEX		
13	NF	Restraining individual desires for organizational goals	XXXXXXXXXXXXXXXXXXXE		
14	N	Self-protection, self-interest first, self-sufficiency	XXXXXXEXXXXXXX		
15	NB	Rejection of established procedures, rejection of conformity	XXXXXXXXXEX		
16	B	Change to new procedures, different values, creativity	XXXXXXXXXXXXXXXXXX	E	
17	PB	Friendship, mutual pleasure, recreation	XXXXXXXXXXXXXXXXXX	E	
18	DP	Trust in the goodness of others	XXXXXXXXXXXXXXXXXX	E	
19	DPF	Dedication, faithfulness, loyalty to the organization	XXXXXXXXXXXXXXXXXXXXXXXXXXXX		E
20	DF	Obedience to the chain of command, complying with authority	XXXXXXXXXXXXXXXXXXXXXXXXXXXEXX		
21	DNF	Self-sacrifice if necessary to reach organizational goals	XXXXXXXXXXXXXXXXXXXXXX	E	
22	DN	Passive rejection of popularity, going it alone	XXXXXXXXXEXX		
23	DNB	Admission of failure, withdrawal of effort	XXXXXE		
24	DB	Passive non-cooperation with authority	XXEXXXX		
25	DPB	Quiet contentment, taking it easy	XXXXXXXEX		
26	D	Giving up personal needs and desires, passivity	XXXXXXXXEX		

Figure 7 Ratings for ENTPs on 26 SYMLOG Values

Note. Bar of Xs = the average rating on each item; E = the "optimum" location for most effective teamwork.

- Having a good time (8) more than ENTJs and ISTJs, who underemphasized it
- Friendship (17) more than ENTJs, ISTJs, and INTJs, all of whom underemphasized friendliness
- Active reinforcement of authority (5) less than ESTJs or ISTJs
- Obedience (20) less than ISTJs and INTJs, both of whom tended to overemphasize obedience

In brief, the ENTP leaders came closer to the optimal profile than their Thinking Judging co-workers on both friendly values and authority-aligned values.

ISTJ Leaders

The SYMLOG values bar graph for the most prevalent MBTI type in this population of leaders, ISTJ, appears in Figure 8. Of 26 items, co-workers' averaged ratings of 107 ISTJ leaders approximately matched the Most Effective Profile on all but eight items, including departures that represented cultural constants (underemphasis on items 3 and 4, and overemphasis on item 14). The ISTJ column in Table 3 shows many differences of three or more standard errors, which are relatively small in absolute terms because of the large number of ratees.

On several values, the ISTJs distinguished themselves from leaders of other MBTI types. Consistent with descriptions of ISTJ leaders as dependable, responsible, detail oriented, and "calm and cool, . . . even somewhat undemonstrative" (Kroeger with Thuesen, 1992, p. 303), their co-workers saw them expressing authority-aligned values relatively often and friendly values relatively infrequently. ISTJ leaders were seen as overemphasizing the following:

- Self-protection, self-interest first (14)
- Conservative and correct ways of doing things (12) more than any other type
- Obedience (20) more than any other type
- Conservative, correct ways (12) more than any other type except INTJs

Overemphasis of authority-oriented values is consistent with ISTJs' dominant Sensing function as well as with the organizational culture. In effect, the culture may have invited ISTJs to express values consistent with their preferences.

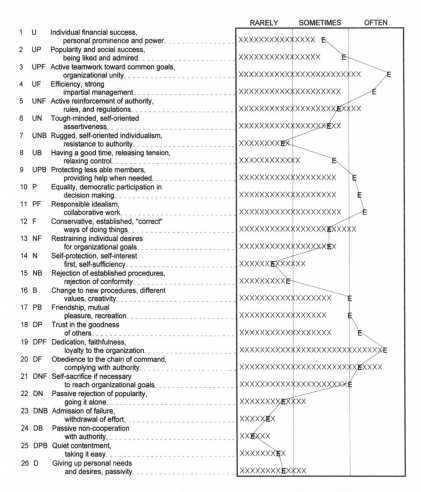

Figure 8 Ratings for ISTJs on 26 SYMLOG Values

Note. Bar of Xs = the average rating on each item; E = the "optimum" location for most effective teamwork.

Compared with the Most Effective Profile, ISTJ leaders were seen as underemphasizing the following:

- Active teamwork toward common goals (3)
- Efficiency, strong impartial management (4)
- Popularity and social success (2)
- Having a good time (8)
- Friendship (17)
- Trust in the goodness of others (18)

Co-workers saw ISTJs express these friendly values less often than ESTJs, ENTPs, and the Feeling types. These perceptions are not unexpected for Introverted and Thinking types, who must work against their preferences to a certain extent to act outgoing and friendly. Also, to express these values, they may have to oppose a culture that overvalues self-interest and undervalues teamwork.

ISTP Leaders

The profile for the 12 leaders whose MBTI type is ISTP appears in Figure 9. ISTP leaders approximately matched the optimal profile on all but six of the values, suggesting that they were seen as highly effective leaders in this culture.

Besides the cultural constants, ISTPs were seen as deviating from the Most Effective Profile on three values. ISTP leaders were seen as underemphasizing:

- Active teamwork toward a common goal (3)
- Efficiency, strong impartial management (4)
- Having a good time (8)
- Friendship (17)
- Equality (10)

  ISTP leaders were seen as overemphasizing

- Self-protection, self-interest first (14)
- Obedience (20) more than INTPs

However, ISTPs were not seen as significantly different from other MBTI types on any of the other values, suggesting that they occupied a cultural middle ground on the values important to teamwork. This in itself is compatible with dominant Introverted Thinking and auxiliary Extraverted Sensing, a combination seen as allowing ISTPs to be observant of their environment, capable of discerning what is acceptable, and acting with necessary restraint (Myers & Kirby, 1994).

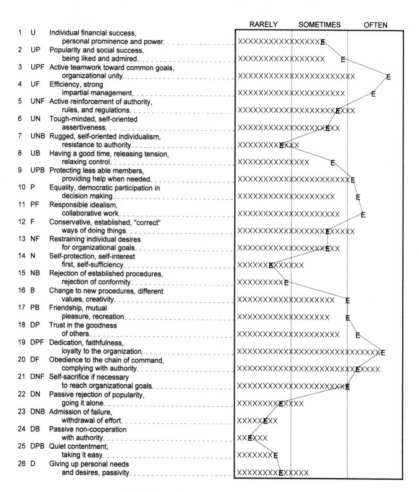

			RARELY	SOMETIMES	OFTEN
1	U	Individual financial success, personal prominence and power	XXXXXXXXXXXXXXXXX**E**		
2	UP	Popularity and social success, being liked and admired	XXXXXXXXXXXXXXXX	**E**	
3	UPF	Active teamwork toward common goals, organizational unity	XXXXXXXXXXXXXXXXXXXXXXXXX		**E**
4	UF	Efficiency, strong impartial management	XXXXXXXXXXXXXXXXXXXXX	**E**	
5	UNF	Active reinforcement of authority, rules, and regulations	XXXXXXXXXXXXXXXXXXX**E**XXX		
6	UN	Tough-minded, self-oriented assertiveness	XXXXXXXXXXXXXXXXX**E**XX		
7	UNB	Rugged, self-oriented individualism, resistance to authority	XXXXXXXX**E**XXX		
8	UB	Having a good time, releasing tension, relaxing control	XXXXXXXXXXXXXXX	**E**	
9	UPB	Protecting less able members, providing help when needed	XXXXXXXXXXXXXXXXXXXXXXXXXX**E**		
10	P	Equality, democratic participation in decision making	XXXXXXXXXXXXXXXXXXX	**E**	
11	PF	Responsible idealism, collaborative work	XXXXXXXXXXXXXXXXXXX	**E**	
12	F	Conservative, established, "correct" ways of doing things	XXXXXXXXXXXXXXXXXXX**E**XXXXX		
13	NF	Restraining individual desires for organizational goals	XXXXXXXXXXXXXXXXXXX**E**XX		
14	N	Self-protection, self-interest first, self-sufficiency	XXXXXX**E**XXXXXX		
15	NB	Rejection of established procedures, rejection of conformity	XXXXXXXXX**E**		
16	B	Change to new procedures, different values, creativity	XXXXXXXXXXXXXXXXXXX	**E**	
17	PB	Friendship, mutual pleasure, recreation	XXXXXXXXXXXXXXXXX	**E**	
18	DP	Trust in the goodness of others	XXXXXXXXXXXXXXXXXX	**E**	
19	DPF	Dedication, faithfulness, loyalty to the organization	XXXXXXXXXXXXXXXXXXXXXXXXXXXXXX**E**		
20	DF	Obedience to the chain of command, complying with authority	XXXXXXXXXXXXXXXXXXXXXXXXXX**E**XXXX		
21	DNF	Self-sacrifice if necessary to reach organizational goals	XXXXXXXXXXXXXXXXXXXXXX**E**		
22	DN	Passive rejection of popularity, going it alone	XXXXXXXX**E**XXXX		
23	DNB	Admission of failure, withdrawal of effort	XXXXX**E**XX		
24	DB	Passive non-cooperation with authority	XX**E**XXX		
25	DPB	Quiet contentment, taking it easy	XXXXXXX**E**		
26	D	Giving up personal needs and desires, passivity	XXXXXXXX**E**XXXXX		

Figure 9 Ratings for ISTPs on 26 SYMLOG Values

Note. Bar of Xs = the average rating on each item; E = the "optimum" location for most effective teamwork.

INTJ Leaders

The profile for 51 leaders whose MBTI type is INTJ appears in Figure 10, which shows averaged ratings by 379 co-workers. The bar graph approximates the Most Effective Profile of values for teamwork on 17 values and departs significantly on nine values, including the three cultural constants.

Co-workers' ratings showed INTJs underemphasizing several friendly values in comparison with the SYMLOG Most Effective Profile. INTJ leaders were seen as underemphasizing:

- Active teamwork toward a common goal (3)
- Efficiency, strong impartial management (4)
- Popularity and social success (2), on which they were also significantly lower than ESTJs, ENTPs, and Feeling types
- Protecting less able members (9)
- Having a good time (8)
- Friendship (17)

INTJ leaders were seen as overemphasizing:

- Self-protection, self-interest first (14)
- Conservative, established, correct ways of doing things (12)
- Obedience (20) more often than any other type except ISTJs

In brief, INTJs were seen as placing relatively little value on friendly, social relationships and as being relatively authority aligned.

INTJs in the present study were perceived much as they were in Thorne and Gough (1991), where they were characterized as overcontrolled, rational, conservative, and as keeping people at a distance. The present organizational culture probably reinforced their auxiliary Extraverted Thinking but may not have provided a way to demonstrate their dominant Introverted Intuition or to develop and use their Feeling function.

INTP Leaders

The bar graph for the 10 leaders whose MBTI type is INTP appears in Figure 11. It reveals that INTP leaders were seen by co-workers as departing from the Most Effective Profile on more values than any other leader MBTI type in this study. INTPs deviated from the optimum profile on 13 values, including several that generally interfere with teamwork.

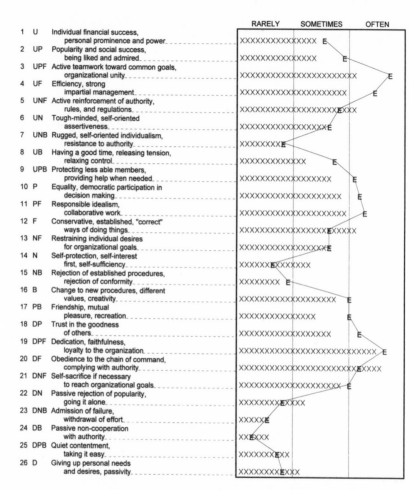

			RARELY	SOMETIMES	OFTEN
1	U	Individual financial success, personal prominence and power	XXXXXXXXXXXXXXX E		
2	UP	Popularity and social success, being liked and admired	XXXXXXXXXXXXXXX E		
3	UPF	Active teamwork toward common goals, organizational unity	XXXXXXXXXXXXXXXXXXXXXXXXX E		
4	UF	Efficiency, strong impartial management	XXXXXXXXXXXXXXXXXXXXXX E		
5	UNF	Active reinforcement of authority, rules, and regulations	XXXXXXXXXXXXXXXXXXXXXXEXXX		
6	UN	Tough-minded, self-oriented assertiveness	XXXXXXXXXXXXXXXXXXXXEE		
7	UNB	Rugged, self-oriented individualism, resistance to authority	XXXXXXXXE		
8	UB	Having a good time, releasing tension, relaxing control	XXXXXXXXXXXXXXX E		
9	UPB	Protecting less able members, providing help when needed	XXXXXXXXXXXXXXXXXXX E		
10	P	Equality, democratic participation in decision making	XXXXXXXXXXXXXXXXXXX E		
11	PF	Responsible idealism, collaborative work	XXXXXXXXXXXXXXXXXXXXXX E		
12	F	Conservative, established, "correct" ways of doing things	XXXXXXXXXXXXXXXXXXXXEXXXXX		
13	NF	Restraining individual desires for organizational goals	XXXXXXXXXXXXXXXXXXXXE		
14	N	Self-protection, self-interest first, self-sufficiency	XXXXXXXEXXXXXXX		
15	NB	Rejection of established procedures, rejection of conformity	XXXXXXXX E		
16	B	Change to new procedures, different values, creativity	XXXXXXXXXXXXXXXXXXX E		
17	PB	Friendship, mutual pleasure, recreation	XXXXXXXXXXXXXXX E		
18	DP	Trust in the goodness of others	XXXXXXXXXXXXXXXXXX E		
19	DPF	Dedication, faithfulness, loyalty to the organization	XXXXXXXXXXXXXXXXXXXXXXXXXXXXXX E		
20	DF	Obedience to the chain of command, complying with authority	XXXXXXXXXXXXXXXXXXXXXXXXXXEXXXX		
21	DNF	Self-sacrifice if necessary to reach organizational goals	XXXXXXXXXXXXXXXXXXXXXX E		
22	DN	Passive rejection of popularity, going it alone	XXXXXXXXXEXXXX		
23	DNB	Admission of failure, withdrawal of effort	XXXXXE		
24	DB	Passive non-cooperation with authority	XXEXXX		
25	DPB	Quiet contentment, taking it easy	XXXXXXXEXX		
26	D	Giving up personal needs and desires, passivity	XXXXXXXXEXXX		

SYMLOG Consulting Group   18580 Polvera Dr.   San Diego, CA 92128   (619)-673-2098
Copyright 1983, 1995 R.F. Bales. All Rights Reserved.

Figure 10   Ratings for INTJs on 26 SYMLOG Values

Note. Bar of Xs = the average rating on each item; E = the "optimum" location for most effective teamwork.

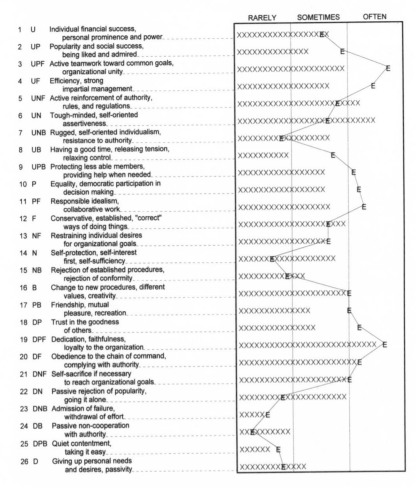

			RARELY	SOMETIMES	OFTEN
1	U	Individual financial success, personal prominence and power	XXXXXXXXXXXXXXXXXXEX		
2	UP	Popularity and social success, being liked and admired	XXXXXXXXXXXXXXX E		
3	UPF	Active teamwork toward common goals, organizational unity	XXXXXXXXXXXXXXXXXXXXXXXX E		
4	UF	Efficiency, strong impartial management	XXXXXXXXXXXXXXXXXXXX E		
5	UNF	Active reinforcement of authority, rules, and regulations	XXXXXXXXXXXXXXXXXXXXXXEXXXX		
6	UN	Tough-minded, self-oriented assertiveness	XXXXXXXXXXXXXXXXXXXXEXXXXXXXXX		
7	UNB	Rugged, self-oriented individualism, resistance to authority	XXXXXXXXEXXXXXXXX		
8	UB	Having a good time, releasing tension, relaxing control	XXXXXXXXXX E		
9	UPB	Protecting less able members, providing help when needed	XXXXXXXXXXXXXXXXX E		
10	P	Equality, democratic participation in decision making	XXXXXXXXXXXXXXXXX E		
11	PF	Responsible idealism, collaborative work	XXXXXXXXXXXXXXXXXX E		
12	F	Conservative, established, "correct" ways of doing things	XXXXXXXXXXXXXXXXXXXXXEXXX		
13	NF	Restraining individual desires for organizational goals	XXXXXXXXXXXXXXXXXXXXE		
14	N	Self-protection, self-interest first, self-sufficiency	XXXXXXXEXXXXXXXXXXX		
15	NB	Rejection of established procedures, rejection of conformity	XXXXXXXXXXEXXX		
16	B	Change to new procedures, different values, creativity	XXXXXXXXXXXXXXXXXXXXXXXXXXE		
17	PB	Friendship, mutual pleasure, recreation	XXXXXXXXXXXXXX E		
18	DP	Trust in the goodness of others	XXXXXXXXXXXXXX E		
19	DPF	Dedication, faithfulness, loyalty to the organization	XXXXXXXXXXXXXXXXXXXXXXXXXXXXXXX E		
20	DF	Obedience to the chain of command, complying with authority	XXXXXXXXXXXXXXXXXXXXXXXXE		
21	DNF	Self-sacrifice if necessary to reach organizational goals	XXXXXXXXXXXXXXXXXXXXXXXXE		
22	DN	Passive rejection of popularity, going it alone	XXXXXXXXEXXXXXXXXXXX		
23	DNB	Admission of failure, withdrawal of effort	XXXXXE		
24	DB	Passive non-cooperation with authority	XXEXXXXXXX		
25	DPB	Quiet contentment, taking it easy	XXXXXX E		
26	D	Giving up personal needs and desires, passivity	XXXXXXXXEXXX		

Figure 11 Ratings for INTPs on 26 SYMLOG Values

Note. Bar of Xs = the average rating on each item; E = the "optimum" location for most effective teamwork.

Like the other Introverts, INTPs were seen by co-workers as under-emphasizing several friendly values. INTP leaders were seen as under-emphasizing:

- Active teamwork toward a common goal (3)
- Efficiency, strong impartial management (4)
- Popularity and social success (2), on which they were significantly lower than ESTJs, ENTPs, and Feeling types
- Having a good time (8), which they were seen expressing less often than Feeling types
- Protecting less able members (9)
- Collaborative work (11)
- Trust in the goodness of others (18)
- Friendship (17)

Co-workers saw INTPs not only as undervaluing friendly social relationships, but also as expressing unfriendly values detrimental to teamwork. INTP leaders were seen as overemphasizing:

- Self-protection, self-interest first (14)
- Self-oriented assertiveness (6) more than any other type
- Resistance to authority (7) more than any other type
- Passive rejection of popularity, going it alone (22) more than any other type
- Passive noncooperation with authority (24)

According to Bales (1990), the particular values overemphasized by INTPs almost always interfere with teamwork.

INTPs have previously been characterized as "rebellious and non-conforming" and as "critical, skeptical, and not easily impressed" (Thorne & Gough, 1991, p. 87). This is not surprising in light of their combination of dominant Introverted Thinking and auxiliary Extraverted Intuition. In the participants' culture, which might be characterized as authoritarian and more focused on self-interest than efficiency, INTPs may have found much to criticize and few allies willing to join in their criticism.

USING SYMLOG WITH LEADERS

An important, practical feature of SYMLOG is that it offers individual leaders the opportunity to compare their ratings against the SYMLOG Most Effective Profile. Usual practice in interpreting SYMLOG results includes not only a set of ratings by co-workers on the individual's actual values, but also the ideal values for that individual to express in order to be most effective. In effect, the practitioner sets up two comparisons involving the leader's values as seen by co-workers: the Most Effective Profile and the ideal profile for the leader in his or her organization.

Using information in this chapter about significant differences between values expressed by different MBTI types may also provide another valuable perspective for understanding and using individual SYMLOG results. Our findings in the present study and our experience in working with leaders from many organizations suggest that various MBTI types tend to be rated in ways consistent with their personalities, even those who have worked at type development. For example, it is unusual for an Introverted Perceiving type to be rated optimal on item 4, "Efficiency, strong impartial management." Knowing the leader's MBTI type may suggest which items are most likely to prompt discussion.

The SYMLOG Feedback Process

While SYMLOG is different from other management feedback instruments in that it measures values (see Chapter 5 of this volume), the process is similar to that used for other feedback instruments. A typical application begins with a planning session in which the leader and practitioner agree that the leader wants feedback and that SYMLOG is an appropriate vehicle for generating it. The leader identifies people from whom he or she wants to receive feedback. Some leaders want to learn how they are perceived by subordinates, peers, and even higher-ranking individuals. Experience suggests that the three perspectives may be different enough to keep separate (different profiles). However, some leaders may want to receive combined, or 360-degree, feedback.

A reliable SYMLOG profile calls for ratings by a minimum of five co-workers. Each is asked to rate the individual's actual values and the values that represent the ideal for greatest effectiveness by that individual. Rating forms are collected in sealed envelopes by someone other than the ratee to assure confidentiality, and then sent to SYMLOG Consulting Group to generate bar graphs and a report. The bar graphs for actual and ideal values resemble those shown in this chapter. The SYMLOG report helps each individual identify current strengths in leadership and areas to consider for personal development.

The practitioner delivers the bar graphs and reports to the leader at a second meeting, with instructions. The first instruction is to read the whole report and to resist skipping over some sections. Thinking types especially may tend to skip over parts of the report that describe how they are seen as matching the optimal profile (what they're doing "right"). Instead, they may skip ahead and read about how they are in departure from the optimal (what's "wrong"). We have found that the Introverted and Thinking types especially need firm guidance toward reading the positive features of their profiles. A second caution is to avoid dismissing the feedback, which is, after all, only a summary of the perceptions of a few co-workers. Other cautions include putting aside the impulse to "shoot the messenger" (raters) or the temptation to rationalize the feedback.

Using SYMLOG Results

After the leader has read the report, the practitioner and leader meet to interpret the feedback and identify specific next steps. The goal is to find two or three practical things the leader can do to improve his or her effectiveness with the people who provided the ratings. The practitioner can help by steering away from the technical details of SYMLOG and focusing instead on its value in helping to develop specific plans for improving teamwork.

One action that usually makes sense is for the leader to meet co-workers and ask for more specific feedback on a few points of particular concern (three or four at most). The resulting conversation may be one of the more valuable outcomes of using SYMLOG. The leader might ask what the co-worker(s) would like to see continued and what they would recommend that the leader do more and less often. It is important in such situations for the leader to listen without arguing. It helps for the practitioner and leader to discuss in advance whether it is best for the leader to meet co-workers one at a time or in a group, or to develop some other plan.

One ENTJ leader, for example, was rated as overemphasizing self-oriented assertiveness. He met his co-workers and asked them for feedback. They said that at most meetings he talked too much and offered his opinion too early. He asked what he could do differently and was told to talk less and ask more questions. He agreed that, in the future, every time he made an assertion at a meeting, he would immediately follow it up with an open-ended question.

As a starting point, the practitioner can suggest that the leader look at values he or she is seen as overemphasizing that also interfere with teamwork. This means looking for departures from the Most Effective Profile that coincide with departures from what co-workers saw as ideal in the leader's situation.

For example, one ISTJ leader was rated high on going it alone (22), and his subordinates indicated an ideal value much lower than the actual. In other words, his co-workers wanted to see less frequent expression of a value that he also overemphasized in relation to the most effective profile. He planned to change this perception by starting one-on-one projects with each of several individuals, emphasizing collaborative work (11), which he also underemphasized.

Using SYMLOG to Improve Team Leadership

Bales (1983) identified eight SYMLOG items that almost always interfere with teamwork:

- Rugged, self-oriented individualism, resistance to authority (7)
- Self-protection, self-interest first, self-sufficiency (14)
- Rejection of established procedures, rejection of conformity (15)
- Passive rejection of popularity, going it alone (22)
- Admission of failure, withdrawal of effort (23)
- Passive noncooperation with authority (24)
- Quiet contentment, taking it easy (25)
- Giving up personal needs and desires, passivity (26)

For those seen as overemphasizing one of these values, the practitioner can help by asking what the leader might do as a positive way to change the perception. A leader who was seen as too high on passive noncooperation with authority (24) might replace that value with actions consistent with an underemphasized value, such as Responsible idealism, collaborative work (11). For one leader, this meant looking for ways to cooperate with a peer whenever he felt the urge to stonewall the boss.

Once the leader has identified two or three areas for development, the practitioner might arrange for a second set of ratings, say, in six months or so, to see whether the leader's plans succeeded in changing co-workers' perceptions.

CONCLUSIONS

Our analysis of co-workers' perceptions of leaders with eight MBTI types suggests three conclusions. First, the eight common MBTI leader types differed from one another and from the SYMLOG Most Effective

Profile in ways consistent with their preferences. Second, the organizational culture apparently discouraged differences among MBTI types that might have emerged on values that represented cultural constants. Third, the culture probably reinforced type development for some types—notably ESTPs, ENTPs, and ISTPs—while inviting others to act out their preferences. For the practitioner, SYMLOG provides a helpful tool for leader feedback, which can be used to identify specific areas of development.

ACKNOWLEDGMENTS

We thank Sharon Hare of SYMLOG Consulting Group for generating the bar graphs and helping us interpret them. We appreciate assistance by Mark Palmerino in developing the original data set, and acknowledge the support of the University of Tennessee Computing Center in statistical analysis of the data. We also appreciate helpful suggestions from Catherine Fitzgerald and Linda Kirby in interpreting differences among leaders' profiles.

REFERENCES

Bachman, W. (1988). Nice guys finish first: A SYMLOG analysis of U.S. Naval commands. In R. B. Polley, A. P. Hare, & P. J. Stone (Eds.), *The SYMLOG practitioner* (pp. 133–153). New York: Praeger.

Bales, R. F. (1950a). *Interaction process analysis.* Reading, MA: Addison-Wesley.

Bales, R. F. (1950b). A set of categories for the analysis of small group interaction. *American Sociological Review, 15,* 257–263.

Bales, R. F. (1958). Task roles and social roles in problem-solving groups. In E. E. Maccoby, T. M. Newcomb, & E. L. Hartley (Eds.), *Readings in social psychology* (3d ed., pp. 437–447). New York: Holt, Rinehart and Winston.

Bales, R. F. (1970). *Personality and interpersonal behavior.* New York: Holt, Rinehart and Winston.

Bales, R. F. (1983). *The SYMLOG key to individual and organizational values.* San Diego, CA: SYMLOG Consulting Group.

Bales, R. F. (1988). A new overview of the SYMLOG system. In R. B. Polley, A. P. Hare, & P. J. Stone (Eds.), *The SYMLOG practitioner* (pp. 319–344). New York: Praeger.

Bales, R. F. (1990). *The new (1990) SYMLOG normative (most effective) profile for the value bargraph.* San Diego: SYMLOG Consulting Group.

Bales, R. F., Cohen, S. P., & Williamson, S. A. (1979). *SYMLOG: A system for multiple level observation of groups.* New York: Free Press.

Bales, R. F., & Koenigs, R. J. (1992). *Images that guide leadership: The SYMLOG reference field diagram.* San Diego: SYMLOG Consulting Group.

Bales, R. F., Koenigs, R. J., & Roman, P. D. (1987). Criteria for adaptation of SYMLOG rating items to particular populations and cultural contexts. *International Journal of Small Group Research, 3,* 161–179.

Blake, R. R., & Mouton, J. S. (1978). *The new managerial "grid."* Houston: Gulf.

Hirsh, S. J., & Kummerow, J. M. (1989). *LifeTypes*. New York: Warner.

Koenigs, R. J. (1990). *A SYMLOG profile of American business: Leaders, teams, and organizations.* San Diego, CA: SYMLOG Consulting Group..

Kroeger, O., with Thuesen, J. M. (1990). *Type talk at work*. New York: Delacorte.

McGrath, J. E. (1984). *Groups: Interaction and performance.* Englewood Cliffs, NJ: Prentice Hall.

Myers, I. B. (1987) *Introduction to type*. Palo Alto, CA: Consulting Psychologists Press.

Myers, K. D., & Kirby, L. K. (1994). *Introduction to type dynamics and development.* Palo Alto, CA: Consulting Psychologists Press.

Thorne, A., & Gough, H. (1991). *Portraits of type: An MBTI research compendium.* Palo Alto, CA: Davies-Black.

PART THREE

Applying the MBTI to Management and Leadership Development

9 | Applying Type Dynamics to Leadership Development

Catherine Fitzgerald

Linda K. Kirby

The *Myers-Briggs Type Indicator* (MBTI) four-letter type code indicates more than the sum of the characteristics of the four preferences: Each of the preferences influences the way the other three are expressed, resulting in 16 dynamic pictures of normal functioning. Type dynamics explains this interaction of the preferences within a particular type.

Much of the value and practicality of type comes from its dynamic theory, which was developed by Carl Jung (1976) and elaborated by Katharine Briggs and Isabel Myers (Myers & McCaulley, 1985; Myers & Myers, 1980). It is dynamics that keeps types from becoming static boxes into which individuals must fit; and it is dynamics that provides the basic underpinning for type development. Understanding each of the preferences is valuable, as people use this level of type to understand the natural differences that occur in people and appreciate their own and others' strengths. However, using the deeper level of type knowledge that is available through type dynamics provides rich rewards in the fuller understanding and more complex uses of type that can be gained from it.

The purpose of this chapter is to present the theory of type dynamics, provide practical examples, and propose strategies and potential positive outcomes for its use in leadership development. Please note that this chapter is aimed at the intermediate to advanced user of the

MBTI, as type dynamics theory is complex and its understanding relies on a working knowledge of the MBTI preferences.

This chapter contains the following:

- A brief overview of the theory of type dynamics, with a particular focus on the use of the two preferred functions—the dominant and the auxiliary
- A description of each of the four functions—Sensing, Intuition, Thinking, and Feeling—in its *extraverted* form (as you are likely to be able to observe it fairly directly) and in its *introverted* form (as you are likely to need to read between the lines to observe) and some suggestions about working with these functions
- Further description of the interplay among the functions, both under normal circumstances and under stress
- Case examples that illustrate the use of type dynamics with managers
- Strategies for using type dynamics in leadership development
- Potential positive outcomes for the use of type dynamics with leaders

INTRODUCTION TO TYPE DYNAMICS

According to psychological type theory, the four basic mental functions—Sensing, Intuition, Thinking, and Feeling—are used regularly by everyone. They are part of being human. Everyone observes reality in the present tense and stores data (Sensing); everyone sees patterns and meanings in facts (Intuition); everyone applies logical criteria in decision making (Thinking); and everyone uses values in making decisions (Feeling). But not everyone uses the four functions in the same way, gets the same energy from them, or gives them equal weight. Instead, there is an order in which people typically prefer, develop, and use the four preferences. Type dynamics suggests a different process of development and use of each of the four functions for each type.

The terms used to refer to the four functions are as follows:

- The *dominant function*—most preferred, first developed, most relied upon and trusted
- The *auxiliary function*—the second most preferred, and developed, providing balance
- The *tertiary function*—normally the third in order of use and development
- The *inferior function*—normally the least used and developed of the four

The Preferred Functions
(Dominant and Auxiliary Functions)

The MBTI was designed to give people access to a knowledge of their own type dynamics—the normal ways in which people of that type develop and use the four functions. The two middle letters of each type code are the dominant and auxiliary functions for that type. In every type, one of these two functions will be used primarily in the external world, the other in the internal world. According to the theory, people use their preferred process (the dominant function) in their preferred world (extraverted or introverted) and use their second favorite function in their nonpreferred world.

For example, the favorite function of ENTJs is Extraverted Thinking. What people see when they meet ENTJs is logical analysis and decisive action. The second favorite function of this type, Intuition, is much less visible to others because ENTJs use it primarily internally. ENTJs see patterns and make connections, but typically they do not express them directly. Instead, these intuitions surface as logical, structured explanations—in other words, in a Thinking form.

For Introverts, the favorite process is used primarily internally. For example, the favorite function of INTPs is Introverted Thinking. INTPs use their Thinking internally to develop clear, logical explanatory patterns for understanding. INTPs typically express these patterns only when something pushes them to, such as someone else giving what is in the INTP's view an incorrect analysis of a situation. What others normally see is the INTPs' second favorite, or auxiliary, function, Extraverted Intuition, which INTPs use to explore and debate ideas.

Table 1 identifies the dominant, auxiliary, tertiary, and inferior function for each of the 16 types.

UNDERSTANDING THE FUNCTIONS

An important aspect of understanding type dynamics in managers involves understanding each of the four functions—Sensing, Intuition, Thinking, and Feeling—in each of two forms, extraverted and introverted. This section provides descriptions of these functions, with a specific focus on the way that they are likely to appear in a management context and with suggestions for working with these functions. Also, to provide an understanding of the four functions in managers and their organizations, we first discuss the relative presence or absence of these functions in management groups.

TABLE 1   Type Dynamics for Each of the 16 Types

	Dominant	Auxiliary	Tertiary	Inferior
Dominant Sensing Types				
ESTP	Sensing (E)	Thinking (I)	Feeling	Intuition (I)
ESFP	Sensing (E)	Feeling (I)	Thinking	Intuition (I)
ISTJ	Sensing (I)	Thinking (E)	Feeling	Intuition (E)
ISFJ	Sensing (I)	Feeling (E)	Thinking	Intuition (E)
Dominant Intuitive Types				
ENTP	Intuition (E)	Thinking (I)	Feeling	Sensing (I)
ENFP	Intuition (E)	Feeling (I)	Thinking	Sensing (I)
INTJ	Intuition (I)	Thinking (E)	Feeling	Sensing (E)
INFJ	Intuition (I)	Feeling (E)	Thinking	Sensing (E)
Dominant Thinking Types				
ESTJ	Thinking (E)	Sensing (I)	Intuition	Feeling (I)
ENTJ	Thinking (E)	Intuition (I)	Sensing	Feeling (I)
ISTP	Thinking (I)	Sensing (E)	Intuition	Feeling (E)
INTP	Thinking (I)	Intuition (E)	Sensing	Feeling (E)
Dominant Feeling Types				
ESFJ	Feeling (E)	Sensing (I)	Intuition	Thinking (I)
ENFJ	Feeling (E)	Intuition (I)	Sensing	Thinking (I)
ISFP	Feeling (I)	Sensing (E)	Intuition	Thinking (E)
INFP	Feeling (I)	Intuition (E)	Sensing	Thinking (E)

Note. This table does not indicate the attitude of the tertiary function. Jung implied that the usual attitude of the tertiary was opposite to that of the dominant function and therefore the same as the auxiliary and inferior functions. The MBTI *Manual* (Myers, I. B. & McCaulley, 1985, p. 18) followed Jung on this, but other MBTI theorists (e.g., Myers, K. D. & Kirby, 1994; Quenk, 1993) have suggested that the attitude of the tertiary function seems not to be as stable or clear as that of the other three functions.

Distribution of the Types and Functions in Managers

Table 2 lists the MBTI types, in order of their representation in a very large sample of managers (N = 37,549) who attended leadership development programs at the Center for Creative Leadership from 1985 to 1992 (Osborn & Osborn, 1994). Table 2 also indicates which functions are extraverted and which functions are introverted for each type. Table 3 then summarizes the data from Table 2, indicating the percentages of managers in the CCL sample who extravert and introvert each function.

What stands out about the relative representation of the extraverted functions in this group is the strong presence of Extraverted Thinking: A substantial 56% of this group relate to the outer world primarily with

TABLE 2   Percentage of Managers of Each MBTI Type Who Attended
CCL Programs from 1985 to 1992

Type	Percentage	Function Extraverted	Function Introverted
10% or more:			
ISTJ	17.0	Thinking	Sensing*
ESTJ	15.8	Thinking*	Sensing
ENTJ	13.1	Thinking*	Intuition
INTJ	10.0	Thinking	Intuition*
5% or more:			
ENTP	8.1	Intuition*	Thinking
INTP	6.6	Intuition	Thinking*
ENFP	5.1	Intuition*	Feeling
Less than 5%:			
ESFJ	3.6	Feeling*	Sensing
ISFJ	3.4	Feeling	Sensing*
ISTP	3.4	Sensing	Thinking*
ENFJ	3.4	Feeling*	Intuition
ESTP	3.2	Sensing*	Thinking
INFP	2.7	Intuition	Feeling*
INFJ	1.9	Feeling	Intuition*
ISFP	1.2	Sensing	Feeling*

Note.*The dominant function is marked by an asterisk.

As reported in N. Osborn and D. B. Osborn, "MBTI, FIRO-B, and NAFTA: Leadership Profiles of Not-so-distant Neighbors" in C. Fitzgerald (Ed.), *Proceedings of the Myers-Briggs Type Indicator and Leadership: An International Research Conference.* College Park, MD: University of Maryland University College National Leadership Institute, 1994.

TABLE 3   Percentage of Extraverted and Introverted Functions
Among Managers who Attended CCL Programs from 1985 to 1992

Extraverted Functions		*Introverted Functions*	
Extraverted Thinking	56%	Introverted Sensing	40%
Extraverted Intuition	23%	Introverted Intuition	28%
Extraverted Feeling	12%	Introverted Thinking	21%
Extraverted Sensing	9%	Introverted Feeling	10%

Note. As reported in N. Osborn and D. B. Osborn, "MBTI, FIRO-B, and NAFTA: Leadership Profiles of Not-so-distant Neighbors" in C. Fitzgerald (Ed.), *Proceedings of the Myers-Briggs Type Indicator and Leadership: An International Research Conference.* College Park, MD: University of Maryland University College National Leadership Institute, 1994.

their Thinking. Extraverted Intuition is the second most common, involving 23% of the managers; Feeling (12%) and Sensing (9%) clearly represent much less commonly extraverted processes. In this group of managers, the introverted functions are somewhat less skewed in distribution, with Introverted Sensing the most common (40%), Introverted Intuition (29%) and Introverted Thinking (21%) intermediate in representation, and Introverted Feeling (10%) relatively uncommon.*

In the following sections, the extraverted and the introverted functions are described. For each function, we do the following:

- Briefly describe the function
- Discuss the representation of the function in management groups and the implications of its relative presence or absence
- Identify potential contributions of the function in a management context
- Suggest issues and dilemmas for managers who extravert or introvert the function, for their staff, and for their organizations

Within each set of functions (i.e., extraverted and introverted), the functions are presented in the order in which they are found in management groups, from most common to least common. In addition, suggestions are made for working with the extraverted functions and the introverted functions.

What Managers Extravert

As we discussed earlier, both Extraverts and Introverts use one of their preferred functions to deal with the outer world. For Extraverts, this will be their dominant function; for Introverts, their auxiliary function. The function that is extraverted leads to some normal differences in the ways managers structure their environment, as the following examples illustrate:

> As project manager for a product development team, Janet is responsible for running the weekly team meeting. Team members quickly learned that Janet ran a tight ship—the agendas were succinct, clear, and logical. Meetings were businesslike, with little chitchat or extraneous conversation; and any-

---

*In the relative order of the types, the CCL sample is similar to that of many other samples of managers. In its distribution of dimensions, the CCL sample is also similar to other samples of managers, with a somewhat higher percentage of Intuitive types than some other samples— particularly retail and state and city government managers. For a variety of samples of type distribution in managers, see McCaulley (1990).

one who tried to stray from the topic under discussion was quickly called back. The necessary meetings took a minimum of time, resulted in clear decisions and directives, and felt like an efficient use of resources. They also seemed to some team members to be rather impersonal. Others were sometimes frustrated by what they saw as a cut-and-dried, goal-focused approach that did not allow enough time for free-flowing discussion, consideration of potential problems, or contemplation of interesting connections they were seeing.

The departmental meetings Bill ran were almost always interesting. Employees could count on hearing the latest things going on in the company, on Bill's sense of how their work fit in and the directions they needed to take, and on Bill's enthusiastic encouragement of their own ideas for improvements. They typically left the meetings with a dozen ideas and insights. For some employees, however, the meetings were confusing. The agenda seemed fluid, decisions were left up in the air, and contradictory ideas were left on the table. They had learned that the next meeting might well involve the same process, with little reference to the discussion at the last meeting. Several had decided that they would simply tune out during the meeting so that they could continue to focus on their own tasks and get their regular work done.

Sarah's meetings had clear agendas and goals. Within that structure, Sarah would ensure that each person could voice his or her opinion, the discussion would include the impacts of decisions on individuals, decisions would generally be made by consensus, and attention would be paid to how people interacted with each other. They left with a sense of having been heard and supported in their work. However, some found the meetings tedious and overly personal, as some individual's particular issues came to dominate the discussion. Others wished that Sarah would "take charge" and make decisions when the group could not agree. And many felt the meetings were not as task focused and efficient as they would like.

Louis' meeting were fun—department members never knew quite what was coming. They might go outside for a walk, adjourn to a nearby restaurant for lunch or a snack, or gather at the place in the plant where they were having a production problem. They could count on Louis to focus the group on immediate problems, arrive at a direct solution, and implement it. And they never wasted time in theoretical discussions. Some, however, felt that they did too many temporary fixes, that there needed to be more consideration of impacts and implications of the problems they were solving, and that overall direction and future issues were seldom considered. They appreciated not having unnecessary meetings, but sometimes felt that their group was without direction.

Each of these brief scenarios describes some common strengths and potential problem areas of managers with different extraverted functions. Janet (like ESTJs, ENTJs, ISTJs, and INTJs) extraverts her Thinking. Bill (like ENTPs, ENFPs, INTPs, and INFPs) extraverts his

Intuition. Sarah (like ESFJs, ENFJs, ISFJs, and INFJs) extraverts her Feeling. Louis (like ESTPs, ESFPs, ISTPs, and ISFPs) extraverts his Sensing.

In the section below, we discuss each of these extraverted functions in more detail in this order, consistent with the representation of that function in type distributions of managers.

Extraverted Thinking

Thinking is the extraverted function for the following types: ESTJ, ENTJ, ISTJ, and INTJ. Extraverted Thinking is the dominant function for ESTJs and ENTJs, and the auxiliary function for ISTJs and INTJs.

Extraverted Thinking is Thinking judgment directed to the outer world. It involves applying logic to decisions in the outer world; analyzing, critiquing, and logically organizing; focusing on truth and fairness; and generally taking a decisive and tough-minded, problem-solving approach to the world. As mentioned earlier, Thinking is the most common extraverted function, typically exhibited by more than half of managers. As the most common extraverted function among managers, its presence is strongly exhibited, supported, and influential.

Extraverted Thinking characteristics have become synonymous with traditional management practices and reflect many management behaviors that are highly valued in organizations:

- Logic
- Decisiveness
- An organizing and structuring approach to the world
- Emphasis on objectivity and fairness
- An analytical perspective
- A critical stance that identifies flaws and strives to correct them

The expectations of people in organizations about appropriate and predictable behaviors for managers have been strongly influenced by the presence of Extraverted Thinking. And, given the makeup of management groups, those expectations are likely to be met: When teams or groups of managers meet, they are very likely to primarily "talk" Thinking. This inclination is well known to leadership development trainers who, to be effective, must learn to deal effectively with (and, hopefully, to enjoy) analytical groups who are outspoken and highly skilled in "finding the flaws" wherever they focus their attention.

Every set of strengths, of course, has a corresponding set of limitations, and the limits of Extraverted Thinking involve the capacity to deal with the "softer" issues: a focus on what the people involved in a team or organization *care* about and value (vs. what's most logical), an emphasis on kindness (vs. fairness) and on being "tenderhearted" (vs. tough-minded), and the inclination and ability to appreciate and support (vs. criticize). Research on why promising managers don't succeed has found that a lack of interpersonal, people-related skills often greatly limits the success and achievement of highly technically skilled and hardworking managers (Lombardo & McCauley, 1988). Much of the focus of management and leadership development training and executive coaching involves teaching Thinking managers awareness and skills associated with the Feeling preference to complement their Thinking skills. The most important developmental task for a great many managers involves this development of these Feeling skills. This needed development creates a dilemma for individuals and organizations because, although organizations express strong desires and intentions about putting people first and nurturing and developing staff, the predominant voice in organizations is typically an analytical, critical, and tough-minded one. As flatter organizations, more focus on team achievement, more work relationships based on influence versus authority, more staff participation in decision making, and more emphasis on knowledge work become increasing realities in organizations, the pressure on managers to have stronger Feeling skills is increasing.

Extraverted Intuition

Extraverted Intuition is the second most common extraverted function in the CCL sample. Extraverted Intuition is the extraverted function for the following types: ENTP, ENFP, INTP, and INFP. It is the dominant function for ENTPs and ENFPs and the auxiliary function for INTPs and INFPs.

Extraverted Intuition is Intuition directed at the outer world. It involves an adaptable, future-oriented, creative approach to the outer world, with attention and energy directed toward observing patterns, seeing the big picture, absorbing new information, and exploring new ideas and new possibilities.

The potential contributions of Extraverted Intuition to organizations include the following:

- A wealth of creative ideas
- The ability to identify trends and patterns
- Enthusiasm about change and innovation

- A willingness to try creative approaches
- Flexibility and adaptability

These contributions are likely to be even more important as organizations confront increasing change and complexity, with faster product cycles and an increasing need for innovation.

Managers who extravert their Intuition create an interesting dilemma for organizations: Organizations greatly—and increasingly—desire and need their enthusiastic and innovative approach. However, there is the usually unspoken expectation that managers will primarily communicate about decisions (which are the natural focus of the more numerous managers who extravert Thinking) and *not* about ideas, insights, and possibilities (which are the natural focus of managers who extravert Intuition). As an extraverted *perceiving* process, Extraverted Intuition is focused more on collecting information, noticing trends, and exploring ideas than on *deciding*. And, yet, the expectations for managers to be decision makers and the tendency to hear managers' words as indicating decisions (and not just ideas) are powerful and persistent.

A common experience for a manager who extraverts Intuition is that he or she will have a discussion with staff in one part of the organization and, in the course of that conversation, will contribute a number of ideas. To the manager, these ideas are simply ideas—a few among the dozens or hundreds of ideas of that particular day. But staff, expecting the manager to talk in terms of decisions, may hear an idea as marching orders. A surprised manager may find out a few weeks or months later that a project to implement the "decision" is being carried out, perhaps with substantial resources! Finding ways to label *ideas* versus *decisions* can be very valuable for managers who prefer Extraverted Intuition and for their staffs.

Another issue for managers who extravert Intuition is that their decision-making function (whether Thinking or Feeling) is introverted—decisions primarily get made privately, during time alone. When staff schedule meetings with managers who extravert Intuition, they may be frustrated that decisions don't seem to happen, that the meetings continue to explore ideas and issues and to generate possibilities. Creating written materials and looking for opportunities to anticipate or even create some private time for the manager can sometimes lead to a decision.

Extraverted Feeling

Extraverted Feeling is a relatively uncommon function in managers: Only 12% of the CCL sample extraverted Feeling, and other distributions of managers often show an even smaller percentage. The following types extravert Feeling: ESFJ, ENFJ, ISFJ, and INFJ. Extraverted Feeling is the dominant function for ESFJs and ENFJs and the auxiliary function for ISFJs and INFJs.

Extraverted Feeling is Feeling judgment directed at the outer world. It involves a relationship-oriented, sympathetic, and interpersonally sensitive approach to the outer world, with attention and energy directed toward appreciating and supporting individual and group development, creating and sustaining harmonious relationships, and structuring the environment to support human values and to meet people's needs.

The potential contributions of Extraverted Feeling to organizations include the following:

- Skill in creating and sustaining harmony in relationships
- An inclination to appreciate and support both individual and collective efforts
- A focus on welcoming and including other people
- A focus on organizing and structuring work environments that support the people within them
- A warm and compassionate approach

Managers who extravert Feeling often provide a genuine and enthusiastic focus on people and their individual and collective well-being and development—a welcome balance in primarily Thinking organizations. As managers who extravert a *judging* function, managers who extravert Feeling *do* talk in terms of decisions, which, as mentioned earlier, is very often expected from managers. However, the Extraverted Feeling decision-making process is likely to be quite different from that of the more common Extraverted Thinking, with much more focus on human values, people, relationships, consensus, and appreciation. Managers who extravert Feeling often report that, to survive in primarily Thinking organizations, they have had to learn how to talk in Thinking terms: to make a logical case for a decision that was made on the basis of Feeling considerations. Managers who extravert Feeling also report that conflict in the organization can be painful and difficult, and that the unkindness toward people of their organization can create real stress for them.

Extraverted Sensing

Although Sensing is typically the most common introverted function for managers, Extraverted Sensing is the least common of all the extraverted functions (9% of the CCL sample). While we think of Sensing as being a common managerial preference, it is interesting to note that types that extravert Sensing are not well represented. The following types extravert Sensing: ESTP, ESFP, ISTP, ISFP. Extraverted Sensing is the dominant function for ESTPs and ESFPs and the auxiliary function for ISTPs and ISFPs.

Extraverted Sensing is Sensing directed at the outer world. It involves an immediate, present-oriented, spontaneous, hands-on approach to the outer world, with attention and energy directed toward experiencing the real world through the senses, seeking variety and vividness in interactions with the sensory world, quickly assessing the status of a situation, and taking action directly and resourcefully to fix the problems that are encountered.

The potential contributions of Extraverted Sensing to organizations include the following:

- A practical and realistic approach
- An action orientation—a focus on doing vs. talking about doing
- Comfort in operating in unpredictable, fast-paced, fast-changing environments
- An immediate, troubleshooting approach to problems
- Flexibility and adaptability

Like Extraverted Intuition, Extraverted Sensing is an extraverted *perceiving* function and tends to focus on collecting information and exploring realities—as opposed to focusing on deciding and seeking closure. As discussed earlier, the expectations that people have for managers often involve decision making. Managers who extravert Sensing can feel strained by the common organizational tendency for substantial and lengthy discussions of possible actions (vs. just *doing* it) and for structure and closure. As a result, managers who extravert Sensing are often drawn to the hectic, fast-paced, troubleshooting parts of organizations and can prefer to work with action-oriented, independent staff.

Working With the Extraverted Functions

The extraverted functions are typically the most visible aspect of the personality—and tend to be much more accessible, observable, and easily discussed than the introverted functions. Practitioners new to the use of type dynamics can learn a great deal about the extraverted functions simply by observing and listening to people who extravert different functions. Observing the topics and approaches that seem to particularly draw people (e.g., managers who extravert Thinking tend to analyze the logic of a situation; managers who extravert Intuition like to discuss possibilities and creative approaches) and listening to the language that is used (e.g., crisp vs. expressive language for types who extravert Thinking vs. Feeling, respectively) can bring the extraverted functions—and their differences—to life.

An understanding of the extraverted functions can be valuable to practitioners in both individual and group interventions. In one-on-one situations, helping managers understand the implications and impact of the functions that they extravert can be very valuable. For example, practitioners can help managers who extravert Thinking realize that their tendency to find and articulate the flaws may be well meant, but may not necessarily be well received. Similarly, helping managers who extravert Intuition recognize that people may be overloaded by the possibilities that they generate and that staff may mistake ideas for decisions can be very useful and can lead to more effective management behaviors.

In addition, it can be helpful in working individually with managers to explore the implications of how common or how unusual their extraverted function is, relative to their subordinates, peers, and bosses. In settings in which their extraverted function is unusual (e.g., managers who extravert Sensing or Feeling), it may be useful to explore strategies for learning to "translate" suggestions and decisions into the language of the majority. For example, a manager who extraverted Feeling reported that he had made an important decision on the basis of his personal values, but he discussed the decision with his primarily Thinking colleagues in the language of criteria and cost benefit. Another potentially valuable discussion with managers whose extraverted functions are relatively uncommon in their role or organization is to explore strategies for making a unique contribution with their unusual perspective by asking questions such as these:

- Where might your colleagues have "blind spots" about which you might be able to provide some valuable approaches and perspectives?
- Under what circumstances do your perspective and approach seem particularly valuable and likely to be heard? Under what circumstances do your perspective and approach seem least likely to be heard and valued?

- How—in current and anticipated work—might your perspective and approach best complement and support that of the majority?
- How can you best introduce and describe your perspective and approach? What are ineffective and/or self-defeating ways to introduce or describe your perspective and approach?

In contrast to managers whose extraverted functions are unusual, managers whose extraverted functions are in a majority may need to be alert to collective blind spots and may want to develop strategies to systematically include the input of the less-heard voices (e.g., Feeling in most management groups).

In group settings, practitioners may find it valuable to be aware of the relative representation of the extraverted functions and to note which perspectives are very common, and therefore may dominate, and which perspectives are likely to be little-used. In addition, practitioners may profitably focus on the representation of extraverted functions in a group and the type of task on which a group is working. A group working on a task that draws on the strengths of a well-represented extraverted function (e.g., a Thinking group analyzing and critiquing a report, an Intuitive group doing brainstorming) may need little help. However, a group working on a task that does not draw on its strengths (e.g., a Thinking group dealing with the anxiety and sadness that staff are experiencing during downsizing; an Intuitive group dealing with a substantial number of specific facts) may need guidance and support. Also, an awareness of the extraverted function of the group leader (versus other group members) can be helpful in coaching the leader and planning for an effective meeting.

What Managers Introvert

The introverted functions describe four different ways that managers relate to their inner world of private observations, ideas, thoughts, memories, emotions, and values. As we discussed earlier, both Extraverts and Introverts use one of their preferred functions to deal with their inner world. For Introverts, this will be their dominant function; for Extraverts, their auxiliary function.

The function that is introverted leads to some normal differences in ways managers remember and reflect, as the following examples illustrate:

> Janet, the project manager whose use of Extraverted Thinking to run a meeting was described earlier, used her Introverted Sensing both before and after the meeting. Before the meeting, she reviewed all the specific, realistic data

and drew on her store of concrete experience to identify all the issues need-ing attention in the meeting, ensuring that nothing was overlooked. After the meeting, she reviewed her notes on the decisions taken and checked them out with her experience to be sure every detail was included. She also used her Introverted Sensing while formulating complete plans for imple-menting the decisions. Her team knew they could count on Janet's covering all the bases before and after their meeting, as the detailed, written imple-mentation plans appeared quickly. However, some felt hemmed in by the structure Janet provided, thought there wasn't enough room for creativity or potentially promising new routes, and felt overwhelmed by the detailed documentation Janet required from everyone.

Sarah, the manager whose use of Extraverted Feeling to run a meeting was described earlier, also used her Introverted Intuition before and after the meeting. Before the meeting, she would spend time reflecting on her sense of where people in her group were in their work and what kinds of issues they might be facing that needed to be addressed. She would also reflect on their overall responsibilities as a group and develop her picture of how her group was doing in relationship to their long-term goals. This confident inner sense of her group and their work provided the context for the meet-ing. After the meeting, Sarah would spend time reflecting on the meeting—how different individuals had responded, tensions she picked up, hunches she had about where the group was—and used this reflection to decide on actions she needed to take next. Her group members knew they could rely on Sarah to keep track of how their individual work fit into the overall pic-ture and to keep them moving toward their long-term goals. At times, how-ever, they were puzzled by the actions she took or the focus of the meet-ings—they wanted more direction on specific, day-to-day tasks and could-n't always understand where she was coming from.

Louis, whose use of Extraverted Sensing to run meetings was described ear-lier, also used his Introverted Thinking before and after meetings. Before he called a meeting, he used his Introverted Thinking to identify an important problem area and to understand the components of the breakdown. After the meeting, he used Introverted Thinking to move quickly and efficiently to systematize the solution they had generated. Some of his group, howev-er, found his focus on problems discouraging. As one said, "We never meet together unless something is wrong." And others experienced his subse-quent Introverted Thinking system-making as ruthless: "He never lets what will happen to the people get in the way"; "It usually seems that he hasn't even recognized the impacts."

Bill, whose use of Extraverted Intuition to run a meeting was described ear-lier, used his Introverted Feeling before and after the meeting. As he pre-pared for meetings, Bill would focus on the mission of his group and the val-ues of the organization to evaluate where his group was. The insights and ideas he would share with his group in the meeting came out of his reflec-tion. After the meetings, he would check out whether what happened in the meeting was congruent with his deep commitments. His department knew that Bill's values were important to him, but they had a hard time under-standing them. It seemed he only articulated them when they had unwit-tingly said or done something that offended him. And when his values were touched upon, Bill was uncompromising and sometimes self-righteous.

Each of these brief scenarios describes some common strengths and potential problem areas of managers with different extraverted func-tions. Janet (like ESTJs, ESFJs, ISTJs, and ISFJs) introverts her Sensing. Sarah (like ENTJs, ENFJs, INTJs, and INFJs) introverts her Intuition. Louis (like ESTPs, ENTPs, ISTPs, and INTPs) introverts his Thinking. And Bill (like ESFPs, ENFPs, ISFPs, and INFPs) introverts his Feeling.

In the section below, we discuss each of these introverted functions in more detail and in this order, consistent with the representation of that function in type distributions of managers.

Introverted Sensing

Although Extraverted Sensing is relatively rare in managers, Introverted Sensing is very common: In the CCL Sample, 40% of the managers Introverted Sensing. Introverted Sensing is the introverted function for the following types: ESTJ, ESFJ, ISTJ and ISFJ. Introverted Sensing is the dominant function for ISTJs and ISFJs and the auxiliary function for ESTJs and ESFJs.

Introverted Sensing is Sensing focused on the inner world. It involves taking in sense data about the world (i.e., what things look like, sound like, feel like, and taste like) and storing it in a very detailed internal database. This private, careful, and continuing collection of experience provides a rich, fine-grained source of data that is accessed to retrieve facts and compare a current situation with a past one. The presence of this private database and the continuous accessing and retrieving of the data tend to make managers who introvert Sensing steady, reliable, and well-grounded in reality. As a continuous "inner historian," Introverted Sensing prompts a profound valuing of personal history and tradition and very often results in a valuing of organiza-tional history and tradition.

Managers who introvert Sensing typically demonstrate these charac-teristics:

- An impressive ability to absorb and remember facts
- Thoroughness and precision
- Realistic and practical approaches to situations
- A valuing of experience as a basis for judgment
- Respect for organizational history and tradition

Contributions that managers who introvert Sensing potentially make to an organization include the following:

- A pragmatic and realistic approach to work
- Institutional memory
- A constant search for and attention to the relevant facts about a situation or problem
- Respect for and maintenance of the traditions of organizations.

Challenges for managers who introvert Sensing arise particularly in situations in which adequate facts are not available and/or in which experience and tradition are not the most useful tools. Changing external environments, revolutionary versus incremental change in organizations, and global competition through product innovation are creating organizations that are less orderly, fact-based, and precise, and more chaotic, inspiration-driven, and approximate. The former organization has been a natural fit for the gifts of Introverted Sensing; the latter is experienced as difficult by many managers who introvert Sensing.

Introverted Intuition

Introverted Intuition was the second most common introverted function in the CCL sample (29%). Intuition as an introverted function was slightly more common than as an extraverted function (29% vs. 23%). Introverted Intuition is the introverted function for the following types: ENTJ, ENFJ, INTJ and ENFJ. It is the dominant function for INTJs and INFJs and the auxiliary function for ENTJs and ENFJs.

Introverted Intuition is Intuition focused on the inner world. It involves a private creative process: seeing possibilities, noticing complex patterns and connections, developing and elaborating theories, generating ideas, and reconceptualizing and reframing. The presence of this constant, internal, creative pattern-recognition process tends to make managers who introvert Intuition visionary, independent-minded, complicated, and creative. As might be expected, the creativity of managers who introvert Intuition is less immediately obvious than that of those who extravert Intuition; with managers who introvert Intuition, the creativity is more focused on things that are particularly important to them and is usually seen over time as opposed to being continuously demonstrated.

Managers who introvert Intuition typically demonstrate the following characteristics:

- A broad, long-range perspective
- The ability to extract the essence of a complex and confusing situation
- An ability to reconceptualize and reframe situations
- An independent view of things
- A facility with theories and concepts
- Depth of understanding

Contributions that managers who introvert Intuition potentially make to an organization include the following:

- Creative approaches
- The ability to deal with complexity
- The ability to look at and deal with situations in new ways
- The ability to apply theories and concepts to organizational issues and problems
- A visionary, long-term perspective

A challenge for managers who introvert Intuition is that their creative process and ideas are private, and they do not usually communicate them until they have done a great a deal of inner consideration. By then, the ideas may be so clear and convincing to the manager that he or she sees them as obvious—and, therefore, not requiring a lot of explanation—and as ready to implement. The private, long-term, visionary perspective of managers who introvert Intuition may require them to do a lot of explaining, selling, collaborating, and specifying to actually make their ideas into a reality. The manager who introverts Intuition may be largely unaware of and/or impatient with such processes.

Introverted Thinking

Introverted Thinking was the third most common introverted function in the CCL Sample (21%); as an extraverted function, Thinking was far more common (56%). Introverted Thinking is the introverted function for the following types: ESTP, ENTP, ISTP and INTP. It is the dominant function for the ISTPs and INTPs and the auxiliary function for ESTPs and ENTPs.

Introverted Thinking is Thinking focused on the inner world. It involves a private decision-making process: a continuously updated inner decision tree that logically categorizes and weighs information. The presence of this inner logical decision tree tends to make managers who introvert Thinking logical, detached, objective, and analytical. Introverted Thinking involves an ongoing search for truth, an ability to

analyze and order information, and a tendency to respond constructively and dispassionately to criticism.

Managers who introvert Thinking typically demonstrate these characteristics:

- A logical and analytical approach
- An ability to critique in a calm and impersonal manner
- An objective stance when dealing with criticism
- A thoughtful and reasonable approach to the world
- Tolerance for a wide range of behavior of others

Contributions that managers who introvert Thinking potentially
make to an organization include the following:

- Logic and objective analysis
- The ability to offer criticism in an objective manner
- A persistent pursuit and valuing of the truth
- An impersonal analytical approach, even in very heated and polar-
  ized situations
- A tendency not to take criticism personally
- A reasonable and tolerant approach

Challenges for managers who introvert Thinking arise because their
Thinking is private: It may be very clear to a manager who introverts
Thinking how various projects and activities fit together into a logical
whole, but he or she is unlikely to talk about the logical connected-
ness—both because it is private and because it is so *obvious* to him or
her. In contrast to managers who extravert Thinking, and who therefore
make decisions externally, managers who introvert Thinking make decisions internally and, as a result, have a tendency *not* to organize and
structure the activities of others to any great extent. This relatively
unstructured approach may be very appealing to staff who enjoy organizing their own work, but can be challenging for staff who would like
more structure and guidance. Also, the objective, detached approach of
managers who introvert Thinking can be valued for its reasonableness
and tolerance, or it can be seen as a lack of interest in people. Like managers who extravert Thinking, those who introvert Thinking often need
to work on their people-related skills in order to be effective.

Introverted Feeling

Introverted Feeling is the least common of the introverted functions in
managers: only 10% of managers in the CCL sample introverted

Feeling. Introverted Feeling is the introverted function for the following types: ESFP, ENFP, ISFP, and INFP. It is the dominant function for ISFPs and INFPs and the auxiliary function for ESFPS and ENFPs.

Introverted Feeling is Feeling judgment focused on the inner world. It involves a private decision-making process based on personal values. This private, value-based decision process continuously filters information and makes judgments in a way that is carefully consistent with inner values, many of which tend to focus on people and their needs and values. The presence of this intensive, subjective decision process tends to make managers who introvert Feeling attentive to people's concerns and values, quietly supportive and nurturing, interpersonally sensitive, and loyal to people and projects that they care about. In contrast to managers who extravert their Feeling and who are often perceived as warm and friendly, managers who introvert their Feeling are likely to take longer to get to know.

Managers who introvert Feeling typically demonstrate these characteristics:

- Quiet concern for those around them
- Focus on praising the good that they see
- Gentle warmth
- A serious interest in helping people fulfill their potential
- Flexibility and tolerance for a wide range of differences
- A sense of loyalty and trustworthiness

Contributions that managers who introvert Feeling potentially make to an organization include the following:

- An interest in the well-being of those around them
- Quiet but persistent support and appreciation for individual and collective efforts
- A focus on the creation and implementation of a people-centered workplace
- A strong, inner barometer that measures the impact of workplace decisions on the people involved
- A tolerance for others and an ability to see the validity in contradictory points of view

Challenges for managers who introvert Feeling arise because their Feeling judgment is very private and personal and can be hard to articulate. As a result, others may not understand the often complex inner process and may be puzzled about the reasons for their decisions. Also, because of their tolerance and flexibility, they may not take a firm stance on decisions that are not important to them and as a result may be seen as indecisive. A manager who introverts Feeling and who may be flexible and easygoing under many circumstances can be unexpectedly firm when a core value is violated. Managers who introvert Feeling may feel concerned about how unkind organizations can be and often need to learn when and how to use "Thinking" language to be successful in predominantly Thinking organizations.

Working With the Introverted Functions

As discussed earlier, the introverted functions are more difficult to observe and to understand than the extraverted functions. However, an understanding of the introverted functions is very helpful in work with individuals and groups and is worth the extra effort required.

Relative to the extraverted functions, the introverted functions have the following characteristics:

- The introverted functions tend to be less conventional and more idiosyncratic than the corresponding extraverted functions because they are more private and therefore have been subjected to less discussion and feedback.
- The introverted functions require observers to notice and to read between the lines. Because some observers are likely to notice and some are not, people often get inconsistent and/or unclear feedback about their introverted function. For example, some observers may see an Introverted Intuitive manager as creative, while others may limit their observation to the day-to-day extraverted judging shown.
- What is particularly important to a person will more strongly influence the focus and content of the introverted function than the extraverted function, which is more influenced by the environment and its demands. For this reason, you can't assume, for example, that an Introverted Sensing type will pay attention to and remember *all* facts; he or she will tend to pay attention to and remember facts that were of particular interest and importance.
- The introverted functions tend to have more depth and complexity than the extraverted functions. Also, from the perspective of a person who introverts a particular function, the extraverted form of that function may appear to be conventional and/or superficial. For example, an Introverted Intuitive type may experience the easily expressed, outer-directed creativity of the Extraverted Intuitive type as superficial and lacking depth.

- People often assume that the content of their introverted function is obvious to others, even though it is very individual and private and they have typically said little about it. For example, Introverted Thinking managers may not tell staff how different projects and activities fit together because it is so clear to them that explaining it would seem to them to be insulting to the intelligence of the others.
- The expression and content of an introverted function is influenced by a person's extraverted function. For example, an ISFJ (who introverts Sensing and extraverts Feeling) will tend to focus more on facts about people, while an ISTJ (who also introverts Sensing but who extraverts Thinking) will tend to focus more on facts about things.

In learning about the introverted functions, it can be helpful to learn about the extraverted functions first so that you can "screen out" the effect of a person's extraverted function. For example, an understanding of Extraverted Thinking will help to differentially focus on the Introverted Intuition of an INTJ manager. Also, a good strategy for learning about the introverted functions is to start with people whom you know well and observe and carefully ask questions about their introverted function. Developing simple language to briefly describe each introverted function can be helpful as a starting point. An example for talking about Introverted Intuition might be the following:

> Introverted Intuition has been described as a private creative process in which people, when they are alone, become aware of patterns and connections, see new possibilities, and have creative ideas. Does this fit at all for you? How would you describe what happens when you're alone?

Listening to the content and even the specific language of people's descriptions of their introverted function can be very valuable.

The following are general suggestions for working with the introverted functions with managers. First, just briefly describing the function and having managers refine and elaborate on the description from their own experience can be very valuable. Such a discussion validates the introverted function and can help managers make explicit something that they may not have had language or license to articulate.

Second, helping people to create practices and procedures in their workplaces for respecting and making space for the introverted function can be useful. Examples include the following:

- Providing written information and agenda items in advance of a meeting

- Allowing time during a meeting for people to collect their thoughts ("let's take a few minutes and each jot down some notes about what we'd like to see happen")
- Using techniques like the *nominal group technique* or *storyboarding* for team problem solving, which allows introverted time to complement team discussion
- Encouraging team norms that respect the value of reflection and the need for some privacy (e.g., an office sign that says, Great Thinking in Process—Disturb Me Only if It's Important)

The following five suggestions are primarily aimed at working with managers whose introverted functions are dominant (i.e., managers who are Introverts). First, an exploration with an introverted manager about how to create the conditions for doing the best work can be important. Introverts tend to work most effectively when their work is of real interest and relevant to their introverted function, and when they have enough time and space for reflection and privacy. If either of these conditions is not in place, some problem solving is important. Solutions might involve a change in schedule to allow for more time alone, a redirection of some work, and/or delegation of some responsibilities to allow focus on more important, interesting things.

Second, managers may need help in communicating and demonstrating the content of their introverted function more in their work. Strategies such as writing, talking first to one or two trusted colleagues or subordinates, meeting in small groups for discussion, and giving staff explicit permission to ask questions and prompt discussions of relevant topics may be helpful.

Third, managers may need help in communicating and demonstrating the value of that which is "between the lines." Others in the manager's environment may need help in seeing—and therefore appreciating—the contribution of introverted functions. For example, an Introverted Intuitive manager, whose creativity and vision are not immediately apparent, may need, at times, to make explicit and label the business results that stem from the inner Intuition.

Fourth, managers may need help in developing effective strategies for managing the demands of their environment for an immediate response, particularly in situations in which they feel that some introverting is important for the highest quality response. Although sometimes demands *are* really urgent and do quickly require the best approximation, in many circumstances in organizations, *some* time for reflection is possible. Finding and using confident (versus apologetic) ways to get reflection time (for example, "It's an interesting and important issue and I'd love to give it some thought—I'll let you know my views right after lunch") can be very valuable and can improve effectiveness.

Fifth, it can be helpful for managers to realize that there is likely to be some variability in the ability of other people to notice the impact and value of their introverted function and that therefore feedback from others about matters relating to that function may be inconsistent and confusing. The variability can be influenced by a number of factors, including how close a relationship a person has with the manager, the extent to which that person works with the manager in small versus large groups, and how generally observant the person is.

In working with managers whose introverted functions are auxiliary (i.e., managers who are Extraverts), it can be important to help them understand the potential contribution of their introverted function to balancing their perceiving and judging. In addition, helping extraverted managers learn ways to regularly access their introverted auxiliary function can be valuable.

UNDERSTANDING THE INTERPLAY OF THE FUNCTIONS

Understanding the extraverted and introverted functions is an important step in developing skill in using type dynamics. Another important step involves an understanding of the individual dynamics of type—the interplay within each type of the four functions. There are three main components to understanding the interplay, or dynamics, among the functions. They include understanding the following:

- Interplay between the two preferred functions, the dominant and the auxiliary
- The role of the nonpreferred functions
- The impact of stress

Each of these topics is addressed in the following sections.

Interplay Between the Dominant and Auxiliary Functions

Understanding the role of the dominant and the auxiliary functions and the interplay between them is essential to understanding type dynamics. This section addresses three related issues regarding the role and interplay of the dominant and auxiliary functions:

- The relative energy of the dominant and auxiliary functions
- The relative importance of the dominant and auxiliary functions
- The contributions of the dominant and auxiliary functions to providing balance

The Dominant Function Is More Energized

The functions described in the previous sections have the same characteristics whether they are the dominant function of a particular type (e.g., Extraverted Feeling for an ENFJ) or the auxiliary function (e.g., Extraverted Feeling for an INFJ). However, the dominant function is the focus of much more energy and attention, and therefore is usually seen in a stronger, more pronounced form than an auxiliary function, which tends to be generally more low-key, less energized, and more like a supporting player than the main performer.

This difference in energy is easier to see in extraverted functions than in introverted ones; the dominant Extraverted Intuition of an ENTP, for example, will tend to be seen as energetic and active: generating lots of ideas; brainstorming with a great deal of enthusiasm; actively seeking out new ideas, trends, and possibilities; talking to others about new ideas with emphasis. In contrast, the auxiliary Extraverted Intuition of an INTP, while still clearly focused on ideas, trends, and possibilities, is likely to be seen as more low-key about them and generally as considerably less active and energized in their pursuit than dominant Extraverted Intuitive types.

For introverted functions, a similar relationship between dominant and auxiliary applies, but is, of course, more difficult to see because the introverted functions focus on the inner world. An example of this is that the dominant Introverted Sensing of an ISTJ is likely to be more energized and active—in the inner world—than the auxiliary Introverted Sensing function of an ESTJ. You may get a glimpse of this in the outer world, when you observe that facts and experience, while very important to both ISTJ and ESTJ managers, are especially attended to and important to ISTJs.

The appendix to this chapter has a description of the interactions of the dominant and auxiliary functions for each of the 16 types.

The Dominant Function Is Overriding

The dominant function is, for most people, the first to develop. According to psychological type theory, as children begin using their dominant function, they find it energizing and enjoyable. This leads them to continue using it on every possible occasion. Dominant Extraverted Thinking children, for example, are often "little lawyers," enjoying quoting rules to others, organizing their schoolmates, and passionately defending fairness in all things. Because they use Extraverted Thinking so much, they become expert in it. As adults, they are comfortable expressing their logical analyses and their reasonable judgments. Most people do not put the same kind of energy into their auxiliary function until later—perhaps in adolescence. The dominant function does not go away at this point, but more attention is directed toward the auxiliary function than has been before.

Because of the early development and refinement of the dominant function, it remains the center of people's identity and functioning throughout their lives, however much they develop other parts of themselves. It is the most trusted, most familiar part, and the one people typically turn to under stress. As a result, a person's overall goals in life tend to be strongly influenced by their dominant function. Although both the dominant function and the auxiliary function are very important, the focus and concerns of the dominant function come first. This can be hard to understand, particularly when dealing with introverted managers, because the auxiliary function is shown to the world and the dominant function is private.

ISTJ managers offer an example of the interplay between an introverted dominant function and an extraverted auxiliary one. ISTJ managers usually show others their rational, decisive Extraverted Thinking. They use this auxiliary function to structure the things they are responsible for—their own environment, their organizations, its systems and processes. Others are seldom aware of the wealth of specific stored data that is in their dominant Introverted Sensing that ISTJs depend upon; however, it is this dominant function that is most central to ISTJs.

Thus, when subordinates or colleagues present new ideas or plans to ISTJ managers, these managers need time to take those ideas inside and compare them with their own experience and internal information. Even when the ideas are presented very rationally and seem to make sense to others, the ideas will be rejected if they don't agree with an ISTJ's internally stored data.

The Dominant and Auxiliary: Providing Balance

In understanding type dynamics, it is important to understand the ways in which the dominant and auxiliary functions of each type provide balance. Two kinds of balance are essential:

- If the dominant function is a perceiving function (Sensing or Intuition), then the second favorite will be a judging function (Thinking or Feeling), and vice versa.
- If the dominant function is extraverted, the auxiliary function will be introverted, and vice versa.

This model of type dynamics means that people who have developed their preferred mental functions have reliable ways for gathering information and making decisions. They also have effective ways to reflect and process internally, as well as to operate in the external world.

The creators of the MBTI, Isabel Briggs Myers and Katharine Cook Briggs, contributed to psychological type theory by clarifying Jung's theory of the balance provided by the first and second preferred functions. Their understanding is included in the full type descriptions contained in *Introduction to Type* (Myers, 1993).

The Role of the Nonpreferred Functions

The tertiary and inferior functions are generally less developed and less conscious than the dominant and auxiliary functions. The normal maturing process for most people includes developing a lot of skills related to those "other" functions. This is especially true when people are in environments that require such skill development. Thus, an ISTJ in a graduate degree program will most likely develop many intuitive skills, learning to skillfully develop mission and vision statements, write papers that clearly spell out the patterns and meaning in data, and so on. Similarly, INTPs who become parents will find themselves developing many Sensing and Feeling skills, as they work to provide an orderly, caring environment for their children.

The inferior function can play a particularly important role in understanding oneself and others. It is the opposite of the dominant function (see Table 1) and, because of this, receives the least energy, attention, and time. Even when people have developed skills related to their inferior function, the amount of energy directed toward the dominant function means that people typically spend little time "in their inferior."

For most people, then, the inferior function is their Achilles' heel—the area where they feel most inadequate and where they make mistakes, overlooking things that are obvious to others. Typically, it is also people's "touchy" area—the place where they react defensively and with inappropriate emotion.

For example, ENTJ and ESTJ leaders, who are dominant Extraverted Thinking types, have Introverted Feeling as their inferior function. For many of these logical, decisive leaders, the piece they overlook is evaluating their actions with internal values. They can then be very effective at achieving goals but may not take sufficient time to decide whether those goals fit with the organization's and their own value systems. And they do not usually respond kindly when others bring this to their attention.

Another example involves INTP and ISTP leaders, who are dominant Introverted Thinking types, and who have Extraverted Feeling as their inferior function. They can devise wonderful logical systems for their organization, but what they may forget to consider is the impact of these systems on the people in the organization. Their elegant system can then fail in practice because they haven't factored in ways to meet people's needs. And they can become very defensive and angry when another person points this out to them.

Table 4 contrasts the eight functions when they are dominant functions—and therefore typically well-developed, primarily conscious, and "adult"—and when they are inferior functions—and therefore typically undeveloped, primarily unconscious, childish, and childlike. Note that the content of the functions as dominant and inferior is similar (e.g., Extraverted Thinking involves judgments based on logic), but the level of development and consciousness is very different.

The Impact of Stress

Under stress, most people report that they look to their most trusted part, their dominant function, to help them get under control. No matter how much other development they have done and how many other skills they have, under stress these tend to be forgotten.

What this means is that the normal balance provided by the auxiliary function is not available to them at that time. When dominant Extraverted Thinking or Extraverted Feeling types, for example, are under stress and out of balance, they can seem to rely exclusively on their extraverted judging. In this case, they will not listen to new information and will not hear it if it is offered, instead plowing ahead to

TABLE 4   Qualities Associated with Dominant Versus Inferior Functions

Function	As a Dominant Function	As an Inferior Function
Extraverted Thinking Dominant: ESTJ, ENTJ Inferior: ISFP, INFP	Competence Truth and accuracy Decisive action	Judgments of incompetence Aggressive criticism Precipitous action
Introverted Thinking Dominant: ISTP, INTP Inferior: ESFJ, ENFJ	Impersonal criticism Logical analysis Search for accuracy and truth	Excessive criticism Convoluted logic Compulsive search for truth

Extraverted Feeling
Dominant: ESFJ, ENFJ
Inferior: ISTP, INTP
	Comfortable inattention
	  to logic
	Sensitivity to the welfare
	  of others
	Sharing of emotions
		Logic emphasized to
		  an extreme
		Hypersensitivity to
		  relationships
		Emotionalism

Introverted Feeling
Dominant: ISFP, INFP
Inferior: ESTJ, ENTJ
	Inner harmony
	
	Economy of emotional
	  expression
	Acceptance of feeling as
	  nonlogical
		Hypersensitivity to inner
		  states
		Outbursts of emotion
		
		Fear of feeling

Extraverted Sensing
Dominant: ESTP, ESFP
Inferior: INTJ, INFJ
	Focus on external data
	
	Seeking sensual/aesthetic
	  pleasure
	Delight in the outer world
		Obsessive focus on
		  external data
		Overindulgence in
		  sensual pleasure
		Adversarial attitude toward
		  the outer world

Introverted Sensing Dominant: ISTJ, ISFJ Inferior: ENTP, ENFP	Solitude and reflection Attention to facts and details Awareness of internal experience	Withdrawal and depression Obsessiveness A focus on the body

Extraverted Intuition
Dominant: ENTP, ENFP
Inferior: ISTJ, ISFJ
	Comfortable inattention to
	  sense data
	Flexibility, adaptability,
	  risk taking
	Optimism about future
	  possibilities
		Loss of control over facts
		  and details
		Impulsiveness
		
		Catastrophizing

Introverted Intuition
Dominant: INTJ, INFJ
Inferior: ESTP, ESFP
	Intellectual clarity
	Accurate interpretation
	  of perceptions
	Visionary insight
		Internal confusion
		Inappropriate attribution
		  of meaning
		Grandiose visions

Note. Modified and reproduced by special permission of the Publisher, Consulting Psychologists Press, Inc., Palo Alto, CA 94303 from *Beside Ourselves* by Naomi L. Quenk. Copyright 1993 by Consulting Psychologists Press, Inc. All rights reserved. Further reproduction is prohibited without the Publisher's written consent.

create the structure they have decided on. When dominant Extraverted Sensing or Extraverted Intuitive types are under stress and out of balance, they can seem to rely exclusively on their extraverted perceiving. In this case, they will continue to act and explore, but fail to use their auxiliary judging process to provide them with priorities, decisions, and commitments. Dominant Introverted Sensing or Introverted Intuitive types who are under stress and out of balance will simply dismiss everything that does not fit with their internal data or picture. The Thinking types will then reject all appeals to reason, while the Feeling types reject all appeals to their concern for others. They can then stubbornly hold on to their internal perception as the only possible way to see things. Dominant Introverted Thinking or Introverted Feeling types who are under stress and out of balance can stop paying attention to any information, insisting that their logical structure or value system is the only possible "right" way to make decisions.

Actions taken while leaders are out of balance are likely to be poor ones. They will be lacking in either enough information or enough judgment. They will be limited and may cause the organization and themselves a great deal of grief.

At an extreme, if the stress and the resulting imbalance continue, a manager's inferior function (as described above and summarized in Table 4) may temporarily take over. (See Quenk, 1993, for a detailed description of the inferior function of each of the types.)

CASE EXAMPLES

Type dynamics may sound abstract and theoretical. However, when understood and used well, it is a very useful, practical tool for helping managers to understand their way of problem solving and decision making and to develop strategies to be more effective, both in working alone and in working with others. The following are examples of the use of type dynamics in work with managers of common managerial types.

INTJs and Decision Making

INTJ is one of the most common management types. In terms of type dynamics, INTJ's dominant is Introverted Intuition and auxiliary is Extraverted Thinking. As described earlier, Introverted Intuition is a private creative process, focusing on hunches, patterns, theories, and possibilities in the inner world, while Extraverted Thinking is an outward-directed, logical, analytical, and critical process. In the outer world, you are likely to see an INTJ manager being logical and decisive. Over time, *if* you were paying attention, you might see the creativity that underlies the logic and notice that certain possibilities and theories were extremely important to the INTJ but were rarely talked about.

A typical situation seen with INTJ managers is the following: When the manager is pushed to make a decision, he or she uses Extraverted Thinking, informing staff in a clear and decisive way about the decision. The staff then starts to implement the decision. However, when the manager has private time, his or her Introverted Intuition—which is dominant and therefore overriding—may be used to entirely reconceptualize the issue, seeing new patterns and new possibilities. The manager, who may have sounded very decisive in announcing the original decision, may come in the next day with a very different approach. Not surprisingly, staff are likely to feel disconcerted by this unexpected change, and, if this pattern happens repeatedly, staff are likely to feel vulnerable and distrusting of the manager's decisions.

It is very helpful—and often a great relief—for an INTJ manager to be aware of this pattern and to see its impact on his or her effectiveness as a manager. Once the pattern is identified, there are a number of fairly simple solutions: The manager can remember to take some private time before making an important decision (e.g., "I'll let you know first thing in the morning"). A second possible solution would be for the manager to alert the staff to his or her decision-making pattern, assure them that the intent is *not* to be difficult, and help them develop strategies for working well with the pattern (e.g., "Consider the decision tentative and do a quick check with me the next day to confirm it").

An ENTJ Banker

Another example involves an ENTJ who was president of a bank that was in very serious financial trouble. To try to resolve the situation, the president was very busy giving orders and using his Extraverted Thinking. When he examined his situation through the lens of type dynamics, it became clear that he needed to make the best possible use of his Introverted Intuition. He was getting an enormous amount of information and events were unfolding very quickly. It was clear that it was very important for him to listen to his hunches and pay attention to trends and to possibilities. The way that ENTJs can access their Introverted Intuition is to spend some time alone. As long as this bank president was incredibly busy interacting with others, he was likely to be using his Extraverted Thinking. After a discussion of his type dynamics, he decided that every day at lunchtime, he would take a half-hour walk alone. He also decided to drive to and from work alone and not to listen to news as he drove.

ENFPs and Decisions

ENFPs are dominant Intuitive types who focus, as described earlier, on possibilities, connections, hunches, and the big picture—all applied to the outer world. For Extraverted Intuitives, possibilities are everywhere. Ask an ENFP how he or she could do something differently, and you will hear many creative ideas and possibilities. What can happen to ENFP managers, however, is that they can get caught up in possibilities and not get clarity about the most valuable course for them and their organizations to take. A solution to this is to help the manager find a situation where he or she can be alone and can come to conclusions, using auxiliary Introverted Feeling. It can be helpful to ask ENFP managers if there is a particular circumstance or activity that they have engaged in alone that has helped them to reach conclusions and make decisions. ENFP managers can typically identify the particular activity that has been helpful for them in the past. Examples of activities cited include the following: walking, jogging, biking, driving in the car with the radio off (or with nature music playing), sitting on the back porch alone, washing dishes, and gardening.

ISTJs and Organizational Change

A current dilemma for many ISTJ managers and their organizations is that, because of their dependability and reliability, they have often stayed in one part of the organization and, as a result, have had fairly narrow experiences. Because of the dramatic and widespread changes in organizations, organizations now often require very different things from their managers than previously. Intuitive managers—even with narrow experiences—can sometimes use their imagination and enthusiasm for new approaches to adapt to a changing organization and environment. But Introverted Sensing managers tend to be more reliant on real experience to adapt to change and can be seen as resistant to change because of this experience-based approach.

An understanding of Introverted Sensing can be enormously helpful in working with ISTJ managers in a changing environment. Often, when first confronted with a new idea or proposal an ISTJ will naturally consult his or her inner database and may say, "We tried that in 1984 and it didn't work." It can be helpful to listen seriously to what happened in 1984, to identify similarities and differences between what was tried then and what is being proposed. Dismissing such a statement as resistance misunderstands the natural process of Introverted Sensing.

An effective strategy for helping ISTJ managers contribute well in changing times is to add to their inner database by prompting them to spend some time—even just a few hours—in an environment in which they are doing things differently. ISTJs can become skilled and careful implementers and even champions of change that makes sense to them. (See Chapter 14 for further discussion of STJs and change.)

STRATEGIES FOR USING TYPE DYNAMICS WITH LEADERS

An understanding of type dynamics can be very valuable to practitioners who work with leaders, either individually (e.g., executive coaching, consulting to the boss in charge management projects) or collectively (e.g., strategic work with senior management teams, designing and delivering executive development programs). The following are some ways in which type dynamics can be especially useful to practitioners.

First, knowledge of the practitioner's own type dynamics can be very helpful in understanding his or her likely approach, goals, and perspective in working with managers. An understanding of similarities and differences in type dynamics between the practitioner and his or her clients may be revealing (e.g., a practitioner who extraverts Feeling working with a team of managers who extravert Thinking) and may lead to more effective practice.

Second, type dynamics provides a number of different specific approaches that may be effective with a manager of a particular type in a particular situation. These include the following:

- Analyzing the impact of the function that is extraverted (e.g., helping managers who extravert Thinking to soften their language and tone when giving feedback to employees)
- Analyzing the impact of the function that is introverted (e.g., helping managers who introvert Intuition try to first write about and then talk about their inner vision)
- Exploring the relative emphasis on perceiving versus judging (e.g., helping managers who extravert Sensing to articulate their decisions)

- Exploring the relative emphasis on the outer world versus the inner world (e.g., when appropriate, helping extraverted managers find times and places that encourage reflection, and helping introverted managers find comfortable ways to communicate about their introverted process)
- Contrasting the type dynamics of the manager with those of another person or group of people (e.g., helping a dominant Introverted Thinking manager interact with a dominant Extraverted Feeling boss, or helping a dominant Extraverted Intuitive manager interact with dominant Introverted Sensing staff)
- Contrasting the type dynamics of the manager with the dynamics of other managers (e.g., helping managers who extravert Sensing or Feeling be successful in a traditional management setting)
- Exploring the impact of the tertiary and inferior functions, both in terms of blind spots and areas that need special attention and in terms of reactions to stress (e.g., helping an Extraverted Intuitive manager pay attention to periodic reports about the facts about his or her organization)
- Analyzing the current setting and demands in terms of its current and potential use of the likely strengths of the type, especially the dominant function (e.g., helping a dominant Extraverted Intuitive manager analyze his or her ability to use Intuition and be creative in a stable hierarchical organization)

Third, in developing a relationship with a manager, type dynamics can provide guidance about where to start and be direct (i.e., using the approach and language of the manager's extraverted function) and where to be more careful, take more time, and watch for cues (i.e., regarding the manager's introverted function).

Fourth, although the common notion about leaders is that they are extraverted, research on distribution of types in managers suggests that Extraverts and Introverts are approximately equally distributed (see Chapter 1). Type dynamics provides invaluable information for working with introverted managers, who might otherwise seem much harder to understand and approach.

Fifth, type dynamics can be a very useful resource for practitioners to use in helping leaders explain their leadership style to their staff—a valuable contribution as staff often devote a lot of time and energy in trying to understand and please the boss.

Sixth, type dynamics can provide an accessible and palatable way to talk to leaders about their limitations and blind spots—an important but challenging task. A clear awareness of limitations and blind spots can be invaluable to leaders and a lack of such can cause talented and committed leaders to fail. An inevitable implication of discussing a manager's type dynamics is that there are functions that the manager is probably not devoting much energy and attention to, in either the outer world or the inner world. Discussion can then focus on the implications of that lack of attention and on strategies to develop awareness and skill in some areas and to deal with other areas through delegation, collaboration, or other similar approaches.

Seventh, type dynamics can provide an understanding of the different reactions of different types of managers under extreme stress. Practitioners can use this understanding to help managers anticipate and deal effectively with their reactions to stress.

Finally, type dynamics can both legitimize and prompt constructive discussion about the inner world, an important arena both for Introverts (for whom it is the most important focus) and for Extraverts (for whom it provides the essential balance of dominant and auxiliary, perception and judgment). In organizations, we sometimes act as if only the outer world—that is, what we directly see and hear and touch—is important to our success and satisfaction. Type dynamics honors the primary importance of the inner world for Introverts and alerts Extraverts to the importance of their inner world for effective functioning.

POTENTIAL OUTCOMES FOR LEADERS

Earlier sections have alluded to the potential benefits for leaders of understanding their type dynamics. The purpose of this section is to summarize and specify these potential positive outcomes, as presented below.

First, type dynamics can lead to a clearer understanding of a leader's central core, the driving force in his or her personality. This, in turn, gives the leaders the opportunity to ensure that their dominant function has space and time to operate in all their important actions. People are typically at their best when they are using their dominant function, and leaders will be more effective if they make a conscious effort to ensure that their dominant function receives support and is used regularly.

Second, type dynamics also points to the importance of using and developing a reliable auxiliary function to provide balance. In decision-making situations, leaders can make it a priority to consciously give time to both information gathering and the application of principles and values.

Third, leaders can recognize the misunderstandings that can result from their failure to make their introverted side clear to others. This does not mean learning to extravert everything, as it is both natural and very important to use the introverted part internally. But it does mean learning ways to communicate whatever is introverted when it affects decisions or actions. This may mean, for an ESFP leader, finding ways to clearly express the values that underlie decisions; for INTJ leaders, it may mean finding the words to articulate the clear inner vision that securely guides them so that others can see it also.

Fourth, understanding the overall pattern of their perceiving and judging (i.e., what is extraverted vs. introverted; what is dominant, auxiliary, etc.) can be invaluable, both for their understanding when confronting various tasks and circumstances and for articulating to others. Some examples might include dominant Extraverted Intuitive leaders saying, when appropriate, "Let me brainstorm about that for a few minutes"; dominant Introverted Sensing leaders saying about something new, "I'd like to take a look at where they've implemented that approach"; and dominant Introverted Intuitive leaders saying, "Let me reflect on that and let you know my decision first thing tomorrow."

Fifth, as leaders become aware of the richness and complexity of their own type dynamics, they are likely to become more aware—and appreciative—of the richness and complexity of other people. This effect may be particularly valuable to technically oriented leaders, who can be intrigued by the elegance, complexity, and accuracy of their own type dynamics and can begin to see other people as more interesting, complex, and potentially understandable.

Finally, as described in the previous section, type dynamics can alert leaders to their likely limitations and blind spots and to the ways that they may be likely to react in times of extreme stress.

SUMMARY

Type dynamics can provide a unique and valuable contribution to leadership development by providing leaders—and the people who work with leaders—with a more refined sense of their characteristic ways of collecting information and making judgments. Type dynamics can give leadership development practitioners a more sophisticated framework for understanding differences in pace, timing, form, and relative emphasis of data collection and decision making in different types of leaders. Type dynamics can also enable practitioners to help leaders be more effective across a wide array of roles, situations, and tasks.

REFERENCES

Jung, C. G. (1976). Psychological Types. In *Collected Works, Vol. 18.* Translated by R. F. C. Hull. Princeton, NJ: Princeton University Press.

Lombardo, M. M., & McCauley, C. D. (1988). *The dynamics of management derailment* (Technical Report Number 34). Greensboro, NC: Center for Creative Leadership.

McCaulley, M. H. (1990). The *Myers-Briggs Type Indicator* and leadership. In K. E. Clark & M. B. Clark (Eds.), *Measures of leadership* (pp. 381–418). West Orange, NJ: Leadership Library of America, Inc.

Myers, I. B. (1993). *Introduction to type* (5th ed.). Palo Alto, CA: Consulting Psychologists Press.

Myers, I. B., with Myers, P. B. (1980). *Gifts differing.* Palo Alto, CA: Consulting Psychologists Press.

Myers, I. B., & McCaulley, M. H. (1985). *Manual: A guide to the development and use of the Myers-Briggs Type Indicator.* Palo Alto, CA: Consulting Psychologists Press.

Myers, K. D., & Kirby, L. K. (1994). *Introduction to type dynamics and development.* Palo Alto, CA: Consulting Psychologists Press.

Osborn, N., & Osborn, D. B. (1994). MBTI, FIRO-B, and NAFTA: Leadership profiles of not-so-distant neighbors. In C. Fitzgerald (Ed.), *Proceedings of the Myers-Briggs Type Indicator and Leadership: An International Research Conference* (pp. 31-45). College Park, MD: University of Maryland University College National Leadership Institute.

Quenk, N. L. (1993). *Beside ourselves: Our hidden personality in everyday life.* Palo Alto, CA: Davies-Black.

APPENDIX

The next four pages show the interactions of dominant and auxiliary functions of type.

Interactions of Dominant and Auxiliary Functions

Dominant Extraverted Sensing

ESTP

Their dominant extraverted Sensing leads ESTPs to quickly recognize the realities of the moment. The auxiliary introverted Thinking then uses that data to arrive at expedient solutions. It is this combination that produces the resourceful, troubleshooting strength of the ESTP. However, at times they can become so involved in stimulating experiences and actions that they ignore their internal evaluating mechanism. They may then forget analysis, evaluation, and commitments in order to live in the moment.

ESFP

Their dominant extraverted Sensing leads ESFPs to generate stimulating and fun activities for people around them. They plunge into action with enthusiasm, energizing people to work as a team. Their auxiliary introverted Feeling makes them responsive to the needs of others, guides their decisions, and creates a warm and caring style in their interactions. At times, however, new people and experiences so engage ESFPs' dominant extraverted Sensing that they put aside their internal valuing process and ignore prior commitments.

Dominant Introverted Sensing

ISTJ

Their auxiliary extraverted Thinking leads ISTJs to structure and organize their outer life, to rationalize their world along logical principles, to seek closure and clarity. When change is demanded, however, they can suddenly appear unreasonable, refusing to apply their thinking logic because their dominant introverted Sensing does not yet have enough data. In spite of their urge to fulfill responsibilities and organize systems, they will resist until their dominant Sensing has sufficient realistic, specific information. Once convinced, however, ISTJs can implement changes and take responsibility for them.

ISFJ

Their auxiliary extraverted Feeling leads ISFJs to express a gentle kindness toward others. ISFJs work devotedly to structure the environment to create harmony. Their dominant introverted Sensing contains complete details about people and directs their service to others into practical channels. However, if their inner store of sensing data includes information about how particular situations should be handled or what certain people need, ISFJs can suddenly become stubborn and reluctant to consider alternatives, insisting that they know how something should be done.

Interactions of Dominant and Auxiliary Functions (continued)

Dominant Extraverted Intuition

ENTP

Their dominant extraverted Intuition leads ENTPs to quickly gain insight into the meanings and connections of what is going on around them. They use the logical principles of their auxiliary introverted Thinking to evaluate, prioritize, and implement these insights with resourcefulness. However, they can sometimes get so entranced by a new idea that they fail to apply their critiquing ability, which leads them to go from one exciting possibility to another without committing to and following through on any of them.

ENFP

Their dominant extraverted Intuition provides ENFPs with unusual insight into exciting possibilities in the people and the world around them. They use their auxiliary introverted Feeling to evaluate these insights in terms of their values and, in combination with their Intuitive enthusiasm, to inspire others to implement these possibilities. At times, however, they get caught up in an intriguing new person or idea, suspending their judgment and their priorities. They may then overextend themselves and not give enough time and energy to the people and things important to them, their inner commitments.

Dominant Introverted Intuition

INTJ

Their auxiliary extraverted Thinking leads INTJs to structure their external lives to provide rational order. They use their Thinking to communicate ideas logically and clearly. Logic is not the final judge, however. If someone's analysis or ideas do not fit with the INTJ's internal intuitive pattern and insights (their dominant introverted Intuition), INTJs will reject them, regardless of how clear and logical they seem to be. INTJs will then stubbornly cling to what they know is right.

INFJ

Their auxiliary extraverted Feeling leads INFJs to focus on values and loyalty to others. INFJs work to structure environments to take account of the needs of others and provide ways for people to realize their goals. However, if something proposed by others does not fit with their inner vision (their dominant introverted Intuition) they will usually reject it forcefully, even when it is suggested by someone important to them and seems to others to exemplify the INFJ's values. They put intense effort into bringing the external world in line with their inner vision.

Interactions of Dominant and Auxiliary Functions (continued)

Dominant Extraverted Thinking

ESTJ

Their dominant extraverted Thinking leads ESTJs to focus on developing and implementing plans that will achieve clear goals as efficiently as possible. They are assisted by their auxiliary introverted Sensing, which stores a wealth of practical information about how things operate in the real world. If the data get in the way of completing their tasks, however, they will put the data aside in favor of a structure that makes sense within their Thinking logic. ESTJs may then ignore new or contradictory information that challenges the external structures they have put into place.

ENTJ

Their dominant extraverted Thinking leads ENTJs to focus on creating logical systems in the world to achieve long-term goals. They are assisted in this by their auxiliary introverted Intuition, which leads them to explore ideas and possibilities and to notice interesting patterns. ENTJs love the stimulation of talking and debating ideas, gathering insights that they can apply to the real world. However, their drive to structure their external environment through logical analysis is so strong that they will find ingenious ways to bring perception into line with their logical system.

Dominant Introverted Thinking

ISTP

Their auxiliary extraverted Sensing leads ISTPs to be observant and tolerant. Others find them egalitarian and easygoing. When they perceive that something is not logical and efficient, however, they may suddenly express their dominant introverted Thinking. Others then realize that the ISTP has been categorizing, analyzing, and critiquing what is going on. Their dominant Thinking will also sometimes lead them to choose and censor which sensing data they will notice and to organize the data to support their conclusions.

INTP

Their auxiliary extraverted Intuition leads INTPs to effectively take in information, process it, and communicate ideas. When an intuition about something important is not logical and reasonable within their internal systems, however, INTPs will generally discount their intuition and go with the logical analysis of their dominant introverted Thinking. These systems of understanding may also influence the information INTPs pay attention to and the way they take in new information.

Interactions of Dominant and Auxiliary Functions (continued)

Dominant Extraverted Feeling

ESFJ

Their dominant extraverted Feeling leads ESFJs to focus on establishing cooperation and goodwill in their environment. They use their auxiliary introverted Sensing to solicit and store detailed information about people and to support others in practical ways. Though they have access to a wealth of specific information, no fact is as important to them as how others are feeling and whether their environment is harmonious. As a result, they can sometimes seem blind to unpleasant facts, especially regarding people close to them.

ENFJ

Their dominant extraverted Feeling leads ENFJs to design and implement ways for people to reach their full potential. They facilitate and encourage development and growth in others. ENFJs use their auxiliary introverted Intuition to "read" people, and quickly assess the needs and possibilities of others. Their focus on cooperation, compatibility, and encouragement, however, can sometimes lead them to ignore signs of conflict and undesirable behavior of people close to them.

Dominant Introverted Feeling

ISFP

Their auxiliary extraverted Sensing leads ISFPs to be finely attuned to their external environment, noticing people and the natural world around them. They are flexible, adaptable, and sympathetic. However, their most important quality is an internal core of values by which they evaluate everything. These values typically focus on supporting people and on practical care for the natural environment. If their core values are violated, they can firmly extravert this inner core, refusing to adapt or flexibly go along with actions they find wrong.

INFP

Their auxiliary extraverted Intuition leads them to be curious about people and ideas, excited about possibilities they see for improving the world. They love to explore new ways of understanding how human beings work. Inside, however, INFPs have a "filter"—a coherent value system through which they evaluate ideas, people, and actions. They commit themselves intensely to people and ideas they believe in, and oppose anything that violates their values. INFPs focus on creating congruence between their inner values and outer lives.

10 | Type Development and Leadership Development

Integrating Reality and Vision,
Mind and Heart

Catherine Fitzgerald

The *Myers-Briggs Type Indicator* (MBTI) has become a key resource in leadership development and is widely used in leadership development training and executive coaching. There are three possible levels of interpretation and use of the MBTI, and the MBTI is being used almost exclusively at the first and most basic level of interpretation. An increase in both expertise and use at more sophisticated levels could make an enhanced contribution to leaders and their organizations.

The three levels of interpretation and use are as follows. Level one involves the *type dimensions,* using the MBTI at the level of explaining MBTI preferences and helping people to understand the meaning of each preference and identify their own preferences. Level two involves *type dynamics,* the interplay of the MBTI functions within each type. Level three involves *type development,* the pattern of development of the MBTI functions across the life span.

Each of these levels of interpretation and use of the MBTI can make a substantial contribution to understanding and facilitating leadership development. Chapter 9 in this volume describes the application of the second level of interpretation, type dynamics, to leadership development. The purpose of this chapter is to describe the potential contributions of the third level of interpretation, type development, to the development of leaders.

My interest in type development began a number of years ago, when I started teaching with cotrainers in the Association for Pychological Type MBTI Qualifying Program. I became intrigued by an expression that was clearly the greatest compliment that you could give to someone who was being discussed: "He's very well-developed"; "That's very good type development"; "She's a very well-developed INFJ." I knew about Isabel Briggs Myers' view of type development (Myers & Myers, 1980, 1994) and had read Grant's (Grant, Thompson, & Clarke, 1983) theory of type development, but the subtleties of a person being judged to be "well-developed" were new and provocative to me. I was also impressed by how much agreement there seemed to be among people who paid attention to this domain about what good type development looked like.

Since my first exposure to this view of type development, the concept of type development has become a critical aspect of my view of leadership and leadership development. The purposes of this chapter are to:

• Give a brief overview of type development theory, elaborating on differences in focus in the first and second half of life
• Address developmental issues in the second half of life in particular, with a focus on midlife as a critical integrative process for leaders and prospective leaders
• Explore the relationship between type development and leadership development
• Discuss implications for practice of the theory presented

TYPE DEVELOPMENT THEORY

Type development theory addresses the process of developing over the life span and builds on the theory of type dynamics, which proposes that

• Above and beyond describing each MBTI preference, there is a dynamic within each type regarding how the preferences fit together.
• The two middle dimensions of the MBTI, the functions, are literally cognitive processes that everyone uses *some* of the time; that is, everyone takes in data about the real world (Sensing), sees patterns and possibilities (Intuition), applies logic to decisions (Thinking), and applies personal values to decisions (Feeling).

- Based on type, there is a particular order and way in which the functions tend to be used.
- Of the two most preferred functions, one will be a perceiving function (either Sensing or Intuition) and one will be a judging function (either Thinking or Feeling); one will be *the* most preferred function (called the *dominant* function) and one will be the second most preferred (called the auxiliary function).
- The two less-preferred functions are referred to as tertiary (i.e., the third most preferred) and inferior (i.e., the fourth or least preferred). The tertiary and inferior will generally be less developed, less conscious, more primitive, and harder to use than the dominant or auxiliary functions.

(For a more complete description of type dynamics and its use in leadership development, see Chapter 9.)

A theory of the process and timing of the development of the functions has been articulated by Grant (Grant, Thompson, & Clarke, 1983). As Grant's theory of type development has been an influential one with MBTI practitioners, I begin with his theory and suggest some modifications to it. Grant's theory addressed the ages at which the functions (i.e., Sensing, Intuition, Thinking, and Feeling) develop. He suggested the following sequence for this development:

- 0 to 6 years   Undifferentiated
- 6 to 12 years   Development of the dominant function
- 12 to 20 years   Development of the auxiliary function
- 20 to 35 years   Development of the tertiary function
- 35 to 50 years   Development of the inferior function

Grant has made an important contribution by addressing the important issue of type development. However, his theory requires modification in two places. First, I have serious doubts that children under six are "undifferentiated." My own experience in raising my two children, in observing nieces, nephews, and friends' children, and in hearing other parents describe their young children, suggests to me that type preferences appear much earlier than Grant suggests. My second problem with the model involves what seems to me to be an overly fast pace of development of the tertiary and inferior functions. If people reach midlife (i.e., mid to late thirties) with their dominant and auxiliary well developed and reliable, it is an accomplishment. Prior to midlife, the tertiary is rarely well developed. A concrete example of this with regard to managers is that, at the start of the midlife process, INTJs and ISTJs do not seem to have better-developed Feeling judgment than ESTJs and ENTJs, even though Feeling is the tertiary of the former and the inferior of the latter.

A way to conceptualize type development that is more persuasive than Grant's model involves an extrapolation from Jung's thinking regarding the first versus second stages of life. During the first stage (through approximately age 35 to 40), the focus is on being a specialist—specializing in a profession or business, a way of life, family roles, and also in the two preferred functions, the dominant and auxiliary. In the second stage, midlife and beyond, the focus is on becoming a generalist, incorporating all of the parts of ourselves that we had put aside in the first half of life. This includes all our neglected, disowned, rejected parts—aspects or characteristics about which we said things like, "My brother is like that, but I'm not" or "That stingy (or irresponsible or spendthrift or . . .) person is like that, but I'm not" or "some people are tactful in situations like this, but I'm not." At this point, incorporating our third and fourth functions, the tertiary and the inferior, becomes an important task. The midlife process, when it works well, is an integrative one in which people become more complex and multidimensional, with an appreciation of a broader range of perspectives and approaches.

THE MIDLIFE PROCESS

Practitioners, theorists, and researchers who are interested in leaders, leadership, and leadership development should be interested in the difference in tasks between the first and the second half of life, and should especially be interested in the midlife process. There are a number of reasons that the developmental process generally, and midlife in particular, are important:

- In terms of age, a great many middle managers and most upper-middle and upper-level managers are in midlife.
- As managers progress through organizational levels, the training and development they receive focuses less on technical issues and more on personal development—and those of us involved in that personal development require a coherent way of understanding the midlife process and providing some guidance and assistance regarding it.
- Organizations can benefit enormously from progress made by their managers and executives in integrating their less-preferred functions.

The midlife process appears to happen something like this: Starting in the mid to late thirties, people begin to get inklings—"taps on the shoulder"—with a subtle but increasingly clear message: "We're back!" What is "back" is an array of feelings, ideas, reactions, and so on, that are experienced as old, somewhat primitive, unsettled, and unsettling, all of which leave people feeling like "It's not me." Jung (1933) described this period in this way:

> We see that in this phase of life . . . a significant change in the human psyche is in preparation. At first it is not a conscious and striking change: it is rather a matter of indirect signs of a change which seems to take its rise in the unconscious. Often it is something like a slow change in a person's character; in another case certain traits may come to light which had disappeared since childhood; or again, inclinations and interests begin to weaken and others take their place. (p. 104)

If people can pay *some* attention *sometimes* to the taps on the shoulder and can begin to let these other parts into their awareness and into an expanding sense of who they are, a rich, though not usually painless or easy, process of integration can begin to take place. This process of integration makes people more open to other perspectives and more aware of both the necessary tension between opposites (e.g., between practicality and vision) and the need to accept and work well with that tension. More genuine collaboration across types is possible in midlife than is possible earlier in life because, as we begin to allow a less-preferred and less-developed function to really have a voice, we realize how valuable and developmentally young that voice is, and we are more genuinely admiring of the giftedness of those who have adult versions of that voice.

The midlife process can at times be painful and tumultuous. Early in the process, and at times throughout this stage of life, people seem to experience a sense of real sadness. Some have attributed this sadness to an awareness of death, but that interpretation is not consistent with my discussions with people who are going through the process. The sadness seems to come from two related feelings. One feeling is that something important is missing in life; that what was fine until fairly recently is no longer satisfying. Exactly what is missing and how to obtain what is missing are extremely unclear to the person experiencing the process. The second feeling involves a sense that "I've worked so hard to develop myself and create my life; why all of a sudden is it not good enough?"

In his discussion of transitions, Bridges (1980) identified three stages of each transition: an ending, the neutral zone, and a beginning. According to Bridges, the neutral zone is a "no man's land between the old way of being and the new," and he argues persuasively that the neutral zone is an inevitable, predictable—and painful—period in any major transition. Bridges described how people experience the neutral zone:

> We aren't sure what is happening to us or when it will be over. We don't know whether we are going crazy or becoming enlightened, and neither prospect is one that we can readily discuss with anyone else. For many people the experience of the neutral zone is essentially one of emptiness in which the old reality looks transparent and nothing feels solid anymore. (p. 117)

During the midlife process, people seem to have periodic experiences very similar in feeling to Bridges' description of the neutral zone. For some, these experiences are fairly mild and fairly brief; for others, they are protracted and intense. For some, they happen early in the process; for others, they are experienced later. Some people make substantial—and surprising—changes in their personal and/or professional lives during this time; others make only minor adjustments.

As mentioned earlier, in midlife, people develop an inner "push" to work on their two least preferred functions. Although they feel pushed from within to incorporate the voices of their tertiary and inferior functions, people usually experience the process as a difficult one, because these functions—in their state of immaturity—present a startling contrast to the generally better-developed dominant and auxiliary functions. People often experience the emergence of the tertiary and inferior as a combination of confusing, painful, exciting, tiring, interesting, and disorienting.

What the Emergence of the Functions Looks Like at Midlife

From discussions with many managers, as well as with colleagues and friends, about the midlife process, I have an increasing sense of what the emergence of the different functions looks like at midlife. For Sensing types, midlife Intuition involves a new desire to pay attention to hunches and patterns and a new interest in things that they had previously thought were irrelevant or tedious. In one-on-one conversations, midlife Sensing managers have revealed a new—and to them surprising—interest in such areas as art, poetry, or psychology. For instance, one ESTJ government manager talked about being drawn to visit art galleries and noted that when she was younger, such places were alien and uninteresting to her. A Sensing manager in a manufacturing organization talked about being drawn to write poetry, which he had never shown to anyone else. An ESTP oil company executive talked with great enthusiasm about his recently developed interest in psychology, which provided a way of thinking about things that he had thought earlier to be irrelevant and strange. What these examples have in common is the midlife Sensor's very new fascination with abstract things that have no immediate practical value.

Intuitives are very familiar with paying attention to their hunches, but Sensing types tend to focus instead on the facts of a situation. In midlife, Sensing types sometimes report paying more attention than previously to their hunches, with results that are often surprising to them. An ISTJ executive, for example, reported with some enthusiasm the midlife emergence of his "hunches." Early in the process, he recalled his staff bringing him a table or chart and his getting a sense, without any facts, that something was wrong with it. Because he did not have facts to support his hunches, he thoroughly researched each hunch and found that hunches very often led him in a useful direction. At the time of our discussion, he declared with pride: "When I tell my staff that I have a hunch about something, they will instantly pursue it!" In general, Sensing types seem to experience midlife Intuition as unsettling, somewhat weird, but often interesting.

For Intuitive types, midlife Sensing involves a desire at times to be more present in the immediate time and place. It seems to take the form of just wanting—for pretty much the first time—to be, to sit in a place and just look and hear and touch and smell. It may involve increased interest in physical comfort (e.g., how a chair really feels) and sense activities (e.g., touching). It may involve a focus on money as something suddenly real and not just a concept. Midlife Sensing sometimes involves a new interest in activities such as gardening, with Intuitive types reporting great delight and a quiet satisfaction in feeling the earth, moving things, and just physically experiencing the garden environment. One Intuitive management consultant, unfamiliar with the manifestations of midlife Sensing, confessed that she was drawn to being in her backyard and was spending her time there just looking—with great interest and involvement—at the bark of one particular tree. Intuitives report this new focus on being more immediately present as both difficult and exciting.

For Thinking types, midlife Feeling involves discovering their "softer side," and, in the process, Thinking types often experience a new desire for intimacy with others and a new tendency to be emotionally touched by certain expressions of feelings. In midlife, Thinking managers may develop a new focus on people issues. An ST manager with a strong technical background, told me: "The technical issues are less important and much less interesting to me than they were earlier. The people issues are what I care about and am primarily focused on now; I realize how much I have to learn."

Thinking types can become unexpectedly—and embarrassingly— tearful about depictions of feelings, even when these depictions are conventional (e.g., long-distance telephone ads). A Thinking manager once told me, "I've become an old softie. I really care so much about the other members of the top management team, but they still think I'm a tough guy." At a leadership development program, an ESTJ military officer heard about my interest in midlife and cautiously raised the topic with me. When I generally described the midlife process and some of its possible signs, he confessed, "I can't sing the 'Star Spangled Banner' anymore." Whenever he started to sing the national anthem, he got choked up and started to cry—a reaction that greatly embarrassed him but which also showed him how much he cared about what the song represented for him. His story illustrates what I often observe and hear from Thinking types about midlife Feeling: that Thinking types can tend to feel somewhat overwhelmed and out of control when they encounter their midlife Feeling.

For Feeling types, midlife Thinking involves discovering their more tough-minded side, what Jung (1933) called their "sharpness of mind" (p. 108). At times, Feeling types discover an inner push to be more objective and more separate from others and to focus on "What I want for myself," as opposed to feeling obliged to respond to others' needs. In midlife, Feeling types are often drawn to be assertive and competitive in a new way in the world. They may begin to feel more sense of their own personal power and authority and let themselves be more challenging. Feeling types report feeling guilty about the urge to do things for themselves versus doing things for others whom they care about. A manager with a preference for Feeling told me, "I used to be a nice person," and proceeded to describe what sounded like a very appropriate, assertive setting of limits with others. In addition to occasional guilt, Feeling types report experiencing a new sense of capability and possibility for impact in the world.

When the Midlife Process Does Not Go Well

The midlife process is challenging for everyone; however, some people seem to ultimately be more open and responsive to the process than others. And some seem to strongly resist the process, with negative consequences. If people do not pay attention to the taps on the shoulder, if they resist change and integration, the taps become more insistent until they become blows. While people are resisting these new inner voices, they become increasingly rigid. Jung (1933) wrote about this misdirection of the midlife process and its outcome:

> The convictions and principles which have hitherto been accepted—especially the moral principles—commence to harden and to grow increasingly rigid until, somewhere towards the age of 50, a period of intolerance and fanaticism is reached. It is then as if the existence of these principles were endangered, and it were therefore necessary to emphasize them all the more. The wine of youth does not always clear with advancing years; oftentimes it grows turbid. (p. 104)

Within organizations, managers who fit the above description are not uncommon. At 50, they are caricatures of themselves at 30; they are experienced as "dinosaurs," have great difficulty with organizational and personal change, and make efforts to limit the horizons and growth of their staff. Not surprisingly, staff will go out of their way to avoid working for such managers. Also not surprisingly, given the need of organizations to respond to accelerating change, to what Vaill (1989) calls "permanent white water," these managers are extremely limited in their contributions to their organizations.

When the Midlife Process Goes Well

In contrast to the rigidity just described, when the process of midlife goes well, people begin to achieve more depth, flexibility, and integration and to become, in type development terms, well developed. Being well developed involves a combination of clarity about oneself and an acceptance of and flexibility about differences. As a first step, good type development involves being grounded in one's type preferences: having a solid, effective, and reliable way to perceive the world and to make judgments about it. As a second step, good type development also involves:

- Recognition of the limitations of your preferences, without in any way discounting, doubting, or rejecting them

- A genuine valuing of both the gifts of the preferences that are opposite to one's own and the people who exhibit those preferences
- Acceptance of one's limited ability to access and use the preferences opposite one's own, while enduring in their pursuit
- Increasing interest in and patience with the expression of perspectives related to one's less-preferred functions

THE RELATIONSHIP BETWEEN TYPE DEVELOPMENT AND LEADERSHIP DEVELOPMENT

The individual process of integration that can occur in midlife is closely related to the process of leadership development—a process that involves the increasing ability to effectively integrate differences within organizations. The purpose of this section is to relate the theme of personal integration discussed earlier with key themes in the literature on leadership. This section assembles a variety of expert views on leadership and links those views to issues of individual development in the second half of life.

Past theory and research in leadership has been criticized as producing a "bewildering mass of findings [that has] . . . not produced an integrated understanding of leadership (Stogdill, 1974, p. vii). Lombardo and McCall (1978) have suggested that this shortcoming is attributed to a "reductionist view of leadership [that] . . . ignores the richness of reality and focuses primarily on what leaders say they do [versus] . . . what they actually do" (p. 7). When writers on leadership look more broadly (i.e., beyond laboratory studies and beyond looking at single dimensions of behavior or personality) and look at what leaders actually do, leadership is very often described as a balancing of a complex array of opposing forces.

Quinn (1988) described how leaders are confronted by change, ambiguity, and contradiction and claimed that they spend much of their time living in "fields of perceived tensions" in which there are no right answers. According to Quinn, the higher a leader goes in an organization, the more exaggerated this phenomenon becomes. He added that "one-dimensional bromides (care for people, work harder, get control, be innovative) are simply half-truths representing single domains of action. What exists in reality are contradictory pressures, emanating from a variety of domains" (p. 3).

In a recent book on leadership, Aram (1990) asserted that "multiple and often-conflicting criteria for action exist in all human organizations." He explained that

> large, hierarchical organizations seeking to accomplish complex tasks have conflicting interests, functions, and values built into their very character. Surely, particular criteria can dominate an organization for a period of time, but long-term success requires a full appreciation for counter or opposing values, interests, and functions. Paradox and dilemma are central features of organizational life. (p. 185)

Johnson (1992) described "polarity management," and argued that leaders and organizations must continuously deal with opposing polarities (such as stability vs. change) that can never be solved, but which must constantly be managed for the organization to thrive.

Koestenbaum (1991) asserted that the "very essence of reality" involves polarization, that

> everything has its opposite, its counterpart . . . nothing is either black or white. For every masculine trait there is a feminine counterpart; opposed to matter there is antimatter. For every right there is a contradiction that is also right. Leadership means coping in that kind of world, a world where answers are actions, decisions, commitments, and risks, not the unambiguous conclusions of mathematical calculations. (p. 72)

Koestenbaum argued that it was essential for leaders to be open to contradictory ideas, conflicting emotions, and the ambiguities of the world.

In summary, these authors—and many of their contemporaries—describe a complexity of forces that need to be focused upon by leaders and emphasize that many of these forces (e.g., stability and change) are in opposition to each other. The following sections examine the content of the opposing forces that leaders need to manage and relate the forces identified to the basic cognitive functions identified by Jung.

Two Key Sets of Polarities: Sensing–Intuition and Thinking–Feeling

If you look at the content of the polarities described by researchers and writers on leadership and organizations, two key sets of polarities are repeatedly described and highlighted. One set of polarities involves the tension between a practical short-term, present-oriented approach—one that focuses on reality and facts—and a visionary, long-term, future-oriented approach—one that focuses on possibilities. The second set of polarities deals with the tension between a technical, analytical, tough-minded approach and a relationship-based, people-oriented approach. These polarities, although described in a variety of ways, are essentially equivalent to the MBTI functions of Sensing versus Intuition and Thinking versus Feeling.

Sensing–Intuition

The Sensing–Intuition polarity appears in a number of different forms. Kanter (1989) critiqued two current modes of leadership, the traditional "corpocrat" and the innovative "cowboy" and proposed a synthesis:

> Without the bold impulses of take-action entrepreneurs and their constant questioning of the rules, we would miss one of the most potent sources of business revitalization and development. But without the discipline and coordination of conventional management, we could find waste instead of growth, unnecessary risk instead of revitalization. . . . Today's corporate balancing act requires a different style from either extreme. . . . [It needs] to both conserve resources and pursue growth opportunities . . . the strength to balance somewhere in the middle, taking the best of the corpocrat's discipline and the cowboy's entrepreneurial zeal. (p. 361)

Senge (1990) suggested that a core task for leaders is to manage the "creative tension" between vision and reality:

> This tension is generated by holding a vision and concurrently telling the truth about current reality relative to that vision. . . . A leader's story, sense of purpose, values and vision establish the direction and target. His relentless commitment to the truth and to inquiry into the forces underlying current reality continually highlight the gaps between reality and the vision. Leaders generate and manage this creative tension—not just in themselves but in an entire organization. This is how they energize an organization. (p. 357)

Kotter (1990) distinguished between management and leadership but asserted that today's organizations need to be high in both management and leadership to be successful. He contrasted management's role of *planning and budgeting* ("to help produce predictable results . . . [by] developing a detailed map . . . of how to achieve the results currently expected") with leadership's role of *establishing direction* ("to help produce changes needed to cope with a changing business environment [by] developing a vision which describes key aspects of an organization in the future"; p. 144). In his study of successful executives, Kotter found them doing both Sensing and Intuitive work: "They were being asked to produce consistent, short-term results to satisfy key constituencies and . . . they were also being asked to help their organizations adapt to changing competition, technology, and markets" (p. 104).

In *Mind of a Manager, Soul of a Leader,* Hickman (1992) draws a distinction between managers and leaders that is similar to Kotter's distinction, while similarly asserting the need for both management and leadership in organizations. Three of the five arenas he used to contrast management-oriented and leadership-oriented approaches contained elements related to Sensing versus Intuition. With regard to external/internal change, he contrasted these actions: duplicate versus originate, plan versus experiment, reorganize versus rethink, and refine versus revolutionize. Regarding competitive strategy/advantage, he contrasted version versus vision, and incremental versus sweeping. Related to bottom-line performance and results, he contrasted performance versus potential, tangible versus intangible, present versus future, and short term versus long term.

In summary, underlying many leadership models is an ability to harness both opposing sides of the Sensing–Intuition dimension. The Sensing side deals with considerations that are:

- present-oriented
- short-term
- incremental
- practical
- tangible
- reality-based

The Intuitive side involves considerations that are:

- future-oriented
- long-term
- experimental/revolutionary
- creative
- intangible
- visionary

Thinking–Feeling

The Thinking–Feeling aspects of leadership have appeared repeatedly in studies of leadership. Summarizing decades of research on leadership in *Stogdill's Handbook of Leadership,* Bass (1981) concluded that "the most frequently obtained leader skill factors tended to involve task or socioemotional performance" (p. 104). Literally hundreds of studies have attempted to identify which approach, task focused, relationship focused, or some combination of the two, is superior.

Recent writings, particularly those focusing on actual leaders, have tended to emphasize the integration of Thinking and Feeling. Vaill (1990) argued that leaders require a "passionate reason" and described it eloquently:

> Three qualities that are much desired in organizational life these days are creativity, courage, and leadership. A little reflection will show, I think, that each of these qualities is an example of passionate reason. Creativity is both a primal energy for what is new and different and a cool understanding of what is indeed new and different. Courage blends the knowledge of the danger one is in with the determination not to be conquered by fear. "Determination" and "resolve" are much more matters of emotion, I believe, than they are logical conclusions. But courage would not be courage if it did not blend rational understanding of the situation with emotional commitment to hold to a particular course no matter what. (p. 338)

Vaill suggested that this passionate reason is "Wholehearted and wholeheaded, and the more profound it is, the less it resides in any one faculty of the human being, the less it is either mental or emotional, either reasonable or passionate. . . . [It] cannot entail the suppression of one part in favor of another" (p. 338).

Srivasta (1983), who has written extensively on executive thinking, suggested that such thinking involves "a union between rational and emotional modes of thinking that produces actions which both appear logical and are bestowed with passion" (p. 299). Aram (1990) emphasized the need for leaders to integrate a "concern for people and a concern for tasks" and a "desire to be fair to all employees and a wish to accommodate the special needs of a few" (p. 185).

Pascale (1990) discussed an "essential tension" between "hard minds" and "soft hearts":

> "Hard-minded" executives include more than those who drive for financial results (although this is the most common by far). It is reflected in a preoccupation with concrete, bottom-line results of all types (e.g., achieving deadlines, or meeting a particular standard or quota). . . . In contrast, "soft-hearted" values pertain to intangibles that are tied to higher-order ideals affecting employees (e.g., treating them with dignity), customer (e.g., fairness), and society (e.g., making a social contribution). These often get short-changed. Soft-hearted values are essential because they act as a counterweight to tangible financial (and other such concrete) goals to which all else is sacrificed. (p. 77)

Kotter (1990) made two distinctions between management and leadership that have components of Thinking versus Feeling. (Note again:

Kotter argued that organizations need both high management and high leadership.) He contrasted the management task of *organizing and staffing* ("creating an organization that can implement plans . . . a process of organizational design involving judgments about fit") with the leadership task of *aligning people* ("getting people lined up behind a vision [by] . . . getting people to understand and believe . . . by communicating . . . to all of the individuals"; p. 147). He also compared the management task of *controlling and problem solving* ("to minimize deviations from plan and thus help produce predictable results . . . [by] monitoring results, . . . identifying deviations, . . . and then planning and organizing") with the leadership task of *motivating and inspiring* ("to energize people . . . [by] satisfying very basic but often unfulfilled human needs . . . and thereby creating an unusually high energy level in people"; p. 149).

Similarly, in discussing management versus leadership approaches to organizational culture/capability, Hickman (1992) presented contrasts that relate to Thinking versus Feeling. He compared authority versus influence, programs versus people, instruction versus inspiration, control versus empower, and consistency versus commitment.

Framed as "masculine" and "feminine," the integration of Thinking and Feeling is implicit in Kaplan, Drath, and Kofodimos' (1991) description of "character shifts" in executives. In a number of studies, Kaplan et al. have investigated "expansive" executives, ambitious, hard-driving executives who are focused on gaining mastery over their environment. They outlined some of the difficulties experienced by and caused by expansive executives who, they argued, may require a "shift in character" to be truly effective in managing and leading. Kaplan et al. outlined the necessary changes:

> For male executives, a shift in character often means a move in the direction of the "feminine," embracing a reduction (even if modest) in their investment in work and an increase in their investment in personal relationships. For men to make this shift at midlife is to redefine themselves as being less thoroughly wrapped up in the quest for mastery, power, and rationality and more concerned with cultivating close, mutual, emotionally expressive relationships. . . . The converse of these executives are those managers . . . whose expansive sides are underdeveloped and whose relational sides are overdeveloped for their leadership roles. They are, to varying degrees, too attuned to how people respond to their initiatives, too reluctant to assert themselves, too eager to please, too self-effacing, too self-minimizing. Their developmental task, the reverse of the extremely expansive executive's, is to rediscover self-assertion and personal power. (pp. 176–177)

In a multidecade longitudinal study, Heath and Heath, (1991) researched the determinants of success in life. Although, like Kaplan et al., their conclusions focus on the notions of masculine and feminine, they appear to deal with the Thinking–Feeling dimension. Heath and Heath concluded:

> If you want a simplified prescription for how to grow up to succeed, the two most noticeable personality strengths would be your maturity and androgyny. More than any other of the numerous personality traits I measured, they predict best who will succeed and be happy. My previous research had alerted me to the importance of psychological maturity. . . . I had had no clue from my earlier research that androgynous, particularly interpersonally feminine, skills would also consistently predict who would succeed. By androgynous, I mean persons whose peers rate them to show many of the strengths associated with both masculinity and femininity. Some stereotypic masculine strengths are self-reliance, independence, and ambition; some typical feminine strengths are sensitivity to the needs of others, loyalty, and compassion. (pp. 18–19)

Surprised by the finding, Heath and Heath added:

> I have to confess that years of studying how we grow up healthily did not prepare me for how much an androgynous character contributes to success and fulfillment. The result—one of the study's many surprises—taught me about a blind spot in my own thinking about growing up. For 30 years, I had taught my students about yin and yang, the feminine and masculine principles, and Carl Jung's notions about the individuation of anima and animus in the adult years. I knew the feminists' arguments that we must become more androgynous to be healthy persons. But I had never really believed such ideas since no one had ever given me the scientific evidence that I require to support my beliefs. So I never studied androgyny earlier. I included measures of it in the middle-age phase of the study to check out Jung's notions, but I never expected they would be useful. Was I wrong! For the first time, we now have good consistent evidence that documents the wisdom of such religious and clinical insights. (pp. 18–19)

In a similar vein, Birren and Fisher (1990), in reviewing research and theory on the topic of wisdom, concluded that wisdom is the integration of "thinking, feeling, and doing." Note that, although neither Heath and Heath nor Birren and Fisher are specifically addressing the topic of leadership development, the similarity of their findings about related human development domains is noteworthy.

In summary, there is a widespread and persistent call for leaders to combine and make the best use of both sides of the apparently opposing qualities of Thinking and Feeling. This call is reinforced by work by researchers in such areas as adult development and wisdom whose findings are remarkably similar. The Thinking preference is associated with components of leadership that are:

- task oriented
- tough-minded
- courageous
- rational
- analytical
- mastery oriented
- oriented to problem solving

The Feeling preference, on the other hand, is associated with components of leadership that are:

- relationship oriented
- tenderhearted
- compassionate
- interpersonally sensitive
- inspirational
- values oriented

The following section elaborates on two models of management/leadership that attempt to integrate both the Sensing–Intuition and the Thinking–Feeling dimensions.

Two Four-Element Models

Two experts in leadership and organizational change, Koestenbaum and Quinn, have each developed four-element models that are particularly relevant to type development, for two reasons. First, the elements of both of their frameworks—both of which were developed *without* reference to psychological type—are remarkably analogous to the four MBTI functions. Second, similar to the perspective inherent in type development, they both emphasized that it is not possible to choose among the elements, that all four elements *together* are essential for success in leading organizations and that, if any element is missing, the leader and the organization are at substantial risk.

In *Leadership: The Inner Side of Greatness*, Koestenbaum (1991) described the four "foundational" dimensions or "strategies" of leadership: vision, reality, ethics, and courage. As they are described by Koestenbaum, they are remarkably similar to the MBTI functions of Intuition, Sensing, Thinking, and Feeling.

Vision involves "maintaining a clear image of your distant goals, . . . moving away from micromanagement to macroleadership, . . . exhibiting a high degree of creativity, . . . having awareness of your possibilities" (pp. 84–85). Reality, which stands "in sharp contrast to vision," involves "the pragmatism of being in touch with the market, with the facts, with the truth," meticulous attention to practical details, . . . to obtain[ing] extensive information, hav[ing] no illusions" (pp. 86, 88–89). For Koestenbaum, ethics means "primarily that people matter to you" and "that you know the power of love and that you act on that wisdom . . . that you appreciate the personal enrichment that comes from being of service" (p. 59). Courage involves "the willingness to risk . . . to exhibit personal autonomy and independence of thought" (pp. 92–93).

Koestenbaum described each dimension as essential to leadership, claiming that they are all needed, although not to the same degree in all circumstances. His model focused on development as a coming to terms with the need for perpetually dealing with opposites:

> The realization that no solution is found either in taking a stand on these opposites or in balancing them opens up the possibility of a higher level of perception, which integrates or synthesizes both and renders a fatuous choice between them unnecessary. This is called maturation, mellowing. It springs from wisdom. (p. 74)

In *Beyond Rational Management,* Quinn (1988) described a lengthy search for the characteristics of effective organizations. After many studies, Quinn observed that the list of characteristics differed from study to study and reported that "it seemed that the more we learned, the less we knew" (p. 47). To resolve the confusion, Quinn articulated the components of four major models that simultaneously coexist in organizations:

- The *internal process model* (the Hierarchy): focused on consolidation and equilibrium; valuing stability, control, continuity, measurement, and documentation
- The *open systems model* (the Adhocracy): focused on expansion and transformation; valuing insight, innovation, adaptation, and growth
- The *rational goal model* (the Firm): focused on maximization of output; valuing accomplishment, productivity, profit, direction, and decisiveness
- The *human relations model* (the Team): focused on the development of human resources; valuing concern, commitment, morale, participation, and openness

The internal process and the open systems models are seen as polar opposites, as are the rational goal and human relations models. The relationship to the MBTI functions, Sensing (internal process), Intuition (open systems), Thinking (rational goal), and Feeling (human relations), is striking.

Quinn (1988) asserted that the models were

> four ways of seeing the world that people hold implicitly and about which they feel intensely. They represent the values that precede the assumptions that people make about what is good and what is bad, the unseen values for whose sake people, programs, policies, and organizations live and die. (p. 42)

According to Quinn, all four models exist at the same time in organizations, and managers are expected to be adept at simultaneously considering and balancing the demands represented by each model. Furthermore, because of the conflicting messages and demands inherent among the four models and because of the desire to be internally consistent, he suggested that both theories of management and the advice given by practicing managers tend not to adequately represent this paradoxical situation.

Like Koestenbaum's, Quinn's model is also clearly developmental. He stressed the need to become a "master" manager and recommended as a first step becoming aware of strengths and blind spots. After that, he advised that

> you must then make a conscious effort to appreciate the importance of your weaknesses. What is it that you tend not to see? What skills do you tend to ignore? This kind of thinking is not easy. It involves a certain amount of cognitive complexity and means experimenting with opposing frames of reference. (p. 24)

The models of Koestenbaum and Quinn are not presented here to suggest that they are reducible to psychological type. They are presented because they are models developed by two very sophisticated organizational theorist/practitioners who have struggled to deal with the complexity, multidimensionality, and paradoxical nature of leadership and, in dealing with that complexity and multidimensionality, have identified four key elements that are remarkably similar to the MBTI functions. It is worth noting that Koestenbaum and Quinn come from different intellectual and practice traditions. Although both consult to leaders and organizations, Koestenbaum is an emeritus professor of philosophy and Quinn is a business professor. Their work was developed independently: Neither author refers to the other; in fact, their supporting references show almost no overlap. The substantial convergence of such different perspectives is provocative and of importance to leadership development practitioners, who increasingly recognize the value of going beyond type descriptions to deal with type dynamics and type development. Practitioners are referred to Koestenbaum and Quinn for a rich source of practical suggestions for working with leaders in a way that is very compatible with psychological type and a focus on type development.

THE MIDLIFE PROCESS AND LEADERSHIP DEVELOPMENT

Jung asserted that the four functions—Sensing, Intuition, Thinking, and Feeling—represent basic human cognitive processes and that each of these processes—and the manner in which they are opposed to each other—inevitably and profoundly influence all human enterprise. It is noteworthy that, more than three decades after Jung's death, these four dimensions should figure so prominently—and so often in the form of opposites—in the writings of leadership.

If successfully attending to and managing these two sets of opposites—reality and vision, mind and heart—is essential to effective leadership, then a critical component of leadership development involves facilitating an increasing awareness, understanding, and valuing of each function and an increasing capacity to deal well with the dynamic tension of each of the opposing functions (e.g., reality and vision). If this integrative capacity is potentially substantially enhanced by—or perhaps even dependent on—the personal integration that is part of the midlife process, it makes sense to provide guidance to leaders and prospective leaders about the midlife process.

Vaill (1990) addressed the issue of the "spiritual condition" of our leaders, defining spiritual condition as "the feeling a person has about the fundamental meaning of who they are, of what they are doing, and of the contributions they are making" (p. 333). He argued that this topic was a difficult but urgent one to address:

> We cannot afford the luxury of silence about the spiritual condition of our leaders. They themselves are experiencing stresses at a deep personal level that many of them cannot cope with; and they are taking actions in their organizations that in many cases reflect their fragile and embattled spiritual condition, and thus others are being affected by their spiritual condition. (p. 333)

Vaill's comments are reminiscent of comments made many decades ago (although not aimed directly at leaders) by Jung (1933) when he outlined the surprise and confusion of the midlife process:

> The worst of it all is that intelligent and cultivated people have these leanings without even knowing of the possibility of such transformations. Wholly unprepared, they embark upon the second half of life. Or are there perhaps colleges for forty-year-olds which prepare them for their coming life and its demands as the ordinary colleges introduce our young people to a knowledge of the world and of life? Thoroughly unprepared we take the step into the afternoon of life; worse still, we take this step with the false presupposition that our truths and ideals will serve us as hitherto. But we cannot live the afternoon of life according to the programme of life's morning—for what was great in the morning will be little at evening, and what in the morning was true will at evening have become a lie. (p. 108)

Do leadership development activities provide some aspects of a "college for forty-years-olds"? Can their contribution to both individual and organizational development be enhanced? Understanding and working to promote type development *can* make a significant contribution to leadership development. The following are some approaches for supporting the midlife process in leadership development settings:

1. We can provide some basic information about the process of midlife, such as the following:

   - Midlife is a normal process that predictably starts in the mid to late thirties.
   - Midlife is a change process, but it needn't be a crisis. In fact, research does *not* support the universality or even the frequency of the phenomenon widely known as the midlife "crisis."
   - A normal sensation is, "I'm not myself anymore"; it's normal to reexamine and reconsider basic life choices.
   - A natural part of the midlife process is a search for meaning, for what is truly important and valuable, both personally and professionally, at this time in one's life.

   Managers seem to find it helpful—and sometimes experience it as a great relief—just to have the process named and outlined.

2. When managers are familiar with their MBTI preferences, we can refer to their type and explain:

   - You are not changing type; your type preferences will not change.

- The midlife process involves your less-developed parts getting a voice, not taking over.
- You are not losing your logic (or your caring, etc.), but are complementing it by developing your Feeling side (or your Thinking side, etc.).
- The process, when it proceeds well, produces personal growth and integration; you have the prospect of making a more integrated contribution to your organization and profession.
- The goal is not perfection, but completion. The goal is not to be perfect at anything but to let all the parts of yourself have a voice and to value and work well with all those perspectives in your work and your life.

Describing in general terms what the midlife emergence of less-preferred functions looks like (e.g., some ways in which Sensing types experience midlife Intuition) can be helpful and reassuring and can open up valuable dialogues.

3. We can provide safe settings in which managers in midlife can discuss their search for meaning and value in the second half of their lives. Either (or both) individual discussions or discussions with small groups of peers can be valuable.

4. We can help people use their preferred modes to develop ways to approach less-developed areas (e.g., helping Thinking types develop logical frameworks to understand people-related issues).

5. We can encourage the search for and interaction with role models in a person's organization or industry—role models who are older and seem to integrate experience and vision and to be able to appeal to both hearts and minds.

6. We can promote conversations and interaction with those who are "experts" on a developing function (e.g., a Thinking type seeking out Feeling types). Collaborations in organizations between people of different types who are increasingly able to appreciate their differences can be very satisfying for the individuals involved and very worthwhile for the organization.

7. We can help people understand and accept that when they try a new behavior that is related to their less-developed functions (e.g., a Thinking type expressing appreciation to someone), they are not likely to do it very smoothly but will learn to do it better and better with attention and experience.

8. We can provide information and encouragement about resources (i.e., books, courses, films) that are available that deal in accessi-

ble ways with meaning and change. Two books that are among my personal favorites are Bridges' (1980) *Transitions* and Pearson's (1989) *The Hero Within*. Two courses that have been very helpful to managers with whom I have worked are the Leadership Development Program (Center for Creative Leadership, Greensboro, North Carolina) and the Management Work Conference (NTL Institute, Rosslyn, Virginia).

9. We can encourage people to take time out—to get away, to take time for reflection, to resist the temptation to stay very busy. Bridges (1980) highlighted the necessity for taking time out to deal with the neutral zone:

> People in transition are often still involved in activities and relationships that continue to bombard them with cues that are irrelevant to their emerging needs. Because a person is likely to feel lonely in such a situation, the temptation is to seek more and better contact with others; but *the real need is for a genuine sort of aloneness in which inner signals can make themselves heard* [emphasis added]. (p. 121)

For practitioners, some things are very important to remember:

- Midlife is a process; we need to start with and accept where people are and pay attention to how we might support the process without being intrusive, prescriptive, or judgmental.
- People have a wonderful capacity for growth during midlife and sometimes do very surprising things. We should not count someone out because he or she seems stuck at some point. In my experience, there are times when almost everyone seems stuck or resistant to the process of integration and change.
- We need to tailor our suggestions and our language to the preferences—and fears—of our clients. For example, with Thinking types, particularly early in the midlife process, we need to be careful about being too "touchy-feely" in our suggestions or language.
- We need to be patient and not make people feel inadequate for being incapable of doing things that may be areas of strength for us. An awareness of our own less-developed, growing edges should serve to keep us appropriately humble and patient.

SUMMARY

This chapter has described the midlife process and has attempted to link effective individual development during the process to key aspects of leadership development. Underlying both individual development and the demands of leadership are four key cognitive functions—Sensing, Intuition, Thinking, and Feeling. Understanding each of these functions, their role in individual development, and their contribution to effective leadership is critically important for leadership development practitioners. Such understanding translated into practice could substantially enhance the impact of the MBTI on the wise development of leaders of all types.

REFERENCES

Aram, J. D. (1990). Appreciative interchange: The force that makes cooperation possible. In S. Srivasta, D. L. Cooperrider, & Associates (Eds.), *Appreciative management and leadership* (pp. 175–204). San Francisco: Jossey-Bass.

Bass, B. M. (1981). *Stogdill's handbook of leadership: A survey of theory and research.* New York: Macmillan.

Birren, J. E., & Fisher, L. M. (1990). The elements of wisdom: Overview and integration. In Sternberg, R. J. (Ed.), *Wisdom: Its nature, origins, and development.* Cambridge: Cambridge University Press.

Bridges, W. (1980). *Transitions: Making sense of life's changes.* Reading, MA: Addison-Wesley.

Grant, W. H., Thompson, M., & Clarke, T. E. (1983). *From image to likeness: A Jungian path in the gospel journey.* Ramsey, NJ: Paulist Press.

Heath, D. H., & Heath, H. E. (1991). *Fulfilling lives: Paths to maturity and success.* San Francisco: Jossey-Bass.

Hickman, C. R. (1992). *Mind of a manager: Soul of a leader.* New York: Wiley.

Johnson, B. (1992). *Polarity management: Identifying and managing unsolvable problems.* Amherst, MA: HRD Press.

Jung, C. G. (1933). *Modern man in search of a soul.* San Diego: Harcourt Brace Jovanovich.

Kanter, R. M. (1989). *When giants learn to dance.* New York: Simon & Schuster.

Kaplan, R. E., Drath, W. H., & Kofodimos, J. R. (1991). *Beyond ambition: How driven managers can lead better and live better.* San Francisco: Jossey-Bass.

Koestenbaum, P. (1991). *Leadership: The inner side of greatness.* San Francisco: Jossey-Bass.

Kotter, J. P. (1990). *A force for change: How leadership differs from management.* New York: Macmillan.

Lombardo, M. M., & McCall, M. W., Jr. (1978). Leadership. In M. W. McCall, Jr., & M. M. Lombardo (Eds.), *Leadership: Where else can we go?* (pp. 3–12). Durham, NC: Duke University Press.

Myers, I. B., with Myers, P. B. (1980). *Gifts differing.* Palo Alto, CA: Consulting Psychologists Press.

Myers, K. D., & Kirby, L. K. (1994). *Introduction to type dynamics and development: Exploring the next level of type.* Palo Alto, CA: Consulting Psychologists Press.

Pascale, R. T. (1990). *Managing on the edge.* New York: Simon & Schuster.

Pearson, C. S. (1989). *The hero within: Six archetypes we live by.* San Francisco: Harper.

Quenk, N. L. (1993). *Beside ourselves: Our hidden personality in everyday life.* Palo Alto, CA.: Davies-Black.

Quinn, R. E. (1988). *Beyond rational management: Mastering the paradoxes and competing demands of high performance.* San Francisco: Jossey-Bass.

Senge, P. M. (1990). *The fifth discipline: The art and practice of the learning organization.* New York: Doubleday.

Srivasta, S. (1983). Improving executive functioning. In S. Srivasta & Associates (Eds.), *The executive mind.* (pp. 297–309). San Francisco: Jossey-Bass.

Stogdill, R. (1974). *Handbook of leadership.* New York: Free Press.

Vaill, P. B. (1989). *Managing as a performing art: New ideas for a world of chaotic change.* San Francisco: Jossey-Bass.

Vaill, P. B. (1990). Executive development as spiritual development. In S. Srivasta, D. L. Cooperrider, & Associates (Eds.), *Appreciative management and leadership* (pp. 323–352). San Francisco: Jossey-Bass.

11 | Enhancing Leadership During Organizational Change

Nancy J. Barger

Linda K. Kirby

Organizations around the world are in the midst of a revolution. Organizational structures developed over the last several decades—from the Japanese model of cooperative management to the more hierarchical organizations in the West—no longer seem to work and appear to be in need of drastic change. Global competition, political and social upheaval, and developments in information technology are driving dramatic market and competitive changes that cannot be avoided by any country or region. The current revolution in organizations is analogous to the industrial revolution in the degree of dislocation, confusion, unforeseeable consequences, and human costs.

Some experts seem to think that if only the correct structures can be found and the most forward-looking systems can be created, organizations will survive and prosper (e.g., Peters, 1994; Senge et al., 1994); but it doesn't seem to be working. This year's model organizations, held up for others to follow, are next year's troubled companies; and many organizations are undergoing their second or third reengineering, searching for the structure that will deal effectively with the challenges. Many of the organizational change experts are recognizing that we don't yet seem to have a handle on what needs to happen for organizational changes to actually result in more effective companies (W. Bridges, personal communication, September 1995; Noer, 1993).

In this chapter, we first discuss two of the primary reasons why we think current organizational change processes are not achieving desired results. Then we suggest and illustrate ways that psychological type can help leaders deal more effectively with organizational change. The information and suggestions in this chapter were developed in dozens of workshops in the United States, Canada, and Great Britain, with employees in a wide variety of organizations—from aerospace defense contractors to hospitals. Almost 2,000 participants in these workshops provided the data we use to explain the impacts of organizational change and the needs of different people.

WHY ORGANIZATIONAL
CHANGES ARE NOT WORKING

Those rethinking current organizational change and questioning the results seem to share a crucial recognition: up to this point, change efforts have focused on organizational structures and systems and forgotten, slighted, or misunderstood the needs of the people in the organization. Expensive programs to train people to work more effectively don't seem to work, and leaders complain that their people continue to use old work values and patterns that sabotage the new structures.

Underlying much of what leaders see as people's resistance to change, in our view, is actually a gap between those who are in leadership and decision-making positions and the rest of the organization—those who do not have much power or control, but must implement the changes and make them work. Leaders are failing to recognize and deal effectively with these factors:

• Impacts of imposed change on the people of the organization
• Differences in people's reactions to change

Dealing With Imposed Change

Responsible leaders recognize that their organizations need to change significantly if they are to survive in the present and future environment. They study the options, consult experts, draw on the ideas of their top people, do cost-benefit analyses, and create a redesigned organization that they believe will provide the flexibility and new systems needed to survive.

The "new organization" is then presented to employees, along with detailed implementation plans, time frames, and retraining programs. For the *leaders,* whatever the external push to reorganize, the new organization they envision is one they have participated in choosing and designing. For the *employees of the organization,* however, this is *imposed change.* They have seldom been given an opportunity to present their ideas and experience, seldom been consulted in developing options, seldom been involved in designing the plans, and almost never given any power to actually influence the changes. Psychological type plays an important role in people's reactions to imposed change (Barger & Kirby, 1995, Chapter 3); but, in our extensive work with people dealing with organizational change, we have yet to find anyone who likes imposed change.

Predictable Impacts of Imposed Change

We realize that leaders see few alternatives to the process outlined above when things seem to be moving so fast. However, change that is imposed on employees has some predictable, difficult impacts on an organization, including the following:

Loyalty questions:

- Is the loyalty I've given to the company through the years being betrayed?
- To whom should I be loyal? The organization? Top management? The "new guys"?
- Does the unwritten contract still hold? Will my past loyalty and productive work still count?

Expertise concerns:

- Do I have the new skills the reorganization requires?
- Does the company have the expertise to implement the plans?

Consistency questions:

- What is the identity of the new organization?
- How will the culture be changing?
- What can I count on?

Credibility issues:

- Who's making the decisions and are they using accurate information and good judgment?

- Are the leaders looking out for their own interests, rather than the organization's or mine?
- What is the hidden agenda?
- Can I trust this organization, these leaders?

And people react predictably to imposed change:

- They feel uncertain.
- They begin to doubt, to lack confidence in the organization and management.
- They are skeptical and suspicious.
- They become cautious, avoid taking risks, "keep their heads down."
- Some feel angry and bitter.
- Many become cynical.
- They experience painful loss issues.

All of these predictable problems interfere with people's motivation and productivity. Just when the organization most needs its people to be creative and energetic, they are feeling off balance and fearful.

Failing to recognize the impacts of imposed change on people and to take action to deal with these problems is a major factor in reorganizations that don't work. In a later section, we illustrate some of the issues related to imposed change.

Systematically Understanding and Providing for Differences

Another important factor in the failure of restructuring plans is the failure of leaders to recognize and develop systematic ways for dealing with the differences between people and the ways they deal with change. Training programs are directed toward changing the way people think and work, but they are designed and run as though people were all basically the same. We have found that psychological type and the MBTI provide a straightforward, systematic, understandable way for organizational leaders to recognize important individual differences during change.

Restructuring the way an organization does business is a complicated process including several stages. Using the MBTI as an underlying guide while planning and implementing the various stages provides leaders with the information they need to take advantage of the strengths of their people, meet the variety of their needs, and create the necessary basis for moving ahead with the reorganization.

Organizational Change That Works

Even well-conceived and thoroughly planned changes will result in an effective, competitive organization *only if* the people who work there also develop new attitudes and behaviors. In the remainder of this chapter, we focus on a number of the challenges leaders face during organizational change and indicate ways that we have used the MBTI with leaders to help them deal with those challenges more effectively. We believe this information will be helpful to leaders and to organizational development professionals who work with leaders.

UNDERSTANDING LEADERS' STRENGTHS AND POTENTIAL WEAKNESSES

The first challenge leaders face is recognizing their own characteristic ways of planning and implementing organizational change. This includes acknowledging how they personally experience and deal with change, as well as understanding their strengths and potential blind spots in providing leadership for others. In other words, leaders need to become aware of the impacts of organizational change on them, along with the impacts of their leadership style on the organization.

While leaders participate in the process and influence the decisions to make organizational change, they still must face their own issues when confronted with organizational change:

- The need to make crucial decisions about the future of the organization without enough information
- Internal questions and doubts about whether they personally have the knowledge and skills needed in the new environment their organization faces
- A sense of responsibility to the stakeholders
- Concern for the well-being of loyal employees
- Criticism, anger, and skepticism from employees about their decisions

Most leaders believe that they need to present a public image of strength, certainty, and enthusiasm about the future, regardless of how they are actually feeling. And, frequently, leaders do not have peers with whom they can talk.

Finally, leaders must deal with their personal orientation to change. They may have had losses in the past—personal or professional—that affect the way they experience current changes. They may be at a time in their life when the additional time and energy required of them during organizational change presents real hardship for them. And they may question their own personal career direction.

All of these factors combine to create stress for leaders who are deciding upon and beginning to implement change programs and are part of the reason we advise leaders to deal first with understanding themselves.

The four mental functions identified by psychological type and the MBTI—Sensing, Intuition, Thinking, and Feeling—play a crucial role, we have found, in how different leaders deal with organizational change and the kinds of challenges it presents to them. Leaders who can recognize their own natural style in the following sections can also begin to expand that style to be more effective. The following sections are presented in the order of the MBTI preference's representation in management groups.

Thinking Leaders

The majority of leaders in most organizations prefer Thinking. Thinking leaders normally bring some very important strengths to organizational change situations:

- Analyzing current problems logically
- Staying detached and objective
- Making the hard decisions
- Developing the rationale
- Moving on—leaving the past behind

Combining their Thinking with a preference for Judging, as is most often the case, these TJ leaders can provide clear, consistent, and strong leadership for organizations undergoing change.

Their very strengths, however, can lead them and their organizations into some serious problems, as the case of Jack illustrates. Jack, who was CEO of a major health maintenance organization operating in several states, announced a radical restructuring of the organization that included selling off whole operations, combining others, moving functions between divisions, and renaming divisions. He had been planning this for some time, but had managed to keep his plans totally secret, at least from employees—they read about it in the paper.

Realizing the concerns the restructuring would raise and having consulted with experts in organizational change, Jack undertook a program to inform and involve employees. He spoke to all company employees across the United States via satellite, explaining the restructuring and giving the rationale for it. He listed the principles that would guide all decisions about personnel changes and expressed his appreciation for past loyalty. He said the personnel reduction and redeployment plans would be communicated to employees in about six weeks. At his direction, divisional leaders then appeared at large meetings at every facility, with all employees invited to attend. The divisional leaders spoke and then responded to questions fully.

Two weeks after the original announcement, when these initiatives had been completed, the company newsletter was published with a lead article by Jack headlined "Now We're Ready to Forge Ahead." The focus of the article was on the ways in which the restructuring would position the company competitively and enable it to meet its responsibilities to shareholders. The article also included strong language encouraging employees to avoid negative thinking and talking.

Jack, whose preferences are for TJ, believed that he had done a thorough job of informing employees and responding to their concerns. He was astonished to hear that his in-house human resources department people thought employees were confused, worried, and uncertain. He heard that employees were spending department and team meetings debating what the changes would mean and passing on rumors rather than focusing on their work. And cynical jokes began appearing anonymously on e-mail. What happened in this situation illustrates a crucial understanding from psychological type: Even with the best of intentions and efforts, it is almost impossible for any individual to comprehend fully the needs of others in stressful situations.

Jack's initiatives provided the kind of process that would work *for him*:

- Logical presentations of the reasons for the change
- Responses to informational questions
- Moving ahead to make the changes

It did not provide the things needed by most of his employees, including:

- Process time
- Emotional support
- Recognition of the impact on employees

Jack's approach points up some potential weaknesses of Thinking leaders during organizational change:

- Difficulty in recognizing that logic does not persuade everyone
- Difficulty understanding and dealing with others' needs for process time
- Impatience with negativity
- Discomfort in dealing with others' difficult feelings

It can be especially difficult for Thinking leaders to understand and accept others' needs for emotional support and process time because the tendency of those preferring Thinking is to bury their own emotions about changes. If they find themselves experiencing emotions, their natural response is to ask themselves, Is it logical for me to feel this way? If the answer is no, Thinking types will typically try to push the emotions away.

This health maintenance organization contracted to offer four-hour workshops for employees on dealing with the changes, followed by structured employee interviews to assess their reactions. We then met with one of the administrative heads of the organization, a woman with ENTP preferences, whose first comment to us was, "Well, are they still whining?" She was not an uncaring person. It was just that she had looked unblinkingly at the realities of the health care environment, recognized that—right or wrong, good or bad—a revolution was under way. She had seen the future, made her adjustments to it, and moved on. She simply could not understand why her employees, many of whom were Sensing and Feeling types, could not do the same.

Sensing Leaders

The proportions of leaders who prefer Sensing or Intuition will be much closer to equal in most organizations than will the distribution of Thinking–Feeling leaders. Sensing leaders bring important skills and perspectives that have been valued for years, and they continue to provide useful leadership during organizational change. These strengths include:

- Giving substance to visions
- Seeing the practical impacts of different alternatives
- Focusing only on the parts that need changing—not on change for change's sake
- Creating temporary structures
- Preserving/conserving traditions and resources during rapid change

Combining their Sensing with Thinking, as is most often the case, these ST leaders provide grounded, realistic, and careful leadership for organizations undergoing change.

Their very strengths, however, can lead them and their organizations into some serious problems, as the case of Ted illustrates. Ted was the director of a wholly owned subsidiary of a major computer software company known for the creativity and inventiveness of its employees. Ted's MBTI type was ISTJ, with most of the employees preferring INTP and INTJ. The creative software designers had been very happy to leave the nuts and bolts of running the company and keeping it profitable to Ted. He, in turn, had recognized their contributions and left them free to pursue whatever "wild ideas" intrigued them.

With the competitive pressure of the global market, the company found itself in financial difficulties. An outside consulting group identified the basic product-development process as a major factor in the company's problems. They recommended a new focus on marketability and quick product development, with new projects to be directed by small teams that would operate outside the regular departmental structure of the organization. Ted led his leadership team in a meticulous design of the new product development process, specifying each step the teams would follow, how progress would be checked, and the documentation required as these teams began to control significant parts of the company's resources.

Within a few months, the restructuring had run into serious problems. The amount of documentation and checks required made the INTP and INTJ team members feel that they had become "paper pushers" and lost their creative freedom. Three different stages of each product's development process were run by three different teams. Ted had ensured that each of the three teams had clear, specific processes to follow; but his plans gave scant attention to interaction between the teams, and this interaction had seriously broken down. And the plans had not provided for the new kinds of interactions needed between departmental managers and teams.

The missing parts of Ted's plans illustrate some of the kinds of problems that can result from Sensing leadership that is not balanced by other perspectives:

- Failing to see all the interactions as part of a whole
- Difficulty in fully comprehending how new structures will work before an experience base is built up
- Changing too little—tinkering instead of revolutionizing
- Digging in, holding on to the past when it is time to let it go
- Not recognizing the validity of intuitive insights—their own and others'

Sensing types, especially the Sensing, Thinking, and Judging combination so prevalent in organizational leadership, have a tremendous experience base upon which to draw. They develop their expertise and practical knowledge with great energy and commitment. However, they can feel lost in a new reality, finding it difficult to see how past experience and expertise can be translated to deal with a changing environment and new tasks. And they can be slow to anticipate interactive effects and the impacts on people of changing roles. (For more information on STJs and organizational change, see Chapter 14.)

Intuitive Leaders

Intuitive leaders have important strengths during organizational change. These include:

- Devoting great energy to exploring new ideas
- Envisioning future directions
- Taking action on their vision with confidence
- Recognizing global impacts and interactive effects
- Persuasively presenting a picture of the future

Combining their Intuition with a preference for Thinking, as is most often the case, NT leaders develop innovative, transformational, and inspirational systemwide solutions to problems their organization is facing.

These very strengths, however, can lead them and their organizations into some serious problems, as the case of Teresa illustrates. Teresa was CEO of a family-owned food production company that had been founded by her late father. Though she was next to youngest of the five adult children, her mother and siblings had recognized her knowledge and skills and strongly supported her leadership. An INTJ, she typically proceeded with confidence to make the decisions needed to keep the company profitable in the fast-paced marketplace. The company itself was like a family—most of the workers had been there for many years, had known the father who started the company, and performed their jobs with expertise and commitment.

As part of her continual search for knowledge and new ideas, Teresa attended a leadership seminar at a major university that was designed to look at the marketplace of the future. The seminar projected the world in 2020 and participants discussed what would be needed to survive in this future. Teresa was tremendously stimulated by the ideas and by the intelligence and foresight of the seminar leaders and participants. She quickly applied these ideas to her family's company and became persuaded that they needed to make transformational changes in order to position themselves for the future.

Teresa returned to the company with a complete restructuring plan. She met with her family and gave a dramatic, enthusiastic picture of the future and how she saw their company changing to meet it. Her siblings (two INTPs, an INTJ, and an INFJ) responded positively and became quite animated about how they could completely redesign the factory and processes, retrain employees, and revolutionize their work.

Their mother, Maria, had ESFJ preferences. She normally did not interfere in decisions about the business, choosing instead to spend her time providing support for her children and for the employees. The employees respected and loved her, and she, in turn, remembered their children, their spouses, their life histories, and their contributions to the company.

At this family meeting, Maria waited until the children were through with their excited brainstorming and then said quietly,

> What's wrong with the way we are doing our work now? We've increased productivity and reduced costs consistently over the last several years. We've changed our product to meet the market requirements for healthier foods and moved into new markets. The people in our marketing and product development departments have demonstrated that they are in touch with our customers, everyone in the plant trusts what they recommend, and we continually make changes based on their information. If we "transform" the company as you are intending, what happens to the employees like Antonio and Joe and Tina, who will suddenly be without a role? What happens to the commitment everyone has to the company?

After their initial surprise at their mother's interjection of her opinion and the passion with which she stated her questions, the five siblings took another look at their discussion. They realized that Maria was exactly right in everything she had said: The company in fact had been incrementally making changes all along as the market changed and had developed new products and installed new machines and processes. They realized that they could not clearly articulate the benefits of the transformational changes they were thinking of initiating and that the disruptions it would cause in the present might mean that the company wouldn't survive to 2020.

What happened with this leadership group illustrates some of the potential problems of Intuitive leaders during organizational change:

- Making "transformational changes" that disrupt or destroy what is now working
- Failing to see all the steps, the time, the resources required for the changes (Since the future vision is so clear, it's difficult to recognize how long it will take and all the difficulties that will be encountered.)
- Failing to recognize and provide what's necessary to take care of business while the change is happening
- Instituting more changes before previous ones have been integrated
- Impatience with those who do not "get" the vision
- Discounting past experience; looking to the new, the novel, even when the old is working
- "Winging" it; going ahead confidently with not enough specific plans in place
- Difficulty in communicating their vision so that it is real for others

Intuitive leaders, in their attraction to new ideas, tend to get bored once the visioning and planning are done. They find it difficult to maintain energy and focus during implementation and often initiate another round of reorganization before the first one is completed, enticed by another interesting vision of the future.

Feeling Leaders

Most organizations have relatively few leaders with a Feeling preference. Even organizations whose culture seems to be Feeling—those committed to serving people's needs—typically have top leadership that prefers Thinking. Nevertheless, Feeling leaders bring some important strengths to organizational change situations. These include:

- Including others in gathering information and decision making
- Appreciating the contributions of others
- Recognizing the need for and providing individual processing and support
- Assessing proposed changes by using the organization's mission and values
- Remembering past contributions

Combining their Feeling with Judging, as they most frequently do in organizational leadership, Feeling leaders can provide caring, committed, and supportive leadership for organizations undergoing change.

These very strengths, however, can lead them and their organizations into some serious problems, as the case of Gordon illustrates. Gordon, whose preferences were ENFJ, led a major division of his company. He had a leadership group he relied on for feedback, processing of his ideas, and reinforcement of his decisions. The group consisted entirely of men with whom he had worked for many years and felt comfortable.

The larger organization for which Gordon worked entered into a radical restructuring, requiring major changes and streamlining of Gordon's division. The VP to whom Gordon reported approached him with concerns that he had been feeling for some time and that became acute with the change requirements.

> Gordon, you've got a lot of dead wood in your department managers. Bob and Dave, for example, haven't had a new idea in years, and Jerry doesn't provide leadership. He just stays in his office and leaves people alone. With the new plans for your division, we've got to either light a fire under these guys or move them out into other positions.

Gordon was upset by this attack on his inner circle. His impulse was to hotly defend each of them by recounting their contributions and years of loyalty. He realized, however, that his own position as leader was being judged and agreed to go along with the VP's suggestion to shuffle leadership. This included adding Kate, an ESTJ on the fast track, as a new department manager.

Gordon's easy, friendly leadership group meetings were over, as Kate advocated new processes, criticized ones in place, pointed out flaws in Gordon's reasoning, and aggressively pursued the goals of the restructuring. Her behavior confirmed Gordon's worst fears. His old group spent their customary Friday afternoon social hour complaining to Gordon about Kate's behavior, using descriptive terms with which TJ women have become all too familiar.

Gordon avoided the situation as much as possible. He tried to smooth things over with his original group, reassuring them of his loyalty to them. He patiently listened to Kate's complaints and tried to appear interested and supportive. He reported to the VP that "everything's great—Kate has really added a breath of fresh air." Nothing changed in the way the division ran, however. Kate and the old group members were hardly speaking to each other, and Gordon was using all his energy trying to negotiate between everyone. He even confided to his wife,

> You know, I think maybe I'm past it. I used to love to go in to work—we were like a family and had some great times. But that's all gone. And the company doesn't seem to want my contributions anymore. Maybe we need to take a look at what early retirement would mean to our plans.

The situation that developed here illustrates some of the potential weaknesses of Feeling leaders:

- Putting excessive energy into inclusion, consensus building, and harmony
- Failing to confront the difficult people and hard choices
- "Playing favorites," that is, failing to see problems in people with whom they feel comfortable and to whom they feel connected, even though they may not be producing or may be causing difficulties for the group
- Wanting the work group to be "a family" and focusing on that to the detriment of needed strategies and tasks that will allow the group or company to survive and prosper
- Romanticizing the past
- Losing trust and motivation—getting stuck
- Feeling personally hurt and bitter about what they see as disloyalty

Feeling leaders can be so overwhelmed by the emotions and needs of others that they back off from intended changes and end up with plans that are overly individualized and complex. They can find disruption of relationships so unsettling that they lose their own motivation; and they can feel bitter and personally hurt by the anger and frustration of others.

Strategy: Balancing the Natural Perspective

The source of the problems we have illustrated is not a particular type preference or a lack of leadership skills. These leaders were operating out of their own natural ways of seeing the world and were sincerely trying to meet their responsibilities. The root of the problems was their failure to balance their natural way of leading, understand and acknowledge their own blind spots, and find effective ways of protecting the organization and employees from their natural weaknesses.

Ideally, every leader would broaden his or her perspective to include all the mental tools identified by Jung and the MBTI. They would use their Sensing *and* Intuition, their Thinking *and* Feeling to ensure that organizational change moved forward more positively. Personal development is certainly possible. Chapter 10 by Catherine Fitzgerald presents the case for such development very eloquently and provides some guidance. In real life and real time, however, complete development seldom happens. After a lifetime of observation and study, Jung observed that in the final analysis, all people are limited by their type—that is, the structure of their consciousness.

There is no quick formula for making use of other perspectives. The following processes require time and energy, but they can help leaders avoid blind spots and increase their effectiveness.

- Recognizing their own strengths and weaknesses during organizational change
- Acknowledging the strengths of their opposites—their less preferred and developed areas
- Actively seeking out those other perspectives, genuinely trying to listen and understand
- Trusting that another's use of a developed preference has as much validity and as much to offer as do their own trusted processes
- Instituting reliable, consistent ways of integrating those other perspectives into their regular work, especially their decisions about, plans for, and implementation of organizational change

Changing is not easy. It means consciously including in your group of advisors people who disagree with you at every turn. It means taking account of critiques of your approach and seeking out those who oppose or don't understand your viewpoint. It means taking positions that may feel more vulnerable than you would like. It's not as neat as the way you would normally operate. And it takes time. Failing to do this, however, means that you and your regular, trusted advisors may share blind spots that could lead you into some of the kinds of difficulties we've identified in this section.

RECOGNIZING OTHERS' DIFFERENCES AND RESPONDING APPROPRIATELY

As people develop their own type preferences and related skills, and as they find these preferences and skills useful and contributing to their effectiveness, a natural type bias develops. The way one understands the world, interacts with it, and makes sense of it seems so natural that it is very difficult not to believe that everyone else would be better off if they could learn to do these things the same way. Even when leaders are sincerely trying to meet the needs of others in their organization, they tend still to be limited by the golden-rule approach: What others really need and want is the same as what I need and want—or should be.

As we have said, there are no easy formulas. However, there are some filters and checks that leaders can use to modify their own behaviors and to supplement their use of advisors with different perspectives.

Here's a brief distillation of the most frequently mentioned needs of people with the different MBTI preferences. (Complete information on each preference and each MBTI type can be found in Barger & Kirby, 1995.)

Extraversion and Introversion

- Extraverts say they need talking, involvement, and action.
- Introverts say they need space for reflection and time for internal processing.

Sensing and Intuition

- Sensing types say they need real data and connections between the new and their experience.
- Intuitive types say they need the big picture and the comprehensive future vision.

Thinking and Feeling

- Thinking types say they need logic, clarity, and competence in decision makers.
- Feeling types say they need consideration of the impact on themselves and others, inclusion in the process, and support.

Judging and Perceiving

- Judging types say they need a plan, goals, and time frames.
- Perceiving types say they need a flexible or open plan, information, and room for revisions.

These basic needs are consistently expressed at every level in a wide variety of organizations. Leaders of organizational change will enhance their effectiveness by ensuring that their change plans provide for these needs. All communications can be reviewed to ensure that they include the needs of different types. In any written or oral information, for example, a leader can check to ensure that both Sensing and Intuitive kinds of information are included, that both Thinking and Feeling concerns have been addressed, and that both Judging and Perceiving needs have been recognized..

Leaders can find a number of ways to respond appropriately to the needs of different people—once they have acknowledged their importance and have committed to taking them seriously. The following sections illustrate some common misunderstandings resulting from type differences and some suggestions of ways to begin taking account of and making use of differences.

Extraversion and Introversion

The most central needs related to this preference are for different styles of communication. It is important to remember that written communication is more usable by Introverts. If the topic is important, leaders will need to be sure that there is also a forum for discussion of the issues, which will assist in meeting the needs of Extraverts.

Leaders can also draw on type knowledge to enhance their understanding of others' reactions and responses to them. For example, in any spoken presentation, Extraverts are likely to react immediately and, as they talk it through, to become clearer about their ideas. Their first responses are not their final decisions, and leaders need to encourage and participate in the process rather than make snap judgments based on the Extraverts' initial statements. In the same face-to-face kind of forum, Introverts are unlikely to express their viewpoints or ideas unless they've had written communication or advance notice of the topics that give them time to reflect. Their failure to respond verbally or nonverbally to leaders' words can throw the leaders off balance and make them feel unsupported or that they are not getting through to their audience.

Extraverted leaders, in particular, may be disappointed, and in their desire for response and active dialogue, they may fill the space with more words when what the Introverts need is some time to digest. Active dialogue is more likely to take place at a second meeting, after time for the Introverts' reflection process.

Likewise, Introverted leaders may be taken aback by the immediate questions of Extraverts in the audience, sometimes even interrupting the planned presentation. This can feel rude and thoughtless to Introverted leaders who have carefully prepared their presentation.

What is needed, especially in times of stress such as that caused by organizational change, is room for both approaches: space and time for reflection, with follow-up opportunities for Introverts' questions and discussion; *and* active dialogues with rapid exchanges supporting Extraverts in their external process of information. It takes a little more time, some planning, and more energy; but as one of our down-to-earth ISTJ colleagues points out, you can take the time now, up front, or pay later in lost motivation and productivity.

Sensing and Intuition

We have observed a tendency in present leadership during organizational change to use an Intuitive approach in presenting change programs, regardless of whether the leader prefers Sensing or Intuition. Intuitive, "transformational" leadership has become the "right" way to deal with the present environment.

Most organizations, especially large ones, will have perhaps twice as many employees who prefer Sensing over Intuition. Especially when presenting changes, leaders need to be sure to communicate Sensing information and validate Sensing concerns. One way of doing this is to clearly and explicitly connect the future to the past. Another is to use practical, grounded, accessible examples and metaphors (such as the pioneer journey along the Oregon Trail, which we use in Barger & Kirby, 1995) to demonstrate how people's past experience is a base for the future.

Expect skepticism, especially from Sensing Thinking (ST) types. They specialize in asking the difficult questions: What's wrong with what we're doing now? How do you know that? How will this future be better? How do you know that? How long will it take? Who will take care of customers in the meantime? How much will it cost? What exactly do you want me to do?

Failure to respond competently and frankly to such concerns can lead the Sensing types to write off the leaders' vision and resist the changes, either noisily and obviously, or subtly. Besides, the information they are seeking is important information for everyone to have. Their concerns need to be appreciated for the substance they can provide for the vision.

Intuitive types typically respond to visions of the future with enthusiasm more quickly than do Sensing types, but there are a couple of potential issues for the Intuitives in the organization. One is that the vision needs to be one that they can "catch onto" or that fits with their own picture. If they have a picture of the future that is different from the leader's, or if the vision does not fit with their own understanding, they can totally reject it, regardless of all supporting evidence. The second complication that Intuitives present is that they like to brainstorm possibilities and see any idea or plan as open to their creative suggestions. As soon as the plan is announced, they will begin changing it, seeing additional patterns, better ways to proceed, and more far-reaching possibilities. It can be hard to rein in this enthusiasm without also taking away Intuitive types' motivation because they feel that there's no room for their ideas.

The best solution for both Sensing and Intuitive types is to involve them early in the decision-making process. Leaders can lay out the information they have and their analysis of the problem, and they can ask employees in small groups to discuss the problem and suggest potential solutions. This process will require opening up the information to everyone in the organization. The Sensing types will pursue the information they need, research what others have done in similar situations, and bring a grounded focus to the discussions. The Intuitive types can add their creativity and insight into patterns and possibilities.

Opening up the process in this way can feel very disorderly, especially to leaders who prefer Thinking and Judging. However, the great majority of employees understand that leaders have to make the eventual decisions and will feel validated that their questions and concerns have been included in the process.

Thinking and Feeling

As we have indicated, Feeling tends to be underrepresented in organizational leadership. This makes it doubly important for leaders to respond appropriately to Feeling concerns and needs, as they tend to stay underground in organizational settings. Failing to surface and deal with them can mean, first, that important issues are avoided, and, second, that many employees will feel disaffected and angry.

Taking Feeling perspectives seriously during organizational change can involve the following:

- Openly discuss the people issues involved in the change. Who will be affected and how? This should be done straightforwardly, with a minimum of euphemisms such as "employee reallocation plans." The people issues need to be presented not only in terms of opportunities and challenges, but also with recognition of dislocation, uncertainties, and difficulties.

- Demonstrate that you have thought about these issues and are willing to discuss and try out several possible approaches (not "solutions"—the Feeling types will want to be involved in the solutions).

- Provide a way for affected employees to be involved in decision making. Leaders will most likely have to set some parameters, but provide as much room for employee control as possible.

- Frequently and publicly express recognition and appreciation for past loyalty, hard work, and contributions to the success of the organization.

- Think through and then present the values that will underlie the ways in which people are going to be supported during the change. Tie these values into the mission and culture of the organization.

Thinking types also want to be involved, but they will focus much more on the tasks to be accomplished. The following are the primary needs of Thinking types during organizational change:

- A reasoned critique of the present system, what is not working and why
- A reorganization plan that is logical and fair
- Demonstration that leadership is knowledgeable and competent
- Respect for their competence and knowledge
- Recognition of their good work—that their ideas and work are used

Organizations and their leaders are typically set up to provide at least some of what Thinking types need but will usually have to stretch to include Feeling concerns and needs in their change process. Interestingly, the rewards for doing so are not limited to Feeling types. Though Thinking employees may not want the emotional processing time that their Feeling colleagues need, Thinking types do recognize and give credit to leaders who demonstrate genuine concern for employee needs. It's also important to remember that Thinking types experience emotions as well.

Judging and Perceiving

Most organizational cultures demonstrate a bias toward Judging—more than half of the employees in most organizations will prefer it. Yet the current environment of continuous change seems to call for Perceiving skills—flexibility, openness to new information, spontaneity, willingness to revisit and revise prior decisions, feeling somewhat comfortable with ambiguity and uncertainty, and the ability to stay motivated in the midst of confusion.

Judging types want firm and clear plans, goals, and time lines, and they want these to be followed. In the present environment, plans, goals, and time lines are changing with such alarming frequency that it's little wonder that the whole culture of organizations, as well as the individuals within them, are in a highly stressed state. Judging types find it particularly difficult to trust that the Perceiving approach will actually achieve results in a timely way.

Leaders need to verbalize the discomfort involved in ongoing change—their own as well as what they see in others. They can speak about the need for skill development in this area, for learning new ways to achieve goals in a changing environment. One effective approach we saw a leader use was to give his people the example of a particular group within the organization that had always had to work in a changing environment—in this case, the emergency room of a major medical center. The leader pointed out that many of the personnel in that department, including the manager, had preferences for Judging, but they had managed to create a basic order within which they could respond flexibly to the unexpected. In another setting, leaders might use the example of a M.A.S.H. unit, which clearly combines order and structure with flexibility and responsiveness to the environment.

Helping Judging organizations and individuals learn to deal with the stress of unpredictability and change is a major task well worth the effort. There are few things more frustrating for leaders than to watch their employees sticking to plans and structures that have become obsolete, insisting on going by the book even when the book no longer applies.

We don't mean to imply that current change situations are easy for Perceiving types. Because of the organizational bias for Judging, many Perceiving types are accustomed to suspicion or criticism from colleagues and bosses. For Perceiving types to be able to use their natural flexibility and resourcefulness, they need to be trusted and supported. They want general time frames, hard deadlines (not the phony ones bosses sometimes give them in their distrust of the Perceiving processes), and freedom to do the job in their own way within those general parameters.

USING TYPE TO FACILITATE ORGANIZATIONAL CHANGE

With these understandings of the normal differences in strengths, contributions, and needs of different types, organizational leaders can construct change programs that will invite and include all of their employees. The programs themselves will be vastly improved by the integration of different perspectives at the same time that employee motivation and performance are enhanced. In this last section, we want to briefly note how this information can influence some of the most important organizational change issues.

Deciding and Communicating About Changes

The key perspective supported by type knowledge is that it is crucial to involve the maximum number of people in the processes of gathering and evaluating information. Leaders need to provide people with the kinds of information they want and with forums for contributing their experience and judgment.

This is a particular challenge to TJ leaders. They frequently say that such a process is inefficient and that there is not enough time. How leaders choose to spend their time is always a question of priorities, however. There is never enough time for leaders to do all the things they need to do, and the things they choose to spend their time on are the things they believe are most important. We hope the information about type in this chapter will have persuaded TJs to change their priorities to make time for a participative process.

Dealing With Loss

This is an area that is crucially important during organizational change, but is most often overlooked or slighted. Employees experience loss issues during organizational change—loss of security, loss of expertise, loss of confidence in the future, loss of colleagues, loss of networks, and loss of power, among other things. Loss leads to emotions associated with the grieving process: anger, bitterness, depression, resignation, and resentment.

If these emotions are not dealt with directly, they stay under the surface, interfering with employee morale and productivity. They are one of the primary reasons that employees get stuck and don't participate actively and creatively in the change process. Yet leaders can find it very difficult to deal with the emotions of people (as well as their own) and choose to deny the experience of grieving employees. This is particularly true for Thinking leaders, who like to use logic to deal with issues and tend to dismiss emotions. It's the "army general syndrome": Yes, there will be some losses, but. . . . The justifications are of small comfort to the foot soldiers!

Thinking leaders who are denying the emotional impact of the changes on employees can exhibit great impatience ("Are they still whining?"). One ENTP leader said to us, "I've decided we just need to slam-dunk the changes. People are going to be unhappy whatever we do, so we're going to just do it." Thinking leaders can also feel beleaguered and misunderstood, getting into a "poor me" syndrome: "Can't they see that this is for their own good? I'm not a bad guy; I care about my employees. Why don't they see that? It's the global market that's driving these changes, but I'm the fall guy."

Feeling leaders are typically more comfortable with recognizing and accepting emotional responses—their own and others'—but they also face some potential problems in dealing with the losses. They can be overwhelmed by other people's emotions and end up questioning and doubting the decisions that have been made. Some backtrack on necessary, well-conceived change plans because there seems to be too much pain involved. When there's not a coherent process for dealing with loss, the resulting difficulties leave some Feeling leaders feeling de-energized and demotivated, questioning their own career path.

The primary need here is to stop denying the losses and provide public and private ways for people to grieve. It will be most effective if leaders participate in these processes (our book on organizational change suggests specific strategies for dealing with losses, as does William Bridges in *Managing Transitions*).

Loss of Identity and Meaning

The final, and in some ways most difficult, issues in organizational change that we will mention are the loss of identity and meaning. The points about dealing with loss apply to these losses as well, but with special urgency in the present and future. Increasingly, we find ourselves working with organizations that are undergoing their third or fourth radical restructuring. Their employees are coming to see ongoing organizational change as the future.

Though different types experience and respond to this differently, it creates serious problems for everyone and for the organization. The emotions associated were expressed clearly by a nurse who recounted all the changes in her work that had taken place in the last few years and the changes she saw coming. She concluded by saying, "I don't like what I'm doing now. And it's not nursing." Her reactions are echoed by employees in a variety of organizations as they come to believe that the amount and kinds of changes are resulting in loss of organizational identity, professional identity, and meaning that was previously found in their work.

It is no accident that books about leadership increasingly emphasize the leaders' role as "meaning maker." We have found the most useful approaches for leaders to be the following:

- Using metaphors for the changes to provide perspective and meaning
- Articulating the vision as clearly as possible
- Honestly acknowledging their own doubts and confusion
- Identifying their primary leadership tasks as listening to and talking with their employees
- Being authentic and honest, dealing with employees with integrity

These requirements are "beyond type." They are available to all leaders who recognize the realities of the impacts of organizational change and who support employees appropriately, while also giving the organization the greatest chance for surviving and prospering in the uncertain future.

REFERENCES

Barger, N. J., & Kirby, L. K. (1995). *The challenge of change in organizations: Helping employees thrive in the new frontier.* Palo Alto, CA: Davies-Black.

Bridges, W. (1991). *Managing transitions: Making the most of change.* Reading, MA: Addison-Wesley.

Noer, D. M. (1993). *Healing the wounds.* San Francisco: Jossey-Bass.

Peters, T. J. (1994). *The Tom Peters seminar: Crazy times call for crazy organizations.* New York: Vintage Books.

Senge, P. M., Roberts, C. E., Ross, R. B., Smith, B. J., & Kleiner, A. (1994). *The fifth discipline fieldbook: Strategies and tools for building a learning organization.* New York: Doubleday.

12 | Using the MBTI With Management Simulations

Betsy Kendall

Sally Carr

Cathy Denton is worried. Her boss and his peers have disappeared into a meeting, just when she desperately needs to discuss a crisis that has arisen at her plant. Not only does the crisis threaten production at the plant in the very near future, it also seems to expose a serious weakness in procedures. Cathy could act alone, but she feels stuck in a familiar bind: To evaluate properly what is going on and decide on the best course of action, she needs to understand how her problem fits in with other issues to be resolved. As usual, the company seems too caught up in putting out fires to consider the big picture. She sighs in combined resignation and frustration, and then gets up and knocks on the door of one of her fellow plant managers.

"Hi, Pat. Do you mind if I just run something by you? Do you have a minute?"

Pat Gleeson looks up from the papers in which he was immersed. A momentary hint of irritation passes across his face and is then replaced by a slightly forced smile of welcome. "Sure Cathy. Come on in. What can I do to help?"

As Cathy explains the problem, Pat's mind is active, taking in the information, relating it to his experience and knowledge. He didn't like having his previous work interrupted, but now that she is here, he gives her his full attention. He listens without much comment, asking occasional questions, such as "So how long has this been going on?" and "Do you know that for sure or are you guessing?"

When she stops, he pauses for a moment, then says, "Well Cathy, this is what I think you ought to do." He goes on to explain how he's handled similar problems in the past, giving some new information and adding some fairly precise suggestions. "I guess in my view, that would just about take care of it," he sums up at the end.

"Well, thanks, Pat!" says Cathy with a broad smile. "Boy, you really know your stuff. I wish I could feel so confident."

Nevertheless, back at her office, Cathy feels vaguely dissatisfied. Yes, Pat's information and suggestions were useful and relevant, but he didn't quite seem to see her point. He seemed perfectly happy to take this problem on its own and just deal with it. He didn't understand her sense of paralysis in the face of all the wider ramifications of the issue. And, if the truth be told, she hadn't really wanted Pat to tell her the answers, anyway. She'd felt a need to talk the problem out for herself, but he appeared to think she wanted him to solve it.

"I don't know what's going to happen to this company if we can't begin to work more as a team," Cathy thinks to herself. "I haven't the slightest idea of what's going on in Pat's area, but the others don't seem bothered at all—why can't they see the problem?"

Pat, meanwhile, returns to his papers and tries to pick up his work from the point when Cathy came in. He feels a little satisfaction at having been able to offer her some help, but he is puzzled as to why she came to him. "I don't get it," he thinks, "she's a smart woman; she knows her stuff. Why didn't she just get on and solve the problem instead of coming to chat about it?"

If this were an ordinary organization, Cathy and Pat would probably have gone on wondering about each other without taking the time to talk about it. But this was no ordinary company. Cathy and Pat were both managers of Looking Glass, Inc., an organization where managers spend as much time reflecting on their actions as they do actually running the company—in fact, a little more. Thus, by the end of the following day, Cathy and Pat had each had a chance to describe the incident and their reactions to it, and they were amused and interested by their differing perspectives.

So what kind of a company has the luxury of being able to sit around and spend more than a whole day discussing what happened the previous day?

MANAGEMENT SIMULATION

Looking Glass, Inc., is a fictitious glass company created as a simulation of managerial work at the Center for Creative Leadership. In this simulation, up to 20 participants choose positions in one of three Looking Glass divisions and receive an in-basket of memos and papers relating to their position. The information in the in-baskets is based on real problems and issues faced by glass industry managers and provides some information about problems relating to the person's position. Participants read their papers privately and the next day come together and simply run the company in whatever ways they choose.

Originally developed as a research tool, Looking Glass' full potential became evident only after the first group of managers took part in the simulation exercise. At the end of the simulation, the researchers, with clipboards full of copious notes on how the managers had behaved, thanked and dismissed the participants. Not unreasonably, however, the managers all asked for feedback about their performance before ending the session.

Debriefing for Leadership Skills Development

The responses of these managers prompted the development of a debriefing structure—a format enabling participants to draw out learning points through reflecting on the process they used in running the company. Typically, three debriefings are conducted.

The first, which occurs soon after the end of the simulation, represents an opportunity for participants to give their initial reactions to and describe their feelings about the experience. The second debriefing focuses on each of the divisions as a team and incorporates data concerning various aspects of team performance, such as number and quality of decisions. Its aim is to draw out for the participants lessons concerning teamwork and management through analyzing what was more and less effective about the way they worked together. The third debriefing is more personal in character. Participants receive feedback from each of the other participants in their division about the impact of their behavior. The process is carefully structured to ensure that feedback is given in a positive and constructive fashion.

Using the Myers-Briggs Type Indicator

The Looking Glass simulation itself is a two-and-a-half day module that can be run by itself, but is more often embedded in a longer development event. The content of other modules is determined by the focus of the workshop and could include strategy, leadership, communication, problem solving, and teamwork. Although we would not always use the *Myers-Briggs Type Indicator* (MBTI) in such programs, we find that psychological type frequently provides a valuable lens through which individuals can examine and understand their reactions.

In the sections that follow, we will describe the main ways in which we use psychological type in combination with the Looking Glass simulation. The same principles can be applied to using psychological type in relation to many other kinds of simulation exercises.

USING MBTI TYPE
TO IMPROVE TEAMWORK

As described above, debriefing a simulation like the Looking Glass usually includes separate sessions focusing on team and individual behavior. The second debriefing in Looking Glass involves examining the processes used by the team in working together to solve problems. The aim is for participants to extract learning points from the analysis of their approach, which they can apply in their real-life jobs.

There are several ways in which the MBTI can be useful in the team debriefing. How it is used will depend in part on when the MBTI is introduced in relation to the simulation. If the participants have been given MBTI feedback prior to taking part in the simulation, then psychological type concepts can be used explicitly by the facilitator to aid the analysis of team behavior. If MBTI feedback is to be given later in the program, then psychological type concepts may still be brought into the debriefing, but the facilitator may choose to refer to them in a less explicit way.

So which way is better? In fact, there are advantages to both: On the one hand, introducing psychological type concepts first is helpful because it enables the facilitator to use the language of psychological type to explain and draw out certain points. On the other hand, there can be a wonderful "aha" experience for groups who go through the simulation without knowing about their own or others' types and then see afterward how their behavior and reactions can be understood in psychological type terms. Introducing psychological type concepts after the simulation also keeps peer feedback independent of the MBTI feedback. There can be a danger that brief exposure to MBTI concepts leads to an erroneous pigeonholing of fellow participants and a subsequent selective perception of their behavior. Thus, like so many questions of this nature, there really isn't a right answer, and, in practice, we have about equal success with programs of either ordering.

The Debriefing Process

Even when participants have been introduced to psychological type before the simulation, we would not usually open the team debriefing with a discussion of type. This would typically seem too theoretical and forced. Instead, we begin by encouraging the team to talk about the ways they worked together in the simulation without imposing any expectations based on psychological type. Various methods can be used to make the team aware of the style in which they set about working together.

A common exercise is to get the team to look back at how they tackled a specific problem by asking such questions as: Who had the information to start with? How was this shared? What options were considered? Who made the final decision? How was this communicated? An alternative method is to focus on a particular aspect of teamwork, such as clarifying strategy or setting priorities, and to provide a structure for the team to examine how they operated in relation to this.

For example, we might split the team into two smaller groups and send them away to consider some specific questions such as the following:

- What was your division's strategy yesterday?
- With 20/20 hindsight, what do you think would be the most appropriate strategy for the division?
- What actions by individuals or the team helped the division's strategy to become clear?
- What else could individuals or the team have done to enable strategy to emerge more clearly?
- What difference might this have made?

The two groups then come back together to present their responses on flipcharts. The degree of agreement is typically high, and participants can quickly draw out key points about the strengths and drawbacks of the way they worked together.

Using Team Type

Once the team is beginning to take a somewhat critical look at their process and to see the roles that different team members played, it is illuminating to look explicitly at the team structure in terms of psychological type. If team members are comfortable sharing type, their preferences can be posted on a flipchart. It is then possible to use a simple but powerful exercise of looking at *team type*. In this exercise, the majority type in each of the preference pairs (Extraversion–Introversion, Sensing–Intuition, Thinking–Feeling, and Judging–Perceiving) defines the team type for that dimension. Putting all four together comprises the overall team type. For example, the following was the structure of a team making up one of the divisions of Looking Glass:

Vice President	ESTJ
Director of Sales and Marketing	INTJ
Director of Manufacturing	ISTJ
Director of Product Development	ISTJ
Plant Manager I	ISTP
Plant Manager II	ESTJ

This team has a pretty clear team type of ISTJ, which is also the actual type of two of its members. Once the team type has been established, team members are in a position to determine to what extent their behavior as a team was typical of that type.

In this case, the team had already recognized in their previous discussions that they were cautious about decision making and tended to focus on each problem separately rather than looking at the overview. The sales and marketing director said that he had felt uncomfortable about working in a vacuum. However, the other team members seemed to have an unspoken agreement to focus on immediate tasks. Although he had made a couple of attempts to voice his concerns, he fairly quickly gave up trying to influence the team as a whole and spent a good deal of the time during the simulation developing a new concept for his role within the organization.

In this example, there is a fairly strong majority type, and, in such cases, it is common for the team to develop an unspoken agreement about how things should be done. The sales and marketing director, as the one person preferring Intuition on the team, had experienced the familiar problem of a minority type trying to influence a majority of opposite types. Although this is by no means inevitable, teams with a heavy majority of a particular type frequently devalue, or just don't hear, the contributions of people with minority preferences. Since their contributions are not rewarded, such people frequently fall in line with the preferences of the majority. Thus, the team may lose the potential value of their different perspective.

The sales and marketing director did what was asked of him; that is, he provided the factual data requested and gave conservative sales forecasts. He stopped offering original ideas for solving problems—there were only so many impatient and withering looks he wanted in one day! As the day progressed, he gradually disengaged from the team and spent more and more time at his desk. The team later found out that he was engaged in crafting a 10-year strategic plan that would have created a whole new focus for the division.

The plan was bold and innovative, but also unrealistic in some ways. However, it was evident that the plan could have made a major contribution to the team's effectiveness if the rest of the team could have worked on it from a practical standpoint. But the sales and marketing director had decided to keep the plan to himself.

Discussion of team type is likely to be most useful when there is a fairly clear majority type and when the team's behavior has clearly been related to this majority type. In practice, however, this will not always be the case. The problem-solving model described below is useful to almost any team, regardless of whether their behavior was typical of their types.

Using the Zigzag Model

The group described in the previous section was not a real-life team. They had come to an open workshop from a variety of different companies and had been put together to make up one of the divisions of Looking Glass. Thus, although they were extremely interested in the relationship between their team type and their behavior, it was not immediately obvious how they would use these insights.

The participants needed some help in translating the learning points from the simulation to a more generalized set of principles that could be applied to their own work settings. There is a tendency to assume that the message we are giving the participants is that they need to know the types of their real-life team members in order to work effectively together. This is *not* the intended lesson. As with any other psychological type application, our emphasis is on using the model to enhance the constructive use of differences. The point is not to discover which type a person is, but to discover how to give space and respect to different approaches. In the case of problem solving, this applies especially to ensuring that all four mental functions (Sensing, Intuition, Thinking, and Feeling) are brought to bear on the problem.

To make this a little more concrete and practical—which often appeals to our usually predominantly ST groups—we find the *zigzag problem-solving approach* very helpful. This model, by now well known, points to the importance of asking questions relating to each of the four functions when approaching a problem. In its original presentation, it took the form of a zigzag, starting with Sensing—gathering facts; moving to Intuition—looking at the big picture and possibilities; evaluating via Thinking—objective pros and cons; and, finally, evaluating via Feeling—consideration of values and impact on people. Some people objected to the apparent rigidity of this ordering of the processes, pointing out that order may not be as important as ensuring that all the functions were addressed. Nevertheless, our experience suggests that, for practical purposes, most groups find it easier to work with the model using the original predetermined order.

The model appeals to managers because of its simplicity and immediate usefulness. When using it in the context of the simulation debriefing, the group may be asked to look at a problem they tackled during the simulation using the zigzag approach. An example of how this works follows.

Gathering the Sensing Information

The facilitator asks, "OK, now we will look at the car-parking problem. First,what do you know? What facts do you have?"

Various group members respond: "We knew the car-parking space was going to be reduced because of the new building. There had been a system of priority parking in the past for senior staff, but that had been abolished because of a desire for egalitarianism. There is a multistory public parking lot near the office, but female staff are afraid to use it after dark."

Other Sensing questions might include: "What do we know about how other divisions of the company have tackled this problem?" "Does anyone have any experience with problems like these?"

Using the Intuitive Perspective

When the basic facts have been drawn out, the facilitator moves on to some of the Intuitive questions, for example,"The immediate problem presented to you is one of finding space for cars to park. Are there any other ways you can look at this problem? Maybe it needs to be redefined or looked at in a wider context."

The participants respond with the following concerns: "Well, for me this issue was a stimulus to question whether our office location made sense, given that parking space is only one of several problems caused by being near a city center," says one. "I thought we should be looking at this as a transportation issue, not just as a question of parking space," says another. "Oh yes, you did talk about that, didn't you? But I'd gone down another track by then," says the participant who had been vice president in the simulation.

Brainstorming can also be a useful way of allowing Intuitive contributions to flow—suspending judgment and recording all ideas, however unlikely they may seem. Other useful questions from the Intuitive perspective could include, "What other issues does this problem relate to?" "How might an outsider look at this problem?" "If we look ahead 10 years, what is our vision of where we want to be then in relation to this problem?"

Using Thinking to Evaluate

When all the ideas brought forward have been recorded, we move on to the Thinking preference. A simple technique here is to list the objective pros and cons of each of the options generated, including costs and time required. It can also be helpful to articulate any objective criteria the solution must meet and then to analyze each possible solution for fit with these criteria.

Although considerations related to the Thinking preference are made explicit, they are *not* used to eliminate options—except perhaps those that are obviously unfeasible—as this would give a preference for Thinking preeminence over one for Feeling.

Using Feeling to Evaluate

A decision must wait until a further set of questions related to the Feeling preference has been asked: "How does this fit with our values?" "Who will be affected by this decision?" "Whose commitment is necessary for this to work?" "What effect will this have on morale?"

Debriefing the Zigzag Exercise

After being led through the zigzag, participants will see that they did cover several of the bases, but usually in a haphazard manner. Facts were brought up, but no one stopped to ask, "Is there anything else we know that's relevant?" Options were thrown out for consideration, but nobody asked, "Are there any other ways we could look at this?" Pros and cons were aired, but nobody ensured that these were recorded clearly.

Not surprisingly, since our groups typically have a majority of members with a Thinking preference, values and impact on people often have received scant attention. In addition, there is often less listening and building on each others' ideas in a team effort and more competition for one person to come up with the best solution. Those with minority preferences may have found it difficult to make an impact because of the unspoken consensus about where the team's energies should be directed. Teams are quick to grasp the principles behind the zigzag and to see the value of asking questions relating to each of the functions. Indeed, in some cases, we have introduced teams to the zigzag model before they have taken part in a simulation exercise (not Looking Glass), with the explicit suggestion that they use the model to help them work together effectively in approaching the problems.

Team Leader's Type

One participant takes the position of vice president of each division, thus becoming the designated leader of the group. The leader's type, especially when it differs from the predominant type of the team, can have interesting effects. In one team, the predominant type was STJ, but the vice president had preferences for ENTP. As the simulation progressed, communication became an increasingly vexed issue. The vice president felt that he was challenging the team to think strategically and consider the global opportunities for the company. His team, however, later reported that they were frustrated by him and did not feel that he gave them any leadership, as they were unclear about what they needed to work on.

Looking Glass also has a position of president, who is the overall leader and works across the divisions. In a program run in-house for a manufacturing organization, the president had preferences for ESFJ—a relatively unusual combination in this company. He spent a lot of time with people at all levels, having one-to-one meetings with plant managers (the lowest hierarchical position) as well as directors and the management team. Just before the president's address, which closes the simulation, he took the facilitators aside and asked if it was okay for him to buy drinks for the whole group. He then opened his address by saying, "I just want you all to know how much I appreciate the hard work you've done today, and I'd like to celebrate." At this point, he brought in a tray with a beer for every team member (and the facilitators!).

Feedback to this president showed that his very tangible gesture of appreciation was a great boost to the team's morale. In this case, although the team had a majority of Thinking types, there was a universally positive response to the way the president expressed his Extraverted Feeling, and many commented on the useful learning they gained from this. On the other hand, some of the team members expressed the feeling that he needed to be a little tougher and more probing in other interactions; they felt that his appreciation needed to be balanced by a willingness to challenge.

Influence of Company Culture on Teams

When working with in-company teams, behavior in the simulation is likely to reflect, in part, the company culture of the sponsoring organization. For example, we have found that managers in the hotel industry demonstrate quick-fire decision making in the simulation, just as they are required to do in everyday life. As William Bridges (1992) has argued in *The Character of Organizations,* this organizational culture may show attributes of an MBTI type, which will often correspond to a majority type in the company. Recognition of the cultural norms of the organization can lead to important discussion of the strengths and limitations of such an approach, which, unless made explicit, can often operate as unspoken and unquestioned truths.

Thinking Cultures

It is not uncommon for there to be no one in a division with a preference for Feeling judgment, and even if there is, they are likely to be in a minority. As a consequence, some such groups devalue the role of the Feeling preference in a work situation, regarding its contributions as an annoyance rather than an asset. A recent division of Looking Glass insisted that one must always be objective and professional in a work situation, implying that Feeling judgment was, at best, unnecessary.

However, an analysis of the way the group worked together during the simulation pointed out very obvious ways in which Feeling issues hampered effective action because they were ignored rather than dealt with. The debriefing enabled participants to see how an initial failure to acknowledge negative feelings had led to a lack of openness and trust, which, in turn, had led to internal splits, distancing, and disengagement from problems. At some level, all these participants had already been aware that they achieve results through people, but this concept took on a new significance after their experience.

Learning From Team Debriefing

We find that few of the lessons from Looking Glass are entirely new ideas for people. Most typically, they represent lessons previously acknowledged in theory, but not necessarily felt at a gut level. The simulation and debriefings provide personal experience of such lessons, thus having far greater impact than intellectual understanding alone. They also provide the participants with a particularly powerful experience of the importance of well-being and trust in a group. The third debriefing, peer feedback, offers a safe environment in which participants share feedback about the impact of their behavior in a supportive manner. Following this, participants usually work together on a task in a leaderless and unstructured group. Over and over again, they report that the group has unusual creativity and energy in this session. Participants recognize that this is related to the trust and respect that develops once the work of openly acknowledging feelings has been done. This experience tends to form a lasting impression and is more convincing of the value of Feeling work than any amount of discussion.

Summary

There are four main ways in which we have found psychological type especially helpful in analyzing team behavior in the simulation:

- We can look at the impact of majority types on team strengths and weaknesses.
- We can show the relationship between psychological type and problem-solving styles and illustrate how the framework can be used to produce more thorough problem analyses and better solutions.
- The impact of the team leader's style may be of special interest, and type allows the group and facilitators to discuss this in a nonjudgmental way.
- Type can help highlight the importance of paying attention to relationship and process variables in a team.

INDIVIDUAL DEBRIEFING

As described earlier, the third debriefing of the simulation entails each participant's receiving feedback from all other group members about the impact of his or her behavior. While the specific goals of the whole program will vary, one important goal will be for individuals to leave with a clear picture of their strengths and development needs. Feedback from the simulation and from self-report psychometric measures is very often combined with feedback collected prior to the program from real-life co-workers. At some point, the participant must integrate these various sources to form a picture of him or herself.

When Behavior Matches Expectations of Type

In many cases, feedback from other sources fits well with expectations based on type. The two participants depicted in the opening paragraphs of this chapter are examples in which this was the case.

Pat's feedback showed that he was seen by others as independent and as someone who focused on the task and saw things through. He kept the boss informed, but didn't do much networking, making contact only when necessary for task achievement. He adopted a relatively low profile, getting on with those activities for which he could gather concrete data. The demands he made on his boss were mainly concerned with specifics, and he didn't push for understanding of the big picture or worry much about the ramifications of his individual agenda. All of these behaviors were consistent with his type—he agreed with his reported preferences for ISTJ.

Cathy was seen by others as very friendly and supportive, spending time creating bonds and networking and being concerned about lack of harmony in the team. She seemed interested in the big picture, but less interested in attending to details. Several of her fellow participants reported that they found her behavior slightly suspect—why was she so friendly and what was behind her desire to make contact? Could she really be as cooperative and agreeable as she seemed? Again, these observations were in keeping with her preferences for ENFJ.

For these participants, the correspondence between their type and the feedback they received gave them a consistent view of themselves. The MBTI framework affirmed the value of their particular style, reminded them of its pitfalls, and pointed out the value of alternative styles and viewpoints. For Cathy, in particular, the feedback that her friendliness could be seen as suspect was a major revelation. Knowledge of how unusual her type was in an organizational context was extremely important in allowing her to take this feedback less personally. It was helpful for her to be assured that others of the same or a similar type often have the same experience. Without this information, feedback that she wasn't entirely trusted—which came both from her co-workers in the simulation and from her real-life co-workers—would have been devastating for her.

When Behavior Does Not Match Expectations of Type

The MBTI was not designed primarily as a predictor of behavior, unlike some other personality instruments. Instead, it was designed to point to underlying preferences that make certain ways of behaving more comfortable and natural. A person's behavior will be influenced by his or her type preferences, but also by the demands of current and past environments. Therefore, although there often is consistency between expectations based on type and actual behavior, it is no surprise to find some occasions where there are apparent contradictions. Although such contradictions make the integration of the different sources of data a little more complicated, they often provide the most interesting insights.

For example, one participant, Carl, received feedback that he seemed overly focused on details and specifics. Fellow participants reported that he appeared anxious and lacking in confidence and that he seemed to deal with this by seeking more and more data. At first, this feedback seems at variance with Carl's preferences for INTJ, and he himself sought to clarify the matter during a one-to-one session with a trainer. During this discussion, Carl discovered that he felt much more at home with and energized by Intuitive perception, but he had never really felt that this was okay. Both his family background and the organization in which he worked (a manufacturing company) emphasized Sensing styles of perception.

Carl had recognized that he was struggling and under stress in his role but had responded by focusing harder than ever on Sensing data. He was surprised to find that he was perceived as too detail conscious, and that this was seen to detract from his effectiveness. Carl's conclusion was that he needed to find opportunities to give rein to his Intuitive side and to explore what would happen if he allowed himself to trust this in safe situations.

In contrast, Belinda was seen as highly competent, but also as intimidating and unapproachable. She was prone to making sharp, witty comments, as if trying to one-up her colleagues in competence. Her style seemed consistent with a rather tough TJ, whereas she had reported and verified preferences for ESFP. During a one-to-one session, she explained her fears that, as a woman, she might be stereotyped if she showed her natural Feeling style. The feedback helped her to see that she was probably overcompensating. Although she was certainly taken seriously, she hated the idea of putting people down or being seen as unapproachable.

Departures from typical behavior can also arise for very positive reasons. For example, Jane, with preferences for ISTJ, asked many excellent strategic questions during the simulation. She did not see this as a contradiction to her type, describing it as a skill she had learned. She knew that strategic thinking was not her own strong suit, but recognized the importance of longer-term and wider vision. Thus, in her case, her behavior arose from self-awareness and personal development.

Different Feedback From the Same Behavior

The type framework can also help participants understand and reconcile apparently conflicting pieces of feedback. For example, Sarah received the following feedback from Calvin:

> Sarah, I really appreciated the help you gave me with that personnel problem, the one at my plant involving Arnold and Tanya. I thought it was great that when you overheard me discussing the problem with Paul, you came right over and joined in the discussion, even though it wasn't really your problem. I really got energized from that conversation, and that interaction set up the easy style of working that I felt we had the rest of the day.

On the other hand, Eileen's feedback for Sarah was less positive:

> At our meeting at 10:30, you came to my desk, sat down, said you had an urgent problem with the mixing process at your plant, and started discussing it. I didn't really like being interrupted, as I was in the middle of writing a report for the vice president. It would have worked better for me if you had given me some notice. I found you hard to follow in that discussion. You seemed to go off on tangents, and it would have been easier for me if you had been more organized. The impact on me was that I was a bit irritated and felt that you weren't thinking very clearly.

Sarah had preferences for Extraversion and Perceiving, as did Calvin. Eileen, on the other hand, had preferences for Introversion and Judging. The same style was seen quite differently by these different teammates. Viewing her type from a psychological type perspective allowed Sarah to see that there was a lot that was good about it but that in certain circumstances and when dealing with certain people, she needed to be more sensitive to her impact and might want to modify her style.

Summary

The power of behavioral feedback can be enhanced by the insights of psychological type in three main ways:

- Providing a consistent and supportive picture when behavior is in line with type
- Stimulating discussion concerning the origin of behavioral patterns when these are not in line with type
- Helping participants understand why the same behavior affects some people differently from others

LEARNING FROM TRAINERS' TYPES

Of course, it is not only participants who differ in type. The task of observing and giving feedback in a complex simulation such as Looking Glass brings out type differences among trainers with some clarity.

Observation Style

At the stage of observing the simulation, the most notable contrast we have found is between Intuition and Sensing. Intuitive trainers typically find it easy to pick up a general sense of what is going on, but have to work harder to tie their insights to specific data. The reverse is true for Sensing trainers, who gather a great deal of information about specific incidents but then have to work to create an integrated picture of what happened. Neither side alone would suffice—data without overall framework would be meaningless and overwhelming, while impressions and hunches without concrete data would be unconvincing.

For example, one ESTP trainer, when she started observing Looking Glass, would take 50 pages of carefully written notes, recording verbatim almost every interaction. Over time, with coaching from her Intuitive cotrainer, she disciplined herself not to write anything for 10-minute periods, during which she would watch, keeping such questions in mind as, What does this interaction suggest about these people's management styles? She also found it important to give herself occasional breaks to go outside and indulge her Extraverted Sensing—six hours of concentration was too much! Even with these modifications, she still found that she did her best Intuitive work at the end of the day, perhaps while swimming in the pool.

On the other hand, an INFP trainer formed very quick impressions about the individuals in her team and had a great deal of faith in these.

For her, the difficult part was to make herself pay attention to and record sufficient behavioral examples to illustrate her insights.

An INTJ trainer, by contrast, tended to see the team as an integrated functional unit and enjoyed tracking how patterns of team activity emerged and impacted the overall effectiveness of the team. Like the INFP trainer just mentioned, she has to discipline herself to note examples of behavior. Her notes tend to consist of diagrams charting activity and ideas for new ways to conduct the debriefing. She is driven by a quest to find the one best way to structure the debriefing discussions and is rarely satisfied that every drop of learning has been wrung from the experience. Even at the time of observation, her mind is already jumping ahead and working on the problem.

Feedback Style

Further type differences emerge during the debriefings themselves. An NT trainer was known for his delight in engaging in competitive debate with participants. Through his speed of thought and cleverness, he would stimulate them to consider new angles and concepts. By contrast, an NF trainer took a highly collaborative approach, creating a warm and safe environment in which participants could explore ideas together. The same NF, cotraining with an ST, suggested to her that when giving individual feedback she might limit the number of behavioral examples rather than feeling compelled to give them all. When giving his own feedback, the NF trainer would pay careful attention to the body language of the recipient, and when he saw signs of understanding, he would stop, even if there were more examples he could offer. He was also prone to using imagery and metaphorical language, which was frequently powerful, but sometimes bordered on the obscure. The ST suggested he might need to be careful that his own delight in imagery not carry him into realms that were difficult for others to understand. Participants reported that both styles had merits—the ST's style was seen as extremely clear and thorough, while the NF's was seen as sensitive and insightful.

Using Trainer Type With a Group

Although it is not the focus of the Looking Glass simulation, there are times in the training when it is appropriate to use the differing training styles as examples to illustrate both the impact and the value of differences. Asking participants to examine what a particular trainer added to their experience, to explore why they may have had difficulty under-standing another trainer, or to recognize the impact of training styles can give them very good information about themselves and their own styles.

Finding Your Own Style

Of course, understanding psychological type is also valuable for the trainer's own development, as the above examples illustrate. To become a management simulation trainer, one must go through an apprentice-ship period, cotraining and learning from others. This usually gives a new trainer an enviable exposure to a wide range of training and facili-tation styles. It also becomes clear that there is considerable diversity and that many different styles can be effective. The difficulty for new trainers can come when they must shape their own style. Adopting some styles is much easier than using other styles, and knowledge of one's type can give insight into which styles may come more naturally and which may be more of a challenge.

A new trainer with preferences for INTJ cotraining with an ENFP was fascinated and somewhat unnerved by the free-flowing nature of the discussion he ran. The discussion was lively and fun, and participants came away feeling good about themselves. A very wide range of issues was touched upon, though not, to the INTJ's mind, reflected on in suf-ficient depth. There did not seem to be any clear direction to the dis-cussion, and so she was all the more impressed at the way the learning points effortlessly emerged. After the session, she became worried that she might be expected to adopt a style similar to that of her ENFP cotrainer. She felt that she didn't know where to begin and was in dan-ger of losing confidence in her ability to become a competent trainer. Here, knowledge of psychological type was particularly useful in giving the new INTJ trainer insight into why an approach that was so effortless for an ENFP felt so foreign to her.

The same INTJ trainer worked in subsequent sessions alongside other trainers whose preferences were closer to her own. Over time, she developed her own style—a style that emphasized calm reflection and encouraged others to consider issues at depth. Her preferred style was also more structured and analytical, and she realized that, for her, it was more effective to work in a slightly more serious atmosphere. In other words, the style that worked best for her was an expression of her preferences. As she grew in experience as a Looking Glass trainer, she learned to adapt her style and developed skills in using the nonpreferred side of herself. She was then able to switch into these different styles when her own didn't seem to be bringing out the best in a group.

Overall, in learning to be a management simulation trainer, it is hard to be fully effective if following a model provided by someone with a very different style. It is important that new trainers be exposed to a range of possible approaches, so that they can find out what works for them.

CONCLUSION

In this chapter, we have attempted to show how valuable the MBTI framework can be when used in conjunction with a management simulation exercise. We have concentrated on Looking Glass because this is where we have the most direct experience ourselves, but we have found psychological type to be just as useful with other simulations and with other experiential exercises. The powerful nature of such exercises and the immediacy of behavioral feedback make the positive, affirming psychological type framework an especially valuable adjunct to management training.

REFERENCES

Bridges, W. (1992). *The character of organizations: Using Jungian type in organizational development.* Palo Alto, CA: Davies-Black.

13 | Using the MBTI Step II*
With Leaders and Managers

Jean M. Kummerow

Richard D. Olson

Effective strong leaders and managers must have a clear understanding of themselves. One way of helping managers discover their own personal style is through the *Myers-Briggs Type Indicator* (MBTI), an instrument that has been used effectively for decades for such a purpose. However, the MBTI type description alone can be somewhat static, in that it does not describe individual differences within a type or take into account type development. The MBTI Step II scoring version can be used to provide insight into individual leadership styles. It takes a very powerful typology, Jungian type, and adds to it behavioral traits. Thus, one can identify how people within a particular type are likely to implement their leadership style.

The MBTI Step II identifies five behavioral components, called sub-scales, within each of the four bipolar MBTI preference scales. Although the four preference dimensions are broader than the 20 behavioral sub-scales in the MBTI Step II, the behaviors identified are very important in defining how people act out their preferences. For example, we know that Extraverts draw their energy from the outside world, yet some Extraverts do not enjoy joining groups and "working the crowd." Such Extraverts may be Intimate Extraverts in MBTI Step II terms. Other leaders, while Introverted (that is, they draw their energy from inside

---

*The MBTI Step II has previously been called the MBTI Expanded Analysis Report (EAR).

themselves), may enjoy expressing their views often. Such leaders may be defined as Expressive Introverts. The MBTI Step II helps us define and explain what may seem like out-of-type behaviors as well as behaviors considered more typical of a particular type.

We believe that good leaders can operate effectively in a variety of styles and behaviors. The MBTI Step II may help define what comes naturally to leaders and what they can build on in their leadership style. It can also point out areas in which the leader may need to develop new behaviors in particular circumstances.

In this chapter, we describe the MBTI Step II briefly and discuss how it relates to leadership and management. Then we provide case examples of how leaders with differing scores may behave and how they have built on their strengths and worked with what they have identified as their limitations.

THE MBTI STEP II

Before relating the MBTI Step II to leaders and managers, we need to provide a brief background and overview of the instrument itself. For those familiar and experienced with it, this section provides a review. If you are less familiar, it provides an introduction.

Subscales

The MBTI Step II provides both overall MBTI type preference and scores ranging from 0 to 10 on 20 subscales. The closer the score is to zero, the more the poles of the subscales defined by E, S, T, or J will apply. The closer the score is to 10, the more the poles of I, N, F, or P will apply. Generally, scores in the middle may share characteristics of both poles, and people may go back and forth in their behaviors. There are no better or worse placements of any of the scores. Circumstances and the situation may define when the particular indicated behaviors are appropriate. Table 1 provides brief descriptors of the 20 MBTI Step II subscales.

Cautions in Interpretation

Neither the preference scores nor the subscale scores measure skills or competencies. Clear preferences or extreme scores are not equivalent to well-developed preferences or skills. In using the MBTI Step II, keep in mind that the subscales are designed to be used to help understand one's style *within* each of the four major preference scales. They are not designed to be used in isolation but rather to help explain and understand the four preferences.

Interpreting the subscales requires additional cautions. Because the subscales are based on relatively few items, one needs to be careful not to overinterpret small differences between them.

Out-of-Pattern Scales

Early in the development of the MBTI Step II, David Saunders, the developer of the scoring system, became aware of the usefulness of the subscales that did *not* cluster with the primary preference. He described these as potential points of stress and development (D. R. Saunders, personal communication, 1987). Scores that are on the side opposite from the primary preference are particularly important in management and leadership development because they often provide the bridge to developing the other side of the personality and to linking up with people who have those opposite characteristics. Profiles in which all subscales are toward the poles of the overall preference are considered *consistent.*

Kummerow and Quenk (1992a) define *out-of-pattern scales* (OOPS) as subscale scores that are outside the norm groups and/or different from the contiguous subscales by five or more points. We would like to add to that definition any scores that are different from those surrounding them, scores that are likely to fall outside the general pattern. An example of this is a score of 7 on the *Intimate* subscale of an Extravert who has all other subscales on the E side. Our cases will illustrate how out-of-pattern scales can be used to round out our understanding of leadership and management styles.

Psychometric Characteristics

Psychometric characteristics of the MBTI Step II need to be examined with respect to both type and the subscales. In using the MBTI Step II, keep in mind that the subscales are designed to be used to help understand one's style (type) within each of the four major preference scales. They are not designed to be used in isolation, but rather in conjunction to help explain and understand the four preferences and the overall type.

TABLE 1   Brief MBTI Step II Subscale Descriptors

Extraversion (E)	Introversion (I)
Initiating	*Receiving*
Sociable	Unexcitable
Active	Reserved
Usually introduces people	Usually is introduced to people
Expressive	*Contained*
Emotive	Controlled
Easy to know	Hard to know
Open about feelings	Keeps feelings inside
Gregarious	*Intimate*
Friendly	One-on-one
Popular	Seeks deep friendships with only
Likes to join groups and activities	a few
Participative	*Reflective*
Enjoys contact with others	Wants space from others
Prefers to communicate by	Prefers to communicate by reading
speaking and listening	and writing
Enthusiastic	*Quiet*
Lively	Calm
Energetic	Enjoys solitude
Seeks spotlight	Seeks background

Sensing (S)	Intuition (N)
Concrete	*Abstract*
Literal	Figurative
Tangible	Symbolic
Likes exact facts	Likes original ideas
Realistic	*Imaginative*
Sensible	Ingenious
Matter-of-fact	Imaginative
Focuses on effectiveness	Focuses on novelty
Practical	*Inferential*
Pragmatic	Scholarly
Results-oriented	Ideas-oriented
Enjoys applied interests	Enjoys knowledge for its own sake
Experiential	*Theoretical*
Realistic	Conceptual
Empirical	Big picture
Facts are valuable experiences	Facts make patterns
Traditional	*Original*
Conventional	Unconventional
Accepting	Idiosyncratic
Values established institutions	Values inventiveness

Thinking (T)	Feeling (F)
Logical (ideal decision-making style)	*Empathetic (ideal decision-making style)*
Impersonal	Personal
Thinking	Feeling
Relies on analysis	Relies on values
Reasonable	*Compassionate*
(actual decision-making style)	*(actual decision-making style)*
Just	Sympathetic
Impartial	Devoted
Emphasizes foresight	Emphasizes sentiment
Questioning	*Accommodating*
Precise	Approving
Independent	Uncritical
Enjoys argument	Likes harmony
Critical	*Accepting*
Skeptical	Tolerant
Offers blame	Offers praise
Wants proof	Takes things on faith
Tough	*Tender*
Firm	Gentle
Tough-minded	Tender-hearted
"Masculine"	"Feminine"

Judging (J)	Perceiving (P)
Systematic	*Casual*
Orderly	Leisurely
Structured	Easygoing
Dislikes diversions	Welcomes diversion
Planful	*Open-Ended*
Concerned about the future	Spur of the moment
Likes things settled in advance	Dislikes being tied down to plans
Early Starting	*Pressure-prompted*
Begins right away	Stress-facilitated
Acts to minimize stress	Works well under pressure
Seeks to avoid emergencies	Accomplishes much in the last-minute rush
Scheduled	*Spontaneous*
Prefers the comfort of routine	Uncomfortable with routine
and tried-and-true methods	Wants freedom to respond to the unexpeced
Methodical	*Emergent*
Organized	Trusts solutions will emerge from the process
Makes plans for the current task	Proceeds without plans
Lists subtasks before proceeding	

Note: For suggestions and strategies for understanding, interpreting, and using the instrument, see Kummerow and Quenk's *Interpretive Guide for the MBTI Expanded Analysis Report* (1992a) *and Workbook for the MBTI Expanded Analysis Report* (1992b).

Adapted and revised from the *Workbook for the MBTI Expanded Analysis Report,* by J. M. Kummerow and N. L. Quenk, 1992b, Palo Alto, CA. Copyright 1992 by Consulting Psychologists Press. Reprinted with permission.

Reliability and Validity

When using a psychological instrument, one needs to be sure that what is being measured is being measured consistently, or *reliably*. Most reliability estimates for the four preferences scales of the MBTI are .80 or higher (Myers & McCaulley, 1985). These are well within acceptable standards. With the shorter subscales, estimates of reliability are, by definition, lower. For a more complete discussion of this, see Saunders (1989). *Validity,* another key psychometric characteristic, is the accurate and meaningful application of the information from the instrument. The focus of this chapter is applying this information in working with leaders and managers.

Polarity Index

The MBTI Step II also contains a *Polarity Index* that is helpful in identifying questionable or invalid profiles. Users need to be aware that a low polarity score (less than 50) suggests a profile that *may be* invalid or difficult to accurately and meaningfully interpret. Saunders (1989) and Kummerow and Quenk (1992a) provide descriptions of the Polarity Index. The profiles we use all have acceptable polarity indexes.

Norms

The MBTI Step II provides a comparison of scores to one *norm group:* those who are the same four-letter type as the respondent. We do not specifically discuss norm group comparisons as part of this chapter, and the profiles we present have been modified to exclude this information. Again, Saunders (1989) and Mitchell (1997) provide descriptions of the norms.

USES OF THE MBTI STEP II IN LEADERSHIP AND MANAGEMENT DEVELOPMENT

The MBTI Step II can be useful in a variety of leadership and management development contexts. First, it is an excellent tool to begin the assessment of the leader's style. For example, one leader who was a Perceiving type was particularly bothered by an assignment to a new position where deadlines were constantly changing and responsibilities seemed to be reshuffled daily. An assessment of his MBTI Step II style revealed that he was an Early Starting Perceiving type who needed to prepare and begin things in advance, something that was difficult given the changing nature of his work. He was transferred to a more predictable environment, his anxiety abated, and he resumed his high level of productivity.

Second, the MBTI Step II is particularly helpful when it is difficult to identify a clear preference on one or more of the MBTI scales. The MBTI Step II identifies a pattern of behaviors within the preference and may help identify the overall preference. One design engineer, for example, scored in the middle on the T–F dimension. While she enjoyed asking questions and debating (typical of a Thinking preference), she avoided interpersonal conflict (typical of a Feeling preference). The MBTI Step II reported her as a Questioning (a T subscale), Tender (an F subscale) person. Her results helped her and others to understand why she asked a lot of questions and to recognize that she would not take advantage of people in pushing her ideas through. It also assisted her in deciding that her MBTI preference was for Feeling—that she was a Questioning Feeling type.

Third, the MBTI Step II helps identify areas of leadership development by pointing out each person's unique pattern. Out-of-pattern styles can be bridges over to the other side—that is, to the nonpreferred functions—and avenues for developing those preferences as needed. They also provide some balance to personality. An Imaginative Sensing type learned about Intuition through accessing his imaginative side; that led him to a greater understanding of the big picture so that he did not focus solely on details. He was continually developing new products that were very much needed in his area of expertise.

Fourth, the MBTI Step II identifies complementary strengths on teams. One office was in the process of remodeling. The ESFJ office manager was providing the organizational leadership to carry it out. The president of the company preferred INTP and provided direction with the overall layout and cost but did not want to be involved in the details.

The office manager was an Early Starter who liked to plan and start working on a project immediately. She was also Methodical and liked to see things implemented in an organized fashion. At the same time, her strong Casual style allowed her to handle the unexpected with a poised spontaneity. For example, when workers got off schedule and started pounding nails in the middle of an important meeting, she was able to handle the situation and the people involved calmly and efficiently. She had highly complementary skills unique to the demands of the situation. Integrating her Early Starting/Methodical style with her Casual side was very important for this task and helped her be a valuable member of her team.

IMPLICATIONS OF SUBSCALES IN LEADERSHIP

The following sections present descriptions of each subscale in a leadership context.

The Extraversion–Introversion Subscales

The Extraversion subscales are Initiating, Expressive, Gregarious, Participative, and Enthusiastic. The Introversion subscales are Receiving, Contained, Intimate, Reflective, and Quiet.

Leaders who are Initiating are constantly linking people up with one another. They may remember details about a person's life, such as names or personal or professional interests. They network easily and connect people who have the same interests. Leaders who are Receiving find themselves eschewing social amenities, wanting to get to the heart of the matter. In groups in which some people know each other and others do not, Receiving leaders are unlikely to do the introductions; the Initiating leaders are the ones who will introduce people to one another.

Expressive leaders like to talk and share what's on their own mind as well as how they feel about an issue. They also like others to readily express what's on their minds, and feel somewhat uncomfortable when people keep their feelings and thoughts to themselves. Contained leaders, on the other hand, will say only what they believe is important and germane to the situation. They tend not to share their thoughts and feelings easily, in part because they feel others may be uninterested or that it will slow the work down. They also like solving issues by themselves rather than sharing them with others; they may not want the help of others.

Gregarious leaders are often comfortable joining groups, interacting with many different people, and working the crowd. They are likely to feel comfortable with the management style of "management by walking around." Gregarious leaders find that they feel stuck if they are unable to roam from group to group, participating in a variety of conversations. Intimate leaders are likely to prefer deep one-on-one relationships with only a few people. These relationships form slowly over time and are likely to be very long lasting. Superficial "get acquainted" conversations are not likely to be pleasing to the Intimate leaders, who prefer more depth to their conversations and relationships.

Participative leaders enjoy communicating in person with others. They would rather walk into someone's office with an idea or a thought than write that idea down. Reflective people prefer to read or write about what's important to them. They may not value people dropping by their offices with their ideas, but would prefer to read them first. One multinational corporation found their Participative managers were particularly bothered by the company's electronic mail system. These managers figured out ways to get around the e-mail system by telephoning or arranging to visit their colleagues in other countries.

Enthusiastic leaders want their work and their lives to be exciting and full of action. They enjoy being the center of attention, whether it's directing a team or giving a public speech. They want to create enthusiasm within those around them. Quiet leaders prefer peace and quiet and serenity. They tend not to put themselves in the limelight and are generally modest about their own accomplishments. Their style is more unassuming than out-front.

The Sensing–Intuitive Subscales

The Sensing subscales are Concrete, Realistic, Practical, Experiential, and Traditional. The Intuitive subscales are Abstract, Imaginative, Inferential, Theoretical, and Original.

Concrete leaders trust and like the facts. They find that before they can proceed in leading others, they must have the facts in place. Abstract leaders read between the lines, using a fact as a stimulus or a jumping-off point for an idea. They are more figurative than literal.

Realistic leaders pay attention to the practicality, the cost-effectiveness, and the commonsensical nature of the tasks before them. Imaginative leaders focus on resourceful and imaginative ways of handling the situations in which they find themselves. They want to be clever in meeting the needs of the moment. One Imaginative leader in computer technologies was quite pleased to be given an assignment in which costs were not a factor, but a brand-new application was the goal.

Practical leaders want their work to be useful. It's how an idea can be used that appeals to the Practical leaders, not what the idea is in and of itself. Inferential leaders, on the other hand, collect ideas and find the life of the mind to be a very exciting place. For them, an idea is useful in and of itself, not because it has a particular application.

Experiential leaders value direct experience, trying things out. They want to build and see and do. Theoretical leaders look for the patterns, trends, and theories that explain what is happening. They embrace theories and will make up their own theories if one is not in place.

Traditional leaders rely on the time-honored ways of doing things. The documentation is read and followed, the procedures are valued, and the institutional ways are most important. Original leaders value newness and change and tend to ignore the standard operating procedures in favor of new ways of proceeding. Relying on what is already in place is very uncomfortable for Original leaders.

The Thinking–Feeling Subscales

The Thinking subscales are Logical, Reasonable, Questioning, Critical, and Tough. The Feeling subscales are Empathetic, Compassionate, Accommodating, Accepting, and Tender.

When thinking ideally about making a decision, the Logical leaders find themselves concentrating on the objective analysis of the data that they have. They want to weigh the evidence and proceed on a logical basis. The Empathetic leaders want to tune into their emotions and the emotions of others as guides to the values of the situation. They want to please themselves and others and to maintain harmony as they think about moving forward in the decision. One Empathetic leader said he allows what he is enthusiastic about to decide his next priority.

Reasonable decision makers actually make a decision based on the logic of the situation. They use standards and criteria and can readily explain these to others. Compassionate leaders make decisions based on what they perceive as right for themselves and others in the situation. They tune into their own values and the values of others as well as the emotional content of the situation.

Questioning leaders feel it's their duty in life to ask questions. They are skeptical and feel that questions will lead them to the information to reduce their skepticism. Accommodating leaders generally feel that questions will exacerbate differences and, since they are attempting to draw everyone together, it is best not to ask questions. When a question is necessary, they express it very diplomatically and very tentatively.

Critical leaders are highly attuned to what is wrong with a situation. They find the flaws and critique them, and find it difficult not to evaluate. Accepting leaders allow all ideas to be possible. They do not start critiquing until they have heard the entire idea. Anything is possible. Middle scores on this scale tend toward the critical behaviors; norms in U.S. society tend to favor the Accepting side.

Tough leaders, once they have decided on a course of action, push their agenda through. There is a one-sided quality to the interaction and, given limited resources, they are aware that someone has to win and someone has to lose. The Tough leaders want to make sure that they are in a position to win. Tender leaders wish to draw all sides together and to conciliate. They use gentleness and affection to help people get along and attempt to create a win-win situation among all participants. As with the subscale above, middle scores on this subscale tend to be defined more by the Tough descriptors than the Tender ones. U.S. norms tend to lean toward the Tender side.

The Judging–Perceiving Subscales

The Judging subscales are Systematic, Planful, Early Starting, Scheduled, and Methodical. The Perceiving subscales are Casual, Open-Ended, Pressure-Prompted, Spontaneous, and Emergent.

The Systematic leaders like to have contingency plans. They have thought of different possibilities that might happen, and they set up plans to avoid having anything go wrong. Casual leaders enjoy surprises, and when things go wrong, they see it as an opportunity to change directions and to have some fun. Casual leaders also tend to create a more casual work environment rather than a formal one.

The Planful leaders feel it is important to have long-range plans. They know where their company is heading, and they are comfortable when the long-range direction is defined. The Open-Ended leaders prefer to keep things open. They want to be able to respond appropriately in the moment, and a plan may get in the way of their taking the correct course of action.

Early Starting leaders want to start in advance to avoid the stress of a last-minute rush. They prefer to parcel out their energy and keep their work flow moving evenly, taking one task at a time. The Pressure-Prompted leaders like to juggle multiple tasks at the same time, often keeping things in the air until the last possible moment. They enjoy the adrenaline rush of pulling things together at the last minute and getting them done right at the deadline. Early Starting leaders often describe themselves as getting nervous watching the Pressure-Prompted leaders' seeming inaction until the final moments.

Scheduled leaders enjoy having routines in place to help them get through their day-to-day operations. They find they can work more effectively when they have good routines operating. Spontaneous leaders tend to find routines boring and restrictive. They want to be able to react to the moment in the way that is best for them, not through a routine. A Scheduled leader often picks the same time to meet with his or her direct reports every week or month. The Spontaneous leader varies meeting times and places. Both may have regular meetings, but accomplish them in different ways.

The Methodical leaders are able to break a task into subtasks and proceed with them in an orderly fashion. They see the component parts of what they must do. The Emergent leaders prefer to plunge in and take an ad hoc approach. They do not enjoy seeing the pieces of what they are doing but rather forge through in their own style.

CASE EXAMPLES

Providing case examples of managers and leaders in action will help illustrate some of the ways we have found the MBTI Step II useful. First, we will present two pairs of cases of the same MBTI type in which one member of the pair has a more consistent profile than the other. Second, we discuss four more pairs, each differing by only one preference and having three preferences in common. Finally, we will point out common out-of-pattern scales we have found in our work, many of which are illustrated in our case examples.

The case examples deal with a variety of MBTI types and with all eight preferences, but we do not include every type. The ones we have chosen are those that illustrate key points about use of the MBTI Step II with leaders and managers. All of the individuals included have reviewed and discussed their four-letter MBTI type as accurate for them.

Contrasting Profiles Within the Same Type

In this section, we will contrast the MBTI Step II profiles of managers who are the same MBTI type. We use two types, ENFP and INTJ, for illustration.

ENFPs With Different Profiles

Both Jack and Carol prefer ENFP, and both work in the human resources area, but their MBTI Step II profiles point out some real differences. Carol, an ENFP human resources manager in a financial service environment, shows relatively clear preferences for that type. Figure 1 shows her MBTI Step II profile. Her Extraverted and Intuitive subscales are clear. Her Feeling preference is somewhat modified by her

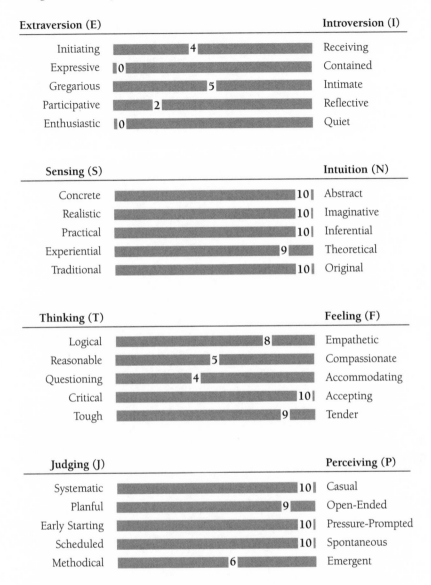

Extraversion (E)

Initiating	4	Receiving
Expressive	0	Contained
Gregarious	5	Intimate
Participative	2	Reflective
Enthusiastic	0	Quiet

Introversion (I)

Sensing (S)

Concrete	10	Abstract
Realistic	10	Imaginative
Practical	10	Inferential
Experiential	9	Theoretical
Traditional	10	Original

Intuition (N)

Thinking (T)

Logical	8	Empathetic
Reasonable	5	Compassionate
Questioning	4	Accommodating
Critical	10	Accepting
Tough	9	Tender

Feeling (F)

Judging (J)

Systematic	10	Casual
Planful	9	Open-Ended
Early Starting	10	Pressure-Prompted
Scheduled	10	Spontaneous
Methodical	6	Emergent

Perceiving (P)

Figure 1 MBTI Step II Profile for Carol (ENFP)

Questioning and Reasonable style. She is not reluctant to ask why a certain procedure is being done. Her Questioning style often leads her to the details of the Sensing side; without this, she might miss some important data. While having a clear Feeling preference, when it comes to day-to-day decisions on the job, she can be very rational and reasonable in her approach. She will often comment on how trying it is to make a difficult people decision, and then she will turn around and do it with ease.

While clearly a Perceiving type, her score toward the Methodical pole reflects her tendency to keep herself reasonably organized and focused. Even in this case, where scores tend to be well defined in the direction of each of her preferences, the MBTI Step II subscales shed additional light on some key aspects of her interpersonal style in the workplace.

Jack, an ENFP, runs a consulting firm that specializes in communications training. Figure 2 shows his MBTI Step II profile. While he is an Extravert, he does have some subscales to the Introverted side. For example, he is an Intimate Extravert. He finds he prefers to work one-on-one rather than with large groups in training situations. He maintains long-term relationships with his clients and gets to know them well. He does not need to be in the limelight, as illustrated by his Quiet score. He is Expressive, and one of the things he does is encourage his clients to express their feelings. Many of them are people who hold back their feelings and do little to reinforce others.

Jack is an Experiential Intuitive type. He is always trying to make his insights work for other people. He teaches communication and problem-solving techniques, and he is constantly pointing out to people how they could change their communication to make it more effective. He is very clear on all of the Feeling subscales. One of his goals in life is to bring Feeling into Thinking organizations.

Jack is an Early Starting Perceiving type. He gets nervous and uptight when there are impending deadlines, and he starts projects far in advance. He dislikes being so organized but finds that unless he is, he becomes very stressed. He recently had heart surgery and needs to avoid stress for his physical health. He uses his Methodical tendency to help him break tasks into manageable steps.

Jack has particularly enjoyed the growth and development opportunities that were pointed out by MBTI Step II. He has become more tolerant of different styles; for example, he no longer expects his clients to be as expressive as he is. He is open about teaming up with people who have different styles than his, and he has encouraged others to do so as well. Without the MBTI Step II, we would have missed important aspects of his personality.

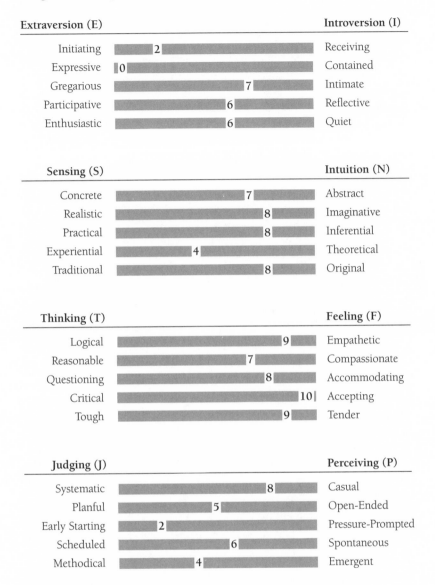

Extraversion (E)   **Introversion (I)**

Initiating   2   Receiving
Expressive   0   Contained
Gregarious   7   Intimate
Participative   6   Reflective
Enthusiastic   6   Quiet

Sensing (S)   **Intuition (N)**

Concrete   7   Abstract
Realistic   8   Imaginative
Practical   8   Inferential
Experiential   4   Theoretical
Traditional   8   Original

Thinking (T)   **Feeling (F)**

Logical   9   Empathetic
Reasonable   7   Compassionate
Questioning   8   Accommodating
Critical   10   Accepting
Tough   9   Tender

Judging (J)   **Perceiving (P)**

Systematic   8   Casual
Planful   5   Open-Ended
Early Starting   2   Pressure-Prompted
Scheduled   6   Spontaneous
Methodical   4   Emergent

Figure 2 MBTI Step II Profile for Jack (ENFP)

Carol and Jack both share ENFP preferences and have many similarities. Yet their MBTI Step II subscales provide insight into the uniqueness of their personalities and help them both grow and develop in ways that make sense for them and that help them to be more effective in their work.

INTJs With Different Profiles

The next cases focus on two INTJs: George, who has a more consistent profile, and Dick, who has many out-of-pattern scales. George is the department head of a government agency. Figure 3 shows his MBTI Step II profile. He is not outspoken, preferring his staff to do their jobs with little direction from him. He prefers one-on-one meetings and likes to stay out of the limelight. All of his subscales fall toward the Introverted side.

He prefers to operate at a policy level, leaving the nitty-gritty details to others. He is continually seeing new things for his department to do; his subscales are clearly to the Intuitive side.

George's Thinking–Feeling pattern is slightly more mixed, although, given the norms of the population, not unusual. He does not try to push his way through, but rather assumes that logic will sway all to his side.

His pattern is clearly on the Judging side, although he does not always like to lock himself into long-range plans. The MBTI Step II confirmed what he already knew about his INTJ style and provided a few nuances.

Dick works in a high-tech industry where he is responsible for obtaining and managing large contracts. Figure 4 shows his MBTI Step II profile. In many respects, he functions as an entrepreneur working within a large company.

He has an Introverted preference. He lives in a secluded house at the end of a one-mile driveway, a choice consistent with his score toward the Quiet subscale. At the same time, he is in meetings all day and seems to know the names of everyone in the plant. As he walks around, he talks to people as if he knew them well. His MBTI Step II results help us understand his Gregarious side and how he uses it effectively in his work. At times, of course, he feels overly stressed by all the people contact. In some ways, he is continually working at the balance between his Gregarious side and his need to have a quiet and calm setting. As an Introvert, he needs time alone to reenergize.

The subscales of the Sensing–Intuitive preference show him to be Abstract, Theoretical, and Original—certainly characteristics of a creative and innovative person. Yet he is Practical. He describes how he likes to implement the projects he designs, and he has brought a great

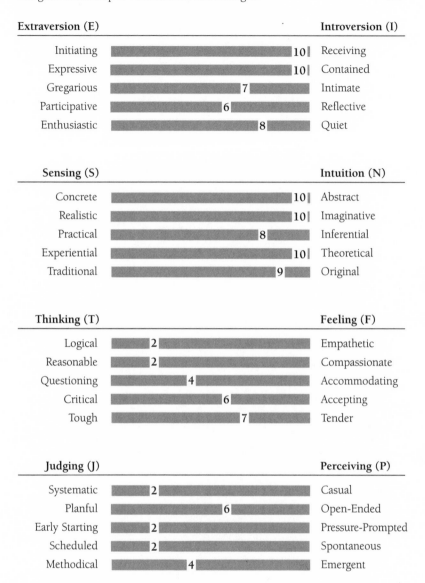

Figure 3   MBTI Step II Profile for George (INTJ)

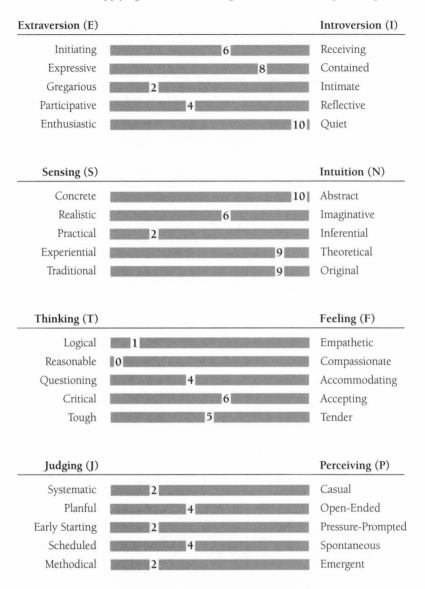

Extraversion (E)   **Introversion (I)**

Initiating	6	Receiving
Expressive	8	Contained
Gregarious	2	Intimate
Participative	4	Reflective
Enthusiastic	10	Quiet

Sensing (S)   **Intuition (N)**

Concrete	10	Abstract
Realistic	6	Imaginative
Practical	2	Inferential
Experiential	9	Theoretical
Traditional	9	Original

Thinking (T)   **Feeling (F)**

Logical	1	Empathetic
Reasonable	0	Compassionate
Questioning	4	Accommodating
Critical	6	Accepting
Tough	5	Tender

Judging (J)   **Perceiving (P)**

Systematic	2	Casual
Planful	4	Open-Ended
Early Starting	2	Pressure-Prompted
Scheduled	4	Spontaneous
Methodical	2	Emergent

Figure 4   MBTI Step II Profile for Dick (INTJ)

deal of profit to his company with his projects. At the same time, his colleagues feel that he doesn't always have his feet planted firmly enough on the ground and that some of his contracts tend to uncomfortably stretch company resources and are extremely difficult to implement. He has been working to access his Practical side even more. His Thinking and Judging subscales are generally consistent with his overall preferences.

George and Dick share the same type and have much in common. The MBTI Step II provides insight into the unique ways in which each uses his INTJ style.

Contrasting Subscales of MBTI Types That Differ on Only One Dimension

Extraversion–Introversion Subscale Differences

Both Pat and Henry have jobs in the legal field. Their type preferences are similar, ISTJ and ESTJ, respectively. Their MBTI Step II profiles further explain who they are. Pat is an ISTJ leader working in law enforcement. His MBTI Step II profile is shown in Figure 5. It shows him to be a Gregarious Introvert. While this is very helpful to him in his interactions with a wide variety of offices and other agencies, it has become a problem in his own office. He leads a small number of people in a rather remote location. His staff's expectations are that they will get to know one another in depth, which is somewhat difficult for him. In addition, he is Contained and rarely shares his feelings and thoughts with others.

Pat is a Theoretical Sensing type, and he is always pushing the office toward using new, even cutting-edge, methods and equipment in the law enforcement field. He does, however, make sure that the innovations work well.

He is clearly to the Thinking side on the Thinking–Feeling scales, and his staff does not appreciate his Critical and Tough behavior. Many of them are Feeling types who want more nurturance than he is likely to give.

He is a Pressure-Prompted Judging type and has multiple projects going at the same time. Many of his staff are Early Starting types, and he creates stress for them by having so much going on.

Part of his leadership development subsequent to his MBTI Step II interpretation has involved developing more in-depth relationships with others and letting people know what's on his mind. To do so, he has agreed to walk through the office several times a day, chatting with

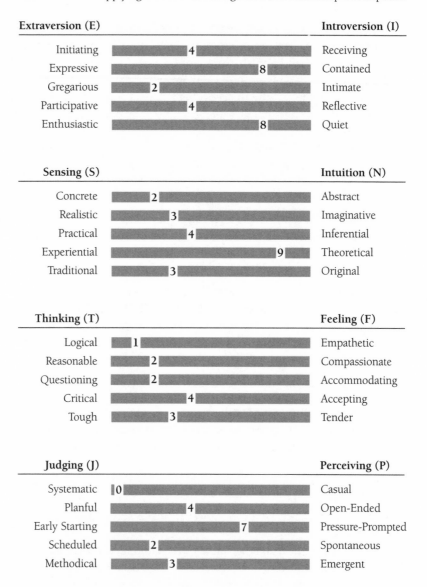

Figure 5 MBTI Step II Profile for Pat (ISTJ)

people, passing on new ideas he has, letting them know his upcoming priorities, and thanking them for the special work they have done. He has also recognized the need to spend more time with individuals in his office, getting to know them on a more personal level. He has difficulty seeing ways to develop Feeling behaviors, but agreed to ask others in his office for ways he could be more supportive of them.

Henry, an ESTJ, is a lawyer who serves as the managing partner of his law firm. His MBTI Step II profile is shown in Figure 6. Note that he has many midscores on the subscales of the Extravert–Introvert dimension, and he may move back and forth between engaging people and operating more inwardly. Initially, he struggled with deciding whether his preference was for Extraversion or Introversion. Most people would likely describe him as a clear Extravert.

On the Sensing–Intuition dimension, he is considered a Theoretical Sensing type. Sometimes he finds this stressful, but his solutions are generally sound, long-term, and practical. He believes in seeing the big picture and structuring it, if possible (note his Judging subscales), and he is a natural when it comes to laying out and implementing a strategic plan for his organization.

While clearly having a Thinking preference, he has strong Accepting and Tender subscale scores. He enjoys working with people and has been heavily involved as a volunteer with youth; he relishes the help he can give teens at a sensitive time in their lives. Yet there is a sarcastic and cynical style that may come in part from his Questioning, Logical, and Reasonable areas. Often this side is more highly visible than the Accepting, Tender side. While he quickly understands what logically needs to be done, he isn't always as quick to get involved with the feelings associated with implementing some of the more difficult people decisions. Defining these characteristics helped him sort through some of his own confusion with respect to his sensitive style and his ability to make very logical decisions.

He is notably clear on the Judging preference and subscales. He is highly structured in organizing his approach to work. In his office, there is not a paper, pen, or pencil out of place. He uses his Judging characteristics to structure problems and to plan and follow through with the implementation of solutions.

On the MBTI, Pat and Henry differ on only the Extraversion–Introversion dimension. The MBTI Step II helps us understand more clearly how they are different on Extraversion–Introversion and also helps clarify how they use their shared STJ preferences differently.

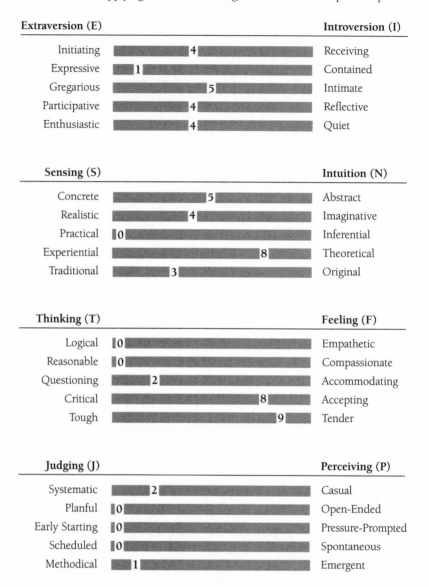

Figure 6 MBTI Step II Profile for Henry (ESTJ)

Sensing–Intuition Subscale Differences

Lloyd, ISFJ, and Jim, INFJ, provide some contrasts on the SN subscales, and some differences within Introversion as well.

Lloyd, an ISFJ, is an executive within the financial service industry. His MBTI Step II profile is shown in Figure 7. He supervises a staff and is also responsible for analyzing information and making investment recommendations. He has no major out-of-pattern scales. He seems to know himself reasonably well, is dependable, reliable, and is seen as a stabilizing factor in his work group. He is not one who becomes easily excited, and he certainly structures his work and focuses on results, reflecting his clear SJ preferences.

In the past, he has had difficulty confronting other people and making difficult people decisions. With a Feeling preference, his strength is in his sensitivity to others. However, his oversensitivity can be limiting at times. For Lloyd, his MBTI Step II profile provided some clues as to how to develop breadth in his leadership style. For example, his middle scores on the Tough and Reasonable subscales of the Thinking–Feeling dimension gave him some clues as to how he might use his logical skills to deal with interpersonal conflict in a sensitive way. He has used these as links to the Thinking side. When a member on his team needed to be confronted about a performance issue, he offered to do it, describing this as a growth opportunity for himself. In the past, he would have been the last person on the team to volunteer for this.

Jim, INFJ, is a senior manager in a nationwide organization. His MBTI Step II profile is shown in Figure 8. Jim is an Expressive Introvert; he is not secretive about his feelings and people do not wonder or feel confused about where he is coming from. At the same time, he is a Receiving leader and not one to pay much attention to social amenities. He connects exceptionally well with people when they are introduced to him, but he is not likely to be the one initiating the connections.

The only preference in which he does not have an out-of-pattern scale is Intuition. One of Jim's great strengths is his ability to identify patterns in information.

On the T–F preference scale, Jim's score is near the midpoint. You can see the mixed patterns in the subscales. He is a Questioning type, quick to question current norms. His Empathetic, Reasonable pattern reflects his value-centered ideal decision-making style. Although he certainly pays attention to the people dimension in decision making, he can be very logical when necessary.

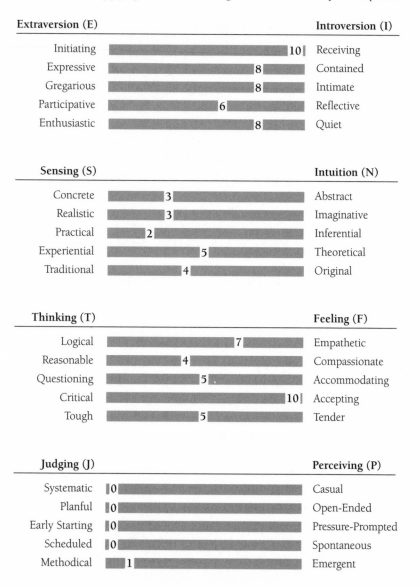

Figure 7 MBTI Step II Profile for Lloyd (ISFJ)

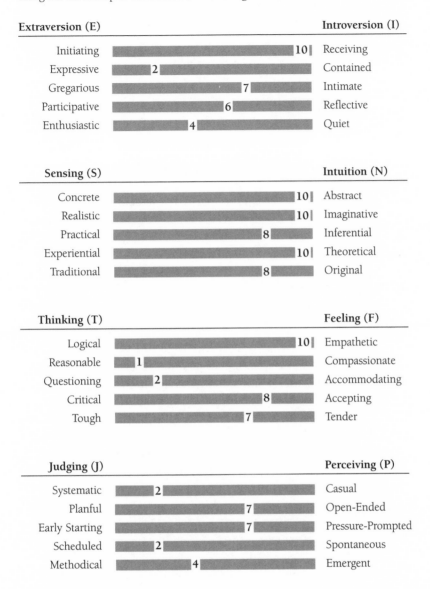

Extraversion (E)   **Introversion (I)**

Initiating   10│ Receiving
Expressive   2   Contained
Gregarious   7   Intimate
Participative   6   Reflective
Enthusiastic   4   Quiet

Sensing (S)   **Intuition (N)**

Concrete   10│ Abstract
Realistic   10│ Imaginative
Practical   8   Inferential
Experiential   10│ Theoretical
Traditional   8   Original

Thinking (T)   **Feeling (F)**

Logical   10│ Empathetic
Reasonable   1   Compassionate
Questioning   2   Accommodating
Critical   8   Accepting
Tough   7   Tender

Judging (J)   **Perceiving (P)**

Systematic   2   Casual
Planful   7   Open-Ended
Early Starting   7   Pressure-Prompted
Scheduled   2   Spontaneous
Methodical   4   Emergent

Figure 8 MBTI Step II Profile for Jim (INFJ)

He is a Pressure-Prompted, Open-Ended Judging type. As part of his job, he has to be able to balance concerns that are arising in a number of different offices and manage them effectively. When he is working on something, he is able to focus and get a lot done, although he is also comfortable with changing direction on a project in midstream.

Jim is a highly effective leader, although he does not fit the stereotypical image of a business executive. He makes use of his ability to see the big picture, his people orientation, and his ability to structure work without being overly tied to that structure. His out-of-pattern scales explain a great deal about his style.

Lloyd and Jim both display very different but effective styles not only on Sensing–Intuition but also in other areas such as their use of T–F. Most organizations expect some Thinking behavior (not many expect Feeling behavior), and both Lloyd and Jim have figured out ways to capitalize on their preference for Feeling while accessing some Thinking subscale behaviors. Without the MBTI Step II, we could not fully understand this.

Thinking–Feeling Subscale Differences

Lisa (ESTJ) and Robin (ESFJ) differ on only one dimension in their MBTI type—the Thinking–Feeling dimension. Their MBTI Step II profiles also reveal other differences, as well as similarities. Lisa, an ESTJ, is a manager in the financial industry. Figure 9 shows her MBTI Step II profile. Her Extravert subscales are clear and, indeed, she is an energetic, outgoing, action-oriented person.

Her Sensing–Intuition subscales show a pattern toward the middle, although in real life she tends to trust the data more than the big picture. She is able to access and use both sides, but she trusts one a little more.

Lisa prefers Thinking overall, but her Compassionate and Accepting behavioral subscale scores convey her sensitivity to people. She asks tough, precise questions to get to the bottom of things. She is able to quickly make tough people decisions (and at times her Judging preference may manifest itself with a rush to judgment). Co-workers sometimes find the combination of compassion and quick people decisions confusing, and she finds it stressful and confusing as she tries to move ahead in a logical way without hurting people's feelings. By better understanding her Questioning and sometimes argumentative style, along with her Expressive, outgoing style, she was better able to leverage her strengths without being perceived as being overly critical of people.

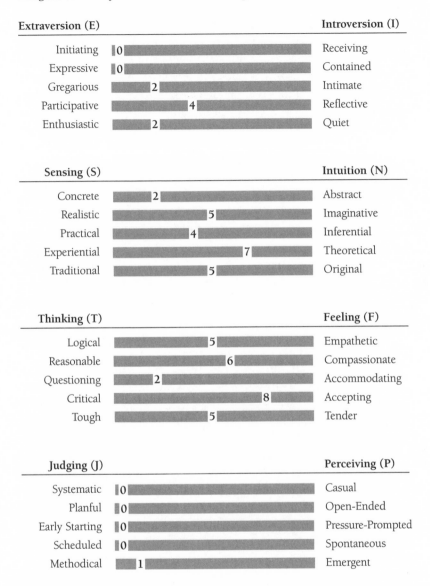

Figure 9 MBTI Step II Profile for Lisa (ESTJ)

Lisa's Judging subscales are extreme. She operates in an environment that is not volatile and that includes a number of fixed rules. She looks for long-term results (see Planful and Systematic) and is less concerned with unpredictable short-term ups and downs. Through observing how several subscales interacted, a greater understanding of her style emerged. What had previously felt contradictory now became understandable and was seen by Lisa as complementary.

Robin, an ESFJ, has worked in management, sales management, and consulting settings. Figure 10 shows her MBTI Step II profile. Her subscales are clearly to the Extraverted side, and she likes to interact with people. Her middle score on the Gregarious–Intimate subscale, however, shows her ability to connect one-on-one with others in sales calls and also reflects her long-term and valued relationships with two close friends from high school.

Her Sensing subscale scores are consistent with her Sensing preference, with the exception of her score of 6 on the Concrete–Abstract subscale. She likes to read between the lines when working with people.

Although she has a Feeling preference, Robin's Questioning scale is out of pattern. She likes to carve her own path and has been described as an independent thinker. Her ability to understand the feelings of other people, along with her ability to structure her work (see her Judging subscales), have been real assets to her career success. Although her major preference scores are quite clear, the MBTI Step II subscales provide additional information about Robin's behaviors.

With Robin and Lisa, there is some similarity of styles, particularly on Extraversion and Judging. Even though both have the same Questioning score and both are seen as somewhat independent, note how the effect of their questions are often different because of the context of their overall preferences. Questioning Thinkers are often perceived as more argumentative with their questions, whereas Questioning Feeling types are often seen as more diplomatic. Questioning Thinking types are often trying to find information to fit into their logical frameworks, while Questioning Feeling types are frequently asking questions to lead to greater harmony in the situation.

Judging–Perceiving Subscale Differences

Deborah (ENTJ) and Carla (ENTP) are both successful leaders who have recently been promoted. They are both seen as having very

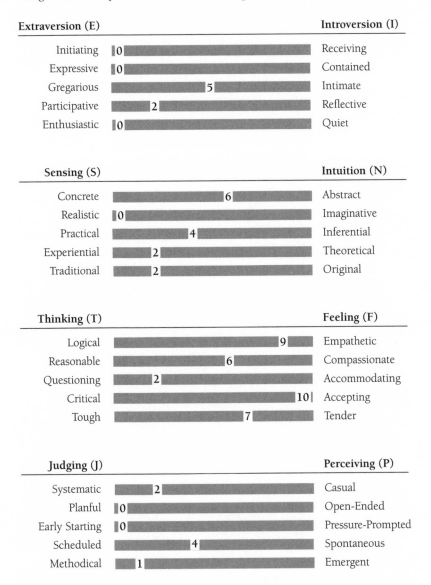

Figure 10   MBTI Step II Profile for Robin (ESFJ)

effective styles in their respective industries. Deborah manages a staff that delivers state-of-the-art electronic systems to other businesses throughout the country. Her MBTI Step II profile, which is shown in Figure 11, is fairly typical of ENTJs. She is out front with her communications (E), focused on new and different ways of proceeding (N), a very logical and firm decision maker (T), and an extremely organized person (J).

Her few exceptions include being an Accepting Thinking type, a very common pattern for Thinking types in general. She is willing to listen to and accept new and different ways of doing things.

She is also somewhat Spontaneous in her lifestyle, although she attributes that to the fact that routines do not work well for her in a constantly changing business environment or in a personal life that includes two small children. Deborah found it particularly valuable to compare her MBTI Step II scores with those of her colleagues and to note the unique behaviors that she brought to projects.

Carla, an ENTP, is an executive in a financial services company. Her subscale patterns, which are shown in Figure 12, reflect her overall preferences, although the slight exceptions help to round out her style. On the Extraverted–Introverted dimension, she uses her understanding of her middle scores on the Gregarious–Intimate and Participative–Reflective scales to lead her to more depth in both her conversations with people and her studies in her field of interest.

She accesses her middle score on the Practical–Inferential subscale of the S–N dimension by asking her co-workers how her ideas (and the ideas of others) can be applied. Her Thinking–Feeling subscales are clearly on the Thinking side, and she is seen as logical and tough-minded. In her case, however, a background in social work and empathic skills help us understand her style. She regularly uses these skills to balance her strong Thinking subscales and to add compassion to her decisions.

While clearly preferring a Perceiving lifestyle, she has recognized the need for contingency plans and has thus worked to develop her Systematic side. While she says she hates long-range planning and locking into plans, she nonetheless has to force herself to do so in her daily work.

Both Carla and Deborah have learned to compensate for the pitfalls in their Judging–Perceiving preferences. Carla, with a Perceiving preference, uses her Systematic style to bridge over her Judging side. Deborah, with a Judging preference, uses her Spontaneous style to link to her Perceiving side. Without the additional information provided by the MBTI Step II, this would not be apparent.

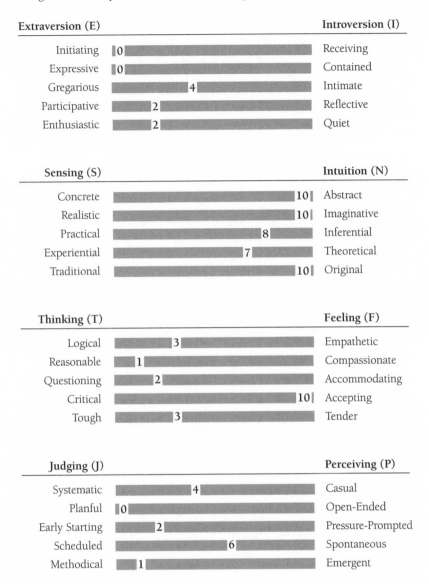

Extraversion (E)   **Introversion (I)**

Initiating   0   Receiving
Expressive   0   Contained
Gregarious   4   Intimate
Participative   2   Reflective
Enthusiastic   2   Quiet

Sensing (S)   **Intuition (N)**

Concrete   10   Abstract
Realistic   10   Imaginative
Practical   8   Inferential
Experiential   7   Theoretical
Traditional   10   Original

Thinking (T)   **Feeling (F)**

Logical   3   Empathetic
Reasonable   1   Compassionate
Questioning   2   Accommodating
Critical   10   Accepting
Tough   3   Tender

Judging (J)   **Perceiving (P)**

Systematic   4   Casual
Planful   0   Open-Ended
Early Starting   2   Pressure-Prompted
Scheduled   6   Spontaneous
Methodical   1   Emergent

Figure 11 MBTI Step II Profile for Deborah (ENTJ)

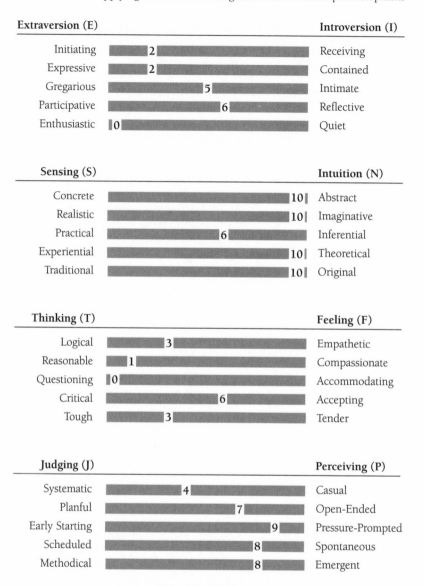

Figure 12 MBTI Step II Profile for Carla (ENTP)

TABLE 2   Common Out-of-Pattern Scales and Case Examples

Out-of-Pattern Scale	Case Illustration
Contained E	
Expressive I	Jim
Intimate E	Jack
Gregarious I*	Dick, Pat
Enthusiastic I	
Concrete N	
Concrete, Practical N*	
Imaginative S	
Practical N	Dick, Carla
Inferential S	
Theoretical S*	Pat, Henry, Lisa
Empathetic F/Reasonable T	Jim
Questioning F	Carol, Jim, Robin
Accepting T	Henry, Lisa, Deborah
Accepting, Tender T*	Henry
Critical F	
Tender T	Henry
Casual J	
Pressure-Prompted J	Pat, Jim
Early Starting P	Jack
Methodical P	Carol, Jack

*Added by Kummerow and Olson to the work of J. M. Kummerow and N. L. Quenk. Original work copyright 1992a by Consulting Psychologists Press, Inc. Reprinted with permission.

Common Out-of-Pattern Scales

Every case we have presented has at least one out-of-pattern scale, and, indeed, in our work with managers and leaders, we have found this to be the rule rather than the exception. Leaders need to be flexible and appreciate other approaches, and the prevalence of their out-of-pattern scales may illustrate these qualities.

There appear to be some common out-of-pattern scales for practitioners to look for with their clients. We are using the rather broad definition of an out-of-pattern scale here for illustrative purposes. Kummerow and Quenk (1992) have noted several common out-of-pattern scales, and we have added to their list in Table 2. The table also contains the case examples we have discussed in this chapter in which out-of-pattern scales occur.

If you have clients with these out-of-pattern scores, do not consider them unworkable or unusual, but rather help your clients see how they can use these different parts of their personality to more effectively lead and manage others as we have illustrated in the case examples we have presented.

SUMMARY

Leaders have many different styles. For decades, the MBTI has helped leaders understand their styles, strengths, and limitations. In looking at many MBTI Step II leader profiles, we have found that very few are consistent or pure types without at least some out-of-pattern scales. These out-of-pattern scales frequently describe important aspects of a leader's style and skills. Without the additional information provided by the MBTI Step II, key leadership characteristics frequently go unrecognized when interpreting MBTI results.

The MBTI Step II provides an added level of complexity to understanding leadership styles. After becoming familiar with and using the MBTI Step II for a period of time, we feel somewhat lost without it. In many of the cases reviewed, potentially confusing aspects of a leader or manager's style were identified using the behavioral subscales and some common patterns noted.

In leadership development, the behavioral subscales can provide clues to the development of the other side of the personality and to appreciating teammates and followers on that side. The subscales can provide a tool to help the leader break through barriers and develop new behaviors, providing greater breadth to leadership skills. The information provided by the MBTI Step II gives a clear and valuable picture of leadership style. It has been used in a variety of leadership and management development contexts. It is useful in appraising style, in building teams, and in breaking down barriers to leadership growth.

REFERENCES

Kummerow, J. M., & Quenk, N. L. (1992a). *Interpretive guide for the MBTI Expanded Analysis Report.* Palo Alto, CA: Consulting Psychologists Press.

Kummerow, J. M., & Quenk, N. L. (1992b). *Workbook for the MBTI Expanded Analysis Report.* Palo Alto, CA: Consulting Psychologists Press.

Mitchell, W. D., with Quenk, N. L., & Kummerow, J. M. (1997). *MBTI Step II: A description of the subscales.* Palo Alto, CA: Consulting Psychologists Press.

Myers, I. B., & McCaulley, M. H. (1985). *Manual: A guide to the development and use of the Myers-Briggs Type Indicator.* Palo Alto, CA: Consulting Psychologists Press.

Saunders, D. R. (1989). *Manual: MBTI Expanded Analysis Report.* Palo Alto, CA: Consulting Psychologists Press.

14 | STJs and Change

Resistance, Reaction, or Misunderstanding?

Susan G. Clancy

W hen I was first asked to write this chapter, the working title was "Helping STJ Managers Deal With Change." I was not surprised to learn that it was the only proposed chapter focused on helping a particular subgroup of types deal with change. Why? Because of what I hear from users of the *Myers-Briggs Type Indicator* (MBTI) who deal with organizational change:

- The conventional wisdom in the type community indicates that STJs have the most difficulty with change.
- It is not unusual for a manager to ask how to get the STJ employees to go along with the massive changes they have under way in the organization, to quit dragging their feet.
- The literature on type and organizations usually identifies ISTJs and sometimes also ESTJs as the most resistant to change.

Since the STJ focus is on preserving traditions and maintaining systems, it logically follows that they will be the most resistant to changing those traditions and systems.

Leaders of change identify numerous behaviors as demonstrating resistance. STJs are said to:

- Argue about the need for change
- Defend the status quo

- Refuse to see or accept the advantages of change
- Vocally oppose the proposed change
- Focus on all the negative consequences
- Ask the same questions, despite repeated explanations
- Ask nitpicky questions or pull discussion "into the weeds"
- Ask detailed questions about implementation that can't yet be answered
- Ask for examples, then argue with their relevance
- Drag their feet about getting on with implementation
- Take overt actions to counter or block proposed change
- Do *exactly* as instructed by higher authority

However, my experience includes many examples of STJ managers who have tenaciously driven massive changes throughout their organizations, steadfastly worked at changing an organizational culture, and demonstrated an unfailing commitment to continuous quality improvement. Those managers do not respond very favorably to being labeled resistant to change, and they can cite many examples of Intuitive types who have attempted to block these changes, either through passive resistance or overt challenges to the authority of the STJ.

So how do we account for this difference in perception? Perhaps it is a coincidence that most of the people who tell me about STJ resistance are Intuitive types, but it suggests to me that we may be experiencing type differences at work. My hypothesis is that the behaviors that are being experienced as resistance are actually a result of STJ type preferences not being thoroughly understood, valued, and incorporated into the change process.

A type lens gives a different perspective for looking at these behaviors. STJ managers are known for their ability to bring stability to an organization. They:

- Tune in on the strengths and values of the organization
- Strive to establish a situation that will support these values and allow them to flourish
- Establish policies and standardize procedures to promote consistency in applying these strengths
- Are comfortable with proven authority
- Place trust in credentials and systems that have previously served the organization well
- Feel a sense of personal ownership and responsibility for their work when supported by the organization

Their drive for belonging often leads to their seeing the organization as a family, and they willingly take on roles that enable them to contribute to the preservation of that family. This can lead STJs to take a challenging stance when changes are proposed. Changes proposed by Intuitive types can seem to threaten the very heart of the organization that Sensing types have worked throughout their careers to build and protect. At the least, the changes will disrupt the short-term ability of the system to produce in a consistent, predictable fashion.

Before supporting a change, STJs want to know why the change is needed, to be assured that both the short- and long-term consequences of the proposed changes have been considered, and to see that the ultimate return on investment will be worth the sacrifices needed to achieve it. They view it as their responsibility to protect the organization and those working within it from reckless and unnecessary change. In their efforts to fulfill this responsibility, STJs are often perceived by others as resistant to change.

Perhaps what is being experienced is not resistance to change as much as it is resistance to being changed—a reaction typical of all types, though demonstrated in different ways. Because they have worked so diligently to establish the way things are done currently, STJs are particularly vulnerable when changes are imposed on them and the systems they feel responsible for protecting. In order to enhance understanding of STJ "resistance," this chapter will examine STJ behavior during organizational change from three perspectives:

- Misinterpretation of STJ reactions and attempts to understand proposed changes
- STJ reactions to the way change is communicated and implemented
- Reluctance to implement a change that the STJ believes is fundamentally flawed

MISINTERPRETATION OF STJ REACTIONS

Despite our knowledge that people are different, we often interpret behavior based on our own perspectives, values, and assumptions, and then project motive onto the other person's behavior based on our interpretation: What would be going on with me if I were behaving that way?

When Intuitive types ask themselves that question about STJ reactions to change, their answer is often that they would be resisting the proposed change. Over time, this projection can form into a negative stereotype: STJs would rather stick with the tried and true than learn new approaches, are slow to grasp the big picture, and value maintaining the current system despite the "obvious" need for change. When one operates out of this stereotype, reactions are easily interpreted and responded to as examples of the anticipated resistance to change. If we expect certain behaviors, we are more likely to notice them and react to them. Our reactions can subtly communicate a disapproval or devaluing of these behaviors, and thus draw even more of the behaviors we expected. Thus, by expecting resistant behavior, we may create a self-fulfilling prophecy of resistance.

Consider how communications about change might differ if, rather than the perspectives just mentioned, they were based on:

- An understanding that the big picture does not come into focus for STJs without a linkage to a solid foundation
- Recognition that STJs want to ensure that a change can be implemented before they agree to throw out the current system
- A valuing of the reality-testing skills of STJs

From the perspective of understanding and valuing the potential contributions of the STJ approach, the questions, comments, and behaviors of the STJ might be interpreted a bit differently.

Defending the Status Quo

When faced with a proposed change, STJs search for evidence that the changes will lead to a future that is better than the past and present. If the current system is working to their satisfaction, STJs will have a very difficult time understanding the need for change. They predict the future based on the past, so saying that things are changing and today's system won't work in tomorrow's world sounds like speculation to them. They are not about to willingly throw out a system that's working based on speculation that it *might* not work tomorrow! They often can point to many previous predictions that didn't materialize and will want to know why this prediction is more reliable.

The following are some questions to think through before presenting a change proposal:

- Where's your evidence that the system needs changing?
- What's the problem you're trying to fix?
- Why is massive change needed? Why wouldn't minor changes to the current system fix the problem you're anticipating?
- What are the consequences of not changing? How do you know that?

The intent of these questions, frequently asked by STJs, is to check out whether there truly is a need to change the system, or if the proposed change is just motivated by a desire to do things differently.

The STJs' experience forms the baseline against which the answers to their questions will be evaluated. Aspects of this baseline will include their own perceptions of the need for change in the current situation, the credibility of the person(s) proposing the change, and their personal experience with previously attempted change efforts. They will be looking for evidence that the change will provide a needed improvement and will not threaten the viability of the organization. Their Thinking function contributes an objective analysis of the evidence, seeking to understand the logic of the proposed change. STJs will test the proposal to determine its soundness and to understand not only why the change should take place but also how it will be accomplished. Changes that result from political maneuverings and do not hold up against the logic standard are particularly difficult for STJs to understand and accept. The following example shows what can happen when confronting STJs with significant changes to a system that has worked well for them.

When John, the CEO of an engineering company, proposed changing the nature of the supervisory role in an effort to flatten the organization and empower employees, he was stunned at the intensity of the reaction he encountered. Line managers, many of whom were STJs, accused him of trying to ruin the organization by changing the role that had been so instrumental in building its reputation. They questioned him on the details of how this new role would work in interfacing with customers, getting projects accomplished, dealing with employee problems, and handling the administrative tasks that consumed so much time. Why was a major change needed? Wouldn't some improvements to the current system fix the problem? What was the "problem" he was trying to fix anyway? They had been very successful, and the company had built a reputation as a leader in their field. Why was he willing to risk all that? Didn't he value the contributions of the line managers? Was it because he just wanted to "make his mark" on the organization?

John knew that the demands on his managers had become impossible. He needed to free them up to provide the technical leadership that would be required to carry them through these changing times. He didn't know exactly what the new structure would look like, but he believed that the "key to the lock" was in changing the nature of relationships between supervisors and employees. He hadn't worked out the details because he had wanted to involve others in creating the new system. Now the very people whom he needed to help him create the new vision had joined forces in opposition to the change. It was evident that they didn't see the threats to the organization's future to be as significant as he did, and now they seemed to have stopped listening. He felt caught in a catch-22. If he had worked out the details, they would have accused him of imposing his change on them, but without the details, he wasn't able to help them see the possibilities inherent in a different paradigm.

To resolve the dilemma, John chose to back off for awhile to let things cool down. Within a year, some of the same people who had argued so strongly against his proposal began advocating change as they started to see evidence that the old system was no longer working as well as it had in the past. Their experience was finally indicating a need to change, and they were ready to explore alternatives.

A different strategy would have been to accelerate the managers' awareness of the need for change by involving them in analyzing the strengths and weaknesses of the current system and in assessing how the environment was changing. Together, John and his managers could then have identified which strengths needed to be preserved and which were becoming obstacles to future success. Once STJs recognize and accept that there is a problem to be solved, they can become very energetic in devising solutions.

Asking Detailed Questions

Once STJs accept the need for change, their focus will shift to an examination of the proposal. They are likely to ask some or all of the following questions:

- Exactly what is being proposed?
- How will it work?
- How will it impact operations?
- Will it solve our current problems?
- Will it create new problems we don't have now?
- Where has it been done before and what was the impact?
- Is it practical? Cost effective? Efficient?
- Will the workforce have the necessary skills?
- Will it fit with other aspects of the current system or require a massive overhaul?
- Will it support or threaten those aspects of the organization that we value most?

- How will it impact the bottom line?
- Can we maintain production or service while we transition to the new system?

Notice that many of the issues that STJs are exploring at this point combine questions about the future state with details about an implementation plan. They are trying to link the proposed end state with their trusted experience base. To do that, they automatically think through what would be required to effect the change. If they can't make the link, then they are likely to view the proposed change as "off the wall," "half-baked," or "too far fetched."

When STJs ask for facts and examples, they usually aren't doing it to distract or irritate; it results from a genuine need to know them in order to understand the big picture. STJs, particularly those in positions of authority, believe it is their responsibility to protect the system from reckless change. They do this by challenging proposers of change to demonstrate that they have thought through the consequences of their proposal. Before committing to a course of action, STJs want to examine these consequences in very practical terms. Feasibility is an essential criterion for an acceptable plan, and this leads to careful consideration of potential obstacles.

Asking for Relevant Examples

Evidence of feasibility will greatly contribute to developing STJ acceptance of an idea. STJs need to be able to see the proposed future state to believe that the change will truly be an improvement. They want tangible evidence—to see how it will work, understand how things will get done, and hear about the problems that will be encountered along the way.

If STJs have no previous experience that is relevant to the situation, they will ask questions about what other organizations have experienced in making such changes. Then they will test whether the examples are relevant enough to be trusted as a useful comparison. Intuitive types, with their focus on connections and associations, may view as germane examples that STJs dismiss as irrelevant. When those examples are rejected by the STJ, the Intuitive type may be inclined to brush off additional requests for examples. If such questions are avoided, the STJ may then become suspicious that such examples either don't exist, because the concept has never been tested, or, if they do exist, that they demonstrate that the change would not work. The following example illustrates this point.

In a course on the Fundamentals of Quality Management, an ESTJ manager from a government research and development organization asked repeatedly for examples of where this new management philosophy had been implemented successfully in government and in R & D organizations. The examples provided tended to focus more on administrative and production-oriented functions, even when the overall organization had a strong R & D focus.

The more the trainer gave examples that did not address the ESTJ's question, the more he argued with the theory. The trainer tried to point out the relevance of the examples and how the principles could be applied to improving any process, but the ESTJ wasn't buying it. In his eyes, the trainer had no experience with organizations like his and was demonstrating a lack of understanding of his situation by the nature of the examples provided:

> You're asking us to change the way we have successfully managed for years, without any evidence that the new way will work better in our situation. Why should we do that just because you say it's the right thing to do? You don't even understand our processes. How could you possibly know these principles would work? I'm open to exploring new management approaches, but I'm not going to change just because you say I should. I want some proof that this new approach will be an improvement if you expect me to invest the time and resources to make this change.

STJs have their view of reality and are not always sensitive to the possibility that alternative views of that reality might be just as valid, though contradictory. Therefore, data provided that do not jibe with the STJ's reality can quickly undermine the credibility of the presenter and the believability of all other information provided. STJs are particularly vulnerable to seeing the world in black and white rather than shades of gray; thus, data either fit or don't fit their framework. The organizing framework of the Thinking function provides a powerful filter for incoming data, causing data that don't fit to remain unseen or rejected as anomalies.

Focusing on What's Wrong With an Idea

Thinking serves not only as the function for organizing and evaluating all of this incoming information, but also as the communication filter through which the information is sought. Thinking types' questions are often posed in a manner that sounds like a challenge. Thinking types tend to target the weaknesses of the proposed change as they attempt to understand the situation. One of the Thinking type's greatest skills—critiquing—is often experienced as an assault by those subjected to defending their ideas. During this process, the Thinking type is not concerned about maintaining the self-esteem of the other person—after all, he or she is focused on critiquing the idea, not the person! When this Thinking communication style is coupled with Sensing, it takes on a powerful ability to unnerve a presenter who has not prepared a detailed defense.

When Thinking types are pointing out the flaws in a proposal, they often are trying to be helpful. After all, how can you fix a proposal if you don't realize what is wrong with it? For STJs, this often includes highlighting all the possible negative consequences that could emanate from the proposed change. They are particularly prone to this style of questioning if they are operating under a lot of stress.

Simply dismissing these STJ projections as catastrophizing is not helpful and may actually increase the concerns. If the potential consequences are recognized, one can at least plan for how to offset them. If they are ignored, however, they can become obstacles that undermine success. Saying "Don't worry, just trust me that we'll work it out later" is a good way to degrade the trust of STJs, particularly if they perceive that the impact of the proposed change has not been sufficiently considered. They often know from experience who the "we" is that will have to work out the problems later.

STJ REACTIONS TO THE WAY CHANGE IS COMMUNICATED AND IMPLEMENTED

If you expect to sell an STJ on changing a well-functioning system because a new approach sounds exciting and full of potential, anticipate a major battle. Change for change's sake is not the way of STJs. There needs to be a good logical reason to undergo the effort of planning and implementing a change. In *Working Together: A Personality Centered Approach to Management,* Isachsen and Berens (1988) described the STJ approach to change: "Do not expect [ESTJs] to become particularly enamored with visions and lofty unproven ideas at the price of achieving what is expected in the immediate future" (p. 186). "ISTJs derive a sense of security from the tried and tested. . . . If a change is deemed important, ISTJs may adjust better if it is presented in terms of the usefulness or practicality of the change" (p. 202).

A frequent mistake Intuitive types make in communicating about change is to assume that the amount and nature of information that convinced them of the need for change will be sufficient for the Sensing type. Explaining the trends and patterns evident in the organizational environment will be helpful to the Sensing types, but won't be sufficient. They are likely to also want to examine the specifics that comprise these trends and patterns. Intuitive impressions are not adequate to change their perception of the facts that support their opinions. The initial attempts at communicating the change is often what stimulates the "Yes, but," the "But what about," and the "How will you handle" comments that are then interpreted as resistance rather than an honest attempt to understand what is being proposed and ensure that it will work.

John, the CEO of the engineering company in the earlier example, ran squarely into this problem when he didn't spend enough time getting people on board with the nature of the problem *before* talking about how he wanted to change things. Based on his reading of the environmental trends, he had come to the conclusion that a new paradigm of management was needed. His managers needed specific evidence that there was a problem with the current system, and he couldn't give it to them in sufficient detail to convince them that radical change was needed.

Often the proposer of a change is at a different organizational level than those he or she is trying to convince about the need to change. Whether the change agent is an executive initiating an organizational transformation or a middle manager trying to sell top management on a new way of doing business, the perspective of the change agent is different from that of those to be convinced of the need to change. Though the patterns and trends have been observed and examined by the change agent at length while devising a strategy, he or she generally tries to communicate briefly about the need for change and is frustrated when the audience doesn't get it. This can be true regardless of the types of those involved, but Sensing–Intuition type differences can widen the communication gap.

If STJs perceive their questions as being ignored or brushed off as irrelevant or picky, they can dig in their heels and initiate a contest of wills. If the change agent demonstrates impatience with the questions, the STJs may interpret this as a sign that the change agent doesn't really care about whether they understand or buy into the change. This can dampen the STJ's efforts to understand what is being proposed, and may later cause resistant behaviors like stonewalling or malicious compliance to emerge during implementation.

Intuitive types are particularly susceptible to falling into a trap caused by a generally unspoken assumption that anything new is, by definition, better than what is or what was in the past. This often leads managers to denigrate the past in the process of explaining the need for change. In the process, they communicate a devaluing of STJ contributions. Lack of appreciation and respect for STJ contributions is also communicated by dismissing discussion of operational concerns as premature and acting as if working out the strategy is the hardest part of change.

One of the worst mistakes that a manager can make is to plan a major change in secret, believing that key players will be too resistant to the change and that involving them will unacceptably slow the planning process. This approach is likely to backfire with all types, not just STJs. ESTJs, in particular, however, are often very skilled at marshalling facts and forces to oppose the proposed plan, thus impeding implementation far more than if they had been involved in the planning. Managers who use such ploys will often diminish the trust and loyalty of the very people they must rely on to successfully implement their plans, as the following example illustrates.

A large corporation had been talking about centralizing their human resources function for several years, pulling resources from the individual divisions into a central office to handle the common processing tasks. The headquarters HR staff announced that they had developed a model for centralization and obtained approval from the CEO of the company. It would mean transferring 60% of the HR staff from the divisions to headquarters. They were surprised by the reaction of the division HR directors, who were angry and resistant.

The headquarters staff admitted that they had purposely avoided involving the division general managers and HR directors because of the resistance they expected—they simply couldn't tolerate the delays in the planning process from dealing with the reactions. A well-respected ESTJ divisional manager called a meeting of many of those throughout the company who opposed the new plan, and together they developed an alternative proposal. This delayed implementation planning as the company considered the merits of the alternative proposal.

In the process of trying to avoid resistance in the planning process, the headquarters staff alienated the very people they would need to rely on for implementation. While the process ultimately resulted in achieving the goal of centralizing the function, it came at the expense of trust and confidence in the headquarters staff and the CEO.

Delaying Implementation of Change

Often managers assume that foot-dragging is a reflection of passive resistance, when many times it is an indication that adequate transition planning has not occurred. Key questions to consider at this point include:

- Do employees feel that their concerns have been addressed?
- Do they know what they are supposed to do differently?
- Do they know how to do it?
- Does the system present obstacles that impede their ability to do it the new way?
- Does the system reward or punish the new ways of behaving?

STJs become expert at working according to procedures they have perfected over time. Introducing a change requires helping them let go of the previous habitual ways of behaving and helping them develop the knowledge and skills needed for the changed approach. Sensing types build their expertise on a firm foundation of experience. It takes time to rebuild their confidence when that structure is shaken.

RELUCTANCE TO IMPLEMENT A CHANGE THAT THE STJ BELIEVES IS FUNDAMENTALLY FLAWED

For STJs, fundamentally flawed change proposals are generally those that have not been thought through. STJs are quick to recognize when a presenter does not have a command of the facts or has not thought through the consequences of a proposed change, and often view proposers of such change as irresponsible. How could one seriously consider implementing a change that would change the work lives of employees and possibly jeopardize the viability of the organization without carefully considering what the impact would be and whether the idea can even work?

Such proposers are viewed as fair game. In response, ESTJs may go on the attack. ISTJs, on the other hand, may withdraw or ask just a few penetrating questions. As Kroeger and Thuesen (1992) have observed,

> Without saying a word, they may give off an aura of being impatient and even disapproving. . . . As a result there's an unwitting "show me" or "prove it" stance to the ISTJ's demeanor: *Show me* how it will be cost-effective; *prove to me* that you're right. The ISTJ's inexpressiveness often results in others feeling frustrated, flustered, or on the defensive. (pp. 304–305)

STJs also have relentless memories, particularly for previous times that management promised "painless" change, instituted a "minor" change without considering the impact on those implementing or affected by the change, ignored employee concerns, or introduced some new management innovation only to lose interest after getting everyone enthused about it. While they may be willing to offer managers a chance for redemption, to forgive and forget is generally not the STJ way. Their vivid memories of these previous experiences underlie the skeptical, and sometimes cynical, reception they give to managers who promise, "This won't hurt a bit."

A frequent mistake of managers is equating questioning and probing with resistance. Creating an environment that encourages lively, and sometimes challenging, exchanges can stimulate critical thinking, improve ideas, and build consensus. Dealing effectively with opposing viewpoints and needs will encourage and reward participation and create the synergy needed for implementation. Giving people of all types a chance to influence a proposed change is important for building commitment. For STJs, that means having an opportunity to voice their opposition. An ESTJ division manager articulates it well:

> When my boss makes a decision I don't like, I always feel like I have to push back one last time, even if he sought my opinion prior to making his decision. If he really listens to what I have to say and still disagrees, then I sign up to his decision and will do my best to represent it as my own. After all, he's the boss and it's his responsibility to make the decision. It's my responsibility to try my best to convince him of what I believe to be the best alternative. I may not always be successful, but I have to try. But continuing to nay-say after that would be disloyal.

Notice that a key factor in obtaining this ESTJ's commitment is giving him the chance to feel heard in arguing his position. If his logic isn't adequate to convince the boss, then it's his failure. But failing to influence the decision is easier to accept than shirking what he sees as his duty to try.

Consider, in contrast, an ISTJ who did not perceive her department head to be open to hearing her concerns about a job placement process he was proposing. She expressed her reservations about the legality of the proposed process to another manager. When encouraged to explain her concerns to the department head, she replied,

> Are you kidding? I saw the look he gave you when you pointed out something you disagreed with. And he values your opinion! No, if I told him what I thought he would just write it off, and write me off, too! No, I'm not

going to tell him, but I'll tell you what, I'm not going to use his new system. I don't believe what he's proposing is legal. I'll just work with my customers to find some way around it if he goes through with implementing this process.

In this case, the ISTJ saw it as her responsibility not to implement a process that she believed to be illegal. But the climate established by the department head did not encourage disagreement, so she was reluctant to voice her concerns. Her sense of loyalty focused on protecting the system in ways she could control, since she perceived that she could not influence her department head.

It's not unusual to hear a reaction like "I just won't do it!" from ISTJs when they are reacting to an imposed change with which they violently disagree. If they are given an opportunity to have their concerns influence an implementation plan, they are likely to come around to supporting it. They may even take on a position of responsibility in the implementation to ensure that it's done right. If, however, their concerns are discounted or ignored, they can dig in their heels and passively resist. They will comply with specific direction given by someone in authority, but they are unlikely to demonstrate much initiative in supporting the implementation of a change they oppose and cannot influence.

There is one more aspect of ISTJ behavior that is important to understand regarding their reactions to and acceptance of proposed change. Isabel Myers (1976) said it best in her original type description for ISTJs:

> They will go to any amount of trouble if they "can see the need of it," but hate to be required to do anything that "doesn't make sense." Usually it is hard for them to see any sense in needs that differ widely from their own. But once they are convinced that a given thing does matter a lot to a given person, the need becomes a fact to be respected and they may go to generous lengths to help satisfy it, while still holding that it doesn't make sense. (p. 14)

The message here is that continued vocal disagreement with a change does not mean that ISTJs will not actively support its implementation.

MOTIVATING STJs TO PROMOTE CHANGE

When STJs believe that the current system is inadequate, they are likely to be receptive to creating a new system. Threaten what the STJs hold dear—the stability and preservation of the organization—and they will quickly become strong advocates of change. When convinced that the future existence of an organization that they care so deeply about is threatened by a competitor or changing environment, the STJ can become adamant about change, regardless of the success of the current system. ISTJs "can be slow to change, but once they see the practical value in making a course correction, they can be quick to implement it and often become zealots of the new way of thinking" (Kroeger with Thuesen, 1992, p. 302). They will then quickly become impatient with others in the organization who don't readily support the change. The following example illustrates.

Phil, an ISTJ business manager of a large company, was charged with downsizing the overhead staff and getting the company's rate structure under control. He convened a team to review how they were spending overhead and make suggestions for where reductions could be made. As a result of that review, he rapidly began instituting changes in the organization.

Others perceived him to be pushing the organization to change too quickly, before they had a chance to sort out how they could change their processes to perform the needed work with fewer resources. Phil, on the other hand, was frustrated that they were not proceeding toward their financial goal rapidly enough: "We need to just get on with it if we're going to be competitive in today's reduced market. We're getting complaints from our customers that we cost too much. We need to just bite the bullet and do what it takes!"

Beckhard and Harris (1987) provide a useful framework for understanding response to change that is particularly helpful in working with STJs. They identify three key factors to be considered in assessing the cost of change:

- Level of dissatisfaction with the status quo
- Perceived desirability of the proposed change or end state
- Practicality of the transition (i.e., minimal risk and disruption)

If someone whose commitment is required is not sufficiently dissatisfied with the present state, enthused about the prospect of the proposed future state, and convinced that the transition process is feasible, then the cost of changing is too great and resistance to the change is likely. For STJs, this translates to the need to help them to recognize the weaknesses of the current system, understand the practical benefits of the new approach, and develop a realistic implementation plan.

Changing the STJ View of the Status Quo

Involving STJs in identifying the strengths and weaknesses of the current system and the threats and opportunities in the organizational environment can be helpful both in achieving a comprehensive environmental scan and in developing the STJs' "database" regarding the need for change. Data are useful in helping to convince STJs of the need to change—provided they are data that STJs view as important, relevant, accurate, and interpreted appropriately.

Your best bet to avoid an argument over data is to involve the STJ in collecting and analyzing the data. ESTJs, in particular, will benefit from an opportunity to participate in individual or group interviews. Data they collect through personal interaction will be far more meaningful to them than information that results from someone else doing the interviews and preparing a written report for the ESTJ to read. The interaction makes it real. For both ESTJs and ISTJs, experiencing the data collection has more impact than reading about it in a report. They are also far less likely to argue with results when they were involved in the process of determining what data to collect, how to collect it, and what it all means. Focus your strategy on building their experience base, but recognize that this approach can backfire if the data do not support the change you want to make.

As dominant Sensing types, ISTJs are likely to consider modifications to their framework when their experience tells them that the paradigm is no longer valid for describing reality. It will be more important to them to fit the framework to the data than vice versa. Of course, they may not readily inform others that they are in the process of reframing their view of reality while they are in the process! Stimulating this reframing for ISTJs is accomplished by first providing them with experiences that refute their view, then offering an alternate paradigm that can explain both their previous and new experiences. It is important to provide time for reflection and observation so the ISTJ can test out the new way of viewing reality. Isabel Myers (1976) described it this way in her original type description:

> [ISTJs] base their ideas on a deep, solid accumulation of stored impressions, which gives them some pretty unshakable ideas. . . . Thus they have a complete, realistic, practical respect both for the facts and for whatever responsibilities these facts create. . . . They do not enter into things impulsively, but once in, they are very hard to distract, discourage or stop. They do not quit unless experience convinces them they are wrong. (p. 14)

So if you can help the ISTJ see that the facts point to a need for change, then they will assume the responsibility to support that change and do what needs to be done to make it happen.

ESTJs are more likely to be resistant to modifying their current paradigm, since it is defined by their dominant Thinking function. Successful reframing of the ESTJ's view of reality is most likely to occur when the ESTJ comes to believe that the logic of their framework is flawed or incomplete. Otherwise, they are likely to assume that data that do not fit their reality result from an inadequate collection or analysis process, thus resulting in their ready dismissal of the contradictions. Myers (1976) stated it this way:

> "[ESTJs] are unlikely to be convinced by anything but reasoning. . . . They live according to a definite formula that embodies their basic judgments about the world. Any change in their ways requires a deliberate change in the formula." (p. 9)

Creating an Understandable Vision of the Future

Based on type stereotypes, one might conclude that STJs, because of their discomfort with free-form brainstorming and futuristic thinking, would not want to be involved in strategic planning. Intuitive types working from this assumption might therefore be tempted to include STJs only in implementation planning once the overall direction has been established.

Yet it is important for STJs to understand the ultimate goal and rationale for pursuing it if they are to forsake tried-and-true methods for the unknown. They need to be able to see how the new approach will enhance the organization's ability to perform or protect its most important values more than maintaining the current course can. The best way for them to achieve this understanding, as shown in the following example, is to help explore the alternatives and create the strategy.

Frank (INTJ), the manager of an Administrative Services Department, had been relying heavily on Anne (ISTJ) to help him design an approach to centralizing delivery of services. Anne had been taking the lead in developing implementation plans, but was continually left out of the high-level meetings in which decisions were being made regarding whether and how to centralize. The decision regarding the general strategy had shifted several times during the course of her implementation planning. As a result, she felt she was trying to solve problems that wouldn't have occurred if the issues had been considered earlier in the decision process.

When she raised her concern to Frank, he could not understand. After all, she had been more involved than anyone in working out how the new system would work. She had a tremendous opportunity to influence how things would unfold. Her perception, however, was that decisions were being made and changed without the benefit of the insights she had gained, and, as a result, she was constantly in a rework mode. It also made it harder for her to develop implementation plans because it appeared that the overall goals of the project kept shifting. If she could just get a clearer picture of his vision for the future, it would help her immensely in designing the implementation plans. But when she had asked Frank to explain his vision for the department, he said he hadn't yet crystallized a new one since things were changing so rapidly. He was just trying to read the political climate and make the best decisions he could for the overall good of the department. She would just have to work with the guidance he had given her about the project.

STJs can be an enormous help in:

- Identifying the key elements of the organization that are most essential to retain
- Examining the practical consequences of various alternatives
- Developing a realistic strategy and timetable

Application of the Sensing type's realism lens in combination with the Intuitive type's free-flowing idea generation provides a far more powerful resource than either can contribute alone. These two functions need to work in tandem throughout the process to effectively develop and implement a future that can become reality.

Developing a Realistic Implementation Plan

This is where the STJ can really excel—if you have succeeded in working with them on the previous steps. Don't let STJs' pessimistic view of the organization's ability to change sufficiently frustrate you. This pessimism can actually be an advantage in anticipating obstacles and negative consequences. Capture these concerns, then brainstorm a list of positive forces and consequences. Focus the group on identifying what would be needed to build on the positive forces and counter the obstacles. In the process of generating a force-field analysis, you will communicate a valuing for the STJs' perspective and concern about issues of importance to them. Get the STJs involved in putting the resulting actions in sequence and filling in the gaps, and you will have tasks needed for the implementation plan. STJs are often not very attuned to addressing the people aspects of transitions, however, so you will want to involve others who can provide additional perspectives.

It may not be possible or practical to include everyone in the planning for a major change to achieve the level of understanding and commitment that stems from involvement in creating the change. But it is important to incorporate processes into the change implementation that provide the opportunity for everyone to understand the reasons for change, get their questions answered about the proposed changes, raise their concerns about the impact of those changes, and offer their ideas about what they will need to implement the changes. STJs are no different from other types in the benefits they derive from participation. While this kind of participation in planning takes time, it will speed up the implementation process immensely. You cannot short-circuit the time it takes to institute change. The question is whether you spend the time on the front end in the planning process, or on the back end, dealing with problems during the implementation.

STJs want plans to be thought through very carefully, test to each aspect, and to have contingency plans. They will be focused on finding ways to introduce change that minimize the risk and disruption to the effectiveness of current operations. They will push for a realistic timetable, building in time for workforce training and practice, pilot testing of new processes and systems, and documentation of procedures. The greatest concern of many STJs with Intuitive leaders is the unrealistic expectations of how long it will take to prepare for implementation. STJs will also be impatient about getting on with it once they have bought into the change. But they will want to make sure that all the "i's are dotted and t's are crossed" to help implementation go smoothly, as shown in the next example.

A human resources organization of a large government agency was developing a proposal for a new approach to handling compensation and performance management as part of the Reinventing Government initiative. The INTJ project manager briefed his staff (many STJs) on the concept plan early to keep them informed of the changes to come. As expected, many of the questions focused on how specific tasks would be accomplished under the new system—details that had not yet been addressed. The INTJ described the plan as being 90% complete; the STJs thought he had not begun to address the issues needing to be worked out prior to implementation, which was less than a year away.

Some were also concerned about who would be able to train them in what they would need to know to operate within the new system since the system was totally new and no one had experience in how to operate within it.

A strong plea was made by the staff not to rush into implementation before giving them a chance to learn the new skills they would need to work within the new system. They described how so many times in the past a plan would be created for a new way of doing business, and they were expected to be able to just jump in and operate effectively. They pointed out that they were very uncomfortable with that kind of situation and that it didn't serve their customers well when they didn't know what they were doing. The manager asked about what personal and professional concerns the staff had as a result of the proposed change, and was surprised when that turned the questions back to inquiring about the details of how the system would work. One ISTJ explained later, "My personal and professional needs are the same. I want to know what I'm going to be doing each day, how I'm going to meet the needs of my customers, and whether the processes that I'll have to use will be efficient and effective."

STJs IN THE WORKPLACE OF THE FUTURE

Much of the literature about the changing workplace suggests that constant change will need to become the norm for organizations to survive. The message to managers and employees is that they need to learn to accept ambiguity and uncertainty and to respond rapidly to change. Jobs are predicted to become more temporary in nature, duties to be constantly realigned, and work groups to form and disband based on specific project requirements. Many employees will work on a contract basis, perhaps for several organizations at a time.

What does this mean for STJs who value security, stability, belonging, preserving traditions, and applying established skills? The key to answering this question lies in understanding the learning process of STJs.

STJs are typically highly motivated to obtain training and education that is directly applicable to their job or life situation. While learning for the sake of learning may not appeal to them, learning for the sake of doing does. They tend to pursue training that will enhance job-related skills and seek educational credentials needed for entry or advancement within their field. While they would generally prefer to refine current skills rather than develop new ones, they will pursue new skills if they view them as essential to fulfilling their responsibilities. They prefer to build on their foundation of experience and benefit most from learning experiences that contribute to their understanding of a current problem or situation.

Assisting STJs

While dramatic change may be painful to STJs when they first encounter it, with experience and coaching they can build the skills and perspectives necessary for coping with it. Their confidence in their ability to handle such change will grow when they can look back at previous experiences and realize that they have encountered similar situations before and survived! Understanding the predictability of reactions to change and transitions can help them feel a little less out of control. Training in creative thinking can provide them with the skills and tools for reframing situations and generating alternatives. Learning how to assess their transferable skills can help them realize that their previous skills can provide a foundation on which to build the new skills required.

Managers can help by reminding employees of situations they've encountered before that required similar changes, coaching them to consider how those examples are similar to and different from the current situation, and examining what they did before that might be useful in dealing with the changes they are facing. While this kind of focus may be frustrating to Intuitive types, it is invaluable to Sensing types in helping them access their experience base differently.

Mentoring can also be useful in shifting perspective. I remember an INFP who always reframed my problem into an opportunity whenever I went to him for help. While it may have been a bit irritating at the time, I realize now that it eventually impacted the way I viewed situations. I also remember a story that an ENFP told me of two little boys who were put into a room filled with horse manure. One moaned and groaned about how awful it was and begged to be released from the room. The other picked up a shovel and started digging enthusiastically. When asked why he was doing this, he replied, "With all this manure, there must be a pony in here somewhere." I frequently think of that story whenever I'm confronted with a change situation that threatens to tear my world apart, and it helps to shift my focus to searching for "ponies." As a manager, I also view it as my responsibility to help my employees reframe their perspective to deal constructively with the changes thrust upon us.

What these examples are really suggesting is a focus on type development to build the skills that can balance those most natural to STJs. When STJs feel capable of adapting to the changing world, they are more readily able to apply their natural strengths to creating the temporary stability needed to perform in the midst of turmoil.

Several ISTJs, when discussing their reactions to the changes occurring in their environment, attributed some of their attitude to age and maturity:

> We've finally learned that it doesn't pay to get all wrung up about it. We've been through it before, and we'll have to go through it again. We know we can manage. Of course, just because we're adapting to all this change doesn't mean we like it! But if we're going to enjoy what we do, we have to get on board with the changes. It just doesn't pay to fight reality.

SUMMARY

Nancy Barger and Linda Kirby (1995) have conducted numerous workshops in which they asked participants of all types to describe what they need during a time of change and transition. Their data provide a nice summary of the impact of type on reactions to change.

ISTJs report that they need:

- Specific, realistic reasons for the changes
- Lots of practical data to support the reasons
- Goals and time lines
- The opportunity to develop plans and structures
- The opportunity to use their experience to assist in the change
- Loyalty from others—above and below them

ESTJs report that they need:

- To know the who, what, when, where, and why
- To understand the purpose of the changes—to be given the logic and data for them
- Opportunities to plan what actions need to be taken, then be able to take them
- Commitment and accountability from everyone
- To be supported by necessary resources
- To just do it!

ESTJs also indicated that one of the ways they contribute to change is by accepting the change *if it's reasonable*. ISTJs have difficulty accepting a change unless they can see logical reasons for it. When they are not supported in a time of change, ISTJs can feel overwhelmed and confused, stubbornly cling to "the way we have always done it," and insist on going by the book.

Perhaps the reason that STJs are perceived as being the most resistant to change is that they are the types that least often are given what they need to accept change! When the data generated by Intuitive types are scanned, there is considerable evidence both of their need to understand the big picture and vision, and of the difficulty they have with focusing on the details. So when change is introduced by Intuitive types, is it surprising that they will focus on providing the kind of information Intuitive types need to accept change?

Even when change is introduced by other STJs, their impatience to "get on with it" may cause them to give limited time and attention to building the understanding required to get other STJs on board. ISTJs report having difficulty reopening things and being patient and tolerant with others. ESTJs report having difficulty with being patient, waiting for others to catch up, and dealing with people who are having a hard time letting go.

Without conscious attention to the impact of type diversity, we all will tend to project onto others the kind of support that we ourselves need rather than focus on their special needs that differ from our own. And when they ask for what they need, particularly if it relates to something that is difficult for us to provide, we may interpret their requests as resisting our ideas or attempting to block them. The type lens provides a means for understanding these differing needs and can help us to hear the questions and challenges as pleas for help. But this can only happen if our understanding of type constructs is coupled with an underlying assumption that all types are striving to give their very best and a belief that ideas and plans are strengthened when diverse perspectives are incorporated.

SOME FINAL THOUGHTS

Sometimes our efforts to advance type theory and its applications lead us to violate the very underpinnings that attract us to it. Studies that attempt to correlate type with ineffective behaviors, such as identifying which types are the most resistant to change, erode these positive assumptions and beliefs and can create a self-fulfilling prophecy. Type theory and the MBTI gain their power from acknowledging the positive qualities of all types and making constructive use of differences. Focusing on the weaknesses of the types will eventually undermine the very qualities that give type theory its power to bridge diversity. Suggesting to STJs that they are the most resistant to change will not endear them to type theory, and may even cause them to avoid its use. Using type constructively and effectively involves focusing instead on:

- Finding ways to demonstrate the usefulness of type as a practical tool to help in management
- Proving that the appropriate use of type concepts can impact the bottom line
- Demonstrating the positive consequences of taking type differences into account in dealing with people
- Demonstrating how to avoid misusing type

When STJs see the practical value of type, they incorporate it into their standard mode of operations. Focusing on understanding how to help each of the types operate effectively, even in situations that place demands on their less-preferred functions, will model the assumptions and beliefs needed to advance beneficial applications of type theory.

Somehow I knew that honoring traditions and values I did not understand, and did not agree with, was not going to be easy but would bring me immediate benefit.

—Marlo Morgan (1994, p. 25)

REFERENCES

Barger, N. J., & Kirby, L. K. (1995). *The challenge of change in organizations: Helping employees thrive in the new frontier.* Palo Alto, CA: Davies-Black.

Beckhard, R., & Harris, R. T. (1987). *Organizational transitions: Managing complex change* (2d ed.). Reading, MA: Addison-Wesley.

Isachsen, O., & Berens, L. V. (1988). *Working together: A personality centered approach to management.* Coronado, CA: Neworld Management Press.

Kroeger, O., with Thuesen, J. M. (1992). *Type talk at work.* New York: Delacorte Press.

Morgan, M. (1994). *Mutant message down under.* New York: Harper Collins.

Myers, I. B. (1976). *Introduction to type* (2d ed.). Gainesville, FL: Center for Applications of Psychological Type.

15 | Integrating the FIRO-B With the MBTI

Relationships, Case Examples, and Interpretation Strategies

Eugene R. Schnell

Allen L. Hammer

The *Fundamental Interpersonal Relations Orientation–Behavior* (FIRO-B) is often used in conjunction with the *Myers-Briggs Type Indicator* (MBTI) as part of leadership coaching and development programs. Practitioners will find that the two instruments converge and diverge in ways that reveal some of the complexities of leadership. The purpose of this chapter is to:

- Briefly introduce the FIRO-B
- Provide examples of how the FIRO-B can be used with the MBTI to enhance leader effectiveness
- Present a general strategy for interpreting the two instruments when they are used together

Practitioners who use the MBTI and FIRO-B have found that both instruments powerfully influence leaders to broaden their view of others. Rather than dismissing others as "wrong" or "problematic," both the FIRO-B and the MBTI promote the recognition of differences as an opportunity to bring together the strengths inherent in diverse ways of thinking and behaving. Both instruments tap key aspects of a person's personality and therefore provide helpful information to leaders about patterns over a variety of activities such as communication, decision making, interpersonal relations, and group dynamics. Finally, by integrating the FIRO-B with the MBTI, the leader can be offered the chance to see that human behavior is complex enough to demand multiple perspectives, yet predictable enough that it can be systematized into understandable models.

THE FIRO-B INSTRUMENT

The FIRO-B was developed in the late 1950s by William Schutz (1958) and has been actively used in a variety of settings, primarily with career counseling and team development. The FIRO-B is based on a simple model proposing that individuals are motivated by three interpersonal needs: Inclusion (I), Control (C), and Affection (A). *Inclusion* represents the amount of belonging, attention, and prominence desired in social settings; *Control* represents the level of influence, structure, and dominance desired; and *Affection* represents the level of intimacy, warmth, and support desired. Schutz also proposed that two dimensions of each need can be identified: (a) the extent to which individuals are likely to *Express* the associated interpersonal behaviors toward others and (b) the extent to which individuals Want to receive those same interpersonal behaviors from others. These interactions form six scales, based on Schutz (1978), measuring the client's orientation to the following statements:

- Expressed Inclusion (eI): I make an effort to include others in my activities, to belong, to join social groups, and to be with others as much as possible.
- Wanted Inclusion (wI): I want others to include me in their activities, to invite me to belong, and to notice me.
- Expressed Control (eC): I make an effort to exert control and influence and to organize and direct others.
- Wanted Control (wC): I want others to provide well-defined work situations and clear expectations and instructions.
- Expressed Affection (eA): I make an effort to get close to people, to express personal feelings, and to be supportive of others.
- Wanted Affection (wA): I want others to act warmly toward me, to share their feelings, and to encourage my efforts.

Table 1 provides a description of behaviors associated with each of these scales.

TABLE 1 Behaviors Associated With Scales on the FIRO-B

	Inclusion (I)	Control (C)	Affection (A)
Expressed (e)	*Behaviors Indicating Expressed Inclusion (eI)* • Talking and joking with others • Taking a personal interest in others • Involving others in projects and meetings • Recognizing the accomplishments of others • Incorporating everyone's ideas and suggestions • Offering helpful information or "tips" to new colleagues	*Behaviors Indicating Expressed Control (eC)* • Assuming positions of authority • Advancing an idea within the group • Taking a competitive stance and making winning a priority • Managing the conversation • Influencing others' opinions • Establishing structured tasks, procedures, policies	*Behaviors Indicating Expressed Affection (eA)* • Reassuring and supporting colleagues, both verbally and physically • Giving gifts to show appreciation • Exhibiting concern about the personal lives of others • Being trustworthy and loyal • Sharing personal opinions or private feelings about issues • Coaching and developing others
Wanted (w)	*Behaviors Indicating Wanted Inclusion (wI)* • Frequenting heavily trafficked areas (e.g., the water cooler) • Wearing distinctive clothing • Decorating the work space with personal keepsakes • Seeking recognition • Getting involved in high-profile projects • Going along with the majority opinion	*Behaviors Indicating Wanted Control (wC)* • Asking for help on the job • Involving others in decision making • Requesting precise instructions and clarification • Deferring to the wishes, needs, and requests of others • Asking for permission and circulating progress details • Raising issues for others to consider	*Behaviors Indicating Wanted Affection (wA)* • Being flexible and accommodating • Listening carefully to others • Displaying an open body posture • Sharing feelings of anxiety, sadness, loneliness • Trying to please others • Giving others more than they want or need

From *Introduction to the FIRO-B in Organizations* (p. 5), by E. R. Schnell and A. L. Hammer, 1993, Palo Alto, CA: Consulting Psychologists Press. Copyright 1993 by Consulting Psychologists Press, Inc. Reprinted with permission.

To measure the three fundamental interpersonal needs across the two dimensions, the FIRO-B contains 54 items. It is easy to administer and requires approximately 15 to 20 minutes to complete. Individual results are reported for six cells of a grid, representing each of the six scales resulting from an Expressed and Wanted score for each of the three needs. The scores range from 0 to 9; scores in the range of 0–3 are considered "low," 4–6 "medium," and 7–9 "high."

Individual cells can also be aggregated across the rows to obtain Total Expressed Behavior and Total Wanted Behavior scores, down the columns for Total Need scores, and over all cells for an Overall Need score. For example, if a person had a score of 5 for each of the Expressed dimensions and 3 for each of the Wanted dimensions, his or her Total Expressed Behavior score would be 15 (5 + 5 + 5), the Total Wanted Behavior score would be 9 (3 + 3 + 3), each of the Total Need scores would be 8 (5 + 3 for each column), and the Overall Need score would be 24 (5 + 5 + 5 + 3 + 3 + 3). A complete development of the FIRO-B model and interpretation of various scores can be found in Schnell and Hammer (1993). Additional information about scale reliability and validity can be found in Schutz (1958) and Gluck (1983).

In comparison to the MBTI, two observations should be made about the nature of the FIRO-B. First, and most importantly, the FIRO-B focuses exclusively on the domain of interpersonal needs and does not represent a comprehensive assessment of personality. Although interpretations about the intrapsychic and cognitive aspects of FIRO-B scores are available (Ryan, 1989), the MBTI is a more direct measurement of these dimensions. Second, the two instruments are drawn from different aspects of personality theory. The FIRO-B is based on the ideas of T. W. Adorno, Erich Fromm, Wilfred Bion, and other interpretations that carried psychoanalytic overtones, while the MBTI is derived from C. G. Jung's theory of psychological types. Each instrument reflects the strengths and biases of its unique perspective. For the benefit of clients, it is not necessary to resolve the differences between the two approaches. In fact, substantial insights can be gained by combining and comparing feedback from these two instruments.

LINKAGES BETWEEN MBTI AND FIRO-B DIMENSIONS

A recent study of the relationships between the MBTI and the FIRO-B (Schnell, Hammer, Fitzgerald, Fleenor, & Van Velsor, 1994) explored

TABLE 2   Correlation of MBTI Continuous Scores With the FIRO-B
National Leadership Institute Sample

FIRO-B Scale	MBTI Preference			
	E–I	S–N	T–F	J–P
Expressed Inclusion	−59***	04	11*	00
Wanted Inclusion	−28***	11*	12*	12*
Expressed Control	−23***	03	−23***	−01
Wanted Control	04	−09	16***	−05
Expressed Affection	−52***	06	22***	07
Wanted Affection	−31***	02	17***	07

Note. *p < .05, **p < .01, ***p < .001. Decimals are omitted from correlations; negative correlations are associated with E, S, T, and J; positive correlations are associated with I, N, F, and P.

From *The MBTI and Managers: Research Findings and Implications for Management Development*, by C. Fitzgerald, 1991, College Park, MD. Copyright 1991 by C. Fitzgerald. Reprinted with permission.

the relationships between each of the dimensions included in the two instruments. Two independent samples of managers were used; all subjects were participants in the Center for Creative Leadership's (CCL) Leadership Development Program (LDP).

The first sample was comprised of nearly 14,000 managers who participated in the LDP between 1979 and 1990 at CCL's Greensboro, North Carolina, site. The other sample involved 386 managers who participated between 1988 and 1990 in the LDP conducted by the National Leadership Institute of the University of Maryland University College. The typical participant was a white male, age 40 to 45, college educated, and drawn from the middle to upper ranks of their sponsoring organization. The most common psychological types in both samples were ISTJ, ESTJ, and ENTJ.

While further studies will be necessary to confirm and explore the findings of these initial studies, the results generally concur with earlier studies reported by Myers and McCaulley (1985) with samples of nonmanagers. Table 2 shows the correlation of MBTI continuous scores with the FIRO-B. The findings are described below.

While we predicted that the Extraversion–Introversion dimension would be related to Expressed and Wanted Inclusion, the research found that Extraversion was related to higher scores on all dimensions of the FIRO-B except Wanted Control. This reinforces the fact that Extraversion–Introversion is a broad concept and that, because of the FIRO-B's focus on interpersonal needs, lower overall results on the FIRO-B can be expected with Introverts. In addition, it should be communicated to clients that FIRO-B dimensions provide elaboration of components of the E–I preference. As will be shown in the case examples, the FIRO-B can add depth and insight to an Introvert's understanding of how he or she interacts in the context of what are typically less intense interpersonal needs.

As predicted, the Feeling preference was positively related to high scores on both dimensions of Affection. Additional analyses of the sample showed that people who prefer both Extraversion and Feeling demonstrated the highest levels of both Expressed and Wanted Affection needs. People with preferences for both Introversion and Thinking had the lowest levels of both Affection needs. Since the Extraversion-Feeling combination is also associated with the highest levels of overall social needs (i.e., Overall Need Scores), FIRO-B results can be used to help managers with these preferences to realize the challenges they are likely to face in trying to satisfy many areas of high interpersonal needs. Not all social contexts will be suitable for fulfilling all interpersonal needs, and people who combine Extraversion and Feeling can use the FIRO-B to help clarify their expectations of different social situations.

Contrary to predictions, Judging was not shown to be significantly related to Expressed Control. Given that the FIRO-B is commonly used to confirm perceptions of dominance, it is important to note this finding. Expressed Control was, however, significantly related to both Extraversion and Thinking. This finding suggests that the control taking of Thinking types may be rooted in the need for a logical and ordered social environment. The data also showed that Expressed Control was the strongest of all interpersonal needs among those personality types with a preference for Thinking. Since Wanted Affection was the second highest need among Thinking types, this may explain a common leadership scenario in which leaders expect loyalty and appreciation (Wanted Affection) in response to taking on the challenges of decision making and direction setting (Expressed Control). As the cases below regarding Control demonstrate, other social needs identified by the FIRO-B and other preferences identified by the MBTI can be used to help leaders understand the patterns they are most likely to use when attempting to influence others.

It is important to note that a preference for Sensing was not significantly related to Wanted Control. This finding is contrary to popular descriptions of the Sensing function, which often posit that a key element of Sensing is a strong desire for structure and direction, and reinforces the need for a clearer and more sophisticated understanding of the Sensing function (see Chapter 14 for a relevant discussion of this topic). A significant association was discovered, however, between

Wanted Control and the Feeling dimension. The highest levels of Wanted Control were found with ISFJs and ISFPs, and the lowest levels of Wanted Control were found with all NT and ST combinations (except ISTJs, whose levels of Wanted Control were not as low as other ST types). These results support the observation that leaders with a preference for Thinking are independent and determined in their goals. On the other hand, one can expect that ISFJ and ISFP leaders are quite different, perhaps requiring more preparation, specification, feedback, and encouragement. Since the Thinking preference is also associated with high levels of Expressed Control, these results also suggest that Thinking types may have difficulty understanding how any person could have simultaneously high levels of Expressed Control and Wanted Control.

Two additional findings are interesting to note. Significant associations were found between Wanted Inclusion and preferences for Intuition and for Perceiving. These findings may be jointly interpreted as indicating that people with these preferences are open to information received from social situations. It may be that individuals with a preference for Intuition remain open to possibilities revealed to them via social interactions. Individuals with a preference for Perceiving might value belonging and social contact as a source of spontaneity and observation. Leaders with these preferences may therefore be attracted to the participative and collaborative aspects of contemporary organizations.

Table 3 presents the one or two highest FIRO-B scores for each MBTI type. It is interesting to note that Wanted Affection was the first or second highest interpersonal need for all 16 types. As noted by Schnell et al. (1994),

> the centrality of Wanted Affection for all psychological types should be discussed in leadership development. There is an increasing need in today's workplaces to acknowledge the role of behaviors that signal listening, appreciation, and openness. In addition, the need for Wanted Affection suggests that there are strong emotional undertones in the workplace that must be addressed by effective leaders. (p. 182)

This brief review of research findings demonstrates that the relationships between the MBTI and the FIRO-B are more complex than might be assumed. The complexity of these results should be kept in mind when helping clients build an understanding of the relationship between these two instruments. It is apparent that a substantial area of overlap exists that can be used to confirm hypotheses about leadership development issues raised by either instrument. It is also clear that each instrument presents a unique perspective that can contribute to building a more complete and complex understanding of the leader.

TABLE 3 Highest One or Two FIRO-B Cell Scores
for Each Psychological Type in CCL Sample

ISTJ	ISFJ	INFJ	INTJ
Expressed Control Wanted Affection	Wanted Affection	Wanted Affection	Expressed Control Wanted Affection

ISTP	ISFP	INFP	INTP
Expressed Control Wanted Affection	Wanted Affection	Wanted Affection	Expressed Control Wanted Affection

ESTP	ESFP	ENFP	ENTP
Expressed Control Wanted Affection	Wanted Affection Expressed Inclusion	Wanted Affection Expressed Inclusion	Expressed Control Wanted Affection

ESTJ	ESFJ	ENFJ	ENTJ
Wanted Affection Expressed Control	Wanted Affection Expressed Inclusion	Wanted Affection Expressed Inclusion	Expressed Control Wanted Affection

From "Relationships between the MBTI and the FIRO-B: Implications for their joint use in leadership development" by E. R. Schnell, A. L. Hammer, C. Fitzgerald, J. W. Fleenor, and E. Van Velsor, 1994. In C. Fitzgerald (Ed.), *Proceedings of the Myers-Briggs Type Indicator and Leadership: An International Research Conference* (p. 186). College Park, MD: University of Maryland University College National Leadership Institute. Reprinted with permission.

CASE EXAMPLES

To illustrate the findings reported above, including some areas still requiring investigation, and to illustrate the power of using the two instruments together, a series of case examples follow. These are actual cases in which joint use of the MBTI and FIRO-B proved to be most helpful. The cases are drawn from a variety of different contexts described in some detail at the beginning of each case. The interpretation of each case is based on the research results reported in the previous section, as well as interpretations constructed from the theoretical frameworks of each instrument and extensive experience in their use.

The Introvert's Dilemma

Leaders with a preference for Introversion offer some of the best examples of the usefulness of combining the MBTI and FIRO-B. These individuals, particularly in a leadership development setting, are often interested in understanding how they can and actually do interact in social settings, despite their general orientation toward the inner world. Introverts, especially in organizations, may come to think of themselves as withdrawn and somewhat antisocial. Using the two instruments can help them overcome these stereotypes. Introverts frequently are well aware of their preferences for solitary tasks but also seek insight about how they can handle interpersonal relations.

A common scenario for Introverts is that a key factor of their promotion into management was their ability to focus on technical expertise rather than relationships. After the promotion, however, Introverts often find themselves taxed to excel in the very areas of interpersonal relations they may have avoided. Because of its focus on interpersonal needs, the FIRO-B is a good means for complementing the MBTI in this area.

Case Example 1: Ben

MBTI Type: I S F J

FIRO-B Results:

eI (5)	eC (3)	eA (6)
wI (7)	wC (5)	wA (8)

Ben was a 45-year-old facilities manager who has served as personnel manager and project manager in his present organization for more than 13 years. In preparing for an internal leadership development workshop for managers, Ben presented two primary leadership development concerns: (a) how to develop a consistent approach to supervision and (b) how to create a better sense of teamwork among his staff. Ben had prior exposure to the MBTI and expressed a sense of conflict between his Introversion and his Feeling preferences. He articulated that while he is generally quiet and reserved, he also has a strong desire for interaction and relationships with others. During a recent reorganization, Ben had acquired responsibility for the largest number of staff in his department (approximately 100 people). He believed his reputation for and interest in task orientation, attention to procedures, and memory for details were at odds with his desire to create a participative workplace.

In an individual feedback session with Ben, the following interpretation strategy was employed. First, the association between Ben's Feeling preference and high levels of Wanted Inclusion and Wanted Affection was pointed out, as was the relationship of these preferences and needs to his interest in building an atmosphere for teamwork. His interest in subjective values and in the personal interests of others—both consistent with his Feeling preference—were identified as advantages he could bring to this task. Since Affection was identified as his strongest interpersonal need, some time was spent clarifying Ben's perspective on teamwork, which emphasized support, encouragement, minimal conflict, and a desire to serve.

Potential difficulties with this perspective on teamwork were discussed (e.g., a certain level of conflict can be beneficial for teams, teams can move beyond support to empowerment), as were alternative views of teamwork that might be of interest to people with different interpersonal needs. For example, individuals with high Inclusion needs are often more focused on interpersonal fairness and equality in relationships, rather than the intimacy and closeness that Ben might encourage. Another particular advantage for building effective teams that was pointed out to Ben was his low level of Expressed Control and his medium level of Wanted Control. Both control scores suggest that he is willing to delegate legitimate roles to teams and to be influenced by them in his own decision-making processes. However, he needed to be aware that his low Expressed Control combined with Introversion and Feeling might be perceived by ETJ types as a lack of leadership.

Another challenge in fostering teamwork that was suggested by Ben's FIRO-B results was a score in the low or medium range for each of the expressed social needs. Individuals with low to medium scores for these needs are often mistakenly perceived by others as being uninterested in collaboration and exchange. Given his dominant Sensing function and his Judging preference, it was easily explained that his reputation focused more on his interest in tasks and details and less on building a strong interpersonal network. Facing a new staff, Ben began planning how he might develop and maintain a different impression.

When asked to describe his decision-making approach, Ben provided an example of a staffing decision in which he personally consulted a small number of trusted confidants (consistent with his Introversion and medium Expressed Inclusion) and delayed a decision until missing information and conflicting opinions of the qualifications of prospective job candidates had been clarified (consistent with his low Expressed Control and his Sensing and Feeling preferences). The relationship between his actions in this situation and his MBTI and FIRO-B results provided him with insight into his decision-making style. This conversation also revealed that Ben had been criticized for being too deferential with subordinates and too laborious when making decisions in a group setting (considering too many alternatives, relying too much on data, attempting to resolve all differences of opinion). Indeed, it was these concerns that underpinned his interest in developing a more consistent approach to supervision. As a development strategy, some time was spent with Ben discussing the strengths and weaknesses of different aspects of his decision-making process and then discussing the types of decisions that might best match different approaches. In addition, the effective use of teams for decision making was discussed.

Case Example 2: Mary

MBTI Type: I N T J

FIRO-B Results:

eI (5)	eC (7)	eA (3)
wI (5)	wC (2)	wA (7)

At the time of the consultation, Mary was a 37-year-old research analyst working for a large government agency. She had recently assumed a two-year interim appointment managing a busy staff of 20 research analysts in a sister government agency. In her previous position, which she accepted immediately after completing her doctoral degree 10 years ago, she had supervised one other analyst. The unit to which she was newly assigned was in a state of turmoil, having lacked a permanent director for five years and, during the same period, having added seven new permanent staff. Mary welcomed a new challenge and hoped to fill the position permanently. After a short time with her new staff, she realized that there were numerous intraunit conflicts and that many staff, given the lack of consistent leadership, were likely to challenge her supervisory authority.

Mary was familiar with the MBTI and requested additional insight about her interpersonal needs, having found the MBTI mostly helpful in understanding her internal reasoning and cognitive framework. Mary was initially surprised at her high levels of Expressed Control and Wanted Affection on the FIRO-B, given her strong identification as an Introvert. Using type dynamics theory, Mary was able to understand how her Thinking preference, as an Extraverted auxiliary function, was used to order and structure the outer world. In addition, since Control was Mary's strongest interpersonal need, the FIRO-B suggested that she would be a leader who stressed deadlines, provided clear structure and instructions for subordinates, stuck firmly to final decisions, set challenging goals, and maintained her legitimacy through skill and proficiency—all things that were consistent with her TJ preference.

In the new work situation, these preferences would help Mary establish a new sense of order, a forward direction for the office, and greater clarity about work procedures. Mary was advised that her greatest challenges would likely involve (a) the preservation of a healthy degree of flexibility, (b) the demonstration of respect for the competence and autonomy of her staff, and (c), given her low Wanted Control score, an occasional willingness to yield to her staff's best judgment. Some time in the consultation was also spent discussing how to assure that she could maintain full staff interaction and group discussion, given that her combination of Expressed Control and preference for Introversion might lead her to minimize interaction or handle staff issues in one-on-one conversations.

The potential changes in Mary's previously established personal relationships with office staff were also discussed in light of her high need for Affection. Like other TJs with high Wanted Affection scores, Mary was sometimes confused and surprised that others perceived her as not wanting or needing Affection. In her past job, Mary had valued the support, loyalty, and honest feedback that relationships with others provided. As manager of the new group, Mary could not expect those aspects of the relationships to continue in the same way. Given the potentially temporary nature of the assignment, the possibility of losing this source of personal support was a serious consideration.

In addition, Mary realized that her need for Wanted Affection might send mixed signals to the staff during her transition period—mixed signals that could interfere with the ease of making the necessary personnel decisions that awaited her. Acknowledging that she had a small group of confidants, Mary emphasized the importance of building a better support network outside of her work group.

When considering a management strategy that might draw upon Mary's strengths, some discussion was dedicated to the potential advantages offered by her NTJ preferences, which involved her interest in making clear plans and interesting others in new possibilities. Her NT preferences and her high Wanted Inclusion suggested that Mary might best engage the group in a collective exercise of planning the future. The plan could serve as a basis for legitimizing the decisions that Mary would need to make so that productivity and intraunit cooperation could increase. From her high Expressed Control and her low Expressed Affection scores, Mary was also able to see that others' first impression of her might be that she was intense, structured, and self-confident. A series of group meetings for the agency planning effort throughout the first months of her transition was suggested to create opportunities for her to represent and communicate her other interpersonal needs for Wanted Inclusion and Wanted Affection to the group.

Learning About Power and Control

One of the common uses of the FIRO-B is to help leaders understand the potential implications of their levels of Expressed and Wanted Control. In any discussion of leadership, issues of power and control are important topics. While the notion continues to fade that effective leadership is rooted in execution of command and control functions, this aspect of leadership has only been diluted, not eliminated. Leaders are still expected to understand issues related to decision making and other aspects of exercising influence, in addition to responding to the demands for high-involvement workplaces and increased delegation in today's flatter organizations. The FIRO-B provides quick access to the issues of control and, when used in conjunction with the MBTI, provides helpful insights on how different leaders learn to exercise responsibility and power.

Case Example 3: Richard, Gavin, and Monique

Richard

MBTI Type: E N F J

FIRO-B Results:

eI (5)	eC (7)	eA (9)
wI (9)	wC (2)	wA (9)

Gavin

MBTI Type: E N F J

FIRO-B Results:

eI (7)	eC (3)	eA (8)
wI (7)	wC (9)	wA (8)

Monique

MBTI Type: E N F J

FIRO-B Results:

eI (7)	eC (0)	eA (8)
wI (9)	wC (0)	wA (9)

This case study of three managers is presented to highlight how the FIRO-B might enhance discussions of power and control and provide insight that complements and goes beyond MBTI results. These managers are all the same MBTI type, ENFJ, but have very different FIRO-B control scores. The implications of the different Control scores are highlighted by comparing leadership issues and styles in these managers who have the same type. The managers in this case were members of a support group for minority managers. The support group involved a broad spectrum of managers from the public and private sectors.

A comparison of these three individuals presented a striking pattern. As mentioned earlier, each showed a preference for ENFJ and, consistent with the research results discussed earlier, had high needs in both the Expressed and Wanted dimensions of Inclusion and Affection, with the exception of Richard, a 30-year-old training and development manager whose Expressed Inclusion fell in the medium range. The most significant differences among these three individuals were the Control scores. The three were close colleagues and well aware of their different control needs.

Consistent with their strong needs for Wanted Inclusion and Wanted Affection, as well as their Extraversion and Feeling preferences, all three individuals emphasized control primarily via interpersonal influence rather than through legitimate authority or expert power. Control for personal aggrandizement or domination over others was scorned by all three. Each believed it was important for a leader to be well regarded and actively engaged with subordinates.

Consistent with expressing a large need for control but wanting little from others, Richard was the most concerned of the three with legitimate authority and accountability for managerial functions (e.g., resource allocation, planning, establishing priorities). However, rather than making unilateral decisions, Richard's view was that leaders must sell decisions and have a high amount of personal contact to ensure acceptance.

Consistent with her low scores on both Expressed Control and Wanted Control, Monique, a 33-year-old safety and security manager, had views most contrary to Richard's. She did not recognize the notion of "legitimate" power and even argued that such an idea was impossible, expressing concern that such institutional controls are coercive and unethical. Monique believed that power was individual and did not like to see herself as a center of power or the distributor of power in her organization. She had a strong facilitative view of leadership and emphasized the importance of individual choice and integrity.

Gavin, a 37-year-old labor relations unit manager, viewed power as completely collective. He emphasized that power arises from consensus and viewed the leader as an articulator of visions and the key source of stimulation and encouragement within an organization. Gavin viewed responsibility as contractual and the product of clear agreements and negotiated roles.

All three reported that their relationships with superiors were nonassertive, as one might expect with their desires for Wanted Affection and their Feeling preferences. While Richard and Monique most desired supervisors who enabled them to exercise a great deal of autonomy (low Wanted Control), Gavin was comfortable accepting a great deal of direction and structure (high Wanted Control). When Gavin once mentioned that it was frustrating when his supervisor did not set deadlines (thereby not satisfying his need for Wanted Control), Monique could not understand the remark, perhaps reflecting her low Wanted Control. She, in contrast, deplored deadlines (low Wanted Control) and found that performing under pressure was very frustrating (reflecting her preference to not Express Control). Richard also disliked deadlines (low Wanted Control), but often enjoyed the sense of pressure and leadership that a "rush job" entailed (high Expressed Control).

With regard to planning, all three of these leaders expressed a great deal of interest and respect for organizational values and guiding principles, not surprising for NF types. Consistent with her resistance to deadlines, Monique showed the least interest in the value of planning and was concerned that many planning activities resulted in rigid and restrictive goals. Although seemingly inconsistent with her preference for Judging, this represented her strongly held NFJ value to allow everyone maximum freedom and opportunity. Richard thought that effective planning was necessary to align resources and generate greater internal and external consistency that would make the organization more competitive (high Expressed Control). Gavin and Monique were not interested in competitiveness (low Expressed Control). Gavin viewed effective planning as a mechanism for specifying procedures and selecting planning indicators that could be used as measurements of progress (high Wanted Control). His view of planning was the most comprehensive, spanning from the determination of a clear mission to the articulation of cyclical goals and tactics.

All three considered themselves self-reflective and had grown as leaders by actively seeking feedback from peers, supervisors, and their own staff members, a product of high needs for both Wanted Inclusion and Wanted Affection, as well as an expression of their Extraversion and their dominant Feeling preferences. All appeared to be striving to reach a consistency between self-awareness and the external perceptions of their co-workers. The most significant development experiences reported were either difficult feedback during a performance appraisal or the insights gained from a formal 360-degree feedback instrument.

Despite their similarities, there were some differences in their leadership development that may be attributed to their different control scores. Richard had sought out a number of assignments that pushed him to develop new skills. This pattern is often seen with high Expressed Control and is most different from individuals such as Gavin, who had spent a large amount of time and money in formal training programs refining specific leadership skills, such as communication and decision making. The pattern of reliance on experts and shaping one's self around formal competencies may be associated with Gavin's high level of Wanted Control. Consistent with the independence indicated by low needs for Expressed and Wanted Control, Monique had avoided both high-risk assignments and formal training programs. Instead, Monique had changed jobs frequently (with about twice as many jobs as Richard or Gavin), each time taking similar positions in different kinds of organizations, both small and large sized, and involving government, industry and education.

These leaders also reported a common set of perceived strengths and problem areas, many of which may be related to their ENFJ type. Perceived strengths as leaders were energy, service-mindedness, conscientiousness, speaking and listening skills, development of staff skills and interests, sincerity, and organizational abilities. The common set of leadership challenges included difficulty in keeping a professional distance, conflict avoidance, and inability to focus and stick to priorities.

Each also reported strengths and weaknesses that are associated with their control scores. Richard believed that one of his major leadership strengths was his entrepreneurial flair and the ability to launch new projects, whatever the odds against him (high Expressed Control). For several years, however, Richard had been trying to learn how to let go and trust others with managing the projects he had started. He was quick to see solutions to problems and was struggling to learn how staff could have greater ownership to solve their own problems without coming to him.

Gavin saw that one of his major strengths as a leader was his ability to continually and incrementally improve systems, but his biggest challenge was to become autonomous. When Gavin had been asked to temporarily assume his supervisor's position, the demand for constant decision making in arenas with no precedents had brought him to virtual paralysis by the time his supervisor had returned from disability leave.

Monique reported that one of her major strengths was the ability to empower others by "giving people room to do their own thing." She was also well known in her organization as a customer advocate whose clear convictions had brought about new consumer-oriented practices. Monique, however, was quick to become frustrated with systems and rules and had been criticized for not quickly bringing certain problem situations under control.

For these three leaders who shared MBTI type, the opportunity to explain differences in their leadership based on the FIRO-B provided a deeper level of understanding. For instance, when an issue was raised, they would first consider whether it was common to the three of them, based on their understanding of the MBTI, or whether it was unique to one person based on the FIRO-B. The resulting small-group discussion uncovered and clarified a complex set of insights.

Managing Change

The role of leader as change agent has become increasingly important in the modern workplace. The pressures of change have required organizations to examine what they do, how they do it, and how they can increase output and decrease costs. Those involved in these change efforts must examine their skills and attitudes to determine how they fit into the new way of doing business—a new way that is likely to be short lived before another shock stimulates further change. For most middle managers, the level of strain during these changes has been extremely high. Middle managers bear the weight of reorganization, downsizing, and rapid growth. These pressures require personal adaptation to new roles while assuring optimal productivity. Used together, the MBTI and FIRO-B can provide leaders with insights about how they are likely to interpret their role as change agent, which strategies they are likely to favor for coping with change, and how they are likely to respond to the human side of change.

Case Example 4: Audrey

MBTI Type: I N F P

FIRO-B Results:

eI (6)	eC (2)	eA (3)
wI (0)	wC (4)	wA (5)

Audrey was a 42-year-old regional manager for a private corporation that manages residential treatment facilities. The position of regional manager had been introduced after a period in which new sites were rapidly added. Site managers (counseling professionals) had previously reported directly to a vice president for operations. As the number of sites grew, the separate facilities competed for a limited number of central services. In addition, the turnover rate of staff in each of the sites was increasing beyond the industry average. The vice president had successfully introduced a regional manager in another division of the company and believed that developing this position introduced consistency, reduced customer and staff complaints, and decreased costs. The regional manager would be responsible for leading the staff of site managers and for overseeing a consolidated administrative function.

Audrey was an experienced site manager who was hired from outside the corporation to fill the regional manager position. She was initially well received by the group. Her highest expressed need score was Inclusion. Thus, she was successful in representing herself as engaging, equitable, involving, and interested in bringing together divergent viewpoints about how to operate under the new organizational structure. Also consistent with her Expressed Inclusion, she had successfully managed to increase the regularity and visibility of the region's staff recognition efforts, which had helped to sustain morale during the difficult transition and confusion created by the reorganization.

During her first annual performance appraisal, Audrey received feedback that, in her words, was "astonishing" and had "blindsided" her. The vice president reported that her staff viewed her as aloof, arbitrary, stubborn, and insensitive to the strain the reorganization was creating. In reaction to their frustration with Audrey's lack of attention to the human side of change, the site managers had established a separate meeting in which they resolved problems and exchanged moral support. The vice president had recently been asked to attend one of these private meetings in which he had gathered the reactions of Audrey's staff.

Given her NF preference, this feedback was very difficult for Audrey to accept or understand. Audrey valued the creation of a family atmosphere at work. Despite her NF preference, Audrey was able to acknowledge by looking at her Expressed and Wanted Affection scores that she was not providing enough encouragement, listening, and appreciation for her staff on a day-to-day basis. By understanding her Feeling preference and the low Expressed Control, she was also able to appreciate how others had viewed her decisions as subjective and arbitrary. When it was observed that Audrey might be willing to accept direction from superiors but not from subordinates (selective/medium Wanted Control), it became easier to see how she had been perceived as stubborn. Audrey added that her preference for Introversion might also have contributed to the perceived stubbornness, since she was inclined to become quiet, reflective, and inward when questioned about her decisions.

Upon examining how Audrey interacted with her staff, an interesting pattern surfaced that was supported by her FIRO-B results and also explained a good portion of the staff's frustration. Audrey had put into place a weekly three-hour staff meeting with the site managers. When asked why she had chosen this length of time, Audrey explained that she wanted to allow enough face-to-face interaction time so that she and her staff could have their privacy during the rest of the week. This sentiment was associated with her Introversion and low Wanted Inclusion. In addition, when asked how the time in these meetings was spent, Audrey explained that they were mostly exchanges of updates and announcements about the reorganization. Audrey reported that she rarely made time to preplan the meetings (consistent with low Expressed Control and her Perceiving preference) and just enjoyed the chance to make face-to-face contact with staff who were geographically distributed (an NF preference). A first intervention with Audrey was to shorten the meetings by communicating some of the information in writing or e-mail.

When asked about her own job satisfaction, Audrey reported a high degree of loneliness. She maintained active contact with her former co-workers at another site but had yet to develop a collegial relationship in this corporation. When the difficulty of fitting in was illustrated by her low Wanted Inclusion score, Audrey was able to see how she had moved to the new corporation physically but not in spirit. This value-based connection to the past is consistent with her NF preference.

Audrey even recalled that when her new employer selected the same date for the annual holiday party as her former employer, she had made the choice to attend her former employer's event.

With regard to coping with the reorganization, Audrey also was frustrated that top-level management conducted open discussion about areas for attention in the reorganization but provided few ideas for resolution. While she wanted to be acknowledged as having an interest in certain issues, she would have rather been presented with a series of optional solutions. This preference is consistent with a low need for Inclusion as well as low/medium Control needs.

Case Example 5: Julian

MBTI Type: E S T J

FIRO-B Results:

eI (7)	eC (9)	eA (7)
wI (5)	wC (2)	wA (7)

Julian was a 45-year-old chief financial officer for a large multinational engineering services firm. Julian had worked for his current employer for two years, having many previous years of responsibility in various financial functions of private corporations. He was well known in professional associations as an advocate for the vigorous transformation of accounting management practices through the effective use of information technology. For a short period, Julian had worked for a consulting firm in the area of business process redesign. Shortly after arriving as CFO, Julian was asked to assume responsibility as team leader for one of two large redesign efforts in the corporation.

Julian's initiation of the project closely resembled what one might expect with an individual high in Expressed Control and whose preferences are for Extraverted Thinking supported by Sensing. Relying heavily on his prior experience, Julian quickly devised a plan for launching a redesign effort. The plan was contained in a series of detailed and logical steps mapped onto an aggressive timetable. Even prior to the CEO's endorsement of the plan, Julian had staff working on various data collection activities for the project. As Julian learned more and more about the organization, staff were continually being added to the redesign team (perhaps related to his high Expressed Inclusion). By the end of six months, the team had grown to nearly 23 people, with each member spending no less than 20% of his or her time on the project. In that same period, Julian's team was successful in the Herculean feat of documenting all financial services, estimating direct and indirect costs for each service, and flowcharting all financial processes in the corporation, which they detailed in 180 pages.

During a strategy session of top executives held at the end of that six-month period, Julian was exposed to a new method of process redesign. In the fast-action mode often seen with ESTJ managers, Julian successfully convinced the top management team to change direction. Upon returning to the redesign team, he introduced a new project plan and distributed new assignments to the team. Shortly thereafter, the CEO began to receive a wave of complaints from team members and their supervisors about their concerns over the direction of the project and the time that was being taken away from their routine work. The CEO then requested that Julian participate in an intensive leadership development workshop.

Julian was quick to understand the relationship between the project's history and his MBTI type. He commented that during this period, his aggressive leadership was stimulated by a need to fit in and be recognized as a deserving member of the executive team (Wanted Inclusion). He also believed that the complaints about the process had been postponed due to his continual encouragement, positive feedback, and emotional support of team members (Expressed Affection). Julian had jokingly referred to himself as the bulldozer driver of change, who also doled out the bandages to the wounded.

Consistent with his need for Wanted Affection, Julian was also concerned about losing support from his staff and being seen only as an aggressive change agent. To his credit, he was able to use his Sensing to see his team's discontent as a fact that had to be dealt with in order to accomplish his goals. Interestingly, Julian viewed much of the structure he provided (plans, time lines, task assignments) as an expression of affection and support to the team. He had justified such an aggressive approach as necessary to help save people's jobs and to save the company from eventually having to downsize in a financial emergency.

His behavior and his rationale for it are consistent with a dominant Thinking perspective, which would indicate that his view of the best way to help someone is to solve their problem and provide them with a logical structure. Through his understanding of the MBTI, Julian was able to recognize that some staff might need to understand the reasons for change, not just the tasks involved. Using the FIRO-B, Julian was able to realize that others might be interpreting his behaviors quite differently from his intentions. For instance, he realized that the detailed plans and time lines were probably not viewed by others as a means of support as much as his personal encouragement and approachability were.

Since Julian's highest Expressed Need was Control, it was not surprising that he first impressed the staff as deadline oriented, firm, competent, and goal directed. He was also able to understand that the relatively large gap (+9) between his Total Expressed needs and Total Wanted needs showed a strong preference to initiate behavior rather than rely on others. This take-charge, action-oriented behavior is also consistent with his ESTJ type. While this had already been demonstrated by his energy and action bias to his staff, it also had created a distance between himself and others that kept him from receiving reliable feedback.

With these insights in hand, Julian returned to his project with a new emphasis. Using his skills as an engaging and organized presenter (Expressed Inclusion and Expressed Control), Julian assumed a training-oriented approach. He broke the redesign team into three subteams, each with its own leader. As each phase of the project unfolded, Julian would visit each team and provide a training session on tools, techniques, and intended outcomes. Julian formed an additional management team to oversee the project. In these management meetings, Julian made a deliberate attempt to emphasize Expressed Inclusion and Expressed Affection behaviors as a means of building a common sense of purpose and support in the project. While Julian often found it difficult not to express Control, the ownership others felt over the project increased and steady progress was maintained.

A STRATEGY FOR JOINT INTERPRETATION OF THE MBTI AND THE FIRO-B

Before making the decision to use the MBTI and the FIRO-B in a leadership development context, practitioners should take note of several conditions that may contribute to the success of their combined use:

- When the client has prior familiarity with and a working understanding of at least one of the instruments. Not all clients shift between the conceptual models of the MBTI and the FIRO-B as easily as a practitioner, whose prior training and cognitive style may favor this type of approach.
- When adequate time is available to respond to individual questions and concerns through one-on-one feedback or small-group sessions.

While clients may quickly see areas of convergence, it is important to help avoid simplistic interpretations and to help clients cope with areas of divergence.

- When the client perceives that the framework of one instrument or the other is too limiting and results in labeling or pigeonholing. A second instrument may provide the opportunity to demonstrate the complexity of human behavior.
- When the client questions the validity of results or perceives contradictions in interpretations. A second instrument provides the opportunity to support inconsistencies and to point out common patterns that may be difficult to accept.
- When an immediate need exists to extend the results of the MBTI to specific interpersonal relations or social incidents that the client is attempting to understand. The FIRO-B permits a quick analysis of complementarity between two individuals and between an individual and a group or social context.

Special attention should be given to the first two conditions listed above. First, while it may be beneficial for a client to have prior exposure to one of these two instruments, circumstances sometimes require introducing both at the same time. Practitioners should be sensitive to overwhelming the client and may accommodate the lack of prior exposure by narrowing the amount of interpretation provided and by checking for confusion and frustration. Practitioners are also cautioned to avoid shortchanging one instrument, and hence the client's own self-awareness, under the pressure of conducting a joint interpretation.

Second, particularly in light of the first point, adequate time must be given prior to a joint interpretation session for both instruments to be adequately processed and digested. Clients should have time to reflect on their results and the interpretations so that questions about the theories, instrumentation, and individual issues can be raised. If the client does not demonstrate sufficient understanding of the concepts and ideas to begin experimenting with them, then the time allocated for a joint interpretation might best be used to deepen the client's understanding of one instrument or the other. Proceeding when the client is not ready will probably generate information overload and dependence on the practitioner that will undermine his or her ability to benefit from either instrument.

If the client has prior exposure to one instrument, there may be a natural interest in readministering that instrument. This provides a chance to look at changes in the client's response to either instrument over time, although this requires more time and effort to integrate. The difference in the results of an instrument over time permits the discussion of life changes, organizational stressors, developmental experiences, and the issues of instrument reliability. Such a discussion might precede a discussion of the new instrument, but in all cases should not be rushed. If a readministration is provided and the results differ from previous ones, the client should be deferred to as the final judge of the accuracy of the results.

With the individual interpretation of the MBTI and the FIRO-B completed, the following process, which consists of six steps, is proposed as a strategy for joint interpretation.

Step One: An easy starting place is to compare the Overall Need score on the FIRO-B with the preference for Extraversion–Introversion. Explore any contradictions with the client. Does it make sense to him or her? For example, some Extraverts with low or low/medium overall interpersonal needs have explained that, while they can be energized just being in crowded places, they have little desire to interact with the others there (e.g., eating alone in a cafeteria, shopping alone in a mall). They are equally stimulated by the sights and sounds of the environment.

Step Two: Look at individual high or low FIRO-B scores and relate them to different MBTI preferences. Refer to the research results summarized earlier in this chapter as a source of links between the dimensions of both instruments. For example, it is consistent with the Thinking preference to have low levels of Expressed Affection. Spend time discussing how these areas of convergence influence the client's leadership strengths and challenges. Clients often find it particularly helpful to see how a point of convergence is matched or mismatched to current challenges facing them in the workplace.

Step Three: Ask clients if they see any other areas of convergence. How do links between the MBTI and the FIRO-B influence their leadership? This step can be important to help judge how the client is integrating the information. This also reinforces that the purpose of both instruments is to stimulate meaningful self-awareness, not conformance to the practitioner's predictions.

Step Four: Point out areas of divergence. Select scores that seem to conflict or do not agree with the research results. For example, Extraverted Feeling types may have very low Wanted Inclusion scores. Ask the client if contradictory results such as these make sense to them. In the example above, a common response is that the leader feels overwhelmed being viewed as the networker and people gatherer. Quite often, leaders' ability to bring together contradictory areas reflects refinement in their flexibility in adopting various leadership strategies and behaviors. Explore whether any of these contradictory results might be related to challenges currently facing the leader.

An INTP manager once explained that his unexpectedly high Expressed Inclusion score represented his interest in exploring how others were understanding complex problems. Indeed, the interpretation session was filled with his questions about "What if?" scenarios about other possible scores, which he used as a means of contrast to interpret his own results. Note that the practitioner should be careful not to suggest that any combination of MBTI and FIRO-B results implies abnormality or deviance.

Step Five: Find out from clients if they see areas of contradiction between the two sets of results. This may reveal a misunderstanding of one instrument or the other, or it may lead to deeper discussion of the links between the instruments.

Step Six: From the FIRO-B, identify the highest Expressed behavior and compare it to the function that is Extraverted (use type dynamics to determine). How are they related or not related? How are these two characteristics working together or in competition to shape others' impressions of this leader?

CONCLUSION

Pictures of the same scene (e.g., the view from the top of a mountain) can be taken from two different perspectives. Each may reveal something not evident by the other. One photo may have something in the foreground or in focus that the other does not.

The same is true for psychological instruments. The MBTI captures one picture of a person's preferences and the FIRO-B captures another. When they are used together, clients are able to receive two perspectives on themselves and their leadership that might complement each other, but have different aspects in focus. When clients observe differences between the two instruments, they can use these differences to better understand their behavior. The rich results from both instruments may reveal a need to bring one or more aspects of their leadership more strongly into focus or to broaden their own view of themselves. In the process, leaders can gain a more complex view of themselves, the nature of leadership, and their influence and needs in the workplace.

REFERENCES

Fitzgerald, C. (1991). *The MBTI and managers: Research findings and implications for management development.* Unpublished manuscript.

Gluck, G. A. (1983). *Psychometric properties of the FIRO-B: A guide to research.* Palo Alto, CA: Consulting Psychologists Press.

Myers, I. B., & McCaulley, M. H. (1985). *Manual: A guide to the development and use of the Myers-Briggs Type Indicator.* Palo Alto, CA: Consulting Psychologists Press.

Ryan, L. R. (1989). *Clinical interpretation of the FIRO-B* (3d ed.). Palo Alto, CA: Consulting Psychologists Press.

Schnell, E. R., & Hammer, A. L. (1993). *Introduction to the FIRO-B in organizations.* Palo Alto, CA: Consulting Psychologists Press.

Schnell, E. R., Hammer, A. L., Fitzgerald, C., Fleenor, J. W., & Van Velsor, E. (1994). Relationships between the MBTI and the FIRO-B: Implications for their joint use in leadership development. In C. Fitzgerald (Ed.), *Proceedings of the Myers-Briggs Type Indicator and Leadership: An International Research Conference* (pp. 177–188). College Park: MD: University of Maryland University College National Leadership Institute.

Schutz, W. (1958). *FIRO: A three-dimensional theory of interpersonal behavior.* New York: Holt, Rinehart and Winston.

Schutz, W. (1978). The *FIRO awareness scales manual.* Palo Alto, CA: Consulting Psychologists Press.

16 | Strategies for Using Psychological Type to Enhance Leaders' Communication

Susan A. Brock

Leading effectively requires skill in communicating both within and outside an organization. To do this, leaders must understand the different needs and expectations of their audiences. Understanding psychological type preferences can provide an invaluable guide for effective communication.

PSYCHOLOGICAL TYPE AND EFFECTIVE COMMUNICATION

Experience with psychological type preference and practical influencing clearly shows that different types prefer communicating in different ways (Brock, 1991). Different types of people prefer different ways of presenting ideas, in effect, different "dialects." Those who lead in organizations need to communicate productively with a variety of people—both face-to-face and in writing—and using a knowledge of psychological type can make them more effective. This chapter will provide information about using psychological type when clear, effective communication is critical.

One important aspect of psychological type, seen over and over by those who use it in their work, is its wide applicability. Knowledge of psychological type and communication can make leaders more effective in various ways:

- Understanding and coaching an employee becomes more straight-forward.
- Presenting a proposal so that staff can best "hear" it becomes as important as the proposal itself.
- Problems that may have been a long-standing source of resentment with a colleague or subordinate suddenly shift and are no longer an issue.
- Creating a media piece that states benefits in ways that various types will appreciate sharpens marketing efforts.
- The steps in presenting an organizational vision and engaging others in committed action become more clear.

In fact, one of the most common reactions of individuals who learn about psychological type in a work context is that suddenly they have a better understanding of people and situations across their life.

There appear to be three underlying aspects of psychological type that are key to enhanced communication:

1. It doesn't focus on what's wrong with a person.
2. It allows interpersonal differences to be consciously understood instead of reacted to.
3. It provides reliable options for how to best approach an individual so that communication and understanding can take place.

Each of these aspects will be considered in turn.

A Nonevaluative Approach

Psychological type is unusual in that it doesn't apply labels of "bad" or "good" to preferences. When presenting the type framework to those working with it for the first time, it is sometimes a struggle to overcome prior conditioning regarding good and bad preferences. Many look for the "best" preference or say, "There must be a bad and good in here somewhere. Some of these preferences must be better than others."

The greatest impact of having no bad or good type preferences is that when fully understood, psychological type reduces the interpersonally corrosive practices of blaming others and worrying about oneself. Upon learning about psychological type, leaders often express sentiments similar to those of one manager: "I've begun to realize how much of the time I have spent thinking, 'If only they were different!' Now I see what a waste of time that is." On a personal level, they may feel a new sense of self-acceptance. No longer are they nagged by the internal worry, "I should be different; maybe I'm not the type of person who can be a leader." Self-acceptance and appreciation replaces blaming others and worrying about oneself. In effect, psychological type nourishes a personal sense of what Carl Rogers (1972) called *unconditional positive regard*. This is a powerful source of energy for personal transformation and leadership.

Understanding Versus Reacting to Differences

Once a level of self-acceptance is present, another transformation can occur interpersonally. Difference needn't signal difficulty. With a heightened sense of self-acceptance and appreciation, suddenly it is easier to understand and appreciate the other person. A person hearing a colleague state, "I plan tomorrow's work while I'm still at work today" no longer perceives it as a challenge to her own method of letting the tasks of the day emerge from a general sense of what needs to be done. She now hears the statement as a difference in tactics. Such a statement can be seen as a perspective to be considered rather than as a threat to oneself.

This shift in perspective can release an enormous amount of energy. Instead of moving into a self-defensive posture complete with reasons for "why I do it my way," or into an aggressive posture of "why the way I do it is the best way," one can simply take in what is being said. We can use our energy to engage and understand the other person, clearing the way for effective commitment and action.

Psychological type can also lead to an altogether different approach to listening. Listening can be part of an inquiry process, as Peter Senge (1990) put it in his "advocacy inquiry" model in his book *The Fifth Discipline*. A stance of seeking mutual understanding is far different from the more typical listening stance of agree–disagree, which is common in many organizations. In *agree–disagree listening*, people listen so that they can mentally decide who's right. They listen so that they can make points or prove their point.

When people receive agree–disagree listening, they sense they weren't really understood. They may try to express themselves again, often in a louder fashion, if they're in an Extraverted mode. Or they may choose an Introverted mode of silence, noting the fruitlessness of communicating with this person. In either case, the desired under-standing isn't achieved.

Psychological type makes it more likely that the inevitable differ-ences that occur when people communicate can be accepted and embraced as a real contribution to the issue at hand. The stance of lis-tening for understanding is essentially no-fault listening.

Creating Communication Options

Once leaders understand their own communication preference *and* the power that comes from appreciating differences, the next questions they often ask are: "How can I be more effective?" "How can I make it easier for others to understand me?" and "How can I listen in a way that puts me on their wavelength?"

Note how different this stance is from the more usual one that asks, "Why don't they say it in a way I can understand?" or "Why do I have to repeat myself?" With an understanding of psychological type, those who lead can modify their communication to present their message in a way most easily understood by the receiver. The shift that occurs moves people from a struggle of me versus them to a striving for mutu-al understanding. Psychological type can then be used as a tool to communicate with others so that we can best deliver the message, engage in dialogue, and work toward mutual satisfaction.

USING PSYCHOLOGICAL TYPE
TO MODIFY COMMUNICATION

The idea of modifying communication to suit the receiver is certainly not new. We write business letters with a more formal address and syn-tax than we use in our more casual notes to friends. What is new is using psychological type to inform us about the way an individual prefers to be dealt with.

For example, when working with the Thinking–Feeling function, participants in type workshops are often surprised at responses to the question, "When you have a troubling interpersonal issue and you decide to talk it over with another person, what do you want most from them?" Those with a Thinking preference most often say they want ideas and solutions from the other person. Those with a Feeling prefer-ence most often say they simply want to be listened to. The two groups are often amazed by the depth of differences this question reveals and by their own passion for what they believe is right. Such experiences, when viewed in the context of psychological type, provide powerful insights and perspectives for working to create effective communication.

Analysis of communication in practical influencing situations such as managing, training, selling, and consulting has shown that different types show predictable differences in how they want to interact, receive information, make decisions, and move to closure.

In day-to-day interactions, however, it is not possible to know the actual type preferences of those we deal with. One strategy for using an understanding of psychological type when one doesn't know the other person's preference is to watch the behavioral cues of the individual, such as body language, the kinds of questions asked, a stance of testing versus harmony, and the drive for closure or continued process. Behaviors generally indicate what response the person prefers at that moment.

Since we all use all the psychological type preferences at various times, we will observe people's behaviors changing as circumstances change. This can be referred to as observing an individual's *type mode*. As a practical matter, it is not necessary to know an individual's actual type preference. It is, however, important to pick up cues as to the person's type mode at a given time, then to shift along one's own range of behaviors to create a closer match during the interaction. Examples of the behaviors that cue us to various type modes are shown in Table 1.

The phrases below each preference in Table 1 are the behavioral cues. The key phrases above each preference are a practical definition of what people operating in that type mode are likely to want in communication.

STAGES OF COMMUNICATION

All aspects of psychological type are important to consider when effective communication is necessary; however, some aspects of psychological type are more significant during certain phases of an interaction. Most interactions have the following basic phases:

• Initiating the interaction
• Establishing shared purpose through investigating needs and suggesting action
• Creating commitment or closure

The length of each stage and its specific character varies, depending on the reason for the interaction and the expectations the parties have of each other and the interaction. Figure 1 graphically shows which

TABLE 1 Behavioral Cues During Communication

Talk It Out *Extraverts*	Think It Through *Introverts*
• Rapid speech • Interrupt • Louder volume to voice • Appear to think aloud	• Pause in answering or giving information • Quieter voice volume • Shorter sentences, not run on
Specifics *Sensors*	**The Big Picture** *Intuitives*
• Ask for step-by-step information or instruction • Ask "what" and "how" questions • Use precise descriptions	• Ask for the purpose of an action • Look for possibilities • Ask "why" questions • Talk in general terms
Logical Implications *Thinkers*	**Impact on People** *Feelers*
• Appear to be testing you or your knowledge • Weigh the objective evidence • Are unimpressed that others have decided in favor • Conversations follow a pattern of checking logic: "if this, then that"	• Strive for harmony in the interaction • May talk about what they value • Ask how others have acted or resolved the situation • Matters to them whether others have been taken into account
Joy of Closure *Judgers*	**Joy of Processing** *Perceivers*
• Impatient with overly long descriptions, procedures • The tone is "hurry up—I want to make this decision" • May decide prematurely • Enjoy closure	• Seem to want "space" to make own decisions • The tone is "let's explore," what are some more factors to consider • May decide at the last moment • Enjoy processing

From *Four Part Framework* (Rev. ed.), by S. A. Brock, 1992, Gainesville, FL: Center for Applications of Psychological Type. Copyright 1992 by S. A. Brock. Adapted with permission.

aspects of psychological type are most significant at each stage of an interaction, though all aspects of type are at play throughout communication.

Initiating the Interaction: The Role of Extraversion–Introversion

When people initiate an interaction, especially when the parties do not know each other well, the dynamics of Extraversion and Introversion are key. It is during this time that the parties are feeling each other out,

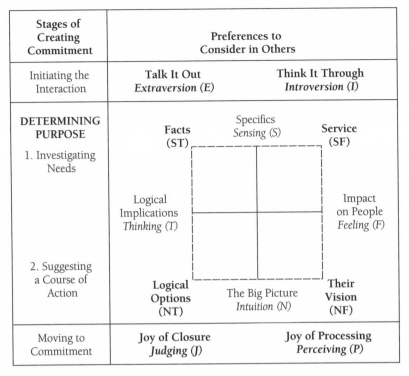

Stages of Creating Commitment	Preferences to Consider in Others		
Initiating the Interaction	**Talk It Out** *Extraversion (E)*		**Think It Through** *Introversion (I)*
DETERMINING PURPOSE 1. Investigating Needs 2. Suggesting a Course of Action	**Facts** **(ST)** Logical Implications *Thinking (T)* **Logical Options (NT)**	Specifics *Sensing (S)* The Big Picture *Intuition (N)*	**Service** **(SF)** Impact on People *Feeling (F)* **Their Vision (NF)**
Moving to Commitment	**Joy of Closure** *Judging (J)*		**Joy of Processing** *Perceiving (P)*

Figure 1 Psychological Type and the Stages of Communication

Adapted from *FLEX Talk®*, by S. A. Brock, 1991, Minneapolis: Brock Associates. Copyright 1991 by S. A. Brock. Adapted with permission.

asking themselves questions such as, What is this person like? Will I find dealing with the person difficult? Is this person believable and trustworthy? Do we seem to be on the same wavelength? Is he or she ready to go further with the task at hand?

In the initial part of an interaction, we quickly pick up behavioral cues to answer these questions. We are especially attuned to facial expression, body language, and voice rate. These are all cues that suggest how a person uses his or her energy, which is a basic component of the Extraversion–Introversion difference.

An Extraverted preference usually results in more outward energy. Thus, we see more animation and hear louder voice volume and a quicker rate of speech from an individual in an Extraverted mode. Energy is coming out into the environment. An Introverted preference is usually shown by cues such as a quiet body and less facial animation. Energy is more contained in the individual.

These are all ways we use to gauge what it will be like to deal with the other person. In general, if we perceive the other individual as somewhat similar to us, we are initially more at ease in the communication. In addition, if the person is generally congruent, that is, the rate of speech, body movement, and facial expression match the message, we find that person more believable and easier to trust.

After one knows an individual, this first phase of initiating the interaction becomes less important and goes very quickly. We know what to expect and we generally get it. With a stranger, we are more aware of the initiating phase, and it generally takes longer. We are learning what to expect and assessing our ability to work together. Although the Extraversion (Talk It Out)–Introversion (Think It Through) dimension is key to this phase of initiating the interaction, it is important to remember that the effects of these preferences actually permeate all phases of an interaction.

Investigating Needs and Suggesting Action: The Role of Sensing–Intuition and Thinking–Feeling

In the next two phases of interaction-investigating needs and suggesting action—the two psychological type dimensions related to the basic mental functions have the greatest effect on how an individual wants to interact. These are the perceiving functions, Sensing (Specifics), and Intuition (Big Picture), and the judging functions, Thinking (Logical Implications) and Feeling (Impact on People).

Reflecting a moment on the underlying idea of psychological type makes this connection more obvious. Jung referred to the perceiving functions of Sensing and Intuition as those preferences related to taking in information, and the judging functions of Thinking and Feeling as those preferences that are used as the basis for one's conclusions. From the point of view of the person receiving information in an interaction, taking in and exchanging information is exactly what he or she is doing when the person communicating is helping investigate needs. Arriving at a conclusion is exactly the process taking place when the receiver hears suggestions for action.

In order to match the receiver's preference during the phases of investigating needs and suggesting action, the first step for the person communicating is to pick up the behavioral cues of the receiver's type mode. Again, as with Extraversion and Introversion, it is not necessary to know an individual's type. It is, however, very important to follow the behavioral cues of the individual and shift along one's own range of behaviors to create a match.

The behavioral cues for a Sensing mode include a focus on specifics:

- How many people will be affected?
- What will the costs be?
- What will the savings be?
- How long will this take?
- Who has tried this before?
- What did they say about it?

The behavioral cues for the Intuitive mode include a focus on the big picture:

- What's the overall purpose here?
- How will this benefit us in the long run?
- What other possibilities are there?
- Do we see relationships or patterns in the situation that should be addressed?

The behavioral cues of a Thinking mode often focus on the logical implications and may include a testing quality:

- What is your evidence?
- What is the logic behind the idea or proposal?

The person in a Thinking mode may also engage in verbal sparring.

The Feeling mode may include cues that focus on the impact on people:

- Will your suggestions help create a good situation for everyone?
- Have others been taken into account?

The person in a Feeling mode is seeking empathy and harmony. This approach uses subjectivity (how people, including themselves, experience the situation) rather than objectivity (standing back from the personal aspects of the situation) in order to arrive at the right conclusion.

Combining the perceiving and judging functions into pairs—ST, SF, NF, and NT—is a good way to help determine what kind of communication the individual will prefer. We will explore the combination of Perceiving and Judging functional pairs in later examples since they form the "dialects" of successful communication.

Attaining Closure: The Role of Judging–Perceiving

In the final step of an interaction, attaining closure, the Judging (Joy of Closure) and the Perceiving (Joy of Processing) preferences seem to have the greatest impact on the way communication is managed. Those in a Judging mode are likely to display a general sense of wanting to move things along. They may show impatience with long descriptions or procedures. Having a timetable is usually important, as is following the timetable to an endpoint or goal.

Those in a Perceiving mode are likely to stay open to suggestions. The endpoint is not necessarily what's important to them; rather, the way in which one gets to that point is what's most interesting. For those in a Perceiving mode, there may be a sense of continued exploration, and often there is no push to closure until the last minute. Thus, the right timing for an action can be very different for those who prefer Judging versus those who prefer Perceiving. "When we need it" might be the Perceiving stance; "As soon as possible" might be the Judging stance. Is it any wonder that "the last minute" can have a very different connotation when communicating across these two type dimensions?

THE DIALECTS OF SUCCESSFUL COMMUNICATION

The central issue in managing communication is often establishing a shared purpose. This means getting on the same wavelength to achieve an agreed-upon end. Because the effects of the perceiving and judging functions in the pairs ST, SF, NF, and NT are most important to creating shared purpose, we'll now turn more specifically to working successfully with these functional pairs.

As we investigate needs and suggest action, it is as if we speak four different dialects. STs want to be communicated with in different words and in a different manner than, for example, NFs. When asked the question, "How do you prefer to be influenced?" individuals with different functional pair preferences show striking differences in their responses.

Predictably, Sensing types want practical facts, with the STs liking an underlying impersonal logic to the way the facts are presented. The SFs like a personal connection or relationship to the fact or to the fact giver. For SFs, the issue of loyalty and service is key.

Intuitive types want possibilities. NTs prefer to test the possibilities and find logical options, while NFs are looking for possibilities that make a difference, especially for people. Table 2 presents the flavor of

TABLE 2 How the Different Function Pairs Prefer to Be Influenced

ST—Facts With Practicality	SF—Service With Loyalty
• Be brief. • Give me the facts, the pros and cons, what it means to me. • Tell me why I should listen to you. • Tell me about competing ideas so I can make head-to-head comparisons. • Be honest and straight to the point, know your stuff, answer questions, support your statements. • Have something I can take away to read, especially objective facts. • Don't say you can do it and then not follow through; be professional. • Give me information in an organized way	• Create a friendly, warm, sincere atmosphere; not stuffy or formal. • Give clear, specific examples. • Explain features and benefits honestly in terms that show what's in it for me. • Give me permission to reflect or get familiar with the idea. • Take time to understand my needs. • Give me the specifics, like costs; be clear, with no surprises. • Let me see, touch, and experience some aspect of the idea, product, or service. • Be there for me; I'll return your loyalty.
NT—Logical Options With Competence	**NF—Supporting the Vision With a View Toward Making a Difference**
• Know your product or field in depth. • Give me the information I ask for. • Learn about my needs/situation. • Answer my questions—*but* don't fudge when you don't know the answers. • Prepare to be tested on your competence. • Check to see if I want to be alone to experience possibilities for the product/service, or if I want you to interact with me to experience possibilities for the product/service. • I want to get the job done—a relationship is secondary.	• Don't pressure me. • Be honest and personal. • Recognize me as a person; listen to me. • Make me feel like I'm special. • Provide possibilities, especially for the future. • Don't bury me in details such as specs and written text; give me an overview, then details as they are necessary. • Be sincere. • Tell me why, in terms that apply to me. • Develop a relationship with me.

these differences in the typical language used by people with each of the four preference pairs.

The statements in Table 2 can be used to think through and design communication strategies that apply an understanding of these communication preferences to everyday interactions. Arenas of particular interest to leaders where a knowledge of such differences can be helpful include:

- Building trust
- Presenting information
- Dealing with interpersonal conflict

Building Trust

Trust is one of the most important ingredients in successful managing and leading. Managers and leaders often experience difficulty in building trusting relationships with staff, peers, and subordinates. Awareness of and skill in interpersonal communication can help in this process.

The Golden Rule, Do unto others as you would have them do unto you, is commonly articulated as a guideline for trusting relationships. The Platinum Rule, Do unto others as they would have you do unto them, may be more effective in most situations. Psychological type provides a framework for stepping out of one's own point of view and moving into what is at least a reasonable facsimile of the perspective of others. Trust is built from a base of respect and when individuals receive the kind of information and treatment they consider important. For each of the functional pairs, a different focus builds trust. Table 3 shows the different elements for the four pairs.

The following is an example of a situation in which trust needs to be built, with some strategies for doing just that:

> A senior management team was faced with the issue of employee skepticism over a major change effort that would move several manufacturing facilities from a traditional hierarchical plant-manager leadership structure to a team-based leadership structure. The senior team had come to believe that the level of profit, productivity, and quality they needed to compete globally could only be achieved through true team-based work. They were prepared to invest considerable time, energy, and resources into preparing the organization for the necessary changes. They also knew that working in a team-based fashion would need to be modeled by senior management, and they had begun to personally confront the changes in their own team that others might experience later. They were now ready to turn their attention to designing methods of interaction and communication to create real dialogue about the proposed changes, modifying the plan as mutual understanding of the relevant factors was achieved with employees, clients, and other stakeholders.

Since a stakeholder group is likely to consist of individuals with a variety of type preferences, the senior management team needs to consider how all aspects of psychological type will affect the communication and dialogue process. They need to be especially aware of the ST, SF, NF, and NT preference styles as they structure input and work to

TABLE 3 Elements That Build Trust for Different Preference Pairs

Type Dialect	Build Trust by
ST	Accurate data, responsible actions
SF	Personalized specifics
NF	Support for a vision
NT	Demonstrated competence

Adapted from *FLEX Selling®*, by S. A. Brock, 1990, Minneapolis: Brock Associates. Copyright 1990 by S. A. Brock. Adapted with permission.

build trust. Some strategies for addressing the needs of each of the functional pairs follow.

Those with an ST preference like accurate data and responsible actions. The senior managers would do well to provide a clear business rationale for the changes. It would be particularly helpful if the management team would provide an example of a similar situation in another company, including why that company moved to action, what they specifically achieved, and what they saw as critical to their success. The information should also include lessons that have been learned along the way, since it isn't logical to expect everything to go perfectly. The STs will want to have or construct a road map or timetable on the phases of work ahead. A known structure is often important, as are regular forums for face-to-face communication with the senior management team. A no-surprises approach will be best for developing the trust necessary to carry the organization through the inevitably bumpy road ahead.

Those with an SF preference like personalized specifics. An overview of a company that has undergone a similar process will be a good starting point; however, actually talking with a work team from that company would mean more to those with SF preferences than any presentation. Could a work team from the other company be brought in? Could representative members from the company's work teams do on-site visits and be the ones who help share new ideas and address employee questions?

Those with an NF preference like making a vision come to life, especially when it will have a positive impact on the people involved. In this particular example, the vision involves considerable disruption of people; thus, the rationale for the changes needs to point to ways a team-based work system will benefit the team members as well as the entire company. What is the underlying philosophy behind the change? How do the resulting practices help people develop? Does the process for considering the changes include room for serious, not cosmetic, input? Will the new practices be fair? Will they rectify any past inequities? What larger goal are we all shooting for here? Can we be inspired by it? Creating forums where such questions can be surfaced and addressed will be critical. The more those with an NF preference can be tapped to create the new possibilities and give feedback on them, the better.

Those with an NT preference focus on competence. Where, from the big-picture standpoint, are we trying to go? Do we have some solid logical business reasons to try this? Though others may have brought about similar changes, what is unique in what we're attempting? How is the senior management group preparing itself for the challenge ahead? Are we starting to see evidence of this preparation, not just in words but in actions? Are we looking at the process of team-based work from a systems perspective? That is, do we have a workable plan that includes all the areas of the plant, such as the pay system, the interaction needs of engineering and manufacturing, or the coordination needs of materials and distribution? What measures, if any, need to be added to demonstrate progress and to fit with our total quality process? A key to building and maintaining trust with NTs is to address these questions and engage them in analyzing how the new possibilities integrate. Since building trust is one of the foundations of leadership and communication, using an understanding of psychological type in this way can be critical to overall success.

Presenting Information

A second application of psychological type dialects focuses on the way oral and written material can be presented to different types. Different types prefer different layouts and approaches. To illustrate this point, we'll focus on type preferences that are quite different from each other: an STJ preference and an NFP preference.

The following approach will make communication to STJs easier, since it focuses on methods that emphasize facts, brevity, and results. The Judging preference adds a component of "get to it and get it done" to the ST practical-facts orientation.

The Extraversion and Introversion dimension is addressed separately for this example because it impacts how an individual wants to interact with the information, not how the material is presented. Those in an Introverted mode like to receive information in written form so they can read it and think about it. This is especially true if the information is new or requires concentration. Those in an Extraverted mode will often want to interact on the spot. Discussion and talking it out are key to an Extravert's understanding and buy-in.

Some specific hints for written or oral presentations that work well with an STJ preference are the following:

- Preview what you're going to say; this is the essence of the "executive overview."
- Provide a clear, practical purpose for reading or listening; for example, state that listeners will recognize the benefits of an idea more quickly when they hear it in their own type language.
- Use bullet points and charts instead of paragraphs where possible.
- Use a logical order; if appropriate, number the points for clarity.
- Use everyday language, not intellectual jargon.
- Keep sentences short.
- Use a goal versus process orientation if possible; for example, "We will achieve 25 to 30% growth this year" versus "We will position the product for 25 to 30% growth this year."
- Use nonpersonal words versus relational words; for example, "We will focus on . . . " versus "We will help you to . . . ."

In contrast, an NFP may appreciate an approach that taps into personal possibilities or possibilities that can make a difference for other people. The Perceiving component adds an element of enjoying the exploration and search process at least as much as, if not more than, the end point.

Those with an NFP preference may enjoy the following approach:

- Use a unique beginning that sets the stage, such as a story, a quote, a poem, or a visualization exercise.
- Provide "human" reasons for action; for example, "We can find common ground and create greater understanding when we factor in how types prefer to interact."
- Suggest interesting possibilities and unique benefits.
- Provide personalized examples that help make an idea come to life.
- Include workshop activities that ask the individual to reflect on personal applications or implications of the ideas.
- Use paragraphs to fully examine or explicate an idea.
- Choose unique words that evoke versus practical words that spell out; for example, "Leadership is an act of stewardship" versus "Leadership moves people toward an agreed-upon result."

- Focus on the future, the larger meaning.
- Envision an outcome that allows for greater empathy or making a difference in the world.

Readers may notice that even in reading the two lists, they respond differently to the words and phrases. The first list has a "Do this and get it done" sense, while the second list is softer and more personal. People may have a negative reaction to information coming in via a less-preferred dialect; that reaction may get in the way of receiving the message that the presenter wants to communicate.

Handling Interpersonal Conflict

A third example of the use of type dialects is aimed at handling interpersonal conflict. When left unresolved, long-standing or intense conflicts waste energy and lead to organizational maneuvering, taking sides, and backbiting. Resolving these interpersonal conflicts may be one of the most potent leadership moves an individual can make.

An example from a topflight consulting engineering firm will illustrate this point.

> The CEO was a highly innovative, articulate individual who found real joy in hearing his customer's needs and designing solutions to meet them. He believed that excellence in listening was the key to successful engineering design. He personally presented training in active listening skills to employees at the twice-yearly new-employee orientation. He was a fine salesperson for the firm and its work. His approach to his business was summarized in his statement: "Our work as consulting engineers is to help clients resolve their pain and achieve their dreams. We must get into their shoes, then build solutions that fit them. They'll know we do an excellent job not only because it works but also because they'll know we care. And what does that mean? It means follow-on contracts and a reputation for excellence that grows our business." Not surprisingly, given this perspective, this CEO verifies an ENFP type preference.

This CEO had a bright articulate senior member (the quality assurance vice president) on his staff. This individual also cared deeply about the organization and its work, yet showed it in a very different way. He verified an ESTJ type preference.

> This staff member looked analytically at a project: What experience do we bring to it? What is already developed that will save our resources and fit this client's need? He also pointed out what was wrong in a project design. He saw it as his responsibility to ask tough questions and have others defend their logic. He described his viewpoint by comparing it to skeet shooting.

"When someone pulls out an idea, I treat it like skeet. I try and shoot it down. If I can't, it's probably a good one."

Given the CEO's preference of ENFP, he was likely to talk out (Extravert) his possibilities (Intuition) and to be especially mindful of how clients were reacting (Feeling). He tended to talk in terms of client needs and how to help them address their problems and achieve their dreams. Notice the personalized tone (Feeling) in his approach. He genuinely enjoyed the process (Perceiving) of playing with ideas and options. Coming to an end point of a contract was less exciting for him than working toward it or seeing the new possibilities emerge for further work once the original contract work began.

The quality assurance vice president's preference of ESTJ led him to find satisfaction differently. He also talked out (Extraverted) his ideas, but these ideas were for logical conclusions (Thinking). It is characteristic of an Extraverted Thinking type to analyze and cite what's not there versus appreciating what is there. This is often a classic case of seeing the glass as half empty versus half full. His specific focus on resources and what has worked well in the past came from a Sensing point of view. The Sensing Thinking combination is often most drawn to analyzing from concrete facts and acting responsibly in terms of what is, not what could be. In addition, there was a real joy of closure (Judging) for this vice president, which drove him to want to move quickly on a project, cut the What if? time, and simply do it.

Not surprisingly, these two people often pressed each other's hot buttons. Both wanted what was best for the company and the client. Both were committed to excellence over the long haul. Both were sometimes critical of the other's methods of doing business. Without a way to achieve mutual understanding, they tended to blame each other and draw others, unproductively, into taking sides.

Since both were dedicated to the business and wanted successful projects, strong client relationships, and good profitability, they had excellent common ground from which to start. They also realized they needed each other's skills and expertise, and they recognized that conflict between them was unproductive for the company. They realized that the business needed the diversity of their preferences and that together they could perform more effectively if they could utilize that diversity.

They agreed to undertake a challenging and different way of interacting. They agreed to listen for understanding, truly striving to see the situation from the other's viewpoint. They realized that in the process, conflicts would arise and breaks might be necessary to maintain their discipline of really listening and not falling back into their old conflicts.

Type preference provided the framework for their listening and understanding. Since type is preference, not destiny, both people understood that they could call on their less-preferred functions as they undertook their new way of working together.

In listening for understanding, the CEO and the vice president came to see that for any project to be successful, it would need the possibilities (Intuition), the specifics (Sensing), the client buy-in (Feeling), and a good analysis of the logical implications (Thinking). They agreed to explicitly use all four of these functions in their work together. They decided to use disagreement, which they often heard as "Yes, but . . . ," as a signal for a time-out. They would then attempt to explicitly track and list the aspects of the discussion that fall into the four functions, as shown in Figure 2.

The vice president agreed to explicitly acknowledge what was "right" about a situation, something that Thinking types often forget to do or see as less important. He could see the logic of this change, given the CEO's type preference, and agreed to make this part of his logical analysis. The CEO agreed to advocate his own position and then explicitly invite inquiry into how the vice president saw the issue. He realized that the positions and insights of others were valuable to the company and important to him. He also realized that communicating in this way was a discipline he would need to practice. He saw this as a developmental leadership move for himself, which fit with his values of continued self-development and modeling good leadership.

Both the CEO and the vice president are now using their type preferences as a basis for doing effective work. Both are explicitly using an understanding of their preferences and values to choose behaviors that further business success and model the consolidated leadership and conflict resolution needed to move the company forward.

USING PSYCHOLOGICAL TYPE
TO UNDERSTAND CLOSURE

The final phase of interaction is attaining commitment or closure. As with the other phases of interaction, all aspects of psychological type affect this phase, but the preferences of Judging and Perceiving have the greatest impact.

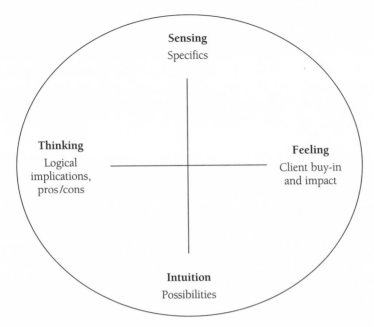

Figure 2 Four Functions in the Communication Process

People in a Judging mode seek closure. They are likely to move through a process quickly to reach the end result. They tend to want clarity about who is in control and assurance that things are under control. Control for them means that they can move forward to a goal or result. For those with a Judging preference, it is this movement to completion that is motivating.

People in a Perceiving mode enjoy processing. They are likely to be more interested in how they get there than in the bottom line. They will resist communication that cuts off playfulness or feels too goal driven. They are interested in options, information, and bringing up interesting issues. In short, they are interested in the process.

An example of managing a work project will help illustrate these differences. It should be remembered, however, that type preference is certainly not the only variable to consider when managing the communication related to a project. Many other factors, such as the readiness of the individual to take on the task, must also be considered.

People with a Judging preference report that when they begin to work on a project, they often feel lukewarm at best. They may even resist beginning work on it. This is the point in a project when nothing is set. They begin to feel more energized as purpose is clarified, resources are known, and time lines are set. As work proceeds and goals are met, they find the sense of productive completion to be reinforcing and energizing. A celebration seems appropriate upon completion of the project.

The following are some strategies to help those with a Judging preference move a project forward more smoothly:

- Communicate the purpose or goal.
- Establish time lines.
- Provide a structure (or, better yet, ask them to do it).
- Clarify resources.
- State overall expectations up front.
- Celebrate completion.

People with a Perceiving preference report a very different pattern when taking on a project. They feel most positive at the beginning. This is the time for exploration. They find the unknown and the lack of structure to be energizing. Their curiosity, playfulness, and attention is engaged. Later, as the project begins to take shape, they report decreased interest. This may result in their attention straying until a deadline is in sight, when they feel a push for completion. The end of a project is often a nonevent. For some, there is mostly a feeling of relief. What is important is the next intriguing project to move to.

The following are strategies for helping those with a Perceiving preference move a project forward:

- Present an unstructured interesting or relevant issue as a starting point; the openness will be more motivating than a project that already has prescribed steps.
- Work through the purpose and clarify resource assumptions only to set necessary boundaries; this promotes a sense of freedom to take off.
- If necessary, set key interim checkpoints.
- As the project progresses, begin to form plans for what's next, contingent on current project completion.

Figure 3 summarizes the four phases of an interaction and recaps some of the ways that psychological type can be used to respond effectively to the type mode of another person. Instead of creating unintended reactions because of the way information is sent and received, a person using the knowledge of type can customize the communication.

Stages of Interacting	What Do You Do?	
Initiating the Interaction	**Extraversion (E)** • Match energy and animation	**Introversion (I)** • Leave time, space for quiet reflection
Investigating Needs and Suggesting Action	**Sensing-Thinking (ST)** • Have the facts • Give the facts • Be practical **Intuition-Thinking (NT)** • Create logical options, unique solutions • Demonstrate your competence	**Sensing-Feeling (SF)** • Personalize interactions • Be warm, friendly • Demonstrate loyalty **Intuition-Feeling (NF)** • Support their vision • Tune into what they value • Create harmony
Attaining Commitment	**Judging (J)** • Move to closure • Work to accomplish goals	**Perceiving (P)** • Be ready for spontaneity • Move in the desired direction

Figure 3 Communication and Practical Influencing for Different Preferences

Adapted from *FLEX Selling® / FLEX Talk® Four Part Framework at Work in Sales and Practical Influencing*, (Rev. ed.), by S. A. Brock, 1995, Minneapolis: Brock Associates. Copyright 1995 by S. A. Brock. Adapted with permission.

Leaders who become effective at managing all the stages of interaction and at communicating across all preferences will have a strategic advantage.

CONCLUSION

Experience with practical influencing, selling, and communication shows that *how* communication is structured and presented has a definite effect on the message received by others. The framework of psychological type gives leaders a way to put this experience into practice. Knowledge of type helps an individual recognize that there is no single correct way to structure communication. Instead, there are preferences that must be taken into account.

Specific aspects of type preference differentially affect the four stages of the influencing process. The perceiving and judging functions combined (ST, SF, NF, NT) have the greatest effect on how to investigate needs and suggest a course of action. It is as if people prefer to communicate via one of these "dialects." Consciously matching the structure of the message to another's preference mode by noting that person's behavioral cues can enhance the dialogue, minimize conflict, and build the trust needed to lead effectively.

REFERENCES

Brock, S. A. (1990). *FLEX Selling*®. Minneapolis: Brock Associates.
Brock, S. A. (1991). *FLEX Talk*®. Minneapolis: Brock Associates.
Brock, S. A. (1992). *FLEX Selling*® / *FLEX Talk*® *Four part framework at work in sales and practical influencing* (Rev. ed). Minneapolis: Brock Associates.
Rogers, C. (1972). *On becoming a person.* Boston: Houghton Mifflin.
Senge, P. M. (1990). *The fifth discipline.* New York: Doubleday.

17 | Type Flexibility in Processes of Strategic Planning and Change

Reg Lang

From a type perspective, many leaders and their organizations face a major challenge: Top management and the organizational culture exhibit a strong preference for STJ, but the organizational environment calls equally for NFP responses. An STJ approach is not wrong—it is incomplete. The STJ way of planning, leading, and managing organizations is more appropriate in an environment of stability, predictability, and order. A rapidly changing, increasingly uncertain, and messy world, however, demands utilization of a complete spectrum of the type preferences: Extraversion, for paying attention to the environment and adjusting quickly to it, alongside Introversion, for reflecting deeply and keeping focused on the organization's core identity; Sensing, for paying attention to the current reality and providing a solid factual base for decisions, alongside Intuition, for seeing the big picture and envisioning new possibilities; Thinking, for analyzing options logically and objectively, alongside Feeling, to factor in personal values and the impacts of decisions on people; Judging, for reaching closure and commitment, alongside Perceiving, for remaining open to new information and emerging strategies. While an STJ approach remains necessary, it is far from sufficient.

Moving toward using both STJ and NFP calls for valuing of type differences. But it also requires using *type flexibility*—that is, making use of less-preferred functions and attitudes when called for in the situation. An expanded type repertoire is especially important in organizations undertaking strategic planning as a means of clarifying their purposes and direction, responding proactively to their environments, and initiating strategic change. Leaders often play *the* key role in these processes. This chapter explores how knowledge of type can contribute to strategic change and, more specifically, how enhanced type flexibility on the part of leaders, managers, and strategic planners may increase the prospects for success.

AN OVERVIEW OF
STRATEGIC PLANNING AND TYPE

There are certain things that all organizations must do: articulate mission, goals, and strategies; align main functions; identify mechanisms of coordination and control; constitute accountability and role relationships; institutionalize planning and communication; relate rewards and performance; and, above all, achieve effective leadership (Clegg, 1992). Strategic planning represents one approach to addressing these imperatives, especially as organizations initiate strategic change.

Strategic planning is a diverse field. It is characterized by competing theories and highly context-dependent practice; hence, strategic planning comes in a variety of forms. It also has a checkered history, having been in and out of favor over the past several decades, and its record of performance is uneven (Mintzberg, 1994). For example, a recent survey of more than 400 executives with strategic planning responsibilities in Fortune 500 companies found strategic planning to be widely recognized as necessary for organizational success—93% of these firms had implemented a formal strategic planning process. Yet only a quarter of the respondents said their process was effective (68% called it somewhat effective).[1]

While it's true that all management tools produce varying degrees of satisfaction and dissatisfaction (Rigby, 1994), clearly there is room for improvement in the use of this widespread and apparently vital method for addressing and generating change. Could type preference be somehow implicated, in the problem and in the solution?

It does seem likely. Strategic planning and personality type are related at a deep level. Central to each are two sets of basic human activities: taking in information and evaluating it to reach conclusions. An understanding of the planning/type relationship, therefore, could help explain why strategic planning proceeds as it does and why it succeeds or fails.

Type's potential extends further. The knowledge and skills associated with type may assist strategic planners—taken here to mean all individuals with responsibility for strategy making, from leaders, managers, and corporate planners to consultants and members of ad hoc teams—to make strategic change processes more effective and less difficult. Use of type could help strategic planning groups deal with the various pressures they face, including:

- Finding a more flexible, adaptive-learning approach capable of generating both deliberate and emergent strategies
- Creating processes leading to shared organizational visions that are equally inspiring and practical
- Interacting with a broad array of interests and treating their inputs as valid
- Assuming facilitative and supportive roles

Responding to these requirements severely challenges planners accustomed to adopting a deliberately rational approach to strategy formulation that relies heavily on information generated by analysis, and it assumes an expert advisor role mostly separated from implementation of strategy (Mintzberg, 1994). To meet this challenge effectively while finding satisfaction in their new work, strategic planners and the organizations they serve need to be able to activate Extraversion *and* Introversion, Sensing *and* Intuition, Thinking *and* Feeling, Judging *and* Perceiving.

Often this range of type responses does not exist in organizations, especially among top managers and leaders. In management, ST appears to be "privileged" over other decision styles, with NT playing the main supportive role (Walck, 1992). Many, if not most, organizations exhibit STJ tendencies, which is also the modal type preference for managers;[2] at higher management levels and among leaders, NTJ becomes somewhat more common (Barr & Barr, 1989; Campbell & Van Velsor, 1985; Kroeger with Thuesen, 1992; McCaulley, 1990; Osborn & Osborn, 1994; Reynierse, 1993; Roach, 1986). My research suggests that many strategic planners probably prefer NTJ;[3] Sensing may show up more in those whose planning roots are operational and in managers responsible for both planning and implementation. Organizations and their planners dominated by STJ preferences may be vulnerable to initiating overly "rational," deliberate, technical planning processes and strategies when the circumstances call for more emergent, innovative, interactive, organizational-culture-oriented responses associated with Intuition, Feeling, and Perceiving.

This problem can be reframed as a further challenge for organizations and their strategic planning groups: to become more type-inclusive, more tolerant and appreciative of type diversity, and better able to make constructive and contingent use of this diversity, recognizing that all preferences are valuable, but not in every situation.

RESEARCH METHOD

I conducted qualitative research to address two questions relevant to the challenge of incorporating all type perspectives into strategic planning and change processes. The first question was concerned with how type information and knowledge are used in processes of strategic planning and change. The second question considered how strategic planners can access their less-preferred functions and attitudes when specific situations make this necessary.[4]

The research method I used is called *grounded theory*. It involves identifying and investigating a particular phenomenon—in this case, use of type in strategic planning—and discovering and developing a theory to explain that phenomenon (Strauss & Corbin, 1990). A distinguishing feature of this method is that the theory evolves out of the data (rather than coming from the mind of the researcher) and during data analysis (instead of afterward). A theory so grounded should be readily recognizable by and useful to practitioners in situations similar to the one studied. The grounded theory can help them make sense of complexity and generate hypotheses for testing and further development.

The main data source for this research was a set of 24 interviews with type practitioners (18 Canadians, 4 Americans, 2 Australians), most of whom also had experience with strategic planning, often in connection with organizational development or training. Four psychotherapists, who use type to help clients "stretch" to their less-favored sides, were added to the data set when the concept of type flexibility began to emerge as important. Although the interviewees' type preferences were skewed toward NFP and NTP, they constituted a good cross-section of experience with organizations of various kinds, sizes, and circumstances.

Data from the interviews, supported by the literature and by my own extensive experience as a professional planner and type user, were transcribed, coded, and analyzed in depth. The next four sections outline the grounded theory that resulted.

APPLICATIONS OF TYPE IN
STRATEGIC PLANNING AND CHANGE

Practitioners apply their knowledge of and information on type to strategic planning/change processes in the following five main ways.

PREPARING FOR STRATEGIC PLANNING.   Use of type assists in the creation of a positive, enthusiastic climate for strategic planning and organizational change. Members of the organization are able to interact more openly around what's happening. Planners and facilitators are better equipped to design situationally appropriate planning processes that, due to type, are exposed to a broader range of perspectives.

BUILDING AND OPERATING THE PLANNING TEAM.   In the formation, development, and operation of teams responsible for spearheading strategic change processes, use of type enables the strength of each preference to contribute to strategic planning. Although individuals tend to be attracted to certain components of strategic planning congruent with their type preferences, no one type has a monopoly on any one component; all types have different and potentially valuable contributions to make (e.g., both Sensing types and Intuitive types have much to offer as an organization defines a practical vision of its desired future). Where type diversity is not present, a prudent strategy is to increase team members' capacity to value type differences and exercise less-preferred functions as circumstances require (Kirton, 1994); accomplishing this removes a key impediment to strategic planning/change. Facilitators identify the type resources on a planning team and, using tools such as the familiar Z-model, determine how to compensate for missing preferences that are needed. The Z or Zigzag model provides ways to integrate all four functions—S, N, T, and F—into the decision-making process (Lawrence, 1993; Myers 1980). Type is commonly introduced in a front-end workshop and then applied, more or less explicitly, as the team carries out its tasks. This approach can reduce tension around differences, improve interaction among team members, enable more open expression of views, build rapport, and assist conflict resolution.

MAKING STRATEGY.   Here, use of type can expand the range of perceived reality, perspectives, and alternatives. Bringing the four functions explicitly into the planning process helps counter the biases of planners and decision makers toward certain data inputs, planning methods, and strategic choices.[5] Type aids planners in addressing the tensions and polarities within strategic issues (discussed later), and members of the planning team gain flexibility as they struggle with strategic decisions.

IMPLEMENTING STRATEGY.   Type can play a valuable role in preparing the organization for the transition from what it is to what it aspires to be. This includes assisting leaders and managers to better understand the impacts of their decision styles and behaviors on others in the change process, to revise their mental models, to develop necessary new management competencies, to break down barriers to change, and to give voice to unexpressed feelings about it. Type also facilitates OD interventions, operational planning, and everyday problem solving.

IMPROVING INTERPERSONAL COMMUNICATION.   Throughout, taking advantage of the nonjudgmental philosophy and vocabulary of type improves communication and relations among members of the organization. Type allows people, fairly quickly and easily, to talk about themselves and their concerns without getting "too personal," promotes reframing to more positive language, and makes interpersonal conflict more manageable. Consequently, diverse individuals become better able to work together in the often stressful climate of strategic planning and change.

Overall, constructive use of type differences can be viewed as foundational to strategic change processes. In organizations preparing for such change, the inclusiveness of type matches the need to open up perspectives, possibilities, and people. Use of type enables members of an organization to see that changes in the external environment are linked to changes within the organization and within each individual. Type offers a pathway, not only to the awareness, understanding, and appreciation of differences vital to the success of the transition, but also to the form of communication that enables this diversity to find expression and be honored.

THE PIVOTAL ROLE
OF TYPE FLEXIBILITY

Type flexibility refers to an individual's capacity to access less-preferred functions and attitudes, enact behaviors associated with them, and work effectively with type differences when called for in the situation. As a strategy, type flexibility involves a conscious choice in response to situational requirements calling for behavior different from that naturally associated with one's preferences. This capability is critical in the contingent use of difference since being more type flexible enables one to be more situationally responsive.

The exercise of type flexibility, here referred to as *typeflexing,* can occur across type dimensions as well as from one function pair to another—for example, from Thinking to Feeling or from ST to NT. Typeflexing involves one person communicating with a different other, adding or subtracting behaviors and using language sensitively so as to better match that person's behavior. Knowledge of type helps us identify and interpret behavior for this purpose, but it is not necessary to know the other's type in order to exercise one's type flexibility. Typeflexing may simply respond to how that individual is behaving in the moment—Susan Brock (1994) calls this *type mode*—recognizing that in a single interaction, each of us may exhibit behaviors associated with various preferences. For instance, as an Introvert, I may observe what looks like Extraverted behavior in someone with whom I am trying to connect (e.g., talks fast, is highly energetic). To typeflex, I access my own Extraverted side and respond in an Extraverted way (answer quickly without long pauses, show energy and enthusiasm).[6] For the practical purpose of improving our communication exchange, it does not matter whether that person is or is not an Extravert. What matters is my willingness and ability to align my communicative approach to the other's type-related behavior.

For a strategic planning team, which is likely to be dominated by certain type preferences and to be missing others, type flexibility serves two main purposes. A more type-flexible team is better equipped to interact with the numerous internal and external stakeholders whose type preferences may run the full gamut. More specifically, team members are better able to close the gaps between preferred and situationally required planning behaviors. Examples include a team of Intuitive types attempting a detailed benchmarking exercise, a predominantly Sensing team struggling with visioning, Thinking types trying to address the impacts their proposed strategies will have on the people affected, and Feeling types confronting the discord strategic change often generates.

Enhancement of type flexibility is a natural process of learning, of "coming to terms with the external world, on the one hand, and with one's unique psychological characteristics on the other" (Sharp, 1991, p. 14).[7] Becoming more type flexible requires awareness, acceptance, and appreciation of type differences. This adaptive process can be visualized as a "type ladder." The first rung, *awareness*, involves becoming conscious of one's type preferences and what they mean. It extends beyond knowing one has certain preferences to comprehending what this implies for one's attitudes and behaviors. The second rung, *acceptance*, goes further in admitting one's type preferences, with their strengths and blind spots, into one's self-concept and frame of reference, and then acknowledging that other people have different preferences. Acceptance, where we recognize that another is different and has a right to be so, is more than tolerance, where we merely put up with the difference. The third rung, *appreciation,* entails grasping the significance and value of one's type preferences, and then honoring preferences different from one's own as similarly worthwhile. Valuing differences is fundamental to the Myers-Briggs philosophy of "gifts differing" and its major challenge—it's one thing to understand and quite another to appreciate.

As an individual moves up the ladder, type preferences are brought into awareness, understanding and acceptance of them is acquired, and there is an enhanced appreciation of type differences. New ways of seeing and being emerge. Type flexibility is implied in this adaptive process, but it requires something else too: Instead of just coming to know, accept, and appreciate what is *most* preferred, the individual also works at differentiating what is *least* preferred. As this happens, there is an increase in personal capacity to make constructive and contingent use of difference.

Although pushed and pulled by contextual forces such as those encountered in an organization's culture, the process of becoming more type flexible is essentially inside out. It begins with the individual who connects with a lesser preference and makes explicit use, however temporarily, of its related behaviors. We begin with ourselves, then flex to another. When people support each other in acquiring greater type flexibility, it becomes a shared reciprocal experience.

Each of the four type dimensions presents a unique set of challenges for increased type flexibility. Often in organizational contexts, the greatest need for typeflexing skills will be from Sensing, Thinking, and Judging to Intuition, Feeling, and Perceiving.

ENHANCING TYPE FLEXIBILITY

Although type flexibility may come more easily to certain types and individuals, it should be achievable by any psychologically healthy individual. Type flexibility involves learned behaviors that build on what people already do without necessarily being aware of it. The aim is not to change the individual's type or preferences but rather to expand that person's behavioral repertoire. This can be accomplished by facilitators and others with suitable skills drawing on the following eight categories of strategies, methods, and techniques.

- *Teaching and training:* Explain lesser preferences and how to use type-flexing;[8] provide specific exercises to enhance and develop less-preferred functions and attitudes; include role-playing to help people experiment with unfamiliar behaviors, vary and rotate roles, and provide for feedback; use humor to dramatize differences and get people in a more playful mood (Smith & Smith, 1995); make available specialized courses such as FLEX Talk®;[9] use versions of the Z-model to show teams how to identify type gaps; locate and create information resources; and throughout, promote self-directed learning using available training aids (e.g., Barr & Barr, 1994; Bayne, 1995; Benfari, 1995; Hartzler & Hartzler, 1985; Kroeger with Thuesen, 1992; Kummerow, 1985; Lawrence, 1993; Provost, 1984; Tieger & Barron-Tieger, 1992).

- *Reframing:* Show people how to redefine boundaries and shift their frames of reference, get a new perspective on their own and others' type preferences, and put new meanings on them so that negatives may be seen as positive and weaknesses as strengths, depending on the context (Murray & Murray, 1988).

- *Imaging:* Use creative visualization and other forms of imagery to help people get in touch with their lesser preferences and access their inner worlds (Keefer, 1995; Keefer & Yabroff, 1995); make use of such related techniques as meditation, active imagination, dream work, and sandplay (Boulangier, 1994; Johnson, 1986).

- *Observing, imitating, modeling:* Assist those individuals who learn best by watching others (e.g., enhance their observer skills); demonstrate what typeflexing and the new behaviors look like (facilitators can do this in workshops); identify individuals in the organization who are typeflexing "naturals" and who can model the use of lesser preferences.

- *Contracting:* Get people to set realistic targets and make contracts (verbal commitments, action plans) to exercise the new behaviors.

- *Partnering and mentoring:* Help different types to assist and support each other's learning of the new attitudes and behaviors; encourage them to consult with persons of the opposite type to improve their understanding of neglected parts of themselves (Myers & McCaulley, 1985).

- *Counseling and coaching:* Work with people one-to-one or in small groups to guide them in their typeflexing efforts (e.g., Lindsay, 1985); provide support and assistance when, inevitably, they encounter difficulty.

- *Rehearsing and practicing:* Encourage use of the new skills along with reflection to complete the experiential learning cycle (Kolb, 1984).

As implied above, strategic planning and change often involve facilitation, a role that focuses on process more than content. Type flexibility is especially important for facilitators, as they too find themselves having to activate their own less-preferred functions and attitudes; a prime example is the NFP facilitator working with an STJ client group, each tapping into the other's less-preferred side. Helping others become more type flexible calls for *reflexivity,* a combination of self-awareness and agency; in other words, the person teaching type flexibility must have and demonstrate type flexibility. Facilitators must know their own preferences well, keep this knowledge in awareness, apply it to enhance typeflexing processes so that they practice what they preach, and use it to address their own needs.

An Example of a Type Flexibility Workshop

This example involves a facilitator conducting a workshop on type flexibility for members of a team about to engage in a strategic planning/change process. First, a workshop climate of permission, trust, and safety is created, which enables participants to experiment with new behaviors. The facilitator then begins by bringing participants' type preferences into awareness, validating them, and generating tolerance and appreciation of differences. Type flexibility is discussed and normalized as something everyone does, in different ways; participants are assured, however, that the objective is to help them learn new attitudes and behaviors, not to change their type preferences. The next task is to stimulate motivation to become more type flexible; this is accomplished by bringing out, in terms meaningful to the participants, the need for a wider behavioral repertoire in the specific planning situations likely to be encountered.

Less-preferred functions and attitudes are then approached via more-favored preferences by beginning where people are at and bridging from strengths to weaknesses—e.g., starting from inside their frame and then gradually widening it. Initially, the facilitator caters to the majority, the types (in this case, not surprisingly, STJ) who are least accustomed to typeflexing because the organizational culture has made it more comfortable for them, compared with the minority types who have been forced to flex just to get along. Techniques used, drawn from the above list, are friendly to all types, however, and the process addresses their typeflexing needs later on.

The facilitator allows for sufficient feedback, processing of what is happening, and positive reinforcement. A special effort is made to prepare participants for "reentry" and connecting with the larger organizational setting so that what is learned in the workshop has a better chance of being applied in the upcoming strategic change process.

PERSONAL AND INTERPERSONAL LIMITATIONS ON TYPE FLEXIBILITY

Exercising type flexibility is a temporary strategy, a coping mechanism that enables us to deal with situational requirements. Typeflexing cannot be sustained indefinitely, and doing it for an extended period can be costly for the individual (e.g., fatigue, stress). Type flexibility has limits, both within the individual and in the situation or context, as well as in relationships between these two levels.

Seven personal/interpersonal factors that constrain type flexibility were identified in my research.

INDIVIDUAL TYPE DEVELOPMENT. "Good type development" generally means knowing and accepting one's type preferences, possessing reasonably clear preferences, having a balance between perception and judgment, and being able to access less-developed preferences when necessary (Brownsword, 1988; Myers, 1980). The degree of type development that an individual has achieved, therefore, can affect how much and what kind of type flexibility is currently possible for that person. It is important to be clear about one's type preferences before "flicking the switch to their opposites," as one of my research participants put it.

At the other end of the scale, one-sidedness or overuse of a function may lead to dysfunctional eruption of its opposite. This relates to the inferior function; views differ concerning the extent to which flexing to it is possible (Garden, 1991). My view is that less-preferred functions *can* be accessed, though with varying degrees of success and within limits. As the most unconscious of the functions, the inferior function is likely to present the greatest flexing challenge, involve the most unpredictability, and require the greatest skill on the part of facilitators and other helpers. Two suggested approaches are the following: (a) use the tertiary function (if it can be accessed) as a bridge to the inferior function (Garden, 1991); and (b) approach accessing of the inferior function in a safe, pressure-free setting and a playful, relaxed manner (Quenk, 1993). Something to avoid is confronting the inferior function directly—for instance, by asking Introverted Thinking types to share their innermost feelings in public.

AGE AND MATURITY. Midlife seems to be a time when many people experience a "window of opportunity" for appreciating difference and accessing previously underdeveloped parts of themselves. For example, Feeling types may discover their tougher assertive side, while Thinking types may begin to notice a soft spot they didn't know they had—e.g., a yearning for intimacy and a capacity to be touched emotionally. Similarly, Intuitive types may suddenly realize a new desire to be present in their immediate time and space, while many Sensing types find they want to pay attention to hunches, patterns, and the big picture (Fitzgerald, 1993). If midlife offers a special potential for increasing one's type flexibility, it may be that younger people are likely to have less inclination and less capacity to become more type flexible.

ENERGY. The most obvious limit to type flexibility is the loss of energy and resulting fatigue that typically accompany the enacting of behaviors associated with less-preferred functions, particularly if this goes on for long. The ability to recharge the depleted energy batteries then becomes critical if burnout is not to result.

ANXIETY AND STRESS. People who are anxious or stressed-out are likely to be less flexible. Anxiety and stress can cause them to fall back on their preferred functions but with diminished facility (Ware, Rytting, & Jenkins, 1994). At the same time, typeflexing can increase anxiety and heighten stress. Ironically, "under stress, people often work more rigidly out of their stronger functions and suppress the third and fourth functions, just at a time when these could be most helpful" (Ruppart, 1991, p. 27). Whether some types are more susceptible to this limitation is an open question. Different types seem to vary regarding how they experience stress (Garden, 1988; Khalsa, 1992), how stress affects them (e.g., Roberts & Roberts, 1988), and how they cope with it (Hammer, 1988; Short & Grasha, 1995).

MOTIVATION, READINESS, AND RESISTANCE Because type flexibility is about learning new behaviors, motivation is a key limiting and enabling variable. Typeflexing must serve a purpose for the individual, either addressing an unfulfilled intrinsic need or responding to an extrinsic demand. And the individual must be ready to become more type flexible. Readiness is linked to a further limitation, resistance to change, which is a natural response to the pressure to do something differently. In a change process, people's resistance is likely to relate closely to what's important to them; for example, SJs can be expected to resist proposed changes that they believe fail to honor the organization's traditions and in-place systems.

TYPE BIAS. Prejudging or stereotyping other preferences is rooted in the tendency to see other types from the perspective of one's own type and hence to resist them and their "strange" viewpoints (Hammer, 1985). Especially problematic in organizations are Sensing–Intuition and Thinking–Feeling biases. For example, Fitzgerald (1992, p. 13) observed that NTs "may make global judgments about the competence of others, permanently writing off people who they see as incompetent (often because that person has a different cognitive style)." Such type bias can be a block to type flexibility. On the positive side, enhancing type flexibility enables type biases to be brought into the open and dealt with constructively (Newman, 1994).

SELF-IMPOSED LIMITS. Most people are likely to have their own limits regarding how far they are prepared to go in enacting behaviors from their less-preferred side. Going too far puts personal authenticity and identity at risk. A type-flexible individual is not a chameleon, nor is type flexibility merely another skill to be mastered to perfection. According to Jung, individuation aims at completeness, not flawlessness. A viable alternative to trying to have it all is "to learn to value the unique contribution of other preferences and work *with* others rather than expecting to do all type tasks well alone" (Murphy, 1994, p. 1).

TYPE FLEXIBILITY IN ORGANIZATIONS

An organization's culture is particularly influential in shaping its members' behavior and in determining whether type differences will be undervalued or appreciated. The culture therefore can either inhibit or support type flexibility.[10] For example, a culture that provides too much comfort for certain types (often STJs) does not motivate them to gain greater capability with less-preferred functions and attitudes; a strategic plan that creates an illusion of stability can reinforce this complacency. Change in the organizational culture, difficult at the best of times, may be required if appreciation of type difference and enhancement of type flexibility are to result. Whatever the approach, greater type flexibility by individuals and in groups requires sustenance from the organization.

A familiar form of organizational resistance to enhanced type flexibility is the lack of continuity and follow-up from type workshops to the workplace. Committed top management along with internal sponsors and champions are needed to counter this constraint. A strategic planning/change process can provide an ongoing setting for applying type and enhancing type flexibility.

While entrenched behaviors related to majority type preferences can block strategic change, careful application of type in an organizational change process can have an opening-up effect that encourages the valuing and constructive use of difference. If this happens, the organization may be better able to counter "defensive routines" (Argyris, 1994), embrace multiple perspectives, work with a wider array of environmental forces, and align with the societal paradigm shift toward greater adaptability (Clark, 1985). Alternatively, in a rather subversive way, the use of type may facilitate micro-level, bottom-up change that is prompted by a widespread desire that people have to find more satisfying work in organizations that listen to their input and treat them with respect. Whatever form the process takes, type flexibility has an important contribution to make, while its absence can be a significant barrier to strategic change.

APPLYING TYPE FLEXIBILITY
TO STRATEGIC PLANNING

Type flexibility, within the foregoing limits, has obvious application to strategic planning and change. In such processes, it is likely that all type preferences and the behaviors that accompany them will be required. It is unlikely, however, that this diversity will be present. Enhancement of type flexibility, along with appreciation of type differences, can help bridge the gap.

Increasing the type flexibility of key participants in a strategic planning process can be accomplished using the strategies and methods described earlier. The potential of such initiatives can be amplified by situating them within a conceptual framework linking type preference to strategic planning and change. Figure 1 presents a preliminary effort in this direction.[11]

Sensing–Intuition and Thinking–Feeling are the intersecting axes at the center of the framework. The underlying assumption is that the four functions and their decision-style combinations are integral to strategic planning because getting information and evaluating it are core planning activities. The Extraversion–Introversion dimension is seen to have

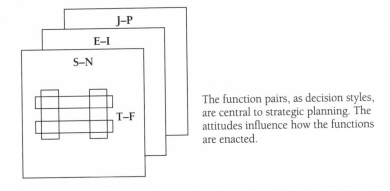

The function pairs, as decision styles, are central to strategic planning. The attitudes influence how the functions are enacted.

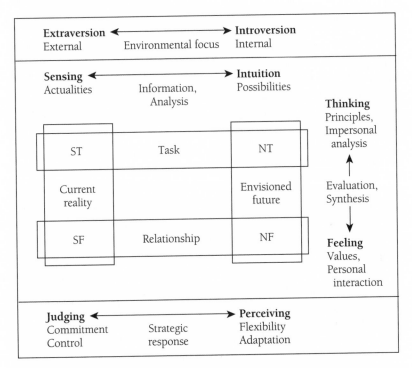

Figure 1 Preliminary Framework for Applying Type to Strategic Planning

its main impact on the environmental focus adopted by the strategic planners, while Judging–Perceiving affects the planners' strategic response. Extraversion–Introversion also influences the ways in which Sensing–Intuition and Thinking–Feeling will be exercised in either the inner or the outer world.[12]

The framework goes further, however, to incorporate an additional characteristic of both strategic planning and type. This is the concept of polarities: interdependent opposites in ongoing tension (Johnson, 1992).[13] A polarity is a recurring issue that, unlike a problem that can be solved, must be re-solved and therefore managed. Prominent polarities in strategic planning include emphasis on the external versus internal environment, the current reality versus the envisioned future, task versus relationship, and commitment versus flexibility. Embedded in these polarities is another set, represented by the four type dimensions. Each dimension reflects one of the strategic planning polarities, as shown in Figure 1. In effect, this results in a next-generation Z-model, with three modifications to the original. First, functions are replaced by function pairs. Second, these are not shown in any particular sequence (in the Z-model, this sequence is S → N → T → F); the appropriate sequence is situation-specific and iterative. And third, the attitudes (E–I and J–P) are included.

A promising application of this framework is as a kind of "mental model" or cognitive/interactive tool that planners can use as they design and conduct a strategic planning process.[14] This would allow important type differences and planning polarities to be exposed, talked about openly, and incorporated into the planning/change process. The framework also reminds planners, managers, and leaders to give all eight type preferences consideration, in accordance with situational demands.

Type therefore offers a pathway to a more complete form of strategic planning. The polarity approach adds depth by turning either/or into both/and, by embracing a multiplicity of perspectives, and by maximizing the best of coexistent opposing forces while minimizing their worst. A constructive and contingent use of type in strategic change is to be found not by seeking balance between opposites, such as commitment (J) and flexibility (P), but rather by learning to manage these polarities.[15] A key to accomplishing this, since it engages the full spectrum of type preferences, is type flexibility.

IMPLICATIONS

Enhancement of type flexibility has implications for organizations and especially for leaders, managers, and strategic planners.

A clear implication has already been mentioned: Organizational support is essential for the appreciation of type diversity and for the development and application of type flexibility. This may seem like a tall order, and for many organizations it probably is. But there are both push and pull factors at work that may render this task less formidable than it appears. One set of forces comes from the organizational environment; a shift toward more Intuition, Feeling, and Perceiving is increasingly being seen (if not explicitly in type terms) as necessary for survival in a fast-changing and unpredictable world.

Another set of forces originates within individuals, especially as they reach midlife and ask themselves, "Is this all there is?" Based on her work with executives and leaders, Fitzgerald (1993) reported a window of opportunity for many individuals who, at this juncture, develop "an inner push" to work on their less-preferred functions, especially Feeling. Wood (1994) echoed this finding, drawing on a survey of leadership training around the world that identified "a very significant trend towards helping individuals come into contact with their [Feeling preference], particularly the role and importance of values and empowerment in the work environment" (p. 131). A pull factor for organizations is the potential value added as they admit new perspectives, turn diversity into synergy, increase their strategic responsiveness, and enhance organizational learning.

Leaders of organizations play a vital role in determining whether the organizational context uses type and encourages type flexibility. Leadership itself "involves the increasing ability to effectively integrate differences within organizations" (Fitzgerald, 1993, p. 14). In addition, the leader is instrumental in managing and changing the organization's culture (Schein, 1985) and in fostering organizational learning (Senge, 1990).

Type flexibility, as an aspect of "good type development," is an essential though often unrecognized element of successful leadership,[16] especially in turbulent times when an organization must be able to muster a full range of capabilities and generate new ones. Such leaders have mastered the art of type flexibility and are able to work effectively with other types in situationally appropriate ways.[17] Barr and Barr (1994, p. 267) provided an example of such a leader, in this case an INTJ:

> Her Introversion sustains her inner-directedness, where she relies on her deep beliefs and values to find direction and meaning in life. She is not dependent upon the external world to validate her. She developed her Extroverted skills to such an extent that she is an outstanding speaker, talented facilitator, and charming conversationalist. Although she relies primarily on her intuitive scan of a situation, she has trained herself to be an astute observer of her surroundings. Her sensing skills are excellent. She developed her abilities to think clearly while feeling deeply to get a full

assessment of a situation. She is adaptable and yet planful. In short, she has worked hard to know her strengths and she works perpetually on developing skills for her least preferred style.

Many managers prefer STJ and work in bureaucratic organizations that support their preferences while undervaluing others. Yet, they may be more susceptible to the call for type flexibility than this picture suggests. As Otto Kroeger pointed out to the 1994 conference of the Australian Association for Psychological Type, many managers experience a parallel reality: mandated strategy-making that calls upon the executive's Intuitive side; increasing demands to engage in coaching, collaboration, teamwork, and other people-oriented activities that require use of the Feeling function; and, as the manager ascends the hierarchy, less control over personal time, especially trying for Judging types. Such individuals may be willing, perhaps even eager or desperate, to find ways to enlarge their coping repertoires.

For strategic planners and their field of theory and practice, there are additional important implications. Planning that addresses and works toward simultaneously managing type and other polarities has gone a considerable way toward a more "complete" form of strategic planning. To proceed further involves covering all the type-preference bases in specific strategic planning/change processes—giving Intuition, Feeling, and Perceiving their due. The most significant challenge this presents for the strategic planners characterized earlier is to appreciate and learn to access and work with Feeling and Perceiving. Some planners may regard Feeling as a threat to their image of the objective, detached professional. Similarly, the Perceiving approach may seem antithetical to planning as they see it. Yet in both cases, planners may be persuaded that it is in their interest, and that of successful strategic change processes, to adopt a more encompassing perspective. Meanwhile, training in type flexibility and polarity management offers pathways to enhanced competence and workable strategies, which ought to be especially appealing to NTs and STs.

An important potential side-benefit of type-complete strategic planning is "synergistic communication" (Covey, 1990, p. 264). As people open their minds, hearts, and expressions to new dimensions of themselves and others, new potentials are released for individuals, groups, and organizations.

For the individual—whether planner, manager, or leader—completion of strategic planning intersects with completion of the self, the bringing of "our whole selves, in all our diversity, to our workplace encounters" (Pearson & Seivert, 1995, p. 301). The press for completion is often from without but the way lies within. Getting to know all the preferences enables one "to develop and maneuver creatively within one's own *Weltanschauung*" (Spoto, 1989, p. 19). The individual gains a capacity for proactive self-direction, a quality especially important for those exercising leadership (Wood, 1994). The ability to respond is enhanced by a larger repertoire of responses to choose from and a greater capability for making choices (Covey, 1990). The kinds of strategic alliances and partnerships negotiated "out there" can also be worked out "in here," between opposite parts of the self. Therein lies the potential for "integration of all the possibilities immanent in the individual" (Singer, 1972, p. 158).

Intrapersonal synergy is the key to interpersonal synergy (Covey, 1990). More complete and more type-flexible leaders, managers, and planners are a route to more complete processes of strategic planning and change.

CONCLUSION

Type can contribute positively to strategic planning and organizational change processes. Fulfilling this promise depends on being able to use type constructively, contingently, and flexibly.

An organization that makes constructive use of type diversity turns it into a positive rather than divisive force and, in so doing, matches external variety with internal variety to increase the organization's response capability. But, because all types and preferences are not equally valuable in all situations, the organization must also be able to create situationally appropriate mixes of preferences and behaviors on its strategic planning/management teams. Since ideal matches seldom occur, type flexibility becomes a central feature of this constructive/contingent response and a key to effective strategic planning and change.

In organizations confronting or attempting to initiate such planning and change processes, a major challenge is to move type flexibility from a quality that is unrecognized to one that is acknowledged and actively pursued. This can be done by individuals and teams in facilitated workshops making use of an array of available techniques and tools. Much of its success, however, depends on the willingness of top management to create a climate of support for appreciation of type diversity and enhancement of type flexibility, which in turn is likely to require shifts in the average organization's norms of conduct and ways of working.

Here, organizational leadership has a decisive role. If context making is truly the fundamental art of management (Morgan, 1994), leaders have a responsibility to reshape organizational contexts so that type diversity may be seen as a source not of conflict but of strength. Leaders themselves must master type flexibility so they may model this quality for others and work effectively with all types.

For leaders and planners alike, type flexibility is a basic survival skill, a key part of what it means to be adaptive learners accessing their own and others' full potential in organizations shaping and enacting strategic change.

NOTES

1. Results of the survey, sponsored by The Planning Forum and the American Productivity & Quality Center, were reported in *Planning Forum Network* (May/June 1994, p. 11).

2. Recent research suggests that line and staff managers may differ in this regard; while (E)STJ was found to dominate both categories, staff managers were significantly more inclined toward Intuition and Perceiving (Reynierse & Harker, 1995).

3. This should be treated as hypothesis when *strategic planner* is widely defined; temporary planning teams vary considerably in their composition and, therefore, also their type preferences. In my sample of 53 strategic planners, two-thirds of whom had professional qualifications in planning, ENTJ was the modal type. Extraversion and Introversion were evenly split, but Intuition was preferred over Sensing 2½ to 1, Thinking over Feeling nearly 4 to 1 (90% of males and 68% of females preferred T), and Judging over Perceiving about 2 to 1. Others have speculated that strategic thinking, planning, and acting is associated with TJ and NT preferences (Hellreigel & Slocum, 1975; Kroeger with Thuesen, 1992; Lawrence, 1993; Mitroff, Barabba, & Kilmann, 1977; Roach, 1986; Taggart & Robey, 1981; Tieger & Barron-Tieger, 1992).

4. The research was part of a doctoral dissertation prepared during the period 1992 to 1995 (Lang, 1995). A 10-page summary is available from the author (Faculty of Environmental Studies, York University, 4700 Keele St., North York, Ontario, M3J 1P3, Canada).

5. For example, research by Haley and Stumpf (1989) indicates that the four decision styles or function pairs display "discrete preferences for modes of gathering data, generating alternatives and evaluating alternatives" and that "these preferences can impact organizational strategies" (Haley & Pini, 1994, pp. 19–20).

6. Type-related behavioral cues and typeflexing responses are provided in Brock (1994) and Kummerow (1985).

7. This is linked to two further processes described by Jung: *individuation*, in which "the reconciliation of opposites and their integration resulting in transcendence is fundamentally achieved by bringing into consciousness the unconscious aspects of our being" (O'Connor, 1990, p. 85); and *differentiation*, whereby preferences are brought into consciousness, with the dominant function being the most differentiated and therefore the most fully adapted (Jung,

1921/1971). Differentiation prepares the individual for adaptation to the external world, such as the organization, where situations routinely necessitate exercising less-preferred functions.

8. The *Expanded Analysis Report* (Kummerow & Quenk, 1992) appears to have considerable potential for assisting typeflexing. Subpreferences it identifies may point to openings for the individual to stretch to the opposite side.

9. Training for typeflexing has so far progressed furthest through the work of Susan Brock. Her FLEX Talk® program is aimed primarily at salespersons and others in situations where one person is attempting to influence another. FLEX Talk® involves knowing one's type preferences and then using knowledge of type to identify, interpret, and respond appropriately to other people's behavior cues (Brock, 1994).

10. An organization's "character," a form of collective personality that is embedded in the culture, can similarly shape expectations and behaviors and affect strategic responses. Bridges (1992) claims that ISTJ and ESTJ are the most common characters of North American corporations.

11. The impetus for such a framework came from Susan Brock (1994) whose FLEX Talk program is underpinned by a framework based on research on type preference in relation to selling. My framework is still speculative; a "work-in-progress."

12. Reynierse and Harker (1995, p. 13) theorize that "the J–P preference represents a broad continuum of entrepreneurism and bureaucracy in which the entrepreneurial P preference tends to initiate and promote change, whereas the bureaucratic J preference tends to encourage the established order and resist change."

13. Similarly, Stroh and Miller (1994) cite "paradoxical choices and characteristics," many of which relate directly to strategic planning. They define *paradox* as a set of conflicting choices or conditions (e.g., stability and change), each desirable in theory but seemingly irreconcilable in practice.

14. Senge (1990, p. 174) uses the term *mental models* to describe deeply held internal images of how the world works—images that limit us to familiar ways of thinking and acting.

15. Johnson (1992) presents a tool he calls a "polarity map" for use in managing polarities. Its application to strategic planning is explored in Lang (1995).

16. Wood (1994, p. 130) reports a conclusion from a series of workshops on creative leadership: "We can find no type that we can confidently predict to be a successful leader, although our observations lead us to believe that type awareness, type flexibility, and a capacity to entertain two opposing thoughts is very important in this process." Conversely, individuals experiencing leadership and management difficulties are often "stuck types" who "seem to rigidly demonstrate the key characteristics of their type without a compensating ability."

17. Anecdotal evidence of type-flexible leaders, representing each of the four temperaments, can be found in a recent four-part series on "leadertypes" in Scanlon (1993, 1994).

REFERENCES

Argyris, C. (1994). A leadership dilemma: Skilled incompetence. In G. Salaman et al. (Eds.), *Human resource strategies* (pp. 82–94). London: Sage.

Barr, L., & Barr, N. (1989). *The leadership equation: Leadership, management, and the Myers-Briggs Type Indicator*. Austin, TX: Eakin Press.

Barr, L., & Barr, N. (1994). *Leadership development: Maturity and power.* Austin, TX: Eakin Press.

Bayne, R. (1995). *The Myers-Briggs Type Indicator: A critical review and practical guide.* London: Chapman & Hall.

Benfari, R. (1995). *Changing your management style.* New York: Lexington Books.

Boulangier, V. (1994). Expressions of type dynamics and type development: Use of the timelines and sandplay in organizations and psychotherapy. In M. Robson (Ed.), *Inner work, outer connections: Type, temperament and the Myers-Briggs Type Indicator in Australia. Conference proceedings* (pp. 23–24). Melbourne: Australian Association for Psychological Type.

Bridges, W. (1992). *The character of organizations: Using Jungian type in organizational development.* Palo Alto, CA: Davies-Black.

Brock, S. (1994). *Using type in selling: Building customer relationships with the Myers-Briggs Type Indicator.* Palo Alto, CA: Consulting Psychologists Press.

Brownsword, A. W. (1988). *It takes all types!* San Anselmo, CA: Bay Tree Publishing Co.

Campbell, D., & Van Velsor, E. (1985). The use of personality measures in a management development program. In H. J. Bernardin & D. A. Bownas (Eds.), *Personality assessment in organizations* (pp. 193–216). New York: Praeger.

Clark, D. L. (1985). Emerging paradigms in organizational theory and research. In Y. S. Lincoln (Ed.), *Organizational theory and inquiry: The paradigm revolution.* (pp. 43–78). Newbury Park, CA: Sage.

Clegg, S. R. (1992). Modernist and postmodernist organization. In G. Salaman et al. (Eds.), *Human resource strategies* (pp. 156–187). London: Sage.

Covey, S. R. (1990). *The seven habits of highly effective people.* New York: Fireside.

Fitzgerald, C. (1992). Introducing type in technical environments: Presenting the MBTI as a "User's Manual" for dealing with people. *Bulletin of Psychological Type, 15*(3), 13–14.

Fitzgerald, C. (1993, March). *The Myers-Briggs Type Indicator and leadership development: Reflections on levels of interpretation.* Paper presented to Advanced Symposium on Leadership, Association for Psychological Type, Crystal City, Virginia.

Garden, A. M. (1988). Jungian type, occupation, and burnout: An elaboration of an earlier study. *Journal of Psychological Type, 14,* 2–14.

Garden, A. M. (1991). Unresolved issues with the *Myers-Briggs Type Indicator. Journal of Psychological Type, 22,* 3–14.

Haley, U. C. V., & Pini, R. (1994). Blazing international trails in strategic decision-making research. In C. Fitzgerald (Ed.), *Proceedings of the Myers-Briggs Type Indicator and Leadership: An International Research Conference* (pp. 19–29). College Park, MD: University of Maryland University College National Leadership Institute.

Haley, U. C. V., & Stumpf, S. A. (1989). Cognitive trails in strategic decision-making: Linking theories of personalities and cognitions. *Journal of Management Studies, 26,* 477–497.

Hammer, A. L. (1985). Typing or stereotyping? Unconscious bias in applications of psychological type theory. *Journal of Psychological Type, 10,* 14–19.

Hammer, A. L. (1988). *Manual for the Coping Resources Inventory.* Palo Alto, CA: Consulting Psychologists Press.

Hartzler, G. J., & Hartzler, M. T. (1985). *Exercises to develop the preference skills.* Gaithersburg, MD: Type Resources.

Hellriegel, D., & Slocum, J. W., Jr. (1975, December). Managerial problem-solving styles. *Business Horizons,* 29–37.

Johnson, B. (1992). *Polarity management: Identifying and managing unsolvable problems*. Amherst, MA: HRD Press.

Johnson, R. A. (1986). *Inner work: Using dreams and active imagination for personal growth*. New York: HarperCollins.

Jung, C. G. (1971). *Psychological types* (H. G. Baynes, trans., rev. by R. F. C. Hull). In Collected Works of C. G. Jung (Vol. 6), Bollinger Series X. Princeton, NJ: Princeton University Press. (Original work published 1921.)

Keefer, K. (1995). Type development: The contribution of guided imagery. In Association for Psychological Type (Ed.), *Diversity and expression of type: Proceedings of APT XI biennial international conference, July 11–16, 1995, Kansas City, Missouri* (pp. 37–43). Kansas City: APT.

Keefer, K. H., & Yabroff, W. W. (1995). Using guided imagery for type development I: The Yabroff method. *Journal of Psychological Type, 33,* 3–10.

Khalsa, K. K. (1992). *The experience of stress by Jungian psychological types: Relationships among the Myers-Briggs Type Indicator, the Daily Hassles Scale, and symptoms of stress*. Unpublished doctoral dissertation, Ontario Institute for Studies in Education at the University of Toronto.

Kirton, M. J. (Ed.). (1994). *Adaptors and innovators: Styles of creativity and problem solving*. London: Routledge.

Kolb, D. A. (1984). *Experiential learning: Experience as the source of learning and development*. Englewood Cliffs, NJ: Prentice Hall.

Kroeger, O., with Thuesen, J. M. (1992). *Type talk at work*. New York: Delacorte Press.

Kummerow, J. M. (1985). *Talking with type*. Gainesville, FL: Center for Applications of Type.

Kummerow, J. M., & Quenk, N. L. (1992). *Interpretive guide for the MBTI Expanded Analysis Report*. Palo Alto, CA: Consulting Psychologists Press.

Lang, R. (1995). *Strategic planning and personality type: Toward constructive and contingent use of difference*. Unpublished doctoral dissertation, Ontario Institute for Studies in Education at the University of Toronto.

Lawrence, G. (1993). *People types and tiger stripes: A practical guide to learning styles* (3rd ed.). Gainesville, FL: Center for Applications of Psychological Type.

Lindsay, P. R. (1985). Counselling to resolve a clash of cognitive styles. *Technovation, 3,* 57–67.

McCaulley, M. H. (1990). The Myers-Briggs Type Indicator and leadership. In K. E. Clark & M. B. Clark (Eds.), *Measures of leadership* (pp. 381–418). West Orange, NJ: Leadership Library of America.

Mintzberg, H. (1994). *The rise and fall of strategic planning*. New York: Free Press.

Mitroff, I. I., Barabba, V. P., & Kilmann, R. H. (1977). The application of behavioral and philosophical technologies to strategic planning: The case study of a large federal agency. *Management Science, 24,* 44–58.

Morgan, G. (1994, Nov. 29). It's all in the water. *Globe and Mail,* p. B28.

Murphy, E. (1994). On the brink of human awareness: Type and human development. *Bulletin of Psychological Type, 17* (4), 1–3.

Murray, W. D. G., & Murray, R. R. (1988). *Reframing—How we look to one another.* Gladwyne, PA: Type & Temperament.

Myers, I. B., & McCaulley, M. H. (1985). *Manual: A guide to the development and use of the Myers-Briggs Type Indicator* (2d ed.). Palo Alto, CA: Consulting Psychologists Press.

Myers, I. B., with Myers, P. B. (1980). *Gifts differing*. Palo Alto, CA: Consulting Psychologists Press.

Newman, J. (1994). Conundrum No. 1: What is introverted sensation? *Bulletin of Psychological Type, 17*(2), 17-20.

O'Connor, P. (1990). *Understanding Jung.* Port Melbourne, Victoria: Reed Books.

Osborn, N., & Osborn, D. B. (1994). MBTI, FIRO-B, and NAFTA: Leadership profiles of not-so-distant neighbors. In C. Fitzgerald (Ed.), *Proceedings of the Myers-Briggs Type Indicator and Leadership: An International Research Conference* (pp. 31–45). College Park, MD: University of Maryland University College National Leadership Institute.

Pearson, C. S., & Seivert, S. (1995). *Magic at work.* New York: Doubleday Currency.

Provost, J. A. (1984). *A casebook: Applications of the Myers-Briggs Type Indicator in counseling.* Gainesville, FL: Center for Applications of Psychological Type.

Quenk, N. L. (1993). *Beside ourselves: Our hidden personality in everyday life.* Palo Alto, CA: Davies-Black.

Reynierse, J. H. (1993). The distribution and flow of managerial types through organizational levels in business and industry. *Journal of Psychological Type, 25,* 11–23.

Reynierse, J. H., & Harker, J. B. (1995). The psychological types of line and staff management: Implications for the J–P preference. *Journal of Psychological Type, 34,* 8–16.

Rigby, D. K. (1994). Managing the management tools. *Planning Review, 22(5),* 20–24.

Roach, B. (1986). Organizational decision makers: Different types for different levels. *Journal of Psychological Type, 12,* 16–24.

Roberts, E. E., II, & Roberts, D. Y. (1988). Jungian psychological traits and coronary heart disease. *Journal of Psychological Type, 15,* 3–12.

Ruppart, R. E. (1991). Careers and occupations. *Bulletin of Psychological Type, 14(1),* 27.

Scanlon, S. (Ed.). (1993). Leadertypes, *The Type Reporter, 51.*

Scanlon, S. (Ed.). (1994). Leadertypes, *The Type Reporter, 52–54.*

Schein, E. H. (1985). *Organizational culture and leadership.* San Francisco: Jossey-Bass.

Senge, P. M. (1990). *The fifth discipline: The art and practice of the learning organization.* New York: Doubleday Currency.

Sharp, D. (1991). *Jung lexicon: A primer of terms and concepts.* Toronto: Inner City Books.

Short, G. J., & Grasha, A. F. (1995). The relationship of MBTI dimensions to perceptions of stress and coping strategies in managers. *Journal of Psychological Type, 32,* 13–22.

Singer, J. (1972). *Boundaries of the soul: The practice of Jung's psychology.* New York: Anchor Press/Doubleday.

Smith, J. H., & Smith, K. A. (1995). Laughing matters: Type, temperament, and humor in the workplace. In Association for Psychological Type (Ed.), *Diversity and expression of type: Proceedings of APT XI biennial international conference, July 11–16, 1995, Kansas City, Missouri* (pp. 105–108). Kansas City: APT.

Spoto, A. (1989). *Jung's typology in perspective.* Boston: Sigo Press.

Strauss, A., & Corbin, J. (1990). *Basics of qualitative research: Grounded theory procedures and techniques.* Newbury Park, CA: Sage.

Stroh, P., & Miller, W. W. (1994, Sept.). Learning to thrive on paradox. *Training and Development,* 28–39.

Taggart, W., & Robey, D. (1981). Minds and managers: On the dual nature of human information processing and management. *Academy of Management Review, 6,* 187–195.

Tieger, P. D., & Barron-Tieger, B. (1992). *Do what you are.* Boston: Little, Brown.

Walck, C. L. (1992). Psychological type and management research: A review. *Journal of Psychological Type, 24,* 13–23.

Ware, R., Rytting, M., & Jenkins, D. (1994). The effect of stress on MBTI scores. *Journal of Psychological Type, 30,* 39–44.

Wood, J. (1994). Leadership and type. In M. Robson (Ed.), *Inner work, outer connections: Type, temperament and the Myers-Briggs Type Indicator in Australia. Conference proceedings* (pp. 127–131). Melbourne: Australian Association for Psychological Type.

Contributors

Nancy J. Barger, M.A., is an organization development and change management consultant working with corporate, government, and non-profit clients. In the last decade, she has worked extensively with organizations undergoing significant change. This work led to her recent authorship, with Linda K. Kirby, of *The Challenge of Change in Organizations: Helping Employees Thrive in the New Frontier* (Davies-Black, 1995). She is also coauthor with Kirby of the chapter on Multicultural Uses of the MBTI for the *MBTI Applications: A Decade of Research on the Myers-Briggs Type Indicator* (Consulting Psychologists Press, 1996) and with Jean M. Kummerow and Kirby of *WORKTypes* (Warner Books, 1997). She has consulted with organizations and delivered organizational change training programs in Canada, the United Kingdom, Singapore, New Zealand, and Australia, as well as in the United States. Nancy is a faculty member in the international Association for Psychological Type (APT) MBTI Qualifying Training Program and teaches advanced applications courses in the MBTI for APT. She also leads qualifying training and advanced applications sessions in Canada, the U.K., Australia, and New Zealand. Her type is ENFP.

Susan A. Brock, Ph.D., is an organization development consultant based in Minneapolis, Minnesota. Her focus is on senior management and teams—specifically interactive methods that move organizations forward in their business agendas. Prior to forming her own consultancy 12 years ago, she held positions in employee relations, training, and organizational development for business and higher education. Her current research is on the practical aspects of psychological type for sales, influencing, and communication. She is a faculty member for the international Association for Psychological Type and was the

Association's second president. She is the author of *Using Type in Selling* (Consulting Psychologists Press, 1994) and the training programs FLEX Selling®, FLEX Talk®, and FLEX Team®. She has a Ph.D. in counseling psychology from the University of Maryland. Her type is ENTP.

Paul L. Busby is a graduate student and doctoral candidate in experimental psychology at the University of Tennessee at Knoxville. He has collaborated on several projects with his mentor, Eric Sundstrom, including a chapter in *Annual Review of Psychology,* "Environmental Psychology 1989–1994." His primary research interest lies in addiction and its implications for the development of the self. He also enjoys teaching, creative writing, and philosophy. His type is ENFP.

Sally Carr, Ph.D., is a principal consultant with Oxford Psychologists Press Limited (OPP), the U.K. distributor for the MBTI. She graduated in psychology from Oxford in 1980 and received a master's degree in clinical psychology at Maudsley Hospital, London, in 1982. She worked as a clinical psychologist in Philadelphia, Vancouver, and Oxford during the subsequent five years. In 1987 she completed a doctorate in psychology at the University of Oxford. She joined OPP in 1987 as a specialist in assessment and counseling with emphasis on the area of enhancing self-awareness and developing interpersonal skills. She has a special interest in longer-term individual development of managers, helping them overcome blocks in order to fulfill their potential. She is a member of the faculty of the international Association for Psychological Type, and is a trainer in several of OPP's qualifying workshops for personality instruments, including the MBTI; she also works with managers on programs run by Sigma, OPP's management development division. She is a senior lead trainer for the Looking Glass simulation and regularly acts as a trainer on Looking Glass programs run by the Center for Creative Leadership (Greensboro, North Carolina). She has been involved in designing and running many of Sigma's tailored programs, including team development and individual counseling projects. The MBTI forms an integral part of many aspects of her work, and is also an endless source of interest and fun in her nonwork life. Her type is ESTP.

Sue G. Clancy, M.A., is the human resources development manager for a large research and development organization of the U.S. Navy. She also consults extensively within her own and other Navy organizations on organizational change and performance development. Building on her background as a physicist, she has focused much of her work on effective leadership of a scientific and engineering workforce. Psychological type provided the early foundation for much of her consulting, and she continues to teach about the application of the MBTI in public workshops and with nonprofit and public sector clients. She was a member of the steering committee that developed the international Association for Psychological Type MBTI Qualifying Training Program and continues as a member of the faculty. Her type is ISTJ.

Catherine Fitzgerald, Ph.D., is principal of Fitzgerald Consulting (College Park, Maryland), which specializes in executive coaching and leadership development. Recent clients have included the World Bank, Life Technologies Inc., the Inter-American Development Bank, the International Monetary Fund, and Citizens Bancorp. She is a faculty member of the international Association for Psychological Type and has also taught advanced courses on the MBTI and leadership and organization development throughout the United States and internationally. She is a faculty member of the National Leadership Institute of the University of Maryland University College, and an adjunct faculty member of the University of Maryland School of Public Affairs for whom she teaches courses on leadership and organizational change. She has conducted research on leadership and was chairperson of the 1994 International Research Conference on Leadership and the MBTI, sponsored by the National Leadership Institute. She is chairperson of the MBTI Research Advisory Board. She has a Ph.D. in psychology from the State University of New York at Buffalo and has completed a predoctoral fellowship in psychology at Yale University. She is licensed as a psychologist in Maryland. Her type is ENTJ.

John W. Fleenor, Ph.D., is a research scientist at the Center for Creative Leadership in Greensboro, North Carolina. He received a Ph.D. in 1988 from North Carolina State University, where he presently serves as an associate member of the psychology faculty. His research interests include the investigation of relationships between personality and leadership effectiveness. His work has been published in *Leadership Quarterly, Journal of Business and Psychology,* and *Educational and Psychological Measurement.* Additionally, he serves as a test reviewer for the Mental Measurements Yearbook. With Roger Pearman, he is co-author of a paper, "Differences in Perceived and Self-Reported

Psychological Type," which received the 1995 Isabel Briggs Myers Research Award. His type is INTP.

Usha C. V. Haley, Ph.D., received her Ph.D. in business administration, specializing in international business and strategic management, from the Stern School of Business, New York University. She also did graduate work in political science at the University of Illinois at Urbana-Champaign, and journalism at the University of Wisconsin-Madison. She has published in several academic journals and has written two books; she currently serves as regional editor, Asia Pacific for *Management Decision* (U.K.) and the *Journal of Organizational Change Management* (U.S.A.). Her current research interests include exploring and improving strategic decision making in large organizations; understanding and influencing organizations' complex interactions with their environments; and doing business successfully in Mexico and the Asia Pacific. She has taught strategic management and international business at major universities and in corporate executive development programs, in the United States, Mexico, Italy, India, and Singapore. She also serves as a consultant for several large corporations in North America, Europe, and Asia. She currently works as a senior lecturer in the Faculty of Business at the Queensland University of Technology in Brisbane, Australia.

Allen L. Hammer, Ph.D., is senior scientist at Consulting Psychologists Press. He received his Ph.D. in counseling psychology from Michigan State University in 1980. He also completed a two-year postdoctoral fellowship in computer applications in mental health at the Missouri Institute of Psychiatry and served as staff psychologist at the Student Counseling Service at Washington University in St. Louis. In his current role he is primarily engaged in research and product development of the FIRO-B, the *Myers-Briggs Type Indicator,* and the *Strong Interest Inventory.* He has authored and coauthored a number of manuals, client guides, and computerized narrative reports for these instruments. His type is INTP.

Betsy Kendall is a director and founding member of Oxford Psychologists Press Limited (OPP), the U.K. distributor of the MBTI. She has primary responsibilities for OPP's psychometric test training program, product distribution, and consultancy activities. Betsy graduated in psychology and physiology from the University of Oxford and is a chartered occupational psychologist. She has been a consultant to national and international organizations since 1984 and has worked extensively in Europe and the U.S.A. She is head of the U.K. Training Faculty of the Association for Psychological Type MBTI Qualifying Program. She also designs and trains many of OPP's personality test training workshops, including the MBTI for advanced test users and psychologists, the MBTI Step II, the FIRO-B, and the CPI. Betsy is also the Managing Consultant for Sigma, OPP's management development division. Betsy specializes in the assessment and development of middle and senior-level managers, in both one-to-one and group settings. She has designed and conducted many of Sigma's tailored organizational interventions involving team development and creative problem solving. She is a senior lead trainer for the Looking Glass simulation, developed by the Center for Creative Leadership (Greensboro, North Carolina) and has worked as an adjunct trainer for the Center for Creative Leadership. Betsy has been studying and working with psychological type since 1985. Her type is INTJ.

Linda K. Kirby, Ph.D., is a writer, editor, and trainer specializing in psychological type and the MBTI. She was coeditor of *Introduction to Type* (5th ed., Consulting Psychologists Press, 1993) with Katharine D. Myers and coauthor (with Myers) of *Introduction to Type Dynamics and Development* (Consulting Psychologists Press, 1994). She works with Nancy J. Barger in designing training programs and workshop materials and is coauthor with Barger of *The Challenge of Change in Organizations: Helping Employees Thrive in the New Frontier* (Davies-Black, 1995). She is also coauthor with Barger of the chapter on Multicultural Uses of the MBTI for the *MBTI Applications: A Decade of Research on the Myers-Briggs Type Indicator* (Consulting Psychologists Press, 1996) and with Jean M. Kummerow and Barger of *WORKTypes* (Warner Books, 1997). Linda is currently director of the Association for Psychological Type MBTI Qualifying Training Program and teaches the qualifying training in Canada, the U.K., Australia, and New Zealand, as well as in the United States. Her type is INTP.

Jean M. Kummerow, Ph.D., is a consulting psychologist with her own firm in St. Paul, Minnesota. She specializes in leadership/management development, career counseling and team building, consulting with individuals and organizations in both the for-profit and nonprofit sectors. She is staff psychologist for the Blandin Foundation's Community Leadership Program. She trains professionals internationally on the use of several psychological instruments, including the MBTI and MBTI Step II. She is an author of *Introduction to Type in Organizations, Interpretive Guide for the MBTI Expanded Analysis Report, Strong and MBTI Career Development Guide* (Consulting Psychologists Press) and *LIFETypes* and *WORKTypes* (Warner Books). She is the editor of *New Directions in Career Counseling and the Workplace.* She received her Ph.D. from the University of Minnesota and her B.A. from Grinnell College in Iowa. Her type is ESTJ.

Reg Lang, Ed.D., is a professor and associate dean in the faculty of environmental studies at York University, Canada. He has extensive experience as an educator, researcher, and practitioner in strategic planning, management, and change. Over the past 10 years, he has used the MBTI extensively in the classroom as well as in his research and professional practice, which currently focus on the role of type preference in planning and learning processes. His type is INTJ.

Richard D. Olson, Ph.D., is founder and president of Olson Consulting Group where he actively works in appraising and coaching leaders as well as in organization and team development. "Focusing on strengths" has been a theme in his consulting and writing for a number of years. A current area of interest involves looking at leadership from a systems perspective. With a background in statistics and psychological measurement, he has developed a number of psychological tests and inventories that are being used in the United States as well as in Europe and Mexico. He serves as a member of the MBTI Research Advisory Board. He received his Ph.D. from the University of Minnesota. His type is INTP.

Paul E. Roush, Ph.D., is a retired Colonel, United States Marine Corps. After graduating from the Naval Academy in 1957, his assignments during his 26 years in the Marine Corps included service in Vietnam and work as a naval attaché in Moscow. He was on the military faculties at the Army Artillery and Missile School, at the Marine Corps Education Center, at the Industrial College of the Armed Forces, and at the National War College. Dr. Roush has master's and doctoral degrees from the American University in Washington, D.C., and received a second master's degree as a Ford Foundation Fellow in Soviet Affairs at the John's Hopkins School of Advanced International Studies in Washington, D.C. As a member of the faculty at the Naval Academy in the Department of Leadership, Ethics, and Law since 1987, he began a comprehensive MBTI program as part of his efforts in the development of leadership programs. His current work is focused on development of a core ethics course to be taken by all midshipmen. His publications and professional presentations have been primarily in the fields of leadership, ethics, individual differences, and women in the military. His type is ISTJ.

Eugene R. "Geno" Schnell, Ph.D., is the associate director, Office for Continuous Quality Improvement at the University of Maryland at College Park. He is coauthor of *Introduction to the FIRO-B in Organizations* and the *FIRO-B Management Development Report*. Geno's research and writing focus on top management teams, organizational change, and executive development. His recent research has appeared in *Leadership Quarterly* and the *Journal of Business Venturing*. He received his Ph.D. in organizational behavior from the University of Maryland Business School. His type is ENFJ.

Eric Sundstrom, Ph.D., is professor of psychology at the University of Tennessee, where he has served on the faculty since receiving his Ph.D. at the University of Utah in 1973. His research interests have focused on the psychology of the physical environment, and more recently on the ecology of work-group effectiveness. He authored the book *Work Places: Psychology of the Physical Environment in Offices and Factories* (Cambridge University Press, 1986) and has more than 60 other professional publications. A licensed psychologist since 1974, he is a Fellow of the American Psychological Association, Charter Fellow of the American Psychological Society, and member of the Academy of Management and the Society of Industrial and Organizational Psychology. He has served on the editorial boards of *Environmental Psychology & Nonverbal Behavior, Population & Environment,* and *Environment & Behavior,* and currently serves on the editorial board of the new journal, *Group Dynamics*. His type is INTJ.

Ellen Van Velsor, Ph.D., is a research scientist and director of the product development research group at the Center for Creative Leadership. In this capacity, she is responsible for development and evaluation research for Center programs and products, as well as the development of the Center test database. Ellen is coauthor of *Breaking the Glass-Ceiling: Can Women Reach the Top of America's Largest Corporations?* (Addison-Wesley, 1991). She has authored numerous other articles and reports, including *Gender Differences in the Development of Managers* (Center for Creative Leadership, 1990), *Feedback to Managers, Volumes I & II* (Center for Creative Leadership, 1992) and "Why Executives Derail: A Cross-Cultural Perspective" (*Academy of Management Executive, 1995*). Before joining the staff at the Center, Ellen was a post-doctoral fellow in adult development at Duke University. She holds a B.A. in sociology from SUNY at Stony Brook and an M.A. and Ph.D. in sociology from the University of Florida.

Christa L. Walck, Ph.D., is a professor of organizational behavior at Michigan Technological University. She uses qualitative research methods and an anthropological perspective to explore organizational culture and management practices and frequently engages in critique of dominant practice. She recently coedited a special issue of *Journal of Applied Behavioral Science* (vol. 31, no. 2, 1995) on "Managing Diversity: Anthropology's Contribution to Theory and Practice," and is on the editorial review boards of *The Journal of Psychological Type* and *The Electronic Journal of Radical Organizational Theory.* Her type is INTP.

Name Index

Subject Index

Affection, as an interpersonal need, 440, *441*
age
  and organizational change, 436
  and type development, 313–320
  and type flexibility, 498
  see also midlife
analysis
  MBTI levels of, *52–54*
  see also factor analysis

balance
  among functions, 295
  situational, 229–30
behavior
  clues from, and psychological type, 387,
    469, *470–74*, 493
  and FIRO-B needs, *441*
  learned, and type flexibility, 494–96
  and MBTI Step II. *See* subscales
  predicting, unsuitability of type for,
    99–100, 374, 375, 437–38
  research on management, 64, 79–83
Benchmarks. See instruments, *Benchmarks*
bias
  corporate cultural, 356
  in decision making, 76–77, 191, *196*
  distinguished from heuristics, 191–92
  input, 192, 194, *210*
    anchoring, 77, 194, 198–99
    availability, 194, 204–205
    perseverance, 77, 194, 201–202
    vividness, 194, 207–208
  operational, 192, 194–95, *210*
    fundamental-attribution error, 195,
      206–207
    illusory correlation, 195, 209
    representativeness, 195, 203–204
    toward imputation of regularity and
      structure, 195, 201
  output, 192, 194, *210*
    functional fixedness, 194, 199–200

bias *(continued)*
  output
    positivity, 194, 202–203
    reasoning by analogy as, 194, 208–209
    social desirability, 194, 205–205

California Psychological Inventory. See instruments, *California Psychological Inventory*
CCL. *See* Center for Creative Leadership
Center for Creative Leadership (CCL),
    95–96, 216
  Leadership Development Program (LDP),
    116–32, 177, 333
    results from, 121–32
    and study of MBTI and FIRO-B, 443–*46*
    type distribution among participants at,
      25, 272–74
  study of MBTI and Benchmarks at, 146
  see also Looking Glass, Inc.
change agents, type and, 85–86
change, organizational, 337–41
  case examples, 342–49 passim, 419–34
    passim
  and dealing with loss, 358–59
  facilitating, 357–60
  failure of, 338–41
  imposed, 338–40
  leadership and, 83–86, 160, 339–40,
    341–42, 455–60
  managing, 85–86, 181, 455–60
  MBTI as a measure of, 115
  motivation and, 428–34
  reactions to, 12, 340–41
  resistance to, 415–16, 426–28
  STJs and, 415–38
  and strategic planning, 491–92
  strategies for, 86, 420, 431–32, 435–36
  successful, 341
  and the theory of opposites, 50–53
  type and, 12, 342–50, 455–60
  type dynamics and, 300–301

527